Praise for Brian Coleman's *Check the Technique* and *Rakim Told Me*

CHECK THE TECHNIQUE

"Brian Coleman has produced the best kind of oral history, getting some of the greatest figures in hip-hop to talk about the music, straight-up. If you listen to it and love it, [or] if you just want to know where it comes from, Check the Technique *is the source-point."*

– Dave Marsh

"What makes Brian Coleman's Check the Technique *unique is his utter faith in the reasonableness and authority of those who make hip-hop, as opposed to those who merely write about it. He asks incisive, elemental questions, and trusts the artists to explain and define themselves, instead of doing the clarification and definition work for them. In a universe where White people relentlessly sort and typecast Black people without consent, his deference has liberatory potential."*

– Harry Allen, Hip-Hop Activist & Media Assassin

"Brian Coleman's Check the Technique *is that rarity in mainstream publishing: a truly essential rap history. Unlike the derivative eggheads, Coleman knows and loves the music. He covers the right albums and artists. He lets hip-hop legends describe how they created the genre's true landmarks and delivers an epic, enthralling, and long-overdue history."*

– Ronin Ro, author of *Have Gun Will Travel*; *Dr. Dre*; and *Raising Hell*

"Brian Coleman's writing is a lot like the albums he covers: direct, uproarious, and more than six-fifths genius."

– Jeff Chang, author of *Can't Stop Won't Stop*; *Total Chaos*; and *Who We Be*

"Brian Coleman gets props for the exhaustive effort it took to interview the writers and producers of three dozen seminal hip hop albums for Check the Technique. *He doesn't merely compile fresh liner notes and anecdotes from stars like Q-Tip, Chuck D and Too $hort. He captures hip-hop's spirit from the '80s to the mid-'90s, when inner-city kids discovered music through samples crammed into SP-1200 drum machines, learned the biz from shady contracts, and built their personae from their stage names up. Most admirably, Coleman sits back and lets these born storytellers talk."*

– Entertainment Weekly

"The rap must-read of the year."

– Boston Herald

"For hip-hop heads, and even casual fans, Check the Technique *is highly addictive reading. Coleman's writing is snappy, but even better is his ability to draw out hugely entertaining and revealing tales from a pantheon of hip-hop artists."*

– Washington Post Express

"The interviews are unfailingly candid, and colorful."
– Boston Globe

"Where others might want to intellectualize the stories of an urban artist's rise from obscurity to legendary status, in Coleman's hands these tales are anything but academic... More often than not, Coleman's introduction to the albums actually outshines the artist-led track commentary, and his enthusiasm and sense of humor are infectious."
– Alarm

"Cliff Notes for Hip-Hop 101!"
– The Fader

"If you read only one author this year, Brian Coleman is your man... Check the Technique *is like the Bible, but better!"*
– Rap Mag **[France]**

"Easy to read and informative... Coleman's volume, covering 400 tracks and 75 [interviewed] artists all told, is a valuable, entertaining inside look at the creative processes behind some of the best-selling albums of their (or any) time."
– Publishers Weekly

"Artists and their work can get paved over and forgotten pretty quickly in these days of cultural amnesia. So a few un-corny hip-hop hoorays are due to Brian Coleman... Deep, informative and hilarious liner notes via interviews with the artists and producers who were there."
– Time Out New York

"Coleman's lengthy chapter introductions are meticulously thorough and informative, putting each album into its proper context. But the real strength of Check the Technique *lies in [the author's] ability to extract the right information from his interview subjects. Coleman writes with the warmth and enthusiasm of a hip-hop addict eager to share his findings with like-minded individuals, rather than with the superior know-it-all smugness sometimes attributed to music experts...* Check the Technique *is a must-read for both old fans who grew up on many of the albums included here, and younger heads eager to learn some history. [Rating: 5 out of 5]"*
– Blues & Soul **[UK]**

"Super-bionic-genetically-enhanced liner notes... Check the Technique *is a fine case of intimate journalism from a veteran writer who has managed to make storied albums [even] more legendary, by providing a looking glass into the genius behind their conception."*
– All Hip Hop

RAKIM TOLD ME

"The idea behind Rakim Told Me *is right on the money – to provide liner notes for landmark Golden Era albums that never had them. Not only were these albums important in their day, but they've continued to grow in importance – which means that the need for loving and intelligent analysis of them has also continued to grow."*

– Bill Adler, author of *Def Jam: The First 25 Years of the Last Great Record Label*; and *Tougher Than Leather: The Rise of Run-DMC*

"Rakim Told Me *answered all the questions I had in my head back when I first heard these albums, and at the same time raised new ones. I bought 10 copies so I could spread the word like a religious zealot."*

– Peanut Butter Wolf, Stones Throw Records

"Rock historiography is full of lore about the making of canonical albums, but there hasn't been much like that for the rap world – until now."

– Village Voice

"This is the hip-hop book of 2005."

– All Hip Hop

"Coleman's project captures the intoxicating mix of genius, charisma and arrogance that's personified by the superintendents of old-school hip-hop... Ounce for ounce, Rakim Told Me *is one of the most intimate glances at the magic behind hip-hop that I've ever experienced."*

– *The Weekly Dig* [Boston]

"'Why the hell didn't hip-hop albums ever have liner notes?' asks Brian Coleman. A damn good question, one that deserves this damn good book in response. Rakim Told Me *is indispensable."*

– *Straight No Chaser* [UK]

"Neither a straight musical analysis nor a total historical or reflective study, Coleman selects 21 albums from rap's past and re-examines them, operating in the same fashion that liner note writers have done for decades with jazz, blues and other genres... [he] blends personal encounters, memories, interview snippets, commentary and coverage, offering rap fans the same type of intricate breakdowns and stylistic dissection that's always been commonplace among music junkies."

– Nashville City Paper

Second Printing

Gingko Press, in association with Wax Facts Press

Gingko Press, 1321 Fifth Street, Berkeley, CA 94710 USA

www.GingkoPress.com
www.WaxFactsPress.com

Book and cover designed by James Blackwell, www.BlackwellSpace.com

Coleman, Brian
Check the Technique Volume 2. More Liner Notes for Hip-Hop Junkies.

ISBN 978-0-9903076-0-0

Library of Congress Control Number: 2014906887

Printed and bound in China

CHECK THE TECHNIQUE VOLUME 2

Brian Coleman

My biggest goal back then was
to be able to one day tell my kids
that I was on a record. Then I could
get a good job at the post office,
and everything would be great.
As long as I was on a record.
– DJ Jazzy Jeff

FOREWORD

By Adam Mansbach

There's product, and there's process. And in this country, we like to obsess over the former and look right past the latter. We define ourselves not just by what we purchase, but the vigor with which we cop it – shout out to all the superfans lined up for hours in subzero temperatures to scoop the new iPhone or Harry Potter joint the day it drops, as if that particular totem of whateverness won't be available the next day, and every day thereafter.

And yet, we'd rather not know how the cow becomes the burger, which is why the same meat-industry exposé has been written every five years for the last hundred (it's like *The Jungle* sometimes), and still shocks us without fail.

The culture industry isn't all that different. Our behind-the-scenes fascination is heavy on lurid details and light on questions that seek to illuminate the black box of artistic methodology. The only place process takes precedent is in rarefied, high-art circles, far from the buzz of mass consumption. If you're paying zip codes for a piece of conceptual art, you can count on being told everything about the thing, from materials to motivations. It's accepted as an article of faith that the object can't be fully appreciated otherwise, though the cynics among us might argue that this is because the shit would be incoherent without that latticework of backstory.

Down here on the ground, meanwhile, artists have learned to lean the opposite way. The cult of the casual creator goes back as far as Jack Kerouac's false claim to have written *On The Road* in one amphetamine-fueled fortnight, on a roll of butcher paper, and it continues through the latest rapper to report that he just strolls into the booth and freestyles his albums, with no preparation or forethought. And every time such a claim is met with breathless veneration – or even credulity – a little more history slips away, and another kid who's nice with the verbs or sick with the paintbrush stops thinking he's gotta build himself a woodshed and actually hone his craft. Because that's not what great artists do, right?

Right. And Rosa Parks was just a nice lady with bunions.

Hip-hop's public relationship to process is particularly fraught. It's only been forty years since Cindy Campbell decided to raise some fresh-gear funds by throwing a party in the rec room at 1520 Sedgwick Avenue, which isn't long for a global takeover. For much of that time, the dominant conversation about hip-hop – volleyed back and forth over the heads of fans and participants alike – had little to do with aesthetics, much less the path that led to those aesthetics.

Instead, hip-hop was a battleground on which fights about race and class, youth and urbanity, were waged. That it was art seemed almost incidental; one could read reams of coverage and seldom come across an insightful description of musical strategies or poetic structures; one might almost conclude that hip-hop was something that came out of a bullhorn. It took time for older critics who understood the brilliance of the form to marshal their arguments, and locate the representative geniuses who'd provide cover to advance them (Melle Mel, then Rakim, and then things opened up). It took even longer for hip-hop generation writers to position themselves in the public sphere and start teaching the world how *we* talked about the music: what the sites of improvisation were, how we evaluated a DJ routine or a sixteen-bar verse, what we meant when we listened to obscure Polish jazz-fusion records and said things like, "Yo, the way Tip caught that is *crazy*."

Meanwhile, as Brian Coleman has pointed out in past volumes of this deeply satisfying series, nobody was writing liner notes. Nobody was asking cats to break down what they'd done or why they'd done it. Those stories were languishing behind closed lips, or being passed around – making their way from borough to borough and then city to city just like Cold Crush tapes or Red Alert tapes or Stretch and Bob tapes, losing fidelity with each re-dubbing. You could learn plenty from parsing the words printed on hip-hop LPs, but it was stuff like which other artists were in the group's social circle, where they'd recorded the album, who the engineer was. That could be illuminating (or perplexing – I remember seeing Big Daddy Kane's name on a Boogie Down Productions shout-out list and being unable to reconcile it with the ongoing BDP - Juice Crew war), but it was a far cry from the thousand words critics like Nat Hentoff and A.B. Spellman and Leroi Jones and sometimes even the musicians themselves routinely dropped on the backs of jazz records in the sixties and seventies. Nobody was checking for hip-hop like that.

Except for everybody who listened to it. We hunted down the songs our favorite producers had sampled, becoming connoisseurs of funk, soul, jazz, reggae and rock in the process – and becoming democrats, too, in the best, small-D sense of the word. Sometimes getting our hands on those records let us get inside the artists' heads; I remember realizing that the spacey, random Turtles song De La Soul sampled for

"Transmitting Live From Mars" (and got sued over) came right after the well-known breakbeat track on the Turtles LP, and imagining the Plugs not bothering to get up and lift the needle after it ended and inadvertently discovering the joint that followed, *hey this shit is actually kinda cool...* I have no idea whether than actually happened, but I sure felt like it did, and that feeling meant something.

What was I talking about again? Oh, yeah. Process, motherfucker. Process. When cats get the opportunity to talk craft, it's amazing what happens. Not only does the story of a record fill out with context and color and anecdote, but assumptions get put to the test. That's especially important in hip-hop, a music that has born the weight of condescension and bogus suppositions about who makes it and how and why and what their influences are since the day it was born. Does it disrupt lazy, received notions of what was going on in New York City in the early nineties to learn that the mad-faced, hoarse-throated, Queens-bred arena-rap quartet known as Onyx recorded their debut platter with the help of a "secret weapon" called LSD, as the last volume of *Check the Technique* reveals?

You're fucking right it does.

Not only do we tend to put artists on a pedestal, we also like to put that pedestal in a box. First we decide who's great, then we decide *when* they were great. It doesn't matter that Louis Armstrong was playing a better trumpet in the '50s than he was in the '20s, or that GZA is a more fully realized, more insightful MC right now than he was on *Liquid Swords*; the box is the box. We stuff the box with trinkets, as if it were the tomb of an Egyptian pharaoh, and then we seal it up. Meanwhile, the artist inside is like, "Hey, this isn't even my stuff. Who told you I was a P-Funk fan? Who told you I was being ironic when I sampled Steely Dan? I fucking love Steely Dan, man! Where's my Steely Dan records? You know, you could have just *asked* me. This is supposed to be *my box*. Also, it's hard to breathe in here."

I'm not suggesting you read *Check the Technique Volume 2* because we need to recalibrate the relationship between product and process, or as a way of supporting the efforts of hip-hop's luminaries to tell their own stories. I'm not suggesting you read it at all – I don't need to, because it's impossible not to tear through this book obsessively, to the detriment of your job and relationship and personal hygiene, if you're a hip-hop junkie. You'll probably read it a few times, if one of your so-called friends doesn't steal it from you first. It's also going to make you pull out some music you haven't listened to in a while, or curse yourself for losing certain LPs the last time you moved, or make you shake your head in astonishment and shame that you've somehow managed to spend this long on the planet without ever hearing the whole ED O.G *Life Of A Kid In The Ghetto* album (yeah, I'm from Boston).

More than that, though, this massive tome my dude Brian Coleman has labored so lovingly to put together is going to add another dimension to your relationship to a bunch of records that already changed your life. And my life. And life in general.

Adam Mansbach is the author of the #1 *New York Times* bestseller *Go the Fuck to Sleep,* which has been translated into forty languages and was *Time* magazine's 2011 "Thing of the Year." His other books include the novels *The Dead Run*, *Rage is Back, Angry Black White Boy,* and the California Book Award-winning *The End of the* Jews. He also wrote the multiple award-winning campaign video "Wake the Fuck Up," starring Samuel L. Jackson. His work has appeared in *The New Yorker, New York Times Book Review, Esquire, The Believer*, and on National Public Radio's *All Things Considered.*

PREFACE

Hello, dear reader.

If you are already part of the *Rakim Told Me* and *Check the Technique* family as a returning customer, welcome back!

And if you are new to our little neck of the hip-hop woods, please come in. You are amongst friends.

As for any guidance you might need regarding what you are about to encounter, it's really pretty simple. You are on the verge of learning many of the things you always wondered about your favorite hip-hop albums. I asked dozens of talented artists about a whole bunch of interesting stuff, so that you didn't have to. You are welcome.

If I missed anything, please feel free ask them yourself, the next time you run into them at one of their concerts, on the street, or at the grocery store. Musicians love to talk about their triumphs. And even, on occasion, their tribulations. Both are revealed here.

As with all volumes in this series, I have had my own set of triumphs – hella enjoyable and engaging interviews – and difficulties – managers, publicists and assorted handlers who blocked me from their artists. Luckily, the triumphs always win. As I have said before: if an artist you love isn't featured in a chapter from one of my books, you can safely assume that it's not for a lack of trying on my end. If you run into Queen Latifah or Dr. Dre at the Whole Foods checkout line, definitely ask them what's up.

I am very proud of the work I have put into the pages you are about to read – prouder than I am of either of my two previous books combined (and that is saying a lot). There are deeper interviews and artistic insights that are even more personal than in chapters past. And you will definitely notice that there are quite a few images that have been included, to help the chapters go down smoother than ever before.

Timeframe-wise, my starting point with these 25 albums runs earlier than in previous editions (beginning with 1981's *Wild Style Breakbeats*) and book-ends with *relatively* contemporary work, pushing up through Mos Def's & Talib Kweli's *Are Black Star* and The Coup's *Steal This Album*, from the late '90s.

This is likely to be my last edition in the series, because I feel that I have put a pretty firm stake in the ground when it comes to creating "invisible liner notes" for hip-hop albums. Perhaps the next generation will add to the fact-finding and discussions, and beat my ass in the process. I would love nothing more than to see that happen.

But enough of my rambling, because these books are definitely not about me. They are about the beauty and the triumph of hip-hop music and culture; and the artists, record label owners and other assorted wild, weird and wonderful people who ushered the artform from Sedgwick & Cedar to where it stands today. The artists in these chapters are true American geniuses, who gave the middle finger to what was expected of them, and carved out their own world instead – a world that many of us can't dream of living without.

Keep digging, my friends, and enjoy *Check the Technique Volume 2.*

Brian Coleman
Boston or thereabouts
June 2014
www.BrianColemanBooks.com

TABLE OF CONTENTS

i ***Foreword***
v ***Preface***
1 **3rd Bass** *The Cactus Album*
32 **The Beatnuts** *Intoxicated Demons: The EP*
42 **Black Sheep** *A Wolf In Sheep's Clothing*
56 **Company Flow** *Funcrusher Plus*
91 **The Coup** *Steal This Album*
114 **Diamond and the Psychotic Neurotics** *Stunts, Blunts & Hip Hop*
125 **DJ Jazzy Jeff & The Fresh Prince** *He's The DJ, I'm The Rapper*
156 **Dr. Octagon** *Dr. Octagonecologyst*
181 **ED O.G & Da Bulldogs** *Life Of A Kid In The Ghetto*
211 **Gravediggaz** *Niggamortis [*aka *6 Feet Deep]*
234 **Ice Cube** *AmeriKKKa's Most Wanted & Kill At Will*
263 **Jeru The Damaja** *The Sun Rises In The East*
278 **KMD** *Black Bastards*
303 **Kool G Rap & DJ Polo** *Wanted: Dead Or Alive*

321 **Kwamé The Boy Genius** *Featuring A New Beginning*
332 **Lord Finesse & DJ Mike Smooth** *Funky Technician*
344 **Mantronix** *The Album*
362 **Masta Ace Incorporated** *SlaughtaHouse*
374 **Mos Def & Talib Kweli** *Are Black Star*
407 **Naughty By Nature** *Naughty By Nature*
419 **Nice & Smooth** *Ain't A Damn Thing Changed*
434 **[Chef] Raekwon** *Only Built 4 Cuban Linx...*
444 **Smif-N-Wessun** *Dah Shinin'*
469 **Stetsasonic** *In Full Gear*
497 **Various** *Wild Style Breakbeats*
511 ***Shout Outs***
517 ***Index***

3RD BASS

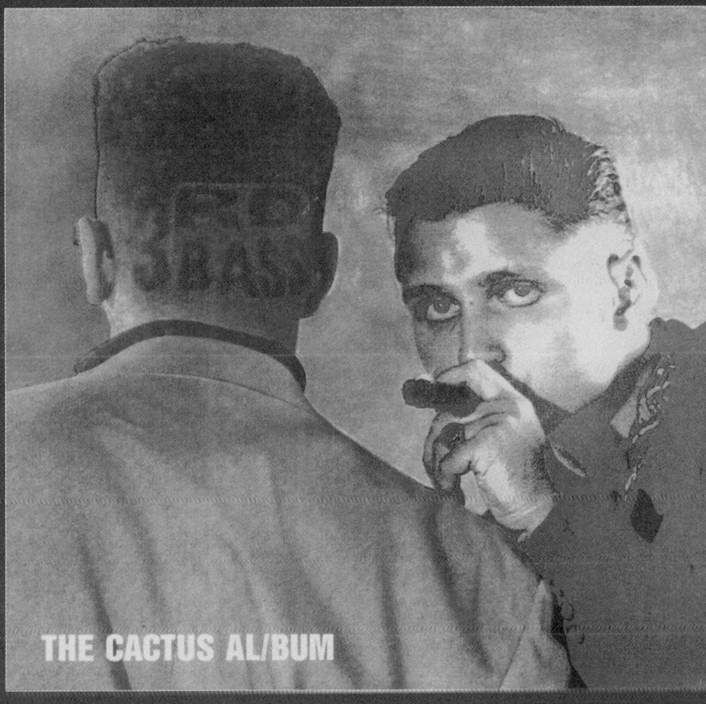

The Cactus Album
Def Jam / CBS, 1989

"It's fun for me to listen to that record, even to this day. It sounds like a bunch of kids having a good time on vinyl to me."

– MC Serch

When the New York duo 3rd Bass – MC Serch [Michael Berrin] and Prime Minister Pete Nice [Peter Nash] – burst onto the national scene in 1989 with the Def Jam single "Steppin' To The A.M.," hip-hop fans jumped on a great, Bomb Squad-produced song by what was assuredly a "hot-off-the-presses" new group. But that wasn't *quite* the case.

Serch and Pete may have been a revelation to the public at large, but they definitely weren't new to those in the hip-hop game, especially in New York. In fact, the release of their first single and the gold album that followed was the result of many years of ups, downs, odd jobs, great music, bad deals and a whole lot more.

The two MCs first met in 1987, but each had been working on his craft for years before that. Serch was born and raised in Far Rockaway, Queens. He explains the household of his youth: "My mom, sister and brother are all music fans, so there was always music in our house. From funk to rock, folk and traditional Jewish songs."

He continues, "I had a talent for poetry from an early age, and my middle school friends in Far Rockaway turned me on to these tapes of guys rhyming. The earliest tape I remember was the Kango Crew [featuring future rap stars Slick Rick and Dana Dane] and a group out of Brooklyn called The Eternal Force. The first time I ever saw hip-hop live was 1981, the Kango Crew in the basement of the High School of Music & Art [in Harlem]. These were the guys on my tapes and they were playing at my high school, doing those skits live. It was an amazing thing to see. I heard 'La Di Da Di' long before it was on record."

Serch, whose love of hip-hop grew throughout the early '80s, graduated from LaGuardia High School of Music & Art and Performing Arts' inaugural class in 1985. His specialty was Singing and Voice.

Ironically, his voice almost landed him on the very opposite end of the music spectrum from where he ended up. He says, "I got offered a Voice scholarship, Italian Opera to be specific, from the St. Louis School of Music. My mom figured that's what I would do, of course. But I was so enthralled with B-Boy culture and everything about it, I just couldn't imagine going there. Being an opera singer was the last thing I wanted to do. I just happened to have a beautiful voice. But I didn't want to do any of that shit."

"So, on my 18th birthday I told my mom that I wasn't going to take the scholarship and wasn't going to college," he explains. "I said I was going to be a rapper. And she said, 'What do you mean? You're going to wrap gifts?'" Serch's mother agreed to let him live under her roof until he turned 21, and at that moment the "hurry up and get a record deal" clock began ticking.

Serch's older brother Henry Blaukopf was in the music business – working at the Stratford One-Stop distributor – and although he got Serch an early meeting with Steve Plotnicki of Profile Records, the confident young MC generally made his own luck. He met producer Tony D [Anthony Dick, not to be confused with the late, New Jersey-based producer Tony D who produced the Poor Righteous Teachers] and, through a great deal of persistence, got a "try out."

"I called Tony for six months, every day," Serch recalls, with a laugh. "And one night in April of 1986 he said I should come over to his studio. I went to Sea Gate, at the tail end of Coney Island. When I walked in, Grandmaster Dee from Whodini and Jam Master Jay from Run-DMC were sitting there. Tony had me under a light-bulb, they were all watching me, and he said, 'OK, rap.' And I did. After I was done, Jam Master Jay was silent for a minute, and then he said, 'If white boys start rhyming like that, we're all finished!' They all wanted me to work with them. Tony gave me a contract and I signed it."

He adds, in a lament often heard from old-schoolers: "It was a really bad deal."

The deal resulted in his first single, "Melissa," which came out in 1986 on Warlock Records. It was produced, of course, by "Grand Wiz" Tony D. "I was really influenced by Slick Rick, I totally bit his style," Serch admits today. "The single was a brick, but I worked really hard promoting it. I was a white boy who danced, so I still got a lot of shows." He says he opened for artists like Run-DMC and Whodini, among others, in New York and even outside of the city.

As a result of the poor sales of Serch's debut, Warlock released him from his contract with the label. For his next move, Serch partnered with Tony D, put up $1,500 of his mother's money and they started the Idlers label, which was distributed by Warlock *[Author's note: The label would go on to put out artists including the Jungle Brothers, Royal House and J.V.C. Force, under Tony D's watch, rather than Serch's].*

According to Serch, there was more bad news to accompany his "bad deal" with Tony: "Tony owned everything with Idlers. I was supposedly part-owner, but I didn't actually own anything."

The MC's second time on wax – this time billed as "McSerch" – arrived in 1987 on Idlers: "Hey Boy!" with the provocatively-titled B-side, "Beware of the Death." This time, the buzz around Serch was gaining more of a foothold. He recalls, "The record did well and word was getting out there that I was a battle MC. I was doing shows and was even doing promos for Red Alert [for the DJ's hugely-popular weekend hip-hop show on Kiss 98.7 FM]."

He continues, "But I was still working three jobs." He says that, among other gigs, he was a bus driver for Yeshiva Jewish children in the mornings and evenings; and was driving a truck for the USDA, delivering milk and food to schools and community centers.

Serch caught another break in the summer of 1987 at the second New Music Seminar MC Battle, which was judged by Red Alert, UTFO's Doctor Ice and Marley Marl. In front of 1,000 people, including more industry big wigs than you could count (in addition to future rhyme partner Pete Nice), he battled and – according to Serch – came in second by a very slim margin.

Serch also simultaneously ruffled feathers and won over new followers by attacking legendary WBLS "Rap Attack" DJ Mr. Magic, after Magic tried to grab the mic from him. He remembers, "I started calling him 'Mr. Tragic' and the radio station 'BL-Fess.' I said Magic was a cokehead. The crowd was going crazy."

One influential audience member in attendance, standing on the side of the stage, was Def Jam and RUSH Artist Management head honcho Russell Simmons. The two had run into each other at various clubs in the past, but weren't close. Nevertheless, Serch recounts that when he walked off stage, "Russell rubbed my shoulders and said, 'If anyone asks you, tell them you're signed to Def Jam.' He told me to come to the office the next day and we'd do all the paperwork."

But there was one problem: "Tony D pretty much owned me at that point. So I had to get away from him."

According to Serch, as per the contract he signed with Tony, it was possible to extricate himself by sending an official severance letter to a Post Office box that Tony rarely used. Serch did this and says that, after a couple months, was free and clear thanks to the cost of a postage stamp. Crisis averted.

At first, Serch – who, according to Pete Nice, didn't officially sign his RUSH contract until June, 1988, a month before Pete – was in Simmons' RUSH Artist Management camp instead of being signed to Def Jam *[Author's note: Some people were both, some were only one of the two; Run-DMC was an example of the latter].* Russell's right-hand-man, Lyor Cohen, set Serch up with a producer named Sam Sever [Sam Citrin], who was a genius drum programmer, known primarily for his involvement with Mantronix as well as programming and writing work on Run-DMC's "Is It Live," from their 1986 smash *Raising Hell.*

One other early player in the 3rd Bass story was RUSH employee Dante Ross, who would go on to later renown as a forward-thinking A & R executive at Tommy Boy and Elektra. Ross was one of the liaisons between artists and producers at RUSH, including Sam and Serch.

Serch recalls, "At first, I was working with Sam at his studio on Canal Street in Manhattan. We were doing some OK songs together, they weren't great. Then one day Sam called me and said, 'Def Jam signed another white kid from Queens *[Author's note: Technically Pete was also signed to RUSH Artist Management at the time].* His beats are crazy. I think you guys should work together.'"

That white kid from Queens was none other than Pete Nice, and it turns out that the two talented MCs had each been doing a bit of "parallel pathing" in the hip-hop world over the past half-decade, unbeknownst to the other. According to Pete, he and Serch had actually already met, briefly, in late 1986 or early '87, at the Latin Quarter, introduced by mutual friend Blake Lethem. Nevertheless, up until that point they hadn't even had a real conversation.

Going back many years before his first meeting with Serch, Pete explains: "My only music endeavor prior to hip-hop was trying to play bass saxophone in the third grade." He was born in Queens, moved to Brooklyn, and then spent his teens in Floral Park, New York ("Technically Long Island, near Belmont Racetrack," he says). His father was a Physical Education teacher, Athletic Director and basketball coach at Bishop Ford Central Catholic High School in Brooklyn, which is where Pete attended. "I lived in Floral Park during high school, but I probably spent more time in Brooklyn," Pete explains.

Pete remembers, "In 1977, I was 10 and my father would coach these teams at the Empire State Games in Syracuse, and he'd have all the best players in New York City on his team. I was the ball-boy, and I would hang out with the players and the younger coaches. They had all the early hip-hop tapes. As a 10 year-old white kid, I had amazing access."

Pete continues, "When I was a junior in high school, one of the guys I went to school with was Jazzy from the group Whistle, before Whistle had started. Kangol Kid from UTFO was his cousin, so we'd get UTFO music before it was out. And I formed a group with a couple other guys, we were called Sin Qua Non, which means 'The Utmost' in Latin *[Author's note: I am not scholarly enough to verify this myself, but the correct Latin for "An indispensable or essential condition, element or factor" is spelled "Sine Qua Non," so Pete's group name was a take on that].* It was just saying rhymes and banging out beats on the lunchroom table type of stuff. It was me, Buddah B, Fresh Fred and Kibwe K."

After Pete graduated, he began putting his amateur experiences in hip-hop – including being a record seeker – to tape, making rough demos. According to him, "From age 10 to 15 I'd listen to classic rock groups, but I was pretty much all hip-hop. Although rock music influenced some of my sampling."

Through a mutual friend from Bed-Stuy in Brooklyn who was in Sin Qua Non, Pete also met Lumumba Carson, son of Brooklyn activist and Black Nationalist leader Sonny Carson, who would later be known as Professor X from X-Clan. As many hip-hop fans know, years before X-Clan's emergence, Lumumba was active as a manager for various hip-hop artists in the mid-to-late-'80s, as well as playing an important managerial and booking role at Manhattan's famed Latin Quarter club.

Pete's Sin Qua group-mates left NYC for college in the mid-'80s, and Pete stayed local – enrolling at prestigious Columbia University. By default, he also became a solo artist. After initially managing Sin Qua Non, Lumumba began managing Pete solo. Pete remembers, "Lumumba was representing Just-Ice, Stetsasonic and Positive K back while the Latin Quarter was going on. He used to drive us to the LQ in his Aerostar, and afterwards they'd drop me off at like five in the morning at Johnson Hall at Columbia."

Although the Prime Minister was meeting a lot of artists and had backstage access at the Latin Quarter, according to him, "By sophomore year in college [fall 1986 – spring 1987], Lumumba wasn't getting anything done and I wasn't getting into the studio. So I basically told him that I was exploring other options and if something came up, I was going to jet."

During his early college years, Pete had met another figure who would strengthen his link with MC Serch: graffiti writer and MC Blake Lethem, aka Lord Scotch, aka Vanilla B *[Author's note: For literary fans, Blake is also novelist Jonathan Lethem's younger brother].* Pete met Blake through their friend Mark Pearson – who would later road-manage 3rd Bass – and Blake started visiting both of them at Columbia. They became quick comrades and soon enough had started an informal group called The Servin' Generals. Pete and Blake MCed, and Blake's friend Shameek would beatbox.

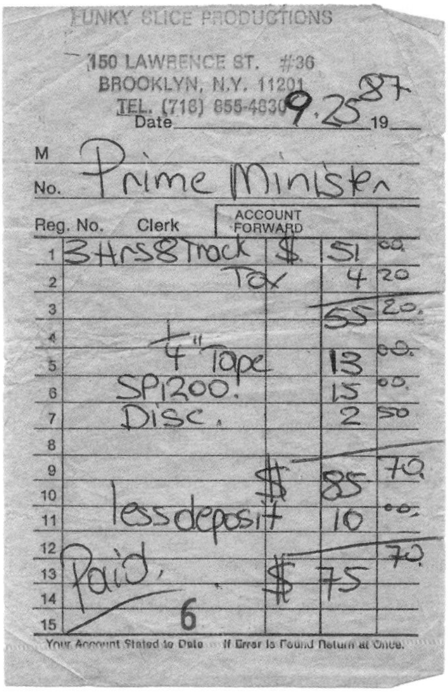
FUNKY SLICE PRODUCTIONS
150 LAWRENCE ST. #36
BROOKLYN, N.Y. 11201
TEL. (718) 855-4830
Date 9.25 19 87
M No. Prime Minister

Reg. No.	Clerk	Account Forward		
1	3 Hrs 8 Track	$	51	00
2	Tax		4	20
3			55	20
4				
5	4" Tape		13	00
6	SP1200		15	00
7	Disc		2	50
8				
9				
10		$	85	70
11	less deposit		10	00
12				
13	Paid	$	75	70
14				
15	6			

Your Account Stated to Date If Error Is Found Return at Once.

Funky Slice Studios bill for Servin' Generals sessions, September 1987.
Courtesy of Pete Nice.

Serch would eventually meet Blake, but at first he was more of an admirer from afar. He explains, "Blake truly was the original white rapper. He went to the High School of the Performing Arts and rhymed with the Kango Crew. To be honest, he was the main reason that I thought I could make it as a rapper, because he was slick and because he just dove in and did it. I'm still friends with Blake to this day. Rap to him was never about getting famous. When he rapped, he didn't care if it was being recorded. It was just part of the culture he came up in."

Things with The Servin' Generals were actually looking pretty good in 1987. Pete recalls, "We booked studio time at Funky Slice Studios in Brooklyn and made a demo. The guys who managed Kid 'N Play, Rich and Lenny, had a production company called Richlen Productions, and they loved us. They were going to put us together with Hurby Luv Bug [the hit-maker known for successes with Salt 'N Pepa, Kid 'N Play and Dana Dane]."

Pre-Funky Slice, Pete explains where he was as a producer: "The extent of our production for Servin' Generals was pretty basic. One of my roommates had a boom box with a turntable in it. You could set it up so that you could rhyme over records, and then record that onto cassette. So it was really just pause tapes, if you get right down to it. Back then I was definitely more of an MC. I was just fucking around when it came to production."

In 1986 and for part of 1987, Pete also did a radio show on Columbia's WKCR, a station later known to the hip-hop world thanks to Stretch Armstrong's and Bobbito

Garcia's 1990s show. Pete says, "By early 1988, when me and Serch started working together, I had gotten kicked off the air at KCR. I was on for about a year-and-a-half. All these hard-rocks were coming in to hang out, and equipment would go missing. The music director liked the show, but we got treated badly by the rest of the station. We were on from midnight to two or three A.M. It was a unique show, we definitely paved the way for Stretch & Bobbito. Clark Kent was our DJ, Blake introduced me to him. And when he would go on tour with Dana Dane, Daddy Rich [3rd Bass' future DJ] would sub for him."

As things continued to move forward in 1987 for Pete and his Generals crew, the fates of hip-hop threw a wrench in the works. Pete explains, "We were all set, contracts were signed with Richlen. But then, within a three-week period, Shameek held up a subway car with some other kid from the projects. And then Blake disappears. Like, disappears off the face of the Earth. So, boom, I was solo again."

The links between Serch and Pete continued to grow during that era as well. This wasn't surprising, since they were both non-gimmicky white rappers with talent: a notable anomaly in the mid-1980s.

Pete explains, "Around the time of the Servin' Generals, I had done a demo song called 'Das Nachleben,' which a professor of mine said meant 'the afterlife' in German. There was an earlier version of that, before the song even had a title, done as a pause-tape over Sweet Tee's 'It's My Beat,' with me and Blake. I remember he ended one verse saying, 'Doomed to failure, you did not succeed / In the garden of rap, you're just a dick-weed!' Then I did another version after that, with just me."

"My roommate SAKE knew Dante Ross and Dante liked that solo demo I did," Pete continues. "So, Dante was hanging out with both me and Serch at the same time, just separately. Serch was ahead of me at RUSH and was already in the studio with Sam Sever. But Dante was definitely important in introducing us. The old story that Russell and Lyor put me and Serch together is the furthest thing from what actually happened."

Through both Sam Sever and Dante Ross, then, a "Pete meets Serch" collision was bound to happen. And, on a night in late 1987, it did.

Pete recalls, "I was on my own at Chung King Studios and had laid down the original version of 'Wordz Of Wizdom.' Then I called Sam and asked him if he wanted to come in and help me out with it. So he did. I might have asked Dante if it was cool if I called Sam, but I already knew Sam, I had been introduced to him separately. Sam liked the track and then he got involved. He played it for Serch and that was really how it all began."

Serch says, "'Wordz Of Wizdom' was the first track that we all worked on together. When I heard the track that he and Sam had been working on, I lost it. I was like, '*That's* the sound! That's what I need to be doing.' I loved Pete's verse. So I started writing my verse, and we all went in to Chung King the next day to record it."

For many reasons, it made a lot of sense for Pete and Serch to join up. First of all, neither of them had yet lit the world on fire as a solo artist. Secondly, in addition to being a heady MC on the same level as Serch, Pete had grown to be a much better producer by late 1987. With the addition of Sam Sever – who also DJed – they had everything they needed to be a self-contained unit.

And there was also the "White MC" thing, which can't be ignored in the equation. Pete says, "We honestly never gravitated towards each other because we were white, it's just the way things worked out. We never really thought about it that much. All my other groups were with black guys."

But clearly, Russell Simmons, who had seen an incredible amount of success with the Beastie Boys, was salivating at the idea of another white rap group.

First, though, they would have to get by a tough opponent: Roz.

Pete recalls, "I remember being in Sam's apartment and Sam had just pitched the idea [of Pete, Serch and Sam working together, as a group] to Serch. Serch was there with his mother Roz, who was an old Vaudeville performer. She said, 'I don't know, I think Michael should be a soloist.' It was hysterical. So, the first person we needed to get by was her. Luckily, we did [laughs]."

As things were now taking shape, the group – calling themselves 3 The Hard Way, with Sam as their DJ – finished their first demo, which included "Wordz Of Wizdom," "Bouncy Bass" [which would later be re-named "Soul In The Hole"] and "Product Of The Environment."

Although they were part of the Russell Simmons umbrella, Russell and Lyor chose to shop the group to other labels, with the understanding that Def Jam would be their back-up. "Honestly, I never knew why Lyor was shopping us to other labels if Russell said we were supposed to be on Def Jam," Serch says. "I never got a clear answer on that."

They were pitched to Arista, A & M – who, according to Serch, passed because they said there was already one white rap group in the world: the Beastie Boys – and to Dante Ross, who was now at Tommy Boy Records. The result: no worthy offers.

Although group members say that the "White MC" specter wasn't a big deal to them, it apparently was to the industry in 1988. Especially in relation to one group who would soon be put in 3rd Bass' cross-hairs: The Beasties.

Pete says, "Honestly, the mere existence of [The Beastie Boys' 1986 album] *Licensed To Ill* held us back for at least two years. After the success of that record, no one knew how to deal with us. Then The White Boys came along [who released 1988's *On A Mission* on Polygram, which featured future in-demand producer T-Ray]. All of that put up a road-block."

"A & R guys wanted the next Beastie Boys, and we weren't them," Pete continues. "Overall, we just felt like they got into hip-hop on a whim, because they were a punk band first. Looking back on it, I really didn't hold that much against them, but we just went after them [on the song 'Sons of 3rd Bass']. We pretty much decimated them on that one [laughs]."

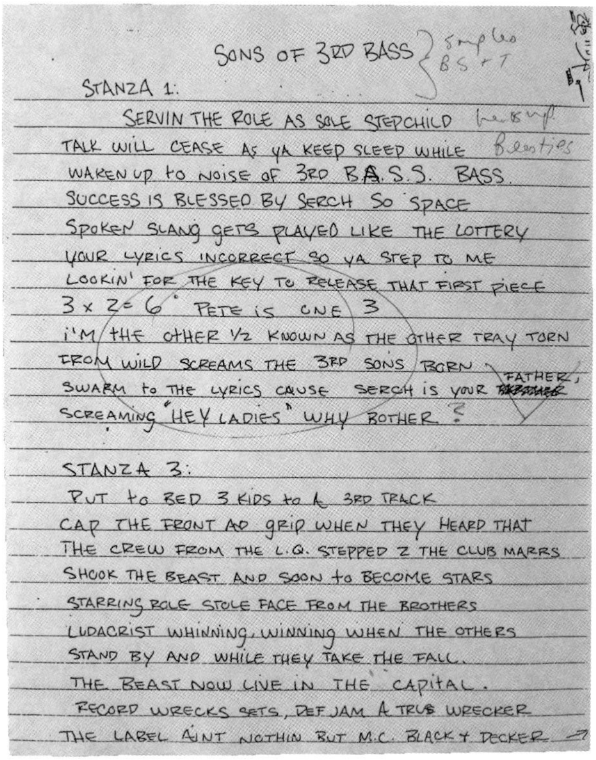
SONS OF 3RD BASS

STANZA 1:

SERVIN THE ROLE AS SOLE STEPCHILD
TALK WILL CEASE AS YA KEEP SLEEP WHILE
WAKEN UP TO NOISE OF 3RD B.A.S.S. BASS
SUCCESS IS BLESSED BY SERCH SO SPACE
SPOKEN SLANG GETS PLAYED LIKE THE LOTTERY
YOUR LYRICS INCORRECT SO YA STEP TO ME
LOOKIN' FOR THE KEY TO RELEASE THAT FIRST PIECE
3 x 2 = 6 PETE IS ONE 3
I'M THE OTHER 1/2 KNOWN AS THE OTHER TRAY TORN
FROM WILD SCREAMS THE 3RD SONS BORN
SWARM TO THE LYRICS CAUSE SERCH IS YOUR FATHER,
SCREAMING "HEY LADIES" WHY BOTHER ?

STANZA 3:

PUT TO BED 3 KIDS TO A 3RD TRACK
CAP THE FRONT AND GRIP WHEN THEY HEARD THAT
THE CREW FROM THE L.Q. STEPPED 2 THE CLUB MARRS
SHOOK THE BEAST AND SOON TO BECOME STARS
STARRING ROLE STOLE FACE FROM THE BROTHERS
LUDACRIST WHINING, WINNING WHEN THE OTHERS
STAND BY AND WHILE THEY TAKE THE FALL.
THE BEAST NOW LIVE IN THE CAPITAL.
RECORD WRECKS SETS, DEF JAM A TRUE WRECKER
THE LABEL AINT NOTHIN BUT M.C. BLACK & DECKER

MC Serch's hand-written final lyrics for "Sons of 3rd Bass."
Courtesy of the Adler Hip-Hop Archives / Cornell University Hip-Hop Collection.

"I agree with Pete, the success of the Beastie Boys really did put up hurdles for us," Serch says. "Anytime we wanted to get signed, people just didn't understand our group thing. They either wanted Beasties sound-alikes, or they didn't want to sign us because people would *think* it was a Beasties sound-alike group."

And so, Serch says, "Putting us on Def Jam was kind of by default, after they shopped us to all the other spots."

"While all the shopping and label stuff was going on, we were still recording a lot," Serch explains. "By the time the album came out in the fall of 1989, some of those songs were two years old. To be honest, we were pretty frustrated waiting around, and there were times that we would drive Russell and Lyor crazy."

Industry frustrations aside, all three group members were gaining momentum as they continued to work together. Serch recalls, "It was such a great, natural progression while we were doing those tracks. When I started working with Sam, I really found my voice as an MC. And when I started working with Pete, I was battling him on tracks, and wanting to be the better MC on all of them. He did the same. It was incredible to be competitive like that."

He adds, provocatively, "I would have been wack if it hadn't have been for 3rd Bass. I really believe that. The combo, the dynamic, it helped me so much. I never saw either me or Pete being the 'lead MC.' We were equal. One of us wasn't more of an MC than the other. That was our strength."

Pete adds, "We would mix it up so that it wasn't always the same order with our rhymes. Sometimes it was tag-team, sometimes it was verse-by-verse. Sometimes we'd bring other artists in. To be honest, there were times that I might be first on a track because Serch didn't show up in the studio on time [laughs]. It was only thought-out inasmuch as we didn't want it to always be the same way each time."

Although Sam Sever was the group's earliest DJ, he soon voiced a desire to stay in the studio and behind-the-scenes, so they went through two early deck-minders before landing on DJ Daddy Rich [Richard Lawson, aka DJ Richie Rich].

"First we got DJ White Nite," says Serch. "He was out of Nashville. But that didn't work out. He ended up getting homesick and was also kinda wack. Then we had DJ Word for a minute, but that didn't last either."

Serch continues, "Then Clark Kent, who had DJed for Pete's radio show, said that he had our guy: Richie Rich. Rich wasn't a part of the making of *The Cactus Album*, he came in as a tour DJ after the album was made. All the cuts on *The Cactus* were done by Sam. Rich didn't record with us until our second album [*Derelicts Of Dialect*]. Rich was in the album photos because Sam didn't want to be a part of the actual group by the time we got to 1989. He wanted to be a producer, and also wanted to work with other artists, since he had just gotten a big publishing deal with Def Jam."

Pete says, "Daddy Rich was going to school at Farmingdale [State College, called SUNY College of Technology at Farmingdale at the time], and I had tried to get him as our DJ from the beginning. But he wasn't in town. So after Nite and Word didn't work out, I said, 'Rich, you've *gotta* be our DJ.' And he was in. The album was already out by then. Daddy Rich is in the 'Steppin To The A.M.' video."

Pete thinks that Rich actually did a couple of the cuts on the album, aside from DJ White Nite, although he's not 100% sure. Pete explains, "Sam could cut, but he wasn't a show DJ. I wasn't ever on the decks, I never messed with that."

DJ Daddy Rich – a "pupil" of DJ Clark Kent, whom Clark often referred to as his nephew even though they are not related by blood – recalls: "I first met Pete on his radio show in 1987, right after I graduated high school. And then me and Pete worked on demos together at Funky Slice in Brooklyn. That was just us as a duo, not with Blake. It was our own shit. We didn't have a name or anything."

DJ Daddy Rich at work.
Photo courtesy of Pete Nice.

Rich continues, "I took a year off in-between high school and college, I got to Farmingdale in the fall of 1988. I was doing a lot of different stuff at the time, including DJing some tour dates for Raheem out of Texas [his album, *The Vigilante*, came out on A & M / Rap-A-Lot in 1988]. When Pete called me to be 3rd Bass' DJ it wasn't a tough decision to leave school, it was a no-brainer. I knew I could go back later, which I eventually did. I think the first show we all did together was at Wesleyan University. Then we did 'Showtime At The Apollo,' got on the tour bus and we were off." He estimates that this was the fall of 1989.

Rich says that he doesn't believe DJ Word did any cuts on *The Cactus Album*, and that he was only aware of Nite as their only other DJ before Rich arrived. He also mentions that Serch knew about his capabilities on the decks before they officially worked together: Serch judged the 1989 New Music Seminar DJ Battle For World Supremacy, and Rich was a competitor.

Overall, Rich states, "I didn't really do any cuts on *Cactus*. Maybe a little work on two or three songs at the very end. It was really already made by the time I got involved. I always thought that Nite did the cuts on the record, and I guess Sam did some as well. I was involved on the remixes for the *Cactus* [*The Cactus Collection* EP, from 1990] and then everything after that."

According to Pete and Serch, most of *The Cactus Album* was recorded at New York's Chung King Studios, and mostly with their go-to engineer, Kevin Reynolds. "We were there in the studio all the time, we lived in Chung King," explains Serch. "Sam programmed all the beats *[Author's note: Using drum machines and manipulating drum samples on a machine like an Akai MPC-60 or Emu SP-1200]*, pretty much. He was 50% of the music, without question. We all contributed, but our contributions wouldn't have been as impactful without Sam. Sometimes Pete would bring in a sample, and Sam would chop it and program everything else around it."

Pete explains, "At the time, I didn't program beats, and Sam was really strong at that. He was an all-around producer, I just had concepts, sounds and basslines that I wanted to use. It was great to work with Sam. Serch would bring ideas, too. Me and Sam had a lot of late nights at the studio, we collaborated really well." Pete says he bought his own SP-1200 sampler midway through the recording of *The Cactus Album*, so he could work on producing at home.

Pete Nice and Sam Sever at Chung King Studios.
Photo courtesy of Pete Nice.

Serch says, "With our recording [budget, from Def Jam], we could stay in the studio as long as we wanted, until we got it right. We could spend 18 hours on a track in a day if we wanted to."

In addition to working in the studio in 1988, 3rd Bass were also performing in the city here and there, building a fanbase as well as their camaraderie on-stage. Serch had been dancing for many years, and the group's live performances were always of utmost importance to him. He explains, "For me, being dope on stage was even more important than being dope on record. I always wanted to spend as much time as I could in rehearsals, getting the show tight. Pete had a relatively easy part in the show, he basically had to hold down the stage and have the swagger."

Serch adds, "My thing was more about the dancing and choreography. When we went on the first U.S. headlining tour, we rehearsed for almost two months. I'm not sure if that was lot more than our peers or not, I didn't care. Public Enemy put a lot of time into their live show, and Chuck D was my inspiration and my mentor. I learned a lot from how they put their show together."

Pete recalls: "We really were a good live group. You just couldn't hold Serch back. We did 'Showtime at the Apollo' around the time of the album, obviously a tougher crowd. It was an excellent show, but Serch was very critical of himself. If there weren't panties flying, he would get so mad!"

As for albums that inspired what the trio of Pete, Serch and Sam were doing, Serch explains, "We really just wanted to make a great album. But I think we expanded our creativity because of De La Soul. They made us want to make a more conceptual album. I always felt like I was an extension of the Native Tongues, even if I wasn't officially in there. I wanted our album to have the organic feel of [De La's] *3 Feet High and Rising*. I wanted it to be a cohesive piece of music."

Pete concurs about the De La influence, and raises Serch a Public Enemy. "We were influenced by De La's interludes a lot," he says. "Going on the road with Chuck D and getting to know him also taught us important things, like being aware of the length of each side of the cassette."

3rd Bass with Prince Paul.
Photo courtesy of Pete Nice.

Serch says, "I think that literally everything that we recorded ended up on the album. We weren't very good at editing ourselves. Faith Newman was our A & R [for Def Jam] and she was a great sounding-board, but we were pretty much A & R-ing ourselves. In fact, Faith at one point mentioned that we should edit it down. But we weren't really listening."

Pete recalls, "We were recording for most of 1988, almost always in Chung King, but

The title "Producer / MC" should never be taken lightly in hip-hop. Most sensible artists do one or the other. Because, quite honestly, it's not easy to be impressive at both. Queens duo The Beatnuts – Psycho Les and JuJu – are both producers first, but they also hold their own on the mic. Their 1993 debut, *Intoxicated Demons*, still stands as one of the more influential musical platters of that era, especially amongst their production peers and beat-digging fans.

JuJu [Jerry Tineo] is a proud, born-and-bred son of Corona, Queens. Hip-hop became an obsession early for him, as he recalls: "I started rhymin' when I was just a shorty, like when Kurtis Blow was out. I was too young to have money for turntables, so I used to just be an MC. Then when I was 14, my sister bought me some turntables and things changed."

JuJu and Les met in their early high school years, through a mutual friend named Moe (aka DJ Loco Moe), who lived in Les' building and went to high school with JuJu. They knew each other, but weren't tight. JuJu says, "Through high school, Les and I weren't really in contact that much. Moe was really the guy I was friends with. Les didn't come into the picture until he started hearing my name on the radio with the Jungle Brothers. At that point he called me to find out what I had going on."

Psycho Les.
Photo © Linda Covello, www.lindacovellophotography.com.

Psycho Les [Lester Fernandez] was born in the Bronx and moved to Jackson Heights, Queens around age 10. He was a DJ first, and his turntable work was the perfect precursor for producing. He explains, "I started out DJing, and once sampling came in, I started producing. I used to buy records for the breaks, and once sampling came in, it let me take all the breaks I had been DJing with to another level. I used to rap, too, but not in public. Mostly just to myself."

Les went to high school and grew into music production with DJ Rob Swift [Robert Aguilar], who in the '90s worked with Akinyele and rose to further prominence as a member of the X-Men / X-Ecutioners turntablist crew. The two friends worked on music together starting in the late '80s, including production on a single for a Philly-based MC named J.M.D. The project was called 2*2*4 [2 Bad 2 Be 4 Real] and they released the "Ill Tempo" single on MADD Records in 1988. As Swift explains, "Les was the 'Prince Paul' [producer] of the group. I was the DJ."

As many old-school fans know, in the late '80s, the Jungle Brothers' extended family was a breeding ground for talented hip-hop stars of the future, including Q-Tip from A Tribe Called Quest and Brother J of X-Clan. JuJu was in the mix as well. He didn't get the shine that other rising rappers in the crew got, but knowing Mike G and Afrika Baby Bam of the JBs was a significant stepping stone for the young producer. JuJu recalls, "I met Afrika at Downstairs Records, when they were on 43rd Street, when the Jungle Brothers had [their 1987 single] 'Jimbrowski' out. We started talking and sharing beats. That first time I met him, he loaned me money to buy a record and we became friends from there."

JuJu continues, "Production on the professional level started for me when I began hanging out with the JBs [Jungle Brothers]." He attended studio sessions with the group, and was known as "Jungle Brother JuJu," and was in the background as they produced their 1988 classic *Straight Out The Jungle*. JuJu would also perform with them on stage. "I learned a lot about production from those guys, especially Afrika and Q-Tip," he says. "I never actually produced for the Jungle Brothers but I'd give them stuff, like the drums for 'Beeds On A String' [from the Jungle Brothers' 1989 album *Done By The Forces of Nature*]. I was just happy to be there and to be involved."

JuJu.
Photo © Linda Covello, www.lindacovellophotography.com.

Once JuJu and Les reconnected and started hanging out more, they quickly realized that they made a great production duo. The two started bouncing ideas off each other and making moves to work with different artists. First, though, JuJu says he had to bring Psycho Les into the laid-back Native Tongues posse. It wasn't always an easy task. He explains, "After a while, when I'd go hang with the Jungle Brothers, Les would go with me. But Les is not too social, so I had to shove him down quite a number of peoples' throats. His personality... well, he's not always the most charming person in the world [laughs]."

Les remembers their reconnection: "Back then, JuJu had dropped out of high school, and I was still going to get my GED. I had JuJu come to my school and we hung out a lot and started working on music. Once I started hanging out with JuJu, I stopped working with Rob Swift and anyone else. Rob went to college anyways, so he wasn't always around."

Although both men had rhymed before and were certainly proficient, in the early '90s they were nowhere near a microphone, focusing exclusively on production. "I was only producing back then," JuJu explains. "I mean, that was my shit, that's what we were known for: beats. Eventually I was showing motherfuckers beats and they wanted me to rhyme on their shit. But I'm like, 'What? I'm a *beat* nut, man, I didn't get into this shit to be rhymin'!' I do it, but I love to produce more than I love to rhyme."

Les adds, "I never thought that I was going to rhyme as much as I did. But then as time went on, I started seeing that it's a part of this shit that we're doing, so I gotta do it. I'm definitely a better producer than a rapper. I rap for fun, for the hell of it. When you hear my rhymes, I'm usually on some funny shit."

JuJu says his earliest freelance production gigs – billed as "Beat Nuts," whether or not Les was involved – were a remix [the "Extremix"] of Shazzy's "Giggahoe" single in 1990; production on the Monie Love song "Pups Lickin' Bone" [from 1990's *Down To Earth*]; and co-production on the Stereo MCs' 1990 album track "Watcha Gonna Do?" He / they also contributed the album track "Heidi Hoe" to Common's 1992 debut *Can I Borrow A Dollar?* and a "Beat Nuts Remix" of Common's 1992 single "Breaker 1/9."

As an actual duo, JuJu says their first real work on production was with teenage phenom Chi-Ali, on his album *The Fabulous Chi-Ali* [1992, Relativity / Violator]. The group was hired for the project by former Jungle Brothers road manager – and future head of Violator Management – Chris Lighty, who was managing Chi.

JuJu says, "Chris probably hired me and Les for production on that album because it would be a lot cheaper than hiring De La Soul or the Jungle Brothers. Plus those guys were probably too busy at the time. We produced every track on his album except for two that Mr. Long [from Black Sheep] did."

JuJu continues, "That Chi-Ali gig was probably the first time we were actually called the Beatnuts. *[Author's note: The album credits them using the spelling The Beat Nuts vs. Beatnuts].* Before that we weren't using it. Afrika from the JBs named us The Beatnuts. We used to call each other the Beat Kings, and in the studio me and Les were always stoned and laughing and clownin' around. So the JBs and De La were like, 'You're not kings, you niggas are *nuts*.' And that shit just kinda stuck, especially after A Tribe Called Quest shouted us out on their album." Les adds, "I never liked any name with 'King' in it, like the 45 King or whatever. So Beatnuts was perfect."

As their production skills and reputation grew, so did their record collections: during that time they frequently went on East Coast vinyl buying sprees to restock raw materials for samples. "Back then, when it came to buying beats, we just lost our fuckin' minds," says JuJu. "I had met Vic [producer Victor Padilla aka V.I.C., of the Ghetto Pros], and that nigga had a truck, so we used to go on *missions*. New Jersey, Pennsylvania, Philly, North Carolina. We used to travel like crazy for those shopping trips." Les adds, "Us and Vic and [fellow-producer] T-Ray used to jump in Vic's truck and take missions out of town and come back with piles and piles of records."

After the Chi-Ali album, the Beatnuts were signed as a group to Chi's label, Relativity, which was also home to Common. Aside from starting to explore their own raps, the group had also added a member, Fashion [Berntony Smalls, later known as Al' Tariq], an MC they knew from mutual friends in their high school years. JuJu says, "Me and Les was always leery about being MCs, you know, so we wanted to have an anchorman. That's what Fashion was there for."

JuJu explains his own rhyme style: "When it came to stuff I rhymed about, growing up I had all kinds of foul shit around me. Selling drugs, all that. And my dad wasn't exactly walking the straight and narrow, so I had all that hardcore shit around me. It just came natural. And when it came to my neighborhood and me rhyming, I was repping Corona to death. I don't think Kool G Rap [who was also from Corona] even put Corona on the map like I did. I would rep my spot in every one of my songs."

And, when queried, Les dissects the duo's production styles: "With my shit, it's got to be funky. I like a lot of funny sounds and shit. Stuff that sounds funny, but is mean at the same time. Like a happy killer clown, who will kill you with a smile on his face.

JuJu's got the serious violin violence beat stuff. Straight hardcore."

L to R: JuJu, Fashion, Les.
Photo © Linda Covello, www.lindacovellophotography.com.

After working on other peoples' albums and songs for years, the time had finally come for the Beatnuts to go for self and rep their own set. JuJu remembers that era fondly: "The recording of that first one [*Intoxicated Demons*] was basically a process of buying records, figuring out tracks, going into the studio and laying shit down, then going out and buying more records. At that time I had no idea about what it was to sell records or be marketable or whatever. I was just happy to be making a record and doing a video. I was thinkin' more about how my peers would like it, like the Jungle Brothers and Tribe. I didn't care if it sold or not. I knew how serious we were about our beats and how serious we were about being original, so we definitely believed in what we were doing."

There was one major event during the recording of *Intoxicated Demons* which altered the group and the release's length as well: Fashion doing a bid.

"He was actually locked up when we started recording," JuJu recalls. "We had gotten the deal and he went in shortly after that. And we didn't really want to rap on a ton of stuff, so the label said, 'All right, instead of a full album, just do an EP.' As we were wrapping up the EP, Fashion got out, and got to get on one or two joints on there, like 'Third Of The Trio.'"

Promotional postcard.
Courtesy of the Adler Hip-Hop Archives / Cornell University Hip-Hop Collection.

The downsizing was a disappointment to the group, and a let-down to their fans, especially in retrospect. JuJu says, "Fashion's problem definitely fucked us up, because think about how good the EP was. Just imagine if we was rocking a full album at that point. Fashion would have been on every track if it had gone as planned."

As accomplished as the tracks were, the men were still learning and growing as producers on *Intoxicated Demons*. JuJu explains, "I had just bought my first MPC-60 [sampler] when we started recording that EP, so all those tracks were like a learning process for me. By the time I got to *Street Level* [their second album, from 1994, also known as *Beatnuts*] I was already nasty with that shit."

JuJu says that although they are both credited equally, he did the main production work on all but two of the *Intoxicated Demons* cuts. "The only songs that Les produced on the EP were 'Reign Of The Tec' and I think 'Story,'" he says. "But with us, no matter who did what, we always put The Beatnuts on it. Back then I might have done more, but now we do everything together."

The cover reflected their love of record collecting and jazz, as it was a clear snag from Hank Mobley's *The Turnaround!* album [Blue Note, 1965]. JuJu explains, "To us that cover was important because a lot of the music we made was jazz-inspired. We wanted to follow the feeling of it, the vibe. We sampled the cover, but didn't sample any Hank Mobley tracks on that one." Les remembers, "We were looking through a Blue Note book and saw that cover and really liked it, so we flipped it, Beatnuts-style."

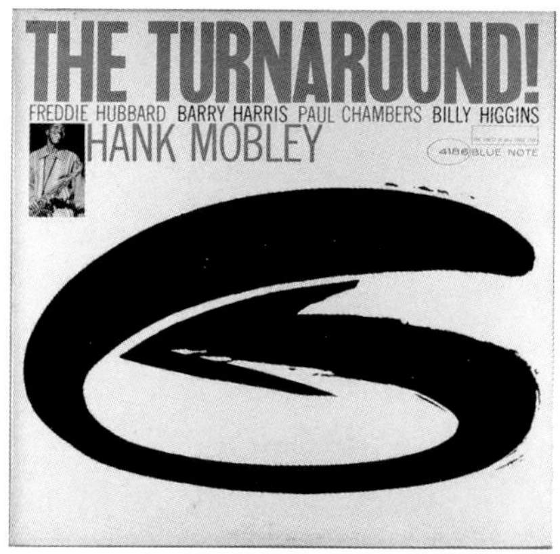

Hank Mobley's *The Turnaround!*
1965, Blue Note.

The guys weren't young pups when *Intoxicated Demons* hit – both in their mid-20s – and the sound of the EP definitely reflected a mixture of their serious natures. There was some twisted humor as well. They released two singles off the EP – "Reign Of The Tec" and "No Equal" – and it went on to be hugely influential, thanks to the duo's innovative, deep-digging samples.

"I'm definitely glad that we put that record out," JuJu says today. "We put a lot of thought into it and I'm just happy that we focused on our music instead of wilding out. Those first two records of ours were really important in establishing us. They had a lot of impact."

TRACKS

World's Famous [featuring V.I.C.]

JUJU: That track is definitely my favorite. Just the way I put that together, it was so tight – the horns and everything, the way it was EQed. The context of the rhymes. It's like: *that's* the Beatnuts, you know? I listen to that now and I hear how young I sounded back then. Vic [aka V.I.C.] rhymed on that, he was a guy we knew from Corona who used to dig with us. He has a group called the Ghetto Professionals [aka Ghetto Pros]. When I first met him, he was producing house records. I wrote those lyrics for him, and it took like 20 fuckin' hours to get him to kick it! Our engineer fell asleep, we was there in the studio until the sun came up. Believe me, after that I never had him rap with us again! Vic loved that Dizzy Gillespie track ["Matrix," from 1970] and he was like, "Yo, this is the shit I want to get on, write me somethin'."

PSYCHO LES: I was in the back of that track somewhere, drunk I'm sure.

Engineer Talking Shit

JUJU: Oh, god, he'd kill me if he knew I forgot his name… it was Rich Keller [the engineer]. I'm sure he was serious about some of the stuff he's saying there, you know, but we told him to do it like that.

Psycho Dwarf

JUJU: I don't know what the title of that one means, but it has the word "psycho" in it so you know who named it. I did the chorus, about fucking and drinking beer.

LES: JuJu produced that one, that track is just some funny shit. I said "psycho dwarf" in my rhyme, and those words just stood out to me, so we named it that.

On The 1+2

JUJU: Either me or Les did the cuts on that. We were both DJs, although when we performed live we usually went off of DATs.

No Equal

JUJU: That was the other single. I don't know who I was riffing on with my rhymes. There was a lot of rappers doing the diggity-diggity-diggity shit. DAS EFX and other people. That shit was just corny to me. I produced that whole track, all that shit. Brett Ratner, the guy who [directed] "Rush Hour," did that video. I don't know what that shit was about, he had us out in the middle of the woods, running around. I don't know... I hated that video. It was some "Blair Witch Project" type of shit.

LES: I was never talking about DAS EFX on that song. I wasn't part of that. As a matter of fact, I liked DAS EFX and I used to always tell those niggas that.

Reign Of The Tec

JUJU: That was the first single, the one that hit radio. When I saw the video for that I was like, "Holy shit! We're on MTV, talking about selling drugs and busting guns!" I believe that video was the last straw, where MTV started banning videos with guns, after it. It was pretty insane. We was bustin' Tecs [Tec-9 "assault pistol"], I had a gun to an old lady's head in someone's living room. An older black woman sitting on the floor in the corner, with a gun to her. And I had the phone, talking about, "I'll shoot your moms if I have to" [lyrics from the song]. Basically, everything bad you could possibly do in a video, we did it. Dave "Shady" Perez did the video, and a lot of it was his idea. He was being really literal about what we was talking about on the record. That beat, it's like, "This shit is real, right here." We were trying to come out as hard as possible on that one.

LES: That's probably my favorite track on the EP. That video was crazy. We had a helicopter scene and all that shit. The director threw in a lot of other crazy ideas that never made it. Parts with me ripping some girl's clothes off. We filmed it, but that shit was just way too raw for TV.

Third Of The Trio [featuring Fashion]

JUJU: Tariq [Fashion] got out of jail right towards the end of us completing the EP. That's why we did that track. Sometimes me and Les are like, "Yeah, I like that shit, but I can't see myself rhyming on that." I don't really know why Tariq was on there all by himself, but he was.

Story

LES: I think I had the story before I came up with the beat. I knew that I needed something slow and funky. I guess at that time I must have been listening to the Beastie Boys, and then that opening sample [from the Beasties' "Paul Revere"] must have just hit me. And the drums, to flip them on some funk shit [hums song]. That shit we're talking about on there is crazy, and it's half true. Because that's all we make: fuckin' lunatic music!

BLACK SHEEP

A Wolf In Sheep's Clothing
Mercury / PolyGram, 1991

"We were the black sheep of the Native Tongues family. Tribe talked about what they talked about, De La talked about what they talked about, and we talked about hoes."

– Mista Lawnge

Sometimes the best things happen by chance. Take Black Sheep, for example.

Dres [Andres Titus] and Mista Lawnge [William McLean, aka Mr. Long] were both minding their own business on an ordinary day in the summer of 1989, when serendipity reared its sly head. Dres recalls, nonchalantly, "Being a rapper didn't really hit me until I bumped into Lawnge on a Manhattan street."

Their chance meeting was even more of a coincidence than it might seem. Both men were born in New York City, but didn't meet and build until the mid-1980s in – of all places – the sleepy town of Sanford, North Carolina, where both of their families had relocated. Dres moved to Sanford in high school and met Lawnge – five years his junior – in the fall of 1984, Dres' senior year.

They would occasionally see each other at a friend's house and mess around with beats and / or rhymes, but it wasn't anything that either Dres or Lawnge thought much about at the time. Lawnge says, "I never went to school with Dres, he's five years older than I am. I only knew him from other people, really. I knew his cousin better than I knew him."

Of those days in North Carolina, Dres recalls, "I didn't really take hip-hop seriously at that point. It was much more of a hobby to me back then. Lawnge was very serious about it. My earliest rhymes, when I would mess around, had lots of storytelling. The stuff I wrote was very visual, with a lot of bragging." Indeed, Dres' later style must not have been too far from his early years, since he became known for his smooth, glib manner and his off-handed tales regarding the pursuit of – as he unapologetically termed them – "hoes."

Even though Lawnge was considerably younger than Dres, his skills were always very mature. Dres recalls, "Lawnge was a child prodigy as a DJ, he was being billed all over the state of North Carolina as a phenomenon. He went by Shorty Doo Wop back then, and people all over knew about him."

Lawnge gives his own early-years rundown: "I started DJing in 1981, because my cousin Ishmael was part of a touring DJ crew and sound system. He was a year older than me, but he was still the youngest DJ around. His crew would go to different clubs around North Carolina, and they always brought their own sound system. At the time I was into BMX bike racing and breakdancing, not DJing. I only started DJing as a competition thing with my cousin. But once I got into it, I found that I had skills."

"My whole thing, even at an early age, was the cuttin' and scratchin' aspect, rather than blending or rocking crowds," he continues. "I was doing tricks and shit. And the leader of the DJ crew, Sammy D, would bring me and my cousin up during concerts to show us off, because we was so young. At that same time, I met this guy DJ Kraze, who owned a record store in Raleigh. He introduced me to the world of DJ battles. I battled at a very young age, and did pretty well."

Lawnge originally used the name DJ Will, and in 1984 or '85 switched to Shorty Doo Wop, a name given to him by Kraze. Lawnge laughs, "I was only like four feet tall back then, so people thought that I was like ten years old."

Lawnge's most important DJ connection came during this same era, when he met New York's famous and influential DJ Red Alert. "I met Red in 1984," Lawnge recalls. "He was DJing for Sparky D at a roller skating place in Raleigh that was called The Rink. He saw me cutting and he was impressed, so he gave me his number and said, 'When you come to New York, give me a holler.' And eventually, that's exactly what I did."

Aside from their loose cipher associations, the duo of Dres and Lawnge were also connected through a local North Carolina release. Dres explains, "My man Mellow Mike, a local keyboardist and musician, produced a song I was on back in 1985, and it was called 'Live Wire.' I don't even think there was a group name on the record. It was some real local, local, local stuff."

"Mellow Mike did the music and he put my name on it, but I didn't actually do anything on it," Lawnge says. "I guess I was supposed to do it but I couldn't make the studio session. I think Mike did the cuts himself. My first thing on wax was actually De La Soul's 'Buddy' [from 1989]. I did some of the cuts on there, even though I never got credit."

North Carolina might have been where the Black Sheep technically began, but – as mentioned previously – both gentlemen were originally from New York. Lawnge was born in Crown Heights, Brooklyn, before moving to North Carolina in the late '70s, after his father passed away; and Dres grew up in Queens – Flushing and Astoria

– before his high school years in Sanford. Dres' stepfather was in the military, and Sanford was near the Fort Bragg military base.

As soon as Dres graduated high school in the spring of 1985, he went back to the Big Apple and enrolled in courses at Queensborough Community College and Hunter College. Lawnge hadn't even started high school at that time, and the two weren't close enough friends to have kept in touch after Dres left North Carolina.

"When I first got back to New York, I was in the street much more than I was into music," Dres explains. "I was always a good student so I was able to find a decent job, but at the same time I would get off work and be in the street real heavy. I was just trying to find my niche in life, and back then I got caught up in different scenarios." Initially living in Queens, by 1987 he had relocated to the Bronx.

Moving ahead a couple years, Dres returns us to the fateful 1989 day when he ran into Lawnge in Manhattan: "Lawnge had just moved to New York and he was trying to do his thing, musically. We had no idea that the other one was even in the city at the time. But we had the foundation from when we were in North Carolina, so it was just like old times."

Mista Lawnge and Dres.
Photo © Koi Sojer.

Lawnge had recently moved to New York, but what Dres didn't know was that Lawnge had been to the Big Apple visiting numerous times in the past several years. "Before I met Red Alert in 1984, I never had any plans to go back to New York," he recalls. "I was too young, and the only person I knew there was my aunt who lived in Crown Heights, and I didn't like her. But, starting in the summer of 1985, I was there each summer, until I moved there for good in 1989."

He continues, "When I got to New York, I was just running around with Red Alert all the time. He was living in Harlem and I'd just head out on the train and hang out with him and follow him around, all day and night. I practically lived with the dude. I was staying with my aunt in Crown Heights, but I'd only really be there to sleep. I'd go back there to Brooklyn in the wee hours, sleep until late morning, and then go back to Harlem. That was my summer routine from 1985 until 1989. I was capturing the hip-hop experience, and I wasn't even trying to DJ at the time. I was just enthused to be around Red, at the radio station [Kiss 98.7 FM], the Latin Quarter and Union Square. Red raised me in hip-hop, he was like an uncle to me. He taught me how important relationships were in the rap game. Stay cool and show everybody respect, and they'll do the same to you."

Lawnge says, "I graduated on June 7, 1989 and on June 9 I was on a bus to New York. When I got there, I was living with a friend's sister in East New York [Brooklyn], because my aunt had all these foster kids and didn't want me to stay there. Then in late '89 I moved in with Dres, so that we could really start shit in motion. As for my game-plan when I got to New York, I was going to DJ in clubs. That was the whole purpose of Red Alert telling me to move up. I was also going to be the DJ for Queen Latifah and for Neneh Cherry. Me and Nice & Smooth even talked about it for a minute, but I obviously ended up forming my own group."

Lawnge mentions his biggest influences when it came to his budding production work at the time: "Creatively, the Jungle Brothers and A Tribe Called Quest molded my sound. I definitely created off of what they was doin', adding to it."

"When we reconnected in 1989," Dres recalls, "Lawnge started introducing me to all these people like the Jungle Brothers and Red Alert. I saw what it could be and said, 'Yeah, let's give this a shot.' Once I saw the environment and that we could make it happen, I definitely got very serious about it." Lawnge says, "At that time, Dres was actually trying to sing. He was more like an R & B dude. But he came back to hip-hop pretty quickly, once I laid out the plan."

Dres describes their next step: "Me and Lawnge started DJing at clubs, because my man Stan in North Carolina had shown me how to DJ. Honestly, Stan would have been the third member of Black Sheep, but he got locked-up for about seven years. Lawnge and I used to DJ at Mars, Power House, The Building, all these different clubs and we were establishing a real reputation in New York for rocking parties. So that opened up the door for us to take things a little bit further."

Lawnge says, regarding their short-lived career as club DJs, "In order to eat, I used to borrow Red Alert's records and we'd go out and do clubs. Our first DJ gig was at Mars. People loved it, our floor was always packed. Dres would be my relief DJ, when I was tired and needed a break. It was a lot of fun, although it really only lasted a couple months."

"After those DJ gigs, we put our money into a demo," Lawnge recalls. "We recorded it at a studio in the Chelsea Hotel, on 23rd Street. There was a song on there called 'Fall Better,' and I don't remember the rest. None of those songs ended up making the album. That original demo got us a 'demo deal' [similar to a production development deal] with Mercury."

Album ad.
Courtesy of the Harvard Hip-Hop Archive.

Considering the company being kept by the two at the time, getting connected with Mercury wasn't an overly difficult task. By late '89 they were managed jointly by "Baby" Chris Lighty [of Violator Management] and DJ Red Alert, and as a result they had entrée to every label in New York City. Dres says, "We were working with Red Alert when we first started, and Red's assistant was Dave 'Funken' Klein [Klein passed away from cancer in 1995]. He really believed in us and made calls about us to four or five different labels, so we could just walk our demo in."

The group's second overall – and first Mercury-financed – demo included two songs that did make their future debut LP, *A Wolf In Sheep's Clothing*: "Try Counting Sheep" and "Butt... In The Meantime." Lawnge recalls, "Nothing else on there made the album. I do remember one that I liked called 'Basically Speaking.'"

Dres adds, "Yeah, the only one that made the album was 'Try Counting Sheep.' *[Author's note: Dres does not remember 'Butt... In The Meantime' being on either demo].* There was a song on there that was pretty dope called 'Listen' that also could have made the album. I think that got knocked off because of sample clearance issues. That was a big thing back then. A Tribe Called Quest used the 'Fall Better' loop on a later track they did."

Lawnge says of their Mercury association back in the first part of the decade: "We were happy being on the label. We were their pet project, since we were the first rap group on Mercury since Kurtis Blow [in the mid-80s]."

As for the group name, Dres explains, "In 1989, once we decided that we were a duo, we started using Black Sheep, before we had anything recorded. The reason we called ourselves Black Sheep is that we were hanging around the Native Tongues, but we were really very different from them, as far as our character. We were all good brothers, but they were wearing beads and dashikis, and that just wasn't us. I was really more of a street kid than a cultural kid, but at the same time I had a diverse upbringing. I was an army kid and had seen a lot, so I was able to always walk on both sides of the fence without stressin' it. That's why I could hang with guys from Diggin' In The Crates from the Bronx *[Author's note: Producer Showbiz is a long-time friend and one-time roommate of Dres']* and Native Tongues at the same time."

Black Sheep's earliest shows were, predictably, Native Tongues-related. Dres remembers a Delaware gig in 1989 with A Tribe Called Quest and also that year's New Music Seminar as some of their earliest on-stage group experiences *[Author's note: Lawnge remembers both shows as taking place in 1990].* Regarding their live show, even in its earliest days, Dres says, "To this day I think we have such command on stage. We live for the show, to rock live! I've always enjoyed being on-stage more than being in the studio."

On record and on-stage, the duo became a simple and effective one-two punch: Lawnge DJed and Dres rhymed. Dres notes that there was another member of the crew who could have brought Lawnge to the front of the stage if things had turned out differently: "Our man Pee Wee from the Bronx used to DJ with us at clubs and he probably would have been the DJ for the group, but he got killed. He was a hilarious brother, he wanted to be a comedian. He got killed for his Red Alert jacket."

Lawnge says, "We was never really the DJ and the MC. It was more like the MC and the Hype Man. Pee Wee was going to be our DJ, and that would have made everything complete."

Although the album didn't hit shelves until October of 1991, it was actually finished almost a year before that, in late 1990. Lawnge recalls, "There was a whole year between when the record was done and when it came out. It got held up because of name clearance for the group and sample clearance. Two other groups had claims on the name – a reggae group and a rock group. Mercury settled it out of court with them, for I think about $40,000. It was tough to wait that long, but during that period I just started remixing tracks, so we used those tracks on our singles."

When it came to production on *A Wolf In Sheep's Clothing*, it was all Lawnge. Dres says, "Lawnge probably did about 98% of the production on the first one. I contributed a few loops, like 'Similak Child' and a few others. But Lawnge did just about all of it. I wrote the rhymes. Those studio sessions were so cool back then. It was a meeting of the minds. Sometimes we had stuff mapped out, but if we didn't, we'd just roll with it. We did it at a time when hip-hop was starting to be monotonous, and we brought life to it."

Looking back on the recording process itself, Lawnge says, "Making that album took almost no time. I did all the beats in our crib, Dres wrote the rhymes, and then we just went in and laid everything down." The album was recorded in Manhattan, mostly at Calliope, with some songs done at Chung King. It was mixed at the Apollo Theater's lesser-known in-house studio. Dres says, "That studio there at the Apollo is one of the best in the world, but it's very expensive."

Mercury Promotional / Retail Pamphlet.
Courtesy of the Adler Hip-Hop Archives / Cornell University Hip-Hop Collection.

Dres said that allies at Mercury helped the group grow during their first recordings. "Dave Gossett and Lisa Cortes [both in the A & R department] pretty much gave us a free hand. They jumped on-board a bit more towards the end, just about the direction of the album. But they really let us do what we wanted to do."

Engineer Lisle Leete was also very helpful on the production side. "Lisle was the house engineer at Calliope and he taught me so much about putting stuff together," Lawnge explains. "He programmed a lot of stuff, too, because I didn't know how to work the samplers. He showed me how to make the samplers sound like live instruments instead of sounding mechanical."

If there are any complaints from Lawnge about the album, they are minor (and fair): "For what it was when it came out, musically I can't complain about it at all. But I do wish that it had come out on double vinyl. There were too many tracks [20 total] for one piece of vinyl. It lost a lot of sound quality and DJs used to complain that the volume was too low. After our record came out, everybody started doing double vinyl."

Although the duo knew early on what kind of a twist they were making on the game, Dres notes how even their close peers didn't always have pom-poms shaking: "On the real, I think everybody around us in the Native Tongues slept on us. They didn't foresee us dropping the album we went on to drop. A lot of people were definitely very surprised."

Lawnge says, looking back on Black Sheep's platinum-adjacent debut [it was certified Gold in 1992 but never officially Platinum by the RIAA]: "We had no idea that the album was going to blow up like that. It's hard to have foresight like that, but I just feel blessed about the whole thing. We was just doing it to have fun. We had no expectations and we didn't follow or care about sales. Because, as we found out, after you learn the business, it becomes a lot less fun."

"As to why it was such an important album, that's simple," Lawnge adds. "Like Dres said, 'If you got a family full of crackheads and you're the only doctor, then you're the black sheep.' We are the black sheep of the Native Tongues family. We just became the black sheep of the industry because people said that we sounded different. Tribe talked about what they talked about, De La talked about what they talked about, and we talked about hoes. That's what made us who we were."

TRACKS

U Mean I'm Not

MISTA LAWNGE: Our first real major tour was with Ice Cube back when the first album came out, and that song [which pokes fun at gangsta rap, and sounds like N.W.A. on steroids] was the reason that we got on the tour. Ice Cube and his producer Sir Jinx actually wanted to use the track in their own live show. They loved it. They took it as funny, not as a dis. Alain Levy, the head of PolyGram, wasn't a big fan of ours at first, because he heard that track and took offense to it. Because of that, they called us in for a meeting. But when he met us, he saw that we were just making fun of that stuff, and we ended up joking around with him.

DRES: De La Soul was a big influence for me on that track. That was something that I couldn't wait to play for everybody, just for a laugh. I wanted to play it for my friends more than I wanted it to be on the album. We always just used to bug out about peoples' perceptions of hip-hop, what's "real" and what's not. That song wasn't supposed to be about N.W.A. specifically, but it does sound like that at the beginning, and I think it was very telling of other gangsta stuff to come in that era. We took the gun stuff to the outer realms of it, just so you could hear how it sounded to us. We did a show at the Apollo opening for Ice Cube back then and that was one of my favorite shows of all time. I thought the rafters and the balcony was gonna break. The whole building was shaking.

Have U.N.E. Pull

LAWNGE: For the single ["Have U.N.E. Pull" is the b-side of "The Choice Is Yours"], we just did a vocal remix to that. The music is really just more of the same sample and we added a couple other things.

Strobelite Honey

DRES: When we was releasing "Strobelite Honey" I had refused, I didn't want it as the single. At first, I even refused to go to the video shoot. I felt that "The Choice Is Yours" was such a street-oriented song and, to me, "Strobelite" was too far in the other direction. I wanted to come out with "Similak Child" next. But the label was going to release it no matter what. It went on to be the #6 dance song in *Billboard* for the year, but at the same time I still felt like it compromised what we was tryin' to do. That's the politics of dealing with a major label. That song was originally called "Strobelite Ho" and it was a one verse skit on the album. They *made* us make it a song. When we turned in the album it wasn't even a song, it was a skit. They liked it that much. And of course we changed the title. It wasn't going to get any play as "Strobelite Ho."

Are You Mad?

LAWNGE: Chris Lighty and the Violators were on that one, messing around. That song was just to say that if you do something that certain people call negative, other people still might like it. You're gonna have haters. Are you mad that people like our group, and that we talk about hoes? People wanted us to make positive records, but we were never that group.

The Choice Is Yours

[album version and single remix, aka "The Choice Is Yours (Revisited)"]

LAWNGE: I actually originally did the music for that remix for Chi-Ali, but Mercury wanted me to write something for a remix of "The Choice Is Yours." I didn't feel like doing all that writing [laughs], so I never gave it to Chi. But I did do the first songs he came out with, on his album [*The Fabulous Chi-Ali*, Relativity Records, 1992; with a majority of the production by The Beatnuts]. I like the remix of "The Choice Is Yours" better than the original. Dave Gossett [Mercury A & R] gets full credit for picking that as a single. That was definitely our biggest hit.

DRES: I've grown to like the remix better over the years. I love the bassline. Changing the verses [from the album version to the remix] and putting new lyrics was Dave Gossett's and Lisa Cortes' idea. They kept the first two verses we had and told us to change the third one, which is the famous one. That was a learning experience for us.

To Whom It May Concern

LAWNGE: I like that song, because I was rhymin' on it. I like the beat, too.

Similak Child

DRES: That's my favorite track on the album, to this day. I love the remix even more than the original. With the dogs barking on the original, that was from a skit we couldn't get cleared that used to come in front of the song. It was a Ramsey Lewis track, covering a Beatles song, "Julia." In the skit I was trying to pick up this chick and every time you heard my voice you heard a dog barking. It was hilarious. We took out the music but kept the dogs. I was just really inspired by that other Ramsey Lewis record [sampled on the album version, "Les Fleurs"]. I made a two-minute pause-tape in the house and just sat down and wrote to it. I was just that inspired.

LAWNGE: For the remix of that song, Dres gave me the bassline on a DAT tape he had recorded it onto, and I just did it from there. I never really loved that song, honestly, but Dres did.

Flavor Of The Month

LAWNGE: That was the last track we did for the album and it was the first single. It definitely did well enough that people wanted to hear a lot more, and that's all that the record company wanted to know. It was just a track about braggin' and boastin'. We didn't have no beef with anybody in particular.

DRES: Some people thought that that song was a swipe at Big Daddy Kane, and people wanted Lawnge to change his first verse, but he wouldn't. We didn't mean for it to be a dis, except for the Vanilla Ice dis. We didn't care about that. But Kane thought we dissed him and we had to explain to him later that it wasn't that way. That came out before the album. When we went to England to meet with Alain Levy, who was the CEO of Mercury *[Author's note: Levy was actually president and CEO of Mercury's parent company, PolyGram]*, he was a great guy, and he told us our album was like nothing he had ever heard before. We told Alain about the sample clearance delays, and that one of them was for that single, a trumpet thing from Herb Alpert. Alpert was just takin' his time clearing it. And Alain said, "What?! Herb Alpert? Fuck that, that's cleared, go ahead. I just gave him [Alpert, who owned A & M Records] $600 million for A & M [laughs]." We put out the single without any clearance paperwork. We knew Alain would take care of it. I remember when I first heard that song on the radio, I was on Grand Concourse in the Bronx and I was explaining to a friend of mine who I hadn't seen in years that I was in the process of making an album. She's looking at me like, "Yeah, yeah, yeah," and as we were talkin', a car rolls by playing that song and I damn near shitted on myself. I was like, "That's *ME*! That car right there at that light, it's playing *my* song!" I couldn't believe it, I was so happy. She was like, "Oh shit!" I'll always remember that.

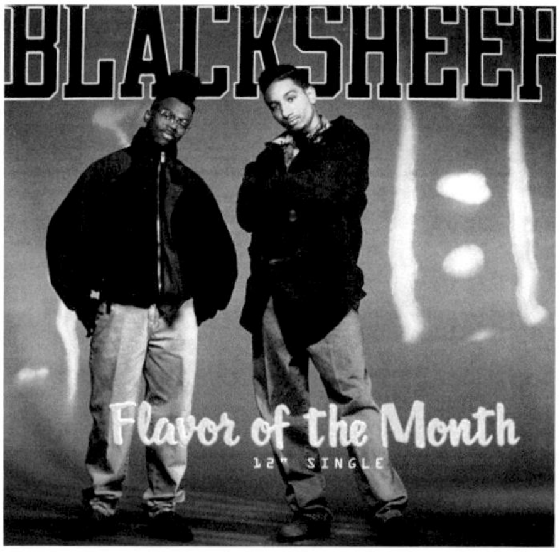

L.A.S.M. (Ladies Against Sexist Motherfuckers)

LAWNGE: I came up with that idea. I saw what was going on and what was going to happen, with women taking offense to all the "bitch" and "hoe" gangsta rap stuff. So I formed a fake organization to strike out against that, and attack us. We weren't gangstas and we weren't outright disrespectful. We were tongue-in-cheek, having fun with all our stuff about women. Those other guys, the gangsta dudes, actually *were* dead-ass serious about it. So I wanted to make the distinction. I had the girl that Dres was seeing at the time and her best friend do the nerdiest voices they could possibly do in that skit, and I think it went down pretty well.

DRES: We didn't take ourselves as seriously as a lot of people did. We really didn't want anyone to take us very seriously. We had fun and we wanted people to have fun. With that track we wanted to do something that was funny but where we weren't so in control. One of the women on there was my girlfriend at the time, Gwen Watts. And another was her best friend, Jennifer Perry. They had just finished college and spoke *so* properly.

Gimme The Finga

DRES: That's one of my favorites. Lawnge did a great job on that track. We were just saying, "Don't be afraid to be who you are." And if you don't like me, you can give me the finger. The world doesn't revolve around us, but we're trying to live our life. We were like, "We dare you to be who you are."

LAWNGE: That was just more braggin' and boastin' shit. We had money and all we did was buy shit. Other people who didn't have money looked at us like, "Fuck them!" They could give us the finger if they wanted, but we weren't going to stop doing what we're doing, just because people were mad.

Black With N.V. (No Vision)

LAWNGE: We did that song on purpose, to twist it up a bit. That was a track we needed to do, to show people that we can differentiate between what's comedy and what's serious. As a group, we had both sides. People were surprised by that track, but were glad that we did it.

Pass The 40 [featuring Chi-Ali, Chris Lighty, Dave Gossett]

LAWNGE: We made Chris and Dave Gossett rhyme on that. They didn't want to. My road manager Big F started to write something for it, but he didn't finish it, so it never made it.

DRES: Chris sounds like a KRS-One reject on that one [laughs]. That one just kinda happened. I don't think Chris wanted to get on like that, and I think he wished he never did it after he heard himself. I think Gossett *did* want to get on there. That track was like coming from the block, at the BBQ. We was like, "Yo, let's bug out with some of the people who are responsible for us being where we are now." We met Chi-Ali through Native Tongues. At that time he was running with Chris Lighty and Red Alert and it was kind of uncanny how well that Chi and I got along. He was 13 or 14 at the time and we were like big brother and little brother. I still love that guy.

COMPANY FLOW

Funcrusher Plus
Rawkus Entertainment / Official Recordings, 1997

"We considered ourselves to be making the most 'hip-hop' records on the planet. I think that what we were doing made people remember and feel the energy that they wanted from hip-hop, it just took a slightly different approach. When you are participating in hip-hop, your job is to come with a new thing – a new style, a new sound."

– El-P

"We just wanted to make music that put a grimace on your face. We were all out to funcrush."

– Bigg Jus

It's fair to say that you always felt like you knew where you stood with Company Flow. If you had a bit of a clue about what hip-hop was really about, they were cool if you were at their party. They might even give you a fist-bump as you walked in the door.

If you were a fan of most major label rap in the mid-'90s, though, you were – best case scenario – getting the stink-eye. Worst case: getting knocked the fuck out.

That's who Co-Flow seemed like – the cool, dangerous kids at school, who smoked cigarettes out front when the final bell sounded. They were iller than you. You approached them with caution.

The New York trio blazed an indie hip-hop path across the country starting in 1995, with uncompromising singles on their Official label. Just as importantly, with the international success of the group's full-length debut in 1997, group leader El-P parlayed the momentum into a full-fledged empire, Definitive Jux, which would rule the underground hip-hop world for the better part of the 2000s.

It all started out with producer and MC bully El-P [Jaime Meline], a Manhattan- and Brooklyn-raised kid who always had a bit of an attitude. "Brooklyn is where I always felt comfortable," he says today. "It's what I knew. All my formative years were spent there."

Although his father was a jazz pianist, he didn't absorb too much – musically or otherwise – from him. "I didn't see much of my father," El explains. "He moved to Key West and I think he kind of went crazy for a while. He was playing piano in bars down there." Young Jaime did take piano lessons ("That was expected of me"), but overall his paternal bloodline didn't play hugely into his own musical work.

His mother and sisters were more influential. "It was a household of records," he recalls. "There was vinyl all over the place, and my older sister would turn me on to new rock records."

Jaime went to two different high schools, but wasn't cut out for the rules that came along with school life. He explains, "I basically got kicked out [laughs]. I could just never connect with [regular / traditional] school, I could never figure out how the shit I didn't like there was ever going to help me. I also had a huge chip on my shoulder, and would get into power struggles with people there."

Although he listened to some rock during his teens, he says, "Hip-hop was something I just immediately loved. It was still relatively new at the time [in the late '80s], it's not like there were decades of history behind it. And I just kept trying to find more of it. By the time I was a teenager, I was full-on listening to hip-hop. I was also writing my own rhymes at about age 13, making demos at home on a used 4-track."

"When it came to school, I ended up getting my GED and went to music engineering school instead," he explains. "Once I got it in my head to do music, going to actual school just seemed like such a ridiculous idea to me. My mother said, 'You're going to get your act together and figure out how to go to school, unless you have a Plan B.' My Plan B, of course, was to become a rapper and producer, which I'm sure is just what a parent wanted to hear from their white child in the '80s [laughs]."

In the early '90s, at age 16 (he told them he was 17), he enrolled at the Center for the Media Arts in Manhattan, and the sailing was smoother from that point on. "Going to school for engineering was definitely a good move, it was effective," he says. "I went from being angry and disaffected to being involved with music every day. Ultimately, I went to that school to become a rapper and a hip-hop producer, and it ended up working."

Things went so well that by early 1993, he was signed to a small record label and was working on his first single. The imprint was Libra Records, which was based in Long Island and run by a producer, rapper, manager and promoter named Anttex [Darren Johnson]. Meline called himself The Lyrical Punisher, or El-P for short. He was also already calling his group Company Flow, even though he was the only member.

That would soon change. At his 18th birthday party in March of 1993, he met a DJ named Mr. Len [Leonard Smythe], beginning a close musical relationship that would last for the next decade. "The group was Company Flow before I met Len," El explains. "I had the beat and the rhymes for the single already. When I met Len, I had him do the cuts, and then I asked him to join Co-Flow."

El-P's new partner, DJ Mr. Len, was born in the Bronx in 1975 and lived in Canarsie, Brooklyn for several years in his pre-teens. "Most of my coming-of-age years were in New Jersey," he says, adding, "But I was still in Brooklyn when I decided I wanted to be a DJ."

Len was raised on funk and soul music, played saxophone and drums in high school and was planning on becoming an engineer [a mechanical one, not the recording kind], like his father. But around 1991, he DJed a house party and caught the bug that would derail any plans he had of a more typical suburban life. "Scratching records was big back then, and I had a unique scratching style," he explains. Like Afrika Bambaataa and DJ Mr. Mixx of 2 Live Crew before him, he would cut in random sound snippets and comedy routines. The crowd dug it.

Len joined a local DJ crew – he was the hip-hop specialist; other members catered to house, reggae and other genres – and they made the circuit throughout high school, becoming popular in North Jersey and making decent money. During junior year, Len and a friend also started an ill-fated hip-hop group: Language Tribe. "I admit, it was very Native Tongues [laughs]. We wore a lot of rayon shirts and black medallions [laughs]."

Language Tribe made a demo that was well-received locally, but beyond that, it never went far. Len even rapped on it, aside from his pause-tape production and scratches. "My rap style wasn't that impressive, I'll admit," he says. "And either way, I always wanted to be a producer. DJing just went hand-in-hand with that."

Len also took his first plunge into the actual business side of music around the same time, at an entertainment management company called Big Arm Management [BAM] in 1991. "I was just an intern there," Len says. "I was learning about things like endorsements and how to deal with record labels. My parents didn't want me to go into music for a career, but my dad said if I was going to do music, I should learn everything I could about the business. He said, 'Don't just be a talented hippy' [laughs]."

According to Len, Libra Records' Anttex was a co-owner of Big Arm before setting off on his own. In the early '90s, the company managed the earliest years of Mobb Deep [who were called Poetical Prophets at the time] in addition to a roster including Isis; Devante Swing from Jodeci; and Ce Ce Peniston.

Len doesn't claim to have gained a great deal of industry knowledge at Big Arm. But for what it was worth, the Anttex connection was what first brought him together with El-P. "Jaime was already working on 'Juvenile Technique' and needed a DJ, and so Anttex introduced us," Len says, matter-of-factly. "At the very beginning, El was calling himself The Roughneck. But when I met him, he was like, 'Don't call me that anymore.'" As mentioned previously, the Lyrical Punisher came into the mix, and then El-P stuck.

"Juvenile Technique" was a trippy, loose-tongued, somewhat laid-back cut which, in retrospect, makes sense as El-P's debut on wax. The hook on the song is Havoc of Mobb Deep rhyming on an Anttex album track from 1991 ["As The World Turns," from *Suburban Etiquette* (Tuff City)], which was Len's way of paying tribute to the man who connected them. It hit record store shelves in 1993 and didn't blow up cash registers. There was no video. But Company Flow was now officially up, running and open for business.

The third and final member of Company Flow, Bigg Jus, also had an Anttex connection, which made the coming-together of the trio seem more than a little bit meant-to-be.

Justin Ingleton, whose MC name has also been spelled Bigg Juss and BigJus, had a very different upbringing than El or Len, and was several years older than both of them. He explains, "Coming up, I was 70 percent in South Jamaica, Queens. The other 30 percent was Esplanade [Gardens] in Harlem, 145th Street and Malcolm X Boulevard."

"My upbringing was a little bit rough," he concedes. "I was adopted, and then my situation fell apart during junior high. I was kind of a ward of the state and had child welfare and truant officers looking for me. Graffiti really saved my life back then. Right before things were going to get very bad for me in New York, I was sent off to a military high school. Riverside Military Academy, in Gainesville, Georgia. That got me out of the city for the next couple years."

As one might imagine, growing up in New York City and being transplanted in the rural South was a shock to the system on many fronts. "It was crazy," Jus recalls. "It was partly like prison, with a lot of psychopathic kids whose fathers were in the military. And then there was me. It was in the middle of nowhere, and there was still KKK around. It was... interesting."

After making it through that experience, he returned to New York, but things weren't any more stable for him. He couch-surfed, and had equal periods of homelessness and mild stability. He eventually headed out to California. "I did a cross-country tour," he laughs. "Kind of to find myself, and kind of to just get out of New York."

During Jus' high school years he always had a love of music, but MCing wasn't at the top of his list. "I honestly never thought I'd be an MC because I'm pretty much a quiet dude," he says. "The early MCs always just seemed to have the gift of gab, shit-talking and all that. That was never me. Where I grew up in Queens, there was IS8 Park, Baisley Pond Park, St. Albans Park. They were throwing park jams in those spots since I was eight. I remember seeing the Disco Twins and Infinity Machine. I was introduced to hip-hop early."

He continues, "When I first starting getting into music, in '87 and '88, I was more into Paradise Garage [the famed house and dance club in Greenwich Village] and the House scene. Honestly, back then that scene was putting out a lot more records than hip-hop was. So my first inclination was to produce House music."

Jus, Anttex and a dancer and choreographer named Shake all hung out together and taught themselves how to make their own tracks in the late '80s, to varying degrees of success. Jus says he produced a demo in the late '80s with Damion Hall from the group Guy and another producer named Dinky, but it wasn't exactly what Co-Flow fans might expect. "I was singing back then," Jus explains. "Aside from hip-hop and graffiti, Prince was maybe the biggest influence on my life. And my demo sounded a little bit like Prince, of course [laughs]. I did a whole album like that, but I ended up trashing it. I thought I was biting too hard." He says he wrote all of the songs and played keyboards.

He adds, "The number one thing that hip-hop taught me was that you had to be original. If I didn't think what I was doing was trailblazing, no matter what genre, I would scratch it." He says that he never released anything during that era; nothing made it past the demo stage.

While he was in California during the late '80s, he tried to make in-roads into the LA music scene but, "All the guys out there in the business were wearing R & B suits and going to fancy restaurants. It was a whole other scene, and I didn't fit in at all."

And so Jus returned to the East Coast in 1991, linking back up with Anttex. By this time, Anttex had formed Libra and Jus started working there. "Libra was mostly a record promotions company," he explains. "They did a lot of payola. We'd stuff CD singles with money and send them out to DJs. Every week we would get a bundle of cash in a PO Box and we would use that to pay DJs to play records. It didn't even seem that shady, that was just the way the music industry worked. The money that was left over at the end of any month was used to put out records on the label. One of those records ended up being Company Flow ['Juvenile Technique']."

Jus recalls El's original demo, the one that got him his deal with Libra: "A lot of the stuff on there sounded like House of Pain [laughs]. I don't know if Jaime would admit that now. But he was still nice, we liked it."

By the time "Juvenile Technique" hit in 1993, Jus and El knew each other well enough to start rooming together, in a lower Manhattan loft space that El's mother owned and rented out. "There were like 13 people living there," Jus recalls. "I would come home from working at Libra [which was based in Long Island] and Jaime would ask me how the record was doing. 'How hard are they working it?' I had to straddle that line and it was really uncomfortable. Because they weren't really working it."

He continues, "At some point I had to decide if I wanted to be an artist or a record executive and I went with the lesser of two evils, and broke off from Libra." This wasn't the easiest thing to do, since it also – on some level – meant choosing an affiliation with his new friend El-P over his way-back childhood pal Anttex. But he did what felt like the right thing for him. He says that after leaving Libra, he didn't speak to Anttex for well over a decade.

"Starting off with El [on what would become their label, Official] wasn't an easy decision for me, because I always tried to be cool with everybody and not rock the boat," Jus explains. "But that was my moment when I had to choose between my childhood friend and a dude who had talent but was a teenager and didn't have the experience I had. Me and El had a hip-hop ethic that we both shared, so I went with him."

"The lack of success for 'Juvenile Technique' had nothing to do with El, he didn't do anything wrong," Jus adds. "It boiled down to the fact that Libra was a promotions company more than a record label. They were trying to get a distribution deal with a major label, too, so they were mostly trying to put out as much music as they could. After a month of working a record, the label was onto something else." For better or worse, Jus says that no payola was used to promote "Juvenile Technique."

He adds, "Jaime was green as hell at the time, and he took it pretty hard."

El-P agrees: "With the Libra situation, I was just a kid. I was disappointed with how things went down, but I got out of the deal after a little while."

El did indeed extricate himself, but it wasn't just a matter of simply saying "Thanks for the memories" and walking away. He explains, "With Libra, I signed a crazy contract. Then it went sour and they were on some 'Fuck you' shit. I was freaking out because these guys were basically saying, 'Your career is over.'"

After a bit of understandable angst, El-P made a very smart move, astutely linking up with someone who could help him learn the music biz from the inside: entertainment lawyer William Krasilovsky, author of the renowned book *This Business of Music*. El says, "I went out of my way at that point in my life to learn everything I could about the music business. I had his book, I called him up, and I said, 'I'll do anything, I just want to learn.' So for a year, in 1993 and 1994, I worked for Krasilovsky, filing papers and shit. And in return, he not only taught me a lot, but he also helped me get out of the Libra contract."

And so, by late 1994, El-P had more life and music business experience under his belt, and was free from any contractual obligations. Ditto with Jus and Len. All three men were still relatively young (El and Len weren't even 20 years old), but all had a pretty solid understanding of the potential pitfalls that might lay ahead in the music business. And, in many ways, that is where the real Company Flow story truly begins.

The one thing that all three knew is that they didn't have a lot of use for major labels. Or, for that matter, indies who acted like majors. As such, it certainly seemed sensible to start their own label. That would become Official Recordings. "At that point, it was me and Jus saying, 'Let's put out a 12-inch, see how it does,'" El explains. "We did the numbers and figured that if we sold 1,000 copies of something, we'd make our money back and maybe even profit a little."

Company Flow, 1995. L to R: Mr. Len, El-P, Bigg Jus.
Photo courtesy of Mr. Len.

Len never wanted to run a label, so he stood on the sidelines, with no regrets. "They offered to have me be part of Official, but I never wanted to," he says. "Even when I started my label [Smacks Records, in the early 2000s], I didn't want to run it. It was just out of necessity." While El and Jus started Official, Len remained with his DJ crew in Jersey. In fact, throughout the '90s he frequently did DJ gigs on the side, whenever he wasn't recording in the studio, working or going to school.

One non-musical thing that happened early on with the group was an event that no one could have predicted: Len had a heart attack. "I was basically just spreading myself too thin back then," Len says today about his cardiac incident in 1994. "I was DJing; I was going to college [Business Management at Kean University]; I had a job at Radio Shack; and I was in Company Flow. I was only sleeping three or four hours a night. So I was like, 'All right, I need to make some choices.' I quit the DJ crew and I quit school, too. Then I just had a job and Co-Flow. Even though Co-Flow hadn't really done anything up until that point."

"Yeah, Len's heart attack was definitely a big deal!," says Jus. "It was a mild one, but at that early age something like that is still very serious. It shook us for a time, until he started coming around again. Then everything was cool. It honestly didn't really delay anything we were doing, we were just worried about him."

The first scheduled Official Records release, in 1995, didn't quite go as planned. With one song produced by El-P ["Dammit"] and another produced by B-Wiz ["Pain To The Brain"], it featured a Brooklyn duo called Dominant Species: MCs Science and Downtown. After production, mixing and mastering, El and Jus went as far as printing the single up on wax, but – according to El and Jus – Dominant Species and their crew didn't like the final sound.

"Those guys were some wild-ass Brooklyn dudes," recalls Jus. "They were from Farragut [Houses Projects], near Ft. Greene." He says they recorded the songs at El's and Jus' loft in Manhattan, and Jus did the artwork for the single. "Jaime and I were extremely happy with that single. It was a raw-ass record, their rhymes were gritty as fuck. It was M.O.P. before M.O.P. But the day we gave them the finished copies, they flipped out on us. They said the snares was too low, they didn't like the artwork. I guess they gave it to somebody who told them that it was mixed wrong, and they took their word for it."

"So we decided to dead it," Jus explains, "and we were left with a bunch of records we couldn't sell. I don't remember if it was 250 or 500 copies. The group didn't want them, I'm not sure where they ended up." *[Author's note: Co-Flow manager Amaechi Uzoigwe says that cassettes of the songs also exist, and were distributed to various press and radio outlets before vinyl was manufactured].*

B-side of un-released Dominant Species 12-inch.

A bit disheartened, but still undeterred, Jus and El made another business decision, this time with a slight twist: They would put out great records, but only their *own* great records.

But since nothing in the Company Flow world ever went as planned, there was a bit of a delay before that happened. Jus left New York for about nine months in 1995, moving to St. Louis and marrying his girlfriend. He also took some of his recording equipment with him. Soon enough, though, they returned, with the newlyweds bunking in El's "crazy loft" that also included – among many others – future MC phenom Cage. Most importantly, El and Jus got back to work recording.

At this juncture, there was another important – and quite significant – development: Jus finally started to MC, after being an observer and reformed R & B singer for so many years.

"I can't tell you where my [MC] vocals came from," he says about his late-bloomer status. "I don't know what to tell you. But on the first joints we recorded together [an un-released posse cut with Anttex, El-P and someone named Jamel; followed by Company Flow's single "8 Steps To Perfection"], I crushed it. I'm just a fan of hip-hop and lyrics, and at the time I already considered myself a pretty decent songwriter. I didn't really work at MCing, I just know what good hip-hop is. Write dope shit, and be original." Once he started focusing on hip-hop, he left his House and R & B singing past behind.

In 1996, the group put out Official's second release, and the first one to actually see the light of day: Company Flow's "8 Steps To Perfection," with the B-side "Vital Nerve." This time around, things went much better, even though El says, "We were just throwing it out there to see what would happen."

Both men worked at Tower Records in the mail order department at the time, which yielded a fortuitous benefit: El worked in the shipping department, and he would mail Official orders out from there, charging them to Tower's account.

Despite his presence on "8 Steps," back in 1996 Jus still wasn't a full-fledged member of Company Flow, which was a decision made by both he and El. El says, "Originally, it was going to be separate. Co-Flow was just me. I came up with it as a group because I just thought it sounded cooler than being a solo artist. The plan was that I would do Co-Flow and then put out Jus as a solo artist. Then I eventually asked him to just join up." Jus backs this up: "In '93 and '94, I didn't really see myself as being in Company Flow. I was really just helping Jaime and Len do their thing."

This is also confirmed by a close look at the "8 Steps" label. It doesn't say Company Flow anywhere on the record, and each side credits "ELP" working with a different MC. "8 Steps" is with "BigJus" and "Vital Nerve" is with "BMS." By the time of their second Official single, "Info Kill" and "Population Control" in 1996, the group had taken more shape. That single even states, on the label: "Co-Flow = DJ Mr. Len + El-P + Bigg Juss."

Another phrase that would be heard in years to come is also present on the "Info Kill" label: "Independent as Fuck."

Being independent didn't necessarily mean being broke, though. El says, "That first single sold more than we could have possibly imagined." He estimates sales of "8 Steps To Perfection" at around 30,000. If you go back to his math for 1,000 units sold, it starts to add up. Maybe being on a major label wasn't really necessary, they thought. Len, who had worked with major label artists selling millions while interning at Big Arm, wasn't as impressed with 30,000 records. But he still saw that they were doing well and was glad that Co-Flow was gaining momentum with each release.

"Info Kill" single, 1996, Side A

Jus says, "By the time '8 Steps' came out, we knew what it took to make a classic hip-hop album. El was a student, he knew his craft. We studied what it took. So once that single sold, we had one goal: to make a classic album. And we kept making songs, usually releasing them, along the way to releasing our *Funcrusher* EP [from late 1996]."

When it came to Co-Flow's music, Len was always on-call for DJ cuts and production input. But he says that sometimes his input was downplayed by El's insistence on being the group's *only* producer. And considering that Len is credited with producing the intro to "Last Good Sleep" on the *Funcrusher Plus* album along with his solo workouts "Lencorcism" and "Funcrush Scratch," (and an un-credited but confirmed co-production on "Lune TNS"), he was clearly more than just the DJ.

"A lot of the production in Company Flow was a grey area," says Len. "Some people might not technically call some of what I was doing 'producing,' but I had a lot more influence than people thought. El's production style definitely changed after I came into the equation. I would ask him to change beats around because of the cuts I would need to do on a certain song. I would need a certain amount of *swing*, I always need a definitive 'one.' That's a lot of what I brought. When El is by himself, it doesn't sound the same. El was never a DJ, so he didn't have that same ear."

[Author's note: Group manager Amaechi Uzoigwe says that El always split the group's earnings three ways, so either way, it was apparently never a money or royalties issue.]

Len adds, "When it came to cuts on the singles and the album, I always had the option to do them or not do them. Sometimes it just wouldn't work out or make sense. I could be in the studio for hours, coming up with something I thought would sound good. But it didn't always happen."

Front of Company Flow promo brochure, 1996 or 1997.
Courtesy of the Adler Hip-Hop Archives / Cornell University Hip-Hop Collection.

El explains, "Company Flow existed before Len and Jus came in, so it was already established that I was doing the music. I don't think we ever had any ego clashes about that. We looked at Len as being an instrument. He wasn't a turntable champion, he was a dude who knew how to cut. An old-school, dope DJ. Sometimes if we didn't use him on a track it was just because we were in New York and he was in New Jersey. It wasn't anything personal, or that we didn't want him on a song."

The group's early indie success was due to many things, starting with aggressive, intelligent and defiant lyrics over truly unique beats. But in many ways, hip-hop fans in the mid-'90s were waiting for a group like Co-Flow to come along. As a result, momentum carried them a long way, as distributors like Fat Beats and Big Daddy were ready to funnel their music nationwide, and local NYC underground / college radio stars Stretch Armstrong and Bobbito Garcia on Columbia University's WKCR were all over them. "Once we made the music, we honestly didn't have to do that much," El says. "The distributors did a lot of it, we just had to keep the records in print. We were one of the first 'hit' groups on the indie rap scene back then."

Jus, who was more of a promotional expert than El, corrects his version slightly: "We made the rounds on the radio, we would go to New Jersey, we went to Wildman Steve's show at Adelphi [on Long Island]. I would go to the *Gavin* conventions and network. I didn't love doing that stuff, but it's something I knew we had to do. And the response to what Company Flow was doing was pretty much all good, across the country. Even though New York was always our stronghold."

Len gives his thoughts about each man's role in the group around 1995: "Jus came from a promotion background, so that's what he did for Co-Flow. Me and El were producing. And I was always out doing something and talking to people. I knew the [Newark, NJ-based hip-hop duo] Artifacts, and they were the ones who first introduced us to Stretch and Bobbito."

When it came to recording their "hit" music, there were two locations. During the earliest days, El had equipment set up at the loft that he and Jus shared in Manhattan. Jus recalls, "For a little while, Anttex, Lou [who had gone to engineering school with El and knew Anttex] and me would just bring equipment to the loft. We pooled our resources." Considering the at-times muddy sonics of the first couple singles, it's clear that they were not done on a 48-track board for $100/hr. And that, of course, was part of the appeal.

From 1996 onwards, they also did a lot of work at a beehive of a studio run out of group manager Amaechi Uzoigwe's Ozone offices ("On Wall Street, across from Goldman Sachs, in a former porn video rental and sex establishment," he says).

Uzoigwe was another significant ingredient to the group's success, far beyond letting them use his recording equipment. Managing the group starting in 1994, he had slick industry ideas but a soft-spot for innovative, left-field talent. Others on his roster – who hovered on the fringes of the company, alongside indie pop groups – included Mike Ladd; the Anti-Pop Consortium; Saul Williams; and Sonic Sum.

Amaechi – who was born in the UK and lived in Africa and Europe before arriving in the U.S. and growing up in Michigan – first met El-P in 1994, when the budding film producer and director had just started Ozone. He recalls, "Our initial grand scheme [for Ozone] was to become a film production company. We thought that by making music videos, we could get attention that way, because there were always artists that needed them."

Eventually, music videos turned into artist management. Although they worked with rock groups, Ozone's early entrees into hip-hop included two videos for Dominant Species (off the aborted Official single) and one for Co-Flow's "8 Steps To Perfection," which was also never aired.

"I remember meeting El-P and being like, 'Who the fuck is this kid?'," Amaechi laughs. "He was super-smart for a teenager, he already had some knowledge of the industry and had a vision for what he wanted to do."

Uzoigwe helped Company Flow as they continued their indie path via Official, and along the way gathered a unique roster of talent, signing spoken-word artist Saul Williams to Rick Rubin's American Recordings imprint and bringing rapper/poet Mike Ladd to a larger audience. This crew was perhaps best heard on the *Eargasms: Crucialpoetics Vol. 1* compilation, which came out as an EP in 1997 and a full-length in 1999 on Ozone Music.

"I wasn't really thinking about any money to be made, and I didn't even know that much about the indie hip-hop movement," Amaechi recalls. "I just knew that I really loved the music that these kids were making. I'm an entrepreneur at heart, too, so that aspect also really spoke to me. That whole crew of guys, including Company Flow, was always challenging each other to step their game up. It was a pretty amazing thing to see."

"Ozone was an all-in company," recalls Len. "They were managing artists, doing artwork, they had a recording studio. I think it was good being around all those guys, because you realized that you weren't as crazy as the world would have you believe. And your problems weren't so unique. For instance, everyone was broke. But everyone's also dreamin'. It was good to know that people you respected were there with you. From the beginning, it wasn't about the equipment everyone was using as much as it was about how you executed your ideas."

One aspect of the group that drew fans like moths to a flame was El-P's unique, raw, murky-but-muscular production style that bore its own path through the bubblegum hip-hop being heard via the major label machines. "When I started off, it was more of a digging [for records and beats] thing, because my only tool was my sampler," El explains. "But I dig in different ways. I took sounds that were unconventional to sample. It wasn't about soul breaks for me. I started blending sounds and chopping loops. I started using 'experimental mistakes,' using things for basslines that weren't supposed to be basslines. Like using a guitar for a stab or even for a bass pattern."

"It was all rooted in the feeling I got from early [Rick Rubin-produced] Def Jam records, and from Boogie Down Productions," he adds. "The Bomb Squad. Records that inspired me. So I'd find my own way to do that. I didn't consider myself to be a contrarian, but at some point when I was writing with Jus, I did start to revel in doing things that... maybe they weren't abrasive, but I had kind of an evil, maniacal grin when I was making them."

El says that, from a technical standpoint, no drum machines were [harmed or] used making any of the songs that appeared on *Funcrusher Plus*, or the singles that led up to it. And that the Ensoniq EPS 16+ "sampler workstation" keyboard was the only instrument used besides a more traditional sampler. "There's no live playing on there either," he explains. "Although sometimes I might sample a note from somewhere and then play that out on the keyboard. You could call that live playing, I guess."

Official's moniker, which first appeared on the "Info Kill" single, summed up their general approach quite nicely. "'Independent As Fuck' really started as a joke," El explains. "We were sitting at the kitchen table in our apartment, cutting and tracing our own artwork to place it on the label. I just said that phrase and it became something we were proud of. We felt like we were beating the system."

There was another way to put it: Funcrushing.

"That phrase was a joke, it was a mistake," says El-P. "Jus was kicking a rhyme he wrote, and I think he said something about being a 'gun-runner.' And I heard 'fun-crusher,' and burst out laughing. He was like, 'That's not what I said!' But it became a running joke. Like, who would want to be the dude who came in and destroyed everyone's fun?"

Jus recalls, "We were walking down the street, we might have been on our way to Ozone, and I think I said 'bum-runner' because I saw someone running down the street. And El said, 'fun-crusher?' And I was like, 'No, but that shit is crazy!' We started cracking up and we would use that term to talk about how we approached music."

One thing that Co-Flow didn't always excel at was performing. Amaechi recalls, "Early-on, they weren't a great live band, their sonics didn't really come across. El was so intense, he yelled a lot. They worked on it, though. Seeing better live acts, like Jurassic 5, influenced them in that regard. They saw what a great live show could do for them. The camaraderie between El and Jus on stage also grew over time. And Len would open the shows and do some DJ stuff, to get people into it. It took a while, but they got better."

That spirit of independence held for the group throughout the mid- and late-'90s. El recalls, "In '96, we had no interest in doing a deal with a major label. When we finally ended up taking meetings with labels, it was them calling us because of how many records we were selling on our own, and we defined our terms ahead of time. We wanted to own the masters [recordings]; we wanted 50% of what was made from the record; and we wanted it to be a one-album deal. We figured no one would agree to that. But if they did, why not do it?"

He continues, "Rawkus said yes."

Rawkus Records was a New York-based indie label without much of an identity in 1996. Founded by Brian Brater and Jarret Myer – with purported early funding by Rupert Murdoch's son James – they had been putting out records since 1992, but to minimal effect, in the press or at the sales register. "At that time, they had been around for a few years but they hadn't really defined themselves," explains El.

"The early stuff they put out was rock, electronic, reggae," El continues. "We were being looked at as having a movement behind us, the leaders of the new guard. And they definitely liked that. I don't think we even got an advance from them. They agreed to our terms and they gave us a bigger platform for our music than we had previously. With them, we had advertising, publicity and the ability to press our records up on a much bigger scale." They had national distribution that wasn't major label-affiliated, but it was bigger than Co-Flow had through their current network.

Amaechi says, "With Rawkus, it was basically a 50 / 50 label. Before Co-Flow, they were doing really shitty dancehall reggae and rock. They had money, but they needed credibility. We knew they could help us get to the next level. The deal was all based on Krasilovsky's advice that he gave El a couple years before: keep ownership and control. And we put Rawkus on the map. It was a good partnership during the *Funcrusher Plus* era. They weren't afraid of the fact that Co-Flow was edgy and left-field. It was always clear that those guys weren't writing hits. Their songs didn't even have hooks a lot of the time! [laughs]."

"When we had our first meeting with those guys [at Rawkus], I didn't like them," Len recalls. "Although I grew to like them, later on. But in the meeting, they pissed me off because they said they weren't going to bother selling Co-Flow to the urban scene. I remember walking out, like, 'So, basically, I can't sell *my* record in *my* neighborhood?' That was fucked up. My neighborhood's sounds were in that record, I put them in there. But either way, Rawkus put in lot of work for the group, I'll never take that away from them."

The group had put out the eight-song, double-vinyl *Funcrusher* EP in late 1996 (on

Official), but after signing up with Rawkus, it was clear that they needed something more. And thus, further work began at Ozone, with impressive results. Later songs recorded for the final full-length included "Blind"; "Lune TNS"; "Tragedy Of War"; and "Last Good Sleep."

Jus says, "When Rawkus came in, we had put out the [*Funcrusher*] EP and it had probably sold 20,000. We were doing a lot of shows and we had a lot of momentum. So we were figuring out the next move. They wanted to do something with *Funcrusher*, so we didn't see why we shouldn't." Len recalls, "Once Rawkus came in and we were doing the album, there wasn't any additional pressure. It was just like, 'Let's do these joints.'"

Above: *Funcrusher* EP demo cassette, October 1995.

Below: *Funcrusher* EP, Side A.

El-P says, "By the time that *Funcrusher Plus* came out, in some ways it felt like it had been out already, with all the singles we had done [as Company Flow and also as the Indelible MC's, a larger posse that also included Juggaknots and J-Treds. The Indelible single gave the album "Collude / Intrude" and "The Fire In Which You Burn"] and the EP. But we felt like making it a full album was what we were supposed to do. We felt like the EP wasn't complete, it wasn't enough. We also knew that putting out a record on Rawkus, with the money behind them, was going to introduce us to a lot of new people. Up until then our audience was relatively small, in the 30,000 range. I think we sold over 100,000 of *Funcrusher Plus*."

When it came to recording extra songs for the album, the group had been working together for several years, but was still perfecting its studio rapport. Jus prefaces his recollections by saying, "Not only is Jaime nasty as a producer, but he's funny as hell [laughs]."

"Company Flow had a recording style that was similar to Wu-Tang," Jus explains. "Very competitive. The verses were always competitive, which wasn't a bad thing. Sometimes it could be a bit of a pain in the ass, because, since he was the producer, El could go back in and do new verses if he got burned. I didn't always have that chance. It could be hard to collaborate, because of that, and because the studio was the size of a shoebox. So I would focus on concepts and song direction and El would make the beats and, obviously, rhyme. Generally, that groove worked."

Jus adds, "When it came to solo or tracks when both of us were on there with other guests, we were always trying to find our voice, together and separately. It was a matter of dictating [by El-P]. Songs were just being made. Sometimes I didn't love a beat, so he'd just have that as a solo song. Our working rapport was established, but it could also be a bit dysfunctional [laughs]. It wasn't horrible, you just had to work within it. By the time the album came out, I wanted to do more production, and so did Len. In the end, I would have loved for *Funcrusher Plus* to have been a more collaborative effort."

"The Fire In Which You Burn Slow" single Ad, early 1997.
Author's collection.

[Author's note: To be fair, the album lists El-P – aka "El Producto" – as the producer, but also clearly lists songs that both Jus and Len produced right below it].

Len recalls, "Up through *Funcrusher Plus*, there was no real ego stuff in the group. All we cared about was: 'Are we killin' it?' [laughs]. We were all trying to do the best we could. My scratches had to be as good as El's and Jus' verses. I couldn't just be normal, I had to be somewhat abstract to match up with what they was doing. It was always a group effort to me, it wasn't about getting producer credit all the time. Although I would say that it should have said that the record was produced 'by

Company Flow.' The songs weren't complete until I added my cuts. That's all I can say."

It could be argued that they went a little bit too far with which songs they included on the album – which hit in July of 1997 – since they packed the double-LP with 20 tracks and the CD with 19. But fans didn't mind, nor did the group members. "It's definitely a long album," El admits. "We actually had to leave 'Corners '94' off the CD because it literally just wouldn't fit [laughs]. Not that we didn't want it on there. It was on the LP and cassette. It's a *crazy* long album. But when a kid is doing his first record, there's not a hell of a lot of editing going on. I don't regret doing it the way we did, even though the kid who made *Funcrusher Plus* has learned a lot about making records. Including appreciating brevity." El notes that his 2013 album, Run The Jewels' *Run The Jewels*, clocks in at a brisk 33 minutes.

Len says, "Honestly, I remember being mad that CDs didn't have more time on them [laughs]. I wanted everything on there. People that knew us, they wanted it all, too. And we went all-in. I mean, a promo for Stretch and Bob's radio show ["89.9 Detrimental"] didn't need to be on there. But that shit's amazing and I wanted it on there!"

The impact of the record didn't put a dent in the sales of Tupac or Puff Daddy in 1997, but to their fans and the group it was a huge accomplishment. It proved that you could stick to your guns as a hip-hop artist, make challenging, intelligent music, and still make a living. Clearly, many fans of the album and its aesthetic became artists themselves in the album's aftermath, in the same way that El-P stood on the shoulders of his idols Rick Rubin, The Bomb Squad and [BDP producer] Scott La Rock.

Amaechi says that the album on Rawkus sold 100,000 units back in the '90s *[Author's note: He also says that the label's main distributor, Twinbrook, went out of business around 1998, and the group never saw any royalties money as a result]* and is at more than 200,000 to the current day.

Ironically – considering that they were managed by a one-time music video director – there were no videos released from the album. After a trashed "8 Steps" video, their next would be "End To End Burners" in 1998, for a song that would never appear on a Company Flow full-length. "I don't regret that," Amaechi says. "Everything just came together so quickly that we never got around to doing any videos."

"*Funcrusher Plus* definitely had the impact that I hoped it would have, without question," El beams. "We knew that people would be shook by hearing some of the songs on the album, because they were abrasive. So we cushioned it with earlier songs we had done, like 'Corners '94,' before things had gotten really weird [laughs]."

El adds, "I didn't have any specific expectations for the record, I just wanted it to be huge. Shit, they were playing it on Hot 97 [in New York], we were in the *Source*, we were selling out shows. It was crazy. So yeah, it was great, it was a dream come true. And it was the thing that made the rest of my career possible."

Company Flow, 1997. L to R: Len, El-P, Jus.
Photo © Eddie Otchere, www.genius-land.com.

Jus says, "I think we accomplished 90% of what we tried to do on *Funcrusher Plus*. I still don't think the perfect Company Flow album was ever made. I'd still love to give it a shot someday. With all the skills we each have now, I think it'd blow our first one out of the water. But when *Funcrusher* hit in '97, the same momentum that we had in New York just spread out all over the world. People loved it, they thought it was dope as fuck. And Rawkus was psyched, it was their first real success. We made an already hot record [the EP] even hotter."

"Part of the greatness of the record was the sheer independence of it," says Uzoigwe. "The slogan, 'Independent As Fuck.' It was a hardcore art record. Hip-hop was so commercialized back then that they just stood apart, they were going in the opposite direction. That spoke to a certain audience in a powerful way. It found its audience. They didn't invent the independent model, they just brought it to the underground in a new and different way. And El hates the 'White MC' angle, but to have a highly-credible MC like him was a real anomaly back then. He was really unique and he had respect."

Looking back, Len recalls, "When the record came out, the first thing I remember thinking was that all of my friends were going to think I was crazy [laughs]. They weren't gonna understand any of this. I enjoyed the fact that there were people out there who were never going to 'get it,' but were going to play it anyways. Like, 'This shit sounds crazy and I fuckin' love it. I'll keep playing it until I understand it!' I didn't really understand the impact that it had with people until much later. And I know for a fact that the people who I didn't think were listening... they were listening. All the shiny-suit people, the haters, the executives. They all listened."

Album ad, 1997.
Author's collection.

Len adds, as he sums it all up perfectly: "*Funcrusher Plus* is an amalgamation of things that you'll never hear again. The mixing of different styles, and genres, and experiences. Three different lives, three guys who came from very different places. It all came together into this one great thought, where our goal was to fuck up everything. And I would say we accomplished that."

TRACKS

Bad Touch Example

BIGG JUS: That was definitely a great one to start with. That sample is a classic J & R Music World dollar-bin record. The cover [for the record that was sampled] was crazy, it was like a child molester record with a cartoon on it. We got home, listened to it, and basically made a song around the sample. That was a no-brainer [laughs]. It didn't take long to make it, we were in the groove at that point. It went something like, "Don't let strangers touch your child." We couldn't help but bug out on it [laughs]. That was the epitome of funcrushing.

EL-P: That's one of my favorites. That song was originally a promo we recorded for Stretch & Bobbito's show on WKCR. I put the beat together and we found this ridiculously creepy sample from a record explaining the difference between a "good touch" and a "bad touch." Our sense of humor was such that we found that hilarious. Apart from "Corners '94," that's probably one of our earliest songs that made the album. That was just an obvious first song. If we were being introduced to anyone, it felt like it was a good way. Because, in our mind, it was the most fucked-up way to start an album. Stretch & Bobbito played that one a lot.

MR. LEN: I was in the hospital after my heart attack when they did that one. When I got out and El played it for me, he asked if I wanted to put cuts on it. I said, "No, it's perfect."

8 Steps To Perfection

JUS: I wrote the beginnings of my rhyme on there while I was in St. Louis, with another joint called "Time To Build." I recorded "Time To Build" with El, just me on vocals, before we did "8 Steps." On "8 Steps," that was kind of "Company Flow featuring Bigg Jus," at first. I wasn't officially in Company Flow. That single sold really well, mostly thanks to Stretch & Bobbito. We had made a sampler CD before anything was on wax. I think Dominant Species was on there, and a J-Treds song or two. They were dope as fuck! And then "8 Steps." I think Stretch and Bob played the shit out of "8 Steps" from that CD sampler before it was even on vinyl. Then once we pressed it, it sold like hotcakes. At that point, we could see that we were onto something. Plus, we only lived a couple blocks from Fat Beats Distribution, so we'd go over there, they'd cut a check and we'd just make more copies. It was easy. I think it sold about 30,000 copies.

EL-P: With the production on that, I was very anti-breakbeat at the time. I would use breaks, but differently than other people. The drums on "8 Steps" are off a break, but you're not going to hear it like that on other records, because I chopped it up a certain way. There's no drum machine on there. I was creating drum kits out of things that had noise in the background. I didn't need clean sounds. A lot of times I was just finding a dope part of a record, hearing a kick and a snare in there, singling them out and going from there. Jus came up with the title. That was his hook and it was perfect. I was like, "I don't know what the hell it means, but let's do it." There's an alternate version of that song, I probably have it on a two-inch reel. That one has cuts on it. Len was cutting Run-DMC saying "perfection," at the end. But we ended up not using that version, even though it was dope. We liked the mix, I remember that. That's one of my favorite tracks.

LEN: The original had cuts on it, but I didn't like the way they sounded. It was Run-DMC and another thing where someone was saying "eight." I did that a lot, I would cut two different things, or the same thing twice, behind itself. I'm a Gemini. But what I had done on "8 Steps" didn't work for me.

AMAECHI UZOIGWE: We borrowed a Super 8 camera and I think a 16mm, for the video. We may have done the whole thing on Super 8, because it was cheap. We did it for like $800. That was the third or fourth video I had done. When I look at it now, I think it's horrific. It's totally cringe-worthy. My old partner thought he'd do a great job… and he didn't. I remember being at El's tiny little studio with all these artists crammed in it, and this girl who was a stripper from a club down the street. She was dancing on a table, with my partner lying on his back with the camera. It didn't make any sense. It was fun making it, it was an experiment for sure. We learned a lot about what *not* to do [laughs].

JUS: The title was something I had. I was reading a book about Supreme Mathematics [a numbers-based system used by the Nation of Gods & Earths] and it was breaking down numbers. It went through eight, nine and then it repeats. There was something about how eight steps towards nine, and so I embraced that and made the chorus around it. We made a video for that, it was really low-budget. I don't remember why we never put it out, but I didn't like it. I look like Kris Kross' older brother in it [laughs]. Amaechi was starting to manage us then, and one of his partners' fathers had a big video production studio in Boston. So I think we borrowed the camera from that studio. But for some reason we didn't like it. Jaime didn't like himself in certain parts, I didn't like myself in certain parts. We had two wardrobe changes [laughs]. That was our only video for the album and we put a kibosh on it, so we never even released it.

Collude / Intrude [featuring J-Treds]

EL-P: I met J-Treds way back, at a party in high school or some shit. He was friends with my friend Lauren, they went to the same college. He and some of his friends were there in the studio when we recorded "8 Steps." I actually did a bunch of demos for J way back, maybe four songs. Some of them are floating around out there. "Collude" wasn't done that early, probably around when we did Indelible MC's, after the *Funcrusher* EP. We were just all friends.

LEN: I cut through that entire song, pretty much. I made so much noise all over that one, I ODed on it! It was just one big, noisy frickin' record. All the cuts on those songs were done on a Gemini mixer, and any DJ who has been around knows that I earned my stripes to pull off some of those!

JUS: I'm not on there, but that's probably my favorite song on the album. I love it, El's verse, J's verse. I was there when it was made, and I wasn't trippin' that I wasn't on it.

Blind

EL-P: That was one of the later songs we did. The song title is from my last verse in the song ["If I have to live on this Earth without sight / I'll be the illest blind bastard, to ever touch a mic"]. Song titles were usually random association or a joke gone wrong. The overlapping rhymes with me and Jus on there were on purpose. The way we started Company Flow was that we were each our own [solo] artist. Then it was a group, but we wanted to keep our own individual identities. So, most of the songs would be each of us doing long verses. But when we were doing the album [post-*Funcrusher* EP], on songs like "Blind" we wanted to be more interactive. With "Blind," that actually came from me remembering an old song by PM Dawn, before they were a pop-rap group. Originally, they were dope. There was an old song off a cassette my homegirl would play me, maybe something that never got released. But the cadence was similar to how we did "Blind." Kinda sing-song. I always remembered it, so it was kind of an homage.

JUS: On other songs, we definitely tended to both have really long verses. We always had problems counting bars [laughs], both of us. I remember with "Blind" it was later in the recording process and it was almost forced, with the concept. It didn't happen as naturally as other songs on the album. To me, the groove is a little bit forced and we didn't quite execute the way we fully wanted to. I love the beat and the chorus, but it's just not one of my favorite records.

LEN: That was dope. I think that was done with a record that Bobbito had lent to El, something that I already had. A Russ Meyer record. El and Jus weren't that big on the record, but I loved it. The cuts on there are all self-referential. I cut up El from [Company Flow's] "Vital Nerve," a fast cut. I always thought that "Blind" should have been pushed more than "Tragedy of War," on the single. But I got out-voted, they really wanted "Tragedy." I really loved the groove on "Blind."

Silence

JUS: I just love that hard-ass, grimy shit, so that one was great with me. That was an ode to my neighborhood, the South Jamaica [Queens] style of rapping. I wouldn't have minded re-doing the vocals on there, I rushed a bit with those. By then, we were at Ozone and it was a traditional session. If you want to go back later and change, it's a pain. I think Jaime came up with the title, there's no "silence" mentioned in the song. I probably couldn't think of what to call it.

EL-P: That's just Jus on vocals, although I produced it. We looked at groups like Brand Nubian, they had "solo" records on their albums. We studied that stuff. So we always tried to keep our identities. Maybe in the back of our heads we knew that we'd each be doing our own things [after *Funcrusher Plus*]. Musically that was just something I came up with for him. We mapped the whole album like that, with solo jams and duos and guests. And since I was producing everything, it was still part of Company Flow.

LEN: That's me cutting Craig Mack and Just-Ice [laughs].

Legends

EL-P: That was one of the last tracks we did, with just me on vocals. I don't think Jus was there when I recorded it. As I recall, I had just written a longer, random verse, and I liked it. I knew we needed more songs for the record and it just sort of happened organically. It was more random than other tracks on the LP, and you can kind of hear it in the production. It's *so* lo-fi, it's barely even sequenced, it's just falling apart. But there's something I like about that. It almost sounds like a demo. We honestly didn't know how to make shit sound good. We were more concerned with it being loud.

LEN: El played that beat for me over the phone. That might be the best track on the album. I was really excited about that one, I was like, "I can't wait to hear that on the album!" For me, that song was a moment where I didn't have to ask El to adjust the beat or anything. It was just right the first time I heard it. And I got to use something that I knew people were going to gravitate to, those Kool Keith lines *[Author's note: From the group Cenobites, with Godfather Don].* "Every rapper on a label should resign and quit." It was perfect. That was the first time I ever used a crab scratch on a song.

JUS: I remember that being real late in the album recording. It was pretty raw, I guess you could say that's the beginning of El's solo sound, his signature.

Help Wanted

EL-P: That movie we sampled for that is "The Holy Mountain" [from 1973, directed by Alejandro Jodorowsky]. My friend Dave Tompkins came over one time and brought that movie, on VHS. It was really hard to find at the time. Watching it just blew my mind. So I sampled it for that interlude or whatever you want to call it.

JUS: I knew that movie, I loved that sample. It was a perfect segue piece.

Population Control

LEN: They were in the studio with RA [the Rugged Man] for that song. I don't have any cuts on there, I might have been on bed rest *[Author's note: Assumedly after Len's heart attack].* I remember hearing it and thinking it sounded really bizarre. I really liked RA but I wasn't sure how he was going to work on that beat. I'm kinda happy he didn't rhyme on it.

JUS: That was one of the earlier singles on Official, after "8 Steps." "Info Kill" was on the B-side. That single sold really well.

EL-P: There are no cuts on there, but it wasn't Len-free for any particular reason. To everyone's credit, no one was insistent on their presence being on every track. The original of that had a totally different beat. By the time Jus came in, after he had already laid his shit down, the new beat was there. That's one of my favorites, it's the core of what Company Flow is all about.

AMAECHI: That was a completely anti-commercial song, but I loved it.

Lune TNS [Produced by Bigg Jus and Mr. Len]

EL-P: Jus is the only MC on that one, and he and Len made that beat. I didn't have anything to do with it.

JUS: That was done later, when cats were producing their own stuff. Lune was a re-writing of an older song I had done about graffiti, I felt I just had to get it out. I wrote [graffiti with the tags] Lune; Lunar; and Looney. TNS was a crew from the Lower East Side, one of the first crews of any notoriety that put me down [let him join], when I was a little kid. That song was very autobiographical. Musically, I like it. I rocked the loop and did something to it, and Len did some cuts, basically [laughs]. I didn't want to get too complicated with the music, because that rhyme style took me a minute to get the flow the way I wanted. So I started with a simple beat and kind of kept it that way. My main thing on there was getting my flow down.

LEN: That was done because we had to add songs for the album. I had a sound I found, it was like someone shaking a spraypaint can. That's a Jus-only record, it's *so* graffiti. It took me a while to figure out what he was talking about. Some of the graf guys he talks about, I had never seen their work. For that one I cut a battle breaks record and a Fat Boys record that was sped-up.

AMAECHI: I love that song, Jus did an amazing graf history on that. To see the reaction it got from writers around the world was great, too. It got a lot of love. He was name-checking dudes who couldn't believe that a rap group was showing them respect. We'd go to Paris or London and writers would show up and Jus would go out bombing with them. I didn't know much about the graffiti world until I met those dudes. I actually got arrested for writing in the subway once, which wasn't fun [laughs].

Definitive

EL-P: In a lot of ways that was my post-"Corners '94" record. It was the last of the three songs that I would ever play anybody from the era before I found my real direction, in terms of being a rapper. "Juvenile Technique," "Corners '94" and "Definitive." I think "Definitive" is closer to the direction that I ended up going in. It was one of the oldest tracks on the album. I knew people liked that one, and if people were freaked out by some of the other songs, that one, "Vital Nerve" and "8 Steps" grounded the record in hip-hop that people might expect.

LEN: That song was so old. That was definitely one of the songs I asked El to swing it. I liked what he had done, even though it was the worst I have ever sounded on a record, scratching-wise. It sounds horrible. On the other hand, it shows growth. Hearing me cut that KRS-One thing, I think, "Damn, you're such a rookie!"

Lencorcism

LEN: That was all me, on production and cuts. That one is at the end of the *Funcrusher* EP. The production on there is *so* simple. It was a piece of "Red Clay" [originally done by Freddie Hubbard], slowed all the way down. El just kept playing it, he loved it. I put it in the sampler and slowed it from there. On that one, with the scratches you can hear how shitty the mixer was, you can hear the clicking.

89.9 Detrimental

EL-P: That's the second Stretch & Bobbito-related song on the album. Obviously their radio show was important to us. They were unquestionably our mentors and our biggest allies, early on. They were really the ones who broke us to the rest of the country. That song was just me, freestyling on their show. I went there and I was just in a zone, so I liked it and wanted it to be on the record. I'm sure I taped the show myself. I taped all their shows, but especially if I was going to be on it.

JUS: With songs like that one and "Corners '94," we wanted to represent the early era of the group. I was probably there for the Stretch & Bobbito freestyle, even though I'm not on that track. I think we did three appearances and I was there for two of them.

Vital Nerve [featuring BMS]

EL-P: When we made that, we knew it was the "head bop" track. That's the one that people freak out to, because it's *so* hip-hop. BMS was a friend I had met through Cage. BMS came up with the hook. He had another part of his rhyme where he said, "Soon you'll see / As I flow fluently and frequently." So I said, "Just say that shit on the chorus, because that's amazing." For the music, that was just me playing with this little bass note, I think Jus had left it up on the sampler. A stock sound that came on an Ensoniq disk. So I just played around and I came up with the rest. Jus isn't on that song, it's just me and BMS. That song originally had other titles – "Automatic" and "Stungunnin" – before we finalized the track-listing on the *Funcrusher* EP. I just changed my mind on it a few times, that's all. It was the same music.

JUS: BMS was kinda rhyming back then. He just had this really dope, crazy-ass rhyme he kicked, and that became his verse on "Vital Nerve." I love that song. BMS was a quiet, humble dude, but when I met him he was Cage's homeboy, so I was like, "Oh no!" BMS actually helped me get Cage out of the loft, so I appreciated that. After that, we got a phone bill and Cage had run up like $700 in phone-sex charges. The phone bill was in my name. That dude was crazy. Anyways, I didn't know BMS could rhyme, he was just a cool dude. Then he kicked this real awkward, mechanical flow, and we thought it was crazy. It was almost like Rammellzee. We liked it and put him on. I think he did his verse over a couple times. I remember it all coming together pretty quickly and organically. It's probably my second favorite track on the album. The crowd always loves that one when we perform it.

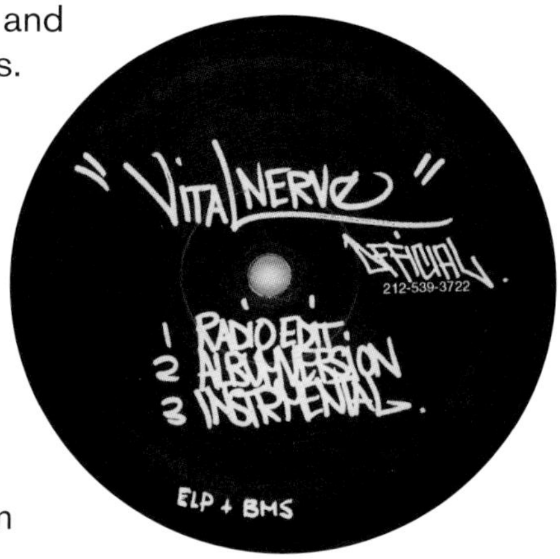

LEN: I was going to actually cut that "New York is number one today" part, but I liked it as a sample, instead of being cut up. It's from a Mister Cee mixtape that got pressed on vinyl. It's Biz Markie saying that.

AMAECHI: That's a classic. It's such a B-boy record. It's brilliant. I go back to that one a lot.

Tragedy Of War (In III Parts)

EL-P: The beginning of that song – the recording of the guy talking, where he says "The parking garage" – that was a live recording that I made from people who had just come out of the World Trade Center when it got bombed the first time, in 1993. I went over there with a portable DAT player and pretended to be a radio reporter. I was interviewing people who were in blankets and covered in soot from head to toe, who had just been rescued from the elevators. So I was catching this conversation between these two guys. It was a weird situation at the time, but I wasn't that affected. How could anyone know what would happen later? I knew enough that I should go out and capture something.

JUS: I remember fighting to get the concept across to the whole group, and Len not agreeing. Jaime was there, but I had to push him along, too. Like, "Are we funcrushing and trailblazing, or are we falling into a routine of being more formulaic?" We needed to keep being different, and I was adamant. Then Jaime did the beat and it was dope. I know El hates his verse on there. I like mine, that's one of my favorites. We were going to do a video for that song, but we never did, unfortunately.

LEN: I always liked that song, but it was so hard for me to do it live, I had to do so much work to pull it off. Even when we were making it, that's what I was thinking about. There were three different beats, but that was the easy part. Connecting them was the hard part, through the sampler and through scratches. There are extra bars at the end of Jus' verse. In the days before Serato, I'd have to remember where the extra bars are, cut stuff in, bring in the next beat and then be able to cut over what was going on.

EL-P: That song wasn't inspired by the World Trade Center recordings that I made, it just worked out that I used those recordings on the song intro. We had the idea to do a three-part song, and I had never done anything like that before. It wasn't easy to do, with the technology at the time. We did the three parts separately, even the mixing, and then patched them together. We decided to do it that way, kind of on the spot. I had the first beat, the one that Jus rhymes over, and he did his verse. And then I did that part in the middle, with Len. Then we were going to go back to the original beat. But, on the spot, I made the beat that I ended up rocking over. People weren't really doing shit like that back then, so we were excited about it. All three of us felt like it was a progression. It was one of the songs where we felt that we had pushed through. That's what was great about working with those guys, we all wanted to see where we could go with things. When shit was special, we knew. That was the B-side of the "Blind" single [which came out in July 1997, near the album release]. At the time, we felt like that was the illest thing that we had done. I think it's considered one of the classic joints on the record, even if it's not exactly a very catchy song [laughs]. My verse on there has always annoyed me, but that song is still one of my favorites.

AMAECHI: We were supposed to do a video for that. I remember scouting locations – there was a "frying pan" boat on the West Side that people had parties on. But the video never came together. That was a very high-concept song, and pretty groundbreaking. I think they pulled off what they wanted to do, artistically, but I'm not sure if it translated to all of their fans. For Jaime, that style was a bridge, with the complexity, it made what he was doing more than just beats and rhymes. It was *composed*. It was his graduation to being more than a beat-maker.

Corners '94 [only on LP and Cassette, not on CD]

JUS: I remember thinking that it'd be cool to have that on cassette, as a mystery track. Then Rawkus asked if we wanted it on the CD and LP and we were like, "Ahhhh." El said he wanted it on there. Originally I think it was more of a mystery song, though.

AMAECHI: That was by far the most commercial song that Company Flow ever made. El didn't want to put it on *Funcrusher* because he didn't think it represented where he was going. But we really wanted to put in on there, we loved it. It's a good song, and including it helped to show the full range. Rawkus really wanted it on there, too.

LEN: I was mad that we couldn't get that on the CD! We wanted it on the CD but we would have had to take off another song and we couldn't figure out which one. That song was done right before my heart attack. I had to ask El for a different beat on there. Those drums are actually based on [A Tribe Called Quest's] "Bonita Applebum." El doesn't even know, I didn't tell him. Slow those down and you can hear it [he hums the guitar part from "Bonita Applebum"]. I was cutting up Jeru The Damaja on there, "The pendulum swings." Even though that song was earlier, I wasn't mad at my cuts on there. In hindsight, I could have left out the snare and just cut the words. You can hear me and El-P starting to get used to working with each other on that song. We might have done that song twice live since it was recorded. It's a very hip-hoppy record to me.

EL-P: That was produced when I was looping shit up. That song and "Definitive" are examples of the fact that I came from the same classic rap perspective that everyone else did. As I went along, I left that and went a different way. That song was smooth and slick. People still like that one, which is funny because it's so different. I was much more on the "trying to be smooth" side [laughs], like on "Juvenile Technique."

The Fire In Which You Burn

[Featuring J-Treds and The Brewin from The Juggaknots]

EL-P: Even though that wasn't very catchy, we put it out as a single anyways, through Rawkus. Rawkus took their cues from me. They would argue their case sometimes, but I wasn't really asking for permission. From a very young age, even if I didn't know what I was doing, I thought I knew what I was doing. But Rawkus let us do what we wanted to do back then. That single blew up, it sold well for sure. Believe it or not, the drums on that song were secondary, and the music on the final is actually a remix. The original beat was completely different, and was a lot more straightforward. I was in the studio, and I had everyone's verses. This is something that I still do to this day, I change things after a song seems to be done. Sometimes you need to make a beat in order to get something going. I was listening and it was cool, but I just started playing with this kick and snare sample in the studio. I muted the original beat and just started playing that pattern [makes sounds of final beat, with his mouth]. To me, it was kind of an homage to [Audio Two's] "Top Billin'," or [Run-DMC's] "Sucker MC's." A take on it, or a rip-off, in a way. And it was just kind of thrilling. Me and the engineer, Pete Bassos, were looking at each other and I said, "Record, record, record!" So I played it and looped it and I had an Indian record in the studio, too. I sampled it at different pitches and layered it, and I was playing it in two different keys at the same time and lifting my finger off at certain points. This weird thing was happening as it was progressing. When the other MCs heard the new track, they were amazed.

JUS: El changed that song up at like 2 or 3 A.M., like Ravi Shankar just called to him late at night [laughs]. I don't even remember the original. I didn't like my verse on it because I didn't like the original beat. I would have liked to have re-recorded my verse, I'm not sure if Jaime re-recorded his. We had to pay for time at Ozone, so it wasn't unlimited. We had to pick and choose what extra stuff we might do. I think the new beat matched the old verses well enough that we just said, "Put it in the can." I loved the new beat he did, though.

LEN: I had to go back in and change my scratches a little bit with the new version, but not *that* much. That new beat he did was actually the easiest beat in the world to scratch over. It's kind of funny, when we did some Company Flow reunion shows recently, I couldn't re-create those scratches. It was because I did something different with my approach on the song. I felt like I had to after El changed the beat. All of the phrasing is backwards. When El re-did the beat, the MCs didn't have to do anything over, but I had to re-do my cuts. When I heard the new version, I was like, "That shit's crazy!" I loved it immediately. I was impressed with myself because for that one I had found a new Fat Boys sound to scratch. It's an interlude off the first Fat Boys album. That new beat is actually all rhythm, I didn't have any issues with it at all. It's Krush-Groove-meets-B-Boy-Records, it's a hybrid. I was always all about snares, so it was perfect.

AMAECHI: They all just showed up one day and started writing. Jaime made the track on the spot, then everyone did their part. To me, it seemed impossible to work that fast.

Those guys were impressive. That's a special song to me. It's got Brewin' and J-Treds, so having the combo of all those voices was great, plus they all have such ill verses on it. That sitar… it's not pure Co-Flow but that is definitely one of my favorites. Indelible MC's were powerful, [with] songs like "Weight." I wish they had done a whole album back then. I remember the first version of the music on that song, but what El did for the final is genius.

Krazy Kings

EL-P: The way that came about was that I had created a demo, but that whole beat is a reverse beat. I had a completely different beat and we were in the studio and we were high. And I played it backwards by accident, I think on a 6-track demo cassette recorder. And I freaked out and re-sampled it, backwards, and built the beat around that. So, originally that beat sounded completely different.

LEN: I was in the hospital after my heart attack when that one was recorded. There's no cuts on there. I never wanted any on there, so it's fine with me.

JUS: Yeah, El changed the beat up, or maybe he added horns to the chorus. There was something he added that made the song pop more. Overall I like that song, I was on the way to finding my voice and determining who I was at that point.

Last Good Sleep

EL-P: That was the first record where I had done any kind of autobiographical shit. It was the first time I had opened up about anything really personal, and the first time I had attempted to really tell a story. It was difficult because, to some degree, I had been trying to write that song for years, and tried and stopped many times. Me and Jus said, "Let's each do a song that is about our lives." He did "Lune TNS" and I did "Last Good Sleep." I wrote it in one sitting. I broke up with my girlfriend, walked back to my apartment, sat on my couch and wrote it. It didn't have any connection with my girlfriend, because I was perfectly happy to break up with her. That song just kind of happened, it just came out. The scary thing wasn't making it, the scary thing was playing it for people, putting it out into the world. I didn't have any real experience being that exposed. I played it for Len, and he played it for his girl and his family and he said they cried listening to it, because they had had a similar experience [with domestic violence]. So I said, "I guess I gotta put this on the record." Over the years a lot of people have told me what that song meant to them. It's a very human song and the process of writing it changed the way I wrote music afterwards. Like, "Oh, I can say something that means something to me?" I had previously figured it was self-indulgent or that no one would want to hear it. Writing it had a profound effect on me. It was real, I was having nightmares about what had happened, for years. I would think I had spotted my ex-stepfather on the street and I'd chase him into the subway and realize that it wasn't him. There wasn't a lot of conversation in my family about what had happened. Me and my mother and my sisters buried it pretty quickly. It happened, the locks were changed, and that was it. So, doing that song felt like a revelation. When I played it for my mother, she just broke down and cried. I hugged her and said, "It's over now." And it was, it was really over. That's when I realized that doing music could be something bigger than just making something that sounded cool. It could mean something. That was an amazing revelation.

LEN: I love that song, but even if I didn't like it, I wouldn't have said anything. That was the only one like that on the album. I never knew that El had played it for me first, I didn't know that. I had already met his mom and had known her for years at that point. So when I heard the song, I remember being kinda angry. Like, "So, why haven't we killed this dude?" You know what I'm sayin'? Like, "We're friends, I'll help you hide the body." I was mad that something like that could happen. The beat on there is a gospel record I had, I had looped it in the MPC-2000 [sampler] at Ozone. And El wanted it for the beginning. I thought that was deep. I was honored he wanted to use it on the song. All of the cuts I did on there were El's ideas. I had that Popeye record, but I couldn't find mine. El had it, too, and I used his. That whole record is about El, though. Behind Shelley Duvall singing, "Until the day I die," is Mic Geronimo from "Masta I.C.," saying "'Til the day that I die." You slow it down and it's like an effect on her voice.

AMAECHI: That was a super-powerful song. I already knew the history of his family, but it was still heartbreaking to hear it. And it was intense to see him perform it at the Bowery Ballroom and dedicate it to his mother. He was choking up on stage, and she was in the balcony, crying. It was deep. You didn't hear songs that were that personal in the world of hip-hop bravado. A song like that is special. Tupac might not have been El's direct influence with that, but he kind of pioneered that, with "Brenda's Having A Baby" and "Dear Mama." Those songs made it OK to be emotional. It was powerful to see El have a catharsis on wax, because I knew what it meant to him, to be able to express it. And it had a lot of impact, a lot of people could relate to it, even if they weren't in the exact same situation.

Info Kill II

EL-P: That final was a different beat than the original. The original version of that was a single on Official, but we knew we could never clear that Queen sample [from the soundtrack to “Flash Gordon”]. On the new version it was still in there, just hidden. But we knew we had to change it for what we’d put out on the album.

LEN: We had Queen and Redman samples on the original. We probably could have gotten away with the Redman, but at the time everyone was scared about samples. When we replaced the Redman sample, we actually used the crowd from a live recording of ours, maybe from Wetlands. I think the beginning of “The Fire In Which You Burn,” with the crowd, is from that same recording. It was off a cassette.

JUS: I love that remix, I like it more than the original. I remember saying, “OK, we’re really funcrushing now!” [laughs]. I guess I do remember us talking about clearing the original sample. I think it’s the same vocals on both versions, just new music, a straight remix. I think we all agreed that it was an old song and it could use a refresh. It was two years old at that point.

Funcrush Scratch

LEN: That song is the predecessor to [the 1999 Company Flow instrumental album, without Jus] *Little Johnny from the Hospitul.* I had a sampler at that point and I went to it. The drum pattern on there was used shortly thereafter by a certain very well-paid producer to make a really big record. I won’t say who it is. The bass on there was from a Novation Bass Station [synthesizer], one of the stock sounds. Someone left it at Ozone and I was going through it and all of a sudden that came up. That was the first DJ-and-scratch record that I had done all to my own devices, with no one else around me. I got El and Jus to say stuff into the sampler. Things that if I had a battle record, that’s what would have been on there. One thing I really love about that song is the drums – the sound and the pattern. It lacks a bit of form, but basically it was us having fun at the end of a funcrushing record. It’s a groove, not a real song. It was a good way to end it.

JUS: El and I are both traditional in that we both know how important the DJ is to a hip-hop group. Adding cuts on our stuff was important. Anytime the record was done and ready for cuts, Len always brought it. He was so good about finding the best stuff to cut in, we never had to wait around for him. He was very professional, he always nailed it. And once he was done, no matter what record it was, it was complete.

THE COUP

Steal This Album
Dogday / Polemic, 1998

"For me, music has always been a retreat from organizing. And organizing has always been a retreat from music."

– Boots Riley

It's a fact: you can count on two hands the list of truly impactful and entertaining political hip-hop groups in the culture's history. It's a unique and delicate line that these artists walk: to inform fans and – when needed – attack injustice, but at the same time keep the grooves grooving. Oakland, California's The Coup is one of these groups, debuting more than two decades ago but remaining a powerful musical force to this day.

Whereas Public Enemy, Poor Righteous Teachers and X-Clan in the late '80s and early '90s shouted funky protests founded in the tenets of Black Nationalism or the Nation of Gods and Earths, The Coup – headed by founder and leader Boots Riley [Raymond Riley] – were Communists. And funky ones at that. They were perhaps the perfect mix of Public Enemy's righteous indignation and Too $hort's laid-back, pimp-strut groove. Feel free to dance, but don't get too comfortable... there's a rally to go to after the show.

The political cauldron of California's Bay Area, centered around the heavily left-leaning cities of Berkeley and Oakland, has always been a hotbed of activism. And from the early '90s onwards, Boots has always been somewhere in the mix.

Riley was born in Chicago and spent his pre-elementary school days in Detroit, before relocating to Oakland at age six. He spent two years, starting around 4th grade, in Stockton, CA, about two hours outside of Oakland. Interestingly, he says, "I went to a school that was mostly white kids, but they didn't like rock. Most of them only listened to soul music. Everybody loved Prince's *Controversy* [from 1981, on Warner Bros.]. That one was really big for me. It was a crazy mix of stuff."

Discussing his political bloodline, Boots explains, "My parents were community organizers. My father, Walter Riley, was in an organization called the Progressive Labor Party. It was a revolutionary organization that he had joined in the early '60s and he made a living organizing for them, until the late '70s. He knew everybody. He was part of the whole SDS thing [Students for a Democratic Society, a student activist group in the '60s], and before that, the Civil Rights Movement, NAACP and CORE [Congress of Racial Equality]. Then he became more radical and joined the Progressive Labor Party."

"We actually moved to Oakland because my father had quit the [Progressive Labor] Party and was going back to school to be a lawyer," he continues. At a young age, Boots went to political rallies and community organizing events, although he admits that the revolutionary fervor hadn't yet struck him back then.

He says, plainly, "I never thought I could stay a Communist because I wanted to be famous. Back then, I just wanted to be Prince."

Moving back to Oakland at age 13, after two years in Pasadena – where he was exposed to the influential Los Angeles-based hip-hop station KDAY – he was a heavy radio listener, soaking in the pop songs of the day, including hits by the English Beat and Depeche Mode. And, of course, more Prince. He explains, "Because of all the radio stuff I listened to in the early- and mid-'80s, that's why I think I always make choruses that you can sing along to."

"When I got back to Oakland, everybody was dressing like they was in [the movie] 'Beat Street,'" he remembers. "That was one thing that Too $hort did for the Bay Area: he made it so that artists could be *themselves*, instead of trying to copy what people were doing in New York or LA."

At age 15, Boots took a break from his Prince studies to work in a summer program that helped farm workers, which got him back to his family's activist roots. "I had to do all this big stuff in my teens," he explains. "Organize a caravan, organize a rally. It definitely made me more mature." During this time, he coordinated a rally of 2,000 students against the School Board of Oakland, which made the papers the next day. "That experience ended up putting me in a position where I had to learn to be very serious about what I was doing," he says. "It also pushed me into organizing much more seriously."

Boots made it through high school and enrolled at nearby Merritt College, where he studied film. He had his first child during his early college years, dropped out support his family, then went back to college in 1989. During the late '80s and earliest '90s he also began to turn his music fandom into action as an MC, joining up with friends who were in the Bay-based groups The 10th Planet and also an early incarnation of the Mystik Journeymen. During this time he says that he was not organizing as actively as he had been a couple years prior.

1991 was a big year for Boots, at least as far as his musical career was concerned. He recalls, "I was working at UPS and I had saved up some money to make a record. I looked around and found the only studio that was open on New Year's Day, because that was my New Year's resolution: to get things started." His ride to the studio that day was fellow UPS worker Eric Davis – who would soon go by the stage name E-Roc. "That's how E got to be part of the group," Boots says. E-Roc would play a significant role in the group as they rose to prominence through the mid-1990s.

The song they recorded on January 1, 1991 was called "Foul Play" [which would later be re-done and released on The Coup's debut album, *Kill My Landlord*] and it appeared on a 1991 cassette compilation called *Dope Lika Pound Or A Key.* The compilation was on the Wax That Azzs label, which was an outlet for local rapper Spice 1's crew, 187 Proof.

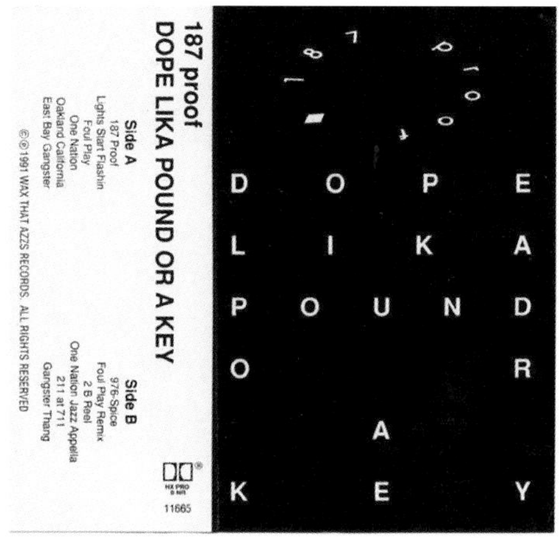

He explains, "Pizo The Beat Fixer was Too $hort's DJ and he was the executive producer of *Dope Lika Pound Or A Key*. I met him at a [University of California] Berkeley rally where I was speaking. He asked me if I rapped because, 'People are into that political shit right now.' I gave him a copy of 'Foul Play' and he put it on the compilation."

Boots adds, "I produced the track, but I had no idea how to do anything. I just brought in an Ohio Players song I wanted to use. We recorded it at a studio in Berkeley. It took us 23 hours to mix the song."

Although they made no money from their appearance on the *Dope Lika Pound* compilation, they were spurred on by the local buzz it created. Boots and E-Roc [spelling his name "E-Roq" early on] kept going, and in October had a release under their own name and on their own imprint.

Simply entitled *The EP*, on their Polemic Records label (partially funded by Boots' father Walter, who is listed as Executive Producer), it was pressed on cassette and 12-inch vinyl and contained six songs: three new compositions ["The Coup," "I Ain't The Nigga," and "Economics 101"]; a re-recorded version of "Foul Play"; and radio edits of "The Coup" and "I Ain't The Nigga."

"*The EP* was done with a different DJ, DJO [listed as Disc Jockey Ouna in the liner notes to the group's 1993 album *Kill My Landlord*]," Boots explains. "He was just a friend of mine. He didn't really have faith in the project and didn't stay with us too long."

On *The EP* it states, "All songs produced by Boots for the Mau Mau Rhythm Collective." Boots says that it wasn't as formal of a group as you might expect: "Mau Mau was just a collection of people in the area trying to put on shows with progressive groups. It was real loose, like Native Tongues."

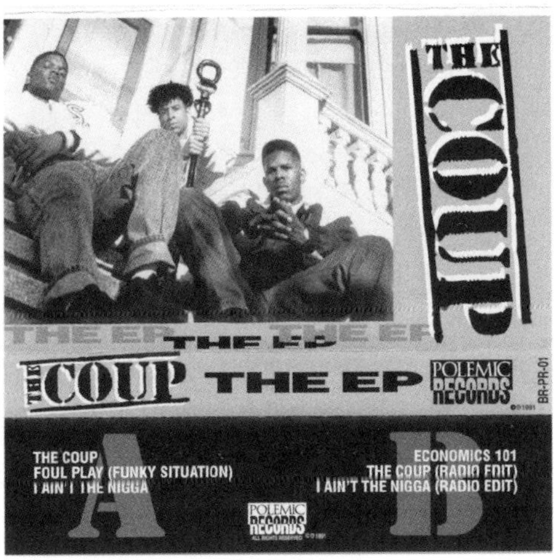

The EP didn't penetrate retail stores until early 1992, but it was popular locally. Featuring a funky, bouncy sound mixed with the fiery political outlook for which they would become known, they were clearly onto something. Public Enemy and X-Clan were hot, but they were from New York. The Bay was a different animal, and required something that fit even better with local fans raised on Too $hort, Spice 1 and the Digital Underground. *[Author's note: Keep in mind that a young Tupac Shakur was just starting to make waves in the Bay at the same time as The Coup, and would embody some of the same characteristics].*

Boots recalls, "We had sold a little over 1,500 copies of *The EP* in 1992 when Wild Pitch called."

As the story goes, Wild Pitch's A & R scouts happened into famed Leopold's Records in Berkeley and asked who their biggest local sellers were. Among other artists, the clerk pointed them to The Coup's cassette. After checking it out, label owner Stu Fine was interested.

"When Wild Pitch called, I was already at work on the next record," Boots recalls. "I was planning on putting it out myself. And I had had some calls from other labels. We honestly had most of the *Kill My Landlord* album done by the time we signed with Wild Pitch."

One unique thing about The Coup's sound is Boots' favoring live playing on albums instead of sampling, which dates back to *The EP*. There are samples used, but they are rarely the backbone of any given song. "The reason I used live instruments was because I didn't have my own [sampling] equipment," he explains. "I didn't know how to make samples sound how I wanted them to sound. Too $hort used live instruments, Whodini did too, so did N.W.A. and Run-DMC. It's not like I was the first. It was just a way for me to get the sound that I wanted. It was basically easier for me to get a good bassline played than it was to EQ a sample of a bassline correctly."

And how did he find his studio musicians? "I would get whoever I could find, usually in a music store like Guitar Center. I'd just ask, 'Who is good around here?,'" he says. He also knew some players on his own, and could pick out some keyboard lines himself. These tactics bore funky fruit, even early on, and led to Boots working with, among others, keyboardist Carl Wheeler, who counted among his credits work with Eric Clapton and Tony! Toni! Toné!

Kill My Landlord album ad, 1993.

After signing with Wild Pitch for a multi-album deal, the Coup's debut *Kill My Landlord* came out in 1993, when Boots was approaching his mid-'20s. Although many fans still love the album for its funky feel and firebrand lyrics – featuring Boots on lead vocals, with E-Roc backing him up – Boots doesn't love it. "I didn't like that record a few weeks after it came out, production-wise," he says. "We just didn't have enough money to make it sound the way I wanted. Whatever we got out of a session, that was it. We generally couldn't go back in and change things. Overall, that album just didn't sound right to me."

The album sold respectably, despite Boots' lack of enthusiasm ("The label was surprised at the number of pre-orders that we got," he says). And they started performing more at the time. "We did a lot of shows back then, but a bunch of them were unpaid," he recalls. "We were able to squeak by on the money we got from Wild Pitch and shows back then, but we weren't making a lot."

During this time, an important part of The Coup's sound came into the picture: DJ Pam The Funkstress [Pam Warren]. Originally from Louisiana, Pam landed in the Bay at age ten ("On the peninsula side") and started DJing in 1988. Her first group, from around that same time, was called Female Funk, and it was no coincidence that they arrived in the wake of Salt 'N Pepa's popularity, not to mention LA's J.J. Fad. Nonetheless, it was a great early experience for Pam. "They were from East Palo Alto," she explains. "One girl had the look and an amazing voice, and the other was light-skinned and soft-spoken, but when she rhymed, she was hard."

Funk Lab All Stars, *Music From A Motion Picture Funktrack*, 1991. Pam the Funkstress top center.

After Female Funk faded out, she joined a group called The Funk Lab All-Stars, fronted by rapper C-Funk. C-Funk, in fact, gave Pam her DJ name. The group, which was unsurprisingly very funk-influenced (but still hip-hop), made one album: 1991's *Music from a Motion Picture Funktrack* [Tandem Records].

In the early '90s, Pam DJed in clubs and did freelance scratches on albums until she ran into Boots. She recalls, "I met him when I was DJing Tupac's album release party *[Author's note: Most likely in 1991 for 2Pacalypse Now]*. Then I ran into him at the *Gavin* Convention in San Mateo, when he saw me DJing for a guy named Jamal."

L to R: Pam, Boots, E-Roc.
Photo © B+ for www.Mochilla.com.

Pam says that she was instantly drawn to the possibility of working with Boots: "I had worked with a bunch of people in the business at that point, but he was different. After we met, he called and was very serious. What I liked about him is what he was talking about. I love all kinds of music, but I could never DJ for Spice 1, Too $hort or N.W.A., calling women bitches and hoes. I listen to their music, but as a female I couldn't let myself be involved with that."

"Boots was very political, he rapped about robbing the rich and giving to the poor," she continues. "He was never disrespectful to women in general, or to me specifically. He really taught me a lot, because I was never that political. Too $hort represents Oakland as far as the pimps, but Boots represents the

Black Panthers and the revolutionary movement."

Pam says that she came in at the very tail end of the recording of *Kill My Landlord*, doing scratches on two songs, including an excellent DJ workout called "Pam's Song." And even though she wasn't as involved with the making of the record, she is pictured on the cover.

"They had another DJ before me [DJO], but that didn't work out, so I joined up," she says. She backed the group on promo dates for *Kill My Landlord* in 1993 and became a more integral part of their work in the studio from that point onwards.

"Not Yet Free" single ad, 1993.

As for Pam's approach to working in the group, especially in the studio, she says: "I always want to make sure that my scratches go with the song, whether it's a rhythm scratch or specific words. It takes time, sometimes hours listening to records, to get the right fit. The Coup has always had a focus on the DJ, and I think Boots has always focused on me like I play an instrument."

There wasn't a lot of time to linger on *Kill My Landlord* for the group, maybe because Boots wasn't head-over-heels about it and maybe because they were now on a record label who wanted them to keep the assembly line running. Next up, after awkwardly having to sever business ties with his father ("He was like a 'stage dad,' it was getting weird," Boots says. "So we paid back his investment with the money we got from Wild Pitch"), they got to work on the album that Boots today considers his first great record: *Genocide & Juice*.

Boots says, "By the time we started the song 'Pimps' [from *Genocide*] I definitely felt like I knew a lot more about what I was doing in the studio. Plus, we could re-do tracks, because we had a better budget."

After several months in the studio, again with E-Roc by his side and again with a mix of live playing and now with Pam's DJing and additional musical input, the record was ready to go. But – sadly, as per usual with The Coup – things weren't super smooth sailing.

"The *Genocide & Juice* era was real weird," Boots explains. "At the time, Wild Pitch's ties with [distributor] EMI were strained. And at the same time, [former member of 3rd Bass] MC Serch grabbed the helm at Wild Pitch. Stu Fine hired him as president of the label, I think. Serch signed all these artists that he had in his stable and put resources behind them, and pretty much told us that he wasn't feeling The Coup."

Genocide & Juice album cover, 1994.

[Author's note: The album says 1994 on it, but Boots says it actually hit stores in January 1995, as a result of the group having to re-record 'Takin' These,' which originally contained an un-clearable George Benson interpolation].

The album produced the group's first hit, the single "Fat Cats, Bigga Fish," with a great accompanying video. "We were getting daytime play in markets like LA," Boots recalls. "We were getting play every hour and selling 5,000 albums a week in those markets." He adds, "With *Kill My Landlord*, I didn't hear people in Oakland bumping it. But *Genocide & Juice* got around, I'd hear it out and about. It should have done way better, sales-wise, but because of EMI's and Wild Pitch's problems, it wasn't distributed well." He says that he thinks *Kill My Landlord* sold about 80,000, and *Genocide* topped out at around 100,000.

On the new album, Pam started to be more involved in the group's sound, in the studio and on stage. "I would put in some ideas on various songs on *Genocide & Juice*," she explains. "I came up with all my own scratches when they wanted them. Sounds that I thought sounded right. E-Roc, Boots and me would all get together and listen to tracks, and Boots would ask what we thought. Boots would make the final decisions, but we definitely all had input."

She adds, "I think *Genocide* is an incredible album. Boots' production skills got even better. It was a more commercial album than *Landlord*, but it still had that same street and revolutionary hip-hop vibe. Everything just got better."

The group continued to perform at the time, but still not with the live players they featured on records. Boots explains, "I didn't start having a live band on stage with us until late 1998. During *Genocide*, I was working with better players in the studio, but their price range was too high for me to bring them out on the road."

According to Boots, after all the label / distributor bickering, EMI bought the master tapes for *Genocide & Juice* from Wild Pitch. Logically, that would mean that EMI would want to make that money back. "So, we thought they'd work the record more," he recalls. "But after they bought it, they told us they weren't going to work it anymore. We were definitely confused about that."

"Fat Cats, Bigga Fish" single sticker, 1995.

This left Boots and his crew still contractually tied to Wild Pitch (who, according to Boots, wasn't going to push them), with a record out that they didn't own and that wasn't being promoted. In other words: no man's land. Boots says, "After that, I was really depressed. I did all that work and it came to nothing. I was 24 years old and I felt like I had wasted most of my adult life rapping, and the rug was always going to get snatched out from underneath me."

According to Boots, Lyor Cohen at Def Jam was a fan of the group, and wanted to sign them after the EMI / Wild Pitch battle, but Boots says that Stu Fine's asking price to release them from his contract was too high. Geffen was allegedly equally interested, and a similar situation ensued.

Boots had completed the song "Breathing Apparatus" [which would appear on *Steal This Album*] when Geffen was courting them. "But after I did that song, I really didn't feel like doing music anymore," Boots says. "So I stopped, in early 1996. I pretty much thought that my music career was over at that point. With Geffen, I made music with them in mind, but I never gave them the tracks that they would have needed to initiate any kind of deal."

He explains, "I had always planned on going back to organizing at some point. The early plan I had was to sell platinum with the first two albums, and then get back to organizing. But somehow it didn't work out that way. So me and some friends started an organization called the Young Comrades, and I got a telemarketing job to pay my bills. I was always good at sales, I had done that in college. I could work one day and make enough money to last me for the week."

"I think I was always a better rapper because of my telemarketing," he adds. "I was always the kid who was knocking on your door when I was 10, selling newspaper subscriptions. I could always figure out what people wanted to hear. It made me listen to people, see where they were coming from, and try to relate. I think it made me more creative."

Boots says of his experience in the Young Comrades: "I was one of the people who formed it, but it was a democratic organization. The people in there meant well, but in the end I left, once we started recording *Steal This Album*. There was always a group of people in there who would stop any momentum we had going. Some people who call themselves revolutionaries just *think* they are because they've read all these texts by people who actually *were* revolutionaries."

In 1997, perhaps at the perfect time, Boots heard a song by fellow political hip-hopers dead prez on a mix-tape *[Author's note: A group who, it's safe to say, had been heavily influenced by Boots' first two albums]*. "That made me realize that political hip-hop could still happen, that it was still viable," he recalls.

By later that year, Boots – who was only fooling himself thinking that he had retired – was back making music again, starting with demos of "The Shipment" and "Fixation." He says, "My goal at that point was to buy a house and have a studio in there, which would also be a central place for organizing."

During the two-plus year hiatus, Pam says, "We weren't doing anything with The Coup because we were just trying to figure out what was going on with the group. I kept DJing, just with other people. I did some shows with [Bay Area female MCs] the Conscious Daughters, and I started getting into production, too. I bought myself a drum machine and started messing around."

Still, she says, "I wasn't 100% sure that The Coup would reform. I just wasn't sure. Either way, Boots was still working on music during the hiatus, even if he says he wasn't. He can't ever stop [laughs]."

One artistic casualty that the group suffered during the hiatus was E-Roc's departure from the group. Boots explains, "He was still my friend and he lived right down the street from me when we were making *Steal This Album*. But he had three kids at the time and he got a job that paid him a lot of money to unload containers off the ships in the [Oakland] harbor. So he was like, 'Man, I gotta do this.' He needed to be able to make steady money. He was on 'Breathing Apparatus,' but that was it. I usually wrote most of his rhymes back then anyways, so it wasn't a huge transition. I didn't write *all* of his rhymes, but most."

Boots continues, regarding E-Roc's absence as they stepped into the *Steal This Album* era: "When he left, the one weird thing was that I had been used to writing lyrics in his voice. It was always good to break things up with another viewpoint. I guess it's like how a method actor sometimes has a hard time just being *himself*. So

at the time were keyboardists Carl Wheeler, Aaron "Moose" Patterson and 16-year-old prodigy Mike Aaberg (mentioned previously as the group's live bandleader).

Most of the album was recorded at Hyde Street Studios in San Francisco, formerly known as Wally Heider Studios, where an impressive list of musicians had recorded in days past, including Neil Young, Santana, Jefferson Airplane and Graham Central Station. And also – most importantly to Boots, since he found the studio's name in their liner notes booklet – funky Bay Area hip-hop pioneers Digital Underground.

Pam says, "I was involved at various stages of *Steal This Album*, even during the hiatus. Boots would play me early stuff over the phone. We put some good time into it and we were happy with it. After being away for a couple years, we knew there was no room for error. We knew it had to be strong."

"The sound of that album changed, because the music had changed," she continues. "The scene around us was different than several years earlier [when *Genocide & Juice* hit]. Boots was always trying to stay at the forefront. I gave him input because he wanted to know what was going on from a DJ perspective, what I was playing in clubs. Boots never listened to the radio in the '90s, he said it distracted him, but he still wanted to know. Back then, tempos were getting faster and there was less sampling."

Boots explains, "The whole budget from Dogday for *Steal This Album* was about $14,000. That was from start to mastering, and back then we'd record on tape, so a lot of that was spent on the tape itself. It was a pretty low budget and it made things difficult. Dogday paid for the studio *time* but nothing else, so that didn't include the musicians' payments. So I had to basically just work with friends who were OK with being paid later, or people who just happened to be hangin' in the studio at the time. Everybody that played on that album basically did it for free, hoping they'd get paid later. I guess that'll teach people to work with me [laughs]."

The cover was unique, showing a modified photo of Boots and Pam trapped inside a human-sized barcode, with the duo looking calm as Boots muscles his way through the lines. "I came up with that idea," Boots says. "We actually had another photograph that would have been better, but at the last minute we changed it to something simpler. Even so, I like the way it ended up working out."

Boots thinks that many fans still prefer *Genocide & Juice*, but he says that *Steal This Album* featured his best lyrics yet. "In Oakland or LA, you would hear black people drive by and bump *Genocide* in their cars," he recalls. "When I played *Steal This Album* for a friend of mine, he said, 'Well, skateboarders will like it.' That was kind of a dis. But pretty soon after that, those kids would become the main hip-hop crowd."

After the album came out – technically in late 1998, although Boots says most stores didn't have it until early 1999 – things seemed to be going well. They were touring with a live band, and had a booking agent getting them gigs. They were also getting attention for something that was clearly important to Boots: lyrics. He says, "With that album, I think it helped to establish me as a lyricist, because we printed the lyrics in the CD and cassette booklets. Before that, I don't think the hip-hop purists paid as much attention, they would just listen to the beats. Their attitude was, 'Yeah, they're like Tha Alkaholiks, but political.' But people, including writers, were paying attention to my lyrics now, and the print media started giving us love."

Unfortunately, according to Boots, just as things were finally going in a positive direction, the Dogday road got twisted up. He says, "*Steal This Album* was selling more than our previous albums. We SoundScanned 60,000 or something like that, when there were still hella stores who didn't report to SoundScan. They [Dogday] never paid me anything and then disappeared at the time. Dogday said they paid more than they did for promotion services, but I found out that those reports were false – the promo people showed me the actual checks they received. They owed other people money, too. I got a $1,000 Christmas bonus one time, and that was it."

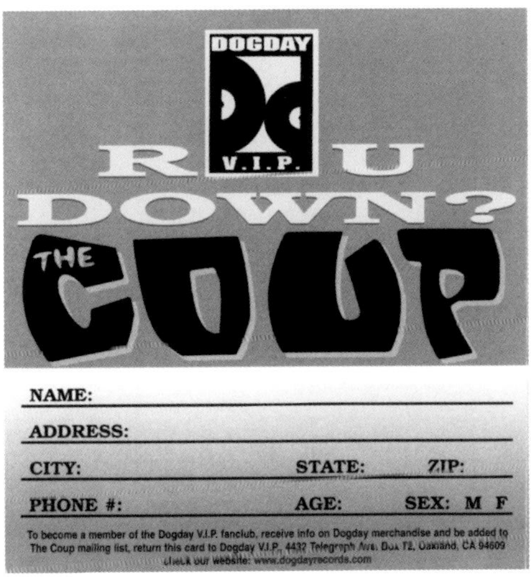

Fanclub postcard from interior of *Steal This Album* CD

He adds, "The Dogday thing was worse than what happened at Wild Pitch, because at least with Wild Pitch we had some advance money up-front to live on. Plus we had more of a studio budget."

"At first it was great with Dogday," Pam explains. "Then all of a sudden, shit started happening. We definitely did go through a lot in the '90s. At one point I was almost like, 'I don't know...' But we just hung in there. There are definitely not many groups out there who can persevere like The Coup."

Partially because of the label issues, there were unfortunately no commercially-available singles from the album, although "The Shipment" and "Me And Jesus The Pimp In A '79 Granada Last Night" both got play on college radio stations across the country. There was a vinyl EP with "a handful of songs" that was sent out for college radio play.

Despite any label drama and bad luck, in the end fans will always have the music on which to focus their attention. And on that front, Boots says, "On *Steal This Album* I was definitely a better producer. And I was a better lyrics writer, too. Some of those songs on there were very personal. Overall, I definitely think that the album was better than anything we had done up until then."

He adds, "I think that my flow got even livelier, too, because I was very aware that it was only me on there. Before *Steal This Album*, I knew E-Roc would come in with something different. Now I had to be more exciting."

"With *Steal This Album*, we reinvented ourselves," Pam says. "It was a new Boots and a new Pam. We were still The Coup, with one less person, but now we had a band to tour with. It gave us a whole new skin and outlook. I think the album was received as well as we hoped it would, and we did a lot of touring behind it. It was a new momentum to push us forward."

TRACKS

The Shipment [co-produced by Pam The Funkstress]

PAM THE FUNKSTRESS: I had a bit more production input on that track than usual. Boots initially had a different kind of beat and groove to it. It just didn't sound right. So I brought in a couple records that added something to the song, for inspiration. And I added the Rakim sample there, the one I cut up. That one is still a staple of the live show.

"The Shipment" white-label advance, 1998.
Courtesy of Billy Jam.

BOOTS RILEY: In late 1997, when I was starting to think about doing another album, I went in and did a demo for "The Shipment," on an 8-track. I used all these musicians who were in the Young Comrades. My demos are always pretty bad. With my production style you really need a lot of imagination at first. We still play that one all the time, even today. That bassline is just the shit. It's similar to a couple basslines from the '70s and it really grooves. Originally my vision for it was a bit slicker than it ended up. My friend Reggie Brown played the bass on there. The song itself is just an introduction for people, it's saying that this "product" is something that they need. There's a Rudy Ray Moore sample at the beginning there. I don't think he'll sue me.

Me And Jesus The Pimp In A '79 Granada Last Night

BOOTS: Originally I had wanted to do a song that talked about how sexism against women hurts mens' lives, too. I had all these different concepts but then somehow that first line came into my head, about how he was smiling like a vulture. I thought of one of those old cartoons, where the vultures are smiling like they're gonna get something. Then the writer in me took over from there, and it just went line by line. I didn't know who he [Jesus the Pimp] was or anything like that, although some of the stories in there happened to people I've known. After a few lines in, I figured out what the story would be. When it came to that being the single, I just chose which song I liked the most. It wasn't really a single, we just put a bunch of songs on wax that we thought that college radio would play. I figured people would like that one the most. And people definitely took to it. The album got a European deal [with Circus Records, from London] because some DJ in New York played that song at a club and the label owner was there and loved it. We still do a version of that in our live shows today. I like the way the video turned out, but it could have been even better. We had a really bad producer and we missed a whole bunch of shots because he didn't get the permits and stuff like that. We tried to do the video literally and that made it more complicated. [Actor] Roger Guenveur Smith was in some magazine saying we were his favorite group, so we got him to be the star of the video. He played Jesus the Pimp. And that was crazy because he's a hardcore method actor, so in-between scenes he stayed in character. We went into this bar called The Serenader in Oakland, and he was acting like a pimp in there. I couldn't tell if he was flippin' out or not. He was giving people attitude and I'd be going to people behind him, saying how he was in character. He was trying to fight with people, picking up chairs. He didn't come out of character until the next day [laughs].

PAM: That song and "Cars and Shoes" are my two favorites on the album. There aren't as many cuts on that one, it's more samples on the chorus, with the Parliament song ["Swing Down, Sweet Chariot" from *P.Funk Earth Tour*, 1977].

"Jesus The Pimp" 12-inch / album sampler. Side A.

20,000 Gun Salute

PAM: I brought in those Beavis & Butthead scratches in [from the beginning of the song]. I love that beat and that production. I had the Beavis & Butthead stuff on vinyl, it was on a scratch record.

Busterismology

BOOTS: I wrote that because I was originally gonna do a song with this dude called African Identity. So I wrote the verse, but I didn't want to use it on the beat he had. I probably even did that verse before "Breathing Apparatus." We haven't played that one live since about 2000, I don't think. There was a group called 3X Krazy, Keak Da Sneak's original group, and we were at some event and I said that rhyme and Keak was like, "Yo, you need to put that on your album." That McDonald's story on there is true to a certain extent. It wasn't a McDonald's, it was an Adidas store. But yeah, that happened. Managers have always treated me like shit. I would define a "buster" as somebody who doesn't play by the code that says that people on the streets stick together. I was relating that to the idea of people who side with the establishment.

Cars & Shoes [produced by Boots Riley and Pam The Funkstress]

PAM: I did some production on that one. Boots originally had something totally different and I was like, "No, dude." It didn't sound beefy enough. So I brought in a new idea for it. We wouldn't sample an old song as much as we'd borrow ideas and grooves and make it our own thing. Boots did modify the style of his vocal on that song, on purpose. He was being funny. That wasn't a political song, so he didn't use his usual voice.

BOOTS: Oh yeah, those car stories are definitely true. Even right now, very much so. That one came from some frustrating, sad shit where I actually broke down on the Bay Bridge. It just makes you feel like shit never goes right. I almost made it into a really sad, introspective song, because that's how you feel when your car breaks down like that. Most of my friends who heard it understand about that. Vocally, I was definitely trying to do a Too $hort imitation on there.

Breathing Apparatus

BOOTS: When Geffen was looking to sign us, they wanted to hear a couple songs and the first one I did was "Breathing Apparatus." Stu Fine had hooked up the Geffen possibility for our third album, because we were still signed to Wild Pitch. I played all the instruments on that demo. And that's why E-Roc is on there, because he hadn't left the group yet. That's the only song on the album with E. That was done before I started the Young Comrades. I'm sure that song would have been on whatever album we were going to do on Geffen. At the time we did it, it felt like a great new direction. If there hadn't been such a hiatus between that song and the rest of the album, a lot of the album would have sounded like that. To me, it sounds different than the rest of *Steal This Album*, but maybe that's just because I know. That has my man Elijah Baker, aka Elijah Hassan, on bass. He was with Tony! Toni! Toné! and played a lot on *Genocide & Juice*, but he wasn't around as much on *Steal This Album*. He had the tightest bass sound, I wish he was on every song I ever did. I actually think the rough mix I did of that song sounds great, maybe even better than the final. We mixed the final in a different room than the rough mix. That was definitely one of the tightest beats on the album. That kind of piano and bassline thing was really more from Spice 1. That was just a staple in the Bay area sound, even if Dr. Dre did it first. E-A-Ski, all that. We tried to do a lot of back-and-forth rhymes on there and we tried to put a lot of everyday speak in there, too, like "Holler at your ace boon coon." Shit you hear just walking down the street. No one really does that EPMD back-and-forth lyrical thing nowadays. It takes too much collaborative writing! There was a crazy sound I put on there that sounded like someone breathing, but it didn't really come through in the final mix. I had the sound first, which led to the song concept itself. [Author asks him if he was trying to imitate Dr. Dre with his vocal delivery]. I wasn't making fun of Dr. Dre on that song. I never thought my vocals on that song sounded like Dr. Dre. If anything, they were more like Tupac, yelling and all that. Musically we weren't trying to do Dre at all. None of that crossed my mind, but I guess I can see why someone might say that.

U.C.P.A.S. [produced by Edifice, featuring F.T.S.]

PAM: I didn't know F.T.S., Boots brought them in to produce.

BOOTS: That group F.T.S. had that song on a demo of theirs, and I wanted to get on it. Then, as we was doing it, I asked them if they wanted to put it on my album. And we ended up doing a whole other beat on it, me and this dude Edifice, who was Erykah Badu's first producer. He was just a dude in my neighborhood. The first group he ever produced had both E-40 and Erykah Badu rapping together. They all went to Grambling [State University, in Louisiana] and Erykah rapped back then. They had the chorus, I might have changed it up a bit, to fit what I was doing politically. My verse on there wasn't one of my favorites on the album, but the beat was pretty tight. Edifice originally just had that bassline and I changed the drums and added a lot of stuff.

B-Side of album sampler.

Pizza Man (skit)

BOOTS: We did that right after we laid our verses on the "Repo Man" track. I've personally never seen that repo method used, but I'm sure that somebody has!

PAM: I go way back with Del. He and Saafir used to come over to my garage, with DJ Platurn. My house was the spot to hang out and listen to music. My dad was hella cool and never minded.

The Repo Man Sings For You [featuring Del Tha Funkee Homosapien]

BOOTS: I'm not 100% satisfied with the lyrics on that. I wrote those right in the studio. There was some jazz horn line that we were using that was doing a kind of Middle Eastern sound and we just pumped it out from there. Me and Del had been talking about doing something for a while, so I played him that beat and he was down with it. I went to pick him up from his house and we really came up with the idea when I was driving him to the studio. He came up with that chorus right there, it was just something to go along with the piano part that we already had. I had heard about Del so much before I ever heard him, because Spice 1 was always talking about him. They had a group together. Del's approach to everything was always very fresh, very De La Soul-influenced. It was something new. And it was inspiring that he was from the Bay.

PAM: That was all right. The concept was cool, but I didn't love the song, not as much as others on the album. That's what you might call filler [laughs].

Underdogs

PAM: That's a good one. A serious song that was well-thought-out, everything about it was great.

BOOTS: I already had that song done, but we were still adding some things. Del was in the studio doing "Repo Man" and I called up this girl I knew from the Young Comrades, who was an actress. She came into the studio to do that part at the beginning. Del was still hanging out, because he needed a ride home. I wrote her part and she was rehearsing it in the hallway. Her rehearsal was actually better than the final, I wish I had recorded it. Del had fallen asleep in the hallway and woke up and she was crying and everything and he was alarmed. He was asking her, "What's the matter? It's gonna be OK!" She was in character, and it was really convincing. Originally the lyrics took shape because I was going through all this shit with a friend of mine who was lying and trying to get over on me. My original verse was kind of to him, about all that. But then it became talking about what he was going through in a more general way. The economic motivations that were making him do some of the foul shit he was doing. In the end it was about those feelings of desperation, which I could relate to. It was definitely a different approach from my usual style. I had stayed away from writing those sorts of things, because there had been attempts at that style in the past that I thought were just super-corny. And as I was writing it, I could see that this was different. I like the way it turned out. I think I tapped into real emotions. I still do that in our live show, a capella.

Sneakin' In

BOOTS: It doesn't matter to me if people sneak into my shows. I mean, I'm already getting' paid! All of those anecdotes on there are definitely real. That was quite an easy song to write. Even before I was rapping, me and my friends always just had a thing about not paying to go to clubs or shows. Just as a rule.

PAM: That's a cool little song, it's not bad. It's a short song, I didn't do cuts on there. I would always have the option to do cuts on a song, but every song didn't necessarily need scratches.

Do My Thang (skit)

PAM: Sometimes, with skits, when we're recording them it seems like it might be corny. But after it all gets put together, it's fuckin' genius. It's funny how different it can be on paper. Those skits take a *lot* of time to do.

BOOTS: [Laughs when title of song is mentioned]. I had "Piss On Your Grave" done and I had "Underdogs," but I didn't have the thing that would connect all the songs together. So we did "Do My Thang." My friend Dawud [Allah] is on there with me, and he's damn funny. I had written it out and we went over it twice in the studio. What you hear on the album is the first time we recorded it. This was before Pro Tools, so we had it recorded, but the timing had to be exactly right, to fit in with the music we already had. As we were doing it, we could hear that we were doing it too slow [laughs] and we weren't going to be on time for when the organ starts. So a bunch of stuff ended up getting messed up. The security guard part was added later. He was the guy who was managing the studio. We skipped lines and messed other ones up. That's why it sounded so real [laughs], because there was a sense of urgency before the organ came in.

Piss On Your Grave

BOOTS: That one was definitely crazy to do, and with all those horn players, they were getting mad. They had to play their parts all throughout the track and keep punching in. It was four horn players, layered on top of one another. That was probably the craziest track on the album to put together. But I love that one, lyrically and musically. Musically the mix could have been better, but I still liked it. The chorus, I don't know how obvious it is, it's some Steve Arrington shit, transposed. I don't know if we ever played that song live. It wouldn't be the same without the horns. We probably tried to do it at some point back then. A song like that is pretty comical, so I can't see anyone taking it too seriously. Although we do advocate a movement taking power that, in the end, would be a violent thing. But I don't advocate any individual thing, like "Kill this rich person, kill that person." I'm more down with a mass movement that fights. Individual violence doesn't accomplish anything. You can't change the system by killing one person. If the president was assassinated, it wouldn't change things radically.

PAM: When Boots does a song like that, I just shake my head. Stuff like that, to me, um… it's pretty strong. That's one of those songs that I'm like, "I don't really want to hear it."

Fixation [produced by Brother K aka Keith McArthur]

BOOTS: Brother K produced that, he was my bass player at the time. I didn't have anything to do with production on that song, aside from him asking me if I thought certain things would work. Basically, he came to me and had this hook-up and was going to have a song on a compilation. It came out cool, so I was like, "OK, let me put that on our LP." That was the second song I demoed for the album, in late '97. The compilation was something that Karen Dere – who runs The Giant Peach [online apparel and music store, based in the Bay] – was doing. The dude putting out the compilation got arrested and the label folded after a while. Planet Asia was on the compilation, too. I wrote that song in like ten minutes, as a reaction to MCs on the "Wake Up Show" [radio show hosted by Sway & Tech] like Eminem, who were rhyming the same sound on every line, even though the subject matter was all over the place. To me, as a writer, I wasn't impressed. I thought it was a gimmick, so I'm talking about it on there. Eminem is cool for a lot of reasons, but back then I thought he was getting a lot of credit for doing these gimmicks. So I did my version of what I thought was tight.

PAM: I like that one. I remember we were in the studio doin' that, and it was an off-beat and abstract record. There must have been a reason for having that be last on the album. Boots was very particular about sequencing. That song was weird, but it was cool.

DIAMOND AND THE PSYCHOTIC NEUROTICS

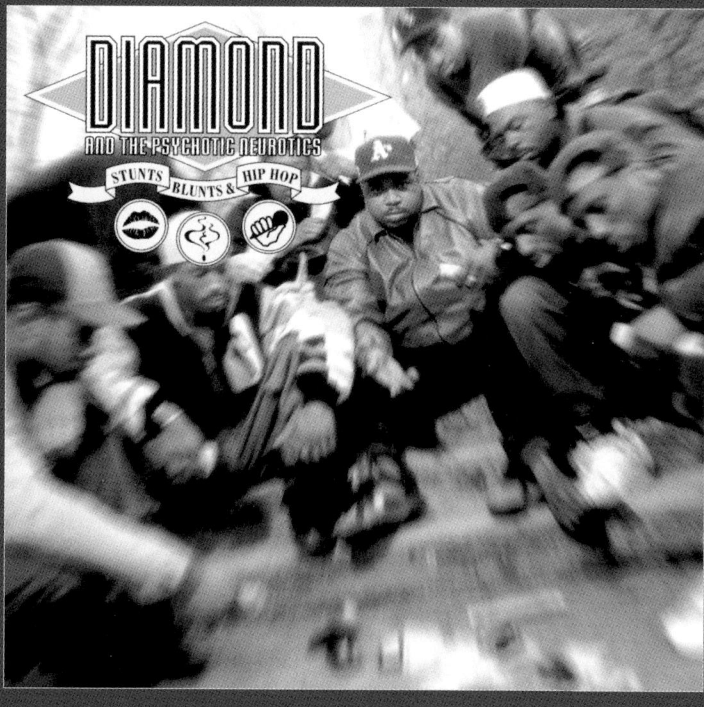

Stunts, Blunts & Hip Hop
Chemistry / Mercury, 1992

Sometimes people make things too complicated. Even hip-hop luminaries. It's an easy trap to fall into, but it rarely achieves optimal results.

Producer / MC Diamond's early '90s solo debut was all about putting the bells and whistles to the side (unless, of course, those bells and whistles were worth sampling) and letting skills speak. If you have any doubt as to his approach, peep a song title on the fourth vinyl side: "Keep It Simple Stupid."

Released just as the West Coast invasion was approaching critical mass via *The Chronic*, Diamond's Bronx-backed masterpiece *Stunts, Blunts & Hip Hop* stands as a textbook example of sonic innovation for both underground and pop producers alike.

Diamond and Dre actually share several similarities, whether or not one of them is a seven-figure savings account. Both are leaders of formidable hip-hop talent stables; both produce and rap; and both believe that less can be more.

Diamond [Joseph Kirkland, aka Diamond D] was born in 1969 and raised in the Bronx's Forest Houses projects. He says, "I was in Forest for like 20 years, until I was 20 or 21." As a child he went to Catholic school, but points out, "That don't mean nothin'. Just because parents pay for their child to go to a private school doesn't mean that the kid can't be a bad-ass. I went to a lot of jams and shows back when I was younger. I wasn't supposed to go, but I'd always find a way."

"I knew that I was going to be doing hip-hop when I was about 11 years old," he continues. "I just knew it, after I heard the Cold Crush Brothers and Grandmaster Flash tapes. Just being in the Bronx at that time [in the late '70s], you were just naturally exposed to shit. I first heard hip-hop as a live thing in about 1980. I was a little kid, and I had a two-block radius where I could go, but luckily the jams would be right in the projects. There was a section [of Forest] called the Blue Courts. We'd all be out there: me, Lord Finesse and Showbiz." Fat Joe was another, younger Forest resident in the mix, who would later work with Diamond and his crew.

Diamond's first hip-hop love wasn't for the mic or for producing. Like many before him, the turntables drew him in. He says, "My first thing was wanting to be a DJ, and that was the main thing for a while. I didn't start trying to be a producer until like 1989. Up until that point I was just DJing, doing house parties. I wasn't jamming out in the park or nothing like that. I had equipment when I was younger. My mother wasn't rich, but she had a good job and bought me turntables."

His earliest and strongest influence on the DJ front was a local deck-rocker named DJ Supreme. Diamond remembers, "Supreme was a pioneer who definitely paid his dues. He was a ghetto celebrity – he didn't have the national recognition of guys like Kool Herc or Afrika Bambaataa. But I looked up to him, and he knew I was an up-and-coming dude. He'd let me look through his records. He knew I was into beats. Supreme never made the progression into making records. He tried one time, but nothing came of it."

Another big influence on the young DJ was the Original Jazzy Jay, one of the most important Bronx DJs of the 1970s and '80s. Jay was the main DJ for the Zulu Nation and Afrika Bambaataa's Soulsonic Force, as well as a producer, involved with Soulsonic's "Planet Rock" and T La Rock's "It's Yours," among others. Additionally, he ran Jazzy Jay Studios, and Diamond would soon become a fixture there, after being introduced by his friend Master Rob.

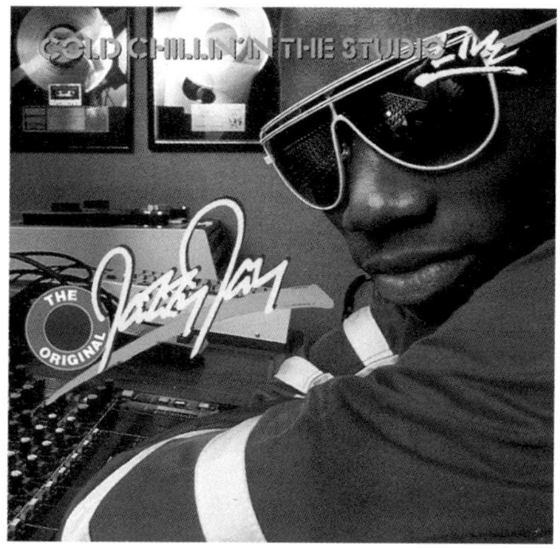

Diamond recalls, "By the time I met Jazzy Jay, the Masters of Ceremony [who released 1986's "Cracked Out" on Jay's Strong City label] were already on the scene. Jay was very well-off, he had like two cars. He was the man at Def Jam at the time. Jay had a vast knowledge of beats, and as soon as I met him, we clicked immediately. He would put on an old-school live tape and I would just sit there and name the breaks they were playing. I was this young kid naming beats that even people his age didn't know about."

Diamond also met many of the people who would be part of the Bronx-based Diggin' In The Crates [DITC] crew in his early years. He explains, "I met Showbiz in 1983 and I knew Lord Finesse before that, because Finesse and I went to the same elementary school, St. Augustine's on Franklin Avenue. He's two or three years younger than me, though, so we didn't hang out that much way back then. Master Rob, Show & Tell *[Author's note: Show & Tell is one person, not to be confused with Showbiz]* and LMD were all there, too, although they didn't stay with the crew in later years."

While he was building his DJ rep in the late-1980s, Diamond made his first stab at production as part of the group Ultimate Force, with his friend, MC Master Rob [Robert Daymon]. Their first song was the single "I'm Not Playing," which came out on UNI / MCA in 1989. Diamond says, "'I'm Not Playing' was my first production, although Jazzy Jay and I actually produced it, together. I didn't know how to program a drum machine or use a sampler, so I just told him what parts of the record to take, and how to put it together. I didn't get any credit on the record, and I didn't rap on it, I just did the beats."

The Ultimate Force recorded multiple tracks during that era at Jazzy Jay's. And although nothing else appeared on wax at the time, their *I'm Not Playing* album, produced by Diamond D with some co-production by Jazzy Jay, finally saw the light of day on Strong City / Traffic Entertainment in 2007.

In the years since his debut, Diamond has built up a truly impressive resume beyond his own solo work, producing tracks for The Fugees, Fat Joe, Busta Rhymes, Mos Def, Xzibit, and many others. He discusses his approach behind the boards, which hasn't changed much over the years: "I've played the drums and keyboards since I was in 7th grade, so I always start with the drums. Always. Drums, and then the bassline. Sometimes I'll arrange the samples and once it's flowing, the bassline will just come to me."

Since the word "Diamond" did not appear on the Ultimate Force 12-inch, the first work to be seen and heard under his own stage name was as part of his elementary school friend Lord Finesse's debut LP, *Funky Technician* [Wild Pitch, 1990]. "I did half the album, five songs, DJ Premier did the other half, and Showbiz did one track," he explains. "After that, I did work on Busy Bee's solo album on MCA [*Thank God For Busy Bee*, 1992 – production on four tracks]. But after Finesse's album, I immediately started on my own record, and that's when I really fell into my groove."

That album was *Stunts, Blunts & Hip Hop*, and for it he returned to his comfort zone: Jazzy Jay's studio.

Diamond explains how his debut came together: "I had recorded the song 'Best Kept Secret' for the Ultimate Force album that me and Master Rob were working on. Capitol Records wanted to sign Ultimate Force and I told them that, just in case the Ultimate Force album didn't blow up, I wanted to have a chance for my solo shot, because I had started rhyming at that point. I wanted that in writing, saying I could do a solo record, and Capitol wouldn't do it. So I was like, 'Fuck that, they must not really believe in us.'

For the [initial] deal with Capitol, I was just going to DJ and produce. Master Rob was going to be the main MC. But I had made 'Best Kept Secret' by then and niggas was feelin' it, so then Capitol wanted me to rhyme."

As for his newfound love of rocking the mic, Diamond explains, "I was always writing stuff, but Grand Puba [of Brand Nubian and, before that, Masters of Ceremony] influenced me to really start rhyming, because I was really feeling him back then on the mic. I probably started writing my own stuff around 1991. My style was very natural, just from being around block parties and park jams."

While he was arguing his case for solo control with Capitol, the Chemistry imprint of Mercury Records, formerly known as PWL America, offered Diamond a deal. He jumped on it. "Before the [*Stunts, Blunts & Hip Hop*] album, I was always setting aside beats that I knew I was going to use for something major," he explains. "I just didn't know what. I was keeping certain beats to myself. Once Chemistry came along, everything just clicked."

Stunts, Blunts & Hip Hop album ad.
Courtesy of the Harvard Hip-Hop Archive.

His deal with Chemistry didn't sit well with Master Rob, of course. Diamond says, "Rob was supposed to be on the *Stunts, Blunts & Hip Hop* album, but at the time he was bitter, because he thought I took the solo deal over our group deal with Capitol. To me, though, it seemed that Capitol was only believing in us like 60%. And if I'm going to go in the hole [as far as recouping an advance] $200,000 for a recording budget, I want to do it with someone who's gonna push the record 100%. I want to get my money back."

Static notwithstanding, with *Stunts, Blunts & Hip Hop*, Diamond had clearly hit his stride. It was a beat-fiend's dream, populated by tracks that manage to be in-your-face and laid-back at the same time. Recorded in a six-month period from late 1991 into early '92 at Jazzy Jay's – engineered by Jay, and mixed by Shane Faber – the LP yielded four classic singles: "Best Kept Secret"; "Sally Got A One Track Mind"; "[Fuck] What U Heard"; and "I'm Outta Here." Diamond perhaps sums up his style best in a lyric from "Check One,

Two": "My sound is raw, don't need a million samples."

And just who were the Psychotic Neurotics, who are credited [and pictured, albeit in a blur] on the album cover? They were his Forest crew and some non-Forest extended family – including Showbiz, Andre The Giant [AG] and Fat Joe. Lord Finesse was in California recording his second album when Diamond's was in production, so he didn't make the cover. By the next year, most of the Neurotics would come under the umbrella known as DITC: Diggin' In The Crates.

"DITC came around 1993, when we all had albums out and when it really started to be about our crew," Diamond explains. "But with Psychotic Neurotics we was just sittin' around, smokin' and drinkin' one day and we just agreed to call ourselves that."

Artistically, the album was a triumph. The only problems Diamond ran across involved label politics, which he says hurt sales in the end. He explains, "At the time the record came out, I was a new artist and I was just happy that someone was feelin' me as a producer and was down with the shit that I was tryin' to do. Chemistry had distribution through Mercury and I was maybe the fourth artist to come out on the label. But by the time my album dropped, the relationship between Chemistry and Mercury had deteriorated, because some of the other albums hadn't done so well. After they heard my album, Chemistry tried to get behind it, but at that point it was too late."

Diamond says, "It's hard for me to listen to my old stuff, since I'm such a better lyricist now." But his fans will always look back on his debut with nothing but a broad smile on their faces. And if you're trying to distill the Boogie Down Bronx sound of the early 1990s into a single set, *Stunts, Blunts & Hip Hop* can't be beat.

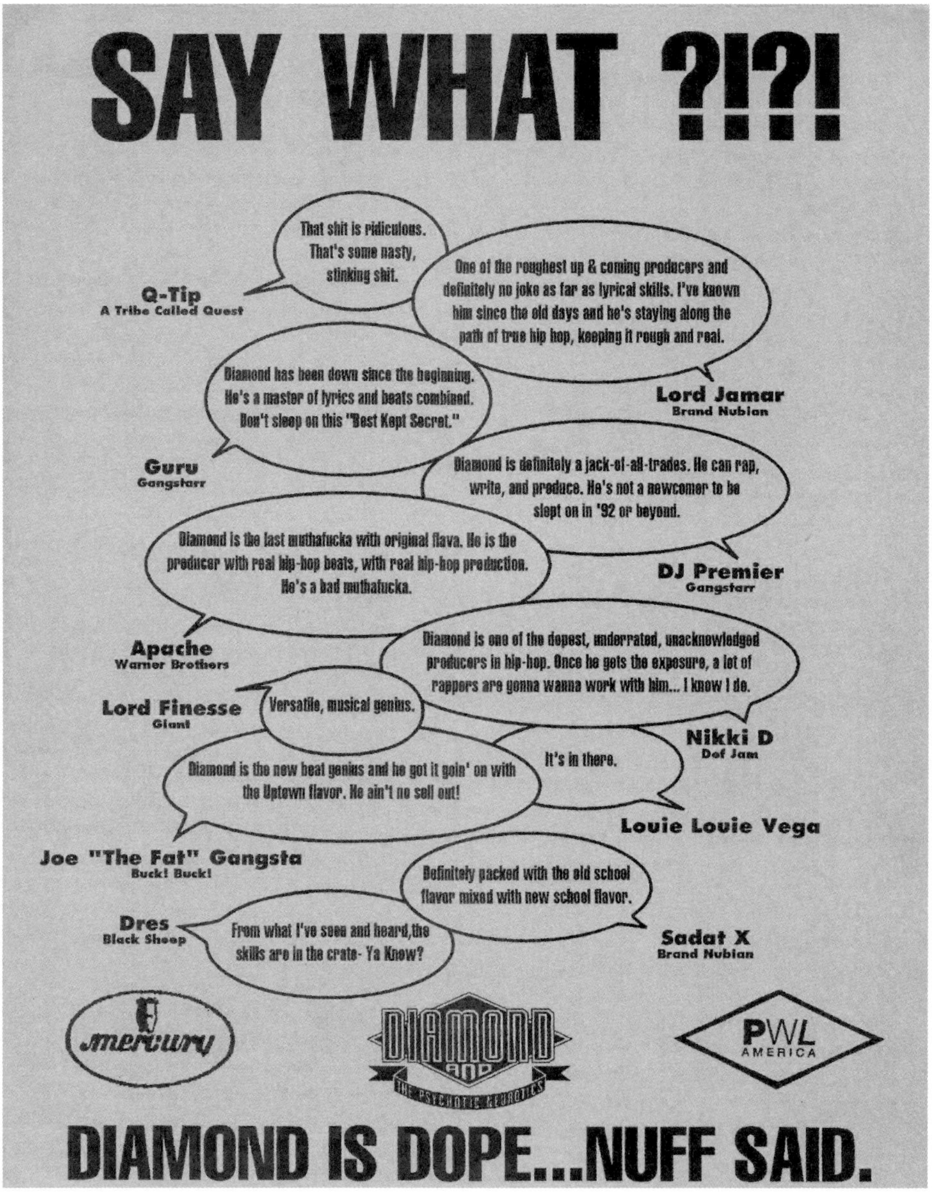

Diamond quote sheet from PWL America / Mercury.
Courtesy of Jamieson Grillo.

TRACKS

Best Kept Secret

[featuring Fat Joe, Whiz One, Bonita and LaReese]

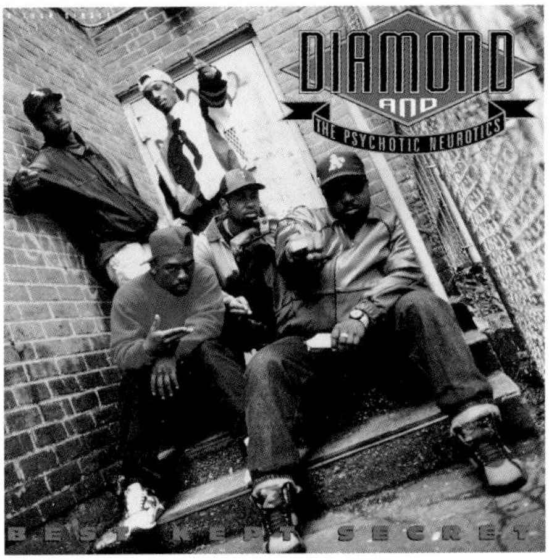

That was the first track I ever rapped on, and it was the one that got me my deal in the first place. It was originally going to be a bonus cut for the Ultimate Force album. Chemistry wanted to sign this guy named Joe Control and I was rhyming on one of the songs on his demo. So they asked him to bring *me* in there. They wanted other songs from me and I gave them "Best Kept Secret." They heard that and cut me a check in like a month. It's kind of fucked up, but that's the truth. I looked out for Joe, though, 'cause I knew how he felt. He was a good sport about it. As for the sample I used on there, Grand Puba had used that same record for MC Lyte on one of her albums. An album track, not a single. I gotta give Puba props on that one.

Sally Got A One Track Mind

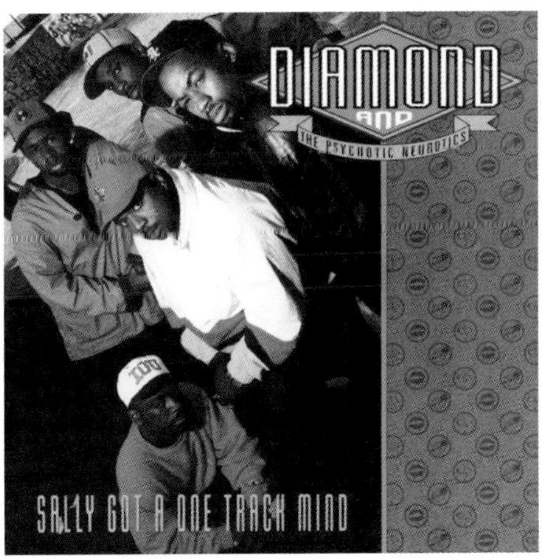

That was one of the singles. On that one I was talkin' about this chick from Brooklyn named Bonita. It's really about her. And it was partially about a girl I knew about named Lisa. We knew each other through mutual friends. They were both runnin' around on the streets, actin' crazy.

Step To Me

[produced by Showbiz, co-produced by Diamond]

I had that beat first, and then Showbiz put it all together. That's me just talkin' shit, because that's the way the track hit me. I added the Delfonics ["Ready Or Not, Here I Come"] on the hook. The drums and the bass and the saxophones were all from Showbiz.

Shut The Fuck Up

[featuring The Psychos]

That one's just the Psychotics buggin' out. That's a rare drum break, for all the beat-heads out there. Some of you probably got that one, but I'll never tell what it is.

"*!*!" What U Heard

That song is just me and Sadat X [from Brand Nubian], hanging out in the studio, getting high. Lakim Shabazz [the solo MC, part of the Flavor Unit] gave me that bassline, so I gave him co-production credit. To me, if somebody gives you a record, you gotta look out for them, because they could have kept it to themselves. I met Lakim through the Zulu Nation, and Lakim has always been nice.

I'm Outta Here

I always loved that one. That story is part fiction, part true. I'm not gonna say which is which. I wrote the lyrics to that in like a half-hour, in one sitting. We were gonna make a video for that song, but that was when things really fell apart with the record label. I was ready to do the video, and we had originally agreed that I would have input on all video concepts. I wanted to be the "John Doe" character of the song in the video, and they wanted to hire an actor. And instead of just sitting down and talking like gentlemen, shit just exploded. I didn't even show up on the video set, so it never got made. This was about six months after the album was out. We had done videos for the other singles on the album at that point.

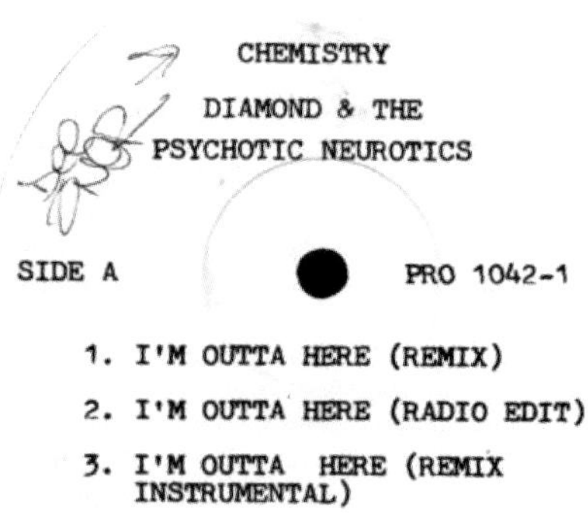

A Day In The Life [featuring Brand Nubian]

I was really into Grand Puba, so I wanted to do something with Brand Nubian. We had to play the original sample over [performed by musicians / engineers Shane Faber and Dave Ogrin], and we played it so good that it sounded like the real thing. Later on, the artist even tried to sue me, but there was nothin' they could do about it, 'cause it was played, not sampled. I won't say who the artist was, they passed away.

I Went For Mine [produced by Jazzy Jay, only on CD and cassette]

That song is on the CD, not on the original LP. Jazzy Jay produced that one. I had to shave some of the songs off for the vinyl edition, even though the album was on double wax.

Check One, Two

That's another one of my favorite tracks on the album. I had that beat for like two years. That was something I was saving. The track itself was some shit that came to me in the studio, and we just put it all together. DJ Mark the 45 King gave me that record the first time, so I gave him co-production.

Lunchroom Chatter

That was another skit. That one has Fatman Scoop on it, it was his first time on wax. He became a big DJ on Hot 97 in New York.

Confused [featuring Michelle Sweeting and Jasmine]

I always liked story rhymes, and that's what that was. I liked that record. Some people got mad about the R & B feel, but I didn't think nothin' of it.

Pass Dat Shit [featuring Whiz One, Maestro, Mike G. Q. and Fat Joe]

That's Fat Joe's first time on wax. Whiz One is a school teacher now. I put that track together, told everyone to come in with their own verse, and it worked out beautifully.

Freestyle (Yo, That's That Shit) [guitar by Shane Faber]

That's probably my favorite cut on the album. Large Professor [who is credited as co-producer] gave me that sample. Shane Faber plays guitar on part of that. I actually did freestyle some stuff on there, which is why I called it that. My usual style is to write all my lyrics down, but not that time.

K.I.S.S. (Keep It Simple Stupid)

Q-Tip [credited with co-production] gave me that bassline. I played him the drums I had picked out for the track and he knew I should put that bass on there. I didn't title it that for any real reason, I just couldn't come up with anything good.

Stunts, Blunts & Hip Hop

That was another ill beat that I was saving for myself. It almost didn't make the album. Other people liked it more than me. I thought it was too happy. But I gave in, in the end.

DJ JAZZY JEFF & THE FRESH PRINCE

He's The DJ, I'm the Rapper
Jive / RCA, 1988

"After all the success of the album and the Grammy, I drove to the McDonald's drive-thru one day, and the girl was like, 'What are you doing here*?!' And I was like, 'Just because I'm successful doesn't mean I don't like McDonald's fries anymore.' We hadn't changed, but peoples' perceptions about us definitely had."*

– DJ Jazzy Jeff

When you think back about hip-hop in the year 1988, a lot of hard, gritty stuff comes to mind. Public Enemy and the S1Ws. Eric B.'s and Rakim's steely-eyed swagger and thick gold chains. N.W.A.'s gangsta tales and sawed-offs.

But that year also saw the release of Biz Markie's *Goin' Off*; Kid 'N Play's *2 Hype*; and Slick Rick's *The Great Adventures of Slick Rick*. The bottom line was: hip-hop wasn't all hard-rocks and beat downs. The genre was breaking out, and there was room for everyone under its ever-expanding tent.

Into that fray entered the Philly-bred duo of Jazzy Jeff [Jeff Townes] & The Fresh Prince [Willard Smith]. They weren't brand-new that year, but 1988 was their indisputable introduction to the world at large. They sold a boatload of records, and even won rap's first Grammy.

They also made a pretty damned incredible album, which had so many top-shelf DJ tracks that it pushed it to become hip-hop's first double LP.

The first part of this musical equation, DJ Jazzy Jeff, was brought up in West Philadelphia, the youngest of six kids in a musical family. His father, who died before Jeff started DJing in the late '70s, was an MC for jazz legend Count Basie, and Jeff says that one of his older brothers played in the legendary Philly soul group The Intruders. "We had tons of old jazz records around the house," he recalls. "And we'd have bands rehearsing in the basement. I was around all kinds of music as a kid, and I took it all in, like a sponge."

Aside from a general love of music, he was drawn to DJing at a young age. His first stage moniker was Mixmaster Jeff, but he changed it to "Jazzy" because the old name took too many letters for a t-shirt he wanted to make (one of his old MCs also used to call him Jazzy). He explains his early history: "My grooming on the turntables came as a non-hip-hop DJ, probably around the same time that the early hip-hop guys were doing it in New York. I was DJing before there was hip-hop in Philly. I used to watch the guys at block parties with the huge speakers, and they were controlling hundreds of people. People were happy because of what the DJ was playing. And I used to just sit there on my bike and watch. I wanted to be that guy."

But there was one small problem. "I never had any equipment of my own," he says. "I was always in crews and they had the equipment. I used to work routines out in my head, because I couldn't actually practice at home. I almost think that *not* having equipment helped me, because DJing became more of a mental thing to me."

He explains, "For all four years of high school, I almost never ate lunch. I would take the money that my moms gave me for food and I would go downtown and buy records with it. I didn't have equipment, but I had records." His vinyl stash continued to grow throughout the late '70s, as did his local reputation as a party spinner. As for his approach, he explains: "My style has always been very rhythmic. I also play the drums, so it has to be about rhythm when I DJ. Plus, I always wanted my mom to think that what I was doing sounded cool. I wanted to sound like a *musician*."

By the early '80s, Jeff and other musical lookouts in Philly could not ignore the heavy rumblings of the new thing coming from New York City, and the Bronx specifically: hip-hop. "When hip-hop hit Philly, it changed all of our DJ styles," Jeff remembers. "And with me and my brothers and sisters, they were older. So I always felt that hip-hop was *mine*. It was my voice." Tapes from artists like the Cold Crush Brothers, the Fantastic Five, Grandmaster Flash and Lightning Lance began to get passed around, from Market Street to Mt. Airy. It was spreading like wildfire.

By the time Jeff had his own turntables, near his high school graduation from Southwest Philly's John Bartram High in 1982, he was already one of the more established party-rockers in town. And even though Philly was a mere two hours from New York, it might as well have been two continents away. "In Philly at that time, we didn't know what was really going on in New York, because we never went there. We had to develop our own scene. We were doing what we *thought* New York was doing. Eventually I saw the difference – in the mid-'80s Philly was still really into DJs. New York was focusing more on rappers by that point."

Jeff is quick to mention other early Philly DJ peers who shared flyers with him: Grandmaster Nell (from South Philly); Cosmic Kev (from Mt. Airy); and B-Force. He also reminisces about his own biggest influence, Kid Destroy. Jeff explains, "Kid Destroy was a genius as a DJ and as a producer. He was Mantronix before Mantronix, and he is the one who got me into the production aspect more than anyone else."

Back in the early 1980s, Jeff's dreams were modest to say the least. "My biggest goal back then was to be able to one day tell my kids that I was on a record," he says. "Then I could get a good job at the post office, and everything would be great. As long as I was on a record." His pre-Fresh Prince work on wax included scratching on local tracks by the Cazal Boys ["Snatching Cazals" from 1985 – Jeff's work is uncredited] and the Korner Boys [1985's "The Saga of Roxanne," with the B-side "Jazzy Jeff Scratch"].

He adds, "No one I knew ever dreamt about being an actual 'recording artist' back then. No one."

As Jeff really started to catch fire as a DJ in early 1985, he met his future rhyme partner in the random way in which these relationships usually begin.

"With the early house party scene in Philly, you knew who all the DJs and MCs were, because there weren't *that* many," Jeff recalls. "And you definitely knew who the good ones were. I saw Will [Smith] in passing at a lot of parties and heard him, and I think he had the same situation with me."

He continues, "Someone was having a party on his block [in the Wynnefield section of northwest Philly], and I got a last-minute call to DJ the party. I called the guy who MCed for me, Ice-C, and he was nowhere to be found. So I ended up just going to the party by myself. When I got there, me and Will recognized each other. I think he knew me more than I knew him. He asked where Ice was, I said I couldn't find him, and he asked if he could rock the mic. So he did."

"It was just weird, we had DJ-and-MC chemistry right away," he explains. "I remember I dropped out the fourth bar [in an instrumental record] like I always did, to give my MC a chance to say their punch-line, and he jumped right on it. Will had seen Ice-C perform with me before, but he was a lot better of an MC than Ice, even that first time we performed together."

The two men hung out later that night and a friendship was born. Jeff was three years older than Will and a lot more experienced in the hip-hop game, but the chemistry was what was most important. Before they could start working together as a duo, though, they both had previous entanglements to deal with.

Jeff had been working with Ice-C for a little while and they had done pretty well at parties around town, including gigs at Wagner's Ballroom in Mt. Airy; the Hotel

Philadelphia; and Jeff's home-base: the 52nd Street YMCA in West Philly. But, Jeff says, "Ice had started to get a big head. The 'local celebrity' thing got to him a bit. He wasn't as available for our shows as he once was, and he'd go to parties by himself and just bask in it. I wasn't with that."

Jeff continues, "So I started calling Will up for shows, and there were even two or three shows in 1985 with both Will *and* Ice as MCs. But it just got to the point where Ice kind of faded out of the picture. And I probably helped him fade out of the picture a little bit, too [laughs]. Basically, I left the guy I was with, Will left his DJ and the other rappers he was with, and we got together." This, Jeff says, was in the spring of 1985, before the "biggest party season of the year" – which meant gigs performing at high school proms and after-parties.

Jeff recalls one specific early performance staple that became their first calling-card: "One of the routines we would do was 'Girls Of The World Ain't Nothing But Trouble.' Will would rhyme the lyrics over the 'Moments In Love' instrumental [by the Art of Noise]. I can still remember watching 500 people in a crowd just stop and stare at Will, hanging on every word of that story."

Until he joined up with Jeff, Will – who had always called himself The Fresh Prince on the mic, and who graduated Overbrook High School that spring – had been in a local group called the Hypnotic MCs. There were two other MCs in the group besides Will: Lord Supreme and Jamie Fresh. The DJ was Groove Damoast, and they also featured an accomplished beatboxer and occasional rapper named Ready Rock C.

When faced with the choice of going along with his neighborhood crew, or teaming up with one of the hottest DJs in Philly as a solo MC, it's clear what would have appealed to a young rapper with ambition. Will joined up with Jeff, and Ready Rock came along. "I was definitely cool with Ready Rock coming into the picture," says Jeff. "He was dope. He wasn't the main focal point of what we were doing, but it was great to have him in the mix."

The new trio, with a name that only featured two of them, rocked all the big high school parties of the late spring in Philly. The group also drew some "industry" attention. Philly was far from a hip-hop hotbed when it came to putting out records, but there was some action going on, with labels like Slice and multiple one-off imprints, some which were based around the Sound Makers distribution company.

The biggest label in town, when it came to hip-hop in the mid-'80s, was Pop Art Records. Pop Art still had bigger things ahead of them, but at the time, they had had indie hits with – ironically – several Marley Marl-produced acts out of New York, including Roxanne Shante and Craig G.

Brothers Lawrence and Dana Goodman ran Pop Art and had gotten wind of Jeff and Will. Jeff says, "They heard a recording of us at one of those parties from '85, approached us and wanted to put us in the studio. The Goodmans lived in Wynnefield, where Will lived, and they were tapped into the scene. Everybody knew Pop Art, it was really the first Def Jam. And it was *the* label to be on in Philly."

After signing a deal for a single – and, as they would find out later, a lot more – they were matched up with local engineer Joe "The Butcher" Nicolo. "I had made a couple records with Lawrence for Pop Art at that point," Nicolo explains. "We had a working relationship, and the next record at that time was their nephew Steady B, who put out 'Just Call Us Def' [in 1985]. When it came to the label in 1985, as far as I could tell, Dana Goodman was more the radio and promotions guy and Lawrence ran the label and did more production."

Recordings were done at Studio 4, on the outskirts of downtown Philly ["3rd and Callowhill, Northern Liberties, near the water," says Nicolo], which was owned by Joe and his brother Phil. Nicolo, who was raised a Beatles fan, looked at Jeff and Will – as later A & R reps would also do – through a pop lens rather than a pure hip-hop one. "It was more about making their early songs like pop records. That's where it started: 'Girls Ain't Nothing But Trouble.' That fit perfectly into the category of people who would say, 'I'm not into rap music, but I like *them*.'"

The single for "Girls Ain't Nothing But Trouble," which featured a modicum of turntable finesse, a whole lot of Will Smith charm and style, and more than a little bit of Slick Rick's "La Di Da Di" storytelling swagger, came out in the fall of 1985. But, interestingly, not on Pop Art. Instead, the label read Word-Up Records [or, in certain pressings, just Word Records, additionally saying it was produced and mixed by "J. & S. Salaam" instead of listing Nicolo or the Goodmans]. It seemed to be the label's debut release.

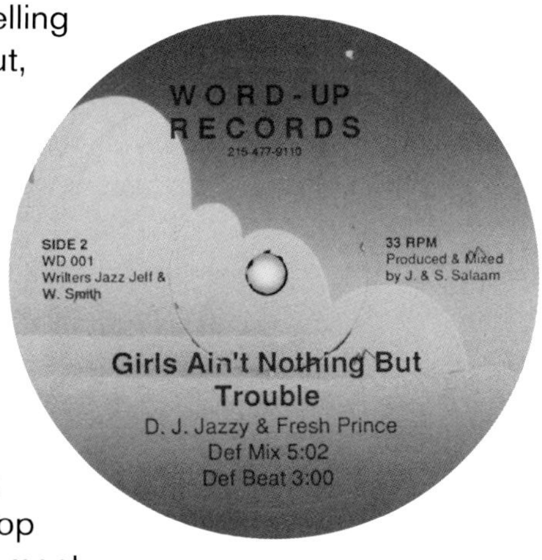

This was a bit of a shock to both Jeff and Will. Jeff says, "I found out later that Lawrence Goodman didn't like 'Girls Ain't Nothing But Trouble,' and that's why it didn't come out on Pop Art. Apparently he and Dana got into a big argument and Dana said, 'OK, I'm gonna start my own label [Word Up] and put it out.'" Joe Nicolo backs up this story from his own recollections about the sub-label's formation.

It turns out that Dana Goodman's A & R inclinations were correct – the song was a hit, propelling the group to the top of the Philly hip-hop scene and getting them out-of-town gigs, including frequent jaunts to New York City. The popularity also meant that Dana Goodman wanted more songs to sell, in the form of a full album. And so back they went to Studio 4.

"When we recorded *Rock The House*, it wasn't a long process, probably just two or three weeks," Nicolo recalls. "We'd cut two or three songs a session. Jeff and Will mostly knew what they were doing, but not completely. The first pass through, we'd put down basic music and Will would do his vocals. He was always quick with those, he was a smart kid. Then on the next session we'd go back to those two or three songs, Jeff would add his cuts, Will would ad-lib stuff or re-cut vocals, and it'd be pretty much done at that point. It was a group effort on that album."

He adds, "Absolutely no disrespect to the Goodmans, because they taught me what real rap was and brought me into the game, but me, Jeff and Will had more to do with that album [from a production standpoint] than Lawrence or Dana did."

Rock The House, original cover, Word Up Records.

Although not given any production or even co-production credits on the album, Will and Jeff were listed as "Assistant Engineers." [Nicolo was listed as Engineer, with no production credit]. Nicolo says, "Maybe the Goodmans did that to make Jeff and Will feel like they participated in molding the sound of the record? It's not much of a credit to boast about, but hey, why not?"

The album cover and credits were indeed a disappointment to Jeff and Will. First off, Dana Goodman somehow thought it was a good idea to rip-off Run-DMC's classic *King of Rock* cover, which had blown up worldwide just one year before. Secondly, sole production was given to Dana ["D. Goodman"]. Jeff says, "Will and I pretty much produced that first album but we only got credit as writers."

[Author's note: The third crew member, Ready Rock C [Clarence Holmes], gets a lone writing credit on the seemingly faked live rap-and-beatbox song 'Rock the House (Live NY Union Square)' on the original issue; but for some reason the writing credit disappears on a later Jive version].

In between recording their debut LP and its release, Jeff managed to shock the hip-hop world by winning his first and only DJ battle, the New Music Seminar's 1986 "Battle for World Supremacy" (taking out 1985's champion, DJ Cheese, in the first round), and then promptly retiring from the battle scene. This was only in part because he had more hit records to make. "I didn't compete in 1987 or after that," Jeff explains. "I had proved what I wanted to prove to myself in 1986. I was never a battle DJ anyways. In 1987 we were touring the world with a hit record, so I just brought those skills to our live show." His championship trophy is pictured on the back of *Rock the House*, with Jeff and Will both proudly showing it off.

Rock The House, original back cover, Word Up Records.

Jeff continues, "Winning that Battle was a validation to me, because Philly DJs didn't get a lot of respect back then. It was a test to see how good I was. Lady B [the legendary Philly radio DJ, who released the pioneering female MC track, "To The Beat Y'all," in 1979] is the one who got me in, over some resistance. After that, I got respect. And my city did, too. Winning the Battle also got us more shows. 'Girls' was blowing up with Will's vocals, and then I was this DJ people wanted to see." That double-headed rap monster would go on to define the group for the next decade.

Concert flyer, Glassboro State College, November, 1986.

Courtesy of Isaac "Iceman" Samuels and Anthony "Antman" Phillips.

But let's get back to the vinyl at hand: the group had another hit on its hands with *Rock The House*, which – although it lacks a release year anywhere on the sleeve or label – was on the market by mid-1986, in Jeff's estimation. It would also be re-issued on two different UK-based labels by 1987: first by Champion and then by Jive. Thankfully, both editions had new covers.

There are some impressive songs on *Rock The House*, from DJ workouts like "A Touch of Jazz" and "The Magnificent Jazzy Jeff" to Will's growinglyimpressive storytelling style heard on "Just One Of Those Days." Jeff dislikes only one song [which Nicolo hates as well]: the "Girls" answer record, featuring Ice Cream Tee, "Guys Ain't Nothing But Trouble." "That was Dana's idea," Jeff says.

"When *Rock The House* first hit, we didn't really care about credits or any of that," Jeff explains. "We were just glad to have an album out. All I ever wanted to do was put out a record with my name on it. And so I doubt we even had time to look at any of the credits. Honestly, people were playing 'Girls' when the single came out, I was like, 'That's it, I don't have to do anything else.'" He says he was more upset about it later on.

Either way, Dana and even one-time non-believer Lawrence Goodman were pushing the record at retail, and by mid-'87 they were rocking live dates from California to "Top of the Pops" in London. Jeff recalls, "We made no money off the record itself, but we did a lot of shows and we made money that way. Next time around, though, we were going to need to get something more."

That next time around came in the form of Jive Records, who had first made note of the duo via Jeff's New Music Seminar victory, but also from the sales they were generating for *Rock The House*. "When we got involved with them, they had already put out *Rock The House* on Word Up," says Ann Carli, who also went by "Tokyo Rose" when writing fanzine reviews or being a radio personality on WBAI in New York.

Carli was in charge of Artist Development at Jive Records in their very small New York office, which was the U.S. beachhead for the London-based label. "At that time, it was just me and [Jive U.S. label head] Barry Weiss, with our offices in a brownstone," she explains. Carli had actually already reviewed *Rock The House* in a small publication called *Hip-Hop Hitlist* (as Tokyo Rose) and was present when Jeff won the New Music Seminar Battle the year before.

As a result of the growing buzz on Jeff and the duo overall, Weiss and Carli brought them in for a meeting. Carli recalls, "During the meeting, Barry mentioned that I was Tokyo Rose and they couldn't believe it. They had memorized the article I had written about them and recited it word-for-word. They told me it was the first review they had ever gotten."

Carli says, "With *Rock The House*, 'Girls Ain't Nothing But Trouble' was already a hit. Since Jive had done Whodini's 'Friends' [from 1984], we already knew that hip-hop could cross-over to pop radio. Plus there were a bunch of other great songs on their record."

Jive was definitely interested, and entered into a deal with Dana Goodman to license

samplers and drum machines including the Fairlight, Synclavier and Linn." Before working with Jazzy Jeff & The Fresh Prince, Harris had played important engineering and production roles on Kool Moe Dee albums beginning with 1987's *How Ya Like Me Now* (on Jive, of course). Further back, he also played a more limited role on Whodini's early Jive releases, considering that Larry Smith was the group's main producer.

Harris, in fact, says that it's not a surprise that there are sonic similarities with basslines and programming between *Kool Moe Dee* [from 1987] and *He's The DJ*. "We didn't change the instrumentation we were using throughout that whole period," he admits. Basically, any keyboard-generated bassline you hear on *He's The DJ* flowed out of Harris' fingertips. He adds, "The tracks we did for the album, which were recorded in Battery Studio Three, were done almost entirely with a Fairlight, with samples I had put in there from all over the place. Sometimes we would use Linn or [Roland TR-] 808 drums, too."

Fairlight CMI trade magazine ad.

"When we were there in London, we basically kept U.S. hours," Jeff recalls. "We would go into the studio around 4 p.m. every afternoon [11 a.m. Philly-time] and work until about 4 a.m. We would fight to stay up until 6 a.m., eat some Corn Flakes at the hotel, and then go to sleep until 3:30 p.m. I barely saw the sun while I was there. I had turntables and my drum machine set up in my hotel room, and every day I would pick up the drum machine and take it to the studio."

Regarding his new recording partners – who weren't requested by Jeff or Will – Jeff says: "When we first started, we said, 'Who the fuck are these guys?' Like, 'Here we go again, we're gonna do all this shit and not get any credit.' But I think Pete and Chuck knew the delicate nature of what we were going through [adjusting to new studio-mates]."

Harris remembers his and New's "briefing" before they met Jeff and Will: "We met in Clive's office and he said, 'I've got these two guys I'm bringing from Philly. They have some great material, and the guy's a great rapper.' The most important thing we talked about, internally, was *crossover*, because that was very hard to get in those days, with rap music. Clive really thought they had crossover potential, because he thought the lyrics were mainstream radio-friendly. But he also said it needed a lot of work to get it there. I do remember that we flagged [their 1985 single] 'Girls Ain't Nothing But Trouble' as an example of that potential."

Jeff says, "When we started recording, me and Will did what we did and Pete Harris had a Synclavier [digital sampling synthesizer] that he would play on the side of the room, with headphones on. I would make the beat and get it how I wanted it, and at some point Pete would turn up a fader and play what he had been working on, to go along with what I had done. He was easing his way in. And in the end, it worked out."

"Being a DJ in the studio, considering all the technology we had [meaning: keyboards and samplers], was relatively obsolete," explains Harris. "So, Jeff would scratch more as a post-production thing. I did always have the sense that Jeff was a bit apprehensive about us being anything more than engineers and twiddling knobs."

L to R: Fresh Prince, DJ Jazzy Jeff and Ready Rock C.
Photograph by Douglas Rowell. Courtesy of the Adler Hip-Hop Archives / Cornell University Hip-Hop Collection.

Harris had – and has – nothing against Jeff as a musician or a person, he was simply coming from a very different background: one of a hit-making pop producer. DJ cuts on songs, or DJ-based songs, simply weren't going to sell the album to pop fans. And, remember, crossing over was his only objective.

One little-known fact about the chronology of the songs recorded for *He's The DJ, I'm The Rapper* is that almost all of Jeff's DJ-centric cuts were actually recorded *before* they arrived in London. These were done with Joe Nicolo at Studio 4 in Philly. The original Jive plan was to put out a 'Scratch Album,' as Jeff calls it, before the group's full vocal-centric debut.

"Initially, Jive wanted to put out my DJ album, because no one had ever done that," Jeff explains. "That was to capitalize on all the attention I was getting as a DJ in 1986 and 1987. We had that album pretty much done and in the can by the middle of '87."

Joe Nicolo backs this up: "We were definitely making a DJ record for Jeff. We recorded it in Philly and me and Jeff flew to Battery in London to mix it there. I remember mixing it on the 4th of July [1987]. It was a full album, not an EP. I don't know where some of those tracks went, but Jive must have them in the archives somewhere. Most of the DJ tracks made it onto *He's The DJ*." But, he notes, not all of them.

Ann Carli explains, "In the early days, Jeff was definitely the star. Will was underrated as an MC and a lyricist, even until *He's The DJ* came out. The way the album ended up coming out, with Jeff's and Will's sides, it was much more of a partnership."

"The DJ-only album was a little limited as a full album," Nicolo admits. "It was kind of like pulling a rabbit out of a hat to make it work. So at the time [that they decided to mix those tracks into *He's The DJ*], I wasn't heartbroken. If that DJ record had come out in 1987 then *He's The DJ* wouldn't have been the same. I think in the end it worked out perfectly."

[Author's note: For confirmation of the original 'Scratch Album' plan, look no further than one of the stickers Jive put on the shrink-wrap of an early pressing of the album: "Two albums for the price of one!," it proclaims. "New studio album plus bonus scratch album."]

Jeff says, "Once we got to London, we all decided that we wanted to mix the scratch stuff in with the vocal tracks. Some of the vocal ones were DJ songs before Will started rapping on them anyways. And then someone said, 'What if we put out a double album? No one in hip-hop has ever done that before.'" *[Author's note: If they had put out Jeff's 'Scratch Album,' it would have preceded the 'Turntablist' movement in the mid-'90s – led by the X-Men and Invisibl Skratch Piklz – by more than a half-decade].*

Jeff says that they did indeed have many of the DJ-centric songs done, mixed and mastered before their London excursion, but adds, "We didn't go over to London with any other songs done. We went and made everything else over there. Aside from the DJ tracks, we recorded and mixed the entire album in one month. We probably recorded for two-and-a-half weeks and mixed for 10 or 12 days. It was pretty quick." Pete Q. Harris backs this timeline up.

Songs completed during these whirlwind London sessions included the album's three singles: "Parents Just Don't Understand"; "Nightmare On My Street"; and "Brand New Funk." All in all, Harris estimates, "We were involved in about 10 songs from the album [out of 18 songs on the 2-LP]. Definitely not all of them."

Songs that were already done, like Jeff's DJ tracks, weren't touched by Harris or New. Or if they were tweaked, it wasn't in any significant way. Harris adds, "The material was fundamentally really good when they arrived, and the working dynamic was all very friendly. We were all there with a common goal: to make a huge-selling record."

Joe Nicolo lists the following songs from the album as being done with him at Studio 4 in Philly (with Dana Goodman in the studio at least at times, although neither Jeff nor Joe say he did any production on them): "Here We Go Again"; "Charlie Mack (1st Out Of The Limo)"; "Parents Just Don't Understand" [an early version]; "DJ On The Wheels"; "My Buddy"; "Rhythm Trax – House Party Style"; "He's The DJ, I'm The Rapper"; "Hip-Hop Dancer's Theme"; and "Jazzy's In The House."

Nicolo says that "Parents Just Don't Understand" was in very good shape before they left for London, and Harris mentions that Will had lyrics for the song ready when he arrived [see song comments, below]. Nicolo also states, "Jeff was a major production factor on *He's The DJ*, there is no doubt about that."

"Honestly, Jeff wasn't the focus of our attention during those sessions," Harris explains. "We had to make Will's lyrics shorter, more punchy, and presented so that they would get to the hook a lot quicker. It was more about *arranging* the music. Taking a fantastic idea or concept and refining it. Jeff and Will already had hits on their own, but the tracks still needed tweaking, especially with their hooks. The basslines they had were, quite honestly, pedestrian. So that's what we did: we made things more musical, more commercialized."

Harris continues, "We didn't create lyrics, but we helped *focus* the lyrics when we found certain topics or approaches to be amusing. For instance, stealing your dad's car and getting caught [from 'Parents']. We've all done dumb, teenage stuff. When we worked with Kool Moe Dee, it wasn't as much work, because he already had three- or four-minute songs ready when he came to the studio."

Jeff says that, overall, the London recordings went well, and that they ended up enjoying their work with Pete Q. Harris, who gets production credit on most of the album tracks. Bryan "Chuck" New, who also gets production credit on most songs, didn't mesh as well with the duo from Philly. "I really did not like that guy, he had no respect for me or Will as producers," says Jeff. "Pete was a keyboardist and he added some things that really helped certain songs. Chuck was *just* the engineer."

Ann Carli, who was not in London during the recordings, says: "Pete definitely added a lot to what the guys were doing. And I think Bryan probably did, too. Those guys created the *sound* of that record. I wasn't there, but I don't think the production credits that Pete and Bryan got were unfair. Although Jeff and Will might."

The third member of the group who was ever heard on wax – Ready Rock C, who was with Will since the early-'80s – had a couple features on the album as well, including the Human Beatbox tracks "My Buddy" and "Human Video Game."

"By the time we got to *He's The DJ*, Ready Rock was just the beatboxer," Jeff explains. "We had that dynamic from before and we kept it all in the mix, but we knew he wasn't going to be on every record we did. Just like there were some records that I didn't do cuts on. When we were doing the records on those earlier albums, he never wanted to make beats. He didn't want to start making beats until later."

Jeff adds, "Ready Rock was great. Doug E. Fresh was the ultimate beatboxer, Biz Markie and Buffy from the Fat Boys did their thing. Ready was very technical, he was our Michael Winslow [the actor from the "Police Academy" movie franchise who did sound effects]. He could do the video games, he could make it sound like he was beatboxing underwater. He was a great showman, too."

Ready Rock feels differently about his role in the production and songwriting of the group. He states, "I was in London for the entire time the album [*He's The DJ*] was being recorded. Even though un-mentioned *[Author's note: I assume he means un-credited]*, I co-wrote 'Parents Just Don't Understand' and contributed many creative factors to the project."

In the end, when it came to combining Jeff- and Will-centric tracks into one double-album package, no one involved is upset with the final product. And, considering the success the album had, how could they be? Jeff says, "That was the best way to do it, definitely. When you have records like 'Parents,' that become hits, it changes everything, because those become the main focus." For whatever reason, many of the DJ-only cuts were sequenced towards the end of the record, although Jeff says this wasn't necessarily on purpose.

"Even despite the hits that featured Will's vocals, I never got lost in the shuffle," Jeff says. "That's where the album title came from. Half of the album is him, and half of it is me." *[Author's note: It should be pointed out that the two biggest hit singles from the album had DJ-centric songs on their respective B-sides: "Parents" had "Live At Union Square, November 1986"; and "A Nightmare On My Street" had "Rhythm Trax-House Party Style"].*

For further proof of the equality of the duo, look no further than the vinyl cover of the album, shot by Doug Rowell with art direction by Ann Carli. Jeff is alone on the front, and Will stands solo on the back. "We wanted to strip the album cover down to who they were," Carli explains. "Both of them had their own personality, and the album reflected that."

Although Jeff was the star as they initially went into the studio to record *He's The DJ*, it was clear that The Fresh Prince had leapt several levels higher before the album was completed. Will's growth as an MC and an on-stage personality had continued throughout his time with Jeff and Ready Rock in the mid-'80s. But by 1988, he had very clearly come into his own, as a rapper who now stood shoulder-to-shoulder with other storytelling masters like Slick Rick and Dana Dane.

"Jeff was great but Will was always the star to me," Harris says. "The ideas, the rhymes, the cerebral conceptualizing of tracks. That stuff seemed to mostly be coming from him." Jeff says, "I've always been a behind-the-scenes guy. Even with Will. I'm the captain of the ship, but he runs the bridge. And I'm cool with that."

Ann Carli has an important recollection from the "Parents Just Don't Understand" video shoot, which helps to sum up how far Will had come in the short time in which she had known him: "We were doing the video transfers from the day's shoot, and me and [director] Scott Kalvert were watching the takes. Up until that point, Will to me had been this loud-mouthed, gangly kid who always had a pimple on the side of his face. He always wore ball-caps, he wasn't ever bothered with grooming his hair. Basically, he was a kid. But we were looking at the footage as it was synched up with the lyrics of the song, and we both turned to each other and said, 'This kid is going to be a star. The camera *loves* him.' Up until then, we hadn't realized it. But it was all of a sudden impossible to ignore."

Regarding the "over-stuffed" status of the album's musical material, Carli recalls: "There was definitely a discussion at some point as to whether we had too many songs. From the record label point-of-view, having the lyric-driven stuff, like 'Parents', was obviously always fine. But we also knew that 'Parents' wouldn't be a big record in the clubs, or in the quote-unquote streets. So the DJ stuff was important for that. Jeff took DJing to another level and we knew what he added to the group's credibility in the hip-hop world, and to the group's identity. So when it came to the album overall, we knew there had to be a mix. It had to be grounded on both sides."

Carli adds, "I really fought for the gatefold cover we did for that record, because it was the first double-album in hip-hop. Jeff and Will came back from London with these incredible songs and I thought the album deserved packaging like that. We had a whole discussion – or argument – about the packaging costs, but it all worked out. It might have only been the first 100,000 or 150,000 copies that had gatefolds because we really had to fight with Jive's parent company, because the packaging cost that much more. And we also included the lyrics in those gatefolds, because that was equally important."

Jeff says this sounds right to him, adding that he thinks the gatefolds and lyrics sheets were only for non-U.S. pressings. "I don't think that was for any domestic [U.S.] versions of the album," he says. "I have signed a lot of records that had those lyrics sheets in them, and at first I was like, 'Where did you get that?' Because it wasn't anything I had seen. I think that usually happened when I was in London or other places overseas, the kids there had the gatefold version."

Ann Carli also remembers another item that proved their connection with fans: "They were the first or second hip-hop group – LL Cool J might have been first – to have their own '900 number' [where fans paid a certain charge per minute to call in and hear recorded messages]. That's actually where they made their first big money, not on their records or touring. I would have to call them when they were out on the road to give us more messages, because the fans couldn't get enough."

The group got by on great music, but their excellent videos didn't hurt. Aside from a sadly shelved, huge-budget video for "A Nightmare On My Street" [see song comments, below], the video for "Parents Just Don't Understand" couldn't have been a bigger crossover hit for the group. And the live performance seen (and heard) on the third single, "Brand New Funk," helped with the more serious hip-hop fans, to remind them that this was a group with a history of rocking shows, not just looking good on a sound-stage.

Album ad, 1988.

Jeff says, "I think we are both a little bit overlooked when people talk about hip-hop history, and I think a lot of that is because of how successful Will has become as an actor. Like, 'Ah, those guys never gave a fuck about that rap shit.' But if it wasn't for rap, nothing else would have happened for either of us."

He's The DJ, I'm The Rapper hit shelves worldwide in March of 1988, preceded by the worldwide smash song and video for "Parents Just Don't Understand." The album went platinum within months and currently sits at triple-platinum status.

Jeff recalls, "I remember we played the album for Russell Simmons when we were on the [Run-DMC] 'Run's House' tour. He said, 'You guys will have a gold album in a month.' And we said, 'Get outta here!' But it went gold in five weeks. We started two acts before Run-DMC on that tour, and pretty quickly we were on right before them."

The group also won the first-ever "Best Rap Performance" Grammy, for "Parents Just Don't Understand," in February of 1989 *[Author's note: Separate hip-hop album and single awards for the Grammys did not begin until 1995].* It was bittersweet, since some members of the hip-hop community – fans and artists alike – felt that a "harder" group, like Public Enemy, Eric B. & Rakim or Big Daddy Kane, should have won the inaugural award.

But that assessment lacked a true understanding of what *He's The DJ* and what Will and Jeff were all about. Jeff says, "That backlash *did* bother me, absolutely. There was very little 'pop' element in the way that Will and I grew up in Philly. Just because we liked to make music that was fun, and just because our music crossed-over to the suburbs, we got labeled as if we were from the suburbs. And I was like, 'I wish I could take you all to *my* neighborhood!' Also keep in mind: 'Girls Ain't Nothing But Trouble' was a huge hit at [New York hip-hop clubs] the Latin Quarter and Union Square. They didn't play crossover junk at those spots."

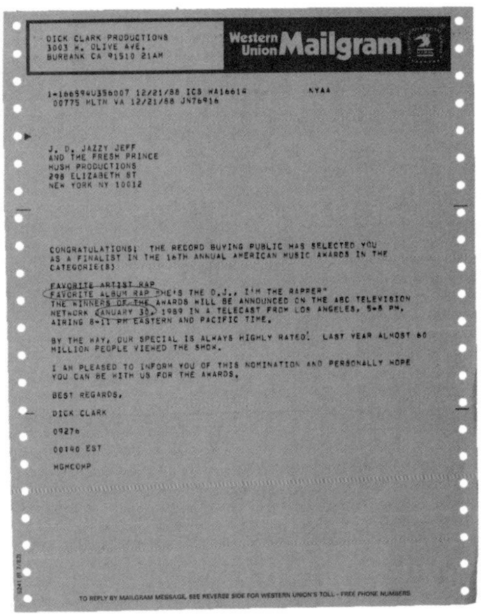

DICK CLARK PRODUCTIONS
3003 W. OLIVE AVE.
BURBANK CA 91510 21AM

Western Union Mailgram

1-166594U356007 12/21/88 ICS WA16614 NYAA
00775 MLTN VA 12/21/88 JN76916

J. D. JAZZY JEFF
AND THE FRESH PRINCE
HUSH PRODUCTIONS
298 ELIZABETH ST
NEW YORK NY 10012

CONGRATULATIONS! THE RECORD BUYING PUBLIC HAS SELECTED YOU AS A FINALIST IN THE 16TH ANNUAL AMERICAN MUSIC AWARDS IN THE CATEGORIE(S)

FAVORITE ARTIST RAP
FAVORITE ALBUM RAP "HE'S THE D.J., I'M THE RAPPER"
THE WINNERS OF THE AWARDS WILL BE ANNOUNCED ON THE ABC TELEVISION NETWORK JANUARY 30, 1989 IN A TELECAST FROM LOS ANGELES, 5-8 PM, AIRING 8-11 PM EASTERN AND PACIFIC TIME.

BY THE WAY, OUR SPECIAL IS ALWAYS HIGHLY RATED! LAST YEAR ALMOST 60 MILLION PEOPLE VIEWED THE SHOW.

I AM PLEASED TO INFORM YOU OF THIS NOMINATION AND PERSONALLY HOPE YOU CAN BE WITH US FOR THE AWARDS.

BEST REGARDS,

DICK CLARK

09276

00:40 EST

MGMCOMP

TO REPLY BY MAILGRAM MESSAGE, SEE REVERSE SIDE FOR WESTERN UNION'S TOLL - FREE PHONE NUMBERS

Congratulatory Mailgram from Dick Clark to "J. D. Jazzy Jeff and the Fresh Prince," December, 1988.
Courtesy of the Adler Hip-Hop Archives / Cornell University Hip-Hop Collection.

Beyond Run-DMC's hits a couple years earlier and the Beastie Boys' raucous 1986 debut *Licensed To Ill*, *He's The DJ, I'm The Rapper* was an important next step in the evolution of hip-hop becoming an *American* phenomenon, not just a New York or a so-called urban one. It featured universal themes, funny and witty rhymes, heavy DJ skills and just about everything else you could put onto four album sides.

"I don't think anyone knew how big that record was going to be," says Ann Carli. "I think that people today forget all the great musical, DJ songs on there. The Jeff stuff. The storytelling, Will Smith songs are why the album sold millions. Because they were stories that kids everywhere, no matter what their ethnicity, could relate to. But a lot of the DJ records kept the hip-hop audience happy. That album just had everything."

"It was really about lyrical crossover," says Pete Q. Harris today. "That was most important. Will's weren't your typical brag lyrics that a lot of rappers were doing back then. His stood apart. And visually, they were also very friendly. Will was a video marketing dream, really."

Joe Nicolo says, "*He's The DJ, I'm The Rapper* was a record that people could *listen* to. It wasn't just for the hardcore rap audience, with two hit songs and then the rest of the album sounds the same. It became one of the first rap albums back then on a *Rolling Stone* list of 'Albums You Should Hear.' It walked the line of credibility and pop factor, and that's not easy to do. It was definitely one of the first rap records to do that."

"We always pushed the envelope," Jeff beams. "We just believed we could do anything. 'Just put us in the studio!' It wasn't good enough to just make a record: we had to make a *double* record. We needed to do more than what other people had done. And I think we did that."

Jeff adds, in summation: "We brought fun and we definitely brought a lot of diversity. There were hits, and there was a lot of skill, too. To me, it was just a very well-balanced hip-hop record. It wasn't ever just one thing. We didn't try to cross over, that was never in our minds. It just happened. It was a once-in-a-lifetime album."

TRACKS

Nightmare On My Street

ANN CARLI: That song was up-front in the sequence of the album, leading the charge, because we were pretty sure that it was going to be a huge hit. We *really* tried to do a tie-in with New Line Cinema [the movie company who owned the "Nightmare On Elm Street" franchise], but that didn't go as planned. Me and Barry Weiss talked to New Line before the album came out, because we wanted to collaborate. But New Line just thought that the Fat Boys made more sense for them. *[Author's note: The Fat Boys did the theme to 1988's "Nightmare On Elm Street 4: The Dream Master," called "Are You Ready For Freddy?" The song played over the end credits and was on the soundtrack, plus was released as a single on Tin Pan Apple Records].* It could have been a huge thing if they had just worked with us. But New Line even sued us. Ironically, Whodini [a Jive artist] did a song for the next "Nightmare On Elm Street" movie, so I worked with them on that. Bob Shaye from New Line testified as part of the suit, it was ridiculous. He was talking about Freddy Krueger like he was his son. Really weird stuff. I had to testify in court and everything. We wanted to make sure that it was viewed as a parody. We changed the monster in the video, we did a lot of things and got a lot of legal opinions before we shot it. It was an expensive video for us at the time. We took all the precautions we could, and they still sued us. They suck for that. I mean, who remembers the Fat Boys record? I might have a copy of that video somewhere in storage. It was an 18-hour video shoot, and part of the set caught fire at one point. That video would have sold *so many* more records for Jeff and Will if it had ever been released.

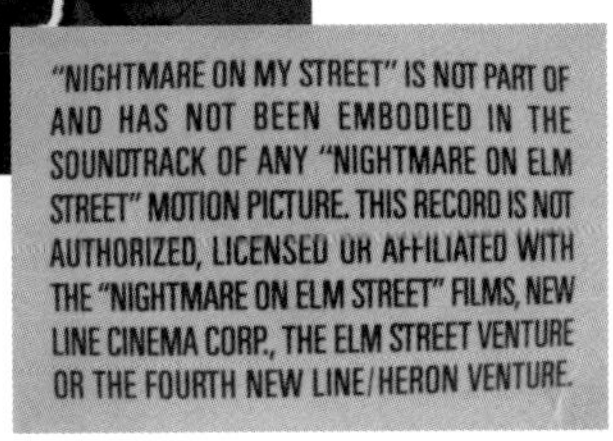
"NIGHTMARE ON MY STREET" IS NOT PART OF AND HAS NOT BEEN EMBODIED IN THE SOUNDTRACK OF ANY "NIGHTMARE ON ELM STREET" MOTION PICTURE. THIS RECORD IS NOT AUTHORIZED, LICENSED OR AFFILIATED WITH THE "NIGHTMARE ON ELM STREET" FILMS, NEW LINE CINEMA CORP., THE ELM STREET VENTURE OR THE FOURTH NEW LINE/HERON VENTURE.

Right: "Nightmare On My Street" single sticker, after New Line lawsuit / injunction.

DJ JAZZY JEFF: If we didn't get an injunction against the video for that song, I strongly believe that we would have sold 10 million copies of the album. That song was bigger and better than "Parents Just Don't Understand," and it would have built even more off the hype from the "Nightmare on Elm Street" movie that year. The single still went through the roof, even without a video. The video was an acted-out thing. We were in a movie theater, we went home, and then Freddy came. I remember the Freddy monster in our video had turntable needles as fingers. It was a glove they had made. It was one of those videos that when you watched it you were like, "Oh my God, we're about to be bigger than Michael Jackson!" It was right after the "Parents" single, so it would have been perfectly timed. The video didn't even have any clips from the "Nightmare on Elm Street" movie.

PETE Q. HARRIS: That song was similar to "Parents Just Don't Understand" in regard to what we did as producers and writers. We took the clap sound on there from Cameo's "Word Up!" [from 1986]. We used that sound all the time, on almost every record that came out of Battery. It's a fantastic clap sound. Unfortunately for Cameo, you can't copyright a sound like that. If the sound of "Nightmare" is similar to other songs that came out of that studio, it's because they were all done with a Fairlight and used sampled [TR-] 808 sounds. We replayed the "Nightmare on Elm Street" theme, we didn't think twice about using samples or re-playing things back then. That's what hip-hop was, we didn't ever think about getting sued. I think I used a Roland D-550 keyboard to replay the theme. And there's a piano on there, too. With the skit type of elements, that was a bit more complicated, but not drastically so. Jeff did the Freddy voice, we just stuck it into a harmonizer and de-tuned it. Which is what they did for Freddy Krueger in the film anyways.

JEFF: That song itself was great. I put that Freddy Krueger piano line in there [from the original theme to the "Nightmare On Elm Street" movie], I made sure we put that violin screech in there, too, because that's how it went in the movie. Pete Harris played that bassline. The album was out and we put the single out. Our lawyer was an entertainment lawyer and he listened to the album and told Jive – and this was before anybody knew anything about what could happen in such a situation – we had some "sample issues" that he thought should be addressed. And Jive basically kind of dismissed him. Then we had our song out, and stations began having "Nightmare" contests on the radio. Which song was the best, ours or the Fat Boys'? And we were killing the Fat Boys record. When we got the first injunction, our lawyers kept trying to explain to New Line that they could just endorse our record, too, because it was helping their movie. They didn't agree. We had to go into court and tried to play it like we were just kids making music. We had to pay New Line some money, we had to pull the single off the shelves. Luckily we didn't have to pull the album off the shelves. But we couldn't show the video we had made. With the video, there might have been four copies of the final version made. I had one of them, and my girlfriend at the time erased it and taped soap operas over it! No one I know has a copy. That song was very big when it came to our live show. I had a pitch-shifter effect for vocals. Will would do the whole song and when we would get to the end, Charlie Mack, our security guy, would dress up like Freddy Krueger, with the sweater and the glove and the hat. He'd come up on the side of the stage, walk up to my DJ riser and he would pretend to kill me. I'd fall behind the riser and you'd hear me screaming. Then I'd turn the pitch-shifter to the Freddy voice and I'd say, "Ha, ha, I've got you now, Jeff!" And people would lose it. I did that distorted Freddy voice on the song, too. New Line sent people to our concerts to get film of us doing it. They said, "Not only are you taking the music, you're also taking the likeness." They pulled out all the stops and there wasn't much we could do. One very interesting thing is that as part of the settlement from New Line, they wanted me and Will to do a movie. They offered us three scripts. The first one was "House Party." As you'll recall, that movie was based on a DJ and a rapper. They kind of made the movie for us, and we turned it down. I forget the other two movies, but we turned those down, too. I don't regret not doing "House Party," even as great as that movie was.

Here We Go Again

JEFF: I brought in that keyboard sample [Bob James' "Westchester Lady"] on the chorus. I made sure to get that hard snare in there, even if the mood of that song was lighter. I was all about drums, making them stand out. The mix on there was good, but the mastering sapped all of the bottom out of that one, and a bunch of others on the album. Pete added those fake horns on the chorus. I didn't mind stuff like that, it was cool for the most part. It was interesting having samples and live playing combined. No one was doing that. I added my own bassline that was completely different than the one in the sample. That was new, no one had really done that either.

HARRIS: That was a great Bob James sample. I played a trumpet sample on that song, from Hugh Masekela, I believe. I worked with Hugh many times, but I don't think I ever told him about that sample [laughs].

Brand New Funk

JEFF: That was a later single, it had the regular and the live version on it. *[Author's note: The single was released as a radio-only promo single and also, separately, as a commercial single, with an updated version of their 1985 song "Girls Ain't Nothing But Trouble" on the A-side].* That was hands-down the best record we had when we performed live in the '80s and '90s. I made that record up in my hotel room in London, I chopped it up and figured out what I wanted to do with it. Then we just recorded it in the studio. Pete Q. Harris played the bassline on that one, after most of it was done. That's Ready Rock saying "Get down!" on there, that's not a James Brown sample. James Brown's people never tried to get money from us on that one. Musically, that track is all me, the London guys didn't really do anything [essential] on there. The only way we were able to get Jive to release "Brand New Funk" as a single was because we asked them to shoot a live [concert] video. They came to the Nassau Coliseum [in Long Island] and shot it, and we had the b-roll from that. The song, the album version, was done already. We actually recorded the live version at a soundcheck, it wasn't during the real show that night. Because we couldn't risk messing up, in case we had to do it over. We went on early in the day. It *was* a live recording, just not with a real crowd. We had to make sure the needle wouldn't jump when I was cutting, that type of thing. It would have messed the video up. Then we played the recording back that night, to get the actual crowd reaction, and I did the extra cuts over the top of it.

HARRIS: Jeff is all over that track. I think there's a Donald Byrd sample, and Pleasure, too. Jeff brought the samples in and we stuck them in the Fairlight. I think that song was mostly samples. It was different from what Bryan ["Chuck" New] and I were doing, and you can hear it. On that song there aren't a lot of our musical ideas, it's mostly Jeff. It's a really great track: a great groove and a great idea.

READY ROCK C: The only bump in the road recording the album was probably when Jeff accidentally erased a James Brown sample on "Brand New Funk." So I had to re-do it using my voice, saying "Get Down!" to emulate that original sample.

JOE NICOLO: I think I remember earlier versions of that song from our work at Studio 4. I believe that it was just re-done in London.

CARLI: I guess I would say that's my favorite song, because that's the one I was always excited for when they did it live. It is definitely the heartbeat of the album. I'm not sure when that one came out as a single, it might have been early. A lot of times we'd put out the "street" record first, then the "radio" record after that. I'm almost positive that we put that one out first, as a promo for the clubs. A "Jeff" record. I agree that "Brand New Funk" is almost the antithesis of "Parents." And the guys wanted that. There was no question that we all wanted to maintain their street credibility, although at some point it became apparent that stuff like "Parents" was going to overtake the other material. [She pulls up video on YouTube as we are speaking]. I definitely didn't have very much money for this video. The whole thing was how Will was coming off harder in that video. We were doing it to show another side, kind of like how we put

"Live At Union Square" on the B-side of the "Parents" single. That was a conscious thing. I haven't watched this video in so long, I love it! I think Scott Kalvert [who also directed the videos for "Parents" and "Nightmare"] must have done this, he was kind of our "in-house" guy for a while.

Time To Chill

JEFF: I loved that George Benson "Breezin'" sample, and I was glad I could make it work as a hip-hop track. I will admit that that one had less substance than other songs on the album, you could say that one was "filler." We had a bunch of those, it was a long album!

Charlie Mack (1st Out Of The Limo)

JEFF: Charlie [Alston] is definitely a very big physical presence; he's 6 feet, 7 inches, 290 pounds. But very light on his feet – he could have been one of our dancers. Charlie was a figure in Philly, people knew him. We would joke that Will and Charlie would go to a club and people would be like, "Charlie! Come in!" and try to make Will pay [laughs]. Everybody knew him, and that song took him to a whole other stratosphere. He could be the menacing guy that you didn't want to fuck with, but he was also the fun-loving guy who was at every event. We'd take Charlie on the road, too, and he's in videos. He's in the "Girls Ain't Nothing But Trouble" video. Everybody knew him: Run-DMC, Public Enemy. So we wanted to give him a song.

As We Go

JEFF: That was about five-and-a-half minutes long, I guess we did have some longer songs on the album. But it was like, "Get the idea out, however long it takes." And back then you didn't worry about how long a song was, as long as it was entertaining. Timing of songs only came in once you started paying attention to radio, and singles. I love the Headhunters sample ["God Make Me Funky"] on there. Believe it or not, we didn't clear that, or any other samples on the record. Our lawyer told Jive that there were "sample issues." And I don't bring it up that much, but the album was a really big turning point in the sampling game. We got sued a lot for that record. Anytime you start to generate a lot of money and you're out touring, that's when it goes from flying under the radar to being in full view. That's what happened with us and with hip-hop culture back then. It definitely messed us up, because a lot of it was just us being naïve. We didn't know the rules, hip-hop was created out of meager means. And at that time it was, "What can you find, and how can you flip it?" Before us, I'm not sure that anyone had ever really gotten sued. It didn't really change until Hammer [with Rick James' "Super Freak"], because he actually sold more copies than Rick James did. Then the original artists would get mad.

Parents Just Don't Understand

JEFF: That was the first single off the album. To me, "Girls Ain't Nothing But Trouble" [from *Rock The House*] and "Parents" were pretty much the same record. Definitely the same subject matter, in a lot of ways. We didn't like having that as our first single, at least at first. Pete Q. Harris said, "This is a smash hit," as soon as we did it. We, of course, wanted a DJ record or something that was a little more "hip-hop" as our first single. But Pete knew, and we went with it. After that song was completely done, Pete played the [Jeff hums bassline to the song] part. He added some spice more than produced anything on there. We thought it was a great record, we didn't hate it. *But* we just didn't want it to be our first single. We didn't think it would get as big as it did, definitely not. I think the biggest reason for the song's success was just how relatable it was. It was relatable outside of hip-hop. And the video definitely helped, of course. But everything just kind of lined up. Everybody has that transition from a kid to an adult, and it sucks. It was a timing thing, too – if that song had come out two years earlier or two years later, who knows if it would have been anywhere near as successful. With the lyrics, they didn't take Will long at all. He used to always say that coming up with a concept is always the hardest thing. Once he had a concept, he could come up with lyrics in 15 minutes. And that's literally how long it took him to come up with those. A lot of those stories were from Will's real experiences. The video director was Scott Kalvert. Different guys gave different treatments, but his was the coolest. The main thing I remember about shooting the video was just how long it took. It was like 18 hours, in a sound stage in New York. When we were touring for the *He's The DJ* album at first, every night I noticed the cheers for us getting louder when they announced us. We were on the road, so we had no idea how the record was doing on the radio. I remember one night we tried something. Will did the first verse and then did the first line of the second verse, but told the crowd to finish it. And I thought, "Oh no, this could be the biggest disaster in the world!" But Will did it and 20,000 people finished

the verse. So we did that for the rest of the tour. When the song got to be so popular, the toughest thing was that the record company wanted another one of *those*.

JOE NICOLO: That was definitely a track we did in Philly that they re-cut in London. The final has the same beat and Jeff's musical ideas, they just re-did the song, with their "Jive sound," pasteurized for your protection [laughs]. That song was really just "Girls Ain't Nothing But Trouble, Part Two." The beat structure on the final was similar, they just added the keyboards. "Girls" was such a hit in Philly and it made a splash everywhere. So it seemed that "Parents" was a logical next step. And they had gotten even better at what they were doing, so it was destined to be even bigger. I think we all knew it was going to be big.

HARRIS: The first day we were in the studio together, they played me an early version of "Parents." It was about nine minutes long and had so many verses. Over a period of a week we worked on that song, along with others. One of the main things for us, as producers, was to focus Will's rapacious rhyme output. He was always writing. We had to fit it all into a three- or four-minute song. That was our biggest achievement in many ways, because many of the other elements were already there in the songs they brought us. Jeff brought a lot of beats to the studio. There's a weird bass sound in the song, and I can't even remember where we took it from. There's that drum-fill sound all throughout the song, that was off another record that I brought in. I can't remember where that one came from, either. I played most of the elements of that track, including the snares, on the Fairlight. There wasn't that much back-and-forth, musically. We put music together when Will and Jeff weren't even there, on occasion. I don't even think that on the original version they had a proper bassline. The one I put on there was really just a doodle that fit with the pitch of the brass samples we were using. We definitely knew that song would be a hit, because we had recently done Samantha Fox's "Touch Me" [from 1986, Harris co-produced the "Extended Version" of the single]. We knew what a hit was, especially a pop hit. And those lyrics on "Parents" are so funny and so accessible to so many people. We felt that it only needed a good bassline. It sounded very commercial to us.

CARLI: That video changed Will's career, and it changed my career, too. It was shot by Scott Kalvert, who went on to do "The Basketball Diaries." It might have been his second or third video. He had done one of Kool Moe Dee's videos for us, either "Wild, Wild West" or "How Ya Like Me Now." We didn't send the song out to a bunch of directors and ask for treatments, because we knew Scott would be great for it. We contacted him when we knew that was going to be a single, so we could work on it collaboratively. He basically followed the idea of the song. I'm actually tagged up on the walls, as "Tokyo Rose," if you look close. That was a one-day shoot, probably 18 hours. It was fun doing all the artwork on the walls for it. We got there early to do that, there was a great artist named Greg Harrison, he was the production designer.

He was the guy that came up with the look on the walls. He designed things for the "Nightmare On My Street" video set, too. There were a lot of influences to the look of the walls. We were in New York, so there were a lot of comic fanzines, Keith Haring, lots of pop graffiti. Some of the characters were Greg's, characters he used in his own work. After the video, we had to repaint the walls immediately. We shot it somewhere in Midtown or Queens. Everybody painted on the wall: me, Jeff, Will, the whole crew. Vanessa Williams – not *that* Vanessa Williams – plays the girl in the video. She's an actress, I think she was on "90210" for a while. I remember the guys being mad at me because she wasn't the "video kind of girl" that they were looking for. But I was looking for an actress [laughs], and she was really good. JL [James Lassiter, the group's road and personal manager at the time] is in it, he plays the cop. Greg Harrison designed all the furniture as well. We had some interesting times trying to get the drawers to open up, using special effects. There's a bit of "Pee Wee's Playhouse" with that. After Scott and I were watching the takes and had realized how impressive Will had become on film, I called two people the next day. The first was Clive Calder, and I told him, "The Fresh Prince is going to be a big movie star and I think we should make a movie with him right away. He's going to be bigger than Eddie Murphy." Clive, who I love to death, laughed and said, "Ann, do you know how to make a movie?" And I said, "No, but two years ago I didn't know how to make music videos either!" Clive thought it was a good idea but he said Jive was still building the record company, so he couldn't get into movies at that time. Then I called Russell Simmons and told him the same thing. Russell laughed at me, and said, "Well, he may be Malcolm Jamal-Warner but he ain't no Eddie Murphy."

Pump Up The Bass

JEFF: That was one of the tracks that would have ended up on my DJ album. That was the real Philly style for sure. The sample of [James Brown's] "Funky Drummer" on there sounds dusty because my copy was just old. That was real static, before people were actually doing static on records on purpose [laughs]. With routines like that – which is really what that track is, a routine – I didn't always retain stuff. I didn't remember what I had done on the fly. So I would try and record everything, because otherwise it'd be gone. I'd go back later and listen and see what worked best, and then I'd build on it.

HARRIS: I definitely worked on that song, somehow. I remember that.

Let's Get Busy Baby

JEFF: I guess that was filler, even though I think it was still a cool record. But keep in

mind, we were also making records that would be good to perform live, and that was one of them.

Live At Union Square (November 1986)

JEFF: That was the B-side of the "Parents Just Don't Understand" single. I think that was Jive giving in a bit, saying, "We've got to give them *some* of what they want." That routine, and the song, wouldn't have been as great if it wasn't for Will narrating and explaining what was going on. He was one of the first rappers to talk about the DJ and explain what was going on with a record or routine. We had been holding on to that for a while, we had a tape of the whole performance. Originally that was from a night at [New York's] Union Square that Mr. Magic was hosting, and Magic taped it. A couple days later he played the tape on his radio show [on WBLS] and people would call in and request it like it was a single. It became a big song, and it helped us get more shows, and gave me more of a rep as a DJ. Honestly, I don't even think I considered putting that on my DJ album, because the album was more of a studio thing. Plus "Union Square" wasn't just a DJ thing, because Will and Ready Rock were on there. We were in the studio trying to figure out what songs would go on the *He's The DJ* album. And somebody suggested that we put the "Union Square" tape on. Not the whole thing, there's a lot more that people haven't heard, because we probably went for 30 minutes during that whole show. I am cutting Whistle's "I'm Buggin'" right where the album version went out, then Ready Rock C did a whole beatbox thing. I still have the original tape. We called Mr. Magic and he sent us the cassette, then we edited it down.

D.J. On The Wheels

JEFF: We did that one at Studio 4 in Philly. Joe The Butcher was just the engineer. A lot of that type of stuff was a drum machine and then I would fly samples in after writing it somewhere else. That wasn't a routine, it was done in the studio, with a drum machine, turntables and a mixer. My drum machine of choice back then was a [Emu] SP-1200. I also used a [Roland TR-] 909 on *Rock The House*.

My Buddy

JEFF: I'm not on that one, we all kind of produced it. That was just one of those routines that we would do live, and we transferred it to a record. There wasn't anything too complicated about recording beatboxing in the studio, it was pretty easy.

READY ROCK: That song is dear to me because it was based on my friendship with Will.

Rhythm Trax – House Party Style

JEFF: That was the B-side of the "Nightmare On My Street" single. We did it again [laughs], putting a DJ record on the back of a pop single, like we had done with "Parents." Philly was definitely an electro town! I was probably one of the first to play it, but "It's Time" *[Author's note: Jeff most likely means "Al-Naafiysh (The Soul)" by Hashim]* was a staple in Philly. Shannon, Cybotron "Clear." We played those and I'd do rhythm scratches over top. Stuff you hear on that track is the real house party routines I would do. My brother used to play that Mandré record on the intro ["Solar Flight," from 1977] all the time.

He's The DJ, I'm The Rapper

JEFF: There was never talk of having *less* of a DJ angle on the album, even after we got into stuff like "Parents" and "Nightmare" [neither of which have a significant DJ presence on them]. Because that's just who we were. A DJ and a rapper. Partners. There was no separation, it was all together. And that's what made it successful. That song is a throwback to groups like the Cold Crush Brothers. That was both of us. One of Will's biggest influences was Grandmaster Caz [a member of the Cold Crush Brothers]. I love that track. I have recordings from not too long ago, from me and Will doing a show, and at soundcheck, I start cutting breakbeats and he goes into "He's The DJ, I'm The Rapper." I told him that if we went somewhere and did that today, people would think it was new, because no one does that style anymore. We can just pick right back up and do it anytime.

JOE NICOLO: That album version is exactly how we did it in Philly, there wasn't any re-recording in London. We wanted to have a freestyle vocal track on Jeff's DJ record. That became the song "He's the DJ, I'm the Rapper." We cut that song in the "B Room" at Studio 4, which eventually became Jeff's "A Touch Of Jazz" room [in the '90s]. What impressed me on that song was the way Will could come up with lyrics off the top of

his head, like he did there. I produced that track and when the record came out there was no production credit for me, not even an engineering credit. Just, "Thanks to Joe The Butcher for helping us make a great album." I was pretty upset. I called Ann Carli and I knew they were building up their guys [Pete Harris and Bryan "Chuck" New]. She said she was sorry and she'd fix it on the next pressing, but it's still not fixed. I don't want to sound like sour grapes. I mean, I've got plenty of credits. But at the time, I was pissed.

Hip Hop Dancer's Theme

JEFF: That was the intro to our live show. The dancers would come out, then Will would introduce me. That song was the beat for all of that.

Jazzy's In The House

JEFF: That was another DJ song that we did in Philly.

Human Video Game

READY ROCK: That was a cool song, because it gave me a chance to show my creativity and versatility.

JEFF: That one was just Will and Ready Rock, it was a routine that they would do onstage. It was interesting to take some of the routines that were so successful live and make them into records. It was almost like working backwards. I don't think those guys actually met in a video arcade, that was just for the song. They grew up around the corner from each other.

HARRIS: With Ready Rock, things weren't always great in the studio. Me and Bryan had a very British, Monty Python-esque sense of humor, and that didn't go over very well with those guys. I remember Bryan was very rude to Ready Rock, he didn't get the whole Human Beatbox thing. It's more of a block party, live thing and we didn't really get it, being from London. It wasn't difficult to record Ready Rock, you would just stick him on a dynamic mic and let him do his thing. Compress the shit out of it, EQ it and it sounded good. Ready Rock was a really good beatboxer, and a real nice guy.

DR. OCTAGON

Dr. Octagonecologyst
Bulk Recordings, 1996; Mo Wax, 1996;
DreamWorks, 1997

"In many ways, that album was a response to the general feeling that in hip-hop at that time, the sun rose with DJ Premier and set with Dr. Dre, as if nothing else existed. Octagon encompassed a lot more."

– Dan The Automator

"A lot of people probably thought I was smoking PCP and was on drugs. Other groups might have needed to be on drugs to attempt a record like that. But I was eating potato chips when we made it. Yoo-Hoos and donuts. It was one big spaceship and everyone was riding. Me and Automator were Mr. Spock and Captain Kirk."

– Kool Keith

Hip-hop in the mid-'90s was at an interesting place in its still-young history. It was clear to all but the most clueless observers that the musical artform and the culture that gave birth to it was the driving cultural force for young people around the world. It was a billion-dollar musical silo. It was here to stay.

But it was also starting to show signs of stagnation. Copycat syndrome had been in effect for the better part of the decade, and "biting" was no longer shunned, especially with the major label machines. Violence and misogyny were not only allowed by many of hip-hop's movers-and-shakers, but in many cases even encouraged, if it meant more sales.

Thankfully, there remained a thriving underground movement which had continued to sprout new branches throughout the decade. This group of creative misfits still held dear the tenets of hip-hop's originators, and practiced them daily: be original, ignore people who don't understand your music, and – if necessary – get weird and push the limits.

In early 1996, an indie duo appeared that left a lot of so-called "heads" scratching theirs, and won over a whole new international audience, from hard-rocks to skate punks. The pair in question was Dr. Octagon: Dan "The Automator" [Nakamura] and Kool Keith [Thornton].

Keith was a member of one of the late-1980s' most influential groups, the Bronx's Ultramagnetic MCs. Their 1988 album *Critical Beatdown* [on Next Plateau] was not a sales juggernaut, but its production – by group member and co-MC Ced-Gee – and lyrical approach influenced countless producers and MCs that followed, from De La Soul to Freestyle Fellowship and Organized Konfusion.

By the mid-'90s, Keith had left his New York home and shipped off to Los Angeles. In the popular consciousness, the West Coast of that era may have been ruled by Dr. Dre, Tupac and others, but it was actually a perfect place for Keith. Underground rappers and producers had always loved his outer-space-leaning, next-level lyricism, and he found himself surrounded by younger artists who were all too happy to welcome him.

He ended up sharing living quarters in LA with Northern California-raised producer Kutmasta Kurt [last name: Matlin; sometimes listed as Kut Masta Kurt], and the two got themselves signed to Capitol Records by 1994. They began work on an album that would later be released on their co-owned Funky Ass label: 1997's *Sex Style*.

"Being out there in California got me more open-minded, musically," Keith recalls. "It wasn't challenging for me in New York anymore. I was on Sunset Boulevard and it was wild: the girls, the pimps, the people, sun, palm trees, going to clubs. It was all so spontaneous, it wasn't like New York. Los Angeles was free-wheeling. Every night seemed like Saturday night. And I also started listening to a wider range of music."

Kurt recalls Keith's cult appeal upon arrival, "When me and Keith got to LA, people kept approaching him to do 'space rap' types of projects. All these rappers with dreadlocks and backpacks, the weed-smoking kids. They all worshipped him."

Up the coast, another young producer, Dan The Automator, was making moves of his own. Born and raised in San Francisco and trained on the violin in the Suzuki method from a young age, he had turned to DJing in his mid-teens. In 1989 he set his sights on producing records, releasing the solid cut-and-scratch 12-inch, "Music To Be Murdered By" [homeBass Records, as "Automator"], during his sophomore year at San Francisco State College. The record didn't light the world on fire, but it was a start.

During the early 1990s he shifted even more towards the studio side of the rap game.

"From 1990 to '95, I was DJing, but after college I wasn't as active with it," Dan explains. "I changed my focus. Earlier, I wanted to have all the newest records, but then I started getting into gear and audio shit. Starting in high school, I had been collecting and using drum machines and vintage keyboards."

Perhaps his most important early association – at least as a studio rat – is one for which he isn't as well-known: being the engineer and de facto co-producer for DJ Shadow, Blackalicious, Latyrx and the Solesides crew. The collective were all based around Davis, CA, but gravitated southwest to the Bay Area, where there was a considerably larger music community. They were introduced through a mutual friend and, as Dan says, "We hit it off, they knew my record ['Music To Be Murdered By']. Those guys basically said, 'We're trying to figure out how to make records. Do you think you can help us?' And I said I could."

DJ Shadow's *Endtroducing* album credits, 1996, listing Automator on engineering duties and The Glue Factory recording location.

Although not properly notated on the crew's earliest releases, their first 12-inch – DJ Shadow and the Groove Robbers' "Entropy / Send Them" from 1993 – states "Thanks to that fool Auto." No recording locations were noted on any early Solesides releases.

Automator says, "Those Solesides records were all done in my parents' basement, which was called the Glue Factory. To be honest, back then we didn't know what to call what we were all doing. For us, producers made the beats. Looking back now, I would say that on those records I was engineering, mixing and doing some production. By the time I was doing the Octagon record, I was still figuring shit out, but I knew I was definitely a producer."

Dan was an Ultramagnetic fan, and says he first met Kool Keith at a BOMB Records party in San Francisco where Ultra performed in 1993 or 1994. Dan recalls, "When I met him that first time, Keith was telling me how he had always wanted to do his own thing." According to Dan, in 1994 Kutmasta Kurt and Dan – who were friends and occasional working partners – both flew out to New York and recorded tracks with Keith before he relocated to California. Kurt produced, Dan recorded and mixed.

By mid-1994, Keith was indeed doing his own thing: in Los Angeles, and with Dan's friend Kurt. After signing to Capitol for a solo deal, the two were working on songs as rapidly as they could get them done. Unlike the more technical rhymes for which Keith was known in his early Ultramagnetic days, his approach had lost its pocket-protector in the California sunshine. One listen to the songs on *Sex Style* shows that the album was a new direction for Keith, who put his unique, sex-obsessed twist on cuts like "Sly We Fly" and the album's title song.

Kurt explains, "The stuff we were working on for *Sex Style* was a totally different direction than what Keith ended up doing for Octagon." He adds, "Dan actually produced two or three tracks that he wanted to get on *Sex Style*, but we didn't end up using them."

Unfortunately, the Capitol deal wasn't all that they had hoped for. Both Keith and Kurt mention that after they finished the bulk of the album in late 1994, the label dragged its feet releasing the material, which annoyed both of them. As a result, they became anxious and were seeking outlets for the tracks that were spilling out of Kurt's apartment-based studio in Santa Monica. "I don't know what the deal was with Capitol," Keith recalls. "We had finished the whole album [*Sex Style*] but they just dropped the project. They fired the urban marketing department or something."

As they waited around for Capitol to release music under Keith's name, a new persona emerged from Kurt's studio monitors: Dr. Octagon. Originally, it was a one-off track which no one figured would go anywhere. Recorded in LA and produced solely by Kurt, "Dr. Octagon" returned to Keith's fast-rhyming heard with Ultramagnetic and added a new lyrical partner: Sir Menelik [Phillip Collington]. Describing a lyrical path for the song is a difficult task considering its abstract, science- and outer-space-drenched beauty. But a Menelik lyric from the song – rhymed under the pseudonym Chewbacca Uncircumsized – sums it up nicely: "We're not alone in the Twilight Zone."

"We were just fucking around, basically," says Kurt. "Those first songs were just fun. Honestly, you could credit major label politics with a lot of the indie records that Keith did back then, like *Big Willie Smith* [an EP that Keith and Kurt put out in 1995 on Funkyass Records, see below] and Octagon. If things had been rolling really well with Capitol, Keith wouldn't have had time, and wouldn't have needed the money."

Kurt sent tapes of "Dr. Octagon" to a handful of DJs he knew, including Stretch & Bobbito in New York; Sway and King Tech of The Wake Up Show, who had just relocated to LA from the Bay; and Mike Nardone, who hosted the influential "We Came From Beyond" show on KXLU. There was no group name yet, so it was natural to take it from the song title. Keith's name was not listed anywhere on the tape.

Aside from the "Dr. Octagon" track, they produced another weirdo cut in that early Octagon era: "Technical Difficulties." The song is a freaky, mid-tempo track, with Keith rapping fast and complex again, mixing mundane and random modern references with outer-space and chemical speak.

To their surprise, "Dr. Octagon" got a great response and Kurt started to hear that listeners wanted more of this new mystery group. And so, the Octagon era began.

One of the people who heard "Dr. Octagon" was Kurt's friend The Automator. Although Dan hadn't been a huge fan of the more grounded and sex-oriented tracks that Keith and Kurt were producing for Capitol, he latched onto Octagon immediately. As someone who was looking for a way to really make a name for himself doing something bold and next-level, an army of light-bulbs began exploding for him. Dan recalls, "Keith and Kurt had done one weird song. I liked it. I saw what Keith was trying to articulate, I took it and we ran with it."

Dan the Automator and Kool Keith.
Photo © B+ for www.Mochilla.com

Kurt says, "Dan was critical of a lot of the *Sex Style* stuff we were doing, but when I sent him 'Dr. Octagon,' he called me and said, 'Tell Keith I want to do a whole project with that stuff.' Honestly, if Dan hadn't gotten involved, we probably would have done an EP along those lines, like the *Big Willie Smith* EP we had just done. Dan saw the Octagon angle as a way to work with Keith on his own."

"Automator knew Kurt, and Dan used to come down to LA to visit," Keith explains. "And me and Menelik had cut that track ["Dr. Octagon"] at Kurt's. It was some spaced-out, crazy stuff. We were in a real elegant part of no-man's land. We were listening to all types of music at that point, [spazz-rocker] Wesley Willis and shit like that. We had basically cut New York out of the picture."

Dan called up Keith and pitched him on the idea of making an entire album around the Octagon "outer-space gynecologist" theme. The basic deal: Dan would produce Octagon at his Glue Factory studio [still in his parents' basement], and Kurt would stick to the non-Octagon material in LA. "I wanted to create something that had sounds from everywhere, for everyone," Dan says. "Keith's flow was perfect for that."

"People were always telling me what I should do and how I should make music," Dan explains. "But I was always doing what I wanted to do. I really didn't care about being popular. And that's how I went into Octagon. I said, 'Maybe no one will ever hear my shit, or care. But I'd rather do it on my own terms.'" Although broke at the time, he scrounged up enough money to make Keith an offer for his rhyming services. Keith accepted.

Keith recalls, "With Kurt and the Octagon stuff, I think he thought we were just joking. But Automator was serious about it, he wanted to run with it. When Automator heard those first two songs, that was his fuel right there. There was no looking back at that point, we went up the ladder from there. Everybody was there for the party, and it was one weird party. We knew that no one was going to try and sneak anything normal in."

According to Dan, it didn't matter to Keith if the record was on a major or an indie, and it was always planned to be an indie project (even if it was later issued via DreamWorks). He says, "With my Keith deal, we partnered on it, so we both made money."

A precedent had already been set for Keith using an alias as he awaited a major label release under his own name: 1995's *Big Willie Smith* EP by Da Beat Terrorists, which Kurt produced and the duo put out on their Funkyass label [later spelled Funky Ass]. It was another way to keep the fires of Keith's rep burning, and make them both some rent money, until Capitol actually put the record out.

Big Willie Smith was a funky, off-kilter brag record, not unlike *Sex Style*. So, to Keith, another one-off record under a second-level-alias – his "stage name" of Kool Keith being the first alias, of course – wasn't a big deal, nor was it a hugely time-consuming prospect.

By mid-1995, recording for the Dr. Octagon album had commenced in San Francisco. Keith made trips up from LA: sometimes alone, sometimes with Kurt. "The recording of the album itself was pretty easy," Dan recalls. "Keith's a hard worker, he likes to work. He was hungry at the time, and we just went into the studio and banged it out, in five or six weeks *[Author's note: Keith remembers it being no more than two weeks of recording, see below].* Pretty much straight-through, with a couple weekends off, when he would go back to LA. Then I mixed it for a month or so."

With the two Kurt-produced songs already done, they merely needed to continue along the freaky path that was unfolding in front of them. Dan says, "We were going for a futuristic, push-it-to-the-limit feeling. Keith brought the space theme into it. We watched some pretty ill movies at the time, to set the mood. Weird horror movies. Sci-fi. And, of course, there was Keith's thing for porn."

"For the Octagon album, I went up to San Francisco for six or seven days," Keith recalls. "I said, 'Let's knock this out.' Automator had all kinds of different beats. He was using [Yamaha] DX7 keyboard, other tiny keyboards, and a Studio 440 [drum machine]. Lots of old equipment, Moogs and stuff. Dan made the beats, I wrote during the day, and we recorded at night. I think the recording was only about two weeks. People thought we was like Quincy Jones, working on the album for like eight months. But it was quick, we just flowed."

Kurt thinks that two weeks of recording seems correct. "I think Keith was up with Dan for three days one time, and then I went up with him for a weekend," he says. "Although mixing and finishing everything after Keith was done took a while." Kurt also mentions that he had ideas for additional Octagon tracks beyond the initial cuts that he produced but, "Dan was like, 'We don't have the budget for that.'"

In a similar way to how Los Angeles had broadened Keith's musical horizons upon his arrival there, San Francisco altered his approach to lyrics. "Being in San Francisco influenced the content of the album a little bit," Keith admits. "That city has an all-year-round Halloween feel. Everybody's weird-looking. You'd see a 7' 1" tranny walking up the block. The city itself is more grimy. Beyond the Rice-A-Roni trolleys, it's grimy at night. It's like a West Coast version of 42nd Street [in New York] in the '80s. I liked that feel."

Although the album remains impressively cohesive despite being about as strange as you can get when it comes to its central motif, even dyed-in-the-wool fans might not have a full grasp on the album's "concept." "It's about pushing boundaries," Dan explains. "When I think about it, that's what I feel. Not hip-hop boundaries. It goes beyond that. The boundaries of the way you make music and art. It was a mentality."

Keith also gives the concept explanation a shot, after a significant pause to consider the question: "It was free and open. It was like that TV show 'The Outer Limits.' It was sci-fi, science and sex. And cannibalism, mixed. Space, sex and 'Psycho,' all at the same time. It really had no boundaries. *Sex Style* was more about sex and Hollywood. It was a lot more concentrated. People definitely got off on how left-field Octagon was."

When it came down to Dan and Keith working together in the studio, Dan says that it was smooth sailing. All recording, aside from "Technical Difficulties" – the Kurt-produced "Dr. Octagon" had to be re-done because of a sample clearance issue with the original music, see below – was completed at The Glue Factory. "Yeah, my parents were around when we were recording," Dan recalls. "Keith got along with them just fine."

Keith says, "Recording with Dan was cool, it was all systems go. We would do a track, give a thumbs-up and then it was on to the next one. Everybody knew their position. It was like the Pep Boys, everybody did their job. We had a rhythm. We'd go out during the day, hang out, go shopping. A lot of producers I work with depend on me to make their song. But with Octagon, everyone complemented everyone else. We didn't have to work hard on any of those songs."

Dan discusses Keith's rhyming approach, which can be tricky for other producers with whom he works: "Keith just rhymes until he stops. You can't tell him how many bars to do. You had to make beats long enough to accommodate him going on and on. We'd work off a beat and then he'd end at the 21st bar, or 14th. He doesn't end where people usually stop. So I would always take that as a personal challenge, to put musical things in there that would bring the song to the next section on a high note. That's why the record is both loose and constructed, at least with the way it feels. It was more than me just making beats and him rhyming on them."

Dan also has an astute take on Keith's approach to rhyming, which helps explain some of the legendary lyricist's mystique: "Most people don't know this, and honestly Keith might not even realize it all the time, but I have seen it in action. The reason his stuff sounds disjointed is because, many times, he will skip his middle thought. He doesn't do it on purpose, his brain is just moving too fast. He brings the conclusion with the assumption that you understand the middle, even if he hasn't given it to you. And I think that helps a listener understand the Dr. Octagon lyrics a little bit more."

"Most songs were done in four takes or less," Dan adds. "But not because Keith isn't good. For the first take, he's working it out. On the second, third and fourth, he's just saying different rhymes on some of them. You never know if those later ones will be better. That's something I learned as we kept going: it's always good to do an extra take, just in case."

Keith says, "When it came to my lyrics, my mind was just so flexible. I can write normal or I can write as a killer. I can play different parts. That album was a movie that me and Menelik wrote. And with Automator's production, it fit like a glove. I couldn't have ever done lyrics like that in Ultramagnetic."

There was an innovative mix of live playing and sampling used on the record, with Dan himself playing violin on selected tracks *[Author's note: The instrument is featured prominently on the single "Blue Flowers"]*, along with other players brought in for guitar and bass work. For Automator fans who have come to his music via Deltron 3030 or Gorillaz, this will come as no surprise. But back then, the varied instrumentation was a different twist, at least in the indie hip-hop world. "It was definitely a 'kitchen sink' record," Dan explains. "Part of the live playing and the jumble of it all related to how I felt about hip-hop at the time. I wanted to go as far away from 'straight' hip-hop as I could."

Most of the album's sampled sources were obscure, which presented those involved in the business side of the album with some grey areas. "We did what we could when it came to clearing samples," Dan explains. "At the time, labels were a bit more liberal about that type of stuff, so we did what we had to. Once Mo Wax and DreamWorks became involved, we gave them the information [about what songs were sampled] and they did what they thought they needed to do."

People usually think of the Dr. Octagon album as a solo release, but Keith wasn't the only hand on deck. He brought along a young, New York MC with him for several tracks: Sir Menelik. Menelik was featured on four album tracks, starting with "Dr. Octagon," [Menelik also came up with the Octagon concept, which Keith and Kurt built upon] and proved to be an excellent super-scientifical, fast-rhyming foil to Keith, pushing him to keep it surreal.

Dan recalls, "Keith brought Menelik in, they had known each other for a while. Menelik understood the direction of a lot of the lyrics. Maybe more than Keith did, at times. The combo worked well, he was a perfect fit for Keith. Keith is a natural MC, and had been doing it for a long time. Menelik was working hard at his craft back then. He was definitely a thinking-man's rapper."

"Menelik was good with words, I liked his style," Keith says. "He was competitive, he would play off what I was doing. He was one of the only fast-talking rappers in New York that I liked. I met him there, we used to hang out before I moved to LA. And then when I was in LA, I invited him out a bunch of times. I needed a person to hang out with that wasn't edgy or anxious."

Foreground: unknown associate. Background, L to R: Dan the Automator, Kool Keith, DJ Q-Bert.
Photo © B+ for www.Mochilla.com

"Keith wanted to help Menelik get his career going," Kurt says. "I even worked on some solo tracks with him. Mostly 'street rap' type of stuff, which was weird, because at first I thought he was a happy-go-lucky guy. He was definitely in the right place at the right time, with Keith and Octagon."

There was one final featured contributor who helped add to the album's next-level sound: San Francisco's DJ Q-Bert [Richard Quitevis] of the Invisibl Skratch Piklz crew, who contributed cuts to half of the album's songs. Q-Bert recalls, "I knew Dan from DJing back in the day, but by the time he had the Dr. Octagon stuff, he had grown so much as a producer. I couldn't believe it. It was almost like he went into hiding with a musical samurai, downloaded a ton of knowledge, and came back and slayed everyone!"

"The work I did on the Octagon album wasn't too difficult for me," Q explains. "Dan would just say, 'Scratch on this track.' Then, afterwards he basically picked the parts I did that he liked and scrapped the ones he didn't. He probably only kept like one percent of everything I did [laughs]. Luckily the beats were mostly hip-hop 4/4 [timing], and not some crazy jazz time, like 7/8 or 5/4. Working with Dan's music was a lot of fun and really let me get loose. And I was always a fan of Keith's, he is a lyrical wizard. He was the opposite of most every rapper out there. People underestimate how great of a musician Keith is, when it comes to abstract division, rhythmically, in his timing skill."

After the month or so of recording, the mixing and mastering wasn't a lengthy process. And after clearing the next hurdle of gathering the cash to actually print up the LPs and CDs, the Bulk Recordings issue of the album was readied.

Aside from the mind-bending music on *Dr. Octagonecologyst*, the album cover also let listeners know that they weren't in familiar territory. Drawn by San Francisco-based artist Pushead [Brian Schroeder] – who was known in the '80s and early '90s for illustration work done with punk and metal bands – a sunglasses-wearing skeleton dressed as a doctor, with a microphone and scalpel in hand, gazes into a skull. It's a perfect mix of sci-fi, horror and Shakespeare.

Dan explains, "Pushead lived in my neighborhood, but I didn't really know him. We got him to do the cover because my manager Toni Isabella dealt with metal bands, so she knew him from back in the day. That was an original piece he did, just for the album. That drawing *is* Dr. Octagon. He told me a while back that, to this day, people still ask him about that cover and it cracks him up."

Back of *Dr. Octagonecologyst* Bulk Recordings LP, 1996.

The back cover is equally trippy, with a crude cut-and-pasted photo of the late actor Don S. Davis – from a cameo on "The X-Files" – holding up a pseudonym-filled cast card detailing the album's musical contributors.

When asked today about how he thought the album would be received, Dan says, "When the record was done, I knew that most 'regular' people weren't going to get it, because it was a pretty big mind-fuck. But I didn't care. I just thought it was a record that should be made. Up until that point, I was just concerned about whether I liked it or not."

The Automator also says that the lack of any mention of Kool Keith's name on the cover wasn't a liner notes error. "It was never going to be 'featuring Kool Keith,' it was always just Dr. Octagon," he explains. "We didn't sell it to the outside world as a Kool Keith record on purpose, because I didn't want people to think it was another Ultramagnetic album. No disrespect to them, but that was barking up a dead tree." Keith himself had no issue with this approach: "I'm not always a fan of being on album covers. Sometimes I don't mind being less in the center. It can be good to be on a great team."

Dr. Octagonecologyst album ad for Bulk Recordings release, 1996. *Author's collection.*

Dan adds, "I don't think that Keith fully grasped the impact that Octagon was going to have for his career when it came out. It wasn't the biggest deal to him, he wasn't taking as much of a risk with it as I was, since I had paid for everything. I didn't think it was going to sell as much as it sold, and I didn't think people were going to care about it as much as they cared. I just knew it was a good record. At the same time, I knew that regular hip-hop fans weren't going to love it."

"We all got an adrenaline rush off what was going on," Keith recalls. "We were giggling as we were making the tracks, because we knew that people were going to trip out on them. It was like we was at a house party and we was making a punch out of lemonade, Pepsi and Welch's grape soda. We was putting everything inside the container: apples, greens, peanuts, cabbage. We blended it all together and we knew people were going to bug out when they tasted it."

The album originally came out on Dan's Bulk Recordings label in early 1996, with the double-vinyl having a slightly different sequence than the CD [it also listed a date of 1995 on the interior vinyl labels on all four sides, despite listing 1996 on the outside cover].

"I definitely remember putting the more banging songs on the outer part of each of the four LP sides," Dan recalls. "Because when you get to the center, it's harder to DJ with them. I wanted those outer tracks to be the loudest in the clubs. *[Author's note: The first songs on each side of the 2-LP set are, as follows: "Intro / 3000"; "Wild and Crazy"; "Dr. Octagon"; and "Technical Difficulties"].* He adds, "The sequencing was definitely very important to me. Everything was in its place for a reason, even if I can't remember all the reasons now [laughs]."

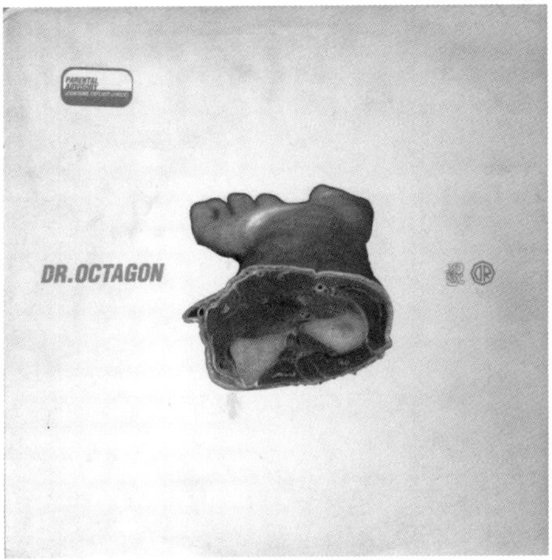

Mo Wax *Ecologyst* 3-LP album cover, 1996.

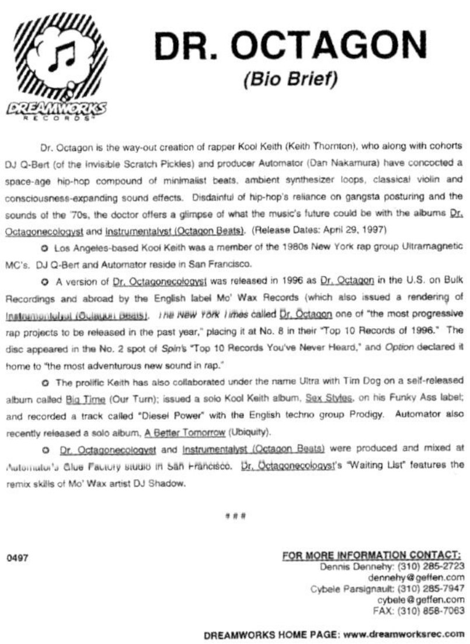

DR. OCTAGON

(Bio Brief)

Dr. Octagon is the way-out creation of rapper Kool Keith (Keith Thornton), who along with cohorts DJ Q-Bert (of the Invisible Scratch Pickles) and producer Automator (Dan Nakamura) have concocted a space-age hip-hop compound of minimalist beats, ambient synthesizer loops, classical violin and consciousness-expanding sound effects. Disdainful of hip-hop's reliance on gangsta posturing and the sounds of the '70s, the doctor offers a glimpse of what the music's future could be with the albums Dr. Octagonecologyst and Instrumentalyst (Octagon Beats). (Release Dates: April 29, 1997)

- Los Angeles-based Kool Keith was a member of the 1980s New York rap group Ultramagnetic MC's. DJ Q-Bert and Automator reside in San Francisco.
- A version of Dr. Octagonecologyst was released in 1996 as Dr. Octagon in the U.S. on Bulk Recordings and abroad by the English label Mo' Wax Records (which also issued a rendering of Instrumentalyst (Octagon Beats). *The New York Times* called Dr. Octagon one of "the most progressive rap projects to be released in the past year," placing it at No. 8 in their "Top 10 Records of 1996." The disc appeared in the No. 2 spot of *Spin*'s "Top 10 Records You've Never Heard," and *Option* declared it home to "the most adventurous new sound in rap."
- The prolific Keith has also collaborated under the name Ultra with Tim Dog on a self-released album called Big Time (Our Turn); issued a solo Kool Keith album, Sex Styles, on his Funky Ass label; and recorded a track called "Diesel Power" with the English techno group Prodigy. Automator also recently released a solo album, A Better Tomorrow (Ubiquity).
- Dr. Octagonecologyst and Instrumentalyst (Octagon Beats) were produced and mixed at Automator's Glue Factory studio in San Francisco. Dr. Octagonecologyst's "Waiting List" features the remix skills of Mo' Wax artist DJ Shadow.

###

0497

FOR MORE INFORMATION CONTACT:
Dennis Dennehy: (310) 285-2723
dennehy@geffen.com
Cybele Parsignault: (310) 285-7947
cybele@geffen.com
FAX: (310) 858-7063

DREAMWORKS HOME PAGE: www.dreamworksrec.com

DreamWorks press bio for album re-release, 1997.

Dan points to one of the big reasons for the album blowing up, critically at least: he astutely partnered with James Lavelle's Mo Wax label in London [which was part of A&M in Europe] to release the album outside of North America in 1996. This was a connection made by Dan's old recording buddy DJ Shadow, who had released his acclaimed full-length debut, *Endtroducing.....*, on the label earlier that year. The Mo Wax version of Dr. Octagon had a slightly different album title – *Ecologyst* – and was spread across six sides of vinyl, with extra tracks.

According to Dan, the album blew up in Europe before it became known in the U.S. He says, "I give credit to James Lavelle. He picked DJ Shadow out of nowhere, and he picked me out of nowhere. He had really good taste. The first big run of press we had was from Europe, which was surreal because I had never even been there."

Domestically, Dan took an offer from newly-launched major label DreamWorks in late 1996, to re-release the album with extra tracks in mid-1997. The new domestic pressing allowed for a bigger press push, as well as the group's first and only video, for "Blue Flowers."

In the end, Dan says that the album – on all labels – sold, "Over 200,000 and less than 300,000. I don't know the exact numbers."

"We didn't tour behind the album," Dan recalls, with some regret. "We got hired to play Lollapalooza in 1997 and then Keith kind of went his own way at that point. He had moved on to the *Black Elvis* stuff. It was a disappointment, but it didn't shock me. To be fair, I knew that Keith would do that at some point, I just didn't know when. DreamWorks was more upset than I was."

In the end, according to Dan and manager Toni Isabella, they never did a single live date together as Dr. Octagon. Keith frequently performed tracks off the Octagon album in the late '90s – many times with Kurt, but without Dan – and still does to this day.

Looking back, Dan still has nothing but good things to say about his first full-length as a producer and musical mastermind. "*Dr. Octagonecologyst* is a classic record for what it is, but it's not a classic *hip-hop* record," he says. "I'm not actually sure if it's considered a hip-hop record at all. We had to do a lot just to get that record out there. That in itself was a bit of a monumental achievement. I mean, we made a record that, ostensibly, there was no market for. A lot of weird people came out of the woodwork and loved it."

Keith agrees that it was never aimed at hip-hop purists: "I knew that the record wasn't going to be an 'urban' record, I knew it was above a lot of heads. It was going somewhere else, although I didn't know where that was. To a lot of people, it was like a haunted house. You go up the steps and something pops out. Then you take a left and something else pops out."

"I like that record a lot," says Kutmasta Kurt. "At the beginning, hip-hop heads were dissing it, because there was nothing else that sounded like it. Once people started to understand what it was about, it became a lot more influential. Like the movie 'The Rocky Horror Picture Show.' I think that people in the hip-hop underground started making weirder and more experimental stuff after [*Octagonecologyst*] came out."

Q-Bert recalls, "When I heard the final album, I was surprised at how great it had become, and I became an instant worshipper of Dan's musical powers. He's been a musical mentor to me ever since."

"It's definitely one of my albums that I'm fondest of," Dan says. "I think the proudest thing for me was just that we got to do it. I've had a lot of ideas that I thought were really good over the years, and it's always nice when you can actually make them happen. That was the first one I really got to implement."

DreamWorks album ad, 1997 – for re-issue of *Dr. Octagonecologyst* as well as instrumentals album, *Instrumentalyst (Octagon Beats)*.

And Keith gets the final word: "When it was finished, I saw it as an album in its own category. It was an audio movie. It wasn't just another Kool Keith album. We didn't make the record for any specific audience, but I think it showed New York City what I was capable of doing, and that I owned that lane. At the time, I think a lot of people out there thought I was more limited. After [*Octagonecologyst*], my future projects were more comfortable. I could do slow stuff, or rap fast. I could do it all. And beyond what it did for me, I think the album helped other hip-hop artists be more open-minded."

TRACKS

Intro

KOOL KEITH: Pornos were signature sounds for me. I guess that rubbed off on Automator, too.

DAN THE AUTOMATOR: I actually brought that porno sample to the mix. It definitely fit in quite well. I can't say which movie it's from, we didn't clear it.

3000 [scratches by DJ Q-Bert]

DAN: I don't know if that was always going to be the first full track, but it was definitely a great way to start things off. The songs and the sequence really just all fell together. We talked about all kinds of ideas, but the lyrics on "3000" were definitely all Keith.

KEITH: I made that on the verge of the next generation. When they hear the album in the future they'll be like, "This album's not old. It sounds new." People put dates in their records, so if I was going to do something, it's got to be wild. I'm a fast writer, I probably came up with that in about 15 minutes. I'd write two or three songs in a day.

I Got To Tell You (A Visit To The Doctor)

DAN: With those interludes and skits, I would tell Keith what I wanted him to do and then he would freestyle it. I'd just say, "Make a commercial for Dr. Octagon's office," and he'd just do it. Keith would do them over the music, that would always be there first.

KEITH: I just naturally made up those skits, on the spot. I'd say shit and Automator would just trip out.

Earth People [additional vocals by C-Note, scratches by DJ Q-Bert]

DAN: "Earth People" was done pretty early on. I think doing that helped us figure out where we wanted to go from there. We got a vibe going and we went with it. I think that's the most influential song that Q-Bert contributed to on the album. No one had rocked pedals with DJ cutting at that point, the wah-wah was pretty monumental. That's me playing keyboards on there. I'm a terrible keyboardist but I'm a good producer, so I can make stuff sound right. I'm not a real keyboard player, though. I can't play horns or guitar but I can play anything else well enough.

DJ Q-BERT: I was pretty influenced by rock guitarists at that time and I thought, "Let's try that wah-wah pedal out on the turntables." And it sounded bugged out, so I started using all kinds of pedals in other tracks I was doing after that. I was watching too many Jimi Hendrix videotapes, I guess!

KEITH: That was me talking to America, with New York and California on two ends. It was me playing a part in a movie, like if I was Darth Vader in "Star Wars." I was telling people to get on another level because they were stuck.

No Awareness

[featuring Sir Menelik, scratches by DJ Q-Bert]

KEITH: I wrote the lyrics first and then we came up with the chorus. There were certain songs that I didn't really want people to understand. The album was based on mental challenges [for listeners]. I love listening to Menelik's rhymes on there.

DAN: That song is great, with Keith and Menelik going back and forth, and then Q-Bert does a back-and-forth scratch solo at the end, his own "turntable conversation," which mimics Keith's and Menelik's back-and-forth vocals. The scratches talk to each other. I love that.

Q-BERT: Back then me and the Invisibl Skratch Piklz [his DJ crew, featuring Mix Master Mike, DJ Shortkut, DJ Apollo, DJ Disk and D-Styles at various times] would do this thing called "Q & A," where we traded bars scratching with one another. So it was just second nature to do it on that Octagon track. I was trying to be different and swing the patterns *super* hard so that they sounded off-beat, but were rhythmically on-beat, in a jazzy way. I don't know if it came off that way, but that's what I was trying to do.

Technical Difficulties

[produced by Kut Masta Kurt, additional vocals by Whoolio E Glacias]

KEITH: After the first two songs, we didn't want to just make a bunch more exactly like them and then call it an album. We [Keith and Dan] just flowed and took each track on its own. Those first two just put everybody in their seatbelts, for lift off. We was in spaceships going straight up, not looking out the window or anything. Whoolio was Kurt's boy, Jason. I have no clue what he's saying on there.

KUTMASTA KURT: We recorded the songs "Dr. Octagon" and "Technical Difficulties" within a couple weeks of each other, around the fall of 1994. My buddy Jason, who was a DJ in Monterey [CA] and the Bay, was one of the guys I had sent the "Dr. Octagon" tape to. He was in town when we were recording "Technical Difficulties." He knows a little Spanish, and he's Whoolio E Glacias on that song. In broken Spanish, he was talking about how he gets drunk and speaks in Spanish, but it doesn't always make a lot of sense, and he knows it. He also did a skit on Motion Man's *Pablito's Way* album [which Kurt produced]. There were elements of "The Twilight Zone" music in the original track we did, so I guess they had to remove those for the album.

DAN: That was the second song they did, Kurt did it. I had to re-do it for the final version, though. I think the original was over a sample of "The Twilight Zone" [TV show]. As I recall, I put the original song aside for a while and then re-did it later. I re-did all the music on that track, but Kurt still got production. It wasn't a big deal to me. I just removed the original sample.

General Hospital (Another Visit To the Doctor)

DAN: All of the skits on the album were there for a purpose, so I guess I directed that one for a specific reason. As an eating analogy, the skits are like the sorbets of the meal. They make it so that songs can work together. With that skit, I'd tell Keith that things are going badly and the patient dies. I didn't have anything to do with him talking about the horse in the hospital. That's definitely Keith.

Blue Flowers

[additional vocals by Miss G and Sweet "P", scratches by DJ Q-Bert]

KEITH: I remember Automator did the drums and then I did the bassline on there. I put that ghost bassline, the rumble, and he kept it on there. That was a euphoric record, for rave children in the fields, swinging their green things around. I don't take pills but I guess it's good if you do, or you're mushroomed up, ecstasy or whatever. I had a psychedelic Woodstock thing in mind when I wrote that song. The music is dreamy, with that electronic element. That's a good song, it sounds big and was mixed perfectly. It was made for people in dreamland. The video was the same way, I liked it.

DAN: That's me on violin. There are samples too, obviously. Q-Bert has cuts on there, I have always had a fondness for those. I love that song, there's just something about it. I wanted to bring a classical element in with the violin. Keith played bass, the first note, on a Kurzweil K2000 [laughs]. Keith came up with the phrase "Blue Flowers." Before that I was playing with some theme about "dancing through the daisies," so he ran with it. That's the only song we did a video for. DreamWorks probably gave us the money. I did want to do a video, for promotion. I'm not trying to make something that people can't find. I don't want to be a rock star, but I want the work I do to get out there.

A Visit To the Gynecologyst [scratches by DJ Q-Bert]

KEITH: That was a movie sample, from Dan.

DAN: That's another porno sample. I found a couple weird pornos to use. I would go shopping specifically for Dr. Octagon stuff. I'm serious. Keith taught me everything I needed to know about porn. He knew all the new release dates. I forget if it's Monday or Thursday, but whatever day, we'd always have to go to the porn shop that day. Not a specific store every time, just any porn store.

Bear Witness [scratches by DJ Q-Bert]

[sub-titled "Q-Bert's Story" on the original LP and "Q-Bert gets biz" on the "Earth People" / "No Awareness" single]

Q-BERT: When I did that one with Dan, I had just finished a mixtape called "Demolition Pumpkin Squeeze Musik" and I did a similar scratch on there, with the same sound. It turned out a little different on the Octagon song.

KURT: No dis to Keith *[Author's note: There are no Keith vocals on the song except for a sample of Keith from an Ultramagnetic MCs song]*, but I think that's my favorite song on the album [laughs]. I have always loved those old-school scratch records, and the way they put that together with Q-Bert was pretty dope. I had known Q for years, so I was happy that he got a chance to showcase himself. It's a cool, different song. I was more connected to the other types of songs on the record, so I guess I expected those. But not as much with "Bear Witness."

DAN: I have loved Q-Bert since high school, so when I was doing a record I wanted to go with the best. He is just the best scratching DJ there is. I think the album fit his style well. I had always wanted to do a track like that. I did the track itself and Q scratched over it. Q was famous within the battle DJ world, but outside of that people didn't know how fucking crazy and incredible he was at the time [1996]. That was probably done around the middle of the sessions. That was always a DJ / production track, there were never supposed to be vocals on it.

KEITH: I loved the intermissions on the album, it was good to take a break. It was like half-time at a basketball game. People could cleanse their minds out.

Dr. Octagon [produced by Kut Masta Kurt, featuring Sir Menelik]

DAN: That was the song that started it all, with Keith and Kurt. The final was pretty similar to the one they did as a demo. That was all Kurt on production.

KURT: We honestly did that first song just to have something of Keith's to play on the radio, because we couldn't play anything we were working on at the time [for Capitol, under Kool Keith]. We were fucking around and made a crazy song to send to DJs, really. If Menelik wasn't around with us in LA, it might not have ever happened. He was up-and-coming and was into some of the outer-space stuff. We were talking about names one day and I think Menelik came up with Dr. Octagon. Since we were working on *Sex Style* at the time, I said "Yeah, Octagonecologyst." And they went with it. Then Menelik came up with his name, Chewbacca Uncircumcized.

KEITH: Honestly, at first when we did that track, I was just playing around. I said, "Dr. Octagon," and Kurt said, "That sounds crazy." It was basically an eight-sided thinker, like how an octopus has eight arms. I can think eight ways. And the name fits the project very well. The "Keep it simple" part in there [on the chorus] was supposed to be a frustrated fan, complaining because it was too complex. But we were going to keep it complex. I had that said to me many times over the years. Like, "You should calm down." I think the best stuff that Menelik has ever done was on the "Dr. Octagon" song.

Girl Let Me Touch You [vocal "harmonics" by Joe Des Cee and Miss G]

KEITH: I could have never made a song like that living in New York. That was a Cali thing. We had the album finished but I wanted to have a song about a girl on there. I took it to another level. I didn't want people to think that the project was so male-oriented, so we brought the ladies in. That's where the masterpiece came in. That song was almost as popular as "Blue Flowers." I still perform that song and women come up and dance. We covered every avenue on the album, so we had to have something for the ladies. That made the album totally complete. Without that song, the album wouldn't have been finished.

DAN: Keith really wanted to be an R & B singer, it wasn't a joke for him. So I said, "Let's do it right." I don't remember actually making that record, but I know DJ Shadow was around. He didn't have anything to do with the production. Keith was serious about the R & B thing, though, so I just tried to do it in a way that worked. And I think it kinda does work, as "out" as it is. I have this plastic keyboard, a Pianosaurus, and Shadow plays the bells from that on the song. I still have the Pianosaurus, it's in my studio to this day.

KURT: I guess that was one of the only songs on the Octagon album that could have also gone on *Sex Style*, although the music would have been different.

I'm Destructive [guitar by Andy Andersen, scratches by DJ Q-Bert]

DAN: That's Andy Andersen [aka Andyboy] from a group called Attitude on guitar. I wanted to do something that was more rock, and that's what we came up with. I'm not mad I did it, but I kind of cringe at the guitar tone on there. At the time, it was the best I could do. I was out of my element a bit. I actually think that's one of Keith's better rhymes on the record, it feels like he's really into it. He even references this one punk band called Spazz, who was hanging out in the studio one day. You can tell that Keith was enjoying it.

KEITH: I think that song shows my versatility. We covered so many angles, and all of them naturally. That song was hard, we was in the Pantera zone, we were competing with rock bands. I like Rush and Korn, I dig rock stuff. I rock on anything, I could even do a song with Elton John.

Wild And Crazy [scratches by DJ Q-Bert]

KEITH: That uses the same drums as [the Ultramagnetic MCs'] "Ego Trippin'": [Melvin Bliss'] "Synthetic Substitution." I think that was a great song, I like my lyrics on there. The pap-pap-pap-pap style. That was very fast, and easy to do. I didn't think you could use "Synthetic Substitution" again, but Automator figured out a way to do it.

DAN: A track like "Wild and Crazy" is just a hip-hop track. At the time I'm sure I was proud of it. But I'm still a bit sorry that there were "regular" moments like that. I still love that song, though.

On Production [featuring Sir Menelik]

KEITH: Menelik is pretty much solo on there. I wanted him to be another voice on the album. He was the "Indian Rapper Guy," like from India or Pakistan.

DAN: Menelik is the main guy on there. Keith is on the chorus. Menelik was a very confident kid, I liked working with him.

Biology 101 [featuring Sir Menelik, scratches by DJ Q-Bert]

KEITH: I played the bassline on there. The vocals with me and Menelik are what I would call "lyrical exercise." Some people go to the gym and stretch their muscles. But that's how me and Menelik warm up. Menelik was my sparring partner.

DAN: That song is about biology, so it's pretty accurately titled [laughs]. It's a good song but not one of my top favorites.

Earth People (Earth Planet Mix aka Demo Mix)

DAN: That was basically where I started with the song, the original version. It's not my favorite mix. I don't hate it, but I like the other versions better.

Waiting List (DJ Shadow / Automator Mix)

[scratches by DJ Q-Bert]

DAN: It definitely made sense to have Shadow be involved with the Octagon album, because we had been working together for a while. I did the original song and he came in and re-did the beats and some other things. No Pianosaurus on that one [laughs].

Q-BERT: I was scratching Kool Moe Dee's "Go See The Doctor" on that one.

Halfsharkalligatorhalfman

DAN: [Laughs when the title is said]. That song is very bizarre for a lot of reasons. It's like one of those alternate universe songs, it just exists. Keith made up that chorus out of the air, randomly, before we brought that sample in. I have no idea where the character Mr. Gerbic [mentioned in the song] came from.

KEITH: That came in late. That was almost a freestyle, after the album was finished. This person was like Dr. Octagon's dad. That was wild. I had that in my mind, but Dan had the sample. An amphibian dude. It was kind of my vision of Hollywood Boulevard, a dream with smog and fog. It was an exaggerated version. I wanted to do a video for it, a dinosaur standing in the middle of Hollywood Boulevard.

1977

KEITH: That was a time-travel thing, like Dr. Who. I liked the ['70s New York hip-hop pioneers] L-Brothers, with Mean Gene, they wore Stetson hats with the feathers. Them and Cold Crush Brothers, especially.

DAN: That song kind of does fit the concept of the album, it's a time-travel piece. We actually recorded that on a 4-track. We added that just for a little something extra for later pressings of the album, with "Real Raw."

Real Raw

DAN: That song and "1977" were the last two tracks we did, those were added late, after the original album.

ED O.G & DA BULLDOGS

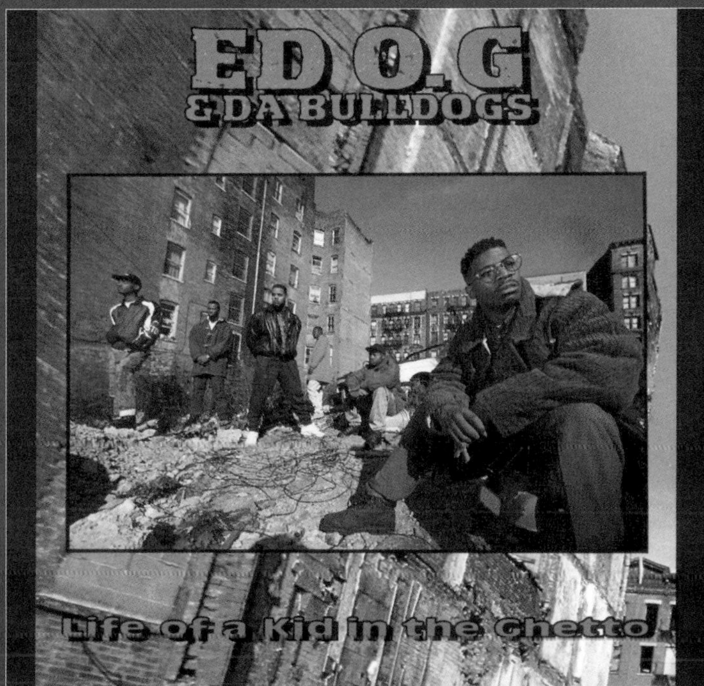

Life Of A Kid In The Ghetto
PWL America / Mercury, 1991

"I didn't want to be in any lane. I was all over the place, but that worked for me."

– Edo G

In the early 1990s, hip-hop was wide open. Gone were the days when you had to be serious on every track; when you had to be a goofball or have a gimmick to sell records; when you had to rock gold chains to be hard; or when you had to dress to the nines just to get attention from the ladies.

Long gone, too, were the days that you had to be from New York to be taken seriously, or to sell records. LA and Miami had long since proven that they had artists like Ice-T, 2 Live Crew and N.W.A. who could be international rap stars. Even Philly came to the plate, with the multi-platinum DJ Jazzy Jeff & The Fresh Prince and, before them, gangsta pioneer Schoolly-D.

So it seemed logical that Boston – who in the '80s had produced the bubblegum of New Edition and New Kids on the Block – was overdue for its own hip-hop star. And that's where ED O.G [Edward Anderson, aka Edo G] came in.

[Author's note: Keith "Guru" Elam – who we love and miss – was born and raised in Boston, but he relocated to New York in the late-'80s, before he became known nationally, thereby disqualifying him from pure Boston hip-hop status.]

"I was born at Boston City Hospital," Ed says today, sitting on his porch, which straddles the Roxbury and Dorchester neighborhood line. He adds, proudly, "And I have lived in Roxbury my entire life."

Ed's early years in school were more tumultuous than they should have been, thanks to Beantown's shameful resistance to educational integration in the early 1970s. He was bused to nearby Roslindale for elementary school. "I honestly didn't really know what Roslindale was actually like," he explains. "I went there to school, got off the bus, and went back on the bus at the end of the day. It was kind of fucked up, we had rocks thrown at our bus and all that. As a kid, I just stuck up my middle finger and stuck my tongue out the window [laughs]. I was so young, I didn't really understand the bigger scope of what was going on."

But there was, of course, an effect. "To be honest with you, it just made me dislike white people at that particular point in time," he says. "Boston was a segregated city then, there weren't many white people where I was. And, honestly, I didn't venture outside of Roxbury much as a kid."

As he entered double-digits in age, he attended Dorchester's Martin Luther King, Jr. K-8 School and started to feel the first rumblings of a calling to showbiz. He remembers, "I was a B-boy at first, a dancer. I probably did my first talent show when I was 10. Breakdancing wasn't even out, we was just popping. By 12 years old I started to feel that I really wanted to do something with my life on stage."

"My first real show was as a dancer was in junior high," he continues. "A guy named Paul, who went by Disco P and is on [the 1986 Boston hip-hop compilation] *Boston Goes Def*, was looking for dancers for a school talent show. From that day on, all I wanted to do was perform." He says that at age 15, in 1985, he also added beatboxing to his performance arsenal.

The aforementioned *Boston Goes Def* compilation, put together by local producer Steve Barry to highlight some of the city's local rap talent, played a significant role in the lives of many Boston hip-hoppers in the '80s. Although many of the groups were only moderately impressive, or guilty of straight-up jacking Run-DMC and other New York acts, there are some shining moments on the collection. "New York was definitely a big influence on how Boston groups sounded back then," Ed admits.

Ed, then known as Edo Rock, is on the compilation, featured as a non-rhyming beatboxer on FTI's "Suzi Q." FTI stood for "Fresh To Impress." The song was catchy, a bit naughty, and well-executed, even despite the fact that it was a clear nod to Doug E Fresh's and Slick Rick's "La Di Da Di," with some "Roxanne, Roxanne" mixed in.

"We had dreams of getting on wax, not being huge stars," Ed recalls. "Having our song on that compilation was a big deal. FTI lived in my neighborhood, Humboldt Avenue in Roxbury, and they really did dress fresh. They had Kangols and everything. Slick Rick was the leader – this is before anyone really knew who the New York Slick Rick was. Rick was older and had the illest rhymes. My boy T-Nyne, from [Ed's later crew] Da Bulldogs was in FTI, too. He was Spoony T back then. He was Rick's cousin and he was 18 at the time. I was only 15 or 16." Ed notes that his future DJ, DJ Cruz, was across town in Cambridge, but he was also down with FTI in the *Boston Goes Def* era.

Ed continues, "I made up the 'Suzi Q' song in my head. Everyone back then had a girl song, that's what could get you a hit. So that's what we did. I had the beat and the hook and everyone came up with their rhymes."

FTI had actually recorded an earlier version of "Suzi Q," several months before the *Boston Goes Def* compilation hit, on cassette, pause-tape style, at DJ Cruz's house. The song was never made available for commercial sale but did well on Boston's only real outlet for local rap talent at the time, WMBR's weekly "Lecco's Lemma" show, with host Magnus Johnstone. "We were number one on Lecco's for several weeks, just as a tape," Ed remembers. "By the time the compilation came out, that song wasn't new, but it was still popular. Plus people hadn't been able to buy it before."

For the compilation, they went in and re-recorded "Suzi Q" properly, with Barry at the controls. They also laid down another song called "Rock Hard," which included Ed's first rhyme put to tape. For better or worse, only "Suzi Q" made it onto *Boston Goes Def.*

Overall, the compilation made an impression in Boston, especially with those already in the scene. But, truth be told, it didn't make many waves nationally. They had an album release party at local rock club TT The Bear's Place, and everyone enjoyed themselves to the hilt. Ed recalls, "I can remember Disco P and the Fresh MC [whose song "Girls" leads off Side One] sitting outside the club in a white limo, waiting to go on. It was hilarious. It was sold out, Body Rock Crew murdered it. I think we made $24 total. We bought some pizza with it [laughs]."

By 1987, Ed had left the FTI Crew – who did not go on to much renown after *Boston Goes Def* – and was working with his friend Shawn Pete, aka Professor Rock, in a group called 3 Def Notes, whose four members included Ed, Pete, Black and Anthony aka A-Train, who was their beatboxer. With their group name listed as A-Train, they had a track on the follow-up to *Boston Goes Def*, 1987's *Def Row*, called "I Can't Hold It Back." Ed says, "That was a dope song. I really thought we was gonna blow up with that one."

They had a second 3 Def Notes song, which circulated on cassette to local radio, called "Black Is Back," which was recorded at "a real studio." It did well on the WHRB show "Street Beat," which was hosted by two Harvard students – Dave Mays and Jonathan Shecter – who would go on to more renown soon thereafter, founding *The Source* magazine in their college dorm room.

Mays, Shecter and the late Kenny Mack were, in fact, managing the 3 Def Notes during that time, trying to get them a record deal with connections they had in New York City. Their efforts on behalf of the group, unfortunately, did not amount to much, except for some attention from another manager, Jay Ellis.

Def Row cassette compilation, Beautiful Sounds, 1987.
Photo courtesy of Pacey Foster.

Into the mix of Ed's adventures and misadventures in the hip-hop world in the late '80s, three new acquaintances came into Ed's orbit who would each have significant impacts on his career. The first two ended up as a business relationship down the line, but things started out as a purely family affair. The gentlemen in question were Teddy Tedd [Tedd Whiting] and Special K [Kevin Bonners], aka The Awesome 2.

Based out of New Jersey, Tedd and K were top-tier movers-and-shakers in New York's rap world, starting with a pioneering and influential early '80s radio show on WHBI, which eventually led to hosting "Celebrity Tuesdays" showcases at the Latin Quarter in 1986. By the late '80s they had parlayed their industry contacts into a management company, Awesome Entertainment, working with groups like Nice & Smooth and Positive K.

It also turns out that the Awesome 2 had a rap star-to-be in the family. Ed explains, "Tedd and K are cousins with each other, and they are both *my* cousins. My grandmother was married to their uncle, and then they had my aunt."

Complicated family trees aside, Ed says, "I wasn't aware of it until the mid-'80s, but once I found out they were in my family, I was all over their asses! [laughs]. I found out around the time we were recording for *Def Row*. They were in town because Tedd was the DJ for The Real Roxanne. That was the first time we met, they came over to my grandmother's house."

Ed continues, "I started sending them my demos in 1987 and '88, and I kept in touch. I'd also go and visit them in New Jersey sometimes."

Teddy Tedd says, of those early demos, "When we heard Ed's earliest stuff, it honestly wouldn't have survived in the climate of the time. We told him, 'It's not ready, you need to go back to the drawing board.' And he did. Once we heard the stuff he was doing with Joe [Mansfield, see below], we were excited, it was hot. We knew it could survive and that we could get it in there."

"Ed came back [with demo tapes] three times," Special K adds. "With the first couple, it wasn't ready. But by the third time, the Joe stuff, it was."

They say that they felt no obligation to manage and shop Ed just because he was family. "A lot of guys come to you and talk about a lot of things and then you never hear from them again," Tedd explains. "But Ed was persistent, and he really honed his craft." Tedd and K both mention that Ed was so anxious to have them hear his new music that he would frequently drive demos down – four or five hours each way – instead of simply mailing them.

The second important new component of the ED O.G equation, entering in 1989, was Joe Mansfield. Mansfield would go on the produce most of Ed's 1991 debut.

"Around 1988, we [Ed's rhyming crew, post-3 Def Notes] were just calling ourselves Da Bulldogs," Ed recalls. "There was no 'ED O.G *and...*' back then. My boy Money 1 moved out to Medford [just north of Boston, about 5-6 miles from Roxbury] and said, 'Man, I found this white dude out here who has a studio and makes beats. You should come and check him out.'"

Ed continues, "I went up there, Joe played me some stuff and I spit a bunch of rhymes. I had tons and tons of them at that point, from all those years. Joe was blown away and I was blown away. So we decided to start working on stuff together. Joe basically just joined Da Bulldogs at that point. It was like, 'You've got tons of beats, and we've got tons of rappers.'" By 1989 they were working with purpose on Ed's solo demo, recording in Joe's basement studio.

Mansfield, a computer whiz at an early age, was born and raised in Medford. "I wanted to be a DJ when I was about 14," he explains. "I'd buy records with DJing in mind. And that got me deeper into music, because I was listening to them more closely." He first got hooked on hip-hop around 1982, with Afrika Bambaataa & Soulsonic Force's "Planet Rock." From that point on, rap was an obsession.

By the mid-'80s he started another lifelong obsession, this time with drum machines, first purchasing a used Roland TR-808. During this era, the final part of the hip-hop production puzzle was solved, at least temporarily, with an Akai 612 sampler. "It had about one second of sampling time," he laughs. "Basically, by 1988, I had enough equipment in my basement so that I could record whatever I needed." By 1989 he expanded, with an [Emu] Emax sampler and an Akai ASQ-10 sequencer.

His first official release as a producer came out in early 1989: Terrors Of A New Breed's "Realm Of Evil," on Too Dope Records. Mansfield recalls, "It was two MCs, a guy Eric Hill who used the name E.Z.E. and another guy Joe Butler, I can't remember his MC name. They were from Chelsea [also just north of Boston, a couple miles from Medford] and I met them in 1988. They already had demos when I met them, but I helped them put everything together." He also acted as DJ for live shows they did in 1989, after the 12-inch came out.

Aside from receiving a smattering a local radio play, the group didn't go on to accomplish much of note after that single. But, Mansfield says, "The important thing I learned from that experience was that it wasn't that hard to put out a record. I learned the ins and outs of manufacturing."

As Terrors was progressing, slowly, Joe and Ed were introduced. Mansfield recalls, "I knew who Ed was before I met him, but he wasn't a star or anything. I knew about FTI and *Boston Goes Def*. Money 1 was living in the projects in Medford, across the way from me. Money was from Roxbury originally, so he knew Ed."

Joe adds, "Basically, when I met Ed, I stopped working with Terrors Of A New Breed. It was definitely my choice. When me and Ed recorded our first stuff together, I knew we had something. What he was doing was what I wanted to do. It was a lot different, it sounded more contemporary. I thought what we were coming up with had a chance to do something."

Regarding Terrors Of A New Breed, Ed recalls: "I liked one of the MCs in that group. I know in some way I kind of pushed them out, but I didn't do it on purpose. Or maybe I did, I was pretty arrogant and aggressive at the time [laughs]. I think that my New York connections just kinda trumped whatever they were doing at the time, and Joe knew that."

At this point it might be helpful to elucidate Da Bulldogs, since it has always been a bit hazy to outsiders, in no small part because none of the group was really heard on *Life Of A Kid In The Ghetto*, despite having billing – and photos – on the cover. Promotional materials from the album list them as "A small nation of talented rappers, writers and producers. Right now, T-Nyne [Terry Smith aka Spoony T], Smooth Ice Gee [Glenn Moore] and DJ Cruz are the most visible."

"That was just our crew," Ed explains. "At first it was about 20 of us. Everybody rhymed and did different things. When we got the deal [with PWL America, for the album, see below], my boys were rhyming on some of the demos, too. But it became mostly me. I hate to say it, but the rhymes they had at the time were not that good, and it was all about putting out the best possible stuff. They were cool, but the songs they were on didn't make the album. So it was kind of like Heavy D & The Boyz, I guess. Da Bulldogs would be there with me rhyming at shows, though. It wasn't a huge issue, because I was trying to get everyone deals back then."

ED O.G with a few Bulldogs.
Photo courtesy of DJ Cruz, who is on far right.

He adds, "I had Da Bulldogs a separate deal with Mercury, but they didn't pursue it aggressively enough. Mercury wanted to hear more songs, but it just never worked out." Rapper Scientifik, who would become part of the posse around 1990 but was never officially considered part of Da Bulldogs, did get a deal, with Chemistry Records – the name PWL America took on – in 1991. His album *Criminal*, would not appear until 1994 [on definite Records], Executive Produced by Ed with multiple producers including Ed, Joe Mansfield and Diamond D. Sadly, Scientifik was killed in the late '90s.

Ed's old friend DJ Cruz, from the FTI days, was the only member who was actually *heard*, doing some cuts on the album and always on the road as Ed's tour DJ. Although Cruz helped with early FTI production work – which was lower-budget, pause-tape style – Ed explains that while Cruz did produce in the late '80s, Joe's beats were the only ones they used on demos given to the Awesome 2. On the other side of the coin, Joe could DJ, but wasn't interested in doing so, so the Joe Mansfield / DJ Cruz pieces within the crew puzzle seemed to fit nicely.

Ed says, "Once me and Joe hooked up in '89, I think Tedd and Special K started to pay more attention." Teddy Tedd agrees: "Joe just had a great ear for abstract loops. His work was definitely very melodic, too. I didn't deal with Joe too much before we started actually recording the album, but I was always impressed."

"I liked what Ed was rhyming about with the new material in 1989," Tedd adds. "He was positive, he was fun and silly. He had a little bit of everything. Back then nobody had really represented Boston yet either."

Before summer hit in 1989, a clear momentum was in full swing and Ed and Joe were riding the wave. Mansfield explains, "By the spring of '89 we were recording so much stuff that it was crazy. We would make songs and Ed would play them for the Awesome 2. They would tell him that we were onto something and said to keep going, so we kept recording. Every week Ed would call me, 'I want to come over, I've got some new lyrics.'"

"I had tons of records at the time, and my family had *tons* of records," Ed recalls. "Some of the stuff we used for the album, like the Bohannon sample for 'I Got To Have It' or the Archie Bell for 'Bug-A-Boo' were from my grandmother's or aunt's or my mother's collection. Me and Joe raided everybody's shit! [laughs]."

Joe mentions that Ed wasn't the only artist with whom he was working in 1989 – Mansfield was also doing demos with local MC Swift, who was also from Roxbury. But, he explains, "I was giving all my best stuff to Ed. We also had the plan in place to sign other rappers besides Ed and I would do beats for them, too." Their production company was called Groovin' Sounds Productions.

"By later in 1989, we had really hit a stride," Ed says. "I sent Awesome 2 a demo tape with a couple songs on it, they loved it and they said they were finally going to shop it to some labels." Mansfield agrees that it took about six months of work until they had songs ready to be heard by labels. "I thought we could compete with stuff that was out at the time," Joe says, looking back.

Mansfield adds, "I don't think that most of the songs on that demo even made the album." Joe would give Ed the finished demos on cassette and then Ed would bring them to Awesome 2. As a result, Ed and the Awesome 2 were more involved in what songs would finally be shopped.

They were indeed clearly onto something, since the shopping process wasn't a long one. "The first label they took the demo to was PWL America," Ed recalls. "And that was it, they signed us up. I couldn't believe it. It was a $75,000 advance, which was a *lot* of money. We were a very low income household."

Ed continues, "Brian Chin from PWL was the guy who signed us. He was a house music guy, but he knew his hip-hop. He signed Diamond D [for the album Diamond And The Psychotic Neurotics *Stunts, Blunts & Hip Hop*, from 1992, on Chemistry], so he gets props for that, too. I think he could see the bigger scope of what I was all about, not just one aspect. He loved 'Feel Like A Nut,' that was the song that got us signed."

Brian Chin has great memories of his first important hip-hop signing for the brand-new PWL America label: "As I recall, Special K brought me four songs, on a cassette, with two or three other Bulldogs besides Ed performing on a couple of them. A song called 'Now You Wanna Know Me' was one highlight, T-Nyne got a good verse off in that one. And 'Dedicated To The Right Wingers' was on there, which appealed to my politics. 'Gotta Have Money' also helped me feel sure enough about Ed to make an offer. We didn't do singles deals, so it was for an album."

Chin continues, "'Feel Like A Nut,' was also on there, and I almost laughed coffee out of my nose when I heard the hook. I recall that my overall impression was that I could listen to Ed rapping for 45 minutes straight, and I hoped America would, too." According to Chin, he made the Awesome 2 a verbal offer for an album deal with Ed & Da Bulldogs and, he says, "I referred them to our attorneys to get a contract signed." It was enough of a green light so that the Awesome 2 and Ed's crew could move ahead recording the album, with PWL's backing.

"I was signed to PWL America, which was an independent label," Ed says. "Mercury was the distributor. For the album, I had to sign contracts with both. In the end, PWL had the final decision about what songs made the album, not Mercury."

PWL America was a new-jack on the block in 1990, looking to break into the U.S. hip-hop scene. Owned by UK-based pop production mogul Pete Waterman – who counted Rick Astley, Kylie Minogue and Bananarama among the artists he had brought to superstardom – the label was a new face on the rap scene, but still had big goals.

Marthe Reynolds was General Manager of the New York City base of operations, and Brian Chin was the head of A & R. PWL America was distributed by Mercury Records in 1991, but was not owned by them, so they did have a certain amount of autonomy.

Reynolds explains, "Pete Waterman was setting up a rap label in the U.S. and we were the ones who were tasked with doing it." Operations started in 1990 and it was a small staff: Reynolds came from dance label Vendetta Records; Chin from Profile [where he had signed Rob Base & DJ EZ Rock, among other talent]; and Robert John Jones was president. Jones' then-wife Margaret also worked in the office. College radio reps included Marc Raybin and, after Raybin left, Jamieson Grillo, who arrived in mid-1991.

"Ed's record was the second or third project we put out," Reynolds recalls. "Pete Waterman trusted Brian Chin implicitly to do the right thing. We all knew Brian had great ears. And I was going to work all of our projects as hard as I possibly could."

She adds, "The Awesome 2 introduced me to every person I needed to know in the hip-hop world back then. All the radio guys, all the writers. Every one of them. I owe them a lot for that." In addition to his obvious talent, Reynolds feels that Ed got heard by a lot of important people because of the Awesome 2's co-sign on him.

By mid-1990, Ed, Joe and the crew began shoring up the tracks that they would be using for the album. As always, pre-production was done at Mansfield's home studio. Mansfield was a semester shy of graduating from the University of Massachusetts Boston at the time [in Business Management], but left and never went back. He explains, "At that point, I had figured out that I could probably make a living doing music, one way or another."

By the summer, they headed down to New York City, where final production and mixing on tracks was completed, at Queens' Power Play studios, thanks again to the Awesome 2's connections. Ivan "DJ Doc" Rodriguez, who had worked with a distinguished list of hip-hop artists including Eric B. & Rakim and Boogie Down Productions, was their engineer and studio godfather.

"Once we got to Power Play, we would lay the tracks down," Tedd explains. "We mixed all the songs and helped produce a couple of them." K adds, "DJ Doc had a unique style. There was great chemistry all around during those sessions."

"I Got To Have It" demo cassette.
Courtesy of Teddy Tedd.

Interestingly, according to Ed, Joe and Brian Chin, neither of the album's most impactful singles, "I Got To Have It" and "Be A Father To Your Child," was on the original demo that got the group signed. So, although the fun and loose "Feel Like A Nut" may have reeled PWL in, the label clearly watched with excitement as even more depth was revealed as the group really got to work.

Chin recalls, "'I Got To Have It' was in the second round of demos, I heard it when I visited Ed and the Awesome 2 at Power Play. By then, Ed was already in command, getting his vocal tracks down perfectly with exact punch-ins. The final contract still hadn't been signed, but at that point I knew we had to do that as quickly as possible."

"I Got To Have It" sample disk.
Image courtesy of Joe Mansfield.

"We were there at Power Play for a couple months," Ed recalls. "It was easy, we just had to get used to being in a professional studio. Everything took a little longer, just because it wasn't as automated back then. But we learned a lot from DJ Doc, he was the best engineer of that era. He brought out my vocals and gave me a new way to present myself on the mic. Plus he pretty much mixed every track on that album."

Mansfield agrees: "Doc pretty much mixed the entire album *[Author's note: Mixing for most album tracks is attributed to Teddy Tedd in the album's liners, not Doc]* and engineered most of it as well. He was really helpful to us when we were there."

While they were there at Power Play – staying in Manhattan at hotels with varying star ratings, none of them terribly swanky – they had numerous hip-hop stars stopping by to check out the new jack on the scene from Boston, thanks to the Awesome 2. Ed says that their top-tier guests included Erick Sermon, KRS-One and Biz Markie, among others.

They also hit clubs when they weren't making tracks. "We met so many people when we were down there," Ed says. "The energy and the vibe we got was amazing. It was just a really pure experience making the record. We were young and having fun in New York. There was no club or party that we couldn't get into."

Mansfield recalls, "Recording at Power Play did seem like a pretty long process, actually. I had to go in there and track all the beats from our demos on their equipment before we really started the harder work. Power Play was a big spot, their equipment was more advanced and it was definitely more 'hip-hop friendly' than the rock studios you would have to record in back in Boston."

Album ad, 1991.
Courtesy of Trevor KARMA Gendron.

"We were there at Power Play for about a month or a little bit more," he estimates. "We'd go down for a week, come home for a weekend, then go back down."

As for how the studio speakers were sounding on playback to the young talent assembled, Mansfield says: "We were making what we liked, music-wise. At times I was even thinking to myself, 'Is some of this stuff really hip-hop? Will people accept it that way?' But [A] Tribe [Called Quest] did it, and we saw that it went OK for them, so we kept going."

When the album finally hit in 1991, the production credit – which was a surprise to Ed and Joe – read: "Produced by Teddy Tedd, Special K and Joe Mansfield for Awesome 2 Productions." This was all fine and well, except that Joe Mansfield had done a majority of the production work, not Tedd and K.

"It was annoying to Joe and all of us at the time," Ed admits. "Joe wanted to be recognized for what he did. He pretty much did all of the beats for that record. We were young and we signed a management *and* production deal with Awesome 2. So they really Executive Produced. Tedd only produced one track, 'Dedicated To The

Right Wingers.' They are my peoples and I love them, but they took credit for a lot of stuff. Tedd was more involved in the studio, and K was more on the business side."

Mansfield explains, "I don't know if the Awesome 2 necessarily took credit for producing, but they did put their names on the album as producers. I didn't really think about it or care that much back then. Honestly, I was just happy to have a record out nationally. And Ed always told everyone that I did everything anyways, it's not like people didn't know. I had nothing against the Awesome 2, they were good guys."

Teddy Tedd says, "We produced the *project*, the entirety of it. I suppose it could have listed us as Executive Producers instead." Special K says, "Honestly, at the time, it helped having our names on there like that. It's no dis to him, but nobody knew who Joe was at the time." Either way, both Tedd and K agree that Joe did indeed do most of the production work on the album.

It's possible that Ed himself could have even gotten a co-production or at least co-writing credit on certain songs, but that was never his concern. He mentions that he gave Mansfield the bassline sample used for "Bug-A-Boo" [Archie Bell's "Don't Let Love Get You Down"], and says, "I didn't feel that I deserved production credit for something like that, because whether I brought the sample in or not, I knew who produced the track. You still have to make the record dope. And that's what Joe did."

"Ed would sometimes bring records and say he liked a loop and I'd do something with it," Mansfield says. "There were only a couple of those that made the album, like on 'Feel Like A Nut' and 'Bug-A-Boo.' Ed was into a lot of 'pretty' soul music, he favored stuff that was more melodic. Ed didn't dig for obscure records or anything, he brought stuff that was popular at some point, or that he heard from someone else."

Envelope sent to ED O.G's fan club.
Courtesy of DJ Cruz.

When the album was completed, the entire crew felt like they had something special on their hands. Ed says, "When it came to lyrics, I really wanted to cover every topic I could. I didn't want to leave anything out. I wasn't worried about the range. It was all about my life, everything I had seen and everything that had gotten me to that point. There's skills rhyming on 'I'm Different' and socially conscious stuff with 'Speak Upon It' and 'Dedicated To The Right Wingers.'"

But which songs were the *real* ED O.G in 1991? "Probably all the stuff about girls [laughs deviously]. I was 20 when I got signed. It was all about girls." After all, he says that ED O.G stood for "Every Day, Other Girls" back then.

Teddy Tedd has this to say about the range on the album: "I didn't see the variety as being an issue at all. People at the label were asking, 'What's his image?' And today that might be more important. But every person is a multitude of things. No one is the preacher all day, and no one is having fun all day. That's what the album represented to me."

"I don't think Ed ever tried to be like anybody else," Marthe Reynolds says. "There was a gritty elegance about Ed and Da Bulldogs, in general and also when they performed live. The album was jam-packed, it was just a great record. It wasn't slick. And with both Ed and PWL America, we were the underdogs, so we just wanted to be heard."

Ed remembers the album cover photo shoot, which was snapped by famed hip-hop, punk and skateboard photographer Glen E. Friedman, but unfortunately not done in Ed's Boston backyard: "We shot that in Harlem, maybe 137th Street. I bought all those clothes in New York for the shoot. Those green boots, they don't even match my jacket. And I was wearing glasses, even though I have 20/20 vision! I guess I was trying to look educated [laughs]. We all looked pretty crazy on there."

"The reason for shooting in New York instead of Boston was solely financial," Tedd explains. "We had a small budget for that and shooting in New York while they were already there meant that we wouldn't have to do flights and hotels for the photographer. Either way, we did get one of the best photographers in the game, Glen Friedman. He did so many classic covers."

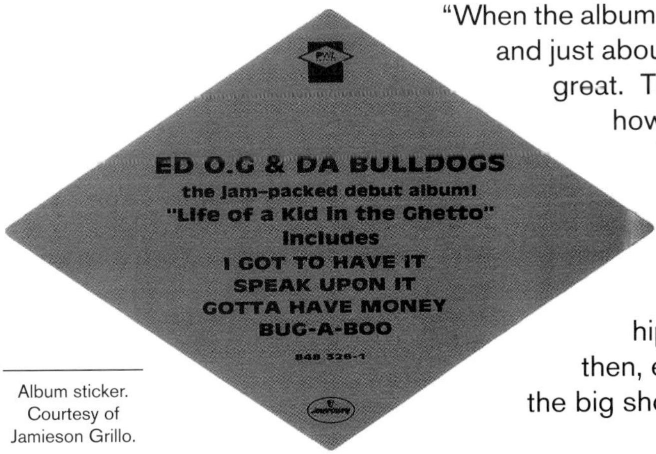

Album sticker. Courtesy of Jamieson Grillo.

"When the album hit, we got a lot of love, in Boston and just about everywhere," Ed beams. "It was great. The only thing that sucked was how violent Boston was at the time. We didn't get any shows in my hometown, so I didn't get to perform 'I Got To Have It' in Boston when it was at its height. No one would book hip-hop shows in Boston back then, even if you had a huge record. All the big shows went to Providence."

Response to *Life Of A Kid In The Ghetto*, which hit in the early spring of 1991, went beyond Ed's wildest dreams, and at age 21 he was living the life. "It was crazy. Everywhere we went, it was huge," he says. "We did a toy drive at Christmas for KJLH in Los Angeles, which was owned by Stevie Wonder back then. It was at a huge place, with Stevie, Ice Cube, all of these huge artists. We did stuff like that all the time."

PWL promotional materials from back then list some of the album's accomplishments and accolades: "'I Got To Have It' went to number one on the *Billboard* Rap Singles chart; number one six times in a row on the *CMJ* college charts; and number one on the *Gavin Report*, which subsequently named the group 'Rap Artist of the Year.' The video also went to number one on the 'Yo! MTV Raps' countdown." The press release goes on to say that the album sold 150,000 copies in only 10 weeks. Tedd says, "They [PWL or Mercury] say it didn't go gold, but it must have by now."

"The album definitely exceeded our expectations," Reynolds says. "The response to the singles 'I Got To Have It' and 'Be A Father To Your Child' was incredible to see. I don't think that any of us could believe how quickly things started moving once 'I Got To Have It' took off. It was a juggernaut. It just had velocity."

Brian Chin, looking back, says: "I got prouder and prouder of the album as it was cut and mixed and readied for release. Once 'I Got To Have It' was chosen for the single and the video was shot, I got even more excited. I wasn't at all surprised when it became number one on 'Yo! MTV Raps' and all the other charts. Ed was totally in control of his talent and his message on the album, and what he was talking about mattered. That's why, in the later '90s, the single and the album were still showing up on 'all-time-best' lists in places like *The Source*."

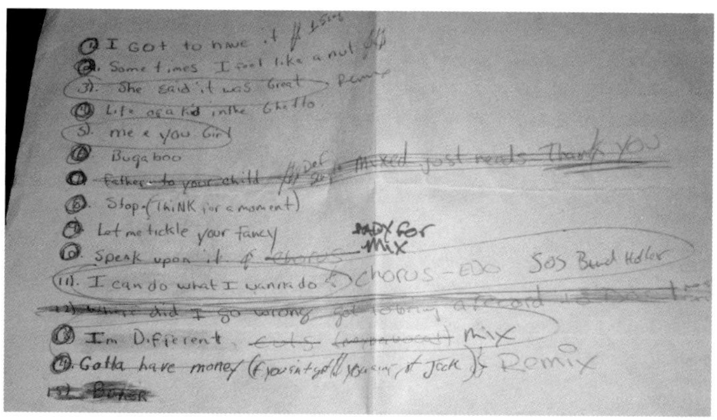

Hand-written album sequencing notes.
Courtesy of Teddy Tedd.

Jamieson Grillo, a hip-hop promotions guru who knew Ed before the album and also worked with him when it was out, says: "Back in 1991, music in general was more fun. After that, it started getting more hardcore or 'hip-pop' with the stuff Diddy was doing. But back then, pretty much everybody was real. You could do goofy, funny stuff but you could be serious, too. That's why Ed did well, because that was him and he arrived at the perfect time. Besides being the first national hip-hop artist from Boston with a number one single, the importance of that album is just the variety. The samples, the messages, it was all just perfect."

"It's not that complicated: Ed has a very unique flow and his lyrics could be very deep," Mansfield explains. "Plus, the music was catchy. It was simple, but also different. The music is unique because we were into a lot of melodic samples. That set us apart. We'd layer those in with raw drums. You can hear the drums cutting through the tracks, they're not smooth in the mix. It was a great combination."

"Ed was the first hip-hop act that Mercury dealt with back then," recalls Teddy Tedd. "He dug the trench for Black Sheep [whose very successful *A Wolf In Sheep's Clothing* came out on Mercury later in 1991]. It was easier for them to have success after we came through."

"There were no bad times about that era for me," Ed says, looking back. "People loved the record, we toured everywhere. It was great. We didn't even have any sampling lawsuits. And when I hear the album today, the three singles – 'I Got To Have It,' 'Bug-A-Boo' and 'Be A Father To Your Child' – stand out to me. They have all stayed pretty relevant and have become classics to a lot of people. Especially 'I Got To Have It.' That song was hard and street, but it also became a club record because of the beat Joe did."

He adds, "If it wasn't for that record, I wouldn't still be in the rap game today, still traveling, still making the music I want to make. We're laying the foundation now for cats who are in their 20s but want to still be doing it 20 years from now."

TRACKS

I'm Different

ED O.G: I probably had those rhymes for two or three years before we actually put them into a song. I had wanted to spit those forever. I think there are four verses on there, it's long as hell. I had to get all of them out! Some of those rhymes might have even been on other [early] demos I had done. The music changes up on there, that's something that Joe was experimenting with at the time. Other people were doing that kind of stuff back then, too. I wanted that song to be first, I wanted people – and other MCs – to know that I could rhyme.

JOE MANSFIELD: That was maybe the last song we did. We had done an earlier version of that, with different music. With the way the beat changes up on there, that might have been Tedd telling Doc to switch some things around. We had a lot of stuff layered in the mix, and I think some of those layers changed around before it was finalized. Of all the tracks that ended up on the album, that one probably changed the most, musically, from the original to the final.

TEDDY TEDD: I think on that song we took out a James Brown sample that we knew wasn't going to get cleared. We changed that around, we put in the M.C. Shan drums [from Shan's 1986 song "The Bridge"], and used some S.O.S. Band. I don't think Ed was there when we did the music for that song. It might have been the last song we did for the album.

Speak Upon It [featuring Ace & Quan and Def Jef]

ED: Def Jef just happened to be in New York at the time when we were recording the album. I can't remember how that song came about, but I had always loved Jef's stuff, starting with [his 1988 Delicious Vinyl single] "Give It Here." His lyrics were crazy, he had metaphors and skill. So he was a super-celebrity for me, and I was really excited to get him on there. We've been friends ever since. He was pro-black, so it was perfect for that song. He slayed it. Ace & Quan were managed by the Awesome 2, they were from New Jersey. They were dope but they never got a chance to put out an album. Quan had a crazy voice, it was in the realm of Smooth Bee [from Nice & Smooth]. I'm not sure whose voice is in that speech in the song, Tedd brought that in. My lyrics on there were about the [racially-charged] Charles Stuart incident in 1989 and 1990, which really made things ugly in town. Boston was still segregated, although Joe [Mansfield] was my boy. He was one of my first real white friends, we'd go to each others' houses. That's how powerful music can be, it can bring people together. Even if it was all black people at hip-hop shows back then. The Charles Stuart thing was fucked up. When the police are randomly kicking in peoples' doors looking for someone, it's crazy. No warrant, they just went into the projects and went crazy. So black people were totally upset, and it took a long time to get over it. A lot of people couldn't understand how powerless it made black people feel. Your home is the place where you feel the safest, and if the police can just kick my door down, I'm really powerless. There was a lot of tension over that, so I wanted to shed some light on it.

BRIAN CHIN: There are so many stories behind that song, obviously, and I still love how Ed tells them, with so much authority and flow.

TEDD: I think Ed had his verse for that and he originally wanted Chuck D on it. I don't know what happened, but we got Daquan [aka Quan], who was another artist we was working with, and Def Jef from the West Coast *[Author's note: Jef was born in New York but was considered a West Coast artist during the late '80s and early '90s].* Ace & Quan was the group, but Daquan was the name of the MC. Having Def Jef on there made sense, because they could all talk about things that were personal to them. I know we wanted it to be a national conversation, talking about racial and social injustice. Ed talked about Charles Stuart. In New Jersey, where we're from, there was a situation where a kid was murdered by a police officer, and the kid who got killed was Daquan's cousin. Jef closed it up, he was in LA, with everything going on out there.

JOE: It was cool to meet Def Jef when we were working on that. Ace & Quan were from around Tedd's way. I was definitely impressed that we were going to have Def Jef on our song, he was the first artist we worked with who was on a real label, and had videos and everything. That beat came about pretty early, and the final was pretty close to the original. It was just mixed a lot better.

Feel Like A Nut

ED: That was the song that got us the deal with PWL America! Brian Chin signed us up after he heard it. He loved it. It's funny that "Speak Upon It" and "Nut" are right after each other on the album, because they are totally opposite from each other.

TEDD: I sequenced the album, so that was a good place to put that song, after "Speak Upon It." It's possible that "Feel Like A Nut" got Ed signed. Honestly, I can't remember. The label might have wanted that to be a single, and we had to fight against it. We liked the song but we knew that "I Got To Have It" *had* to go first. The label didn't see that, but they weren't in the rap game like we were. "Feel Like A Nut" was a good record, it was fast-paced. But Ed wouldn't have been able to have the career he has had up to now if that had been his first single.

SPECIAL K: I remember that PWL was hyped on that song, for how commercial it might be.

JOE: That wasn't one of my favorites [laughs], but Awesome 2 definitely loved it and that one got us signed. "I Got To Have It" hadn't even been recorded yet. PWL just loved that song, for some reason. I think that song was going to be a single until they heard "I Got To Have It." I think Ed wanted to use [Bob James'] "Mardi Gras" on there, and I added a bassline. That didn't change too much from the original demo, it was pretty much the same. We used "Mardi Gras" and the horns were from another Bob James song, on a different record. The bassline was Chambers Brothers, I think. Originally I didn't want to use "Mardi Gras," just because it had been used so many times. But Ed really wanted to, so it was fine. The bassline had a weird time signature, so it was hard to get the drums right on it. So we just ended up using the "Mardi Gras" drums on the song.

I Got To Have It

JOE: That's definitely my favorite song on the album and it might have been the last song we recorded before the album came out. It was my favorite before it blew up, partially because of the journey we went through putting the song together. I think there was a consensus with everyone that it should be the first single. One day, Ed suggested we scavenge though some of his family's records to find samples. I came home with about 50 records, most of them by artists I had never heard of before. After needle-dropping through a few records I came across Bohannon's [album] *Stop & Go*. The album had endless amounts of material; I could make beats for days with it. And I realized all this before I even got to [the song which is sampled for "I Got To Have It"] "Singing A Song For My Mother." I could not stop listening to that song. "I Got To Have It" originally started in 1989 with a beat I did with just the Bohannon horns on it. The horns were the main part of the beat, and Ed really liked it. He wrote lyrics for it – different ones than appeared on the final version. For the next part of the production, I was listening to that same [Bohannon] song and trying to find different samples, beyond the horns. I loved the bassline, the organ and guitar, but I couldn't isolate those parts. There was always something else there. Then, somehow I heard a way I could grab it, by sampling different sections, starting at the back and going to the front. It took a week of listening and trying to figure it out. I must have come up with 20 different versions of the beat. With today's technology it would have been a lot easier, but back then it wasn't quick. The sample just wouldn't start on the downbeat, it would start on the three, then the sample would loop around to fill in. You can't hear it when it's mixed, but that's the way it came together. The horns were never in the song until we got to Power Play. Doc [Rodriguez, the engineer] took the sample and bounced it so that we filtered everything out except just the bass. That gave everything a really nice bottom. The James Brown sample [on the chorus, saying "I got to have it,"] is from "I Don't Want Nobody To Give Me Nothing" [1969, King Records], on 33 instead of 45. In the opposite way, the Bohannon samples on the final track, the sax and guitar and organ, are sped up from the original. So, after a lot of work, I had what I thought was the perfect loop. It had the sax and organ, a bass drum sound from my 808 [drum machine], tambourine from my Roland R8 [drum machine], and some heavy drums. I played it for Ed and he went crazy. I remember the Bohannon sample on there was tough to clear. Bohannon didn't want to clear it because his song was about his mother and he didn't think Ed's lyrics were respectful of a song like that. But eventually they worked something out.

ED: DJ Doc brought out the sub-bass on that one, and it just amazed us. I think the song did so well because the beat was catchy as hell, and people could relate to what I was saying. I wrote those lyrics and then went to Joe's and he played the beat and I was like "Oh, yesssssssss, this is it." That was probably mid-1990. We sent it to Awesome 2 and PWL, we was already signed at that point. On the third verse, I was talking about my cousin, one of my best friends. I said, "I don't have to pump jumps to clock Gs." Because he was out on the block at the time, hustling, while I had chosen music. Later on, he ended up leaving that alone and came along with us. The first time I actually performed that song in my hometown was in Cambridge, late 1991 or maybe '92. I reached out to [fellow Boston rap crew] Almighty R.S.O., we were doing a show at a middle school, in the auditorium. I had R.S.O. open up, I was trying to unite everyone. And then they stole a bunch of our equipment, so we couldn't perform [laughs]. It was crazy back then. We still performed, though. We shot the video for that song in December of 1990. It was freezing out. We did it all in black and white. That's Cathedral Projects [in Boston's South End, near Roxbury] at the very beginning, and the parts with the steps and columns, that's on Cedar Street. It's a church now. That's right down the street from my house. It was big for me to shoot in Boston, you see the A Nubian Notion sign, you see Orchard Park Projects. Little things that let you know this is home. That video was number one on MTV ["Yo! MTV Raps," not regular

MTV rotation] and BET for weeks. At that point I was annoyed with Mercury a little bit, because they made us shoot the album cover in New York, when I had wanted to shoot it on my block. So I was like, "I'm not shooting a video in New York." I had to put my foot down. Although, of course, every other video I shot after that was in LA or New York [laughs]. A lot of people don't know, but Guru and DJ Premier are in the video. They're in the part with the first hook, it's quick. They were doing promo for their album [*Step In The Arena*, 1990, Chrysalis] at A Nubian Notion [a popular Roxbury record store] and we had to get them on there! Scientifik was in that video. He was around back then in 1990, even though he wasn't in Da Bulldogs. The rest of the people in the video are just our crew.

MARTHE REYNOLDS: The album came out after the New Year in 1991. But because "I Got To Have It" was the first single, I knew we needed to get it out over the holidays. Def Jam always had a record banging in the clubs from Thanksgiving to New Year's, and I wanted that. I fought with the pressing plant, and it was a heavy fight to get me the single by mid-November. In the end, I got the vinyl, but only as white labels, without any printing on them. So I went around the block from our office to a printing shop, and had rubber stamps made. We had 1,500 white labels of the single delivered to the office and for multiple days and nights we took the vinyl out of the sleeves, figured out which was Side A and Side B, and hand-stamped each one. Then we mailed them out, and that's how the single blew up. From the middle of November [1990] until January 1, it was *the* biggest fucking record in the New York clubs. We used that time window and made it blow up. Me, Marc Raybin and our office people worked our asses off. Boston was one of the hardest markets, because there was one station up there that prided itself on *not* playing black artists. And we had to fight with them on it. I mean, Ed was from Roxbury! They weren't called JAMN back then, I don't remember the name. But they eventually played the single.

TEDD: The way that Joe put that song together was crazy. So creative. A lot of people couldn't even hear it, they didn't even know what the original song was. The original doesn't play like that. That was just a great song for anybody going through something in their lives. "Black people unite, and let's all get down," lyrics like that. "You wasn't down when we was ridin' the bus." A lot of people can relate to things Ed said on that song. That was the catalyst of the movement behind the album. That's my favorite video from the album, because Ed got to shoot it in Boston.

SPECIAL K: Ed was so clever with his rhymes on there, and he was talking about where he came from. He really repped Boston on that song. It's a classic for sure. The beat for that was so hard and Doc EQed it so well, people hadn't heard a sound like that in a long time. It made people pay attention and it drew people to the album.

JAMIESON GRILLO: That's such a classic, timeless song. I remember being at shows and that beat would come on and it was pandemonium. No matter where we went. Other songs got a great response, but "I Got To Have It" was the shit. I'm pretty sure that song charted higher than "Be A Father To Your Child."

ED: I'm still best known for that song, even today. Maybe not younger cats, but most people. The song has been re-done and sampled by a bunch of people. Aceyalone did it, when we was both signed to the same label, Ground Control [2000, on Aceyalone's album *Accepted Eclectic*]. Royal Flush from Queens did a cover. Mary J Blige [sampled] it. Heavy D did something that Pete Rock produced, I think it's on the *Blue Funk* album. A group called Intro sang it on a song called "Let Me Be." When we were in the 3 Def Notes in 1987 or 1988 we went to New York and met with this guy Jay Ellis. Dave Mays introduced us to him. I rhyme about him in that song, "Jay Ellis get jealous," in the third verse. He managed Antoinette, and he was going to shop our demo. We was doing that fast DAS EFX type of shit back then. We performed it for Jay and Antoinette and they was amazed. Then we heard her next record and she's doing the same style. They bit our shit. Jay never ended up doing anything for me and that's why I dissed him. He actually sued me back then for defamation or slander or whatever, but they threw it out of court.

She Said It Was Great

ED: Back to the girls! [laughs]. We came up with that one when we were at Power Play. I came up with the sample, a Bernard Wright thing ["Haboglabotribin'," from 1981], brought it to Joe and he made the beat around it. I came up with the hook, too, I had always wanted to sample that Slick Rick part [from Rick's "The Moment I Feared," 1988]. It's a true story on that song, everything I'm talking about. With storytelling rhymes like that, you just had to have that style in your arsenal. That just came natural, from influences I had coming up. There are cuts on the end of that, that's DJ Cruz doing those.

JOE: That sample had been used before and the Slick Rick was Ed's idea. Anything like that, on a chorus, is always Ed's idea. We never built a song around a chorus, but he was good at bringing stuff like that in. The beat was Bernard Wright, I didn't think too much of it. I was trying to get it to fit in with the sample. I never had the Bernard Wright record, so that must have been from one of Ed's relatives, or maybe even DJ

Cruz's uncle, he also had a bunch of records.

Dedicated To The Right Wingers

ED: I think that's the only song on the album that Joe didn't produce. Teddy Tedd did that one, that's his only one. I love that song. No one had really used that Funkadelic [technically Parliament, "Dr. Funkenstein," from *The Clones Of Dr. Funkenstein*, 1976] up until then. We had only met Marquis from 2 Live Crew up until that point. We had gone to Miami to do a show at Luke's Club [Pac Jam]. We was chillin' with Marquis and another dude, Luke wasn't there. That was when they was going through all those problems with their records. I was trying to stand up for our rights as artists. I was into politics, I'm interested in what's going on in the world. And what happened to 2 Live Crew could happen to me, too, with censorship. So I wanted to support them. We went to perform there in Miami again after the record was out, but we never got on stage. They said, "You can't perform until Luke gets here." It was like 4 a.m. and we just bounced. I never met Luke! Marquis was appreciative of that song, though.

TEDD: We brought the P-Funk in for that one, yeah.

JOE: Tedd had some input on that one. I think I did the drums. I think Ed might have brought in the [P-Funk] sample. There wasn't much to hook up on that one, just the main sample and the drums underneath.

Gotta Have Money (If You Ain't Got Money, You Ain't Got Jack)

[featuring Pure Blend]

CHIN: I was definitely sorry that we didn't get to do that song as a single or video. But our distributor, PolyGram, told us they were done with the project after [the third single and video] "Be A Father To Your Child" failed to sell enough additional albums. I love that song, though.

JOE: I like [R & B vocal group] Pure Blend, that stuff was good. It added to the song, which was just a loop and some drums. Gang Starr used that loop later on [The Delfonics' "Trying To Make A Fool Of Me"]. The additional vocals were the only real difference between how that song was in my basement and the final version. We didn't arrange those vocals, Doc definitely helped get that straight, as far as how they sounded on the track.'

ED: That's another record about girls. Coming up, you'd see drug dealers with fly cars coming through, and girls were attracted to that. So those lyrics on there were just me being a frustrated, broke kid. It was all about my experiences getting no play because I didn't have a car. I'm sure it's even worse for younger kids today. I talk about how living the right way can make it tougher to get ladies. I had stopped being out in the streets at that time, trying to live a more wholesome life. I wanted to be around for 100 years, I'm not trying to get killed by selling drugs. As a younger person I had sold drugs and gang-banged. My neighborhood, Humboldt Avenue, is still caught up in that. Music was my chance to get out of that. Gang Starr used that sample at the same time as we did, I think ours is better, Preem [laughs]. Pure Blend sang on that, a lot of people don't know them. They sang on Nice & Smooth stuff, too. They were also under the Awesome 2 umbrella with us. I loved R & B, I wish I could have had *more* singing on the album. But at that time, you couldn't have too much of that. Pure Blend were real singers, there was like four or five of them.

TEDD: That was actually an underground favorite, I've always loved that song and sample. It was a great mix, the sample was melodic and Pure Blend extended it. We didn't manage Pure Blend but we worked with them on Nice & Smooth's [hit single, from 1990 on Fresh Records] "Funky For You." That style wasn't done too much in hip-hop, so we knew that it could make Ed's project even better. I don't think that Pure Blend ever put out its own record.

K: That was [DJ] Kid Capri's favorite joint, he was mixing it on WBLS. He played it a lot.

Let Me Tickle Your Fancy [featuring Pure Blend and Horace Fly]

TEDD: Originally that had a different beat. We put in that James Brown ["Your Love"]. Horace Fly was the keyboardist, we also worked with him on some Nice & Smooth stuff.

ED: That's another funny record about girls. I loved Digital Underground, I banged [their 1990 album] *Sex Packets* so many times! So I wanted to sample that. I loved how that one turned out, it's one of my favorites. Horace Fly came through Awesome 2, he was an R & B dude who played and sang and produced. That song had samples and live playing on it, a lot of people weren't doing that combo back then. I think that track was ahead of its time, musically. We were talking about chasing ladies, even if we had a little fame and it was a little easier. We were still chasing.

JOE: That one is kind of in the same vein as "Gotta Have Money," with that James

Brown sample, and tightened-up vocals. The original demo was a James Brown sample with Ed rapping over it, and when we got to Power Play we added the keys and the vocals. I like both versions, I guess the keys took some of the rawness out. But I got out-voted. It's still a cool track.

Be A Father To Your Child

JOE: That was one of the later songs we recorded. I had a bunch of Roy Ayers records, I liked how melodic they were. So I had made a bunch of beats off that Roy Ayers song ["Searchin'"]. I made the beat first, and then I think Ed already had the lyrics and he knew they'd fit well. It was a really unique message. There were so many demos we recorded over that year-and-a-half, there were other songs that had similar lyrics to those in there. We used Roy Ayers on another song that didn't make the album called "I Love My Mother" [released on ED O. G & Da Bulldogs' *Life Of A Kid In The Ghetto: Demos And Rarities*, Direct Records, 2008]. That was a great song, too. "Be A Father" probably bumped that off the album.

ED: That was the third single off the album. That basically came from me seeing at the time how it was supposedly cool to tell a girl that the baby was *not* yours. It was the thing to do. And I'd see tons of girls pushing carriages around with no father. I didn't have a kid back then, it was just what I was seeing. No one was trying to step up, so I wanted to speak on it. I didn't think it would resonate like it did, but it got me on BET "Video Soul" with Donnie Simpson. That was bigger than being a *Billboard* number one, because that show was on daily. All the big celebrities were on that show. So to do an interview on there, that's when I knew I had made it. That record propelled me to a whole other level of people I could perform for. I was a spokesperson for Big Brothers and Big Sisters and they played "Be A Father To Your Child" as part of a campaign. We shot commercials and they played them on the East Coast. After the success of the first two singles, I was pretty sure it was going to do well. So many people, even hardcore dudes, have come up to me saying, "Man, that record made me step up to the plate." That's when I knew that music could have an impact on a person's life. Of course, that can mean positively or negatively. We did a talk at Harvard University with [scholar, activist and author] Dr. Benjamin Chavis, who had steamrolled all the rap tapes in Harlem because of all

the negativity in music. So we were chosen as the artists to go against him in this debate, me and Scientifik. Dr. Chavis broke it down, how it can be negative or positive, but it *does* have an influence. He killed us in the debate, and it had a big effect on the way I thought.

REYNOLDS: One thing that we did once Mercury got on board [later in 1991, once the album was selling] was that we put together plaques that had the lyrics to "Be A Father To Your Child," and sent them to radio and TV. We made a good number of them, and sent them to places like BET, because we felt the lyrics were so important. We didn't get anything but a positive response for that song. Donnie Simpson from BET "Video Soul" was a huge supporter. The lyrics of that song definitely transcended hip-hop. It was just a big urban record. I'm glad to hear that being on "Video Soul" meant so much to Ed. When you're a promotions person you can forget how the artists perceive the results you get them. With that song, Ed also had to take his own advice, because he had his daughter around that same time. That video and "Bug-A-Boo" were both shot in LA, in May of 1991. There was a big blow-up on the set of "Be A Father To Your Child." People from Mercury wanted the group to wear white suits in the video, and the guys definitely didn't want to. Mercury wanted to clean them up. It was a war and it got ugly. Once the hits came in, we started to lose control with Mercury. They wanted to come in and act like they were heroes. Things blew up at the video shoot and the photo shoot, all about the suits. But it just wasn't them. They weren't Boyz II Men.

ED: Yeah, I remember those suits. We took some photos in red suits and Mercury, who were trying to take over at that point, told us that they wouldn't use them for any main promo pictures. Then they used them anyways. We didn't want to wear those suits at all. I remember they also wanted us to wear these suspenders outfits on [the TV show] "Soul Train" [when they were performing "Be A Father To Your Child"] and we were like, "Are you fucking crazy?" We said we weren't going to perform on the show if they were going to insist on that. It was a huge blow-up on the video set. Glenn [Smooth Ice Gee] had to go to The Gap at the last minute and buy us some jeans to wear on the show, because we refused to wear the suits. We got hats from the swap meet with bulldogs on them [laughs]. In the end, they knew we couldn't be controlled. Those Mercury people were all coked out, they was crazy [laughs].

TEDD: We always knew that we wanted that song to be the third single off the album. The fact that the theme was so different than most hip-hop songs back then was something that we were both attracted to. There was silly stuff on the album, but there were also really positive and uplifting songs, like that one. It was Ed's first album, so no one had any expectations for him yet. It was one of those songs with a message that you could use in a lot of different areas.

GRILLO: I never got any feedback that people thought it was a "soft" song, only that people appreciated the positive message. Guys dug it and female DJs *really* supported it. I think people wanted to get behind it. No one had ever done a song like that, from what I can recall. In fact, a lot of hip-hop out at the time was the opposite. The sexism in hip-hop was starting to get worse right about then.

Stop (Think For A Moment)

JOE: Black Moon used that Grover Washington song ["Hydra"] a couple years after us, but I didn't consider it a bite. When people used the Bohannon after "I Got To Have It," I thought that was more of a bite, because no one had used that before we did. But lots of people knew that Grover Washington, it was a known break. Ed brought me the Guru chorus sample on there.

ED: I love that beat, it's one of my favorites. That's another record I brought [to sample], especially for the hook. I loved Guru, and that part of [Gang Starr's 1989 single] "Words I Manifest" was always so dope to me. Guru was my boy, but that was just a dope sample, no matter who it was. Plus the "Stop" part was by itself, with no music underneath. So it all made sense, and I could build lyrics over that.

Bug-A-Boo

TEDD: As I recall, PWL and Mercury picked that single because we had picked the first one ["I Got To Have It"]. That was a cool record, but... I don't know. Honestly, we didn't want that record as the second single. At the time I think we wanted "Gotta Have Money" or "Stop (Think For A Moment)." "Bug-A-Boo" was a good record, but we wanted to go somewhere different. It wasn't a good follow-up to "I Got To Have It." As far as the video goes, our main work was getting some of the celebrities that were in it. Kurtis Blow, TJ Kirkland, Tone Loc. We got all of them for cameos.

JOE: Ed had the Archie Bell [& The Drells] bassline ["Don't Let Love Get You Down"], I just hooked it up. The drums were a combination of a sample from Lee Dorsey and also an X-Clan sample. That was a really catchy song, but it was never one of my favorites. I didn't think it should be a single. I like the remix better. I thought the original was just too gimmicky. I did the remix, it's called the "Awesome Remix," I'm not sure why. I did all the remixes, including "Be A Father To Your Child." I wasn't in the video for that, I was only in the video for "I Got To Have It," and just for a second.

REYNOLDS: That video definitely drove that song's popularity. It was never a radio record, it was just them fucking around. It was all about the video.

ED: I didn't necessarily think that was going to be a single when we did it. I loved the sample, it's Archie Bell [Ed pulls out his iPhone and plays the original]. It's a great song. I used to just listen to the original in my room. I don't remember who I stole that record from in my family [laughs]. They weren't listening to these records in the '90s anyways. "Bug-A-Boo" was about people sweating you. I was looking in the dictionary for words, and I came across that one, so I figured I could coin a new thing.

It was a fun song and the video captured that. People sweating you, bothering you. My man Glenn [Smooth Ice Gee] says "I'm buggin' who?," on the chorus. Joe did some dope remixes on the 12-inch. There are a lot of people in that video. Afrika Islam, Kurtis Blow, Tone Loc, Muhammad Ali's daughter. We shot that in LA, and "Be A Father To Your Child" too, within a week. We were there doing promo, "Soul Train" and "Party Machine." Mercury had us out there for two or three weeks. The video was great, I was in awe of a lot of the people in there. Tone Loc was huuuuuuge at the time, and he had his son in there, and his son cried at the perfect time. There were a lot of models who weren't in the video but who were there on set, so that was great, too. And yeah I was wearing Lakers gear in the video. First of all, we shot the video in LA. But at the time I was a Lakers fan. I was a big Magic Johnson fan. I just was not a Celtics fan at that particular time. But I have had to answer for that, many times, over the years. A lot of kids loved "Bug-A-Boo." We could do clubs but we also weren't too scary to audiences, so we could go to a school and perform that song and talk to kids. We did a huge contest in New York for us to come to your school if you won and we went to this place in the Bronx. I think the records we made let us get into places that other rappers couldn't get into. I guess I was a little surprised that the song did well, because it wasn't my choice for the next single at the time. I don't remember which one I wanted, but I don't think it was "Bug-A-Boo."

Life Of A Kid In The Ghetto

ED: All of the stories in that song are true, the whole thing. That was written when I stopped gang-banging, after my friend Lee had got killed. That's when it got super-real. You weren't getting jumped or stabbed anymore, you were getting *shot*. It was a whole new level. That happened a year or so before we were doing the album. A lot of people were getting killed, and that was it for me. So I wanted to talk about it, and the song was dedicated to everyone in my neighborhood, because they knew every single detail. I wrote it right after Lee got killed, late '89 or early '90. It made sense to have that also be the album title, it just fit. We sample Erick Sermon on there and he was actually in the studio at Power Play when we were doing "Be A Father To Your Child." He heard the instrumental and said, "Yo, where is that sample from?" And my man Black, this guy [points to him on album cover], was like, "Yo! Don't be bitin' our shit!" And I was like, "Shut up, man, that is fucking *Erick Sermon*, don't be saying that!!"

JOE: That was done later in the recording process, there weren't any major changes from the demo to what we did at Power Play. I like that song. There wasn't any particular reason for the long outro on there, I'm sure we didn't give it any deep thought either way [laughs].

TEDD: That was last in the sequence because it summed up what you had just heard on the album. It was Ed's life. That's one of my favorites, and as the B-Side of "I Got To Have It," it made that 12-inch so strong.

REYNOLDS: I loved that song, it was such a real way for Ed to express his life.

GRAVEDIGGAZ

Niggamortis [aka *6 Feet Deep*]
Gee Street / Island, 1994

"A lot of people still talk to me about that record today, they still have me autograph it and they say how much they love it. I guess it just took a long time for people to fully appreciate it. But I'm like, 'Wow, where were y'all in 1994 when I was in tears, trying to figure out why people hated me?'"

– Prince Paul

Looking at it with more than two decades of hindsight, it might seem like the Gravediggaz would have been jocked unanimously when the group's demo was circulated to industry A & Rs. Just check it out on paper: produced by legendary super-producer and imagineer Prince Paul [Huston], it created its own genre – "Horrorcore" – and featured rhymes by a trio consisting of The RZA [Robert Diggs]; Poetic [Anthony Berkeley, who passed away in 2001]; and Stetsasonic heavyweight MC Frukwan [Arnold Hamilton, aka Fruitkwan].

But it wasn't that way at all. In fact, when Paul first got his graveyard quartet together, it was the exact opposite. "We were a bunch of misfits," he says today. "It was a time when I felt like I had to prove myself, and I felt like I had to help the other guys prove themselves. People thought I had fallen off, they were on to the new, hot guys like Pete Rock. I had lost some footing in peoples' eyes. And I was like 'Yo, I'll show them!'"

Dew Doo Man business card, early '90s.
Courtesy of Prince Paul.

The first spark for the Gravediggaz began in early 1992, after Paul's Dew Doo Man Records label – a deal with Rush Associated Labels and their parent company at the time, Columbia – was deaded before it really had a chance to have any impact. That death included a shelved album by the group Resident Alien.

Beyond Dew Doo Man, the luster for De La Soul's daisy age – which Paul helped usher into the world, on 1989's *3 Feet High And Rising* [Tommy Boy] – had, sadly, lost some shine in the public's eye. At least as far as record sales went. And either way, Paul over the years had been slowly pulling away from his production work with De La, so that they were less tied to each other in fans' eyes.

So, the producer started making tracks. Not for a specific project, but, "Because that's just what I do." He recalls, "I was feeling all sorry for myself and so I was just making these sad, slow, hardcore tracks. I was in a dark, angry mood." He adds, stating the obvious: "I knew I couldn't MC, so I needed to find some guys. That's when I gave everybody a call and got them together."

Much like an army commander calling his troops to active duty, Paul set about assembling a team.

His Long Island compatriot Poetic was first, since Paul had been talking to him recently, hoping to sign him to Dew Doo Man [in a duo called The Brothers Grimm, with Poetic's brother Brainstorm]. Before the possibility of a Dew Doo Man deal, Poetic had been dropped from Tommy Boy Records after putting out the excellent 1989 single "Poetical Terror" [as Too Poetic] and recording an album for the label that never saw the light of day.

"I heard through the grapevine that Poetic was pretty much homeless at the time, so it wasn't even easy to find him," Paul recalls. "I always felt he was extremely underrated, and I knew he wanted to experiment and branch out his style. His rhymes were very crafty, plus he was easy to direct, which is different than a lot of MCs."

Next was the man we now know as The RZA, another Tommy Boy reject, who had put out "Ooh I Love You Rakeem" under the name Prince Rakeem on the label in 1991. Paul had first met RZA in 1989, and the two even worked on demos back then. "I had always thought Rakeem was dope," Paul says. "I didn't even know him as a producer back then. His rhyming is what stood out to me."

Finally, Paul called upon Frukwan, an old associate from the days of Paul's first notable crew: live-band legends Stetsasonic. Frukwan had left the group before their final album, 1991's *Blood, Sweat & No Tears* [Tommy Boy], and Paul definitely wanted him on-board: "I always felt that he was amazing, but underrated. In Stet, he always got overshadowed by Daddy-O."

Paul, who clearly had more pull than he figured, explains the result of those first calls: "RZA, Poetic and Frukwan were the first three guys I called and they all said yes. They came over to my house and we started making a demo."

Frukwan, the group's veteran, recalls, "The whole challenge at that time was to come out not mimicking anyone else. We wanted to create a new diversity in hip-hop. We had to figure out what other MCs could match the new chapter that we were going to put out. Who was creative enough?"

Frukwan, who had met Poetic before but not Rakeem, adds, "Honestly I think we all felt like we were starting from scratch, from ground zero. Me and Paul couldn't do another hip-hop band like Stetsasonic. There were a lot of solo MCs back in the early '90s, but there weren't as many groups. And it was an awkward mix of guys. But Prince Paul was one of the top producers of that era, and he already had some beats. So we all agreed to see what we could do, to fit concepts and lyrics on what Paul already had."

The Gravediggaz name was agreed upon first, and Paul says there has been some debate within the crew as to whether RZA or Poetic came up with it. "At first there was no concept at all," Paul recalls. "I was just in it for the beats and rhymes. But once we sat down and talked, we realized that the name would be most important. So we came up with Gravediggaz and built the concept around it. The guys' personas had to come right after the group name, of course. Rakeem said, 'Yo, I'm gonna call myself The RZArector,' and then that became RZA for short. So that's the first time he used that name."

"Then Poetic said he'd be the Grym Reaper because he had had The Brothers Grimm group," Paul continues. "And at first I was like, I'll be the Pall Bearer [laughs], but then I chose The Undertaker, because I was the dude who prepped everything. *[Author's note: Frukwan was The Gatekeeper].* After all that, we knew we'd be coming from a dark place. And my tracks at the time were already there."

Importantly, and potentially unwittingly, Paul and the crew were creating a new sub-genre within hip-hop at the time, which would come to be known as "Horrorcore." This was, of course, a post-album marketing construct more than anything. But, Paul explains, "Gangsta Rap had already been so exploited at the time, so we went with horror. And then the guys would drop some non-horror hip-hop jewels in there from time to time. Basically, all three guys were in full character at recording sessions, starting from the earliest days. I didn't have to keep reminding them."

"As for the image," Paul adds, "I left that to the MCs. My whole focus was the music and the arrangements. Once the name and concept was set, I left it open, because I had MCs that I loved and knew they would come up with the dopest stuff possible."

Frukwan explains, "Sometimes it was a challenge to stay on-point and not go off-course. We talked about that while we was putting the record together. I grew up with knowledge of self, and taught consciousness and cultural awareness, so I didn't want to go away from that. We basically set it up that the world was deaf, dumb and blind. People were mentally dead, and we were digging in their brains to wake them up out of their ignorance. It wasn't about worshipping the devil, or eating brains or any of that."

The group initially centered their work around Paul's home studio in Long Island – aka Paul's Coffee Shop – for their demo. They sometimes laid down vocals to Paul's sound creations on the same day, and vocals were also occasionally spliced together by Paul later on.

At first, things were off to a good start, since Paul also remembers: "That first day we met, we did a song called 'The House That Hatred Built.' It didn't make the album, but that set us up for everything else to come. We were in the graveyard, with bones and all that."

"The way that a song went was basically the first one who finished their verse, they were first on the track," recalls Frukwan. "It was that simple. Everybody had the music and everybody knew what time we was supposed to be at the studio. In a way, it was a battle, because the person who rhymes first is probably going to be the most-remembered one for any song."

He adds, "Every verse we did and liked was always accepted, there was never any argument about whether we should re-do anything. We just knew. We were in-tune. We became tight pretty quickly, because we was all we had when we were recording those early songs."

Other early-on tracks included: "Freak The Sorceress" [which was not on the album, but turned up on the B-side of the "Nowhere To Run, Nowhere To Hide" single]; "1-800 SUICIDE"; "2 Cups Of Blood"; and "Pass The Shovel [And Step]," the latter which only appeared on the UK CD pressing. Paul adds, "There were a few other unreleased ones, I still have them on cassette somewhere."

A death-defying demo was done by late 1992, with approximately six tracks on it. "I thought that what we had come up with was *amazing*, and I shopped that demo for a year," Paul explains. "But *nobody* would bite. Jive was interested at one point but someone there said, 'Why would you want to sign *them*? They're old and played out.' That was pretty depressing."

Paul continues, "Either way, I was still making beats the whole time it was being shopped, and some of those ended up making it onto the album." During his year of shopping he was also helping De La Soul with their underrated third full-length, *Buhloone Mind State*, which was released in the fall of 1993. Ironically, on Tommy Boy.

Scott "Scotty Hard" Harding, a young studio wizard and producer who had just engineered the shelved Resident Alien album for Paul, remembers the demo well, even though he was not involved in its creation. "Believe it or not, I actually like the demo songs even better than the later ones they did, the ones I actually worked on," he says. "'Pass The Shovel,' 'Freak The Sorceress,' those songs were amazing." Harding also recalls a song called "Don't Be Afraid Of The Dark," which did not appear on the album or any singles. He would go on to engineer most of – and mix – the album-to-be.

Despite the industry apathy to the Gravediggaz demo, all was not lost. He remembers, "It was literally a week before the time we agreed that we were going to give up, in late '93, that Jon Baker at Gee Street came through. I think that Poetic was working at a bread factory at the time, and he was just planning on just staying there."

Gee Street Records' founder Jon Baker recalls, "I felt that the Gravediggaz record was *perfect* for us." This might seem like an odd statement since, before the Gravediggaz, most hip-hop fans – at least in the U.S. – knew the label for relatively less-aggressive groups like PM Dawn, the Stereo MC's and New Kingdom.

But, Baker reasons, "You can't tell me that that record would have easily fit at any other label of that era either. Gee Street was the definition of left-of-center, alternative hip-hop in 1993. We weren't trying to be Def Jam."

Baker does have a point. And his ears were indisputably good ones when it came to A & R. Starting Gee Street in London in 1985 after a half-decade in New York [where he worked as a bouncer at downtown hotspots like Negril and the Roxy], by the end of the '80s he was helping groups on the Warlock / Idlers and Tommy Boy labels blow up in the UK and continental Europe by licensing their singles and albums.

By 1991, PolyGram and Island Records had bought 50% of the label; made Baker one of their heads of A & R; and moved his operation to Island's Manhattan homebase at 4th & Broadway. He didn't know Prince Paul well on a personal level before he signed the group, but they both had a great deal of respect for each other.

Prince Paul recalls, "Jon was really into the concept of the record, and at first he even wanted to downplay the fact that RZA was in the group *[Author's note: Assuming this means wanting to focus on RZA's character in the Gravediggaz, The RZArector, instead of relying on his Wu-Tang Clan association]*, to keep all of that separate and sell our album without Wu-Tang fans."

"At first, when we signed it, I was more attracted to what Paul was doing than the fact that RZA was in the group," Baker concurs. "Wu-Tang was starting to blow up while I was talking to Paul [in mid-1993], but it wasn't fully there yet. For me, the attraction was the chemistry that all four guys had together on the demo that I heard." Baker doesn't recall the album track and single "1-800 SUICIDE" being on the demo he heard, although Paul remembers it being one of the first six or seven tracks they produced and included.

Paul says that songs from the demo that Gee Street signed were the same as they appeared on the final album. "We didn't redo any of the demo songs," he explains. "They are on the album the same way. Tascam 8-Track cassette and [Akai] S900 samplers, straight up." Scotty Hard has the same recollection.

Gravediggaz in the studio, 1993.
Photo by Prince Paul.

After the ink on the Gee Street contract had dried, more sessions were embarked upon – from late 1993 into May of 1994, continuing the vibe that was already in place. Paul recalls, "For all of those album sessions, everybody was open for the most part. Towards the latter part, RZA started getting really busy because Wu-Tang was steaming up. That was the only thing that made scheduling a little bit more difficult."

Most of the additional album recordings were done at Firehouse Studios in Brooklyn and GLC Studios in Manhattan. "GLC was almost on the West Side Highway, at the end of Christopher Street," Scotty Hard recalls. "It was a weird place and it wasn't known for hip-hop, but it was cheap." Paul and Scotty both agree that mixing for almost all tracks was done at Greene Street Studios.

And while there were many outside guests on the Gravediggaz album, those paying close attention might have noticed that the three members of De La Soul were notably absent. Paul explains, "I guess part of it, at that point, was me setting myself away from them, having an identity that was me without them. At least on my record."

Paul explains a producer technique he used, to get the most out of his motley crew of MCs: "I used to play those guys against each other, to push them. Poetic would rhyme in a normal way, and I'd be like, 'C'mon, man, you can't let RZA outdo you!' Or I'd tell RZA, 'Yo, Poetic ate you up on his verse.' Then they'd come back with something closer to what I wanted. I'd tell each of them that the other one was better – especially with RZA and Poetic – and they'd battle right there on the spot."

Paul continues, "Frukwan was more like 'I'll beat you up' than he was likely to rhyme against someone. But the competition made him step up his game as well. When it comes down to it, all MCs are the same: you never want to be the wack guy on a song."

"I do remember that technique Paul used," Baker says. "It was almost like a reality show, how he would push them with their verses."

Paul also employed different ways of getting vocal contributions, using a "Have DAT, will travel" approach and even using the United States Postal Service as an accomplice [see song comments below]. He says, "With guys like Biz Markie or Serch [both MCs are on "Defective Trip"], I would go to their houses and record them. I was kamikaze recording a lot of stuff with a portable DAT machine. I'd just tell them what to say or what to talk about. And then throughout the production process, I had to edit a *lot* of voices together. Old-school style, sampling and splicing."

Paul points out, when asked to compare RZA's role in the Wu-Tang Clan and the Gravediggaz: "He had full control in Wu-Tang, but when it came to Gravediggaz, he wasn't production-first. He was more about lyrics. If you recall, he only does vocals on a couple of songs on [the Wu-Tang Clan's late-1993 debut] *Enter The Wu-Tang*. When he came in for Gravediggaz sessions, he was always into it and down for anything, he wasn't distracted by what was happening with Wu-Tang. I don't think Gravediggaz ever took a back seat."

"The ironic thing about RZA back then is that Gee Street was ready to sign the group without him and I *demanded* that he be in it," Paul notes. "RZA was a little apprehensive because Wu-Tang was starting to take off, and he didn't want to be locked down to anything. So I told Gee Street that we wouldn't all sign until they worked it out with him, because we were a group. Then, of course, RZA blew up and Gee Street was like, 'Fuck Prince Paul, let's deal with RZA!' [laughs]." Paul says that the deal they signed was for two or three albums, but, "I was only concerned with that first one."

Although the group was two years old by the time their album came out in late summer of 1994, a bit of serendipity – or was it karma? – helped these misfits attract more ears to their sound. Paul says, "A lot of Wu-Tang fans were checking the Gravediggaz record out because we were kind of an affiliate, so that wasn't a bad thing." Additionally, RZA brought in guest MCs from his orbit who contributed to Gravediggaz songs with which they were involved, including Scientific Shabazz [David Collins, aka Shabazz The Disciple] and Killah Priest [Walter Reed].

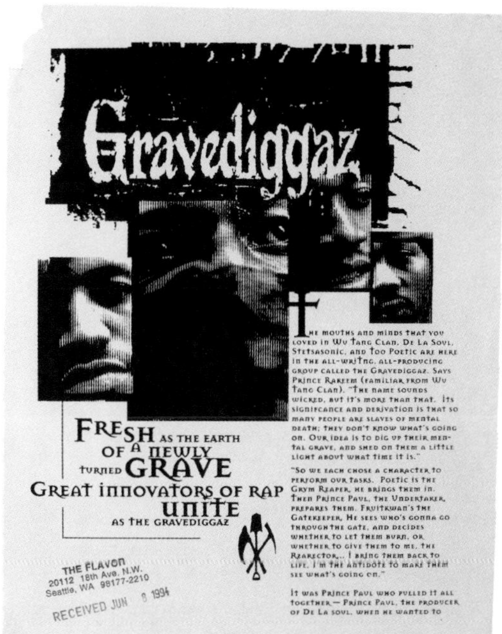

Gravediggaz

Fresh as the earth of a newly turned grave

Great innovators of rap unite as the Gravediggaz

The mouths and minds that you loved in Wu Tang Clan, De La Soul, Stetsasonic, and Too Poetic are here in the all-writing, all-producing group called the Gravediggaz. Says Prince Rakeem (familiar from Wu Tang Clan), "The name sounds wicked, but it's more than that. Its significance and derivation is that so many people are slaves of mental death; they don't know what's going on. Our idea is to dig up their mental grave, and shed on them a little light about what time it is."

"So we each chose a character to perform our tasks. Poetic is the Grym Reaper, he brings them in. Then Prince Paul, the Undertaker, prepares them. Fruitkwan's the Gatekeeper, He sees who's gonna go through the gate, and decides whether to let them burn, or whether to give them to me, the Rzarector... I bring them back to life. I'm the antidote to make them see what's going on."

It was Prince Paul who pulled it all together — Prince Paul, the producer of De La soul, when he wanted to

THE FLAVOR
20112 18th Ave. N.W.
Seattle, WA 98177-2210

RECEIVED JUN 8 1994

Album press release, page one.
Courtesy of the Adler Hip-Hop Archives / Cornell University Hip-Hop Collection.

The way the group was marketed was also unique. They were presented according to "Horrorcore" themes you might expect, with plenty of splattered blood, weaponry [both modern and antique] and dirty sneers for the camera. But with crisp photography by Christian Witkin on stark white backgrounds, the visuals approached elegance. Jon Baker explains, "We didn't package them with a full hip-hop sensibility. It was a different approach. And beyond the visuals, we managed to communicate in various ways that this was not shock and horror just to get a rise. There were messages behind certain songs, like 'Diary Of A Madman' and '1-800 SUICIDE.'"

Reg Reg Askew, who was in charge of promotion at Gee Street during the *Niggamortis* years, recalls their marketing approach: "Within the company, the discussions were never, 'Is this too violent or too much?' It was more trying to define what 'Horrorcore' was. Otherwise, it was just about selling the record to core Wu-Tang fans because of RZA, and getting the word to vintage hip-hop fans who were into Stetsasonic and De La Soul. Overall and most importantly, everyone at the label was very excited about promoting the record, because Wu-Tang was on fire at that point."

Askew, who had worked with Poetic before [at DNA International, who partnered with Tommy Boy for the Too Poetic release] and knew RZA, adds, "I didn't really expect a record like *Niggamortis* from Prince Paul, but I definitely did from RZA. It was a really fascinating album. And when we went on the road to promote it, the fan excitement was real, it wasn't hype. Everything about that record was pretty unique from a promotional perspective, because I didn't have to do many outgoing calls. People were calling *me*, asking what was next with the Gravediggaz. That's very rare." He says that the singles off the album – "Diary Of A Madman"; "Nowhere To Run, Nowhere To Hide"; and "1-800 SUICIDE" – got "lots of mix-show and college radio play, but nothing much at mainstream."

As fans of the album know, there is great deal of insider humor embedded in some of the group's tongue-in-cheek, graveyard-laden lyrics. Paul points to the line, "Who killed Tommy's boy?" from "360 Questions" as one of his favorites, since all four group members had various connections with the Tommy Boy label. Either way, Paul explains, "I didn't even care about the jokes as much, because I thought that, bottom line, the music had to be great, and the rhyming had to be great. I was only caught up in making sure that it was an innovative record."

Even if there was some humor involved, certain segments of the public took the group a bit too seriously. "I guess in the context it was placed in, people didn't know whether they should take it seriously – whether we was buggin', or if it was a gimmick," Paul admits. "Phil Donahue or somebody back then wanted us on their show because somebody's son tried to commit suicide and they wanted to blame it on our record ['1-800 SUICIDE']. It was pretty absurd. Someone even told me that they saw C. Delores Tucker on TV in the early 2000s, years after the album was out, holding the cover of our album up."

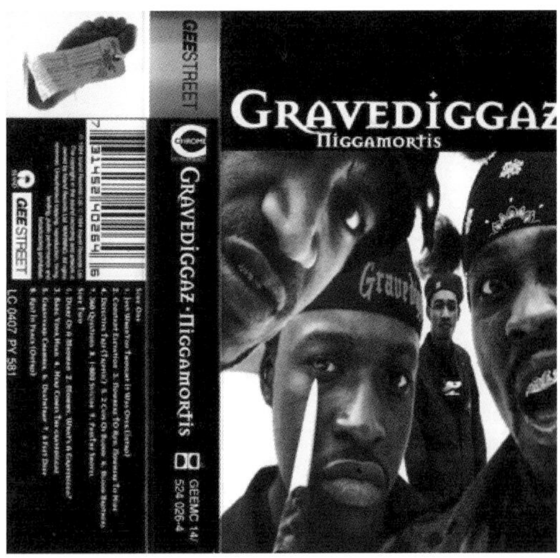

The album had two different titles, depending on where it was purchased. For most of the world, including Gee Street's birthplace in the UK, it was *Niggamortis*. In the U.S., it was changed to *6 Feet Deep*. Paul says, "We had to change it in the U.S., but it was cool everywhere else, I guess. I think they figured that the title *Niggamortis* wouldn't fly at places like Target or Wal-Mart. But it was always *Niggamortis* to us."

Released in August of 1994, the album reached number 36 on the *Billboard* "Top 200" album charts and sold quite respectably, driven almost exclusively throughout its push at retail by the single and Hype Williams-directed video for the song "Diary Of A Madman."

There was actually another Horrorcore competitor in the game that year: The Flatlinerz, who featured one of Russell Simmons' nephews on the mic [Jamel Simmons, sometimes incorrectly listed as Jamal]. The Def Jam album *USA* – which stood for "Under Satan's Authority" – didn't make much of a splash by most accounts, which to the Gee Street team proved that shock alone didn't sell. There needed to be some substance behind it, as well. Askew says, "That album did nothing because Gravediggaz had so much hype around it." Baker adds, "That Flatlinerz album was wack."

Paul says that he shopped the Gravediggaz demo to Russell Simmons and Def Jam A & R reps in late 1992, which would have given them plenty of time to drum up their own splatter-hop group, if you are into conspiracy theories. "I thought it was a bit strange, because the Flatlinerz were so similar," Paul says. "But that's the music biz for you." It didn't matter: the so-called "has-beens" in the Gravediggaz are the ones that fans remember today. After 1994, the Flatlinerz faded from view.

To add to the group's profile in 1994 and '95, the Gravediggaz toured with the Wu-Tang Clan at various times. "It was us and Wu-Tang on one bus," Paul recalls, with a laugh. "That was pretty intense. With our live gigs, to match the imagery on the record we just wore dark clothes. It wasn't very complicated [laughs]." During those same years they also toured with Ice Cube, House Of Pain, Korn and the metal / punk group Biohazard on different bills. This proved their broad appeal, which also spilled over into the rock and metal arena.

"They would do a lot of shows with Wu-Tang back then and RZA would pull double-duty," Askew recalls. "He'd do a full Gravediggaz set, change, and then go back out for Wu-Tang. The Gravediggaz actually put on an incredible live show, they had lots of energy. It was the anti-sexy rap thing, the Wu-Tang mentality. Poetic always stood out on stage, he topped them all."

Paul estimates sales of *Niggamortis* at around 400,000. Gee Street's Baker counters, "By 1995, I would think the album sold 200,000 or 300,000 in the U.S., but at this point it has definitely gone Gold [500,000 units] in the U.S. We probably didn't officially certify it. By the mid-2000s, I bet it had sold a million worldwide." Baker attributes the perennial and consistent sales to RZA's continuing relevance in the worldwide marketplace, beyond the fact that the album has gained underground classic status thanks to Prince Paul's involvement.

July 1994 album release party invite.
Courtesy of the Adler Hip-Hop Archives / Cornell University Hip-Hop Collection.

Either way, Paul says, "It broke the Top 40 charts and that was pretty good for an album without any hooks on it [laughs]."

More than sales, though, Paul wanted respect, since that was why the album was made in the first place. He explains, "Production-wise, it's probably my favorite record that I have ever done, and if I had to do it again, it would have been the exact same. When it came out, I was jocking myself on how good it was: the music, the lyrics, the sequencing."

"On that album, I actively played the role of producer," Paul explains. "I'd suggest stuff, I'd make people do verses over. It was the epitome of producing and arranging. When I was doing [De La Soul's] *3 Feet High And Rising*, I was directing the production, but I didn't know what I was talking about most of the time. By the time I did Gravediggaz, I knew what I wanted, and I knew how to get to it."

Scotty Hard says, "The MCs in Gravediggaz didn't seem disgruntled when we were making the tracks I was involved with on the album, but I know Paul was going through a tough time, especially after shopping the demo. I think some of the negativity and aggression came out in the tracks Paul made, because he's not generally a dark guy at all. At the same time, he was also combatting his 'Daisy Age' image [from De La Soul], so it made sense to go in that direction. In the end, it all led to a really unique record."

Paul has an extra sentimental view of *Niggamortis* because of Poetic's presence on it, and how he was – in many ways – the lyrical leader of the group. He says, of his friend who passed away in 2001: "I miss him, he was my man. To me, Poetic was always a wordsmith and a true rhyme guy. We just got along, and I was able to really pull amazing stuff out of him. Right before we got the deal with Gee Street, he was having some hard times, and I was really glad that he got some money from the deal. It was important to me that he was able to do what he loved."

"I think that Poetic surprised me the most as an MC on that record," Frukwan explains. "He had an ill flow. I'm more conservative, but thorough. And RZA comes from north, south, east and west. That was just a groundbreaking record, we all did what we set out to do."

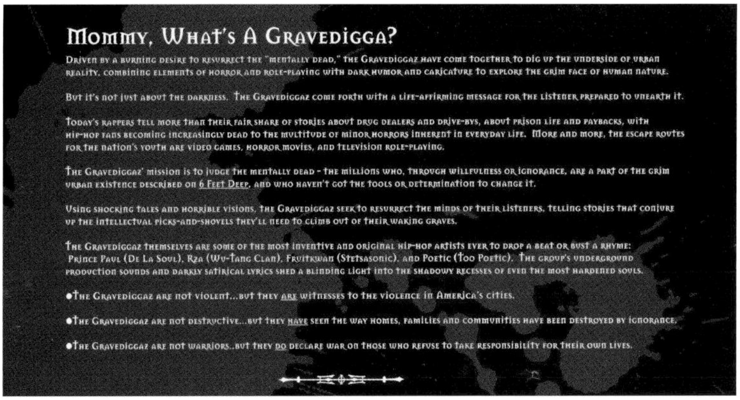

Mommy, What's A Gravedigga?

Driven by a burning desire to resurrect the "mentally dead," the Gravediggaz have come together to dig up the underside of urban reality, combining elements of horror and role-playing with dark humor and caricature to explore the grim face of human nature.

But it's not just about the darkness. The Gravediggaz come forth with a life-affirming message for the listener prepared to unearth it.

Today's rappers tell more than their fair share of stories about drug dealers and drive-bys, about prison life and paybacks, with hip-hop fans becoming increasingly dead to the multitude of minor horrors inherent in everyday life. More and more, the escape routes for the nation's youth are video games, horror movies, and television role-playing.

The Gravediggaz' mission is to judge the mentally dead - the millions who, through willfulness or ignorance, are a part of the grim urban existence described on 6 Feet Deep, and who haven't got the tools or determination to change it.

Using shocking tales and horrible visions, the Gravediggaz seek to resurrect the minds of their listeners, telling stories that conjure up the intellectual picks-and-shovels they'll need to climb out of their waking graves.

The Gravediggaz themselves are some of the most inventive and original hip-hop artists ever to drop a beat or bust a rhyme: Prince Paul (De La Soul), Rza (Wu-Tang Clan), Fruitkwan (Stetsasonic), and Poetic (Too Poetic). The group's underground production sounds and darkly satirical lyrics shed a blinding light into the shadowy recesses of even the most hardened souls.

• The Gravediggaz are not violent...but they are witnesses to the violence in America's cities.

• The Gravediggaz are not destructive...but they have seen the way homes, families and communities have been destroyed by ignorance.

• The Gravediggaz are not warriors..but they do declare war on those who refuse to take responsibility for their own lives.

Snippet from Gee Street marketing / retail promo brochure.
Courtesy of the Adler Hip-Hop Archives / Cornell University Hip-Hop Collection.

Jon Baker states, "That whole era was just amazing. You had Biggie, you had Bad Boy Records on the rise. It was an exciting period in hip-hop, and the Gravediggaz were right there in the middle of it. They were older in relation to other artists coming out at the time, but they still connected with younger fans. And when you connect with the youth, you sell records [laughs]. Paul really had a conceptual vision, and that album was his baby. Then RZA took it to another level, somewhere that Paul might not have even expected. A place that was even more hardcore. It was amazing to watch it happen."

"What impressed me was that it was just a *real* hip-hop record," says Reg Reg Askew. "There wasn't anything commercial on there. And for us at Gee Street, we had gone from PM Dawn to Gravediggaz without missing a beat. It made people look at the label differently."

"First of all, musically the album still stands up," Scotty Hard explains. "It wasn't just a gimmick that fell apart. People weren't doing concept records like that back then, especially in hip-hop. And it really drove home the point that whoever you are in rap, you're probably playing a character of some type. It could be gangsta or it could be flower-power. And Gravediggaz, it took it to the edge, to make it so obvious. It was like pro wrestling: let's make sure people know that we're kidding. The lyrics are so extreme, but also classic. It just couldn't be real, the stuff they were talking about. But it made people say, 'Maybe other rappers I listen to are playing a role, too.'"

Paul concludes, "That's probably the most fulfilling record I have ever made in my career. It stands right next to *3 Feet High And Rising* and [Paul's experimental 1996 solo album] *Psychoanalysis*. For me, Gravediggaz was done to show the world that I wasn't wack. And to prove the same thing about the rest of the guys, too. People weren't looking out for me, Poetic, Frukwan or RZA in late '92. What I hear now when I listen to it is the camaraderie, how all of these guys who didn't know each other got together and made one thing. Everybody was on the same page, and we were all very dedicated. It was all about achieving something collectively and gaining common ground. It was creative and it was harmonious."

Album ad, 1994.

TRACKS

Just When You Thought It Was Over (Intro)

[featuring Mr. Sime, Bimos, Biz Markie, Chino]

PRINCE PAUL: With all the vocalists on there, that was me doing kamikaze recordings with my DAT. I'd go to them and say, "I need you to say 'Gravediggaz.'" Then I'd edit it all together. This is before Pro Tools, mind you, on an [Akai] S-950 sampler and a sequencer program called Master Tracks Pro 6, I think. It wasn't easy.

Constant Elevation

PAUL: You can't beat Poetic when he starts things off like that. I'm pretty sure "Constant Elevation" is the first song we recorded when we were in a real studio, after we finally got signed the deal. Poetic really landed on his style there. That was the only way I could think to start the record. I remember Poetic re-did those vocals a bunch of times, before he locked in with that style. We also wanted to keep all the verses short. And RZA came into the session late, that's why he's on last. RZA did another verse for that song that didn't make it, it was more street type of stuff. That verse is on *Hip-Hop Gold Dust* [a compilation of Paul's work, released in 2005 on Antidote Records]. That's the one I really liked, it was the "Prince Rakeem style. He was trying to get away from that style, though, so the verse on the album was his "new" style. He hated that Rakeem era.

Nowhere To Run, Nowhere To Hide

[with Kurious, Don McKenzie, Gerald Whalley]

PAUL: I think that was the second single we put out, and that was one of my favorites. I remember RZA had that phrase, "Nowhere to run to, baby," from some session he had done, and he wanted to use it for the hook. I originally put a Cold Crush Brothers [live] tape sample on there, but I had to take it off later. Grandmaster Caz couldn't give me permission because he said Tuff City owned the rights to his vocals, even on a live tape that was never released! That's what Caz told me, at least. Later pressings of the album don't have the Cold Crush stuff on there at the beginning. I didn't even know that myself until I bought a cassette later on and realized it had been removed. There were some other changes like that on the album, but that's the most notable one. I threw that [Wu-Tang] "Protect Ya Neck" thing in there because RZA messed up part of his vocal, and there was a blank space. He said, "I'ma come back and fix it," but I threw that in there and he really liked it and wanted to keep it. I liked messing with him like that.

FRUKWAN: I think that's probably my favorite song on the album. We really nailed that one.

JON BAKER: That song really stood out to me when I heard it on the demo. It was clever and the hook was great. It definitely ended up being one of the strongest songs on the album.

Defective Trip (Trippin') [with Biz Markie and MC Serch]

PAUL: On that one, Serch is saying "Old Fat Ned, from a crackhead." And Biz says, "Got a piece, little man?" Those vocals were on DAT, they weren't done in a studio. That song was supposed to be dreamy and funky, like a drug trip. We cut in parts from [De La Soul's] "Plug Tunin'" on the hook. Things fell into place. The guitar sample was off some soft-rock '70s album [John Ussery, "Listen To The Melody," from 1973].

2 Cups Of Blood

PAUL: That was on the early demo we did, on a Tascam 8-track cassette. Frukwan wanted to get on there and I told him, "Nah, man, it sounds good the way it is!" [laughs]. Everybody didn't have to be on every song, it was good to switch it up sometimes.

FRUKWAN: I didn't mind not being on any given track. It was what it was. I was on enough tracks.

Blood Brothers

PAUL: When I first put the group together, I had copies of songs that all three guys had done, and I gave a copy to each MC, so they could hear more about the other guys. "Blood Brothers" was a song that Frukwan had, so we re-did it, and everybody was down for it.

FRUKWAN: I had the concept for that, but not the music. I brought it in, and everybody took to it. RZA and Poetic added on. I hadn't had the lyrics to that for too long before I brought it to the group.

360 Questions [featuring Vernon Reid and Djinji Brown]

PAUL: I remember we recorded that at GLC Studios. The Muslims had these books, *360 Questions To Ask A Sunni Muslim* and stuff like that. So I turned that into a Gravediggaz thing by just asking dumb questions. We were all giggling and having fun. Killah Priest had this 'hood chick in the studio, and we had her ask the one about the Herculonious Period [laughs]. Vernon Reid was there, too. Everyone just came up with their own thing. And the "Who Killed Tommy's Boy?" line was because we were all ex-Tommy Boy *employees*.

SCOTT "SCOTTY HARD" HARDING: That song was different than other tracks on the album because most of those people recorded their vocals at GLC instead of on DATs. Vernon Reid is the guy who asks, "Y'all eat eggs?" All of that shit was so funny and so stupid.

1-800 SUICIDE

JON BAKER: I loved that song, it's one of my favorites, next to "Diary Of A Madman." I remember we did Public Service Announcements and campaigns about youth suicide behind that.

PAUL: That one was done very early on. It was recorded at my house and then mixed at a regular studio. I just *knew* that song was going to get us a deal. Like, "Oh, man, this is so excellent, it's so *crazy*!" The beat, the rhymes. It hurt me to my heart that I had to shop it to labels for a year [laughs]. That was maybe the third or fourth song on the demo. And I think that ended up being the third single. Everybody liked the song, but it was pretty controversial. It was so outlandish. You'd need to be on serious drugs to take that song seriously. I knew that we'd get talked about, of course. I wasn't afraid of the publicity. But sometimes I give humans more credit than they deserve. I figured people would get it and have a sense of humor, but it's not always like that [laughs]. Sarcasm requires a certain amount of intelligence, I guess. I don't remember recording any PSAs about teenage suicide, but if we did, it was probably because the record was getting a lot of heat from the PMRC [Parents Music Resource Center, headed by Tipper Gore] and other places like that.

SCOTTY HARD: That was my best "Ferris Bueller" impression on there *[Author's note: In the middle of the song, Harding speaks one of the lines from the popular '80s movie: "... If you don't stop and look around every once in a while, you might miss it."].* The original demo of the song had the actual movie quote on there, but we knew we'd never be able to clear that. So Paul just had me replace it. "We need a bland, white guy voice to go in and say these lines." Paul always thought shit like that was hilarious. I think overall that's my favorite track on the record. The lyrics are dope and I think it sums up the album really well.

REG REG ASKEW: Jada Pinkett actually directed that video. It also has scenes from the [1995] movie "Demon Knight" that she was in. C. Delores Tucker was really going after Snoop and gangsta rap overall at the time, and the topic of suicide was always touchy anyways. Island Records was the distributor for Gee Street and they were a bit hesitant to push that song to radio, so we did issue it as a single, but didn't really push it. It wasn't available commercially as a single.

Pass The Shovel *[on CD version of Niggamortis only, not on 6 Feet Deep]*

FRUKWAN: I think that was the song where we really bonded and confirmed that this was going to work. It was one of the first ones we did, and it was on our demo.

Diary Of A Madman [produced by RNS and RZA, co-produced by Prince Paul; featuring Scientific Shabazz aka Shabazz The Disciple and Killah Priest]

PAUL: That was the first single off the album. With the production on there, here's the full story: RZA had the beat, he played it for me and thought it would work for Gravediggaz. His man RNS from Staten Island did it. So I asked what we had to do to get it for us to use. RZA said we could give RNS some money and a credit. RZA gave me the original beat on a cassette, it was a real bad version. And RNS would never tell us what the song [he sampled] was. So I programmed the beat around what they gave me. Then Shabazz and Killah Priest came in and laid down their rhymes. And all I remember is that RZA didn't know what rhyme he was going to do behind it. And I was thinking, "How am I going to make this cohesive with the rest of the record?" RZA and Frukwan laid their rhymes and Poetic was hurt about it but I told him there were already too many people on there [laughs]. When I listened to it, it was just missing *something*, it was a random record with no hook. So I came up with the courtroom thing, and I started seeking out voices. I wanted Wildman Steve, a radio DJ out here in Long Island, he was on WBAU at the time, but that didn't work out. So I pieced it all together and RZA was like, "Yo! That's *crazy*!" Some people say I didn't do much on that track because the album says "Co-produced," but trust me, I did plenty! I didn't care about the credit, I just wanted to make it work. Those verses were done in a different order, and I put everything together like a puzzle *[Author's note: Ironically, this was similar to the way RZA pieced together Wu-Tang Clan verses for their debut single, "Protect Ya Neck"].* It wasn't always that way on the album, but definitely with that song. We didn't have a concept at first, it was just rhymes. Shabazz came in with his rhyme, after he heard the beat. And he set the bar *high*. Cats were intimidated. His is first, that's the only one that's in the right place. The lawyer voice is [journalist, producer and WordSound Records label owner] Skiz Fernando, because I knew he sounded shady enough for that role. I think the judge was an engineer at GLC Studios. He had an ill voice. I can't remember his name, but he's in the credits somewhere *[Author's note: The small print lists Ted "The Judge" Gannon].* I recorded them on DAT after telling them what to say, and I pieced it all together. When the album came out, a lot of people said that song was a gimmick. Biggie Smalls and Craig Mack "Flava In Ya Ear" were out at the time, so we must be some kind of gimmick. But we got redemption when it was number one most requested song on Hot 97 in the "Battle of the Beats" competition they would do, where listeners who would call in and vote. And I was like, "Yo, my record doesn't even have a hook!" That made me feel good.

SCOTTY HARD: The judge on the song is this strange guy who was an intern at GLC named Ted. Paul always told me that I had a weird voice, and I was like, "If you think I have a weird voice, you really need to hear *this* guy!" That was really the way he talked, and Paul was like, "We *have* to use him!"

JON BAKER: That video is definitely what kicked the album off. It encapsulated the entire album, Hype Williams did an amazing job on it. I remember it was a 27-hour shoot, on the Lower East Side, in a synagogue. We all put our hearts and souls into that, and the result was incredible. The video was banned, it was written about. But the fans understood it, they got it.

ASKEW: That song did the best of the album singles, by far, and drove most of the album's sales. That one got rotation on Hot 97 [New York's influential R & B and hip-hop powerhouse], and that was pretty important. At that time, the station was innovative in how they played hip-hop in prime-time hours, not just on mix-shows. Them putting Gravediggaz into rotation didn't surprise me, because they were down with Wu-Tang, too. And after Hot 97 got on it, other stations, like JAMN in Boston, put it in light rotation.

PAUL: That was definitely the biggest hit on the album. We did a video for it, although nobody would show it. It was Hype Williams' first major production. MTV wouldn't play it because they said it had too many graphic images. Of course they were playing booty videos all over the place back then. The video just followed the storyline and implied a lot of bad things, but it didn't *show* anything. And even when we edited it and chopped stuff out, they still wouldn't touch it.

Mommy, What's A Gravedigga? [featuring Scott Harding on bass]

PAUL: That was purposefully done as a short song. The original loop was something that Pos [from De La Soul] found and was used on a De La remix. I always loved it. So I flipped it and had Scotty play bass on it. I remember that Frukwan set how that one would be rhymed, and I remember debating with Poetic, telling him he was rhyming too soft. But he and RZA liked that style, so I was outnumbered, because Frukwan was neutral. I still like it, but I do wish that Poetic had come from a different angle. That's my voice at the beginning [saying, among other things, "Walking in the shadows / You realize that life / Is just a form of animated death"]. I was dark back then. That female vocal wasn't anyone I knew. There was this guy, MC Goldilocks, I had met him and I told him to send me a cassette tape of him and his friends saying "Gravediggaz." It was just random vocals and I put it all in place. The album is truly cut-and-paste, that stuff happened all over it.

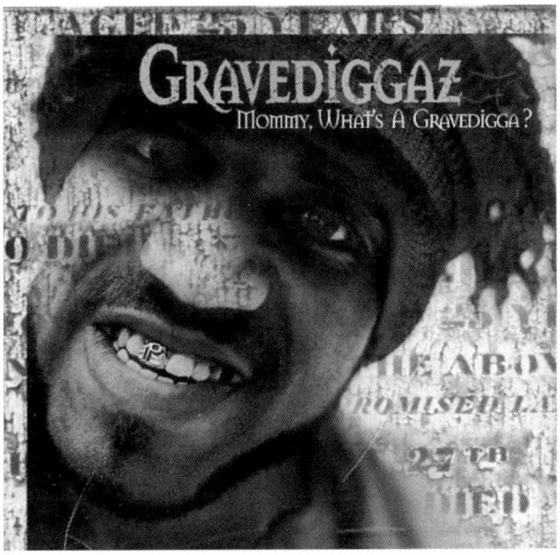

Bang Your Head

PAUL: RZA came up with that title. I had originally made that beat for the Cold Crush Brothers, believe it or not. They came by my house and we had some ideas, but it never came to fruition. I always loved that beat, though, I did it on my Juno 106 [keyboard]. RZA was recording the Wu-Tang album, the song with "Better go to the wall and bang your head." *[Author's note: On Wu-Tang's "Da Mystery Of Chessboxin'," U-God's verse includes the words, "You might as well run into the wall and bang your head."].* So that phrase was in his head, and I was like, "Cool."

Here Comes The Gravediggaz [produced by Mr. Sime]

PAUL: With that one, the beat was done by this guy Pedro Sime, who went by Mr. Sime. I was pretty hands-off on that one. He was Poetic's homeboy, he had produced the demo for Poetic's group the Brothers Grimm. I always liked Sime's style, he could program beats really well. They had that beat, so I wanted to use it for the album. That "Grave – Diggaz" at the beginning, that was this guy Chino from California. It was another random dude on a cassette tape. That "Get Off Nigga / Gravedigga" is RZA, sampled from the first song we did as Gravediggaz, "The House That Hatred Built," which didn't make the album.

Graveyard Chamber [produced by RZA; with Scientific Shabazz aka Shabazz The Disciple, Killah Priest and Dreddy Kruger]

PAUL: That was fully RZA's track. I remember it was done in some other studio we hadn't really worked in. He had this ASR-10 keyboard and some sounds in there. I left because it was too late for me, and when I came back, it was just a crazy track. It was that classic RZA sound, everything all over, the quality was bad. But it just *worked.* That's one of my favorite songs on the album, lyrically for sure. Working with RZA during that era really grounded me, because he was so unorthodox. He didn't care about *anything* – sequencing, timing, quality. Random snares all over a four minute track. Who does that? But it sounded right, he was onto something. It's about how it *feels*, not about how technically beautiful it is.

Deathtrap [featuring Masta Ace, with Don Newkirk on keys]

PAUL: I had Masta Ace do the intro there, I didn't think he would fit into the concept of what we were doing as Gravediggaz beyond that. I was always a fan of Ace, because he did [1993's] *SlaughtaHouse* and called out Wu-Tang. I had that beat for years, I had always liked it. It samples part of [The Whole Darn Family's] "Seven Minutes Of Funk," a part that no one uses. The album version, with the bongos. That's the one I remember Afrika Bambaataa using when I heard him DJ, when I was a kid.

6 Feet Deep [produced and mixed by RZA & Gravediggaz]

FRUKWAN: I was on guitar with that one, yeah [laughs]. I had messed with guitar before, but I didn't really know how to actually play. With that song we just started going, to see what would happen. The flows for all the MCs on there were awkward, but we had the magic, so we did it.

PAUL: I believe that was the last song we recorded. One day we were in GLC and they had a "live" room, with instruments. We were waiting for our engineer Scott, so we just picked up random instruments. I think I was playing drums, RZA was on keyboards, Frukwan was on guitar. So we just played random stupid stuff and ran a DAT of it. Every once in a while, as "off" as we were, we'd catch a groove. It was so much fun, we were cracking up. Then RZA took the DAT and pieced together that song. I never got the DAT back. Then they laid vocals down on it. RZA came up with the lyrical style on there, but he couldn't finish the chorus. He was stuck on, "Gravedigga, nigga, can't you see?" And I was like, "Man, that sounds cheesy!" So I suggested "Six feet deep" and that was it.

SCOTTY HARD: I honestly don't remember that one, but I must have recorded it. I was probably pissed when I did it! RZA took bits of it, put it in his ASR [sampler] and made the track. It almost sounds like a Tom Waits song.

Rest In Peace (Outro) [featuring Mr. Sime, Bimos, Biz Markie, Chino]

PAUL: That was a random instrumental, and we just ended the album with dialogue. RZA wasn't there at first, and we were trying to figure out how to do it. Then he walked in, picked up the headphones and just ran it down, one take.

Freak The Sorceress

[B-side of "Nowhere to Run, Nowhere To Hide" single, not on album]

FRUKWAN: I think that was the first song we did. We did it just to test the waters.

PAUL: That was one of the first tracks we made, right after we formed. It was on the demo we shopped, but we didn't put it on the album because I don't think RZA liked that song. He didn't want to disrespect women like that. I was more reckless, I was like, "I don't care!" So I found a way to put it out, on the B-side of a single.

The Reincarnation Of Freud

[B-side of "Nowhere to Run, Nowhere To Hide" single, not on album]

PAUL: I don't even know where that song name came from. Poetic might have come up with that. It was just a production piece, I made it on the SP-12 [sampler / drum machine]. As if everyone would be so impressed! [laughs]. It would have never made the album, it didn't fit anywhere.

ICE CUBE

AmeriKKKa's Most Wanted
Priority Records, 1990

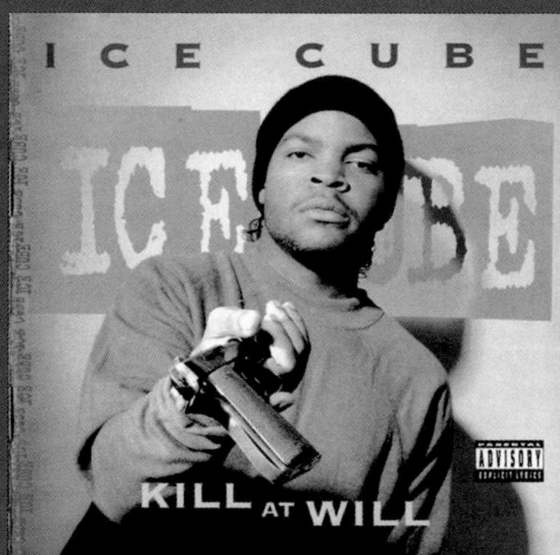

Kill At Will
Priority Records, 1990

"I was making my solo move before a lot of people even realized that I was out of N.W.A. People were pretty surprised when they heard I was working on the record."

– Ice Cube

"I have always tried to communicate rebellion, and you can't convey that in a harmonious atmosphere. You have to create an atmosphere that is conducive for agitation."

– Hank Shocklee

To say that 1989 was both an exciting and chaotic time in the world of rap music would be quite an understatement. Numerous groups throughout the '80s had pushed and pulled the hip-hop artform in different directions, bringing it from the streets of New York City to the world. It had morphed and moved from party-time music to drive-by music, and encompassed every sound and emotion in between. It never stopped moving.

In the same way that the truism "sex sells" works in advertising, you could say – then as now – that "chaos sells" in the world of rap. And as the "Me Decade" inhaled its last breath, music headlines rang out that two of hip-hop's most popular, bombastic, and talented groups, Public Enemy and N.W.A., were showing signs of internal chaos and potential implosion. Fans buzzed as they waited for the latest updates.

In May of 1989, Public Enemy leader Chuck D expelled group member Professor Griff in the aftermath of anti-Semitic remarks made during an interview with the *Washington Times*. At the same time, the most infamous band in popular music, Los Angeles' N.W.A., was slowly coming apart at the seams, with chief lyricist Ice Cube threatening to leave the group. (Producer and rapper Dr. Dre would soon follow.)

After more drama in both camps, later that year two incredibly talented forces of musical nature – Public Enemy's Bomb Squad; and Ice Cube, with his homie Sir Jinx – came together in New York City to create the first classic hip-hop record of the 1990s: *AmeriKKKa's Most Wanted*. And for all parties involved (including fans), it was nothing but wonderful, beautiful chaos.

Let's begin with the colorful list of players involved: in the West Coast corner there was Ice Cube [O'Shea Jackson], 19-years-old in 1990; and Cube's long-time associate, Sir Jinx [Anthony Wheaton], 18. From the East, there was the Bomb Squad: pater familias Hank Shocklee [James Henry Boxley III]; Chuck D [Carlton Ridenhour]; Eric "Vietnam" Sadler; and Keith Shocklee [Keith Boxley].

Cube and Jinx had worked together long before Cube's N.W.A. days, in two different groups: The Stereo Crew and C.I.A. The third member in both groups was K-Dee, aka Kid Disaster. Cube and Jinx first met when Jinx moved two doors down from Cube's family in the mid-80s, on Van Wick Street, in South Central LA. "Me and K-Dee went to Taft High School in Woodland Hills. We got bused there," Cube explains. "Jinx went to Washington High, which was right up the street from where we lived."

"I started DJing before I had come to the area where Cube lived, in fourth or fifth grade," Jinx says. "Then Cube got into rapping in eighth grade. We just wanted to be entertainers." Cube recalls, "Jinx had DJ equipment and we was cool. But we wasn't *that* close because I was trying to go out with his sister. So I was closer to her. Once I started rapping, we starting hanging out a lot more. He really showed me how to put the skills I had to the beat, and make it flow."

After making demos in primitive studio situations, the Stereo Crew were actually signed to Epic Records in 1986, and put out one single: "She's a Skag" [produced by Dr. Dre – Andre Young – and Alonzo "Lonzo" Williams]. At the time, Jinx – who is Dr. Dre's cousin, five years his junior – rhymed alongside his two partners. They were managed by Lonzo, who also managed, and was a member of, Dre's first group: the World Class Wreckin' Cru.

"We didn't like the label situation with the Stereo Crew," says Cube, "But everything else to us was positive. We was getting a chance to hang out with Dr. Dre, and we learned with him. We were all trying to figure out what was gonna work."

The group C.I.A. had the same lineup, but boasted a harder, naughtier edge. Jinx explains, "After the Stereo Crew, 'La Di Da Di' [by Doug E Fresh and Slick Rick aka M.C. Ricky D] was big in LA, so we started doing parody raps, with curses. [Run-DMC's] 'My Adidas' became 'My Rubber.' 'Pee Wee Herman' *[Author's Note: Assuming he means either Joeski Love's "Pee-Wee's Dance" or MC Boob's "Do The Fila And The Peewee Dance"]* was 'VD Sermon' and

[Salt-N-Pepa's] 'I'll Take Your Man,' became 'I'll Fuck Your Friend.'" Cube says, "With C.I.A., it was the same guys, but our content changed. We were starting to do harder music, finding our niche."

"And then," Cube adds, "Eazy started coming around."

C.I.A., like the Stereo Crew, was short-lived. The group put out a three-song, Dre-produced single on Kru-Cut Records in 1987 (the *Cru' In Action!* EP), which did have some regional impact. It could, in fact, be argued that the trio's work led directly into the raunchy, provocative hurricane that N.W.A. would soon become.

Local hustler and future rapper and music executive Eazy-E [Eric Wright] entered the picture as C.I.A. was enjoying its brief period of success, plucking Ice Cube for his writing abilities. Their first collaboration was the 1987 Eazy-E single "The Boyz-N-The-Hood," which christened the Ruthless Records label.

"Boyz" was produced by Dr. Dre and was originally supposed to feature vocals by a group from Riverside, CA, called H.B.O. After that plan fell by the wayside, the tune was recorded with Eazy on vocals and – just like that – the N.W.A. era was born. "N.W.A. was an all-star group in a lot of ways," Cube says. "After we started it, we couldn't have really gone back to what we was doing before, with those previous groups."

As N.W.A.'s popularity continued to rise in 1987 and 1988, Cube became fully ensconced in the group. During this rise, truth be told, Sir Jinx as a rapper, DJ and producer was pushed to the side. Nevertheless, he remained in the mix. "I was on the road with N.W.A. in 1988 and 1989, traveling everywhere with those guys," Jinx says. "It was great. You want to know what I did? Every time you saw an N.W.A. show back then, you saw yellow police tape across the front of the stage. That was my job! [laughs]. I knew where all those damn ribbons was, under the bus.

I'd carry bags, set up turntables during sound-check and put up tape. Then, a year later, once Cube came out, I was setting up my own tables for soundcheck."

Aside from his N.W.A. police-tape duties, during 1988 and '89, Jinx had continued to build his skills as a DJ and producer, working out of a studio in Long Beach owned by Calvin Anderson. There he made demos with MCs including Dazzie Dee, Ice Cube's cousin Del the Funky Homosapien and Tajai from Souls of Mischief.

By the fall of 1989, as the group was becoming one of the hottest groups in all of music, Cube became agitated with his standing in the N.W.A. universe. He felt that group manager Jerry Heller and Eazy-E [who both owned an interest in the group's label, Ruthless] were short-changing him on royalties, and he wasn't planning on being quiet about it.

"When you catch someone with their hand in the cookie jar, they can do two things," Cube explains. "They can say, 'Yeah, you caught me, let me make it up to you.' Or they can say, 'My hand wasn't in the cookie jar!' And that [the latter] was their position. If they'd have come clean with me, then they would have had to come clean with everybody in N.W.A., so they took the stance that I was the outsider. I was forced out, in a way."

He continues, "But I didn't want to just be gone. I had made a name for myself in the group, so as long as I could get a record company behind me, I knew I'd have a shot. The key factor was Priority's position *[Author's note: Priority Records distributed N.W.A.'s smash 1988 album Straight Outta Compton].* Would they force me to stay in the group by not giving me a solo deal, and not letting me out of my contract? Or was they gonna roll with it and put out both records [the upcoming N.W.A. EP, *100 Miles and Runnin'*, and Cube's solo debut]? Luckily, they was smart."

But, Cube adds, his first choice was not to leave the group. He explains, "I had wanted to work it out with the group, it's not like I just washed my hands of it and I was gone." Still, relying on his old crew to help with his solo project wasn't very likely. "When I left the group, I was still trying to get Dre to produce my album," Cube recalls. "I didn't have any hard feelings like that. It was a business decision when I left. But Jerry Heller stepped in and vetoed Dre working with me."

This left Cube with a tough decision: now that his friend and producer Dre was off-limits, who could produce his solo album? "With N.W.A., we had toured with a lot of East Coast groups: De La Soul, Public Enemy, Salt-N-Pepa, LL Cool J. So I knew the hot producers," Cube says. "We was all fans of the Bomb Squad, as you can tell by the samples that we used on *Straight Outta Compton*." In addition to being a fan of Public Enemy on the music side, Ice Cube respected Chuck D's outlook as an elder in the still-young hip-hop game.

Cube explains, "I initially called Chuck because I wanted his advice about me leaving the group. He was actually encouraging me to find a way to stay in N.W.A., because the group was so meaningful to so many people. At the time I never asked him if the Bomb Squad would do my record, I was just talking to him about what I should do next. I had also talked to Lyor Cohen and other people I knew, because if Priority was gonna front on me, I was gonna go to Def Jam."

"The one thing I definitely remember from those days was trying to stay out of the middle of the N.W.A. and Ice Cube beef," Chuck remembers. "I had just had the Griff thing happen with my group and I had done shows with N.W.A. in the summer of '89. I didn't want to get in the middle of that group's implosion. But Cube kept reaching out to me, he kept saying he wanted the Bomb Squad to at least do a couple tracks with him. He knew that even if Dre was able to do his record, he would keep getting his release date pushed back, because Dre was so busy."

Ice Cube, 1990.
Photo © Debra DiPaolo, www.debradipaolo.com.

In January 1990, Cube traveled to New York to meet with Chuck's first producer recommendation, Sam Sever [producer for 3rd Bass and other artists], at Def Jam's offices. The meeting with Sever never transpired, but the trip wasn't a loss. Chuck D happened to stop in the office that day, and invited Cube to a Public Enemy recording session that night at Greene Street Studios in Manhattan for their upcoming *Fear Of A Black Planet* album. The result of that session was the song "Burn Hollywood Burn," featuring Big Daddy Kane. And, a last minute addition: Ice Cube.

"That was my foot in the door," Cube smirks.

According to Chuck, the story unfolded like so: "Cube went to Hank [Shocklee] and us and said that he had mentioned to Dre and Eazy that the Bomb Squad might produce his album. And when he did, Eazy had rolled his eyes, and Dre said, 'Well, then you'll barely go gold.' When that was heard, we assembled." [Cube would not confirm or deny who from N.W.A. said what. Although, he says, "I think Hank took that as a challenge. Like, 'They laughin' at us?!'"].

"I was always a fan of N.W.A., but I had never met Cube before," explains Hank Shocklee. "I remember getting a call at the studio, and the person on the line said he was Ice Cube. He wanted to come and talk to us about doing a record. At first, I didn't believe it was him on the phone, honestly. And if it *was* him, I couldn't believe that he wanted us to do a record. I figured if he was serious, he'd come out [to New York]."

Eric "Vietnam" Sadler recalls, "The first we ever paid attention to any of those West Coast guys was Eazy-E, his first stuff. Except for Darlene [the cover model for Ice-T's early albums and singles on Sire]. But when *Straight Outta Compton* came out, I was like, 'Whoa, this is some great stuff.' I was definitely surprised when I heard that we might be working with Cube. At the time, though, I had no idea he had left N.W.A."

"I was shocked that Cube did come out, but he did," Hank continues. "And I said to him, 'Before I work with you, I have to see what you're all about, as an artist. I know your records with N.W.A., but I don't know *you* as an artist or as a person.' I have always believed in tailor-making music. When I first talked to him on the phone, I told him that I didn't like to do *pieces* of records. It wouldn't be worth bringing the Bomb Squad to the table unless we were doing a full album. He knew that from day one."

Chuck says, "Before we started anything with that album, I told Cube to pick up a notebook and start writing ideas down. We talked about different theories I had, like never doing the same thing twice, and making sure you can back up anything you say. Cube was already *there*, I was just reassuring him that he was on the right track." Cube remembers it similarly: "Chuck had me working in a notebook, making notes about what I wanted on the record. We had our antennas up. We wanted to make something that had never been heard before."

Hank has memories of Cube's notebooks as well, but different ones. "I realized this could be a really good project when Ice Cube showed me six or eight composition books full of rhymes," he remembers. "And they weren't the 90-page ones, they were 200-pages, filled up! That was what got me really excited. To me, that's the mark of an artist – how much material can you bring to the table? I already knew we had an album's worth, now we had to figure out how to condense it into something cohesive."

Shocklee adds, "Doing a single artist can be a liability, because you only have a single voice, a single sound repeated over 10 tracks. So, how do you make that interesting to the listener? That's where an artist's imagination and material come into play."

"We knew it had to be the best of both worlds," Chuck explains. "Cube was the chief writer in N.W.A., so he had to deliver the gangster thing. But he was also going to have to deliver some things that made more sense. [N.W.A.'s song] 'A Bitch Iz A Bitch' ain't gonna work, you know? [laughs]. Just be *believable*. You don't gotta become conscious overnight, but you also have to grow. And I definitely think he did that."

Cube's next move was now in place. To work on his debut, he would trade his sunny Los Angeles homeland for the cold streets of New York City in the dead of winter. Aside from warm socks and a sweater or three, he packed essential personnel: his old pal Sir Jinx, with Cube's Lench Mob crew members J. Dee and T-Bone in tow for good measure.

"What I really remember is that when we got there, it was snowing and hella cold," Jinx recalls, with a grin.

"Cube took me to New York to keep an eye on things," Jinx continues. "I wasn't there to produce no tracks, because we were thinking about producing other tracks [for the album] when we got back to LA. I was there just to document stuff – who did what, and who needed what credit. When we got to New York for that album, there was no real entourage. I had never been there before. We had an apartment in Manhattan, by the Hudson River."

"Jinx was kinda in the wings on the N.W.A. projects," Cube admits. "He always felt like, 'What is my role here?' And me leaving N.W.A. disrupted what Jinx was doing at the time. But there we were, back together, in New York, figuring things out. Jinx was a good producer, but we both needed more work to figure out how to put a whole record together, song by song. Jinx's role was to hang and keep the record where it was supposed to be, as far as the West Coast influence. We had to make sure we stayed in our element. I would say that he was an overseer on that record, more than an executive producer."

Arriving in New York in late January, Cube and Jinx didn't go straight into Greene Street Studios, where final recordings would be done. Instead, they took a two-week trek to Public Enemy's rehearsal space, pre-production studio and clubhouse at 510 South Franklin Street in Hempstead, NY. Strong Island. "We first went to the basement of that Church," Jinx recalls. "That's where I first met Busta Rhymes, he was hanging out there." *[Author's note: 510 South Franklin was actually a commercial building, not a church, with a dentist's office in the basement].*

"They had us come out to Long Island first, we stayed in a hotel out there," Cube says. "We just sat there for four or five days before we even went to 510 South Franklin, because Public Enemy was doing shows. At 510, they basically had a warehouse full of records. They eventually showed us around and then said, 'Go find your album.' They told us to go find what records we wanted to use, and we'd go from there."

510 South Franklin Street at night.
Photo courtesy of Eric "Vietnam" Sadler.

Hank says, "When Cube arrived, he told me that he had come with the one-way ticket [laughs]! I had to applaud him for that. When he got in, I let him get up in 510 South Franklin and go through all my records. He stayed there for days. I wanted to feel where he was coming from, musically. He was into a lot of funk, stuff from the Steve Arrington era. Slave, Con Funk Shun. Mostly, though, he liked a lot of the underground funk, like Betty Davis. He liked a lot of slow stuff. I understood where he was at after that. Cube slept on the floor of 510 going through all those records. He had a hotel, but he was working around the clock."

Bomb Squad friend and affiliate Sugar Bear inside the Bomb Squad's lair at 510 South Franklin Street.
Photo courtesy of Eric "Vietnam" Sadler.

Cube says that this approach showed a marked difference from his work with Dr. Dre, right from the jump: "With Dre, it was like, 'Here's the sound, I'm gonna do this beat and we're gonna like it together.' [laughs]. He's open to ideas, but he's gotta like 'em. If he don't like it, then it's a bad idea. But with Bomb Squad it was like, 'We can't go to the real studio until we fill these two crates up with records that *you* like.'"

"As a producer, I manage from a different perspective," Hank explains. "I want to make sure that artists are empowered. I tell people what I *don't* want to hear, as opposed to enforcing the things I do want to hear. There has to be a give-and-take when you produce. You have to interact."

"It took us a week or 10 days to listen to records and find stuff," Cube says. "Loop that, sample this, listen to some of Jinx's beats. After those two weeks in Long Island, Eric Sadler was putting 'bottom beats' together for us on an 8-Track."

Sadler, the Bomb Squad's true secret weapon and musician-in-residence [he plays guitar, bass and keyboards, in addition to being an excellent drum machine programmer], recalls: "Before they got to New York, Chuck had sent Cube a tape of 60 or 70 musical ideas I had put together. Not full songs, just grooves and rhythms. I told him to let Cube know that I wanted them to listen to those ideas, but also that I wanted us to all write together when they were here."

Sadler also mentions that Cube and his Cali crew weren't left *all* alone in Long Island upon their arrival – merely that Sadler was their initial Bomb Squad contact, and Cube wasn't aware of his central role. He says, with a chuckle, "When I picked them up at the airport, Cube was like, 'Who is this guy?' He thought he'd only be working with Hank, Chuck and Terminator X on the album. He didn't know that I did 99% of our music."

After their pre-production was completed at 510, operations moved to Greene Street Studios in Manhattan. "Being in New York just gives you an attitude," says Cube. "I was hanging around some of the most famous rappers of the day there: X-Clan came by and I heard songs from their first album before it came out. Flavor Flav would drop by every now and then. I was meeting hip-hop royalty. I left N.W.A. just when the group was getting embraced, so when people heard about me and the Bomb Squad they were just trying to imagine how crazy that was gonna sound. It fueled anticipation of the record, but it also made us work harder, because we knew that people wanted to see how it would turn out."

As for the division of labor in the sessions, there are many sides to the story. The one indisputable fact is that the Bomb Squad couldn't have been busier at the time. They were halfway done with recording Public Enemy's third album, *Fear Of A Black Planet*; they were working on Cube's debut; and also putting in production, mixing and remixing work on Bell Biv Devoe's smash debut *Poison* [MCA Records, 1990].

Additionally, as Sadler recalls, "There was also some turmoil within the Bomb Squad at that time. Not everyone was talking to one another, although I was talking to everyone. It wasn't the best time for us. But we always made sure that the work we had on our plate got done."

"Vietnam would do the bottom beats, the rhythm," Cube explains. "Keith and Hank would add onto that, like the salt and pepper, to season it. And Chuck would come in with the dessert, saying where we should scratch things in or put samples in different places. Chuck was the master of that. But everyone had their role and no one took credit that they didn't deserve. I came in-between a lot of things they were doing and I think all the Bomb Squad guys contributed as much to my record as they would have for any Public Enemy record."

Jinx claims that he and Sadler, along with Cube, did the yeoman's work on the album, with Hank, Keith and Chuck there, but not as often. "I'm definitely not saying that Hank and them did nothin'," he states. "But me and Eric put the foundation in. The other guys put in the windows of the house. I was at Greene Street all day, every day. Chuck was in the studio a lot, when he wasn't on tour."

"Eric's job at the time was to be the nuts-and-bolts guy," Shocklee explains. "He's not the conceptual guy, he makes sure that the timing is right and those types of things. My thing is to zoom out and see what kind of picture I'm getting. If it wasn't for Eric and Jinx executing, we would never have gotten that record done so quickly."

Sadler adds to Hank's assessment: "I was the chef, giving ingredients and saying what would and wouldn't work, from a musical perspective. It always has to make musical sense, even if it's dissonant. Otherwise, it's just *noise*."

"One thing I definitely remember is that I thought the music they picked from the original ideas I gave them, and also from 510 South Franklin, was some very strange shit," Sadler says. "It wasn't stuff that I thought was hot. So I was curious to see how we were going to make it all work."

He adds, "When operations headed to Greene Street, which we locked down for four weeks, we had about 15 songs that we were thinking about."

As a result of Hank and Chuck not being in the studio all the time, Jinx took advantage of some down-time and was able to spread his wings as a front-line producer for the first time. "Eric and Keith definitely listened to me with production ideas, and that's something that Dre would never do," he says. "Eric was kind of like me, he didn't care about the fame. He cared about making things sound the best that they could. He made a lot of different sounds work."

"I didn't know that Jinx was there to enforce the West Coast sound aspect," Hank says. "When Jinx arrived, it seemed like he was new to being in a studio environment. I knew he was Ice Cube's guy and Cube was part of our family now, so it was great to have him with us there either way. Jinx was talented."

"We couldn't have done *AmeriKKKa's Most Wanted* without the Bomb Squad, but the record couldn't have been finished without me" Jinx adds. "Without me it would have been a much more East Coast record." Hank disagrees slightly, explaining, "I wasn't going to let that album go out if it didn't sound like it could have come from the West Coast. That was in my mind from day one. To me, the artist's viewpoint is always front-and-center. And that record would have been inauthentic if it sounded like it came from the streets of Queens or the Bronx."

"We knew that Jinx and the Lench Mob were there to keep the West Coast feel, and we knew that the album couldn't be straight New York," Sadler adds. "It had to have LA in there, too. Jinx's work was especially helpful to keep the Cali sound there. I loved working with him."

And regarding J. Dee and T-Bone from Cube's Lench Mob, who Sadler says were in New York for several weeks during pre-production and recording, he recalls: "Those motherfuckers were definitely pretty rough. They were the real deal, real gang-bangers. They'd sleep on the concrete floor, when there was an empty couch right next to them. I had never seen shit like that [laughs]."

"The Bomb Squad would generally only work from 6 p.m. to 6 a.m., so sometimes you'd go to sleep, wake up and they'd just be there, still working on shit," Cube says. "Like, 'Who did all that? This is dope!' All of those dudes was mad scientists to me. No one has ever been able to put samples together better than they did back then. It was just all these people around the album like bees, working on one thing. Living, breathing and growing."

Sadler does remember one moment of conflict during the Greene Street sessions: "As we usually did, me and Keith would lay down the tracks and basic vocals, before Hank and Chuck would come in to deconstruct and re-assemble everything. And we worked pretty fast when we first got to Greene Street. We probably had 14 songs laid down in the first week. Then we were just waiting for Chuck and Hank to come in and do their thing."

He continues, "But then Cube started to get mad. He wanted us to start finishing stuff. He really wanted to get his shit out as soon as possible, to beat Dre and them [N.W.A.]. And he was yelling and cursing at *us*, even though we were just waiting for the next stage. So me and Keith and Jinx started finalizing more tracks than we usually would. Chuck and Hank started coming in more after that, so Cube stopped yelling at us [laughs]."

With all recordings completed in just over a month's time, *AmeriKKKa's Most Wanted* was a true triumph in bringing two coasts and six imaginative artists together for one purpose – to let Ice Cube express himself in his own words, with his own voice. It is interesting to note that despite understandable animosity between Cube and his old bandmates, there is not one anti-N.W.A. dis on the album. Jinx says, "Me and Cube looked each other in the eye when we did the album and we said that it wasn't going to have no reflection of N.W.A. We chose not to do a track like 'No Vaseline' [the harsh dis track from Cube's 1991 *Death Certificate*], and that was beautiful. There was no dissin'. That would be almost impossible now."

"I didn't have 'No Vaseline' when we was recording the first album," Cube says. "I never planned on dissin' N.W.A., there's no mention of them on the whole first record. I never even talked about dissing them, because I was happy. I had money, I was solo, and I just didn't care."

"That was the foundation of the record, for us at least," Chuck recalls. "When things first started, we said that we wouldn't have any of that [dissing other members of N.W.A.]. We wanted to give Cube an open door to go back to N.W.A. if he wanted. We just had all of that chaos with Griff, so I was very experienced with group beefs. After that album, Cube still could have come back to record with them. Even though, behind the scenes, that situation in 1990 was hotter than people knew."

After the New York recording, mixing and mastering sessions were finalized in late winter – Shocklee says that everything was mixed before the LA crew departed – Cube and Jinx left to go out on tour. "We didn't even go back to LA," Jinx says. "Nobody in LA knew what that record was going to do. We were out on tour when it was released."

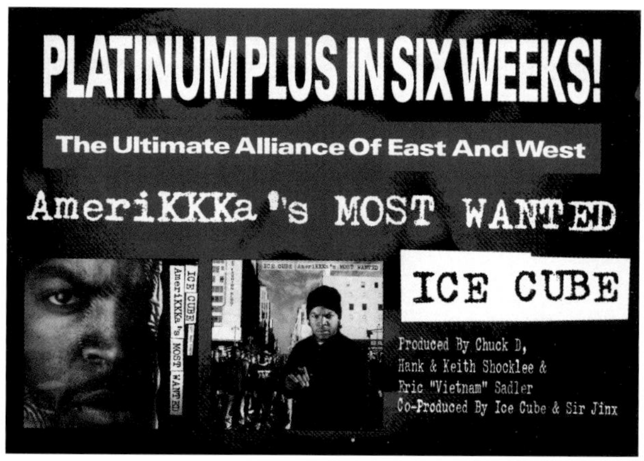

AmeriKKKa's Most Wanted hit stores in May of 1990, and was certified gold in three months' time. A year later, it would officially pass platinum status. Credit for most productions were shared by all six parties involved, with Jinx and Cube sharing co-production on tracks that were led by Bomb Squad, and vice-versa.

"Once I heard the album all finished, I was very confident about how it would do," says Cube. "We had learned from Dre, who is the master, and we learned from the

Ice Cube "900 Number" ad, November 1990.

Bomb Squad. Chuck taught us how to put a record together from start to finish, how to keep it flowing. I knew we had a record that flowed all the way through and stayed interesting. The rhymes was right, and the beats was cutting edge. It was West Coast enough and it was East Coast enough. We just knew we had it."

"As for East and West, I just wanted to make a great album," Sadler explains. "I didn't care about geography, I cared about textures, tempos and sequencing. After working on that album, I learned that Cube and Chuck were the exact same type of person, even though they were different in other ways. But their writing notebooks looked so similar. And they were both so professional. That especially shocked me about Cube, how 'down to business' he was. That's how we were, but I figured he'd be coming into the studio with women and drinking 40s. It wasn't like that at all. Plus, of course, I learned that he was a lyrical genius."

"It was actually one of the last times that The Bomb Squad ever came together as a team," Chuck says, looking back. "That record was all six of us, together. And the important thing was that in the end, Cube was the one who took it into the end zone. We were the foundation, but he built on that and finished it. It was the first step in the rest of his career."

"I don't think the East Coast and West Coast have ever been as glued [together] as they were on that album," Chuck adds. "It tied us together. I really think that record also gave Dre the energy to go into that second or third gear as a producer, leading to [his 1992 solo debut] *The Chronic*."

Eric Sadler states, "*AmeriKKKa's Most Wanted* is one of the works that I'm proudest of. You always want something to turn out a certain way, but it rarely does. Cube's record was about 98% of what I hoped it would be. It couldn't have gotten much better. It was a joy to be part of it."

"If Ice Cube didn't have the material and the vision, I wouldn't have done the record in the first place," says Hank Shocklee. "But it was just a pleasure to work with someone who could hold his own. Cube didn't have any confidence issues going in, but afterwards he knew he could now make a whole record, on his own. And Jinx now knew everything he needed to do to complete an entire product, too. To me, Cube was the underdog, and I always fight for the underdog. That was a challenge, and the fact that we were fighting for him helped form our bond, even though we were only there together for a short time. At that time, everybody was rapping, but only a select few were doing it at a higher level. Cube was young, but he was already there."

When asked to rank the album against others in his catalog, Cube does not hesitate. "To me, *AmeriKKKa's Most Wanted*, that's the best," he says. "I woke up one day

All Access tour laminate, 1990.
Courtesy of Eric "Vietnam" Sadler.

and that record was a phenomenon that you couldn't get away from. It's better than *Straight Outta Compton*, because that was a shock record. *AmeriKKKa's* had more good songs than *Compton* did."

Cube continues, "Puffy once told me that he studied *AmeriKKKa's Most Wanted* before doing Biggie's first album, and to me that's a major statement. It shows that *AmeriKKKa's* was the blueprint for how records were put together for a long time after that, with the skits and the whole record being one *thing*. It all sounds like it was made on the same day. It set the tone for a lot of records to come, for probably 10 years after that."

Here are some tales about the making of this classic, from robbing Son of Bazerk to getting jacked by Mister Rogers.

TRACKS

Better Off Dead

ICE CUBE: Jinx helped put together so much stuff on the record, including the skits like "Better Off Dead."

HANK SHOCKLEE: It was important to me that the album had a glue to it. The most underrated part of that album was the skits. I've always made albums as mixtapes, starting with *It Takes A Nation Of Millions to Hold Us Back*. Everything should just meld into each other, you can't let anything die down. Once you've got listeners engaged, you want to keep them there. At the same time, skits are just that, they're skits. And when they become too long, you're gonna lose the listener. I get bored easily and I know that listeners do, too.

The Nigga Ya Love To Hate

CUBE: That was originally supposed to be a song for N.W.A. *[Author's note: He means lyrically, not the music, which was done by the Bomb Squad].* I felt like mainstream America hated us [N.W.A.], like they thought we was the worst thing to come out to America since... Columbus! [laughs]. And that fired us up, because it meant that we was being heard. That was the most important thing. I mean, rap is the blues, especially gangsta rap, because you're hearing our pain, whether you agree with it or like it or not. You're hearing what we've got to say. If not, then you're voiceless, you're not even a number to a lot of these... people in high places.

ERIC SADLER: I wrote that music originally for a friend of mine named Howard Eady, who also went by "The Baanleader." He was in bands with me and he was a singer, not a rapper. A James Brown type of cat. That one is a Steve Arrington thing *[Author's note: The song samples Arrington's 1983 hit "Weak At The Knees"].* Howard got on the beat and had it for a while, just for himself. He didn't release it. Then Cube heard it at 510 South Franklin and wanted it, so we gave it to him.

HANK: That was done after [the song] "AmeriKKKa's Most Wanted," they were both done early in the sessions. I'm a big Steve Arrington fan, so I loved that one. Back then, very few people would mess with Steve Arrington samples. Even on the West Coast back then, people had their list of people you should sample, and Steve wasn't on there as much. The Bomb Squad would always take music that wasn't typical, and make it fit within the genre. With Ice Cube, we got to use a lot of tracks that we wouldn't use for Public Enemy because they were too melodic. We got to show people that we weren't always just noisy.

CUBE: We had different choruses for that song. One went, "Love, hate" and then other things in there. And we was trying to find stuff that we could scratch in. I thought about it for a long time, like a whole day. And then I came up with, "Fuck you, Ice Cube!," like people were mad at us for doing hardcore rap. And everyone in the studio thought I was crazy, like, "How you gonna say 'Fuck yourself' on your own record?!" We talked about it for a long time and then Chuck said that it was dope, he liked it. So we did it.

HANK: I remember talking about the chorus. When I heard the final version, what it said and the way it was recorded, then I could feel how it worked with the song.

AmeriKKKa's Most Wanted

CUBE: I stole that track from [Public Enemy extended family member] Son of Bazerk! Originally the Bomb Squad had just the beat, and we put everything else on top of it during the sessions: me, Jinx and Chuck. Chuck put a lot of the – you know – *stuff*, on top of it. All those beat changes, too. Chuck came in one day and just sliced that song up. When I first heard the beat I just loved it, and I was like, "When is Bazerk's record coming out?" They didn't know, so I told them I had to have it. I had been thinking about what the album title should be for a long time. I really liked that one a lot, and it was done pretty early in the album process. So it just grew on me.

SIR JINX: That was the first single off the album, and me and Cube used to argue about it. I always said that "Once Upon A Time In The Projects" [the single's B-side] sold that 12-inch, but he thought it was "AmeriKKKa's Most Wanted." The single came out before the album. "AmeriKKKa's Most Wanted" was a Bomb Squad track, I didn't have nothing to do with it. Maybe I synched up the vocals from the guy from home on there.

SADLER: Way before Cube got to New York, Son of Bazerk heard the music for that at 510 and wanted to use it. Bazerk recorded a version, then Cube heard it and wanted it. Basically, with us, it was whoever gets a deal first can use it [to release]. The Bazerk song did have vocals on it, it was done just as a demo at 510. Once Cube wanted it, I left it up to Hank. He was more the decision maker for stuff like that.

HANK: By the time we hit Greene Street, I knew that the body of work was there, I just needed two lead-off singles that people was gonna get into. At the same time, the album had to have an underground quality. Those two singles were "AmeriKKKa's Most Wanted" and "The Nigga Ya Love To Hate" *[Author's note: The latter was never released as a single].* They were the pillars; everything else was in the middle. And both of those were done pretty early on. After we finished "AmeriKKKa's Most Wanted," I knew we had something. If we can duplicate the vibration of that one nine more times, then we're good. As I recall, the lyrics on there were from three different songs that Cube had. I wanted to make sure that they built in intensity. You should be hot at the beginning, but you should be super-hot at the end.

CHUCK D: That was the first thing we worked on together. That and "The Nigga Ya Love To Hate."

What They Hittin' Foe?

JINX: That one has live musicians on it. Al "Purple" Hayes [says his name in a fond, reminiscing way]. I think he was a New York guy, because the guy I used in LA was Hami Wave [Marquis Dair]. Hami worked on other stuff with us.

SADLER: I had played with [guitarist and bassist] Al Hayes since we were like 14 years old. He grew up listening to Hendrix and Ernie Isley, just like me. We used to play in bands together and Al would slide on his knees and play guitar behind his back, with his teeth. He was from Freeport, NY [Long Island], he grew up down the street from Flavor Flav. Al was my dude.

You Can't Fade Me

CUBE: Anything you hear with P-Funk in it, like there on the chorus, me and Jinx brought that in. I got a lot of heat for the lyrics on that one. I didn't expect any of it, but it didn't piss me off. I really just thought it was a dope rhyme, so I was cool taking the heat for it. A lot of people liked that track, so it wasn't all bad. When it came to the "Kick her in the tummy" line, I didn't do that to upset people, it was just part of the flow.

I mean, men just got sick minds, man! [laughs]. I've heard men say shit like, "That bitch pregnant, I feel like going and kickin' in her god-damned stomach!" [laughs]. It's just real. Whether they'd do it or not, I doubt it. I've never seen nobody do it, but I've heard mo'fuckas talk about it. So, for me it wasn't nothing to put it in a rhyme. I never had any paternity suits back then, fuck no. Man, come on. I mean, I listened to that rhyme called "Jimmy Hat"! [Boogie Down Productions' "Jimmy"].

HANK: I really liked the way that one came out, musically. Music and vocals have to work together, so the tempo of that one wasn't important. Once I heard the music and lyrics together, it made sense and really worked.

JD's Gaffilin'

SADLER: When Cube and his crew arrived, I had just bought a portable DAT player and I just started recording their conversations. All day long, I would just record them. And that's from one of those. It was important to get that aspect on the album, about how those guys talked and interacted with each other.

HANK: One important thing about the album was when Chuck went to LA and he brought back J. Dee with him. Those cats [in the Lench Mob] helped to bring the experience of the LA lifestyle to the record. Because none of us sound like we're from LA.

CHUCK: I remember editing one of the skits on the album, by one of the Lench Mob brothers who I won't name. He was talking about something he jacked and he gave the actual street. So we had to take that out, because somebody could get yo ass if you put it on record! [laughs].

Once Upon A Time In The Projects

JINX: That was the first song I produced for the record. Bomb Squad had nothing to do with that *[Author's note: The album's liners credit Bomb Squad with co-production]*, the credit is wrong. There's two sounds on that song – a loop, the bassline, and a guitar, maybe some drum stuff. But I did all that. Cube wrote the words to that one for Eazy, but the music was originally supposed to be for Tajai and Adam *[Author's note: Aside from Tajai, assuming he means Adam "A-Plus" Carter from Souls of Mischief]*. They originally rapped on that beat. But when I went to New York, that one just worked for Cube. It was a free beat!

CUBE: I can't remember if I had originally written those lyrics thinking that Eazy would do them. Jinx looped the music for that one. He had the beat, and we did that one day when the Bomb Squad was tired. We just jumped in there and did it. When it came to storytelling, I liked Schoolly-D, and Just-Ice used to tell a lot of stories. Storytelling is always the most-clever form of rhyming. It's rap at its finest, telling an interesting story. Heavy D, Too $hort, all those guys inspired me. Was any of the stuff in that song true? There's always true experiences mixed in there, man. But nothing I'm gonna self-snitch about! [laughs].

HANK: That's my third favorite track on the album. Jinx brought that one to the table and that was really perfect for Cube. That one was done about halfway through the recording. Musically I love it, that's Betty Davis ["Shoo-B-Doop And Cop Him"], one of the classic underrated funk albums of all time. Back then, no one knew that record.

SADLER: That was Jinx's song, 100%. We did help with the production on that one, maybe more than with other Jinx songs. That's why we got co-production credit. But it was Jinx's song for sure.

Turn Off The Radio

CUBE: We was just fed up, because we wasn't gettin' no love on the radio. It ain't like how it is now, they wasn't playing no kinds of records with no kind of gangsta nothin'. It wasn't until *The Chronic* that the mainstream media decided to jump on the bandwagon. MTV helped hip-hop more than radio did back then. But there's always been a tug-of-war with artists and radio. We [N.W.A.] never figured we'd get on MTV because at the time they was playin' [Jazzy Jeff & The Fresh Prince's] "Parents Just Don't Understand." We never thought much about MTV either way. But radio *could* play us, and they were still our biggest nemesis in 1990. Then one day they started playing *The Chronic* and that made it better for what's called Gangsta Rap. Before then [pauses, exhales], nothin'.

JINX: Chuck D did that one. He took that on tour and would work on that in different studios, when he could. The radio voice guy on there also did "W-Balls" for Dogg Pound *[Author's note: "W-Balls" from Snoop Doggy Dogg's Doggystyle, from 1993]*, his name is Ricky Harris. He did all the stuff like that for Snoop. That dude got very popular for talking like that, so when Dre went over to Death Row, he had a job.

Endangered Species (Tales From The Darkside)
[featuring Chuck D]

CUBE: Jinx helped with the concept on that one. I like the *Kill At Will* [EP released on Priority Records, also 1990] version better, because it's thicker. But the original there, that was my chance to do a PE kind of song with Chuck. The beat is damn near [pauses], you know, psychotic! [laughs]. You know what I'm sayin'? With the feedback and all that shit. I remember putting all those sound effects on the end of the song, and Hank Shocklee running all that shit. For me, the original is more sentimental than the remix, because Chuck wasn't there when we did the remix.

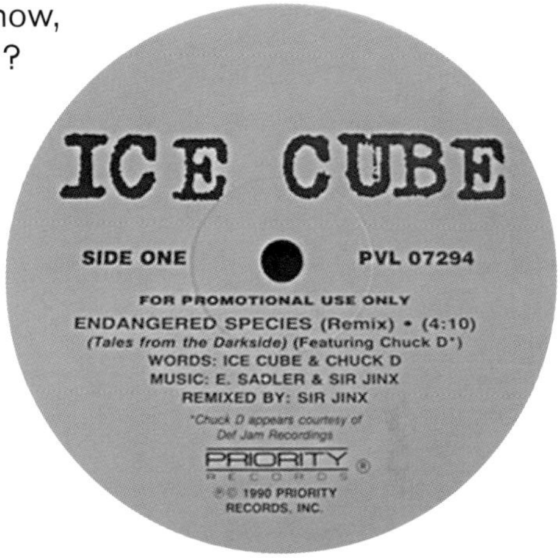

CHUCK: Once we talked about the concept, that song just came into Cube's head. My job on there was to co-sign and back things up that he believed in.

A Gangsta's Fairytale

SADLER: That's one of my favorites on the album. We had actually already recorded that with this group we worked with called True Mathematics. But they had done a pretty bad job on it, they stabbed it to death. I had put that music on the tape Chuck sent to Cube before he got to New York, but honestly I never thought he would pick it. It was too goofy. But Cube got on it and I was blown away. It's always about the combination, music and lyrics.

JINX: That one was just Eric Sadler. He had that beat and it was incredible. On that song, Mister Rogers tried to sue us! Here's how you know who the true fans are – the first 200,000 copies of the album have a piece on the beginning of "A Gangsta's Fairytale" that's like Mister Rogers [Jinx sings a version of theme song with gangsta drawl... after "Won't you be my neighbor?" he makes sounds of gunfire]. The second version just starts out with, "And now, in the black part of the city." If you got the version with the dude singing Mister Rogers then it's probably worth some money! Ultimately we had to pay Mister Rogers five cents a record, he got paid off of that. After the first 200,000, we took it off. That mean-ass man! [laughs].

CUBE: We had that "It's a beautiful day in the neighborhood" thing in the beginning of the original. Did Mister Rogers sue us? Damn.... [pauses, trying to remember]. Actually, yeah, I remember. He told us we couldn't use it, we took the song off the album and he sued us anyways. I think they made us give him damages because we mention his name one time.

JINX: The reason that we made that album so fast was because Cube had written a lot of his raps already, some of them for Eazy. Half of the tracks on the album, I bet. That album has two colors: the Public Enemy color and the "pure nigga" color. The "pure nigga" shit was the Eazy-E type songs, like "Gangsta's Fairytale." Just listen to it, it sounds like the shit that Cube wrote for him. And the reason Cube wanted to do them on his record was so that Eazy wouldn't put them out. He wanted to pull the rug out from all that.

CUBE: Jinx helped me put together that track, as far as concepts go. The lyrics on that one were written initially for Eazy. N.W.A. and Eazy never had them, I hadn't given the lyrics to them. It's not like I was trying to beat them to the punch or anything. They was just songs I was writin' while I was still in N.W.A., for the second album. I wrote them while we was on tour in 1989. That little kid on there is one of Keith Shocklee's girlfriends' kids. We wanted to get a little bad-ass kid on there, so we brought him in to talk shit. Keith knew he'd be good. The kid wasn't really that bad-ass, but he sounded like it.

SADLER: That song ended up being brilliant; it's one of my favorites. I have to say, though, that it did cause me some grief later on. I dealt with a lot of record labels, and dealt with a lot of women at those labels. And some of them stopped talking to me because of the fact that I was involved with records like that one for Cube, and also Bell Biv Devoe. They were pissed. I had to take stock of what I was getting involved with, even if I was just doing the music. I mean, it's not like I was saying the lyrics. But I rationalized it to myself as if it was a film. It's just a story. Cube ain't like that in real life. Overall, though, I was really happy with that song, I'd give it a 94 out of 100 if I was rating it. I do remember listening to the song at home while we were still working on it, after I had just gotten married. And after the part where the kid starts talking about "the kids," my wife said, "Oh, you're going to hell for that one!" [laughs]. And I said, "Yeah, it kinda feels like that." [laughs].

I'm Only Out For One Thang [featuring Flavor Flav]

CUBE: I wanted to do a song with Flav, and that was one of the last songs we did. It was kinda like a throw-away track, we didn't think we'd finish it because Flav was hard to track down. But we caught him one day, he was coming in to talk to Hank and Eric on his way to the airport. So I was like, "Flav, what's up?!? You said you was gonna jump on my shit!" So we put the track up and he was running late, so we knew we'd only have one take. When we messed up at the end, we just kept movin'. I had my lyrics written out, and his on there was just a rhyme that he had in his head.

CHUCK: I always loved that one. That was where Flavor was at, and that was a place that Cube could get with, too [laughs]. That was definitely an interesting record.

SADLER: I love that one, with Flav. It's quirky.

HANK: Here's one thing that nobody seems to understand about Flav – he's the hype guy, not a main artist. He can come up with something lyrically, but it'll take him *so* long. Unless you force him, he's not going to come to the table with something. That's why it took him so long to get on that track with Cube. You don't even understand how long it took us to even get the intros to Public Enemy songs! I don't think Flav wrote anything out for that song. Cube wrote it out and Flav just said it.

JINX: That's one of my beats, it's a pretty short song. That track was at the end of the recording sessions, we already had 10 great, locked-in-fo-sho tracks at that point, so that was a good one to break up some of the harder songs. Flavor came in for that after they was on tour. At the time, Flav and Griff weren't getting along and Griff would be in the studio a lot, so that might be why Flavor wasn't there too much. Flavor was really explosive as a talent, and he's still like that. He was great to work with, he's a musical genius. He plays like five different instruments. He actually used to live around the corner from me in LA. If you want to compare people that Cube collaborated with, Flavor wasn't anything like Eazy-E. Eazy was a gangster, and Flavor was an entertainer. The stuff that people saw from Eazy-E on his records, that was actually the furthest end of his spectrum. Because he wasn't a rapper or an entertainer, he was a hustler.

The Drive-By

JINX: Each of those in-between [skit] things was supposed to be a part of the album's story, about why Cube was "America's Most Wanted." But the concept got too time-consuming. Those inserts aren't easy to make – musical versions of visual stuff. We had three of those planned, but "The Drive By" was the only one we used on that album. My voice is on there, but we had to limit a lot of the ad-libs by Eric because he sounded like he was from New York. It was an LA album! You can't jump out of a 6-4 and yell, "Shoot them niggas, yo!" That don't work, it made us cringe a bit. So we had to play down his voice.

SADLER: I had no clue what to say on that type of thing [laughs]! That's why those guys had to step in. I didn't even know what they were talkin' about.

HANK: I thought that skit was funny more than anything else. And the production made you feel like you was in it.

CUBE: There were other skits we did that didn't make the album. As I learned from Chuck, it's all about the *flow*. If a skit or anything else disrupts the flow, then take it out.

Rollin' Wit The Lench Mob

CUBE: We were coming together at that point, and we needed a crew to make it all work. We wanted to give an identity to the new people I was with. People from *my* neighborhood, not from Compton. I come from South Central and I was always with all these dudes from Compton in N.W.A. So this was a chance for me to put together my own clique of people I hung around with. T-Bone, J. Dee, Shorty. T-Bone came to New York for a couple days when we was recording but the other dudes didn't have no money. I came back to LA two times, during weekends, and we'd get a studio out here and do those little parts, like "JD's Gafflin'." Then we got back to New York and just put it into the tracks.

JINX: We didn't bring no hype man with us to New York, so basically Cube and Chuck flew to LA one weekend and told J. Dee, T-Bone, Shorty and Robin Harris to do some fills on the album, vocal stuff to use in the background. If you listen close, you can hear that none of those are on-beat, because they didn't do them with the tracks themselves. I still have the tape with all of those vocal parts on there. My job was to put them in the right places.

Who's The Mack?

JINX: When I first got to New York, that was one of the tracks I ended up doing. That was really one of the Bomb Squad's songs. But the other guys would get sleepy and leave. Me and Eric are the same, we're techies. I was excited, I was young and there was a 24-track in front of me. That was the second single off the album. Me and Eric Sadler knocked that one out. I slid that Marvin Gaye on there and there was more live playing on that track, guys from New York. Son of Bazerk is on there, too, I used to just love his fuckin' voice! If people don't remember, Bazerk was the original rapper in Public Enemy, when Chuck was still on the radio and Terminator X was just Norm. Bazerk would come to the studio and his voice was so deep, I had to get him on that track.

SADLER: That song was really an idea of Hank's, then Jinx gave it the feel. But I would say it was more Hank, Keith and Jinx than me. The live flute on there was those guys' idea. I had some issues with that song, it was a bit clunky, musically. It took a lot of work, but Jinx had the feel on it. We used this piece of equipment called a Publison Infernal Machine 90 to get everything in the right key. It made it so that you could change the speed of a sample, but not the pitch. It would have been a lot easier to do that kind of thing today, with the latest technology, that's for sure!

CUBE: Jinx helped build that track. We wanted to do one of those cool, laid-back kinda songs. Do some storytelling, some preachin' about what's going on. Basically trying to make an analogy for a mack as a pimp or a mack as somebody who can get you to do what *they* want you to do. Just trying to break it down like that. And that beat was just dope. If you remember, Chuck did that Sly & The Family Stone thing on *Fear Of A Black Planet [Author's note: Assuming he means either "Reggie Jax" or "Polywannacracka"]* so it was kinda like that, an experimental kind of flavor.

It's A Man's World [featuring Yo-Yo]

CUBE: Jinx did that track. We were shopping Yo-Yo's deal before we recorded *AmeriKKKa's Most Wanted*. We had put a demo on her together, just songs we had done in my bedroom with Jinx. But "It's A Man's World" was definitely her coming-out party. I don't think that track was on the original demo we did, although initially we were planning on putting it on her record. She wasn't signed at that point, but it was getting close. We felt it was good to bring her out attacking me, because I had done "I Ain't The One" [on *Straight Outta Compton*] and that was big for me. It was cool to have a girl come back at me. People always liked that song when we did it in our live show. I didn't mind what she was saying in there at all, I was glad that female fans liked it. I told her to approach it that way, like, "It *is* a man's world, you bitches is in the way." [laughs]. And she was like, "What? Aiight...," and that's all I needed to do. She went to high school with Jinx and we used to go over to their school and rap all the time, on the quad. Jinx would be like, "There are some motherfuckers over here that you guys gotta rap against!" So we'd get our rhymes together and head over.

JINX: Me and Yo-Yo was rivals, we went to the same high school – Washington High in South Central. That song was supposed to be on Yo-Yo's album, but we couldn't come up with anything better for Cube's record, so we snatched it and put it on Cube's. Yo-Yo's record [*Make Way For The Motherlode*, Atlantic Records, 1991] came out a little while after Cube's. With the music on there and all the changes, I just love it when music drops out, when you go through a complete roller coaster in three or four minutes. There were so many elements on that song. I made that music because I loved Soul II Soul. That's how long I had that beat! The DJ on that one at the end was probably Chilly Chill [Derrick Baker]. He lived in Inglewood.

HANK: Yo-Yo came out to New York to cut the vocals on that. I really liked that song, it was something that Cube wanted to do. That was more his creation. Everybody Cube brought in was great, we all got along and they all gave us respect.

CHUCK: I always really liked that song.

The Bomb

CUBE: Jinx did that track.

JINX: I produced that one, DJ Chilly Chill did almost all of that beat. He was one of my apprentices and I told him to do one for the album, although he thought Cube would get mad. I was actually supposed to rap on that, but I chose not to. I didn't want to write to a song that fast. I always told people that Chilly produced it, but that's just how they did the credits *[Author's note: The album credits do not list Chilly].* There's a lot of stuff that people didn't get credit for in that situation, and I think a lot of that was [Ice Cube's manager at the time] Pat Charbonnet. She was smart as a motherfucker, but she wasn't smart for me.

EXTRA CREDIT

KILL AT WILL EP

CUBE: By the time we got to that EP – after learning from Dre and the Bomb Squad – me and Jinx was like, "We got this, we know what we're doing." We did it ourselves, without any help from anyone. EPs were just sellin' back then. That came after an EP that N.W.A. did [*100 Miles And Runnin'*, 1990]. We had some of those songs left over, songs with longer versions, and we just threw together an EP. Priority was *beggin'* us to come back out again, and quick. So we figured it out. We didn't have anything to prove, we just did it because we could. We knew that "The Product" and "Dead Homiez" were hits. We did all those tracks after *AmeriKKKa's Most Wanted* was done.

JINX: That was just supposed to be our remixes, because we already had "Jackin' For Beats." So "Jackin'" had to have some friends. I just stayed in the studio on my own to do all of those remixes. And ultimately, I didn't even get paid for doing those.

SADLER: I have to be honest, at the time I wasn't really happy with O'Shea [Ice Cube]. I figured that we would also be doing their next album. I was a little bit hurt, because I think we did a great job on *AmeriKKKa's Most Wanted*. But I knew that it came down to money with Cube, and if they did it themselves they could keep more of it. But I kind of turned *Kill At Will* off in my mind at the time.

Jackin' For Beats

CUBE: That was after *AmeriKKKa's Most Wanted* was done. I had thought of that concept, because at the time so many dope beats had come out. I just wanted to rap over all that shit. Chilly Chill was there when I was thinkin' about it, in our demo studio, and he started helping me put it together. But Jinx helped him pop the song off, when we got to the big studio. He helped him with all the hooks and stuff. We had all the tracks, the beats, but we didn't know how the hooks would go. I chose all those tracks to use. I'm not going off on anyone in that song, I just want their beats! I mean, I use a Public Enemy beat in there. D-Nice's beat was dope! X-Clan and EPMD, too.

JINX: Cube didn't always give too much input on production, but he made up the concept for that song. Cube came up with that idea, and me and Chilly made it happen. After we got off tour, we started remixing the records. That new song and the longer version of "Endangered Species" were the beginning of *Kill At Will*. At the time, I was trying to make up a DJ crew, and one of those guys was Chilly Chill. I wanted a trick DJ to go on the road with Yo-Yo, and Chill knew how to do beats as well. When I went into the studio to do "The Product," I had Chilly put together "Jackin'." He did it mix-tape style, but in the end we put it together the right way. Chilly Chill became Yo-Yo's DJ, he's the dude standing with his back to the camera on the inside of *Make Way For The Motherlode*.

Dead Homiez

CUBE: One of the homies in my neighborhood had got killed – a guy named T-Bone. Not the one from Lench Mob. T-Bone from Lench Mob was from another 'hood, but he went to school with me. With the one who got killed, I was feeling real bad about it, because I was friends with his younger brother, Little T-Bone. It really messed me up, so I wrote the song that night. That song was easy to write just because it was so personal. I think I wrote it in about 90 minutes. I was already writin' when I heard about his death, so I put what I had been writin' down and went into that one.

JINX: It's not credited on the EP, but I did the music for that track. T-Bone [from Lench Mob] gave me the idea for the loop.

JERU THE DAMAJA

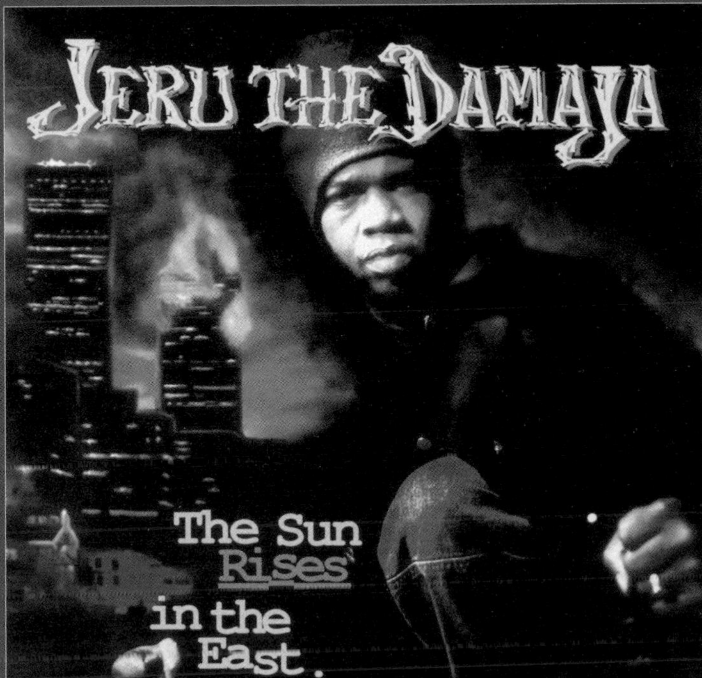

The Sun Rises In The East
Payday / FFRR, 1994

"When I hear a beat, it sounds like something to me. Because everything in life is beats. Some beats are hot, some are cold. This beat might sound like an airplane to me, this one might be a spy theme. It all helps me write my lyrics."

– Jeru The Damaja

In 1993, after the rise of Dr. Dre's rap tsunami *The Chronic* [Interscope, 1992] and Snoop's *Doggystyle* [Death Row / Interscope, 1993], hip-hop's birthplace was fighting an important battle: for ears.

But all was not lost. The Wu-Tang Clan, Black Moon, Gang Starr and a young upstart named Nas were doing everything they could to bring the rap world's attention back to New York. And, as dope singles and albums volleyed back-and-forth from coast to coast, onto the scene burst another powerful and intelligent new voice from the East. Specifically, Brooklyn's roughest-and-ruggedest spot: East New York.

Jeru The Damaja [Kendrick Jeru Davis] was ushered into to the hip-hop world at large through the auspices of Guru's and DJ Premier's Gang Starr Foundation umbrella, bringing a compelling mix of consciousness and street lessons to the game. But his wasn't an overnight success story.

"I've always moved in the 'hood," Jeru explains. "But I have always stood for righteousness. That is always needed. I mean, Jesus was righteous and he hung out in the 'hood, with murderers and thieves. The balance comes when you know the difference between right and wrong."

Although he didn't "go pro" until later in his teens, Jeru started home-schooled lessons on the microphone from an early age. "I was always an MC," he says. "My aunt, who went by Sweet G, was an MC, she had a crew and a DJ from our block, a guy named David. They'd do parties and I'd always be there, because my aunt was also my babysitter. And I just fell in love with hip-hop. Once I saw rhyming like that, that was it. That's what I wanted to do."

Jeru continues, "They'd let me on the mic to bust rhymes back then, around age 10, as a joke. But at the time it was real to me. So I always prepared and had lyrics ready.

When I was 13 and 14, we'd use the radio room at our church to make demos and do routines. My man would beatbox and we'd be rhyming. We'd make tapes and run 'em off."

Jeru grew up with a lot of MC talent near him in East New York, including several members of the legendary hip-hop band Stetsasonic; Wu-Tang affiliate and producer True Master; Jemini The Gifted One; Lil' Dap of Group Home; and his future rhyme partner Afu-Ra. "There were a lot of dope MCs from my neighborhood," Jeru recalls. "Me, True Master and Jemini would stand on the corner for hours, just rappin'. We'd have freestyle sessions that would last from eight at night until three or four in the morning. We'd be drinkin' beer, smoking weed, shooting dice and rhyming. My style was never just one style, never just one flow, because I had so many people around me that rhymed. And we was rhymin' every day. You always had to come up with something new."

Jeru decided to take MCing more seriously around 1987. Soon thereafter he came in contact with rapper Guru [Keith Elam] of Gang Starr, a recent transplant from Boston who was doing his best to break into the New York rap game. "My boy Shab [King Shab, who was part of Guru's original group, Gang Starr Posse] was from Boston, but he went to my high school," he remembers. "He told me that Guru was coming down and that we should meet."

Guru met Jeru's DJ, Tommy Hill, and friend Lil' Dap while he was building the 2.0 version of Gang Starr, which would become locked-and-loaded once DJ Premier joined. "I was too busy in the streets when Guru first got here," Jeru says. "I was trying to be a criminal. I was a little gangsterish." But eventually Jeru was down, appearing in Gang Starr's "Words I Manifest" 1989 video, the same year that he graduated from Brooklyn's Franklin K. Lane High School.

DJ Premier [Christopher Martin], another New York transplant – from Texas – recalls: "I first met Jeru at the 'Manifest' video shoot. We shot it in late '88. I met him and Lil' Dap through Guru. You might not see Jeru too well in the video, but he's there, in the crowd."

Despite his skills and growing ambition, Jeru says that his association with Guru and Premier at the time was a social one – more about hanging out than plotting to take over the hip-hop industry. "By the time I met Guru and Premier, it wasn't even a rhyming type of thing," he explains. "It was more just friendship. We were just homies, bullshitting around. Guru didn't give me rhyming lessons or anything, as people might think. We'd just get drunk in the house and rhyme all night."

Premier, who until 1989 was still back and forth between his Texas home and crashing at a college classmate's family's spot in East New York, has the same recollection. "Keep in mind that back then, I was still new to the game as a producer and Gang Starr had just put our first record out," he says. "With Jeru and everyone else except Guru, it was more like, 'Let's see how this all develops.' Jeru was part of the crew and we'd all hang out."

Premier continues, "Back then, Jeru used to call himself 'Porky The Pimp,' because he was a little chubby. He also called himself 'The Fat Mack.' He would tell people, 'I'm down with Gang Starr and I'm going to be famous one day.' He was always very confident, and he always had that dope voice."

By 1990, Jeru had worked on one or two demo songs, with producer and East New York neighbor PF Cuttin' [Felix Rovira, later known as one half of Blahzay Blahzay]. Premier remembers one of the songs well: "The first Jeru demo I remember was the one I think he did with PF Cuttin'. The music was slow and you could hear Jeru's voice really clearly. He used to drive around with this guy Mr. Dave in a burgundy Jeep Wrangler, and they'd play that demo all the time. I think it was called 'Tray Pound.' It was a loud system, too. They'd play it over and over [laughs]."

Gang Starr built an air-tight rep in the rap world from 1989 through 1992, releasing the albums *No More Mr. Nice Guy* [Wild Pitch, 1989]; *Step In The Arena* [Chrysalis, 1991]; and *Daily Operation* [Chrysalis, 1992]. With the latter full-length, Jeru got his first real chance to shine, rhyming as a guest – alongside his pal Lil' Dap – on the track "I'm The Man."

Premier recalls, "At the time, our manager, Patrick Moxey, said we should put out some of the artists in our 'family.' Big Shug from Boston had just gotten out of jail after three years, and he was one of the original guys in Gang Starr Posse, with Guru [before Premier was part of the group]. So Guru started working on some production with him. And we talked about Jeru and I said, 'Let me work with him. I think I'd be better to give him some music that won't shake his style.'"

Premier continues, "By '92, we were working on *Daily Operation* so that seemed like a great time to start showcasing people. So for 'I'm The Man,' I changed the beat up with each new guy who got on the song [Guru, Jeru and Lil' Dap], so they all kind of had their own track."

"That song was the first time I got to really bust," Jeru beams. "I had done demos before that, and I was supposed to be on [Gang Starr's] 'DWYCK' [featuring Nice & Smooth, which appeared as the B-side to 1992's "Take It Personal" single, and finally landing on Gang Starr's 1994's *Hard To Earn*], but it didn't work out. So I just patiently waited in the cut."

Premier remembers the moment that he knew Jeru was really ready for the big-time: "We performed at the Apollo Theater around Easter *[Author's note: Assuming in 1992]*, with Eric B. & Rakim, for the show they did there every year. We were so excited to open up for them. We brought Jeru on to do 'I'm The Man' with us and the crowd went *crazy*."

In 1992, Guru produced a Jeru demo that Jeru himself shopped – "None of those songs ever came out," he says – around the time when "I'm The Man" was out on *Daily Operation*. "We walked all over New York City with that demo," Jeru laments. "Me, Tommy Hill and Lil' Dap. We was definitely getting meetings with labels because of Guru's name, but people just wasn't hearing it." Jeru's profile was also raised by touring with Gang Starr. "Mostly to do my verse on 'I'm The Man' and carry records," he says.

After the touring and demo shopping, Jeru and DJ Premier made the track that was to become the MC's no-turning-back breakthrough: "Come Clean" [for more info on the song, see below]. The song was sent out to national radio and selected press as part of an unassuming three-track vinyl EP, with one song each from Jeru [billed as Dirty Rotten Scoundrels]; Big Shug; and Group Home. Guru pressed it up in early '93, and it was called, simply, *Gangstarr Foundation Sampler* [Ill Kid Records].

The other two cuts on the EP have mostly been lost to the sands of time, but "Come Clean" was an instant underground smash. "We mailed 'em out to everybody and the next week 'Come Clean' was on every radio station," Jeru says. "They all played it, from college radio to [New York's R & B and hip-hop powerhouse] WBLS."

"After the sampler, that was it," Jeru continues. "From there a lot of labels wanted me. I went with Payday because we was trying to keep it in the family. [Gang Starr manager] Patrick Moxey owned the label, so we knew we'd have more control if we went with them." Payday released "Come Clean" as an official single in mid-1993 and it continued to blow up nation-wide, setting Jeru up for ears to hear his impending debut.

Jeru and Premier worked on the album in late 1993 and early '94 at New York's D & D Studios, for what Jeru estimates was about two months. Guru wasn't as involved with the album-making itself. "He was pretty much working on other shit at the time, so basically it was just me and Premier," Jeru explains. "Guru didn't care or get jealous that he wasn't involved, because we was all just homies."

Premier backs this up: "Guru didn't mind that I took over production for Jeru, he gave it his 100% blessing. I actually think he was happy that I wanted to take the time and work with him. I was just starting to produce outside artists at that point. Guru was in-and-out during the album sessions, he knew things were in good hands. He and I both had a 50 / 50 cut in what we made on Jeru, so it was all good to him. It was still Gang Starr Productions at the end of the day."

Premier adds, "After 'Come Clean,' Patrick Moxey said, 'As long as you [Premier] do the album, then it's a green light.' So we got to work. I knew that with Jeru's voice and the different style and flow that he had, it could be a hit record. And it was."

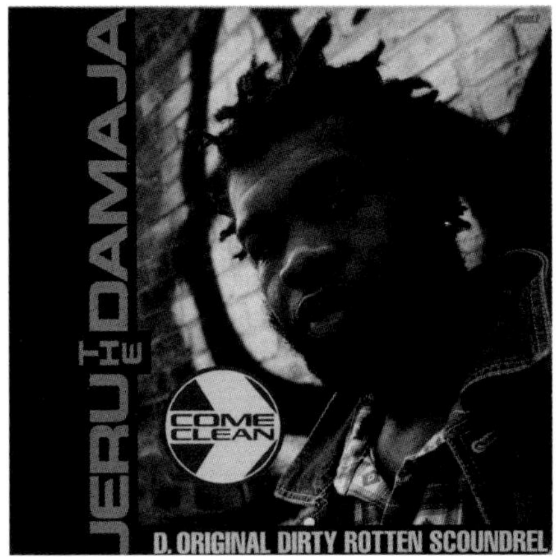

"Recording the album was definitely very natural," Jeru recalls. "There wasn't any pressure either, because with me and rhymin', when you do something all the time, it's just second-nature."

Jeru continues, expounding on his writing style: "Whatever lyrics you hear on one of my songs, they're a direct result of that music. If you want to know how a beat made me feel, just listen to the lyrics. No rhymes on any of my albums were written ahead-of-time. I do have rhyme books, but I always write to a beat. That's why every record I do has a different flow."

Premier describes the album recording process from his standpoint: "I always make tracks on the spot, I never do beat tapes. So those Jeru beats were done just for those songs. Then the writing process would start. Sometimes there were *concepts* before the beats, but never lyrics. We would sometimes listen to records [to be sampled] at my crib, but it was usually at the studio."

Premier adds, "From when I first met him until we did 'Come Clean' and then the album, Jeru's development as an MC was gradual, and I was definitely impressed each step of the way. It was helpful that I knew him as a person before we worked together in the studio. He was head-strong from day one, he always wanted to be a great MC and make a classic album. He was always reading books and was into knowledge of self. And I noticed that he also did a lot of martial arts and karate by '92, and had lost some weight as well. By the time we did the album, he was ready to make a classic."

Jeru mentions that, in his eyes, the album was a dual production. "I wrote all my lyrics to a specific beat," he explains. "Premier didn't just give me beats and I'd choose and match lyrics I already had to the music. I mean, me and Premier would just listen to records together for *hours*. If I would like a certain sound or a certain thing, then *boom*, he'd do his thing and hook it up. It wasn't just like him saying, 'I got a beat for you.' A lot of people don't know that. It was a group thing. Everything on that album came together as one thing."

Premier doesn't exactly agree, at least as it pertains to how the roles were listed on the album's credits. "I got upset because the first pressing of the album said 'Produced by Kendrick Jeru Davis and DJ Premier,'" he recalls. "Jeru had a lot of input, but I'm the producer, no question about it. I was really pissed off, it should say, 'Produced by DJ Premier for Gang Starr Productions.' I don't know who wrote it that way the first time, but I made them change it." Premier has no issue with Jeru being credited as co-producer, as he is on later pressings.

"Knowledge Is King" by Elika Burns, 1994.
Courtesy of Elika Burns.

Jeru's lyrics on *The Sun Rises In The East* were a breath of fresh air, mixing 'hood smarts with true philosophical consciousness in a way that harkened back to KRS-One's rise to prominence in the late-'80s. He explains his outlook and approach to life: "My philosophy came from reading books, living life, the influence of my pops, and all kinds of different stuff. I grew up in a very conscious type of household. My father started the first Nyabinghi [Rastafarian] organization in New York, over 30 years ago. So I also grew up with that."

"Even when I was out running in the streets, I still had a conscious side," he adds. "That's the balance everyone has. Me and Afu-Ra and a guy named Asheru used to sell books with True Master on the street in Manhattan. We had a table, selling materials on knowledge of self, science, mathematics. We always had loads of knowledge."

Jeru's debut album hit at retail in the spring of 1994, a lean, mean platter featuring only 10 full vocal tracks, with three interludes. As with all great albums, it was a matter of quality, not quantity. "We were used to the days where albums had 12 or 13 songs," Jeru says. "When you put too many songs on an album, it's overkill. What does it matter if you've got 20 tracks when only 10 of them are good? We just worked and how it came out is how it came out. If we sat back and listened to it and had felt that it needed more tracks, we would have made some more. But we listened to it the way it was and said, 'This is it.'"

Album ad, 1994.

Premier agrees: "It was perfect, it was never supposed to be any longer than it was. You can just tell when something's done. Those tracks were all we needed."

And as to whether the album title was an early volley in the "East Coast vs. West Coast" battle that consumed the hip-hop world later that decade, Jeru has this to say: "The title of the album had nothing to do with the East *Coast*, because there wasn't any coastal stuff going on back then. Not with us, at least. We listened to Dr. Dre and N.W.A. when we drove around. The media created the East vs. West stuff."

He continues, "People took the title to mean East Coast after the media got involved. But I come from East New York, and if you're in Brooklyn, they called my 'hood The East. It was about me being a son of East New York, but also a physical sun, shining the light. It was saying: 'Boom, the dude from the 'hood is coming up to shine his light. The dude who the principal thought wouldn't make it, and who people thought was gonna end up on the wrong side of the gun, is now doing something worthwhile.'"

The album was instantly jocked by fans of true-school hip-hop around the world, aided by more touring with Gang Starr in the summer and fall of '94. Additionally, the album's singles – "Come Clean," "D. Original," and "You Can't Stop The Prophet" – featured some of the highest-quality and most-compelling videos of any hip-hop artist that year.

Jeru looks back on the album very fondly: "Everything about that album is great to me.

I was just trying to make real hip-hop, and hip-hop was the best it has ever been back then. Without sounding conceited, I'm an MC and I thought the album was the shit. I knew that if people liked 'Come Clean,' they'd really like the rest of it as well."

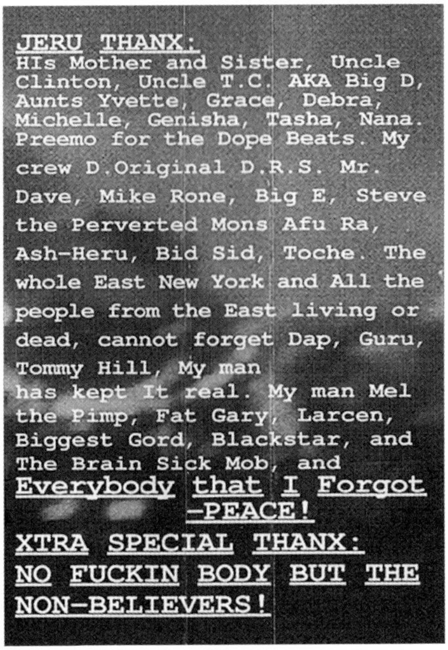

JERU THANX:
HIs Mother and Sister, Uncle Clinton, Uncle T.C. AKA Big D, Aunts Yvette, Grace, Debra, Michelle, Genisha, Tasha, Nana. Preemo for the Dope Beats. My crew D.Original D.R.S. Mr. Dave, Mike Rone, Big E, Steve the Perverted Mons Afu Ra, Ash-Heru, Bid Sid, Toche. The whole East New York and All the people from the East living or dead, cannot forget Dap, Guru, Tommy Hill, My man has kept It real. My man Mel the Pimp, Fat Gary, Larcen, Biggest Gord, Blackstar, and The Brain Sick Mob, and Everybody that I Forgot -PEACE!

XTRA SPECIAL THANX:
NO FUCKIN BODY BUT THE NON-BELIEVERS!

Thank-yous from *The Sun Rises In The East* cassette interior.

"I think it's one of the most classic albums in hip-hop history," boasts Premier. "It's one of my greatest accomplishments as a producer."

And Jeru adds, "For most artists, their first album is the accumulation of everything that has happened in their life up to that point. You get a chance to get it off your chest right there. And that's what I was doing. Because it's like, 'I don't know when I'm going to get this chance again.' Every song on there was huge to me, because they were all just different experiences. Everything was perfect back then, nothing went wrong. And with Premier and Gang Starr, we were a family, just having fun."

TRACKS

D. Original

JERU THE DAMAJA: That was the second single, it came out when the album hit. The video for that one was just some 'hood type of stuff. Walking around the neighborhood, taking the train. I actually get killed in the video at the beginning, then my ghost comes out and rhymes. It says, "Rest In Peace, D. Original," with no real explanation when it starts. I get up from the dead body and just start rhyming. Ralph McDaniels' [from Video Music Box] partner The Vid Kid [Lionel Martin] directed that one.

DJ PREMIER: At that time, me and RZA had a bit of a competition. RZA and GZA used to come to my house before Wu-Tang, they had the whole concept but no records out. So we were all watching it happen. And RZA said, "Yo, man, I got this ill piano record called 'C.R.E.A.M.,' wait until you hear it." I did my piano record with Jeru, "D. Original," to go at RZA. But when I heard 'C.R.E.A.M.,' I was like, "Goddamn it!" He got me on that one, even though ours was a dope record, too. I used to cut up that Guru part from "I'm The Man" [off *Daily Operation*] all the time, and I knew that was perfect to use on "D. Original." The group DRS, which stood for Dirty Rotten Scoundrels [which was the same name as Jeru's teenage neighborhood crew] did a song "This Is For My Homies" *[Author's note: Technically, the song is called "Gangsta Lean," a single and album from 1993 on Capitol]*, and that's why the song was "D. Original," to make it clear just who was screaming Dirty Rotten Scoundrels first. Jeru was using that name in the '80s. In "Come Clean," Jeru says, "D. Original don't sing no R-and-B," that was referencing DRS, too. We respected that record, but we knew they weren't making anything like us.

Brooklyn Took It

PREMIER: That's one of my favorites. Of course we had to do a song about Brooklyn. I lived on Washington Avenue, between Lafayette and Greene, and we used to see

[The Notorious] B.I.G. and the whole Junior M.A.F.I.A. on Fulton Ave all the time. I remember Biggie would always say, "Yo, if Jeru ever does a video for 'Brooklyn Took It,' I want to just stand next to him and look *hard*. I don't even want to say nothin'." Unfortunately for him, we never did a video.

JERU: That song's easy. Brooklyn always represents Brooklyn. You can go anywhere in the world – and I've done this – and if you ask, "Is Brooklyn in the house?," you're going to get a, "Yeah!" That track wasn't even about the rhyming, it was like, "If it's gone then you know Brooklyn took it, because we're there." That's the reputation we have: to take things, to dominate. Geography and pride is still important in hip-hop. I mean, Jay-Z still always shouts out Brooklyn. And those Down South dudes say where they're from. I remember when I wrote that track I was walking down the back street of my crib, in the projects. I was coming home at like three in the morning one night and it just hit me: "Brooklyn Took It." That's one of my favorite songs off the album.

Mental Stamina [featuring Afu-Ra]

JERU: Afu [Aaron Phillip] was my rap student. We grew up together. When all of us would be outside rhyming, Afu knew everybody's rhyme, but he wasn't rhyming at the time. So one day I just told him to start writing on his own, and he did. Even though I say he was my student, I never really "worked" with Afu. We was just homies, we lived together and everything. This is how we do: we set you off and then you make your own way from there. Back then there were a lot of people who didn't think Afu would be good on a record, but I knew it'd be crazy. And it definitely came off. He brought his own unorthodox technique, and with that song it was time for him to show it.

PREMIER: I didn't know Afu could rap at first. He was always around, and we'd hang with his brother, too. On that song, I told Afu he could spit but I told him that if he didn't rip it, we weren't gonna keep it. That's why there's that shit at the beginning about "No turning back." But when he spit, I thought it was very creative. I like the noisiness of the sample, too. The way they're going back and forth on that, lyrically, is like a sparring session.

Da Bichez

PREMIER: Jeru told me he wanted to make a record about women, without dissing them. He had the general concept, and then I looked for a [musical] vibe that matched the idea.

JERU: Some people wrote how that song was misogynistic, but it wasn't like that at all. People just didn't listen. When people hear "bitch" or "ass" or "pussy," that's all they hear. It didn't upset me, because most people got it. You know what they say in show business: no publicity is bad publicity. It all worked for the greater good at the end of the day, because I could sit down and explain to people what I was talking about.

You Can't Stop The Prophet

JERU: That was the third single on the album. I love that video. That was one of the hardest ones I've ever done. Daniel Hastings did that one. He and this dude Chris Cortez did the artwork for the video. We sat around for days, figuring out how to do all that stuff. It was really fun seeing it come to fruition. That one took the longest of all my videos. With my lyrics, I always just think of a concept and then I make it happen. That one was definitely one of my most conceptual rhymes. I mean, that record is like my life. Every day I had lived, up to the day I wrote that record, prepared me to write it. It was me showing how I felt about life, all the things I fight against. Hatred, jealousy, deceit, envy. These are all things that we deal with on a daily basis. When I first heard the music all put together, I was like, "This is some super-hero shit."

PREMIER: Jeru told me he wanted to do a record where he was a prophet and a super-hero. Daniel Hastings did that video, and he did all the artwork for the album. He did artwork for *Moment Of Truth* and *Ownerz* covers for Gang Starr, too, as well as [Jeru's second album] *Wrath Of The Math*. I think "You Can't Stop The Prophet" was his first video. The Pete Rock remix of that song on the 12-inch is amazing. I'm very picky about anyone remixing me, really just Large Professor or Pete Rock [have his blessing]. So I knew it was going to be good. If it hadn't have been, I would have told Pete, definitely. I'm a very opinionated dude, I can't help it.

Perverted Monks In Tha House (Theme)

JERU: The thing about Perverted Monks comes from kung fu movies. That's the way I felt. I was on the path of righteousness but at the same time I had things about me that weren't correct. It's the balance. Yin and yang, light and dark. You can't have completely one or the other. Dirty Rotten Scoundrels is a name we used for the crew since I was 14 or 15. That was just the name of the clique, all the brothers from the 'hood. It wasn't a group. Perverted Monks was more like age 19.

Ain't The Devil Happy

JERU: I always wanted to be remembered not just as an MC. I wanted to be remembered as a person who made a change, who took a stand. Who said, "Fuck the status quo, I'm doing *this*." I grew up listening to Public Enemy, KRS-One, [Big Daddy] Kane, Kool G Rap. All of them influenced the way I thought. Same with Bob Marley and Stevie Wonder. Social commentary, with a hint of righteousness. And one important thing I believed was that righteousness doesn't mean I'm better than you. Or that I always do the right thing. It means, "I see things that are not right and I don't just turn my head. I speak up about it. I can't sweep it under the rug."

PREMIER: Those lyrics came after he heard the track. I remember we loved "Tearz" [by Wu-Tang Clan] and there was that "Ha ha ha" laughing part in the song. I used to cut that up on WBLS. So when he said the title of the song, I knew it would blend in perfectly.

My Mind Spray

PREMIER: I have always loved [Bob James'] "Nautilus," and so many artists have used it. Run-DMC, Lord Shafiyq. I had always wanted to break down my version of it, so when Jeru mentioned the title, it just went from there.

Come Clean

JERU: Every night on tour with Gang Starr, in '92 and '93, Premier would sound-check with that Onyx sample [from their 1992 hit "Throw Ya Gunz"], that "Uh oh, heads up, 'cause we're droppin' some shit." He'd cut that up, and I said "Yo, when we get back let's do a song with that as the hook." With that Onyx sample we weren't dissing them at all. Those are my boys. We used it because we were dropping some shit, too. I always had a really good relationship with Onyx. So we went to Premier's crib and heard a lot of records, then we heard that intro [the percussion drops, which are heard at the beginning and throughout the song]. We looped it up, and the rest is history. That song was calling out any gangsta rappers who was fake. They knew who they were. I wasn't speaking to anyone directly, but whoever took it that way, they did so for obvious reasons. I'm not a gangster, but I'm real. I grew up in the street and I've stared down the barrel of guns and all of that. I've been shot at. With that song I was just standing up for what I thought was right. I grew up with a lot of real gangsters and I've seen dudes get killed right next to me. So I was saying, "Don't promote something if you're not a gangster." Like on TV, when they say, "Don't try this at home." Same thing. We were trying to be different with that track, of course. We knew it was dope but we didn't know that it would catch on like that. We wasn't thinking on the level of whether it would be a hit. We was just trying to make dope hip-hop. We didn't know what to expect. After we signed to Payday, they put the song out as an official single, in '93. It was spring or summer. I remember because when we did the video for it, it was hot out.

PREMIER: We did that single and it took off *immediately*. When we finished it, we knew then that it was a banger. I knew that no one had ever made a record that sounded like that before. There wasn't any build-up, DJs just threw it on the second they got it. We didn't think that Onyx would take it as a dis, because we [used the sample] in a 'hood way. If you do it in a way that people in the 'hood can relate to, you don't have anything to worry about. It wasn't always seen as an anti-gangster song anyways. Like with Public Enemy, they'd say, "Shame on you if you sell drugs." But those same drug dealers were like, "Yo, I love Public Enemy!"

Jungle Music

PREMIER: The music came first for that one. Once he said he liked the music, I started looking for extra sounds to add. I had a disk with jungle sounds on it, I just saw that floppy disk the other day. It literally said "Jungle Sounds" on it. It had stuff like [makes sound of a gorilla] and birds and shit. So once I knew what he was going to call the song, we started with those sounds. He wrote his lyrics right there, on the spot.

JERU: With that track, I was still just trying to hit every different part of my life, lyrically. I don't remember exactly what happened to start those lyrics, but whatever it was, it made me think of Africa, about where music came from. The beat and my inner feelings just made me write it.

Statik

JERU: That's one of my favorites on the album. One day Premier was looping some shit, and what he was looping had a lot of static on it. It wasn't even the record we ended up using for the song. But I said, "Yo, we should do a record and I'm just gonna rhyme on the static." And he was like, "Word up." With most of the shit we did, that's exactly how it happened.

PREMIER: Once we heard that sample, it just had so much dirt in it that the title and subject came quickly. That was the second time I had used scratchy vinyl on a track. The first one was [Gang Starr's] "The ? Remains" [the B-side to the 1994 single "Suckas Need Bodyguards," on Chrysalis]. We used the dirt in the record on there, too. With "The ? Remains," I had a clean copy [of the original record that was sampled] and a dirty copy, and for some reason the dirty one sounded so much better to me.

KMD

Black Bastards
Elektra, 1994 – un-released; Readyrock, 2000;
Metal Face / Sub Verse, 2001

"After Doom got his check [from Elektra], he looked at it and said, 'Yo, I should get dropped more often. This is more money than I've ever gotten in the music game.' I know he must have been devastated, but he didn't seem like it. He was almost Zen-like. I didn't see him much after that."

– Dante Ross

There are few releases in hip-hop history with as much mystery behind them as KMD's second full-length, *Black Bastards*. The album, whose cover boldly depicted a cartoon "Sambo" being hanged, didn't even receive the insult of being shelved or pushed back by Elektra Records upon its completion in 1994. Instead, it was outright refused, with very little above-board explanation as to the reason, or even much of an apology, as they ushered the group's leader out the door.

And while the aftermath of Elektra's decision caused the group's only remaining member unimaginable distress, the album didn't stay buried forever. Years later – much like the artist formerly known as Zev Love X, who would shed his old name, image and vocal style and emerge as MF Doom – the album would be resurrected and released on multiple labels.

But let's start at the beginning. KMD – sometimes written "K.M.D.," but not always – was, at its core, two brothers: Daniel Dumile [Zev Love X, aka MF Doom] and the two-years-younger Dingilizwe Dumile [DJ Subroc, aka Raheem or Heem]. Their family moved around Manhattan and the outskirts of New York City growing up, although they spent most of their high school years in Long Island. Even though they were separated by two years, Doom says, "It always seemed like me and Sub was twins. Or it might have even seemed that he was older. Like his spirit was older."

Doom, who was born in the UK shortly before his family moved to the U.S., says, "We grew up in a lot of places. We went to school in Manhattan and in Mt. Vernon [NY]. Every year we was in a different town. Manhattan was always the focal point, though, because we were either going to school there or cutting school to go there."

Aside from Manhattan, one geographical locale that had significance to the Dumile brothers was Long Beach, NY: a town technically in Long Island, but just outside of the

Queens borough line. Importantly for their musical career, it was also a stone's throw from Far Rockaway, the home of 3rd Bass' MC Serch. Doom says that they were firmly planted in Long Beach when he was in junior high and early high school, and they also kept roots there throughout the mid-'90s.

In Doom's mid-teens [Sub's early-to-mid teens], the brothers were into graffiti as much as music, and the decision about their group name – instead of the larger ESP ["Every Sucka Pays"] crew with whom they were connected – flowed directly out of a can of Krylon. "With KMD, those three letters just sound great, the way they ring together in that order," Doom explains. "When we first figured out the name, that's all we wanted. Then we built it from there. It was really more of a graffiti crew at first. It just looks ill when you write it."

He continues, "At first, it stood for 'Kausin' Much Damage.' Then it was more like, 'Kause in a Much Damaged Society.' Like a positive cause *[Author's note: See the bottom of their 1991 single "Peachfuzz" as well as the upper left of their debut album Mr. Hood for the use of this phrase].* We used the letters to make sense of what we was trying to do, musically, at any given time."

Similar logic went into the elder Dumile's first stage name: Zev Love X. He explains, "I started with X and also liked Z and V. Then I added 'Love' in the middle. It was always about the illest combination of letters, and not many people used Z or V in graffiti back then. X always posed a question. In algebra, it was a mystery. And it also spelled out 'X Evolvez,' backwards."

Although visuals and language consumed their young minds, they also went beyond graffiti and tags. "We started making actual music in about 1986, just hooking up double tape-decks," Doom explains. "I used to DJ, too, but I always took hold of the vocal aspect. Subroc had more of the technical side sewed down."

They also met a future rhyme partner, Onyx [Alonzo Hodge], around this time. He was a neighborhood acquaintance and appeared as a secondary MC on their first album, *Mr. Hood*, but was not on *Black Bastards*. "He was my man from down the street," Doom says. "He used to build and bug out with us back in '86. Everyone else in our neighborhood wanted to have beef, and he was the only dude who would talk to us. We had the same views and ideas about life. He was in between me and Sub, age-wise."

The last important piece to the KMD music puzzle came into play during the mid-to-late '80s as well, in Long Beach. Doom recalls, "I met [MC] Serch there around '85. Back then it was pretty basic: everybody didn't rhyme like they do now. If you were an MC or did beats or were a DJ, there were only a few of you. So you stuck together, or eventually met each other. Serch used to do talent shows, I think I met him at one of those."

"One day, probably in'88, Serch came through and was like, 'Yo, I got a record deal,'" Doom continues. "He asked us if we wanted to be on a track."

That track ended up being 3rd Bass' smash single "The Gas Face," which appeared in 1989 on Def Jam and featured Zev as a guest on vocals, alongside Serch and his 3rd Bass rhyme partner, Pete Nice. The entire song was, in fact, based on a term that Zev himself had coined. With the addition of being in the song's video, he was quickly vaulted into the public eye, despite still being in high school. *[Author's note: For more commentary on "The Gas Face," see the 3rd Bass The Cactus Album chapter in this book].*

Pete Nice, who would go on to co-manage KMD through the mid-'90s, says, "Serch met the KMD guys before I did, through 3rd Bass' dancers, Ahmed and Otis. They lived in Long Beach, too. They were all in the GYP, Get Yours Posse. Those guys [Zev and Subroc] were very young when 'Gas Face' was out. They were both at a lot of our sessions for *The Cactus Album*, and then they toured with us after the album came out. So it was definitely a family thing; they were like our little brothers. And they were like Siamese twins with each other. Zev and Sub were so connected."

After the impact of "The Gas Face," record labels were more than open to the idea of a KMD album. And while Zev was the leader, at least as far as most people could see, Subroc remained a strong, silent partner. "He was just quieter than me, I guess," Doom says. "Subroc was usually the guy to fix tracks after I had left them half-done. He'd get it tight and set the pace. He was my partner in crime. And on the mic, he started coming with his MC shit right around the time of the first album [*Mr. Hood*, in 1991]."

Doom explains, "'Gas Face' was the first thing that we had ever put out, but the KMD music we were working on was piling up. Even so, we weren't necessarily looking for a deal." Nonetheless, by late 1990 they had one, signed to Elektra by hip-hop A & R impresario Dante Ross – a man who already had an impressive history in the game, having worked at RUSH / Def Jam [with 3rd Bass, among many others] and Tommy Boy before landing at the major label. He would go on to sign some of the most influential rap acts of the early '90s, including Brand Nubian, Pete Rock & CL Smooth and Leaders of the New School.

During the first album, KMD was managed by Serch's and Pete's R.I.F. Productions. "It wasn't a super serious company or anything," Pete explains. "But we had a lot of connections in the industry, so we figured why not?" He explains that it wasn't a tough sell to get Dante Ross to pick up KMD at Elektra, and the group's initial advance was raised slightly by some interest shown by Def Jam during the shopping process.

"I first met Doom and Subroc when they were kids, really," remembers Dante Ross. "Doom was in that post-teenage, almost-a-grown-up age, still young. And Subroc was a kid, honestly. They were both really endearing and charming. I met them through 3rd Bass, probably through Serch. They really were like twins, they were so close."

Pete Nice and Zev Love X on stage, 1989.
Photo courtesy of Pete Nice.

He adds, "By the time I was at Elektra and building the label's hip-hop roster, I got to know KMD even better. We dug each other as people, and I loved their music. I guess you could say that they were somewhere in between Brand Nubian and De La Soul [two artists with whom Ross had worked]."

"Honestly, we didn't talk to anybody over at Elektra besides Dante," recalls Doom. "He was a regular dude. He made beats, too, and he was open to the creative direction that we were going in back then. We had total creative control making that first album." The song "Peachfuzz" was their first single, and the first time that Sub and Doom had ever been on wax under their own group name.

One of the people who helped KMD harness their musical ideas early-on was John Gamble, a friend of Dante Ross' and a partner in the Stimulated Dummies production crew and studio, with Ross and Geeby Dajani. Gamble engineered the entire *Mr. Hood* album, which he says was initially made – over the course of four or five months

– as a full album demo. These first recordings were completed at the Dummies' SD50 Studio, located in the basement of the Westbeth artist's building where Gamble lived. After that, with Elektra's green-light, final album tracks were completed at Calliope Studios, after another two months of work.

Gamble says, of the *Mr. Hood* sessions: "At first, I had no idea how the stuff they were looping was going to make any sense. But then I saw the genius of those tracks, as I watched them unfold. They were truly on some *next level* shit, even at a young age. It was all mapped out in their heads."

Zev Love X.
Photo by and courtesy of Pete Nice.

"Doom was much more verbal at first, Subroc didn't talk much," Gamble recalls. "Although Sub got to be more outgoing by the end of *Mr. Hood*. Sub was more of the technical guy. I seem to remember that, more often than not, it was Sub who had the records and ideas of what was going to be sampled. They also never really argued about anything, or even had conflicting ideas about the music. Maybe they had already had those discussions before I saw them, but I never heard them fight about anything. Those were the best and most fun sessions I have ever done, to this day."

Zev Love X, Subroc and Pete Nice at Greene Street Studios.
Photo courtesy of Pete Nice.

Doom explains what "Produced by KMD" meant back in the *Mr. Hood* era: "Me and Sub would do whatever we could do. It wasn't necessarily sectioned off. It was really just for fun, in a lot of ways. I would dig in the crates, find the loops, and come up with a concept. Then, I'd usually get close to finishing it, but I'd be too lazy. I never liked messing with computers or programming drum machines and samplers. I left a lot of beats half-done. And Sub would come in and finish a lot of them. Onyx was only vocals, he didn't fuck with the music at all. He added a lot of humor to what we were doing. His was an ill angle."

He also points out that – in addition to behind-the-scenes production and technical work – Subroc started rhyming on *Mr. Hood*, notably on the song "Subroc's Mission." "That shit is retarded," says Doom.

Mr. Hood came out in 1991 and featured three singles: "Peachfuzz," "Nitty Gritty," and "Who Me?" Album artwork and single covers showed a cartoon Sambo image, drawn by Doom. It was a startling and evocative graphic, and it would come back to haunt him less than three years later.

Mr. Hood was successful, at least for a debut album by an abstract-leaning trio who made catchy music, but whose lyrics were too complicated for cross-over smashes. "I thought the album was promoted well," Doom recalls. "And the wreck [praise / sales] we caught off it was good enough wreck for me." Most parties involved agree that the album sold in the neighborhood of 130,000 to 150,000 units.

Back of "Who Me?" single, 1991.

"*Mr. Hood* actually drove me crazy, because they did the demo in our studio," Ross says. "So I couldn't even use my own spot for like three or four months. But besides that, I never liked the way that the record *sounded*. I thought the drums were funny on a lot of the tracks. There was a lot of 'demo-itis' on that record. Maybe they wanted it to sound lo-fi. Either way, there was a lot of innocence on that record, because the guys were pretty innocent back then."

"Their image and lifestyle was definitely much different on the first album," Pete Nice recalls. "They were both devout Muslims back then, in 1991. They were still kids. We would go on the road and they would have their prayer rugs during Ramadan. They didn't drink or do any drugs."

Despite Ross' feelings about the sonics of the record, and with only moderate apprehension from Elektra higher-ups as a result of the sales numbers, Ross convinced the label to green-light a second album. He explains, "We didn't recoup on the first record, so when it came time to talk about another one, the label wasn't sure. I convinced them that they should, but they set the budget at $200,000, which was a lot less than *Mr. Hood*."

Mr. Hood album ad, fall 1991.

KMD toured with 3rd Bass and other like-minded artists after the release of *Mr. Hood*, working on their follow-up album whenever they could for the next two years. "We were on the road a lot and we were always working on stuff," Doom says. "We always had the [Akai] MPC with us. The road was the most fun shit and it was even better for working on music, because we were there with so many different musical minds."

Doom and Sub had added new friends to their extended family during the *Mr. Hood* era. Most notably the Constipated Monkey crew, including vocalist Kurious, whom Doom met via 3rd Bass in 1989. "We had been down with them for a while," Doom explains. "They were from Uptown and they had a similar thing going on to what we were doing. So we met up and joined forces, the way culture grows. It's like plants. Kurious, Bobbito [Garcia], Tone Greer, those are my fams."

Doom says that they started recording the follow-up to *Mr. Hood*, "Upstate, at Dr. York's studio, where the photo on the back of [MF Doom's] *Operation Doomsday* [from 1999, on Fondle 'Em Records] was taken." Dr. Malachi York is the controversial leader of the Nuwaubian / Nubian Islamic Hebrew Mission spiritual movement and the Holy Tabernacle Ministries. York and his ministry operated out of several locations starting in the late '60s, including Brooklyn; Liberty, NY [near the Catskills, about 90 miles from Manhattan]; and, starting in 1993, rural Georgia.

In addition to being a religious and spiritual figurehead, Dr. York was also a recording artist, beginning in the early '80s. Doom and Sub had an association with him during their teenage years and, according to many accounts, followed his spiritual teachings. "Doom and Sub would go and visit Dr. York in Brooklyn on the weekends," Ross recalls. "He had a lot of influence on them."

Demo recording locations for KMD's second album, which would be known as *Black Bastards*, included multiple spots: 4-track demos at home; MPC tryouts on the road; and hip-hop hotspots like Chung King and Calliope in Manhattan. Clearly the location wasn't important, and inspiration came from just about everywhere. "Sometimes we would just start recording in a big studio, staying in there all day. Music would just come to us, chilling and digging in the crates," Doom says.

As they began their sophomore effort, another musical collaborator entered the mix: engineer Rich Keller. A jazz bassist who first entered the hip-hop game engineering the Beatnuts at Chung King Studios a year or two earlier, he was brought into the *Black Bastards* project by Pete Nice. "I was there pretty much from the beginning of those sessions," Keller says.

Dr. York *New: York* album cover.
1985, York's Records.

Although many people reasonably assumed that final tracks for the album were recorded at Chung King – since that is the only studio listed on the album's sole single ["What A Niggy Know"] – Keller says that almost every song on the album was actually recorded at his home studio in Livonia, NJ.

"I had full set-up there," he explains. "It was a well-known spot. Onyx [the Queens-based group, not the ex-KMD member], Run-DMC, and Wu-Tang would record there later on. I would always go to other studios to mix records, we only tracked music and vocals at my place. When KMD was recording, a lot of times they would just crash at my house, for days at a time. We worked very steadily on the album and were very productive over that winter, late 1992 into the spring of '93. They came with the music in their samplers and we'd build the records. I helped with technical shit, and sometimes I'd play bass or a guitar lick to fill something in, to connect sections. But it was Doom and Sub who had all the ideas."

"What impressed me about those guys more than anything was Doom's passion," Keller adds. "He *lived* the music, every song was a proclamation that he had to get out. I was inspired by his dedication to the music."

Keller, who had just met the duo in 1992, has an interesting recollection about Subroc, who was clearly coming out of his shell by the *Black Bastards* era: "Subroc was different than Doom; he was more animated and outspoken. He acted more like the rapper of the group during our sessions. I know Doom was the main MC, but Subroc acted like he was. He had the machismo and had more attitude. Doom was more about the music and 'the mission' when I was with them."

Doom describes the transition from *Mr. Hood* to what would become *Black Bastards* in the following way: "*Mr. Hood* was like all the ideas we had from 1986 through 1991, when I was 17 and Subroc was 15. We both grew up a lot between [when Doom was] 18 and 21, being on the road, and having a career in music. The truth doesn't change, and we were dealing with the truth. The messages don't change, they just sound different. Maybe our attitudes towards things, or towards women, changed. We both had children by the time that we were making *Black Bastards*, too."

By *Black Bastards*, Subroc's voice – which was quieter on *Mr. Hood* – appeared on multiple tracks, solo and duo, including "Gimme!"; "It Sounded Like A Roc"; "Suspended Animation"; the single "What A Nigga Know"; and the bonus track, "Q3 119." He was 19 years-old, and as an adult he started to stand shoulder-to-shoulder with his older brother, becoming a more front-and-center part of the group.

Pete Nice agrees: "A major change with *Black Bastards* was Subroc coming to the forefront. He rhymed and did a lot more production. Sub was very involved with *Mr. Hood*, but he wasn't *heard* as much. By *Black Bastards*, he had come into his own. He had a big influence on the sound. In fact, he was so quiet during *Mr. Hood* that it was surprising to hear him rhyme. He was still young, but his lyrics were strong. He and Doom built *Black Bastards* together."

"I think a lot of the musical ideas on *Black Bastards* were Sub's," says Ross. "He was a boy genius, extremely insightful and intelligent. And there was an immense change with the guys in-between records, both as people and as artists. They were hanging out in the city a lot, often with the Constipated Monkeys, and they were experimenting with a lot of mind-altering drugs. Like, a *lot* of them. Even so, I still felt good about what might become of the record."

Pete Nice also mentions the marked change in the Dumile brothers between albums: "They had been really devout and serious before. By the time they got to *Black Bastards*, they were still Muslims, but they were drinking 40s. And musically, things got more serious. *Black Bastards* was more dense with imagery and complexity. *Mr. Hood* was more straight-forward. They were becoming adults, and were also influenced by the developments of other groups they admired, like De La Soul, Tribe Called Quest and the Jungle Brothers. Doom had a pretty intense focus back in '92 and '93. I love both albums, but I like *Black Bastards* more. They were just getting better at what they were doing."

When queried as to whether *Black Bastards* is an angry – or at least less innocent –

album, Doom replies: "On *Mr. Hood* we did take a less aggressive approach. There was some of the same subject matter on *Black Bastards*, but we went at it a bit more aggressively. I guess you could say that. Either way, people had type-cast us on *Mr. Hood*. To be honest, if I had wanted to come *real* angry with shit, I could have been much angrier than what you heard, considering what was going on in the world back then. There were still plenty of jokes and funny shit on *Black Bastards*, so I wouldn't call it an angry album."

One interesting side-note is Doom's and Subroc's obsession with one singular album, which was sampled multiple times on *Black Bastards*: ex-Last Poet Gylan Kain's fiery, black power treatise *The Blue Guerrilla* [1970, Juggernaut Records]. "We used to listen to that album a lot, and it was ill," Doom explains. "It matched a lot of funny stuff we was trying to say, and it helped us get our points across. That album was definitely an inspiration."

Ross says that John Gamble hipped Doom and Sub to the album initially, and that they knew Kain's son. Pete Nice was also aware of the Dumile brothers' obsession with the album. "I think that their love for the Kain record helped make *Black Bastards* more intense," he says. "Everything they were doing ended up having a double or triple meaning."

After many recording locations, road miles and wild samples, *Black Bastards* was just about finished when an almost unthinkable tragedy struck. On April 23, 1993, Subroc was killed by an oncoming car as he was trying to cross the Long Island Expressway on foot. He was only 19 years old.

Still reeling from the tragedy two decades later, Doom recalls, "The album was almost completely done when he was killed. I had to finish off a couple things here and there, but it was really almost done. And the album was due, so I had to go right into it. I had no time. I had to just finish it."

Keller agrees that the album was almost completed when Subroc died, and mentions that Doom was – understandably – in bad shape for some time afterwards, occasionally calling him or stopping by to borrow money, recording equipment or even pillows and bedding for his siblings. "He was trippin' for a little while," Keller says.

"I think some part of Doom was gone when Sub died," says Ross. "Sub's death, understandably, made Doom a very angry person."

Pete recalls, "I remember that at Subroc's wake, Doom set up a boombox right next to the casket and played pretty much the whole *Black Bastards* album. It was intense to hear it in that context."

According to all accounts, Doom did not take excessive time to mourn. Even so, he worked slowly, finishing the album – which Keller says was mixed at Chung King and mastered at Masterdisk in Manhattan – by early 1994.

In April of '94, less than a year after Subroc's tragic death, the first single, "What A Nigga Know [modified to "Niggy" for the radio version]," was released on Elektra. A video for the song was also shot and readied.

Advance cassettes for *Black Bastards* were circulated to press VIPs, and interviews for features about the album were completed with outlets including *The Source* and *4080*, among others. The release date for the album was set and printed on Elektra marketing materials that were sent out to press and retail: May 3.

But, sadly, Subroc's death turned out to be merely the first blow in a one-two punch that would force Doom into a deeper depression, and out of the public eye for several years.

"It was totally out of the blue," Doom recalls. "'What A Nigga Know' was out and doing well, and we were at a session. We got a call from Elektra, they wanted to see us there at the office the next day for a meeting. I didn't really think much about it, honestly."

"We got there and they had the [cover] artwork proofs out on the table," he continues. "There were a couple of people in the room, including one old dude I had never seen before. He

In Memory of Subroc of KMD

In late April, **Subroc** of **KMD** was tragically hit by a car and killed in Long Island, only a few days before the new KMD album was fully completed. Although plans are still in effect to release the record, Subroc will be missed by all of those who enjoyed his music. The following is an excerpt from his eulogy:

Subroc was born **Dingilizwe Dumile** on August 3, 1973, at Nassau County Medical Center in East Meadow NY, to Ashlyn Thompson Dumile and Daniel J. Dumile. He was raised primarily in Long Beach, NY.

Subroc's family was always an important

DOOM AND HIS LATE BROTHER SUBROC

part of his life. He was a sweet son and nephew, he was the illest brother and best friend. He touched the lives of everyone he came in contact with and influenced many through his music. He made a difference. He was always there with a smile to lend a kind word and a helping hand. He was kind, caring and could make anyone laugh in any situation.

Subroc was a member of the **Nubian Islamic Hebrew Mission**, he was a good follower and a great leader, a good student and a great teacher, he *was* KMD along with his brother **Doom**!

Subroc was academically, musically, mechanically, and artistically inclined. He was very skilled, talented, thoughtful and able to master everything he put his mind to. He thought what others couldn't perceive to think. He knew what others couldn't begin to know. He understood what others couldn't begin to understand. He did what others wouldn't try to do. He was what no one else could be. And now he still stays one step ahead of us.

KINETTA POWELL-DUMILE

Feature on Subroc's passing, *The Source*, July 1993.

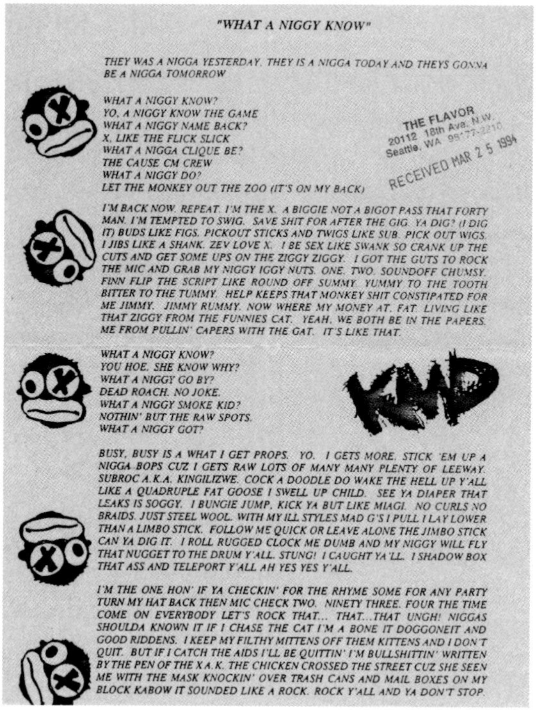

"WHAT A NIGGY KNOW"

THEY WAS A NIGGA YESTERDAY. THEY IS A NIGGA TODAY AND THEYS GONNA BE A NIGGA TOMORROW

WHAT A NIGGY KNOW?
YO, A NIGGY KNOW THE GAME
WHAT A NIGGY NAME BACK?
X, LIKE THE FLICK SLICK
WHAT A NIGGA CLIQUE BE?
THE CAUSE CM CREW
WHAT A NIGGY DO?
LET THE MONKEY OUT THE ZOO (IT'S ON MY BACK)

THE FLAVOR
20112 18th Ave. N.W.
Seattle, WA 98177-2210
RECEIVED MAR 2 5 1994

I'M BACK NOW. REPEAT. I'M THE X. A BIGGIE NOT A BIGOT PASS THAT FORTY MAN. I'M TEMPTED TO SWIG. SAVE SHIT FOR AFTER THE GIG. YA DIG? (I DIG IT) BUDS LIKE FIGS. PICKOUT STICKS AND TWIGS LIKE SUB. PICK OUT WIGS. I JIBS LIKE A SHANK. ZEV LOVE X. I BE SEX LIKE SWANK SO CRANK UP THE CUTS AND GET SOME UPS ON THE ZIGGY ZIGGY. I GOT THE GUTS TO ROCK THE MIC AND GRAB MY NIGGY IGGY NUTS. ONE. TWO. SOUNDOFF CHUMSY. FINN FLIP THE SCRIPT LIKE ROUND OFF SUMMY. YUMMY TO THE TOOTH BITTER TO THE TUMMY. HELP KEEPS THAT MONKEY SHIT CONSTIPATED FOR ME JIMMY. JIMMY RUMMY. NOW WHERE MY MONEY AT. FAT. LIVING LIKE THAT ZIGGY FROM THE FUNNIES CAT. YEAH, WE BOTH BE IN THE PAPERS. ME FROM PULLIN' CAPERS WITH THE GAT. IT'S LIKE THAT.

WHAT A NIGGY KNOW?
YOU HOE. SHE KNOW WHY?
WHAT A NIGGY GO BY?
DEAD ROACH. NO JOKE.
WHAT A NIGGY SMOKE KID?
NOTHIN' BUT THE RAW SPOTS.
WHAT A NIGGY GOT?

KMD

BUSY, BUSY IS A WHAT I GET PROPS. YO. I GETS MORE. STICK 'EM UP A NIGGA BOPS CUZ I GETS RAW LOTS OF MANY MANY PLENTY OF LEEWAY. SUBROC A.K.A. KINGILIZWE. COCK A DOODLE DO WAKE THE HELL UP Y'ALL LIKE A QUADRUPLE FAT GOOSE I SWELL UP CHILD. SEE YA DIAPER THAT LEAKS IS SOGGY. I BUNGIE JUMP, KICK YA BUT LIKE MIAGI. NO CURLS NO BRAIDS. JUST STEEL WOOL. WITH MY ILL STYLES MAD G'S I PULL I LAY LOWER THAN A LIMBO STICK. FOLLOW ME QUICK OR LEAVE ALONE THE JIMBO STICK CAN YA DIG IT. I ROLL RUGGED CLOCK ME DUMB AND MY NIGGY WILL FLY THAT NUGGET TO THE DRUM Y'ALL. STUNG! I CAUGHT YA'LL. I SHADOW BOX THAT ASS AND TELEPORT Y'ALL AH YES YES Y'ALL.

I'M THE ONE HON' IF YA CHECKIN' FOR THE RHYME SOME FOR ANY PARTY TURN MY HAT BACK THEN MIC CHECK TWO. NINETY THREE. FOUR THE TIME COME ON EVERYBODY LET'S ROCK THAT... THAT...THAT UNGH! NIGGAS SHOULDA KNOWN IT IF I CHASE THE CAT I'M A BONE IT DOGGONEIT AND GOOD RIDDENS. I KEEP MY FILTHY MITTENS OFF THEM KITTENS AND I DON'T QUIT. BUT IF I CATCH THE AIDS I'LL BE QUITTIN' I'M BULLSHITTIN' WRITTEN BY THE PEN OF THE X.A.K. THE CHICKEN CROSSED THE STREET CUZ SHE SEEN ME WITH THE MASK KNOCKIN' OVER TRASH CANS AND MAIL BOXES ON MY BLOCK KABOW IT SOUNDED LIKE A ROCK. ROCK Y'ALL AND YA DON'T STOP.

"What A Niggy Know" lyrics sheet, sent to radio with 12-inch in early March, 1994.

Courtesy of the Adler Hip-Hop Archives / Cornell University Hip-Hop Collection.

Black Bastards advance cassette j-card.

Courtesy of DJ Platurn.

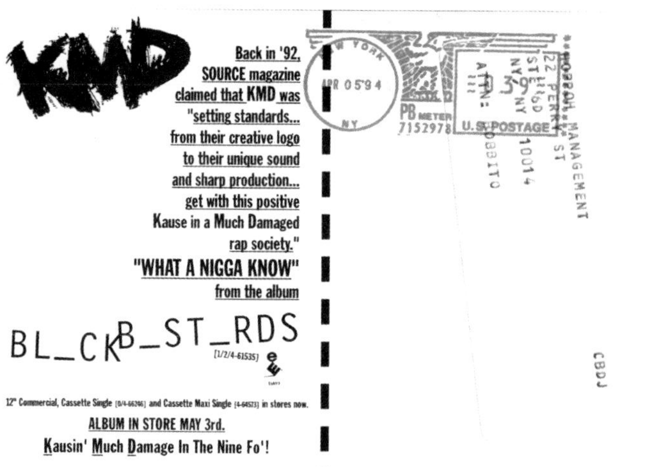

Black Bastards promotional postcard, sent early April, 1994, announcing May 3 album release.

Courtesy of the Adler Hip-Hop Archives / Cornell University Hip-Hop Collection.

was speaking on behalf of Elektra. It seemed like they had everything planned out already, like they knew how everything was going to end before we said anything. And they said they weren't going to put the album out. They didn't even want us to change the cover *[Author's note: Which depicted their trademark Sambo character, this time being hung by a rope on a makeshift gallows]*."

This came as a huge shock not only to Doom, but also to Dante Ross, who had been KMD's biggest booster at Elektra since day one. "The album got mastered and turned in, and the artwork had gone through the Elektra system," Ross recalls. "No one had ever questioned it. Then, all of a sudden the artwork got leaked to Terri Rossi at *Billboard*. At the time, a lot of older, bougie black people weren't feeling hip-hop. I'd put her [Rossi] in the same bag with C. Delores Tucker or Dionne Warwick. She just didn't get it."

Ross continues his recollection of why the Elektra meeting had come about: "Terri Rossi rallied against the album and she never even listened to it *[Author's note: Rossi's anti-KMD article, from February or March 1994, was technically in her "R & B Rhythms" column in the Airplay Monitor, a Billboard spin-off newsletter]*. She never asked Doom what the album or artwork was about. He was never allowed to explain it, or defend himself."

Original planned *Black Bastards* artwork.
Courtesy of the Adler Hip-Hop Archives / Cornell University Hip-Hop Collection.

It's somewhat understandable that Rossi would be more reactionary against, and out-of-touch with, hip-hop, as she was chiefly an R & B writer. But hers was not a lone, dissenting voice. Havelock Nelson, *Billboard*'s hip-hop columnist at the time, also spoke out against KMD's use of the "N-Word" and the Sambo graphic as it pertained to their single. In the April 16, 1994 issue of the magazine, he stated, "Regardless of what the group was attempting to achieve with this imagery and the term, many in the black community will find them offensive. It's inexcusable that the executives at Elektra allowed these images to slip through."

"We had used that Sambo character before, on *Mr. Hood* graphics," Doom explains *[Author's note: The group had, in fact, used the image – sans gallows – as far back as 1989]*. "It was kind of like our logo, our mascot. We were about deading [getting rid of] the whole stereotype thing. It was a mockery of a mockery. And we took it to the next level on *Black Bastards*, by hanging the dude. But minds were just closed. It had to be more than the cover [when it came to Elektra not being pleased] because then we asked what if we changed it, and they weren't hearing it. I guess what we were doing was going to make waves in places where they had financial interests."

The Sambo character was drawn by Doom, who was a talented artist in addition to his lyrical and production skills. Sub may have had a hand in it as well. "Doom generally did all the artwork for KMD, like the Sambo character," Ross says. "And I think Sub might have helped with some of what appeared on the *Black Bastards* cover. They had a symbiotic relationship, even with the artwork."

"My boss, Bob Krasnow, understood what Doom was doing [with the cover] after I explained it to him," Ross continues. "But Bob was in no position to help us, because of some internal politics over there. He ended up getting fired less than a year later."

Ross says that a meeting was even set up at one point with some of the powers-that-be at Elektra and WEA – including Sylvia Rhone, Vincent Davis, and even Terri Rossi – but it was cancelled at the last minute. Seeing no other good option, Ross says he convinced Krasnow to release Doom from his Elektra contract, give him his master tapes, and some "walking money" for his trouble.

According to Doom, Ross and Pete Nice, the album had cost somewhere around its $200,000 budget to complete, including sample clearances and the video for "What A Nigga Know," which was never released. And now, for better or worse, Doom had it all tucked under his arm, on his way out of the Elektra Records doors.

"They were like, 'We'd rather you just keep the album,'" Doom says. "I would have changed the cover at the time, but I'm glad I didn't. The whole jewel of that album is based on the cover."

Clearly, the 1992 Ice-T and Body Count "Cop Killer" controversy had rattled Elektra, and they were willing to take a significant loss rather than put out the album. "This was all definitely tied in to the Body Count fiasco, and they gave Ice-T his masters back in that case, too," Ross explains. "Basically, I think Elektra knew that the [KMD] album wasn't going to be a huge hit, and they didn't want black people mad at them, in the community and at the company. So they figured they should just cut their losses."

"It wasn't just the cover," says Pete Nice. "And it was definitely a direct result of the 'Cop Killer' stuff, not anything else. I mean, the record was called *Black Bastards*, the single was 'What A Nigga Know.' Unfortunately, everything added up against them being on Elektra. And it wasn't Dante's fault at all, either, he did everything he could."

To make things official, Elektra released a statement which appeared in *The Source* magazine's "Weekly Word" newsletter on April 8, 1994. Attributed to "Bob Krasnow, chairman of Elektra Entertainment," it read, "The groundswell of reaction produced by the cover imagery of KMD's new album has exacerbated existing concern within Elektra, and the decision has been made that it was best that the record be taken in its intended form elsewhere."

And so, with another tragic occurrence under his belt within a year's time, Doom walked off into the sunset. "The album advances were sent out to a lot of people, they were out there," Ross says. "And the single had already been out. So lots of people in the industry had it, and liked it. But the final album never got pressed."

Despite now having the album under his control, things weren't looking anywhere near up for Doom. He was, of course, still reeling from his brother's death. And now he had a blacklisted album to try and sell to another label.

"It was a dead album, everybody was scared of it," Doom recalls. "We shopped it and everybody shot it down. Believe me, I would have wanted something to do with the business if the business wanted anything to do with me back then. It just seemed that, all of a sudden, motherfuckers didn't want to fuck with me anymore."

"As soon as we got the record back from Elektra, I immediately tried to get it on Sony," Pete Nice says. "Kurious was on the label, so I already had that connection. And they passed on it. That record just had a black mark on it after all the controversy. At that point, Doom kind of disappeared, which was understandable."

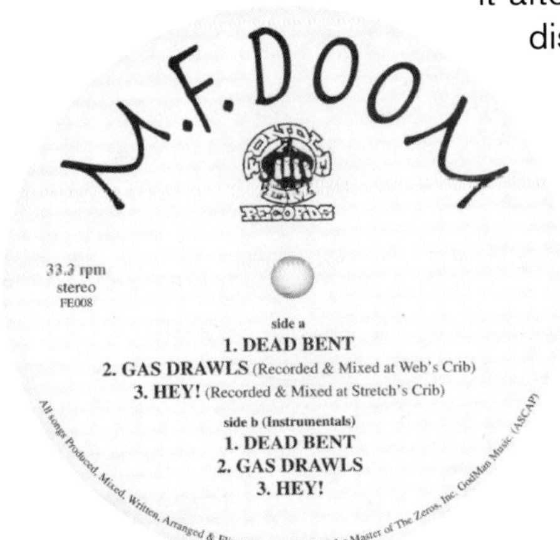

Doom faded from view for a couple years, moving from New York to Georgia. It was there that his MF Doom persona began to take shape, in private. By 1995, Doom's old friend Kurious suggested that he approach radio impresario, artist manager and journalist Bobbito Garcia to release some of the new, non-KMD material he had been building, on Garcia's ultra-indie label Fondle 'Em Records.

The first MF Doom single, "Dead Bent," [with "Gas Drawls" and "Hey!"] was one of Fondle 'Em's earliest releases, and garnered attention in the now-churning underground hip-hop scene emanating out of New York City. It bolstered Doom as he embraced a new era of music-making.

"I think Doom enjoyed putting out stuff the way we did it, with no politics or any of that," recalls Garcia. "No record sleeves, no CDs. Just put the record out and it will speak for itself."

As he continued to release intermittent singles on Fondle 'Em as MF Doom from 1996 until the end of the decade, the former Zev Love X decided that it would also be a good time to finally revisit *Black Bastards*. By 1999, he had released three KMD-related platters: the *Black Bastards Ruffs + Rares* EP [which included four album songs, plus the song "Popcorn"]; the "What A Nigga Know" / "Constipated Monkey" single; and "It Sounded Like a Roc," featuring the late Subroc on lead vocal.

Garcia says, "Once people were hearing the Doom stuff, he told me that he owned the masters to the KMD album 100%. So I was definitely down. He selected all the tracks he wanted to put on those singles, I wasn't involved with any of those decisions."

Black Bastards Sub Verse issue, 2001, CD booklet back.

Interestingly, Bobbito says that the KMD releases didn't sell as well as Doom's "Dead Bent" single, despite the fact that KMD had been a known, major label entity earlier in the decade. On the full-length releases front, Doom's non-KMD work also led the way: in 1999, he released *Operation Doomsday* [as MF Doom, also on Fondle 'Em] to much acclaim in the indie hip-hop world.

In 2000, Doom finally released the full KMD *Black Bastards* album, rejected artwork and all: first on the California-based

Readyrock label; and then a year later on his own Metal Face Records [via Sub Verse], with two extra tracks. The 2000s cover had been slightly modified from the 1994 version, but not in any significant way.

Black Bastards Sub Verse issue, 2001, CD booklet interior.

Doom describes those years in the late 1990s: "I went from real pain to being ultra-broke, and then back up." His new MF Doom persona was a rebirth for the rapper formerly known as Zev Love X: still witty and ultra-charismatic, but now with a choppier lyrical attack that was perhaps even more abstract than his previous incarnation. That and the fact that – although the world had seen him many times in videos and promo shots – he now wore a metal mask, seemingly 24/7, on-stage and off.

"The way things go is the way things are supposed to go," Doom says, looking back. "I try and go with the flow and see what's good with it. You can always find some things in any situation that are to your benefit."

And Doom says, looking back on those days with his dearly-departed brother Subroc: "*Black Bastards* was a dope album and it feels right that it finally came out, no matter how that happened. I look at it now and say, 'OK, I definitely see what we was trying to do.' I just wish more people would have seen the same thing back then."

"With that whole album, I was always impressed with the music they drew from to sample," says Rich Keller. "It was traditional, *real* music. It was deeper than a lot of their peers. Working on that album was like working with a great jazz band."

Pete Nice muses, "As it ended up, you really couldn't forecast a worse disaster for an artist or a group than what happened to KMD. If *Black Bastards* had come out in 1994, I think it would have been a huge underground classic. KMD always had the potential to hit the level of A Tribe Called Quest, they just never quite got there. They were still so young, even when *Black Bastards* hit, they had so much more to accomplish. I think the record would have definitely done Brand Nubian and Leaders of the New School numbers, which were more than acceptable to any label in that era."

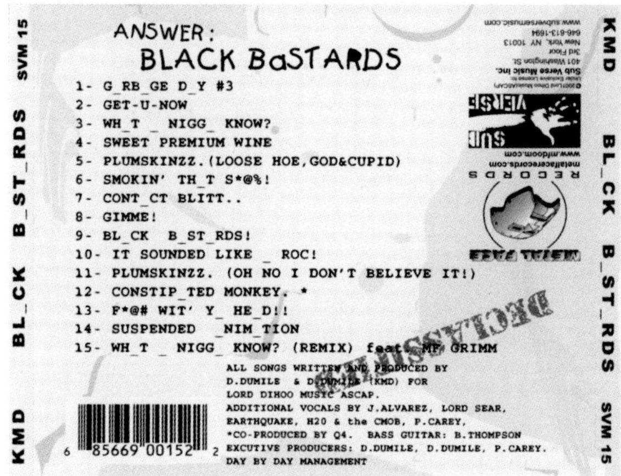

Black Bastards Sub Verse issue, 2001, back of CD.

"When I listen to *Black Bastards* today, I think it's amazing: insightful, expressive and just great," says Dante Ross. "It's very complicated, too, since the frustration of Doom's life is on that record. In a lot of ways, his innocence was gone. But it was the shining moment of KMD. Doom was a better rapper, the beats were 100 times better, the mixes were better. His vocals were so much tighter, he knew his pocket and his style was so much better. I just think that those guys had stepped up their game 100 percent. There was a good feeling about it with people who heard it when it was finished back then. I would say that, aside from Large Professor's record [*The LP,* recorded for Geffen in 1996, and not released until 2009], *Black Bastards* is probably the greatest lost hip-hop record of all time."

TRACKS

Garbage Day #3

MF DOOM / ZEV LOVE X: That's got all those movie samples on it. We really got that style from listening to the radio, especially WHBI 105.9, the World's Famous Supreme Team Show [from the early '80s]. Just Allah [aka Jazzy Just] the Superstar and Se'Divine the Mastermind were the DJs. They had a section of the show where they'd play beats and would put shit that sounded like Monty Python behind the records. Ever since we heard that, we would do a similar type of thing. That track was Subroc's idea, he put that whole thing together. It was movie pieces from the '60s and shit like that. They had a different style of speakin' in those days. Sub did the beat and all the vocal samples. He just happened to stay up all night one time and recorded most of those movie things used on there. It was like, "Watch cable all night, keep the DAT player recording, and catch all the illest lines." Then we stayed up all night the next night just cutting 'em up. The "It's not the three of us anymore" part on there is a reference to how Onyx wasn't on the album.

DANTE ROSS: We never cleared any of those movie snippets, or even that Jody Watley joint ["Looking For A New Love," sampled on the single "What A Nigga Know"] [laughs].

Get-U-Now

DOOM: That was me talkin' about if you was real, real broke, what extreme would you go to? How far would you go, with the heat? Robbing people, just to eat. It's a real extreme song, about how wild it can get.

PETE NICE: That and "Suspended Animation" are my two favorite tracks on the album. Those guys had a lot of pent-up anger, and it came out on a track like that.

What A Nigga [Niggy] Know?

ROSS: That was the first and only single off the album. There was a video, but that got pulled pretty quick. I don't remember it being stunning, but it was pretty cool. That's definitely one of my favorite tracks on the album. We [Elektra] didn't pull the single from retail once the album got dropped, we just stopped promoting it.

DOOM: That preacher type of thing at the beginning was Gylan Kain. Subroc was using his Dead Roach alias on his verse there. He used that alias a lot, but not really on any records. That was out before the Elektra shit happened, I think they had pressed about 20,000 copies. We even did a video for it. That was a filtered bassline, Sub was using that technique a lot. A lot of those were sampled notes, played in a certain order. We made a video for that song. It was real ill. I know I got a copy of it somewhere.

PETE: We had to change the title of the single to "Niggy," or that would have never made it out. That was the only single that we had figured out up until that point. I'm not sure what would have been next.

Sweet Premium Wine

PETE: A song like that would have definitely never been on *Mr. Hood*! They weren't drinking back during the first album.

DOOM: That's one of my two favorite tracks on the album, and that would have definitely been our second single, if we had ever gotten the chance. We already had it planned out. I was drinking a lot of Manischewitz wine back then. White Concord grape stuff. At the time, let me tell you, it was a stressful situation, and that's when niggas started drinking. It was a fun drinking time back then. But eventually, you slow down. When we was on the road, half of us would be drinkin', half of us would be against it. But that wine came in handy sometimes.

ROSS: I'd always have these bottles of wine in my office and Doom would just come in and drink them. I didn't even drink wine, so I didn't care.

Plumskinzz (Loose Hoe, God & Cupid)

DOOM: If you listen to the end of that version, there's a recording of a girl, and she's sayin', "You're so Goddamn stupid!" So I picked words [for my verse] that made sense, but still rhymed with what she said. "Loose Hoe" was a reference to her. God, that's me. And Cupid came in between and got me fuckin' with a loose type of woman. "Peachfuzz" [from *Mr. Hood*] was about how girls see the guys, and "Plumskinzz" was more about how we see them. Like fruits, like succulent plums, all rounded when they get ripe.

ROSS: That was the first demo I heard from them off *Black Bastards*. I think they wanted to play me the song they thought was a hit. Eric B. & Rakim used that same loop later on, for "Know The Ledge." Nice of them to take a song that never came out! That's a Pharoah Sanders loop.

Smokin' That Shit [featuring Kurious, Earthquake and Lord Sear]

BOBBITO GARCIA: We used to play that song on my show ["The Stretch & Bobbito Show," on WKCR], because it had Kurious and Sear on it and those were my boys, too. That song is hilarious. I love Sear's banter at the end.

ROSS: Lord Sear was a little less crazy back then, but he was still as funny. Jorge [Kurious] was the leader of the gang they all hung with, with Zev [Doom]. Grimm was the more street dude, and he led Doom down that road a bit. Those guys were all very heavily into psychedelic drugs, and ... I dunno, some of that shit might have contributed to Sub's death. Sub had a bad acid trip a few months before he died, and was pretty spaced out at that time.

DOOM: That was Earthquake and them on that. I don't know what happened to that dude. Quake was from Freeport, Long Island. We tried to do for Quake what Serch did for us. I met Lord Sear uptown, through Kurious. Sear was Kurious' DJ.

PETE: They were always hanging out with [Kurious] Jorge during that era, they were very close. And Cage, too, they spent a lot of time together. Especially Subroc. Earthquake was another kid from Long Island in the crew. Jorge was definitely the leader of the Constipated Monkeys, he was a big influence on those guys. He and Doom were always together.

Contact Blitt

DOOM: That was a totally true story. We was on tour, in Cali. The album is kind of our initiation into manhood. "Sweet Premium Wine" was when we was just starting to drink. "Blitt" is when we first started to get introduced to smokin' weed.

Gimme!

DOOM: I think that's my favorite track, that's my shit. Some Subroc solo shit.

Black Bastards

[Author's Note: Originally titled "Black Bastards and Bitches," on the advance cassette]

DOOM: More or less, that was about identity, and how people have problems with whether they're black or they're white. There's always a black or white issue. That song is about the whole color thing and about how it's not such a big deal. It really don't make no difference. It was also about how a lot of white MCs were coming out of the blue at the time. Like, "Now you're on TV so you can rhyme, all of a sudden!" There was this guy Parker Lewis, I talk about him on there. That was a true story, it happened at Ed Lover's birthday party. He was so wack, I had to put it in there [Doom continues to go off on him for a while...]. At the party, they applauded him because he was on TV. We take this game for real, though. Cats eat off this game.

ROSS: That was a really great song.

It Sounded Like A Roc

DOOM: Between that and Subroc's thing on "Gimme!," I don't know which one is iller. They're both so well-written. That's some solid shit, it could come out today and still be dope. Sub started coming with his MC shit around the time of the first album. He had a solo joint on there called "The Mission" ["Subroc's Mission"] that was retarded.

PETE: That was Subroc's solo joint. They both did the music.

ROSS: Sub did most of that one. That song is definitely sentimental to me.

Plumskinzz (Oh No I Don't Believe It!)

ROSS: When I heard that, I knew those guys were onto something. Although I thought the first version that was on the album ["Plumskinzz (Loose Hoe, God & Cupid)"] was better.

Constipated Monkey [co-produced by Q4]

ROSS: Q4 was their man from Long Island.

DOOM: That's the last song I laid down vocals for on the album, after Subroc was killed. My other brother Dim is two years younger than Sub [therefore four years younger than Doom], he found the drums for that song. For years he'd say, "You know I found those drums, you gotta give me co-production credit!" That "constipated monkey" sample was another one off the [Gylan Kain] *Blue Guerrilla* album. Constipated Monkey was our crew. It was a vast crew, but we always stuck together. All the drums on the album are sampled or programmed, but if they're programmed, it's to mimic the sound of real drums. The only live instrumentation on the album was on that song, my cousin Brian [Thompson] played the bassline.

Fuck Wit' Ya Head!! [featuring Hard 2 Obtain]

DOOM: That was with H2O [Hard 2 Obtain] and CMOB, they were my boys from Long Island. They had an album out, I forget the label [Atlantic Records, 1994, with several songs produced by Dante Ross' Stimulated Dummies crew]. That song was to show how versatile we were, beat-wise and lyrically. That T La Rock "It's Yours" sample was the basis for the song, because it was true. Some musical rhythms *can* fuck with your head. Different sounds affect the body in different ways.

Suspended Animation

PETE: That was my shit back then, because it was Subroc's first full effort at rhyming on a track. The atmosphere on that song is just so surreal. I still remember being at Subroc's wake with the album playing, and that song really moved me more than anything else.

DOOM: That poem was another Kain sample. I used to listen to that album so much, for real. I was trying to figure out what he meant: "Casting shadows over the sun." If you're higher than the sun, you're *real* high. So I made it all about trees.

What A Nigga Know? (Remix) [featuring MF Grimm]

ROSS: I think Doom did that because he just wanted Grimm on a song, to change it up. Grimm started fuckin' with them between the first and second albums.

DOOM: That remix was done after the rest of the album was recorded, but before I mastered the album. The day after we did that song, Grimm got shot up [and was paralyzed]. He was standing up when he did that track, and the next day he got shot. A friend of mine, Jay, who was at that session, he got killed that same day. We released that as the B-side of the original single.

BONUS / EXTRA SONGS

Q3 113

[B-side, with slightly different title, on Elektra's "What A Niggy Know" single from 1994; not on 2000 ReadyRock album; Originally listed as "Untitled" on 2001 Metal Face / Sub Verse CD]

DOOM: That was actually called "Q3 119." *[Author's note: The 2001 version of the album lists this song as "Q3 113" although the 1994 song title on the "What A Niggy Know" single lists it as "Q3 119"].* That was another one of Subroc's names, his aliases, and that's some of his freestyle solo shit. I don't know what that means, he named it. I never got a chance to ask him...

Popcorn

[from Fondle 'Em *Black Bastards Ruffs + Rares EP*, not on other versions of *Black Bastards*]

DOOM: That was a *Mr. Hood*-style track, but it was done after the album was out. And then it was too early for *Black Bastards*, so it didn't make it there. It was kind of in between.

KOOL G RAP & D.J. POLO

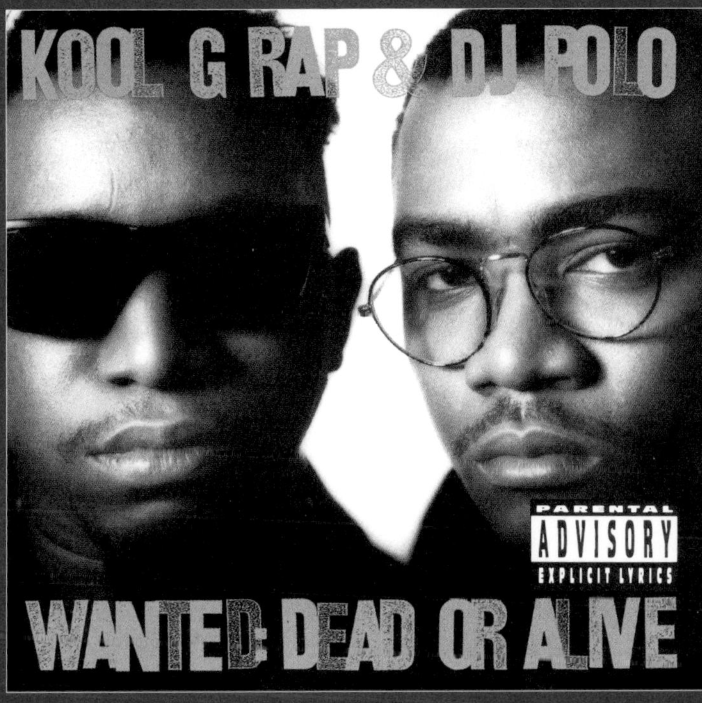

Wanted: Dead Or Alive
Cold Chillin' / Warner Bros., 1990

"I was always a day-dreamer kind of person, and ever since I was young I had a knack for writing," says one of the illest MCs of all time: Queens-born Kool G Rap [Nathaniel Wilson]. "I used to write little short stories, like three-page novels, when I was in sixth and seventh grade. Little horror stories and shit like that. So when I started getting 100 percent into rap music, I just brought that with me."

Known for his vivid storytelling about street life, cautionary jail tales, and gangsta flossing – which were perfected years before his lyrical sons Nas, Mobb Deep and the Wu-Tang Clan hit – he brought a sharp, hard edge to the rap game in the late '80s, one that still scares kids straight today.

Kool G was born in Jamaica, Queens and raised in Flushing and Corona. He explains, "I repped Corona, although a lot of people thought I was from Queensbridge, because I was down with the Juice Crew."

Always possessing lyrical skills, he linked up with fellow Queens resident Eric B. [Barrier] around 1985, and in turn met Eric's mutual friend and G's future musical partner, D.J. Polo [Thomas Pough]. "I knew of Polo ever since I was a kid, because we was from the same 'hood," G Rap says. "He was the DJ that used to do jams out in the park. And Polo knew of me, too, because I was a known rapper in Corona."

G describes his early style and influences: "I was most influenced by Melle Mel, but also Kool Moe Dee and a rapper named Silver Fox from the Fantasy Three [the latter group was known for their 1983 single "Biters In The City," on C.C.L. Records]. My earliest stuff was definitely more on the brag side."

D.J. Polo is a Corona, Queens diehard, born-and-raised. He was a DJ from a young age, and before his mid-teens had a solid deck rep in a neighborhood full of DJs [LL Cool J's DJ, Cut Creator, lived around the corner]. "I always DJed and I listened to all kinds of music," he explains. "And every time I got any money, I would put it towards new equipment. I was doing stuff in the parks and I was even DJing at a strip club at the age of 13. They had to build me a special booth. In my family, music was always around. Basically, by 1984 and '85, I was established."

Polo also grew up with another legendary DJ and producer: Marley Marl [Marlon

Kool G Rap contact sheet. Photos © B+, for www.Mochilla.com.

Williams]. In fact, the two went to high school together. "We was in the same 600 school *[Author's note: A "600 school" in New York is one for children with behavioral problems, among other issues]*," Polo says. "PS 4 in Queens. It was a bad school, where people think that since you got kicked out of class by teachers that you was gonna be nothin'. They had already counted us out. There were a lot of Spofford kids in there [the infamous juvenile detention center based in the Bronx's Hunts Point]."

But Polo and Marley were not without hope. Music bonded them and would lead to future successes for both men. Polo remembers, "We used to cut out of school, go to [electronics store] Sam Ash and play with the turntables."

Polo met aspiring hip-hop DJ Eric B. during this same time, in the mid-'80s, when Eric was dating Polo's niece. "I brought Eric into the game, and he used to even live with me," he says. "Then he started living at Marley's after that." Even though Marley's and Polo's future home, Cold Chillin' Records, had yet to be launched, Marley was on New York's WBLS by 1985, scratching for Mr. Magic's "Rap Attack" show. He had also started producing records, for the Pop Art label out of Philadelphia and Nia Records out of New York, for artists like Roxanne Shante, MC Shan and MC Craig G.

Forging a similar path as his friend, Polo put out a one-off single in early 1986 under the group name The Terminators, on the Snowflake label. The song was produced by Marley. The A-side was "Forever Dis," an attack on Run-DMC; the B-side was a Polo tribute, simply entitled "Polo." His MC was a local rapper named Frosty.

"I had a white Benz at the time, and then Jam Master Jay [who was, of course, also from Queens] got one," Polo recalls. "We saw him one day and we waved out to him, but he ignored us. So we figured we'd do a Run-DMC dis. I mean, fuck them. The B-side was about me. It wasn't a huge single, but people knew about it." *[Author's note: "Forever Dis" lists a sole writing credit to Shawn Moltke, better known as M.C. Shan].*

The Polo / Frost partnership wasn't long-lived, and by mid-1986 the DJ was on the lookout for another MC. Luckily, one was right around the corner. "I met G Rap at a place called the Elmcor in Corona," Polo says. "Eric B. was there and he said, 'Polo, you're looking for a rapper, right?' And I was, so Eric introduced us. At first I thought his name was 'Gucci Rap.' That would have been dope, Polo and Gucci! [laughs]."

"Elmcor is a spot that everybody in Corona knows *[Author's note: The full current name is Elmcor Youth & Adult Activities, Inc.]*," explains G Rap. "It was actually a rehabilitation center, a lot of people needed it as a result of the heroin epidemic in the '70s. There were a lot of addicts in Corona and that was like a methadone clinic. But there was a gated section right outside the building and they used to have events there. We used to call them 'jams,' before hip-hop was even in clubs. I was probably 16 [in 1984] when I first got on the mic at one of those."

"I met Polo there, and then right away I met Marley Marl through him, so a lot of things happened pretty quickly," G continues. "I think that if we didn't record our first song the next day, it was definitely within three days [of him meeting Polo]. The first time I met Marley, we started tracking stuff at his apartment in Queensbridge that night. It wasn't even supposed to be a real song or single, it was called 'It's A Demo' because that's what it was [laughs]. But they liked it so much that they wanted to put it out."

"That song was about us, as a crew," Polo explains. "Not one guy or the other guy. I had the music already, and right after I met him at Elmcor, G Rap came to my house. I think he put those rhymes together in less than 30 minutes. When we went to companies to shop it, we didn't have a name for the song, so that's why we called it that." He says that they recorded their 1987 single "Rikers Island" [which would appear on *Wanted:*

Dead or Alive in 1990 instead of 1989's *Road To The Riches*, for some reason] during that same first session with Marley Marl.

"It's A Demo," which had indeed been recorded in Marley Marl's living room, was released as a single later in 1986 on the recently-minted independent Cold Chillin' label [it was Cold Chillin''s second release, after M.C. Shan's "Jane, Stop This Crazy Thing"].

As Polo notes, their first two singles differed from future releases in how the duo's name was presented. Initially it was listed as "D.J. Polo & Kool G. Rap." He says, "I never wanted an MC to get on and then cut his DJ out. I saw how LL did that with his original DJ [Cut Creator, who was replaced by the West Coast-based DJ Bobcat in 1987 on Def Jam's *Bigger And Deffer*]. I was smarter than that."

Polo gave the same advice to his friend Eric B. for *his* debut in 1986 with a then-unknown rapper. The group listing for the single "Eric B. Is President" and "My Melody" read: "Eric B. featuring Rakim." Eric B kept his front billing on future releases, whereas Kool G had moved to the front by their third single, 1988's "Poison."

Polo says that after they did that first session, a bond of friendship was formed quickly. "Me and G Rap started hanging out and doing shows together right away," he remembers. "It was just on after that." And, G Rap says of the Marley Marl connection: "I was fun working with Marley, he was just a real cool cat. And he was really good at what he did. He made us sound great."

"It's A Demo" [and the B-side, "I'm Fly"] was a hit on New York radio and the duo was off and running, in a whirlwind of funky hip-hop lyricism. Next came 1987's powerful "Rikers Island" and by 1989 they had released a Marley Marl-produced full-length, *Road To The Riches* (on Cold Chillin', of course).

"I wouldn't change anything about that first record, not for the time when it came out," says G Rap, looking back. "I did that album from my heart and that was the kind of music that I was feeling at the time." He thinks that the album moved in the neighborhood of 300,000 units, which was more than respectable for an indie hip-hop platter in the late '80s.

G Rap also explains his lyrical process in those early years: "I never really thought about concepts too much, and never thought mechanically about songs. I would just wait for an idea or thought to hit me, and then the lyrics would flow naturally."

Looking back on *Road To The Riches*, D.J. Polo says: "I love that record, we were really on a roll back then. We was makin' a lot of money, and doing a whole lot of crazy shit. We were just glad to be making music. Cold Chillin' was jerkin' us like dogs, but we enjoyed doing what we was doing."

By the time they approached their sophomore effort, G Rap and Polo had started moving away from the Marley Marl production umbrella. But, G Rap explains, it wasn't in bad blood. "I think people just started growing," he says. "I always had a knack for production, so Marley never had to do everything for me anyways. I knew what music I wanted to rap on, I just didn't know how to work all the equipment. I would come into Marley's studio with the records and I would tell him what I wanted. [Big Daddy] Kane and Biz Markie did the same thing. The cats [from the Juice Crew] that Marley really produced from scratch was MC Shan and [Roxanne] Shanté. Everybody else pretty much had an idea about what they wanted to do."

Warner Bros. trade magazine ad from 1988, touting Cold Chillin' Records and Ice-T (who was on Sire Records).

Marley's friend and school-days running partner Polo agrees. "It's not like Marley did everything for us," he says. "We brought him our records and gave our ideas, and he put it in his drum machine. It's not like we couldn't do that with no one else."

There was another, more practical reason for thinking about using another producer: time. "Marley at that time was doing stuff with a *lot* of other people," Polo explains. "He was really busy. We wanted to get into the studio when we wanted to get in there, and we also wanted to start making our own money as producers. I think Marley was a little upset about it, but we had to do what we had to do."

Aside from switching producers, there was an occurrence that happened between albums that was about as dramatic as any one person or group can live through: in mid-1989, Kool G Rap was hospitalized for several months.

"I had a severe case of Sinusitis," G Rap says today, with a calmness that belies how serious his condition was at the time. "Going back to my youth, I always had issues with my sinuses. And then later on I wasn't makin' it no better by sniffin' coke and stuff like that. But my surgeons said that the coke wasn't what caused it. It was an infection, and when you don't address it over a long period of time, it just gets worse and worse."

"The more money we got, the stronger the cocaine that we could afford was getting," Polo says. "It was closer to pure, and it could fuck you up a lot more."

It got worse and worse to the point where G Rap was rushed to a New Jersey hospital one night by his girlfriend, and had to have a Craniotomy. "I told my mom, 'I don't care if they cut my fuckin' head *off*.' That's how bad the pain was," G recalls. "I didn't care about dying, I just wanted the pain to stop. So they opened up my head and had to clean everything out, then they put my skull back in place. It was crazy. I almost died. They said that if I had went to sleep that night, I probably wouldn't have woken up the next day."

The recovery from this very serious surgical procedure took several months. "I lost coordination in my left side, and I write with my left hand," G says. "I had to learn to write and tie my shoes all over again. I still recovered pretty quick, even though when I first arrived the doctors said I had less than a 50% chance to survive. At first, I was definitely concerned about whether it was going to affect my ability to write and rhyme." As *Wanted: Dead Or Alive* proves, his concerns must have quickly melted away once they got to the studio.

"That was really scary, it was crazy," Polo says. "They cracked open his skull and afterwards his head got huge on one side. He looked like Mr. Met [the New York Mets mascot]. But I was really happy he made it through. We all came and visited him at the hospital whenever we could – me, Kane, Marley and a bunch of other people."

G Rap adds, able to laugh about it more than two decades later, "I used to tell people that they put a microchip in my brain."

As they prepared to enter the studio for their second album, the group's approach was a slightly new one. Polo was active during 1988 and 1989, but not always with group activities. "I was DJing in clubs and parties a lot back then, I didn't produce as much," he explains. "I was making other money and getting caught up in that [see song comments for 'Money In The Bank' for more about the 'other money' Polo was making]. I was bringing my expertise as a DJ rocking parties to the table in the studio. I knew what people wanted in the club."

"I was young when we recorded that first record *[Author's note: He was 20 or 21 in 1989]* and the hip-hop game was young at that time, too," reflects G Rap. "I didn't know as much about what direction to go with, what to make for a single. I was basically just going from my heart. But with the second album, I was more conscious of what kinds of songs to do and all that. It was still from the heart, but in 1990 I really saw who G Rap was to the public, and to myself."

Enlisting a very young Queens producer named Large Professor [William Paul Mitchell], who was signed to Eric B.'s Lynn Star production company at the time, Kool G set off into another rhyme chapter. This new look displayed an even harder street edge and an even more vivid and developed style of storytelling. "I wanted to come across a little more gangsta, that was the main thing," he explains. "And Large Professor just had such a new sound to me. It was inspiring."

"I met Large Professor through Eric B," he adds. "Large was just a young, hot producer. After we did a few tracks together and they were what we were looking for, I didn't see any reason to stop. It was incredible watching him at work in the studio, he would work *so* fast. He'd press buttons and move shit on the SP-1200 [sampler] so fast that it was crazy. He was like a secretary on a typewriter." Large Pro was only 17 years old at the time.

Despite lead production claims on six tracks credited to Eric B., alongside a litany of other production and co-production listings including Kool G, D.J. Polo, Anton *[Author's note: His last name was Pukshansky, although for some reason this isn't listed anywhere on the album, he is merely "Anton"]* and Large Professor, Kool G Rap says: "There was really just one producer on that record – Large Professor. Eric B. would come by the studio to hear how everything was coming along and would just be amazed. But Large Pro was there in the studio every day, not Eric. He really did the whole album, he was just working under Eric B.'s production company." *[Author's note: Large Professor declined to be interviewed for this chapter].*

"To be honest, I didn't give Eric B. any production credit on the album, so I don't know why it says he produced anything," says G Rap. "I didn't even know that Large Pro was under Eric's production company. I told the label, 'Produced by Large Professor' and

I remember Eric B. saw that and got upset."

"Large Pro had beats and he was trying to get on, so we sat there with him and worked things out," recalls Polo. "Large was hungry and he had a different sound from Marley, definitely. And right then, we needed a different sound. I produced two tracks ["Jive Talk" and "Polo Club," both co-productions with Anton Pukshansky]; Biz did one ["Erase Racism"]; and Large Pro did pretty much everything else. Eric B. didn't have shit to do with the production."

One final piece of the *Wanted: Dead Or Alive* puzzle was a "stunt DJ" who entered the mix during the sessions: Dr. Butcher [Andrew Venable]. It's a lesser-known fact, since he was left off the album's credits, but a majority of the scratches on the album were actually done by Butcher. "I brought Butcher in and made him an affiliate of ours," G says. "It wasn't a mutual agreement or anything with me and Polo. Butcher was a cut-master and he did pretty much all the scratches, except for 'Polo Club,' I think."

G Rap adds, "I think Butcher did a great job on the album. I was actually hanging out with Butcher more than Polo at that time. He was just nice with cuts and scratches, and I wanted that element affiliated with what I was doing. It was important to me, even if there weren't cuts on every track *[Author's note: There are only cuts on six out of the album's 13 tracks]*. We didn't need cuts just to have them. Only where they were needed. And Polo didn't have the same skill level with that kind of stuff. Polo never expressed to me that he was mad about having Butcher in the mix."

DJ Dr. Butcher was born in Brooklyn, but landed in Corona, Queens around age eight and was raised there through his 20s. He lived within a block or two of both Cut Creator and D.J. Polo, and was hanging out with LL Cool J and his posse via Cut Creator when James Todd Smith was first blowing up, in 1985. He met Kool G around this time and even introduced the rapper-on-the-rise to LL. Interestingly, early on, Butcher was known much more in Corona as an MC [calling himself Drew Ski]. As another side note, he almost became Polo's first MC in 1986, instead of Frosty. So, he had known both men for a many years by the time they were all in the studio together.

By 1989, Butcher was a sophomore in college and had become a technically impressive DJ. A female friend of his was dating G Rap and suggested that he check out Butcher on the wheels of steel [keep in mind that, up until that point, G Rap had only known Butcher as a rapper]. Kool G had always wanted a DJ named Dr. Butcher [as proven by G's 1988 song "Butcher Shop," from the "Colors" movie soundtrack, with cuts by Marley Marl instead of Polo] and so he gave Venable that name.

Dr. Butcher says, regarding coming into the fold for *Wanted: Dead Or Alive*: "G Rap was like, 'I'm the illest rapper, and I want a crazy DJ behind me.' So he brought me along. I never heard Polo say anything about *not* wanting me there, so I was under the impression that he was OK with it."

Butcher adds that he definitely did scratches on the following album tracks [the only possible exceptions being "Play It Again, Polo" and "The Polo Club"]: "Talk Like Sex"; "Kool Is Back"; "Play It Kool"; and "Death Wish." He also appears on the remix of the song "Wanted: Dead Or Alive," which appeared on the B-side of the "Erase Racism" single. That remix is the only song where Butcher's name appears anywhere pertaining to *Wanted: Dead Or Alive*.

"Butcher was a good DJ and could do all the fancy tricks," says Polo. "Different DJs do different things, just like different rappers do different things. I never worried that Butcher was going to replace me or anything. I mean, I brought G Rap in, and my thing was always that DJs had to be an important part of the group. I liked Butcher, he lived across the street from me in Corona. He was a part of what we were doing at the time and there were times when I wasn't there in the studio, so he would get on and do his thing. He was eager and looking to get on, so he was ready to do scratches for $10, or free, or whatever. He even did some live shows with us, he'd do tricks there, too."

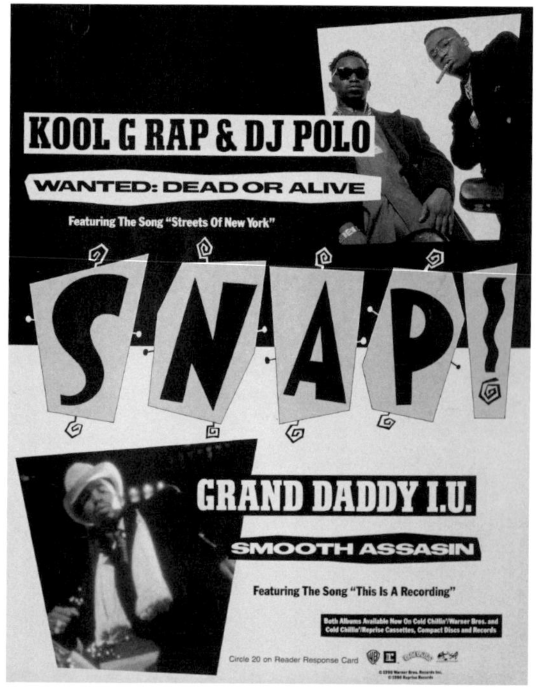

Wanted: Dead Or Alive album ad, with Cold Chillin' label-mate Grand Daddy I.U., 1990.

Courtesy of the Adler Hip-Hop Archives / Cornell University Hip-Hop Collection.

The album was recorded at Power Play Studios in Long Island City, Queens, over a period of three or four months, from – according to Butcher – around November 1989 to the spring of 1990. Polo explains, "It wasn't quick, we went through a lot of shit and a lot of ideas."

Besides scratching duties on selected tracks, Butcher says that he also helped dig through records and find pieces that they could potentially use for beats and samples. "I was there for probably 80 or 85 percent of the sessions," he recalls. "I would bring my records or I would go through Large Professor's records to find stuff and show him."

Another interesting duty of Butcher's was to act as a de facto chauffeur for Large Pro. He says, with a laugh, "I would basically drive him right from the studio to his high school in the morning, after our all-night sessions would get done. And then we'd be back at the studio that same night. I'm not sure when he slept. It was just amazing to watch Large work back then. He didn't even have his own equipment back then. He was basically learning as he was producing that album."

Even though the group's second album had little or nothing to do with their former musical partner Marley Marl, they were still reaping rewards being part of the Cold Chillin' universe. "Being with Cold Chillin' and the Juice Crew back then meant that we was at the top of the list in the rap game," says G Rap. "Def Jam was doin' their thing, too, and were maybe even bigger. But the streets belonged to the Juice Crew. Def Jam was more commercial. The Juice Crew was the first Wu-Tang, we were from the streets."

Wanted: Dead Or Alive, cassette interior.

The album, which hit in the fall of 1990, had three very different singles, which all showed a different aspect of *Wanted: Dead Or Alive*'s range: "Streets Of New York"; "Erase Racism"; and "Bad To The Bone." G Rap says he believes that sales were in the neighborhood of 200,000 units.

Regarding the serious-looking cover, with both men ice-grilling their audience, Polo explains: "If you're in the crew, we joke around all day. But if we don't know you, we don't play. That was our look for strangers."

Dr. Butcher has a lot of great memories of being around the *Wanted: Dead Or Alive* sessions. "Early on, everybody knew that Large Professor was going to be the guy to produce that record," he remembers. "It was just a great connection, and those sessions were really fun to be in. I think that's why the album has the feel that it does. Plus, when G Rap went into the hospital, we didn't know if he would ever be the same again. I mean, he was paralyzed on his left side for months. But he proved that he hadn't lost anything, and he actually sounded even better. That's what 'Kool Is Back' is all about to me. He was still here and stronger than ever."

Polo sums up the album succinctly: "G Rap was able to really be himself on that album. And he was really stretching out."

And Kool G says, in closing, "That one is very high up on my own favorites list. It is just monumental, which is not to take anything away from our first album. But *Wanted* had 'Talk Like Sex.' No one had ever done a song like that before, in hip-hop or anywhere else. Right from the gate, I always wanted to be considered the best, or one of the best. *Wanted: Dead Or Alive* really solidified me in the game, and let people know that I was here. It made me a force to be reckoned with."

TRACKS

Streets Of New York

KOOL G RAP: That was the first single and it's definitely my favorite song on the album. That record carried a lot of emotion. That was my version of Marvin Gaye's "What's Going On" [laughs]. It was pretty big right away because, at that time, people was definitely lookin' out for G Rap. It was my biggest hit during that era, it was big everywhere, on the rap charts and all that. Large Professor made the beat right in front of my eyes, he came up with a loop and we just started adding to it from there. I had that rhyme already, before I heard the track, and I said it to Large Pro and he made the track, customized to my words. I mean, how perfect was that? There's live piano on there, that was this guy Anton [Pukshansky], he was the engineer at Power Play, and we found out that he could play the fuck out of the keyboard. He had a lot of participation and input in the album, because he was our main engineer. When we first did that song, I was blown away by it, honestly.

D.J. POLO: That was the biggest song on the album, definitely, and that didn't surprise us at all. I knew it was a hit when we was playin' it live. That's all real shit on there [musically], no samples. Anton, the engineer, played keyboards on there. I don't know what happened to him. We gave him a shot and he was great. That was a different song for us, we reached deep for it. "Jive Talk" had a similar kind of groove. We weren't trying to do what we had done on the last album the second time around.

Wanted: Dead Or Alive

G RAP: With all my lyrics on there, that was just what I had seen growing up. I'd been through it and I was still livin' in it. Even back in 1990, I was still pretty much in the streets, I just wasn't doing the same things as before I had started making records. I'd say that the best thing I ever got from the streets was street smarts and just an instinct for survival. The streets definitely make you a survivor.

Money In The Bank [featuring Freddie Foxxx, Large Professor and Ant Live]

POLO: I go way back with Freddie [laughs]. I knew Freddie since the pimp days. Freddie had like ... [pauses] ... six girls [prostitutes] back in the day. I had 15. This was all real stuff we was talkin' about. We was for real. Ice-T talked about how he was this and that, but we was for reeeeeallll. Large Pro rhymed on there. Both Freddie and Large Pro were good, but they weren't ready for G Rap. They still had more practicing to do [laughs]. They were our people, we wanted them on there. Eric B.'s brother, Ant Live, is on there, too.

G RAP: Yeah, that's Freddie Foxxx on there. That was the crew back then: me, Eric B., Freddie Foxxx, Rakim. We all hung out together. That was the first track I ever did with Freddie, he was still coming up at that point.

Bad To The Bone

POLO: We were definitely living the life back in that era. We bought gold because nobody else could really mess with it. Truth be told, we had rope chains before Run-DMC and them, no doubt. We bought gold because it showed that we're here. The ones we was wearing at the time was going for about $8,000. We went to Jamaica Ave. [in Queens] to get some pieces and I think G bought a gold Jesus for like $2,500. I was looking for a horse, something different. If someone ever robbed me or I got killed, I'ma make sure people would know that's my fuckin' piece. I paid $7,000 for an Isis bracelet, like the one Wonder Woman used to have, with POLO in diamonds. People knew that was mine! I had a horseshoe that was a necklace and I made it into a ring [laughs], just to show people. Road to the riches, man!

G RAP: That was another single from the album, talking about some gangsta lifestyle stuff. I was pretty flashy back then – gold chains, gold teeth. I was even wearing diamonds back then.

Talk Like Sex

G RAP: I don't think that was ever a real single from the album, because of the [explicit] content. But it was still definitely popular. It says on the album that I produced it alone, but that was all Large Professor, just like the rest of the album. Nothing really made me do that song, particularly, I just wanted to do a song about... [pauses] fucking. I got in much more trouble for "Truly Yours" [from *Road To The Riches*] because I mentioned homosexuals on that one, and because that was being pushed as a single more than "Talk Like Sex" was. When we did that live we had blow-up dolls and all that on stage [laughs].

POLO: It was definitely all about girls with us back then, no doubt. G Rap was just talking about how he crushed girls on that one. When we did it live, we'd bring sex dolls out. We did some fundraiser for BET [laughs like an evil genius] and brought those on-stage, with the mouths open [laughs]. Guys were pumpin' on 'em [laughs]. At a fundraiser. We did it on purpose, so that people would talk about it. I didn't realize that there were no cuts on the previous songs on the album [in the album's sequence]. After a while I wasn't trying to cut on every track. I wasn't just a DJ, I was part of the group. People ask me why I don't do all the fancy tricks and I'm like, "Nigga, I ain't no trained monkey! I'm cool already, I don't need to dance around the turntables for you to know who I am. I'm the man behind G Rap!"

Play It Again, Polo

POLO: I don't think I got my full due as a DJ back then, or now, but I don't give a fuck. People didn't put me here, I'm here because this is what I love to do. My mom taught me this: we might not have had the money to wear the expensive sneakers, but I was cool like a muthafucka in the cheap sneakers. I never stayed home all day and learned how to slice records and do tricks. If I do a party and slice and keep cuttin', nobody can dance.

G RAP: I think D.J. Polo got his props as part of the impact that we had. Just for that reason alone his name got out there. He never got props for being one of the illest DJs out there, because he wasn't. He was never a Jazzy Jeff or DJ Cash Money type of skills guy. Those vocals on that track are pretty damn fast – I could never do something like that in one take! I had to do some punch-ins, definitely. I mean, there was no breathin' space [laughs].

Erase Racism [featuring Big Daddy Kane and Biz Markie]

G RAP: Biz Markie might have produced that one. I don't think that people expected me to do a track like that at all, but I was doing a lot of things from my heart, just like when I was rapping about the streets without making them animated. Not like how rappers do it today, they talk about that stuff because everybody else does. That track came from the heart because a young boy, Yusuf Hawkins, had got killed in Brooklyn [in August of 1989] and I was upset about it. That was a way for me to express why I was upset.

POLO: One day we was in the city, coming out of our record label and I think we had a check for like $50,000. We went to the bank and cashed it, and had the money on us. Then we tried to get a cab. We'd never drive to Manhattan because police would always fuck with us. I actually had to ride around with my album cover in the car, to show police. So, we tried to get a cab, and none of them would stop for us, they'd keep going by. Then a cab went past us and picked up a white lady ahead of us. So we kicked the fuck out of the back of the cab. We wanted to do a song about how shit like that happens all the time. Yusuf Hawkins' death was also around that time, and that shit affected us.

Kool Is Back

G RAP: Butcher killed the cuts on that track. I love that song, it was just rhyming, it's one long fuckin' verse through the whole song. That is just one of my all-time "prove a point" songs, along with "Men At Work" [from *Road To The Riches*]. Songs that show your lyrical capabilities, like [Big Daddy] Kane's "Raw"; "Lyrics Of Fury" for Rakim; and "My Philosophy" for KRS-One. For a song like that, we weren't thinking about song structure or any of that shit. With our earlier albums, we didn't ever think about choruses or jingles on our songs.

DR. BUTCHER: That was the first song I did scratches on. G Rap brought me in to show Eric B. what I could do. When I walked in, they had that song on, and I just started scratching to it, and going crazy. Eric didn't act too impressed, but then they used my scratches on the album.

Play It Kool

BUTCHER: I definitely did scratches on that song.

Jive Talk

POLO: That was one of the two songs on the album I produced *[Author's note: The album lists D.J. Polo and Anton as the song's producers]*. I love that song. You know why it's called "Jive Talk"? It's like when you're a kid... my mother, my father and my uncles, all sittin' around, playing jazz and talkin' shit. It's a loose song, I copied that vibe in my mind. In the middle of the song I just started playing drumsticks on the mixing board. I just wanted to do that. After that part of the song, we EQed G Rap's vocals different. We did that on purpose. It's "Jive Talk"! There's no cuts on that one either. Anton EQed and mixed that one down. G Rap wasn't even gonna rhyme on it, but I asked him to do some stuff.

BUTCHER: That's actually me rhyming at the end of that track. We were just bored one night and started acting stupid. Those were old rhymes, I was actually surprised they kept my stuff on there. I didn't get any credit, of course. Large Pro was tapping on the floor with the drumsticks for that weird sound you hear.

The Polo Club

POLO: I still get so many people who run up on me about that song! It was a hip-hop club song. I DJed in clubs, but I didn't just play hip-hop. I would do gigs on the side when we wasn't on tour. Back then my go-to song was "Set It Off" by Strafe [from 1984, on Jus Born Records]. People lose they mind when you put that on in a club! When you know what you're doing, you can make a mix sound better than the original songs. We got Spanish heads and dance heads who liked Kool G Rap & Polo because of that song.

G RAP: That track [which features a "hip-house" beat] wasn't my idea! [laughs]. That was Polo's. He liked house music and I didn't. I liked raw, hardcore hip-hop. That's why that one is at the end: it's his own record, by himself.

BUTCHER: That was the last song we did. I remember G Rap saying he didn't even want it on the album. I think I tried to figure out cuts on it, but what I was doing wasn't really fitting. I know I did scratches on it, but I'm not sure if they are on the final version.

Rikers Island *[on CD and cassette versions of the album, not on original vinyl]*

G RAP: That was an old track that wasn't on the first album, so they just tacked it on, I guess. Marley Marl produced that one. I was never in jail, but I learned all that shit being around so many people who had been. I used to hear a lot of vivid stories [laughs].

POLO: That came out as a single in 1987 but it didn't go on the first album. I guess we just considered that a bonus track.

KWAMÉ THE BOY GENIUS

Featuring A New Beginning
Atlantic, 1989

When your back-in-the-day synapses fire about Kwamé The Boy Genius [Kwamé Holland], his trademark polka dot wardrobe and blond streak are most likely what come to mind. But that's a bit unfair to the man, who was even more of an all-around artist than his peers in producer Hurby [also spelled Herby] "Luv Bug" Azor's late-'80s talent stable, including Salt-N-Pepa, Dana Dane and Kid 'N Play.

Kwamé's lyrical approach, like fellow Queens ambassador LL Cool J, encompassed everything from aggressive battle rhymes to love songs. Also similarly to LL, he rocked his lyrics on wax before he was old enough to vote, debuting at the age of 17.

He was raised through his mid-teens in East Elmhust and Corona, Queens. Some very interesting family connections – Kwamé says that his grandfather, Kenneth Drew, founded the pioneering African-American paper *The New York Voice* – allowed him to rub elbows with a range of famous houseguests, including family friends Stevie Wonder and jazz legend Lionel Hampton.

"It wasn't strange to see the mayor of New York comin' to my grandfather's crib, or Malcolm X," he recalls. "Lionel Hampton actually gave me my first set of drums, when I was nine years old. That's what got me into the whole beat thing." His father was also friends with respected jazz pianist Abdullah Ibrahim [formerly known as Dollar Brand]. Kwamé explains, "My father was just... *down*. He wasn't a musician, but he knew a lot of them, and I was just always around heavy cats, especially jazz cats."

His house might have been hopping with politicos, activists and musical legends when he was young, but as he entered his teens he was also hob-nobbing with younger stars from his neighborhood. "My area in Queens was filled with rappers and producers," he explains. "Kool G Rap, Eric B., Kid 'N Play and Hurby Luv Bug were all there. I lived on 97th Street, Eric B. lived on 96th Street and Kool G lived on 103rd. They were older than me, but they were just guys from around the way. Everybody knew each other. I came up at a great time."

Back in his early teens, though, he wasn't figuring that music was his way to make it in the world. "I was one of those cool nerds when I was growing up," he says. "I hung out with the cool dudes, but I wanted to be a scientist or an astronaut. I never saw the reality of making a career in music." But as he dreamt about his future NASA exams, he also learned to play drums and piano.

He was drawn to hip-hop around age 10 as a fan, but a specific neighborhood connection eventually ushered him into the rap world: Hurby "Luv Bug" Azor. Steve Azor, Hurby's younger brother, was one of Kwamé's best friends growing up [in addition to being Salt 'N Pepa's lead dancer] and both boys watched as Hurby became one of hip-hop's first "super-producers," by the mid-'80s.

Initially, though, he was just Steve's older brother. Kwamé does recall an important day that shifted his attitude: "Me and Steve used to break into Hurby's room and practice on his equipment. But the day I really decided to close my options and make this music thing my career was when Hurby came home with a Mercedes, a fat rope [gold chain], gold teeth and like five shopping bags full of stuff that no one I knew could afford. I wanted that."

The House That Rap Built compilation, featuring Hurby "Luv Bug." Sound Check / Next Plateau, 1987.

There was another moment that cemented his career dreams for the next several years: "I tried to see Slick Rick and Doug E. Fresh in Harlem in 1985 or so and the show got shot up, so it never happened. But a couple months later I finally saw them and when Rick came out, the girls lost their *minds*. I said, 'This is definitely what I want to do, forever.'"

Thus, Kwamé's life course turned from science in the lab to science on the mic, and he started actively following his dreams of being a rapper and producer. As mentioned previously, he didn't have to go any further than his neighborhood to find connections, although it wasn't as easy as just walking into the game. "I used to just be that little kid who wanted to get on," he remembers. "I was younger than everybody and I was in awe of all those cats that Hurby was working with, like Dana Dane and Salt-N-Pepa."

"I'd go over to Steve's house [which was, of course, Hurby's as well] when Hurby was doing tracks with them, just wanting to find out more," he says. "Trying to find out how to be like that. Hurby knew I could rap, and he'd ask me to write rhymes for Salt-N-Pepa and, later on, Kid 'N Play. My influences were Kool G Rap and Slick Rick. I was the story dude with all the slick, witty stuff."

In 1987, when Kwamé was 15, his parents divorced and he moved to Englewood, NJ, with his father. He remembers, "I was disconnected from all my Queens people at the time, but I was also connected with a whole new neighborhood. Sugar Hill Records was in Englewood. Redhead Kingpin was also there, and we were close friends." He would still return to Queens frequently, and started doing talent shows at the popular United Skates of America in Jackson Heights. Master Ace, Father MC, and Superlover Cee & Cassanova Rud were some of the people he shared stages with there, as he continued to get noticed.

Later in 1987, Kwamé changed high schools, ending up at one that was brimming with future hip-hop stars: Manhattan's High School of Art & Design. Aside from his future A New Beginning crew [including A. Sharp, B. Flat and Peek A Boo], other classmates included Pharoahe Monch and Prince Poetry [of Organized Konfusion]; Sticky Fingaz [from Onyx]; and Prodigy and Havoc of Mobb Deep.

While he was in New Jersey, he worked at a grocery store in Englewood and, he says, "Saved every paycheck for studio time." His first self-produced demo, recorded at the Music Building in Jamaica, Queens in mid-1987, included two songs: "She's Not Just Another Woman" and "Mind Power." The latter song, he says, sampled Stevie Wonder's "Superstition" and didn't make his first album because it couldn't be cleared.

"I gave those demo tracks to Hurby but he didn't like them," he says. "I also brought them to P-Fine's show on WNYU and he said he wanted to help get me signed. But I didn't care about a record deal. I just wanted to get the demo played on the air. I told him, 'You just *gotta* play it on the air, because I'll get mad girls if you do!'"

It's unclear as to how many girls he got from his WNYU airplay, but Kwamé knew he was on the right path. And by the earliest days of 1988 he had a second demo in hand, again made at the Music Building in Queens. This time, though, there was a new twist – his latest work was engineered by Paul C [McKasty], who was starting to make waves at Studio 1212, working with artists including the Ultramagnetic MCs. "I was the producer, he engineered," he says.

He continues, "Paul actually engineered half of my first album *[Author's note: The album's liner notes credit Andre DeBourg as the album's engineer, with no mention of Paul C, even in the thank yous; Kwamé says that some of the second demo tracks were re-recorded at Bayside Studios, so DeBourg's involvement in the album may not have been mis-stated]*, although we didn't know those would be album tracks when we were doing them. Songs like 'The Rhythm'; 'The Mic Is Mine'; a different version of 'Mind Power'; 'Keep On Doin''; 'The Man We All Know And Love'; and a song called 'A New Beginning' that never came out."

"I remember that it was Christmas Eve [1987] when we recorded the second demo, because that was the only studio time I could get," he recalls. "I came out of there with like six joints. I wrote the songs, recorded and mixed them in a 10-hour period."

Kwamé dropped off a copy of his latest work to his idol, Hurby Luv Bug. To his surprise, Azor was very impressed this time around, and in a short time had started shopping the demo to different labels. Kwamé says that Epic, Atlantic, Sugar Hill [under the label name Bon Ami] and Columbia were all interested in signing him. He ended up on Atlantic, and says that the original plan and deal was for a six-track EP.

"Sylvia Rhone and Merlin Bobb signed me at Atlantic when I was still 16 years-old," he says. "I was still that semi-weird kid in high school. Everybody was wearin' jeans and sneakers and I was the dude wearin' Armani suits, tryin' to be fly, with big gold chains and a crazy flat-top."

One distinctive feature of Kwamé's self-produced music was his frequent use of live playing mixed with samples – something unique for the time. It was especially impressive considering that Kwamé was usually the artist performing the music, rather than hiring session musicians. "My production style has always been the same: 50 percent samples, and 50 percent live playing," he explains. "I was The Roots before the Roots. That was the only way I knew how to do it. I considered myself a scientist of sound. All I ever wanted to do was go in the studio and try something new."

By the fall of 1988, his father had moved to Virginia and Kwamé was back in Queens, living with his mother in Forest Hills and beginning his senior year in high school. This semester, though, he had a new part-time job: recording his debut album. "I was going to high school and also recording my album, at Bayside Sound in Queens," he says. "It was a pretty simple 24-track in a garage, but Hurby and Full Force and other people recorded there. It was owned by David Eng. The album took no more than a month to record, and all that was mostly after school. I'd get to the studio at four p.m. and leave at three or four a.m."

He adds, regarding the studio's not-so-welcoming location: "Bayside was predominantly white and pretty old-school, so black kids walking down the street were prone to being chased, or having things thrown at them. I'd have to make a mad dash to the studio once I got off the bus. Or my mom would drive me and I'd do my homework in the car."

As if he wasn't under enough pressure during the sessions as a 16- and 17-year-old, Kwamé makes an interesting claim: Hurby, the album's nominal producer, was rarely at the studio. "Hurby never showed up, so I was really the full-fledged producer of the album," says The Boy Genius. "But I'm not mad at him for that. What I give Hurby credit for is being a supervising, or executive, producer. I did 90 percent of the production and then Hurby would come in and orchestrate the mix-downs. As for the Invincibles

[Hurby's production stable, who are credited with co-production] – Steve Azor, Ron Lawrence, and Prince Charles from Queens – they didn't deliver."

One executive production decision that Hurby made was to modify Kwamé's style in spots, before finishing the album. Kwamé says, "Before the first album, I was very lyrical and more intense, like a little Kool G Rap or Big Daddy Kane. I was purely into hard lyrics. But Hurby's vision of me was to be a bit softer and smoother. He tried to tone me down." The modification – which Hurby used on many of his acts, especially Kid 'N Play – clearly helped to bring Kwamé to a broader, pop audience.

Kwamé tells an amusing story about the album's cover shot: "Back then, I was always trying to say that I was one or two years older than I really was. So on the first album cover shot, I made the make-up lady give me a [fake] moustache, and a little beard. I wanted to be older. On the back cover, everybody in the shot had painted-on everything. Sideburns, mustaches and beards. I was like, 'Yo, I want to look like a grown-ass man so that I can get some grown-ass women!'"

He adds, regarding the album cover shot [where he is seated at a computer, looking longingly or exhaustedly at the screen, with his lyrics and an electronic piano nearby]: "I was making beats with a computer, something people didn't start doing for years after that. The premise of the cover was that I was supposed to be up all night, working. When we did the cover, the song 'Boy Genius' was done but the intro to the song wasn't. So the photo inspired the intro. Hurby did that."

Kwamé says his debut was released in February or March of 1989, during the waning months of his senior year in high school. Classes would have to wait, though, as he was soon on a national tour opening for fellow Luv Bug-produced rap sensations Salt-N-Pepa. Kwamé says the album sold a half million copies, enough for gold status. Although, he points out, "I never got a plaque."

Featuring A New Beginning album sticker.

The album was a funky, smooth, entertaining and lean affair, boasting three singles drawn from only eight tracks – "The Man We All Know And Love," "Sweet Thing," and "The Rhythm." Kwamé explains the reason for being selective with the songs they included: "At that time, you didn't get paid royalties if you had more than 10 songs on a record. And our philosophy was that classic albums all had from nine to 12 cuts. So, as far as we were concerned, any more than 10 songs and you're just wasting your efforts."

By the time the album hit in '89, his single "The Man We All Know And Love" and its accompanying video was out, which started the image that still haunts Kwamé to this day: polka dots. "Back then we did a show at a mall, and everyone was wearing polka dots, with blonde streaks in their hair [like he has in the video for the song]," he remembers. "And it kept happening, even though I was never wearing polka dots at my shows. But the fans kept rocking that style everywhere we went, and they expected me to as well. So I just gave in and did it. I mean, people expected Michael Jackson and that glove; Prince to wear purple; and Kwamé in polka dots. It just got crazier and crazier, so we started including it in our visuals from then on out."

Featuring A New Beginning back album cover.

TRACKS

Boy Genius

Salt from Salt-N-Pepa was actually the one who came up with the Boy Genius idea. We were all brainstorming about image and how I should be presented and she said, "He records, he writes, he does the beats. He's a Boy Genius!" So I went with it. I wrote most of that song, but Hurby did the intro and he put his Fingerprints writing company down for co-writing credit. There were a lot of live instruments on there, just like the rest of the album. Hurby used a lot of live stuff in his productions and we both learned a lot from each other.

U Gotz 2 Get Down!

The only record that Hurby ever produced 100% for me, without my help, was the remix for that song, the one that they used for the video. And to this day, I *hate* that song. Hate it! The original beat was hard, to match the lyrics. And he made it into some soft, bubblegum, go-go record, just like he did with all his groups. And now, that's the only video of mine that they show on that channel VH-1 Soul. I gotta call and have them pull that shit off! The video treatment I did was some Star Trek shit, where everybody got beamed down to this planet of girls or something stupid.

The Rhythm

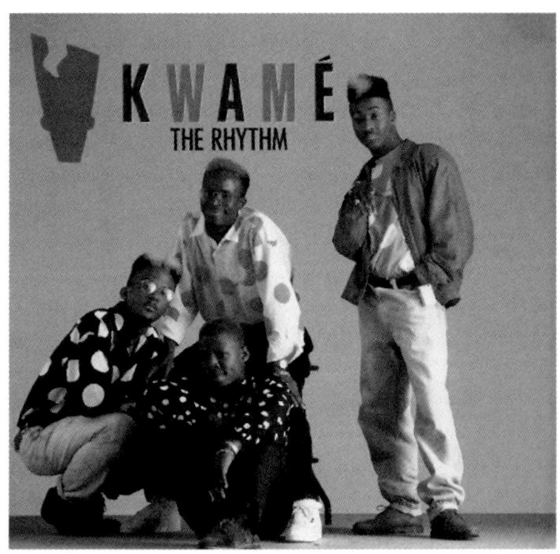

The final album version of those lyrics is pretty laid back and slick. The original ones, on my demo, were similar but approached things in a harder way. Hurby softened things up, as he did with all the singles. That single came out first as a 45, then it got pulled, then it was on the B-side of "The Man We All Know And Love," and then it finally got its own single release, a double A-side, with "U Gotz 2 Get Down!" For that double single we shot two videos, it was supposed to be one long-form video. On the production side, that track was very innovative. I was the first producer to actually use "chopped" samples *[Author's note: This claim*

can be disputed, since producers like Ced-Gee of the Ultramagnetic MCs and Paul C used "chopping" on sampled tracks as early as 1986 and 1987]. Most people would just loop a record, but I combined samples, piecing them together and making them sound like one whole beat. "The Rhythm" was four samples, chopped-up. The first kick and snare were Lyn Collins' "Ain't No Sunshine"; the middle was James Brown's "Funky Drummer"; and the end was the Staple Singers' "I'll Take You There." The loop under it was a Bob James record. Nobody was sampling like that back then, except of course The Bomb Squad, but they were using samples in a different way. And on top of all that, I played the bassline and the Fender Rhodes [keyboard].

The Man We All Know And Love

I was cool with Slick Rick and Dana Dane back then, and that track was definitely influenced by them. That song was never supposed to be a single, though. That was me just buggin' out, doing the storytelling thing like Slick Rick. If you look on the record, or maybe on the single instead of the album *[Author's note: It is also listed on the album version]*, it says that someone named "HeeMe" wrote that record. That was an alter-ego of mine, my storytelling and bug-out side. It wasn't supposed to be a reflection of Kwamé, really. The original demo of that was much more stripped-down on production, and it was very explicit [vocally]. It had the same stories, but they was just straight-up raunchy, with lots of shock value. Hurby and I both toned it down, even the rhythm. The single version of that is different than the album version. There's three stories on the album [version], and only two on the single. The night before the video shoot for that song I had a girl I knew whose sister was a hairdresser and I went over to her house and asked her to put a big blond streak in front of my head. She was like, "Why?" and I said, "Just trust me." I knew that when that video hit, everyone would know who I was, I'd be distinctive. Spinderella [from Salt-N-Pepa] was one of the leading girls in that video and it was weird because I'm like, "This is practically my sister and I have to act like I'm into her." All these people were in that video. Kid 'N Play were waiters; Dana Dane was a maître d in the restaurant; Malcolm-Jamal Warner was there. In one scene, a bedroom scene, I had a polka dot shirt on, and that's where it all started, with the polka dots. That was never supposed to be the image that I wanted. I mean, the cover of the album [in a t-shirt with a polo shirt on top] was how I actually dressed. But I knew the importance of image, just like

Kid's [from Kid 'N Play] fade.

The Mic Is Mine

There's a lot of Kool & The Gang on that track, and on the album all around. Any Kool & The Gang that I sampled was from their *Jungle Boogie* album, because that was the oldest record in my stash. I had had it since I was two years old! Every night you had to play that album for me to go to sleep. I was giving them back some love, because they held me down when I was growing up.

Keep On Doin' (What You're Doin' Baby)

That was partially a cover of a Bobby Byrd song that James Brown produced. I always believed in giving credit where credit was due [Bobby Byrd is credited on the album for the song, among others, including James Brown and Fred Wesley]. I knew that if I was bustin' my ass in the studio that they had to have done that, too.

Pushthepanicbutton!!!

That's my favorite track on the album, maybe next to "The Rhythm." But "Panic Button" is probably my favorite. I love the rhymes, I love the beat. It was just a raw record and I wanted to be represented that way, too. I wanted to put that out as a single but I was persuaded in softer directions. My DJ at the time, B. Flat, did the cuts at the end. He was replaced later on by DJ Tat Money out of Philly.

Sweet Thing

The formula for making hit records back then was this: a rock joint, a reggae joint, a love joint, a hardcore joint, and a radio joint. I wasn't gonna do a rock record and I definitely wasn't going to do a reggae record. But the love thing was cool. Plus it was a true story, about this chick that I was strung out for in summer school. I wrote that in summer school in '86 or '87. The Rufus & Chaka Kahn original that I sampled is one of my favorite records, so two and two came together and that came about. I hate performing that track now, though. I just feel like a wimp. But I still do it. On the original version of that, I was rhyming hard and Hurby was like, "Yo, you're supposed to love this chick, you're not gonna beat her up!" So we chilled it down into what became the final version.

LORD FINESSE & DJ MIKE SMOOTH

Funky Technician
Wild Pitch, 1990

"I would travel anywhere to rhyme against people back then. It was a rush to me, to write the rhymes and go out there and see the expressions on peoples' faces when I rocked them."

– Lord Finesse

"Name me one song on that album that isn't solid as a rock..."

– DJ Premier

"Back in the day, to make my mark, I went to different schools, different projects, different talent shows, all kinds of block parties," says Bronx lyrical legend, the appropriately-named Lord Finesse [Robert Hall]. "A lot of my reputation was made off the streets. It wasn't about the money. I was just trying to prove that I was one of the baddest niggas on the planet. I got so wrapped up in it that it was crazy."

He continues, on a roll (as usual), "I was brought up learning the lyrical stages of the game and how to perform and rock parties, as opposed to making records." And while he claims that translating his street-honed battle skills onto wax was "extremely hard," you'd certainly never know it by listening to his debut album, *Funky Technician*. Finesse's trademarks were his gritty, mid-tempo, funky-fresh beats [provided by DJ Premier, Diamond D and Showbiz]; his complex similes; and his punch-line knockouts that ended most verses. And battles.

Raised in the Forest Houses projects in the Bronx along with longtime friends and DITC [Diggin' In The Crates] members Diamond and Showbiz, by the later 1980s Finesse was a DJ in training and an MC on the rise, influenced by lyrical masters who preceded him. "Back then the standards for rap were extremely high, with [Kool] G Rap, Rakim, Kane and KRS-One," he explains. "I wanted to be affiliated in that group of people and nothing less than that. I wanted people to dissect my rhymes and go, 'Damn, this is a work of art.'"

He continues, "Rakim taught me the importance of *explaining* your whole rhyme to the audience. And Kool G Rap helped me create my formula for words and patterns. I just loved playing with words. Because of that culture, I've never really looked at myself as just a rapper. I look at myself as an MC."

"I started really forming my own technique around 1989," Finesse says. "Before that, I was more like G Rap, Kane and Rakim." He says that his first live show dated as far back as 1985, at a club called 371, alongside the group Ultimate Force [MC Master Rob & Diamond D]. "Diamond had Ultimate Force in the mid-'80s, so I had to wait for him to finish that part of his career before he could finally work with me," he adds.

For liner notes watchers, Finesse's first studio session and appearance on wax was heard – featuring his "Grandpa Finesse" voice – on Raheem's Diamond D-produced "I'm The King," a track off the underrated compilation *Cold Chillin' In The Studio Live* [Uni, 1989, under the artist name The Original Jazzy Jay, since all tracks were produced at the legendary DJ's studio].

One of Finesse's biggest battle assets in the late-'80s was his finely-tuned punch-lines, which were not something he took lightly. "I listened to guys that came before me and I was influenced by them, but I knew that I needed my own niche," he explains. "The way people bugged out when I used punch-lines made me know that I had something that was uniquely different. When I heard the oohs and aahs, I just went with that, and got wittier all the time. Stuff like, 'Rhymes more fresher than a virgin in a refrigerator' [from his song 'Bad Mutha']."

"I was definitely influenced by Eddie Murphy on the comedy side, too," he adds, "because shit always has to be funny. And once I got into the rhyme patterns *[Author's note: By Finesse's definition, this means rhyming several words within one or two lines, not waiting until the final word of a line. An example: 'I'm teachin' the masses, join up for classes / You're blind to the truth, so I'ma get you some glasses' on the song 'Slave To My Soundwave']*, it got really crazy."

Even while he was destroying mics throughout the Bronx as a teenager, Finesse was still thinking that DJing would be the way for him to gain fame. His friend Mike Smooth, who also became his DJ and occasional producer, actually drove him towards the mic. "Me and Mike go way back, we were childhood friends," he says. "He was the big brother that I never had. And the world should thank him for Lord Finesse because honestly, I wanted to be a DJ. I didn't want to be an MC. DJs did parties, got the money and got the girls. But Mike stayed on me about my rhyming, until I got nice."

He adds, "Even so, I was still DJing and doing mixtapes when the first album came out. They had 'Apollo Rap Night' every Monday and I won the DJ competition there four weeks in a row, in 1990 and '91. Even today, if you put me up against half these radio DJ 'personalities,' I'd bust them on their ass."

Lord Finesse, 1990.
Photo courtesy of Lord Finesse and Slice Of Spice Records.

A major turning point in Finesse's rhyme career outside of the Bronx was the New Music Seminar's yearly MC Battle, which – along with the equally popular DJ competition – was heating up in the mid-to-late 1980s. He recalls, "I got turned onto the Seminar in 1987 or '88 by a friend. All these MCs and DJs were involved with it: DJ Cash Money, [DJ] Jazzy Joyce, King Sun, Melle Mel. When you went to that event, you was actually witnessin' the dopest MCs in the world go against each other. It instantly became my main goal, because all I cared about was being the best, and that's where you could go to prove it. I went in 1988 [as an audience member], it was in midtown Manhattan, and it was the most incredible thing I had witnessed in my entire life."

"After 1988, the New Music Seminar is all I wanted to do," he continues. "It wasn't even about making a record, it was about winning there. I knew if I entered that I'd end up getting a deal anyways. But the trick was that you had to be signed first, because that was the only way you could get into the Seminar."

Finesse started sending his demo tape to a slew of indie labels. Fortunately, he caught the ears of both Guru [from Gang Starr / Gang Starr Posse] and DJ Word, who were helping owner Stu Fine do a bit of A & R for Wild Pitch Records at the time. One of Finesse's future producers, DJ Premier [Christopher Martin], remembers: "Right before I joined Gang Starr, Guru had heard my demo and Finesse's demo. This is probably 1988. Guru suggested that the two of us come in to Wild Pitch. He wanted Stu to sign Finesse."

Finesse was indeed signed to Wild Pitch in 1988, which was great on two fronts: first, he was going to put out a single. Secondly, and more importantly to Finesse at the time, he could now enter the New Music Seminar MC Battle.

Premier would also be signed to Wild Pitch, as part of Guru's new, NYC-based duo version of Gang Starr [after leaving his early Boston version, Gang Starr Posse]. Gang Starr's debut album, *No More Mr. Nice Guy*, was recorded in late '88 and would hit streets in the spring of 1989, bolstered by forward-thinking tracks like "(Words I) Manifest," "Jazz Music," and "DJ Premier In Deep Concentration."

In the spring of 1989, Finesse finally got his wish, wowing the audience – which included Premier – at the New Music Seminar MC Battle. Anticlimactically, though, he didn't win. Finesse says, "Towards the end of an early round, I went up against the 1988 winner, Mikey D, and I was like, 'I don't want no beat, just start the timer.' I did my rhyme a capella and beat him. That was my first real introduction to the world, right there."

"Lots of people heard about me in the industry after that Battle," Finesse adds. "I got taken out in the next round because the judges said I stumbled on a rhyme, but I had already made my mark by beating last year's champ. Freshco ended up winning that year."

Premier recalls, "I was there for that Battle. I was back and forth between Texas and New York at the time, but Stu Fine told me I should definitely go. I remember that Finesse made it a long way before he was eliminated. He was the youngest kid in the battle, very skinny and full of attitude. He had so many punch-lines, he was so witty."

Work on *Funky Technician* started in 1989 while the buzz from New Music Seminar was still fresh in the air. "We started work on the album probably a week after the Seminar," Finesse recalls. "I remember it was right after [Gang Starr's] *No More Mr. Nice Guy* came out."

The album production was led and overseen by DJ Premier, and also included top-shelf work by Diamond D, Showbiz and Finesse's DJ, Mike Smooth. Finesse says that recording took place from July through October or November. "That was my first production outside of Gang Starr," says Premier, who produced six out of 13 tracks. "I was excited about it. I'm into voices, and once I hear a good voice – like Finesse's or Guru's – that's all I need."

Premier adds, ruminating upon his production peers on the album and his own status in '89: "Showbiz and Diamond were Finesse's people and he wanted to bring them into the fold. And Mike Smooth was there, too. Finesse also introduced me to AG and Fat Joe back then. I was never supposed to do all the tracks on the album, definitely not. It's not like I was a [production] master back in 1989. I was glad to work with another artist to improve my production style."

"Me and Finesse both grew a lot on that album, we were still young," Premier continues. "My sound with non-Gang Starr productions wasn't really to be reckoned with until about 1992, when I was working on KRS-One's *Return Of The Boom-Bap* [1993, Jive Records]."

L to R: Mike Smooth, Finesse and Andre the Giant (AG), 1990.
Courtesy of Lord Finesse and Slice Of Spice Records.

Regarding the array of producers, Finesse explains: "I just stuck with my whole clique, the people that I was comfortable with. We didn't have money to hire [bigger producers of the day like] Mark the 45 King or Marley Marl, so we did it ourselves. No one cared who produced what track on the album, they was just like, 'That's a dope song.' That's all that mattered."

He adds, "Half that album was written on the way to the studio. I would incorporate old rhymes into new stuff I was doing, to make everything work."

Work was done at Brooklyn's Such-A-Sound, where Premier had just recorded *No More Mr. Nice Guy*. "Premier and Schlomo [Sonnenfeld, the owner and engineer of Such-A-Sound] really worked hard with me on that first album," Finesse recalls. "Premier really should have been Executive Producer, credit-wise. He made me do a lot of stuff over and pushed me. I have a lot of respect for him, then and now."

Premier says that while Finesse might not have been listed as a producer for any tracks on *Funky Technician*, he contributed more than your average MC to the album's sound. "Finesse wasn't really producing back then, but he had an ear," the super-producer remembers. "He knew what he wanted, he knew records and he knew breaks. He brought most of the records in that were looped up. Plus, he was very tough on what music he would accept to rhyme over."

Premier points out that *Funky Technician* was the launch of the Diggin' In The Crates [DITC] clique that would rule head-nod hip-hop for the better part of the '90s. He also references a future classic with which he was also involved. "I guess you could say that *Technician* was an *Illmatic* [Nas' debut, from 1994] type of situation, with a bunch of dope producers and a young MC," he states. "*Funky Technician* was just on a smaller label. But it had an *Illmatic* feel to it. There were no songs that you ever wanted to skip over."

K-Solo and Lord Finesse concert flyer.
Courtesy of Lord Finesse and Slice Of Spice Records.

The album, which was released on February 6, 1990, had a huge influence on both producers and fellow MCs, especially in New York. "There wasn't heavy promotion on that album, it went mostly by word-of-mouth," says Finesse. "But once it started, people passed that shit around like drugs."

Finesse continues, "As much as people use punch-lines today, they weren't using them back then like I was. That was my mark in the game, and that's definitely what I want to be known for. A rhyme ain't a rhyme unless the shit is intricate enough where you can break it down and go, 'Damn, this nigga is really *thinkin'* when he rhymes!'"

"Back with *Funky Technician*, my confidence was high, because when we started, Finesse wasn't as well-known," Premier reminisces. "And neither was I, even if people liked [Gang Starr's] '(Words I) Manifest.' So it was almost a guinea pig situation. Me and the other producers knew that we could all try things and get better. In our world, that record was a hit. It was such a solid hip-hop album. Plus, Finesse and AG were doing so many battles, they were destroying a lot of people. Their presence was felt everywhere they went."

TRACKS

Lord Finesse's Theme Song Intro [produced by DJ Premier]

DJ PREMIER: Finesse pretty much had everything for that song, I just hooked it up for him. I wouldn't even say I produced it, because he had all the ideas down. The horns and the drums are part of the same [sampled song], we just chopped different pieces. Finesse might not want me to disclose it. In the black community it's a well-known independent film, even though the soundtrack was on a major label. We sampled it off the wax.

Baby, You Nasty
["New Version" and original 12-inch version; both produced by DJ Premier]

LORD FINESSE: The average record right now is about 48 bars of lyrics, broken up into three 16-bar parts. I never broke my rhymes up into that formula. If you listen to that song in particular there are like 82 bars. That was the first single off the album, before the full-length came out. The album version, the "New Mix," was different, more like a remix. We stripped the drums down and added a James Brown loop ["Coldblooded"]. That vocal sample on there is Eddie Murphy, off an album of his. It was a skit where he was talkin' about his grandmother. Eddie Murphy was definitely an influence on me and my style.

PREMIER: Finesse would come over to my place in the Bronx where I was back then and we'd go over beats. Every beat I would play, he'd be like, "Naaaah." I'd say, "What's wrong with it?" And he'd say, "It's not *fonnkee* [extra emphasis on "on"]." He was tough on my beats. Then I played him the beat for "Baby, You Nasty" and he said, "*That's* fonnkee." So we went and recorded it. The 12-inch version is different than the album version. By the time we got to doing the album version, I found that James Brown sample. I did the new drum pattern but the original vocal didn't match the new tone of the sample, so he re-recorded the vocal. The album version of that one is my favorite song on the record that I did. Finesse brought in the Eddie Murphy thing we sampled on there. That was the first video Finesse put out. There weren't that many videos out back then. I'm in it, Fat Joe's there, all of us. Wearing Dapper Dan and all that. Strictly Roots was in it, Kid Capri, Guru. Dancers with door-knocker earrings. Finesse wearing Ballys, all that.

Funky Technician [produced by Diamond D]

FINESSE: The album was always called *Funky Technician*, just like that song. Because my whole thing was being funky. James Brown always said, "Make it funky." Diamond produced that track, and he was the biggest James Brown fan around. He was always a great guy to hang out with. We used to cut class and go to his house, way back. That was the first song Diamond ever produced for me. That music was actually originally supposed to be for Raheem [a friend of Finesse's and Diamond's, who did the 1989 song "I'm The King," referenced earlier], but he had gotten locked up. So I told Diamond, "I'll use that one." Diamond was going to do Raheem's whole album, he could have been the next Rakim. He had a big influence on my style. Raheem taught me how to flow and use compound words.

PREMIER: Guru gave me a copy of Finesse's demo tape the first time I met him, in 1988, at the Wild Pitch offices. I still have it. It has a different version of "Funky Technician" on it, which Finesse did with breakbeats and two turntables. I just ran across that demo tape the other day.

Back To Back Rhyming
[produced by Showbiz, featuring Andre The Giant aka AG]

FINESSE: Showbiz did that one, and it had my man Andre [Barnes aka AG] on it. I battled him way back, when he was calling himself Infinite. It was in the school-yard where he went [AG lived in the Patterson Houses, in another part of the Bronx], and we just came to a standstill. I was just rhymed-out after that 'cause I had been there all morning. But I had never met a dude with his talent. Me and AG lost touch for a minute, but we was re-connected because he was dating a girl who lived directly across the street from me. I was DJing at the time along with MCing, and he needed a DJ, so his girl sent her brother to look for me. When we came face to face we both bugged-out, seeing each other again. I told him I was a DJ, but that I also had my album to work on and told him to come down to a session we were having that next day. That's when we did "Back To Back Rhyming," and that's how it started. Like me, he also had a lot of great punch-lines. AG battled Percee P's partner and then set me up to battle Percee, for our famous showdown. Me and Andre just used to run amok.

Here I Come [produced by Diamond D]

FINESSE: That's a slower track, but it didn't matter. I'd rap over anything. If I felt it, I'd rhyme over it. I generally wanted up-tempo stuff, but slow tracks were fine. And radio was playing just about anything back then, no matter how fast or slow it was.

Slave To My Soundwave

[produced by DJ Premier, co-produced by Mike Smooth]

PREMIER: Mike Smooth was very involved with that, he had the scratch ideas. If I did any scratches on tracks, it was just because Mike wasn't there in the studio that day. That's faster than some other tracks on the album, but everybody had fast records back then. That was really an extra song. It wasn't supposed to be on the album, but Finesse wanted to add one more song, and he loved that sample and the drums. He brought that to me and I hooked it up. Mike helped, too, so we all shared credit. That "Slave to my soundwave" sample just wasn't working initially, and I just kept pushing the cuts to get them to go into the beat so it wasn't clashing. The reason I worked so hard was because Mike would have to do those cuts live. I liked the way Finesse approached that track. It was a great song to round out the shape of the album.

FINESSE: Mike brought the loop for that, so he got co-production credit. Most of the idea was Mike's, but Premier put it together. If you listen to that first verse on there, that style is definitely Rakim-influenced. I shout out Ice-T and Rhyme Syndicate at the end there, because I met them at the New Music Seminar in 1989. He told me to call him if I ever needed management, and after the first album, I did.

I Keep The Crowd Listening [produced by Diamond D]

PREMIER: That's definitely my favorite song on the album that I didn't produce. The sample, the scratches, the change-up on the hook. It's so *fonnkee* [imitates Finesse saying the word].

FINESSE: That was definitely a Rakim influence, too. I wrote lyrics to that song after hearing the music, just like I did with most of the songs on that album. I got that Grandpa Finesse [a character on the song, done by Finesse] from listening to Marley Marl stuff *[Author's note: Marley does a similar "funky uncle" character at the beginning of "The Symphony"]*. Premier did the cuts on that one. He was like an artist with his scratching. He added almost as much melody as the loops did when he cut. His stuff was just so intricate.

Bad Mutha [produced by Diamond D]

FINESSE: I talk about my younger years rapping on there. I wasn't always more advanced than cats who were around me. But as rap evolved, so did my style, until I found my niche.

Keep It Flowing [produced by Diamond D, featuring Andre The Giant aka AG]

FINESSE: Me and AG talked a lot of shit on that track, wow! I let AG go first because I respected him. It was about genuine love, not ego. At the time, me and AG was out battling people in the street, and that aggressiveness definitely rubbed off on that track. When niggas tell you you ain't nice, it makes you angry and more focused to get even more aggressive and talk even more shit. We was just arrogant. AG is still so dope, to this day.

A Lesson To Be Taught [produced by DJ Premier]

PREMIER: That was definitely [Big Daddy] Kane-influenced, very much so. Finesse brought the samples for that song, too. He was definitely the leader of that album. Most of the time I just hooked things up how he wanted them.

FINESSE: That was a lesson track that was partly a Big Daddy Kane influence and also partly the label's influence. Stu was saying I was talking all this shit but I didn't have enough concepts. They wanted a positive record that touched people. Kane had a lot of great concept records, like "Word To The Mother (Land)" [from 1988]. So I tried to talk about some important stuff there.

Strictly For The Ladies [produced by DJ Premier]

FINESSE: That was the other single off the record. To this day, a lot of people don't know that Premier produced that song [even though he is credited on the album]. One of my first real live gigs was at the Zodiac Club, in 1987 or 1988, when my style was getting more developed. Back then I was doing that song as a routine. I figured you can never lose talking about the ladies. That routine worked well because it wasn't disrespectful. I never wanted to do an "I Need Love" [by LL Cool J] record when it came to the ladies, it had to be more arrogant and slick-talking. When I met females I always had slick shit to say, and that rhyme grew out of that. When I did it live I'd point out females in the crowd, just having fun. We did a video for "Strictly For The Ladies" and the budget must have been about $3,000 from the way it looked [laughs]. But we were like, "Fuck it, it'll get played somewhere." The last rhyme on there was from an old routine of mine.

PREMIER: At the time, the album version of that was my favorite one of mine on there. It's close between that and the album version of "Baby, You Nasty." All those samples on there were mine. With that one, I played Finesse so many beats and he didn't like any of them again. "Nope, nope, that's not *fonnkee*." It took a while, but eventually he liked that one. The album version is a different mix, I like it better than the 12-inch version. I added more bottom to the album version.

Track The Movement [produced by DJ Premier]

PREMIER: That has a sample for the main drums, and a drum machine over top. I used an SP-12 [drum machine, by Emu Systems], not the [newer] SP-1200. And I did the cuts on that one.

FINESSE: Those where some of the rhymes that I used at the 1989 New Music Seminar. That was the B-side of "Baby, You Nasty." It was just me, flowin'.

MANTRONIX

The Album
Sleeping Bag, 1985

[Author's note: This is an expanded Mantronix *The Album* chapter. A considerably shorter version appeared in my 2005 book *Rakim Told Me.* Enjoy!]

"Our sound wasn't based on old music. It was more original."

– MC Tee

"The first Run-DMC album sounds pretty dated now. Mantronix doesn't."

– Will Socolov, Sleeping Bag Records

The mid 1980s was one of hip-hop's most interesting, experimental and important phases. The genre was making an at-times awkward transition from early party- and live-based musical forms into the oncoming rule of drum machines, sampling and the advent of the "master producer." One crucial bridge between the Furious Five, Afrika Bambaataa, Run-DMC and the advent of both Marley Marl's Juice Crew and Public Enemy's Bomb Squad was the group Mantronix.

Mantronix was influenced and informed by early '80s electro-boogie and the spirit of the garage disco scene popularized in New York by Larry Levan, but was even more firmly rooted in the kick-drum thud and decay of the recently-popularized Roland TR-808 drum machine. And although, at-times, they may have sounded like a full 808 orchestra, Mantronix was only two men: producer Kurtis Mantronik [Curtis Khaleel, aka Kurtis Khaleel, known as Kirk to family and close friends] and rapper MC Tee [Touré Embden]. Together, they dropped a sonic bomb on the music world with their 1985 debut, *The Album*.

The album's title was simple, but the music was not. Intricate, ever-changing drum programs, the crackle of high-volume handclaps, and thick analog basslines ruled the group's sound scheme, buoyed by edits from production masters like the Latin Rascals [Albert Cabrera and Tony Moran] and always iced by MC Tee's glib, loose, party-moving rhymes.

"I was a nerd and really into technology, so I was into production from the start," explains Kurtis Mantronik. "I always used the latest technology, like the 808 drum machine, because I just loved the bass *[Author's note: "Bass" = kick-drum / bass-drum sound]* that it gave." He says that he never played musical instruments as a child, and taught himself how to program both the Roland 606 and 808 machines.

It remains unconfirmed as to whether Mantronik was born in Jamaica [Mantronik himself refused to comment upon his country of birth] or was simply heavily-influenced by that part of his heritage, since his closest bond was with his Jamaican mother. As for his earlier years, he lived with an uncle in Canada at some point in the '70s, and by 1980 – in his mid-teens – had landed in New York City, to live with his mother.

"When I was growing up, I listened to a lot of rock music," Kurtis says. "I loved Kiss' 'Beth,' for instance." But his tastes changed soon enough, and he got his dance music jones fulfilled working at Downtown Records, located in the Chelsea neighborhood of New York, in addition to frequenting the multi-floor Danceteria club, which wasn't far from the record store.

And while he did DJ later on, production is where Mantronik started. He explains, "I wasn't a DJ before I became a producer. That came later."

Mantronik's future lyrical partner, MC Tee, was born in the Bronx, and his family roots were also from Jamaica. After his earliest years in the Big Apple, he moved to Jamaica with his mother, from ages 10 to 15, and then returned to New York. "We moved a lot, I lived in every borough," he says.

The young Touré was actually a child actor for a brief time, foreshadowing his future performance-based career. "I started acting when I was about seven years old," he recalls. "My mom signed me up for a 'Tiny Tot' contest and I won. I did 'Sesame Street,' I did Campbell's Soup commercials. That was before we moved to Jamaica."

Artistically-inclined from a young age, Tee went to Manhattan's High School of Art & Design and even took classes at Parsons School of Design in Greenwich Village after high school, before leaving to get a 'real job' and pay some rent in the mid-'80s.

"When I met Kurtis, I was living in Long Island with my father, and my mother was in Brooklyn," Tee says. "I was working for a company called Burns Telecommunications in Manhattan, selling equipment for businesses. Downtown Records was near my office and I would probably buy $30 worth of records there each week, because I was practicing to be a DJ. Kurtis was the guy who played records in the store for people. That's how we met. I remember that he was going to school for music, I think to do production. Kurtis always wanted to be in the music industry, from early on."

Tee says that he even helped come up with Kurtis' stage moniker: "He was trying to come up with a DJ name, and I suggested Mantronik. Like, 'You're a man who is electronic.' He didn't really have a DJ name before that one."

Although MC Tee was considering being a DJ himself, he wasn't dead-set on it. "I knew that if I couldn't fit in with a crew as a DJ, I could probably fit in as an MC," he says. "I was practicing and writing rhymes all the time." His genre of choice was always hip-hop, from hits of the day to the breakbeats that made up the music's backbone. On the rhyme side, Melle Mel was his favorite, and he listened to Mr. Magic's WBLS "Rap Attack" radio show religiously.

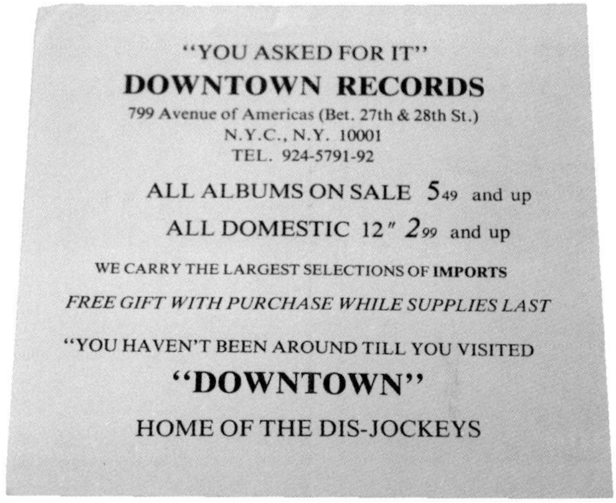

Downtown Records flyer.
Courtesy of the Adler Hip-Hop Archives / Cornell University Hip-Hop Collection.

Tee remembers the day that the group Mantronix was truly born, on the sales floor at Downtown. "Kurtis loved showing off and he was very ambitious, and we both talked about wanting to do a record," Tee remembers. "He wanted to put something out like [Davy DMX's 1984 DJ-based single on Tuff City / CBS] 'One For The Treble,' just his own version of that. And I told him he should put me on the B-side, rhyming. So I went to the DJ booth in the store and busted a rhyme to a beat he played. He really liked it, and we were on after that." Tee says the rhyme he used that day didn't appear on any songs the group recorded later on.

Shelling out what Kurtis says was $80 for studio time, Mantronik and Tee cut the original demo for the song "Fresh Is The Word" in one day. Tee says it was recorded in a studio that was part of a school Kurtis was attending or affiliated with at the time, but he can't remember exactly which one. "Some fashion institute or art school," he says.

Tee adds, "Neither of us knew how it was going to turn out. We didn't know what we were doing. We produced it and mixed it, it's not like Kurtis did everything. We sat there together and made that first song. It wasn't even at a real studio. That original demo for 'Fresh Is The Word' wasn't like how the single turned out. It was a lot rougher around the edges."

Aside from Kurtis and MC Tee, the other person most responsible for the rise of

Mantronix was Will Socolov, the owner of Sleeping Bag Records. Launched as an avant-garde dance label in 1981 [co-founded with producer Arthur Russell], by 1984 they had established a bit of a foothold in New York's club scene. Around town, Will was known for his forward-thinking A & R ears.

"The first time I met Kurtis was on the street, actually," recalls Socolov. "I was doing a record with Mark Kamins, who was a DJ at Danceteria. [Fellow Danceteria DJ] Freddy Bastone was coming to the studio to hear what we were doing. Freddy knew Kurtis, and saw him on the street, so we were all talking. Kurtis started begging, '*Please* let me go with you guys to the studio!' Freddy made him promise to be cool if he did, and so he came along."

Socolov continues, "Kurtis told me about this record he was working on that he said was hot. I asked Freddy about it and Freddy said, 'Will, whenever I put that song on at Danceteria, the place goes crazy.' The song was just an instrumental at that point, and it was only on cassette. So I went to Danceteria [located at 30 West 21st Street], which was Kurtis' favorite club, and Freddy was right. People loved it. But it needed a vocal, and Kurtis wanted me to hear one, too."

Kurtis Mantronik's club of choice, Danceteria, on West 21st Street.

Socolov adds, "So Kurtis asked me to go to Downtown Records, which was a weird store. It was on 6th Avenue at 18th or 19th Street. When I got there, MC Tee was in the store and they did ['Fresh Is The Word'] live, with Tee rapping over the instrumental. There were probably 20 kids there and they were all grooving to it. I signed it immediately. It was hot."

Neither Tee nor Socolov could recall where the vocal version of the 'Fresh Is The Word' demo had disappeared to at the time, which made the instrumental the only version available when Socolov and Kurtis first met ("It was really just the drum machine sequence – the drum machine and the cowbell," Socolov says). But the end result was the same: Mantronix was onto something, and Sleeping Bag was behind them.

The first thing they needed to do, then, was to re-record "Fresh Is The Word." For that, Socolov made a call to his go-to spot at the time: INS, located on Murray Street, not far from the World Trade Center. "Ian North owned it, that's why it was called INS," Socolov says. "I used them pretty often for Sleeping Bag projects, so it was natural that we would go there for Mantronix."

The engineer for that first "real" Mantronix session was John Poppo. And having a good engineer was of utmost importance, as Tee explains, "The engineers were key for Mantronix during that first album, because they knew the equipment. Kurtis was learning each time he went into the studio, a little more with each song we did. But the engineers helped us find the sound that we were looking for."

Kurtis Mantronik, 1985.
Photo © Geoff Spear, www.spearphoto.com.

MC Tee, 1985.
Photo © Geoff Spear, www.spearphoto.com.

Poppo, who was more of a rock and pop fan and specialist, was fresh out of SUNY Fredonia [near Buffalo, on the other side of the state from New York City] in 1984, with a degree in Audio Engineering and Performance. INS was one of his freelance home-bases on the engineering front. "Back then, I was learning from the artists and producers as much as they were learning from me," he says. "And when it came to INS, those were mostly hip-hop and dance artists. INS was a small room that sounded really good. But it was too small for rock bands."

Poppo's earliest engineering work in hip-hop was with Doug E. Fresh and the Sugar Hill Gang, and it didn't always go the way he was taught in school. He recalls, with a chuckle, "My first hip-hop mixes were sonically clean and perfect, and the guys would be like, 'No, no, you gotta distort this, you gotta dirty this up!' Following their directions, I was mixing the bottom so heavy in records that I'd have to call Herb Powers at the mastering plant and ask him if it was OK. It was all analog, and the needle was literally jumping out of the record."

But he adjusted quickly enough, and by 1985, the fresh-faced duo of Kurtis and

Tee were standing in front of him, with an 808 – which was either freshly-purchased with Socolov's modest advance money, or borrowed from a friend – and some lyrics in hand. "I remember that Kurtis had that demo of 'Fresh Is The Word' with him, which he had done at school," Poppo says. "Kurtis wasn't a technician in the studio back then by any stretch, but he was deep into the music, and hip-hop culture. He was more of a beat guy than a producer. As I recall, he didn't even produce Tee's vocals, really. Tee pretty much had that part figured out himself."

Poppo adds, "Will Socolov was usually there with Kurtis and Tee, too. He was very hands-on and deserves a lot of credit for those songs as well, besides merely recognizing Kurtis' talent early on. I was impressed that Kurtis and Tee did all of that being as young as they were. But honestly, it was almost a trio. Will was like the Clive Davis of the indie hip-hop and dance scene. They all just enjoyed making music."

There was also one last [unpaid] member of Mantronix, who doesn't get as much credit or fanfare: the Roland TR-808 drum machine. "The 808 was still pretty new back then *[Author's note: The machine was introduced to the market in 1980, but didn't catch on in hip-hop circles until 1982 or '83]*, and it was a strange machine," Poppo explains. "You would program it as much visually as musically. It had all these lights, and you programmed and sequenced right in the machine. Hip-hop kids were playing with it like it was a fun toy. But the sound was amazing, the bottom on that machine was tremendous. It was the staple for hip-hop, just like the [TR-] 909 was the staple for dance music."

Regarding the group's working relationship and pre-production locations, Tee says, "Kurtis would work on beats and we'd meet up at his apartment, or at the Sleeping Bag offices. I think Kurtis lived on 72nd Street, about 10 blocks from the label [Sleeping Bag was at 1974 Broadway, near 67th Street]. He didn't have a lot of equipment at his house, just a basic drum machine and turntables. We were both pretty broke back then."

"Kurtis lived on 71st or 73rd Street, it wasn't 72nd," Socolov recalls. "He and his mother lived in a small studio apartment, and when Kurtis would play me music at his place, we would have to listen to it in the bathroom so we didn't disturb his mom. I would sit in his bathtub and he would play me the drum beat he was working on, with headphones. He didn't have his own 808 back in 1985. He had a Roland, but a lower version. *[Author's note: This was most likely the Roland TR-606 Drumatix]*. That's what he used to program all those beats before he would transfer them to an 808 for what we would record in the studio."

"I'd pick a beat I liked, take home a copy, and write to it," Tee continues. "There were times when I would even finish rhymes at the studio. Kurtis would make suggestions about topics sometimes, but all the rhymes were mine. Once I started writing, things went pretty quickly. And that was good, because we had some pretty long songs!"

Tee adds, "Recording in the studio wasn't bad, although it could be nerve-racking at times, because you had to be so quiet. You had to breathe a certain way and you couldn't move around when you were rhyming, because the microphone would pick it up. But the rhyming itself was no problem. I definitely liked performing live more than being in the studio."

John Poppo has this to say, regarding any sonic contributions he may have had on the songs on which he worked: "I was there to give suggestions or advice when asked, but I wasn't the producer. I mixed the record. Kurtis did the arrangement, which was really pre-arranged since it came right out of the 808. 'Fresh Is The Word' was just a beat and a rap. I made it sound good. Honestly, I would say there is some doubt as to whether there even was a producer on that first session at INS [laughs]. But, if anyone produced it, it was Kurtis and Tee *[Author's note: The single lists the artist as 'Mantronix with M.C. Tee,' and the producer as Mantronik]*. Tee worked on his vocals, so he produced that aspect."

The re-done version of "Fresh Is The Word" hit stores on Sleeping Bag Records by the summer of 1985, and took off like a rocket in both the dance and hip-hop worlds. Socolov says that sales of the group's debut single broke 70,000 units, a considerable number for an unknown group who were not making simplistic, bubblegum music.

With single sales of that magnitude, Socolov was quick to exercise his right to have the duo record a full album. According to the notes on the back of the LP, two tracks were recorded at INS [both with Poppo as engineer]: the group's first two singles, "Fresh Is The Word" and "Needle To The Groove."

Another four songs – or possibly five; no one interviewed could remember where the "Mega-Mix" was actually edited together by the Diamond Two – were completed at a location listed as: "Al Cohen Studio."

"Al lived in the Chelsea Hotel and he recorded music in his apartment," Socolov explains. "We were paying $45 an hour at INS, and Al definitely charged less than that. He was a good keyboard player, so Kurtis would tell him what to play on certain songs. I think they recorded on an 8-track for all those songs."

"Al Cohen Studio" was known as A.C. Music Productions at the time, at least to its owner. And it would prove to be a fruitful – if unlikely – recording location for Mantronik and Tee. Their work together for *The Album* would be the first of many Cohen / Mantronik collaborations in the years to follow.

Cohen, a guitarist [and occasional / casual keyboardist] with a degree in Composition from Boston's Berklee College of Music, says that those remaining songs on *The Album* were indeed recorded on a Tascam 8-track. He did not know Mantronik before they worked together, nor did they have any mutual friends. To his best recollection, Kurtis simply answered Cohen's weekly ad for recording services in the *Village Voice*.

As previously mentioned, Cohen's studio was in the infamous Chelsea Hotel [alternately known as the Hotel Chelsea] on West 23rd Street, which included a long list of provocative past residents with artistic inclinations, from Dylan Thomas to Bob Dylan to Sid Vicious. It wasn't swanky by any stretch, but it was artist-friendly for sure.

"I had one large room, with a loft bed in the back, behind a wall," Cohen says. "The Chelsea was still an artist haven in the mid-'80s. I made noise with my recordings, but my landlord allowed it. I really built the studio to record my own music, but I would take on outside clients to pay for the up-keep and to get new equipment."

Cohen continues, "I think Mantronix was the first hip-hop group I had worked with back then, and Kurtis was also one of the first cats I knew who used MIDI [Musical Instrument Digital Interface, a standard electronic language that can link different instruments and computerized devices together]. Recording with him was the first time I had hooked up a drum machine to a keyboard and locked them together."

Cohen's studio was the ultimate example of making the most out of what was in front of you. He explains, very matter-of-factly, "I didn't even have a vocal booth. Here's what we did: I would say, 'Tee, you go on that side of the room with the microphone, and I'll be over here, with the 8-Track.'" Using an AKG 412 condenser mic and some engineering acumen, they made it work.

Cohen says that all tracks done at his studio were the final versions – no extra "re-touching" or modifications were done at other studios before mastering. And as for why they worked so well together (and why they continued their producer / engineer association for years after Cohen's work on *The Album*), he says: "Kurtis was always ahead of the curve, he was a very progressive cat. He constantly tried new things and wanted the newest equipment. And I was always looking for new equipment and ideas as well. For example, I was one of the first guys at that time to have the Akai S612 [one of the earliest professional samplers, released in 1985]. We just had a great chemistry. We were comfortable with each other and trusted each other."

Consisting of only seven songs, *The Album* was still a beefy platter, since the songs were longer than many hip-hop tracks at the time. Some of them pushed seven minutes in length, with Mantronik's musical assaults filling in the spaces where Tee wasn't rapping. "The songs weren't supposed to be long on purpose, they just came out that way," Kurtis reasons. "'Rappers Delight' [by the Sugarhill Gang, from 1979] was long, and so were other club tracks back then. It wasn't out of the ordinary, at least outside of the hip-hop world."

Aside from their sound on wax, another important aspect of Mantronix in 1985 was their live show. "We were one of the first crews to bring a drum machine out live," Tee points out, with pride. "We played our first gig at the Roxy [in New York], which was the first time I had ever performed on-stage. We brought out the 808 and people were amazed at how Kurtis was scratching over the beat. No one had really seen that before. Pretty much every other group back then just performed off records."

The Album, back cover.
Photo courtesy of Geoff Spear, www.spearphoto.com.

Tee also reminds us that one of Mantronix's musical peers, Run-DMC, was situated very differently in the industry: "Run-DMC had a whole team behind them, with Russell Simmons and their label [Profile Records]. Compared to them, we were a couple of guys beating on cans. We had to work a lot harder on our own to get heard, we didn't have huge budgets or major tours. Which really sparked Kurtis, because he was very competitive. He always wanted to be better than whatever was hot at the time. Plus, he knew the competition because he worked at the record store."

Socolov agrees with Tee about the relatively limited resources that came from being on Sleeping Bag. "If Kurtis was marketed properly, he could have been *huge*," he admits. "Although I don't think he would have gotten there with Tee. But Kurtis' appeal had the potential to be very broad."

From Sleeping Bag's perspective, *The Album* was a huge success. Socolov says, "In America, the album did OK, maybe 150,000 units. But it was *massive* in Europe, it was more than double our American sales over there. It might have sold more than 500,000 in Europe, with at least 200,000 in the UK alone. That album was definitely our biggest seller up to that point, and it only cost about $10,000 to make. Maybe less."

He continues, "The response in Europe versus America didn't surprise me. I knew that the hardcore New York hip-hop guys weren't going to jump on all of the tracks, because they weren't hard enough. But that album was so innovative and it crossed a lot of stylistic boundaries. As a result, it found a big audience around the world."

John Poppo, who had a ringside seat for the earliest adventures of Mantronix on wax, has this to say about the album and the group: "There was something special about Mantronix on a couple of different levels. First of all, they were innovative; they weren't trying to be like anyone else. They were making their own sounds, and they were one of the first groups to really feature the 808. They managed to make a lot of noise on a very low budget. Overall, it showed a lot of artistry, risk and creativity."

The Album, cassette cover.

"Kurtis wasn't following what anyone else was doing back then," Al Cohen states. "He would try anything. And whatever he tried, it always had a lot of rhythm to it. The sound they made was just a revolution. It was rap, but it was all very new, it didn't sound like what had come before it. There was *music* going on."

Kurtis Mantronik himself muses about how important he thought *The Album* was back then: "I guess I was surprised at how people reacted to it. I just made music because it was cool and fun. As long as I got a sound to move the crowd, nothing else mattered."

"We just wanted to be a part of the scene and to have an influence on the sounds that were going on back then," says MC Tee, looking back. "We didn't even care if the songs were hits. When you put a lot of love into something, I think it holds up over time. And we really put a lot of love into the songs on that album. We were just making music, and not thinking much more about it at the time. But I think it just so happened that we were ahead of our peers."

TRACKS

Bassline ["specially edited" by the Latin Rascals]

KURTIS MANTRONIK: I think I played that bassline on a Juno [keyboard, most likely the Juno 60]. The track itself came together pretty quickly. I think it took us only a day to record the whole thing. I think it was Will's idea to get the Latin Rascals to do the edits, but I wanted those guys also. They had a name on the street from their radio show on WKTU. They only did edits. I think that doing hip-hop edits is a lost art these days, which is a shame, because you can really do some cool stuff with them. Things that you can't get from regular production. Aside from the Latin Rascals [Albert Cabrera and Tony Moran], Omar Santana and Chep Nunez were the most popular guys doing edits back in the '80s.

WILL SOCOLOV: I always knew that "Bassline" and "Ladies" would have more limited success in the U.S. Those songs were different, they were beyond hip-hop. There was definitely a huge buzz on the group in Europe. Kurtis brought in the Latin Rascals, he loved edits. Them and the Diamond Two [Chep Nunez and Charlie Dee]. Editing wasn't Kurtis' strength, but he loved it, so he would bring other people in to do that on his tracks. Chep became his main guy eventually, because Kurtis didn't work with the Latin Rascals for too long. We even had an editing suite with equipment in the Sleeping Bag offices, and the Diamond Two would just work there [instead of paying to work in a recording studio]. I think that the Latin Rascals might have worked at Downtown Records with Kurtis, at least one of them. It was a big thing back then to have someone do your edits, especially those guys.

MC TEE: I said "Tee Ski" in my rhyme on there, but I never really used that name. People would just add "Ski" to their name back then. Everybody had different names. When I tagged [graffiti], I would write "Crime Master T." That song was really about how we had confidence in ourselves, how we were able to shine. I liked some of the edits that they had on there, even if a lot of that stuff was new to me. It was a cool addition, although sometimes those would be put on there without my input, and I didn't like that. Kurtis and Will [Socolov] would figure it out. On the first album, it was all fun, but later on I didn't appreciate that as much.

AL COHEN: I think I played that bassline on there. Or maybe Kurtis did. I mean, it's not much of a bassline, only three notes! It was most likely on a Juno 60. Kurtis did everything else, all the programming. For the edits that the Latin Rascals did, I would just give them a bunch of different versions of the song [on tape], so they could use them and edit. One version with vocals; an instrumental; one with a lot of echo; one with a lot of drop-outs *[Author's note: Similar to a "dub" version, in the '80s hip-hop sense]*. We would mix all of our songs with instrumental versions, in case they wanted to extend them later on. It would all be mixed down to ¼-inch tape and then edited from there, with razor blades. I did some edits, but not the ones on that song. You had to do a lot of takes and versions when you were doing edits, because if you screwed up and didn't have enough music, you'd be in big trouble.

Needle To The Groove

TEE: That was me on the vocoder [voice effect], of course. It wasn't that difficult to adjust to it. The engineer did most of the tweaking of the sound, I just said the lines. The vocoder was in the studio, Kurtis didn't have one. It was just something the engineer [John Poppo] wanted to try out. Kurtis originally wanted to use reverb to make the vocals sound like there was more than one voice. But then we tried to vocoder and that worked.

SOCOLOV: That was the second single, and it didn't do as well as "Fresh Is The Word." "Needle" might have done about 50,000 units, which is still a great number. It wasn't really about sales, and we weren't really competing with Run-DMC and Whodini in the hip-hop world. We were going a different way, we weren't going for the rap charts. "Needle" was already showing Kurtis' movement into a different feel.

MANTRONIK: That's Tee on the vocoder. I changed up the beat and the drum programming on that because it just felt better to keep it moving. Beck took that for one of his hits ["Where It's At," from 1996] and never gave me credit or money for it. It bothers me when I'm not even acknowledged, but it's even worse when they sample your shit and you don't get any credit, like Beck and Snap. Some people give props. DJ Shadow and the Chemical Brothers have both said nice things about my music.

JOHN POPPO: For that song, they had written the music and rhymes before they got to the studio. It seemed like they had already worked on everything together. Kurtis did the music, Tee did the rhymes, I don't think either guy helped the other one out too much. They stuck with their specialty. We used the vocoder on there, but it wasn't a big deal. You can trigger that effect with a keyboard. So with Tee's vocals, we just added the effect afterwards. He didn't hear his vocals like that when he was recording them. It's definitely a lot more difficult to do a vocoder vocal live, but that's not what we did on there.

Mega-Mix

["specially edited" by The Diamond Two: J. "Chep" Nunez – incorrectly listed as "Chet" on the back of the album – and Charlie Dee]

MANTRONIK: That was done at the end of the record. I've always had mega-mixes on my records because it's so much a part of where I come from. It's that cool hip-hop cut-up thing that good DJs do to hype the crowd. I don't think The Diamond Two did too much together other than this track, maybe a couple other things. Charlie did a bunch of other solo edit stuff in the '80s. And Chep died in a fire later on *[Author's note: Nunez passed away in late 1990]*.

TEE: I definitely said to Kurtis that every record on the album didn't have to have [new] rhymes on it. So it was cool to have a song like that, a different mix.

SOCOLOV: I know that Kurtis was very proud of that one, they worked very hard on the mix.

Hardcore Hip-Hop

TEE: That's my favorite song on the album. We was at Kurtis' apartment and he had that beat. We came up with this hardcore sound and we really liked it. The more we messed with it, the more excited we got. We wanted to get in the studio and record it right away, we could feel the vibe and the energy. That one never got the radio play it could have gotten. It should have been big. The lyrics on there were me saying, "I am who I am because of you," to guys who came before me. "You guys created me. Here I am."

MANTRONIK: That's about the roots of hip-hop. A lot of the sounds and change-ups on there were really done just because they sounded cool and we were all experimenting to top each other with new shit. Not only in clubs, but also on records. I never had any musical training, I always liked learning things for myself, so experimentation came very naturally from that.

COHEN: Kurtis must have done the cuts on there. He brought in a turntable and we'd just hook it up.

Ladies

MANTRONIK: That song was written with a special lady in mind. That's why I've always had a soft spot for it. It's definitely my favorite track on the album, still today. Our music back then – and my music now – is all about being different, not like today where people are too busy trying to be like this or like that. Back in the day it was better when you *didn't* sound like anyone else. Otherwise you were considered a "biter."

TEE: The hip-hop industry was much more respectful to women back then. All content was controlled, it was just a rule for the radio that people stuck with. We also tried to keep cursing out of the rhymes. Kurtis and I were young and into the glamour and the females, but we both grew up with respect. We never had that "Women are bitches" attitude. When we put that song together, we knew it had a cross-over sound, that it could get some non-hip-hop radio play. That was a single later on [in 1986], we thought it could even get daytime radio play. Back then, hip-hop was never played in the daytime. Although in the end we didn't get that much radio on that song. I guess we didn't always have that kind of [record label] muscle. If we were on Capitol back then [the group was signed to Capitol later in the '80s], "Ladies" would have done a lot better.

SOCOLOV: That was very different – it was Kurtis trying to make a category that no one else was in. He didn't want to be Run-DMC, nor did MC Tee. I'm not sure they could have even pulled that off, but they didn't want to, so it didn't matter.

Get Stupid "Fresh" Part 1

COHEN: That was a free-form track. It was called "Get Stupid," so there you go. You can hear them using my sampler on there, an Akai 612. That had just come out.

SOCOLOV: I guess it's fair to say that that song is less "inspired" than others on the album. It was done in one night. I had told them how many tracks we needed [for the album] and that one got us to seven. But I'm not going to bad-mouth my own artist!

MANTRONIK: That one was done on the spot, but I usually don't like taking a day to do a track either way. I usually think about what I want to do beforehand, based on the technology available. We always goofed around a lot in the studio, but we always got things done.

TEE: That was Kurtis doing his thing, and me going along. It wasn't as put together as I would have wanted it to be. We didn't always agree, we'd fight sometimes. That song was album filler, it wasn't as strong.

Fresh Is The Word

MANTRONIK: That was the first song I ever had on wax. I used the 808 a lot back then because I loved the bass. When I used it in a show at the Roxy with Tee – the first time anyone used an 808 on stage – the crowd freaked when I hit that first kick. I had a good amount of cutting on there, too *[Author's note: The single's label says "Scratching by Louie L. and Mantronik]*. It was all about capturing the hip-hop vibe you heard in clubs, but making it *bigger*.

JOHN POPPO: Honestly, when they first came in with that record, I looked at Will like he was crazy. I had worked with hip-hop groups before, but they didn't sound like that. I said, "Clearly you're going to do more production on this, right? It's not finished, is it?" It was so sparse and empty. Will looked at Kurtis and said, "No, that's it." If I had produced it, I would have added a bunch of stuff, and it wouldn't have sounded as cool as it is. Kurtis had the vision to say, "This record is about what we *don't* do." And Will backed him up, and they deserve a lot of credit. He felt that that was enough, and he was right. Sometimes the hardest thing for a producer is what *not* to do, or add. From the original demo Kurtis had, we stepped it up into professional-level recording and production, at INS. Kurtis added some programming to what he had on the original. But the basic core of the record wasn't really changed. He walked in with an 808, plugged it in and we recorded it to multi-track, and added the vocals. We got Tee on multi-track and got a great sound for him. Then we mixed, EQed and balanced everything. By the time it came out of the speakers, it was *pounding*. The room was shaking.

SOCOLOV: That was the first single, it sold 70,000 or maybe 80,000 copies, which was amazing. That was one of the most "street" hip-hop records that Kurtis ever did.

It was so stripped-down. At the end of the day, the biggest songs in Kurtis' career weren't hard hip-hop tracks. The day we were booked to record the single version of "Fresh Is The Word" was the last day that INS was open before they were doing a bunch of renovations. They were going to be closed for two weeks after that. So we had to do the record in one session, because they were about to tear everything apart. Kurtis did the 808 program and other embellishments, and then Tee did his vocals. We started at about 8 p.m. and it was now about 4 or 5 in the morning. But we needed a B-Side, which was going to be a dub version ["Fresh Is The Beat"]. Kurtis started falling asleep and he said, "Will, you finish it." It was already mixed, but nothing was edited together yet. So I started editing pieces of the song that had already been mixed. When we were doing the final edits, there were construction guys literally dismantling the studio as we worked to finish. They were pushing us out of the studio so they could tear it apart. It was like being in a restaurant and the waiter is taking food off your plate as you're still eating [laughs]. It was hysterical. And Kurtis was asleep in a chair with his coat wrapped around his head, because the sun had started coming up. We added a bunch of reverb and delays from the music that had been done on the A-Side. We were doing ½-inch tape and razor blade edits. The 2-inch tape and the machine it had been on was already disconnected and removed. By the time we were finally kicked out of INS, we were on an MCI half-inch machine. We played it back and there was a guy with a small sledgehammer whacking the doorway, to demolish it. But we were done.

POPPO: The bottom of that record, the bass, was the biggest challenge for me on there. How were we going to get that big, giant kick to really come through? Back in those days we had all kinds of tricks. I used to run a 40 Hz sine wave out of the console oscillator, and I would gate it and trigger it with the kick drum. I would tune it to the key of the song. In this case, there was no key, so I would just match it to the kick drum tone. So, every time the kick would play, the 40 Hz gated sound would create what was basically a sub-frequency synthesizer. So you got this *thud* thing happening underneath. That's what the 808 really was, it adjusts the decay in the same way. But we had done that before the 808 was being used. Either way, we used the 808 *and* the 40 Hz trick on "Fresh Is The Word." After recording the song, we still had to make it "workable" when it was mastered to vinyl. There were limitations to the cutting lathe and how much bass frequency you could put in the groove. So I worked very closely with Herb Powers, the mastering engineer. If it wasn't done properly, the engineer would do their own approximation and it could sound very "tinny." Most times, the producer [or engineer] of the song wasn't in the mastering session, so the mastering engineer would "fix" things that didn't sound right to them. You had to work within the bounds of technology, but you also wanted to reach the boundaries of the imagination of the artist. It's a hard balance sometimes. I wasn't used to that much low end, to the point where it was unbalanced with the rest of the mix. I would ask, "Why does it have to rumble the speakers that much?" [laughs]. But if you went to a hip-hop club, you realized why.

MASTA ACE INCORPORATED

SlaughtaHouse
Delicious Vinyl / Atlantic, 1993

Brooklyn's Masta Ace [Duval Clear, aka Ase, aka Ase One] first became a hip-hip household name in 1988, thanks to the Marley Marl-produced posse masterpiece "The Symphony" [Cold Chillin' Records]. He then co-produced and controlled the mic on his debut, 1990's highly under-rated *Take A Look Around* [Cold Chillin' / Reprise].

But by late 1991, things weren't as rosy for the MC, through no lack of talent and through no fault of his own.

The harsh realities of the music industry hit him one day, out of the blue. "I was recording my second album for Cold Chillin', with about 10 tracks done," he recalls today. "And Warner Bros. [who distributed Cold Chillin'] handed down the law that a certain number of artists had to be dropped because the label had too many artists that weren't meeting their sales quotas. They drew a line. If you were above the line, you stayed. If you were below the line, you had to figure out something else for yourself. My name was just below that line. They showed me the list."

"After that, I had to start completely from scratch," he continues. No small task. But Ace wasn't the giving-up type. Plus, he had already been standing on his own two feet in the recording studio for years. Nevertheless, it was a daunting task and a completely new journey for the MC. It would take more than a year, and a bi-coastal partnership, to complete it.

Ace was born and raised in Brownsville, Brooklyn. Like many New Yorkers, hip-hop wasn't ever far away in the late '70s and early '80s. He remembers, "Nobody in my neighborhood was making records or was well-known in hip-hop in the late '70s, but there was lots of cats who DJed and rapped. Those cats were my early influences, I would watch them do their thing in the park. DJ Pistol Pete was from the Langston Hughes Houses and DJ AZ was from my projects. Charlie Wop, a rapper, was in my building."

Ace was drawn to the mic from those experiences, and throughout the 1980s he continued to perfect his craft. He eventually met "super producer" Marley Marl after winning a rap contest at Queens' United Skates of America. As Marley explained in the book *Rakim Told Me*, "The grand prize was to go into the studio with me. I liked Ace's style, so I kept him with me after the demo."

Marley then gave Ace a coveted place on a posse cut that would go on to become legendary: "The Symphony." On it, he stood shoulder-to-shoulder with top-tier MCs including Kool G Rap, Big Daddy Kane and Craig G. At age 22, it was his first appearance on wax, and his famous turn did not go unnoticed by fans. Ace also got a solo shot on Marley Marl's 1988 album *In Control Volume 1* [Cold Chillin'], with the song "Keep Your Eye On The Prize"; and a 1989 Marley-produced single on Prism, "Together / Letter To The Better" [as Ace & Action].

"Everything happened so fast for me in '88," Ace recalls. "MC Shan was the man at that time, and Kane and Biz were on the cusp of super-stardom. Eric B. & Rakim was hittin', and they was so ill. The pop audience for hip-hop wasn't even on-board yet, the kids in the suburbs weren't there. If you didn't have skills then you weren't being checked for. 1988 was such a crucial year, and I was just glad to be in the mix."

The Juice Crew was on fire at the time and Ace patiently waited his turn for a full-length. By 1990, he had his wish. *Take A Look Around* was everything fans of Ace and the Juice Crew could want. Intelligent rhymes, funky beats, and a mix of fun – for example, the hit single "Me And The Biz" – with depth, positivity and soul-searching ["Take A Look Around"]. As Ace wrote in the album's liner notes: "The title track is a message to all ghetto dwellers who may not realize the clock is ticking."

When it came to working with the legendary Marley Marl in the studio, Ace has nothing but good things to say. "Overall, I learned a lot. He never did anything detrimental to me," Ace explains. "He was the cat that was on, so it was always a given that he'd make the most money on any deals that were done. I got co-production credit on the first album, but not co-production money. Almost every beat on *Take A Look Around* was from my mother's records, I would bring them over to Marley's house. He would put his twist on it, he would throw on a drum track, chop it up and make it sound extra."

Ace's only quip with *Take A Look Around* was the "Me And The Biz" single. He sighs, "I didn't want that as a single at all, especially not as the first single. But Warner Bros. wanted to go the gimmick route. Benny Medina [the album's Executive Producer] really wanted it. I dealt with some backlash after that, mostly puppet jokes *[Author's note: A reference to the single's cover, plus the video, which featured a fake Biz Markie doll]*."

Considering where Ace was at, post-album-release, it's obvious why the pink-slip news in late 1991 would have hit him so hard. After several years of praise, solid record sales, and next-level rhymes and music, Ace was all of a sudden a dope MC without a contract. "Cold Chillin' said they'd put out my album on Prism [a singles-only off-shoot of Cold Chillin'], but I wasn't feeling that idea," he says. "Everybody else on the label was managed by Superstar Management, which was basically Cold Chillin', but I had my own. So my manager did her thing to get me out of the deal. Unfortunately, Cold Chillin' owned the songs I had recorded already [for the next album]."

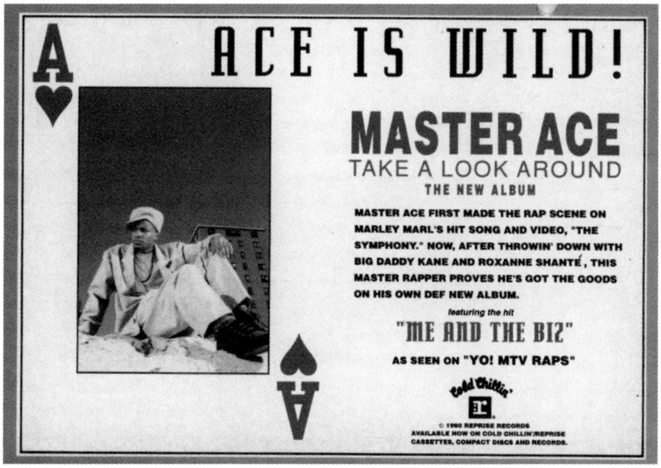

Magazine ad for *Take A Look Around*, late 1990.

Despite his bad run of luck, Ace did have a couple things going for him: a mind full of ideas; a strong will to succeed; and a lawyer in LA who wasted no time making calls. Soon after the outreach began, Delicious Vinyl – a heavily West Coast label, boasting acts including Tone Loc, Young MC and the Pharcyde – expressed interest. Their first step was to include him on their upcoming, Brand New Heavies-backed *Heavy Rhyme Experience Vol. 1* album [1992], with the track "Wake Me When I'm Dead."

"That was the testing ground for me," Ace says. "They liked it and I had a deal from there."

Back on track and – for better or worse – putting his previously-recorded songs behind him, he began work in Brooklyn with his newly-assembled Masta Ace Incorporated. The crew featured brothers Uneek [Shawn McFadden] and Eyce [Courtney McFadden] – producers and MCs who were together known as Eyceurokk, or Ice U Rock – as well as Lord Digga and Paula Perry. Latief and Witchdoc rounded out the production team.

Ace wanted a crew for a reason: "At that time, groups were selling way more than solo artists. The best way to appeal to an audience was to have a lot of characters with me. If a fan didn't like me, maybe they'd like somebody else in the crew."

"Digga and Eyce went to high school with me at Sheepshead Bay High, although I was older than them," Ace explains. "Uneek was the youngest, he was in junior high when I was in high school. Eyce and Uneek always rhymed, Digga didn't rhyme at all back then. He was just a cat who wanted to be around the scene and get down with music in some way or another. He was funny, so we liked having him in the mix."

Masta Ace, cruising.
Photo © B+, for www.Mochilla.com.

He explains that his production relationship with Uneek actually went back to his first album: "He produced and rhymed on 'As I Reminisce' *[Author's note: The credits on 'As I Reminisce' read 'Concept and Performance' by Ice U Rock]*. They gave the co-production credit to Mister Cee because Marley didn't want to have a no-name cat with production credit." And, Ace adds, "Going back beyond that, I probably met Uneek in '82 or '83. His oldest brother and me are the same age. Uneek had a cheap little 4-track at his house and I'd go over there. He'd have these raw beats, making at least one a day."

SlaughtaHouse was the only Delicious Vinyl album recorded outside of Los Angeles during that era, and a very New York-tinged album to boot. But geography wasn't a concern to Ace either way. "I was just happy to have a deal," he admits. "I wasn't thinking about anything in terms of coasts. That East Coast / West Coast thing hadn't even really come about yet."

Did it worry him that after his Cold Chillin' affiliation, he was now working with relative no-names? "It didn't matter that people didn't know Masta Ace Incorporated," he says. "In '93, most people didn't have cats in their crew who were known, so it wasn't a big deal."

SlaughtaHouse was recorded at Firehouse Studios in Brooklyn – run by Shlomo Sonnenfeld and Yoram Vazan – where Gang Starr, the Audio Two, MC Lyte and the Wu-Tang Clan recorded in the late '80s and early '90s. And although he had help with production, it was still clear who was the leader. "It was a crew, but I was the director," he says. "I knew what I wanted on the album. I left those 10 tracks I had done for Cold Chillin' and started brand new. I had gotten new energy from records that had come out between those older tracks and when we started recording my next record. Redman, Cypress Hill and DAS EFX had a big influence on me back then."

Backed by thumping, sometimes jazzy and generally dark beats – a definite departure from his previous work on Cold Chillin' – Ace vented about a lot of things on *SlaughtaHouse*, especially his disdain for wannabe gangsta rappers. "Part of what I was doing with the album was attacking all the N.W.A. copycat dudes," he says. "I just thought that was all way overdone."

"Slaughtahouse" single ad, fall 1993.

But he wasn't only mad at fake gangstas. "I was a lot angrier overall when I recorded *SlaughtaHouse*," he says, openly. "I was really upset with the way the Cold Chillin' thing went down and I channeled that anger into the album. I was just mad at everybody."

Many times, as on the album's title track and "Boom Bashin'," Ace walked a thin line with his verbal attacks, with overly realistic parodies of derivative MCs. In fact, it could be argued that some of the satirical work on *SlaughtaHouse* was walking the exact same lines as the uber-witty Gravediggaz [overseen by producer Prince Paul, with RZA, Frukwan and Poetic], who would debut a year later, in 1994 [*Niggamortis / 6 Feet Deep*, Gee Street / Island].

"The jokes on the album went over a lot of peoples' heads," he admits, adding, "And the album was too dark for a lot of people. You have to remember that *The Chronic* dropped around the same time. That album was clear and crisp, and the most amazingly-mixed album ever. And then here's my shit – sounding dark, dirty, grungy and just gutter. So you was with one or the other. And most of the people in the world jumped on the whole Dre sound."

Album sticker.

There was also an excellent smattering of boom-bap, party-moving jams, like the hit "Jeep Ass Niguh"; the jazzy "Mad Wunz"; and the excellent posse cut "Saturday Nite Live." Once the album was out, he toured with Mic Geronimo, the Alkaholiks and the Pharcyde. "Mostly just spot dates," he says. But he had survived and re-invented himself, without missing a beat, which was a triumph in itself.

The album had a wide range, but was stronger because of all the bases that were covered, and iced by the fact that Ace's lyricism – whether telling stories, schooling fakers or philosophizing about the woes in his urban environment – never faltered. He explains, "I was saying, 'This is how it is, but it shouldn't be this way.'" And as dark as the content could be at times, he says, "It was fun recording that record. And when it hit, I got respect from both coasts. So I was nothing but glad."

TRACKS

A Walk Thru The Valley

My plan was to do a poem on each album. That was my second one, and the intro to the record. I wanted to set the tone with the gunshots, and paint a picture of the neighborhood. I was going a step further than a group like N.W.A., saying it shouldn't be like it is. In the poem, I actually name several of the song titles from *Take A Look Around*. Not every song, but quite a few. At the end, with that classroom scene, that was actually Uneek as the teacher, and it was an actual class of his that he was talking to *[Author's note: Ace says that Eyce and Uneek both became teachers after the album was released]*. A summer school class or something like that. I would love to be reunited with some of those kids today.

Slaughtahouse ["starring MC Negro & The Ignorant MC"]

That was the second single. Uneek produced that one and he was also MC Negro on the song. After that came out, I was doing shows in the Midwest, and there's the portion of that song where MC Negro comes on, before I come in. On the single, him and The Ignorant MC have their own three-minute song ["Murder Mix"], and I have extended rhymes on the single, too ["Death Mix"]. People out there thought that their part ["Murder Mix"] was a real group and a full single. People had their rap on some kind of countdown in St. Louis. I went to a car show in St. Louis and there was a wet t-shirt contest and they was playing *that* record for it. It's like a Weird Al Yankovic parody and the people in the crowd at the show have got their hands in the air, saying "Murda murda murda, kill kill kill." With the humor in that type of song I was definitely walking a thin line. I don't know if it's true or not, but I heard that the Westside Connection [group] was created because of the

SlaughtaHouse album. The whole purpose of their group was to defend West Coast gangsta rap. Somebody told me it was said.

Late Model Sedan

I love that track, the beat especially. Latief did that one. He should be famous right now. The rhyme on that was actually based on a flow that Ice Cube did on one of his albums. "Ghetto Bird," I think. After that song and "Jeep Ass Niguh," the album definitely started getting darker.

Jeep Ass Niguh

That was the lead-off single for the record. It was a double A-side, with "Saturday Nite Live." We did videos for both songs. When I perform that today, people just start jumping around. It never blew up like it could now, but it was a good underground, hip-hop purist record. Cars were just something that I was into. I had recently bought my first Jeep, when my first album came out, and I just kept buying tons of car magazines and was figuring out how to hook the thing up with a giant sound system. Driving around Brooklyn just became part of what I did. Not too many people were making songs about cars on either coast. "Jeep Ass" was definitely one of the first.

The Big East

That's one of my favorite cuts on the album. The Beatheads produced that. They was some cats from Connecticut. I didn't really know them, but they reached out to me and I really liked the music they played for me. I was really into slow, funky tracks. That's my A & R guy, Orlando [Arguillen] who says, "Don't even think about trippin'" on there.

Jack B. Nimble

Before I was anything else, I was a storytelling rapper, that's how I got on in the first place. Like "La Di Da Di" type of joints. When I won the contract to work with Marley Marl at a contest, it was with a story rap. It was a fun way to paint a picture. When Uneek gave me that beat, the story just came to me. His beat is a chop of the original "Symphony" beat, a small tiny piece he looped up. Those lyrics were originally recorded over a different beat for my second Cold Chillin' album, the one I started but never came out.

Mad Wunz

That's another one of my favorite tracks. That probably should have been a single. I perform that song now and people wild out. I remember Jon Shecter [co-founder of *The Source*] told me one time that if that song would have been released as a single, my whole career would have been different. That was the song that was getting all the spins when the album came out. It was more of a joint rather than making any kind of statement. At the time, I was trying to be more artistic and creative, but that was just a cool track.

Style Wars

I produced that one myself. It was a chopped up B.B. King thing. A remix of that was on the flip of the "Slaughtahouse" single. I called it "Style Wars" because I was really influenced by that graffiti documentary [with the same title, from 1983, directed by Tony Silver]. It made sense as a title because rap is about style too, and about MCs battling with rhyming. I didn't write [graffiti] a lot back in the day but I definitely started bombing again when the album came out. I wrote "Ase."

Who U Jackin'?

That's a thing with me and Paula Perry. I met her through Uneek. She's from Fort Greene [Brooklyn]. Uneek and Eyce were recording demos with her. I heard them and definitely wanted a female to be on the record, and this was kind of her introduction. She played more of a role later on. There's nothing too involved about the concept on that track [about a guy trying to stick up a woman and her talking back to him], I just thought it was a funny idea. It was too easy to do a love rap kind of thing, so I made it about a stick-up.

Rollin' Wit Umdadda

That's one song that I listen to now and I wince a little bit. I don't like the way I sound on it, or the way the beat came out. There was a different beat on there originally and I think I started to over-think it. I produced that one, too. A lot of people still don't know that I produce, even to this day. The title of that song is really stupid, too. Back then we were trying to make up different slang, and it was like, "Yo, I was rolling with like umdadda niggas" [meaning: a lot]. It became a song title because guys started saying it all the time. The end of the song, when we're stepping on stage at the club, sounds live, but we did that in the studio.

Ain't U Da Masta

Lyrically, that's one of my favorites. With that one I was going at the press a little bit, because it had been a minute since I put the last album out, and I felt like people were counting me out of the game. I kind of felt like the press was going to dis the record, so I was giving them permission ahead of time.

Crazy Drunken Style

That's one of my favorite beats on the album. Lord Digga's on there. He wasn't really so scary, but he was good at acting rough. He's a nice dude, really.

Don't Fuck Around (Outro)

That wasn't Paula Perry singing, that was some chick that Eyce and them knew. I wasn't very experienced with what good singing was, and I kind of wince when I hear that one. I didn't want it to be taken seriously anyways.

Saturday Nite Live

That was a single with "Jeep Ass Niguh," a double A-Side. Our whole crew was in that video, everybody we grew up with. That was fun. We all had baseball bats and big sticks, being real rugged. That was the whole Naughty By Nature influence. We were in an abandoned building and a highlight was that a famous graffiti writer, Cope 2, was in it. I had never met him, but he was famous to me. He came to the set and did a couple throw-ups, and one of them is in the video. That set was pretty ill, too. One time the cameraman stepped into a hole and fell. One leg went into the hole and he got pretty hurt, but he kept filming. The abandoned building on the cover is the same one where we shot the video. It's in Crown Heights and it's all re-done and condos

now. I put that song last on the album because it starts with such a great mood and because I also wanted the album to end on an "up" note. Lord Digga wasn't supposed to be on that [as an MC] at first. At the time, early in the album, he wasn't writing good quality stuff yet, lyrically. He was just starting to rhyme back then. We all did our verses and he was sitting there with a sad face. Up until that time he tried, but we'd never put him on. But on that one he got it together and we all agreed it was dope.

MOS DEF & TALIB KWELI

Are Black Star
Rawkus Entertainment, 1998

"I was listening to a lot of jazz at the time, and I wanted to give our work that same sophistication, while still keeping the raw energy."

– Yasiin Bey [formerly known as Mos Def]

"The reason that the album has held up is because they both wanted to be mouthpieces for the struggle. And they were."

– Shawn J. Period

The late 1990s was an at-times tumultuous – and frustrating – era in hip-hop. There was the East Coast / West Coast feud (real or imagined); the tragic murders of Tupac and the Notorious B.I.G.; and the continuing spread of wack major label artists and producers, with color-by-numbers formulas for hits (Puffy and Jermaine Dupri, with their artist stables, come to mind).

Equally important, though, was the rise of a disaffected-but-bold indie hip-hop underground, which began manifesting itself in the form of groups like Company Flow, Dr. Octagon, Lootpack and the Solesides family [DJ Shadow, Blackalicious, Latyrx].

In the middle, somewhere between the anti-establishment party crashers and the pop charts, stood Mos Def [now known as Yasiin Bey; birth name Dante Terrell Smith] and Talib Kweli [Talib Kweli Greene]. They sympathized more with the underground than with charting rappers, but they made music that wasn't grating, and wasn't necessarily trying to overturn the entire apple cart. They wanted you to make your own decisions about where you stood in the hip-hop world of 1998. And that was precisely why they became such a phenomenon.

Oh, it should also probably be noted: they could rap circles around most of their peers, with content that was both of-the-moment and timeless, exposing both the struggles and triumphs of young African-Americans.

The real mover behind what became known as Black Star – and who will be the first to point out that it *wasn't* supposed to be a group, as you'll see below – was Talib Kweli, known as Kweli or "Kwa" to friends. Born and raised in Brooklyn [Park Slope, East

Flatbush, Bed-Stuy, Ft. Greene], he had one brother and was brought up in a family of educators. Both parents were college professors [his mother: humanities, English, and writing; his father: sociology].

"When I first started listening to hip-hop, what I was immediately drawn to was the messaging," Kweli recalls. "The music was always around me in New York, but honestly I didn't pay as much attention to it until 1987 or '88, other than bigger records by Run-DMC and the Beastie Boys. It was party music when it started, and it didn't really gain a foothold as something that would be 'conscious' or uplifting until later."

Raised with learnings and discussions about Marcus Garvey-inspired Black Nationalism and Pan-Africanism in his home, Kweli was instantly drawn to political and socially-conscious rhymes. "When I started listening to [popular NYC hip-hop radio DJs] Red Alert and Mr. Magic, groups like Public Enemy, Boogie Down Productions, Big Daddy Kane and Rakim really caught my attention," he explains. "Especially Kane and Rakim – they had party songs, but they were rooted in 5 Percent philosophy. That matched up well with the images that were around me in my house when I was younger."

He continues, "All of a sudden, the things I learned at home were being talked about on records. It all came together. I'm a writer, that's what I do. I just happen to be a musician. So I put my writing to music."

This, of course, was happening while Spike Lee's pro-Brooklyn, pro-Black movement was being celebrated in movies like "Do The Right Thing" [1989] and "Malcolm X" [1992]. Many fans of Public Enemy, Rakim or X-Clan, especially in the suburbs, were rebelling by bringing these albums home. For Kweli, though, it was something you could put on the living room stereo, then discuss pros and cons with your parents at dinner.

In the earliest 1990s, Kweli left his home of Planet Brooklyn for the suburban backdrop of Connecticut. Although, not by choice. He was sent to the Cheshire Academy in the central part of the state, about two hours from New York City, where he eventually earned his high school diploma. "I got sent to boarding school," he says, "because I just refused to go to regular high school in Brooklyn [Brooklyn Tech]. It wasn't a challenge to me. I would skip school and go to a Blackwatch event that X-Clan was having instead."

"I'm glad I went to Cheshire, it was a great move on my parents' part," he continues. "It was an international school with kids from all over the world. It was a better place for me to learn. I'm blessed that my parents sacrificed to make it happen. Education was their number one priority for me."

After Cheshire, Kweli returned to the City and enrolled at New York University. There he became roommates with someone who would help him as he later strove to climb the music business ladder: rapper and producer John Forté [who would later be known as part of the Fugees' extended family]. The two both went to boarding schools in New England [Forté at Phillips Exeter in New Hampshire] and would travel back to New York together on occasion, so they had already known each other before landing in the same dorm at NYU.

Kweli recalls, "Forté had one toe in NYU and the rest of his body was in the music business. He was immersed in the world of hip-hop and he was one of my best friends, so I was soaking up a lot of game from him." With Forté helping Funkmaster Flex and a [pre-Puffy] Sean Combs promote parties and pass out flyers in 1994, Kweli was learning tricks of the trade and important lessons that would serve him well in the mid- and later-'90s, as he cemented his own career in the music business. One of Kweli's other roommates, Omari, hailed from Cincinnati, OH. This connection would also come into play later on.

Another important link in Kweli's – and Yasiin Bey's – history from the early '90s throughout the 2000s was Nkiru Books, a historic African-American bookstore in the Boerum Hill neighborhood of Brooklyn. Kweli worked there starting in the mid-'90s, and many of the people he met there would go on to influence him in later years. Kweli and Bey would, in fact, go on to purchase the store together in 2000, converting it into a non-profit organization [the Nkiru Center for Education and Culture], although it is no longer in existence.

Beyond Nkiru, it seems inevitable that Kweli and the former Mos Def would meet, considering their shared interests and associates, as well as their budding music careers. "When I was in boarding school, I was coming back to New York every weekend and spending time in Greenwich Village," Kweli explains. "At that time, in the early '90s, Mos was really more into acting than rapping. He was on a TV show with Nell Carter ['You Take The Kids,' 1990-91] and was on that Malcolm Jamal-Warner show ['Here and Now,' 1992-93]."

He continues, "We were casual acquaintances, and I really respected him as an artist. I was working at Nkiru with the mother of my children and became friends with the mother of [Yasiin's] first two children. Our families would get together from that connection. And that's really where Black Star was born."

"I lived in Brooklyn from my birth until 2005," says Yasiin Bey today. He grew up in a large family in Bed-Stuy, Brooklyn's Roosevelt Houses projects, and by his mid-teens in the late '80s had started acting, sometimes appearing as Dante Beze, sometimes as Dante Terrell Smith. Soon he graduated to TV shows, including the two aforementioned programs, and then 1994's "The Cosby Mysteries."

Easygoing and soft-spoken, but fiercely intelligent and decidedly pro-Black, he had attracted a range of musicians and spoken-word artists into his orbit by the mid-'90s. He was doing as much poetry writing and spoken-word as he was performing straight-up hip-hop.

"I first met Kweli in the Village," Bey remembers. "There were a lot of creative young people hanging around Washington Square [Park, near NYU] back in the early '90s. I heard Kweli's demo and I liked his style a lot. It was unusual. I liked the way he put his ideas together. So we just started kickin' it from there. We were both from Brooklyn and on a similar vibe and frequency, so we became easy friends."

During that time, Yasiin was the first of the crew to become known on the mic. After one indie release, in 1994 Bey along with two of his siblings – who went by DCQ and Ces [Denard Smith and Frances Nieves] on the mic – was signed to Payday Records, a label run by artist manager Patrick Moxey. The trio put out three singles in that era under the name Urban Thermo Dynamics [UTD]: "Hardcore Nights" (1994, self-released); "My Kung Fu" (1994, Payday); and "Manifest Destiny" (1995, Payday).

Yasiin recounts his UTD experiences, which were both good and bad: "I was young, 18 or 19, when we started doing the group [in about 1993]. I was new in the business, but I was grateful for the opportunity to make some money. It was my first recording experience and my first time with a record label. There were ups and downs. Eventually we got dropped and the album we recorded never got released. So I was sour on the record industry after that. Plus it kind of dissolved the group, and there were some hard feelings. But I was also determined to go on with music. I just knew I had to find another way to do it."

"When I first met Mos, I knew him from UTD," Kweli says. "They were on Video Music Box. Their records might not have been hugely successful, but for us in Brooklyn it was big. People were excited. Those records were super-creative, they were on some 'other' shit."

Bey points out an important Nkiru-related bonding experience that both young MCs shared. "I would visit Kweli at the bookstore and hang out with him during his lunch breaks," he recalls. "And in that era he started doing these poetry readings there at the store called Foundation. It was really cool, there was a whole 'Brooklyn Moon' scene, a lot of spoken-word."

Makeba Mooncycle, a friend of both Talib's and Mos' throughout the '90s, says, "Talib had worked at another bookstore in Manhattan, near NYU, before Nkiru. But Nkiru was such a great place, there was a great vibe there. So many good books, and not just by black authors. It was a central part of the underground rap scene back then, too. Everybody went to buy stuff there and hang out. And those Foundation nights really got everybody together. They were about loving our people, without anger. We didn't separate poetry from rap. Everybody could just do their thing."

Bey agrees: "Foundation was unique, because it was more dynamic than most spoken-word back then. It included hip-hop MCs. A lot of the spoken-word scene back in the mid-'90s was just about quote-unquote poets, and they had a dismissive, even hostile, attitude towards hip-hop. Rap was seen as being a real 'hood-and-hooligan affair. But at Foundation, the best of hip-hop and poetry was showcased, side by side, in a positive way. It was serious because it was at a bookstore, but it was also a youth event, with MCs and producers there."

"Kweli," Bey adds, "was such a great *connector*." Talib would also perform his own spoken-word compositions at Nkiru's Foundation nights, and the two men continued to build friendship and respect for each other as artists.

Talib's first crystallized hip-hop association was during the early '90s, in a prototypical inception of the group Da Bush Babees, with Mister Man [later known as Mr. – or Lord – Khaliyl]. The group continued when Kweli went off to boarding school and would later put out two albums on Reprise, in 1994 and 1996. Kweli acknowledges that if he hadn't gone to Connecticut he very well might have ended up as a member of the group.

By 1995, Kweli was trying various avenues to become known as an MC, with varying degrees of success. He continued to hang with John Forté, but had dropped out of NYU and was looking for a way to get his voice heard. He was managed by Makeba Mooncycle, who had started her career helping road manage X-Clan and had formed a management company with MC Lyte and Isis called Duke Da Moon, working with many artists on the indie scene, including early Rawkus Records signing The Rose Family. She would go on to work at Gee Street and Blunt as the decade wore on, and she was always in Talib's camp.

Kweli's first demo as a solo artist, he says, was done with John Forté as a producer and, "recorded in a very basement studio in Brooklyn." He made more demos in the mid-'90s, usually with producer Self and Self's production partner Goldie. "People were starting to pay attention," he recalls, "but nothing was really breaking through yet." He had begun to register on the radar of the popular "Stretch & Bobbito" underground hip-hop show on Columbia University's WKCR as well.

"Unfortunately, Talib wasn't talking about things that were popular at the time," Mooncycle explains. "Mobb Deep was popular back then. He was too intricate. But we all knew something was going to happen. I always believed that he was the next KRS-One. He had consciousness but with personal reflection about what was going on around him." She also mentions that before he landed on using Talib Kweli as his performing name [which is his first and middle name], he called himself Eternal Reflection and had a song with the same name, in about 1994. "He only called himself that for about six months," she says.

"I was making demos and meeting a lot of people, but honestly, in around 1995 I was getting tired of the New York scene," Kweli remembers. "It seemed stagnant to me. So my friend Omari [from NYU] invited me to go Cincinnati. He knew guys in this group called MOOD [rappers Donte and Main Flow, with producer Jahson]. I'm honestly not sure what made me go; I guess I was just bored. I was working, and had dropped out of NYU at that point. So I went out there and met them."

Kweli continues, "The guys in MOOD were hustlers, street hustlers, who rapped really well and made beats. And they all had their own money, cars, studio equipment. They looked up to me since I was from New York, but I was really impressed with them, because I was still scrounging back there, living hard. I guess the meeting was great for both of us."

From that point on, Kweli and MOOD would visit each other in their respective hometowns. Soon, Kweli would meet his future production partner, DJ Hi-Tek [Tony Cottrell], a friend and collaborator who worked with MOOD. And MOOD would sign an album deal with New York-based Blunt / TVT Records via Makeba Mooncycle's connections. The group put out the album *Doom* in 1997, with guest vocals on almost a half-dozen of the CD's tracks by Kweli.

During trips to Ohio, Kweli met and built with Hi-Tek – a relationship that would soon become an intensive one from a production standpoint. "I went out to Cincy one time and I came back with three songs that Hi-Tek had done for me," explains Kweli. "And that's when people started taking me more seriously, with that demo."

"Kweli told me how he was going back and forth to Cincinnati, to link up with those guys," Bey remembers. "He'd play me the stuff he was doing with them and I could see that he was on his grind, that he was asserting himself as an artist. I had a lot of respect for that. I mean, I wouldn't have done that. I didn't have the motivation to take a bus to Cincinnati [laughs]."

"Before that [Hi-Tek demo], people gave me respect, but were like, 'That's that guy who's always with John Forté,'" Kweli says. "But after I met Tek, Danny Castro and Anthony Marshall from [popular hip-hop performance series] The Lyricist Lounge finally let me get on by myself, instead of being part of a cipher. Things definitely changed, and it was all up from there."

Looking back, most attentive people – fans and those involved with its recording – would agree that DJ Hi-Tek was the glue that held the *Are Black Star* album together, from a production standpoint at least. But in many ways, it went beyond knob-twiddling. Born in 1976 and raised in Cincinnati all his life, he has a quiet confidence that undoubtedly kept both Kweli and Mos Def at ease during the album sessions.

"Music has always been in my family," Tek says. "My father was the lead singer in a group called the Ditalians. Him and my uncle Larry, with some other guys, also started a group who, after my dad had left, went on to become the group The 24-Carat Black [known to hip-hop fans for their song "Ghetto (Misfortune's Wealth)," sampled by Eric B. & Rakim on "In The Ghetto"].

He grew up on two sides of Cincinnati in the '70s and '80s: the suburbs and the projects downtown. The adjustment from green grass to concrete wasn't an easy one, but Tek says, "Being in the projects made me who I am today. Because I learned hip-hop there."

Originally allied with a local rapper named Vicious Lee, Hi-Tek taught himself to produce, "at age 14, with three tape decks in my bedroom, doing pause-tapes with a Casio SK-5 keyboard. I think it had a two-second sample time." He adds, "Later on, I heard what Pete Rock and Premier were doing, but I was flying blind, I had no one to teach me what to do. So I figured it out myself."

Eventually gathering enough equipment and clientele, with help from Lee, he ran his own studio during the early '90s, working with local MCs and singers from many musical genres. He and Lee made a demo in 1994 and attended the New Music Seminar in New York, hoping to get discovered. But soon, after they returned home with no deal in hand, Lee did the first of two stints in jail. The time apart made it difficult to keep their momentum going as a duo.

During the unfortunate soap opera of Lee being in and out of jail during 1995 and 1996, Hi-Tek started working with MOOD. He points out that he was never a member of the group, although he did some production for them, including work on 1997's previously-mentioned album *Doom*. After a New York trip in 1996, Main Flow and Donte from the group brought back a demo from an MC he had never heard before: Talib Kweli. "I thought that shit was incredible," Tek recalls.

As a result of continued conflict between Vicious Lee and Hi-Tek ["Lee would get jealous when I was over at MOOD's studio," Tek explains] and Lee's jail bids, Tek started to gravitate more towards MOOD's side. Tek produced a remix for their self-released single "Hustle On The Side," which came out in 1995 [Tek says the original came out in 1994 on Below-Zero Records] and featured Lee on vocals. As MOOD began to negotiate with Blunt on their album deal, Tek even considered joining up.

But, he says, "When I found out I didn't have to be in the group and could still get paid for the beats I did, I was good with that. I produced about 50 percent of the album and they signed one of the worst contracts you could ever sign. So I was glad to *not* be part of that."

Most importantly, he met Talib Kweli during these back-and-forth Cincy-to-New York excursions, and the two began working on tracks together more consistently. [At this point Lee had gotten arrested again, this time for a longer bid]. "I was always looking for the right person to work with," Tek explains. "MOOD was already a group, and Lee wasn't taking the rap thing seriously."

When asked why he was drawn to work with his musical partner from the Buckeye State, Kweli says, "Tek has a rare ability to have his shit be knocking and soulful at the same time. He was the next in line from Premier, Pete Rock and Diamond D. Those guys are the ones that me and Mos grew up on, so it worked out perfectly. The other producers on the *Black Star* album, like Shawn J. Period, 88-Keys and J. Rawls, had beats that were really dope. But Hi-Tek had a *vision*."

Tek and Kweli never re-did songs on the demo that had first caught Tek's ear [which was produced by Self], they started anew with their own music. Tek recalls, "Kweli came to Cincy to work with me, we were in my studio for like two days straight. That's when everything was born. I had all these beats, and Lee wasn't being serious. Kweli was hungry. I had been waiting."

Tek says that the demo, from 1996, included two or three songs, including "What's Going On In The World" and a song called "Verses" *[Author's note: This could also have been spelled "Versus"]*. Neither was released during that era. Tek also points out that the first Reflection Eternal single, "Fortified Live," was *not* on that original demo.

By mid-1996, both Kweli and Mos were fully ensconced in the indie hip-hop explosion that was underway in New York, centered around the Lyricist Lounge night; Stretch & Bobbito's radio show; and Fat Beats Records and Distribution. Into this fray, alongside a slew of smaller indie labels, came Rawkus Records.

Kweli was already well-aware of Rawkus, thanks to his friend and running partner John Forté, who Kweli says went to high school at Phillips Exeter Academy with label founders Brian Bater and Jarret Myer. After Exeter, Brian and Jarret both attended Brown University. Kweli says, "When they got out of Brown, they contacted John and said, 'We want to start a record label.' Not a hip-hop label, per se, just a record label, for a bunch of genres. So John was actually their first A & R guy, in about 1994. They put out a bunch of rock, reggae, bass music, trance. None of it worked. Then they moved on to hip-hop."

"Mos took a meeting with Rawkus, he was going to do a single with them," Kweli continues. "And I was still shopping my demo to major labels. He said to me, 'Yo, these guys at Rawkus have money, you should fuck with them, too.' And that's what I did, after a little while. Initially, I wanted to go with a major label, but by the time Mos met with them, I was warming up to putting out records in that indie scene."

"It actually wasn't that long after the Payday experience with UTD that I started talking to Rawkus, probably in 1996," Bey says. "I knew I didn't want another record deal, or to do anything with a major label. Then De La's *Stakes Is High* [Mos Def was featured on one track – 'Big Brother Beat'] and Da Bush Babees [Mos is on three tracks on *Gravity*] happened. I made money on those, and my work was getting out there. I had been on my own since I was a teenager, making my own money. I was always fine with being a 'working artist.' I never wanted to be super-famous, I just didn't want to live at home with my parents."

Makeba Mooncycle has two recollections about Yasiin back in the mid-'90s: "He definitely never wanted to be in a group. And back then, even more than music, Mos really wanted to be a successful actor. I think that was more his passion. Music was his hobby, and he just happened to do it better than most others."

"I remember I told De La and [their manager] Chris Lighty that I wanted a one-album deal or nothing, and they laughed at me," Bey recalls. "They said, 'Ain't no one gonna give you a one-album deal.' But that's what I wanted. And I heard that Rawkus was giving deals for singles where they didn't require a long-term contract. They were looking for people like me, and I was looking for people like them."

As fans will recall, Talib's and Mos' first efforts on Rawkus were not as a duo. First came Mos' "The Universal Magnetic" in June of 1997, produced by Shawn J. Period. Then Talib's "Fortified Live" [under the name Reflection Eternal], which featured Mos Def and Mr. Man, and was produced by DJ Hi-Tek.

"I already had the song 'Fortified Live' recorded as a demo when I went to Rawkus," says Kweli. "They fell in love with the song and offered me a single deal. So we recorded that at Platinum Island and put that song out, right after 'The Universal Magnetic.'"

"Hi-Tek was so dope," Yasiin says, "I loved his tracks. They had 'Fortified Live' and I just loved what they were doing."

At the time, Hi-Tek had moved to New York and was crashing on Talib's couch. He would go back and forth between New York and Ohio as the Rawkus relationship continued to develop, in 1997 and 1998.

Next was the single that cemented the Kweli / Mos partnership, in Rawkus' eyes and their own: early 1998's "The Lyricist Lounge Vol. 1 presents: Body Rock." The A-side, produced by Shawn J., was Mos Def with Q-Tip and Tash [from Tha Alkaholiks]. The B-side was Talib's and Hi-Tek's "Manifesto" [with "Kweli" listed as the artist, not Reflection Eternal]. Taken from an upcoming compilation that would highlight the Lyricist Lounge scene of which they were both an important part, it seemed like Reflection Eternal might have to take a back seat as Mos and Talib revved up as dueling MCs.

While Mos was fine with putting out more singles, Talib was thinking full-length, since he and Hi-Tek had been working towards that goal with their own studio time together since 1996. "Reflection Eternal was my group with Hi-Tek, and I tried to sell Rawkus on an album with Reflection first," Talib explains. "But I was doing a lot of shows with Mos at the time, so Rawkus thought it was perfect to put us together."

"After we had success with 'Body Rock' and 'Universal Magnetic,' Rawkus wanted to do an album with me," says Bey. "But I was hesitant, because there was a certain amount of freedom that I wanted to maintain. Because of that, singles appealed to me. But Jarret and Brian from Rawkus said, 'The album budget [advance] would be a lot bigger than the single budget.' And I said, 'Oh, yeah, that does sound nice!' Either way, though, I didn't want to do more than one album."

With the understanding that a Reflection Eternal full-length would happen *after* an album released with Mos Def [which did happen, in the form of 2000's *Train Of Thought*, on Rawkus], both Mos and Talib capitulated. "It was great with me," says Kweli. "By that time we were spending a lot of time together, and we were fans of each others' music. People expected to see me at his shows and him at my shows. So it was a natural thing to do."

[Author's note: Moving forward in this chapter, when the album itself or the music contained in it is referenced, this will read Are Black Star or Black Star. If references pertain to any combination of the group of people who made the music on the album, it will be written Black Star *[un-italicized], even though – as previously noted – they were not an official group using that name].*

Hi-Tek is actually glad that the *Black Star* album was done first. He says, "It didn't bother me, really, because in my heart I knew that I wasn't ready to do a full album. Doing *Black Star* first took some of the weight off my and Kweli's shoulders, because we wasn't ready. After we did that album, I felt ready, and we went right into working on Reflection Eternal, with an even bigger budget than we would have gotten before."

Possibly because of Mos Def's independent feelings at the time, Kweli never actually saw the duo as a full, dedicated group. "People think of Black Star as a group, but honestly I don't think either of us thought of it that way," he explains. "We became a group, especially the way we look back at it now, but it wasn't really that way when it

Talib Kweli & Mos Def [Yasiin Bey], 1998.
Photo © Eddie Otchere, www.genius-land.com.

was happening. It was like, 'We're doing an album.' You can see that in the way the album title reads [Mos Def & Talib Kweli *Are Black Star*]."

Bey had a similar understanding of the group dynamic. "The album was unique because me and Kweli didn't have to both be on every song," he says. "We agreed that we would each show what we were doing in a different light. We were individuals who were working together. People responded to us as a group, but that wasn't our intention."

He continues, "Our identities as individuals weren't dependent on us as a group. That's what made it special. It was a place of positive creation and no pressure. We weren't trying to compete with anyone or to live up to anyone's expectations. We were doing what we wanted to do. And both of us have been able to stand strong, as individuals, in the years since it came out."

Makeba Mooncycle adds, "I don't think either of those guys could ever be in a group. Talib was definitely always made to be a soloist."

"As we were starting to work on the album, Kwa was more lyrical than Mos, but he was still trying to find his voice," says Tek. "They are a lot like Outkast, if you ask me, with Mos as Andre 3000. When we would do shows, Mos was the shining light, but Kwa was the lyrical fire. Mos wasn't as lyrical. In the end, it was a great balance."

Producer Shawn J. Period, who worked with Mos on his early Rawkus singles, states, "They both had such a great mutual respect for each other. Talib prepared a lot, but he wasn't so tight and rigid that he couldn't get creative. And Mos prepared, too. He wrote stuff ahead of time. But when he was in the studio he just let it flow a little bit more. If there was an instrument lying around, he'd mess with it while the engineers were prepping. They weren't trying to change each other. They were two individuals coming together, with a common goal. Both of them wanted to articulate struggles that they saw, and different perspectives on urban living."

Kweli says, "The way we named the project was pretty telling of how our dynamic was. Mos said we should call it Black Star and I was like, 'Yes, Marcus Garvey.' And he said, 'Yeah, I guess, but I was thinking of it more as a celestial phenomenon.' That's why the first [full] song is 'Astronomy,' because that's where he was at with it."

As they prepared to record the album, Bey recalls his state of mind, at least from a musical perspective: "I was listening to a lot of jazz back then, and there was a John Coltrane and Milt Jackson album I heard *[Author's note: Assuming he means 1960's Bags & Trane, on Atlantic]* and I thought it'd be cool to do that with a hip-hop artist. A collaboration, in the jazz spirit. We could both stay as solo artists and both keep pushing. So we started doing it. We'd write together at each others' cribs, and we started doing more shows together."

Kweli explains, regarding the division of labor when it came to getting things done: "The contract with Rawkus was mostly with me. I'm not even sure if Mos signed it, honestly. It was an extension of my Reflection Eternal deal [which, Talib says, was for two albums, with *Are Black Star* being the first]. Like, 'We're doing a Reflection Eternal album, but before that we'll do this quick Black Star project.'"

For better or worse, quick it was not. There were two phases to the album recording – the first ended up being more of a bonding trip to Los Angeles, in late 1997. The second consisted of sessions completed over the course of about four months, mostly at Brooklyn's Funky Slice Studios, with a side-trip to Chicago.

"The idea we started with was that when it came to production, it was going to be mostly DJ Hi-Tek – my guy – and Shawn J. Period, who was Mos' guy," Talib explains. "But at that time, Shawn decided that he didn't want to do certain types of hip-hop songs. He didn't want to do songs with cursing and also didn't want to sample anymore. So, he took some time away and re-learned his craft. Unfortunately, that happened right as we started to put the album together."

Bey says, "I didn't know how many tracks that Shawn would end up doing, we were just playing it by ear. Hi-Tek [who produced six of the album's 13 tracks, compared to Shawn's two] was just around a lot. Which doesn't mean that Shawn wasn't, but... Tek was just in the mix, because he and Kweli were in the planning stages for Reflection Eternal's album."

Hi-Tek agrees that the initial plan was for around a 50 / 50 workload split on production: "If you look at the album cover, at the bottom, in the center of the crowd you can see me and Shawn J, both there in the front. As for how many tracks I ended up doing, it was all about whatever worked best for what Mos and Kwa were doing."

"Shawn was the next dude who would have hit it big before he changed his path," Tek adds. "He was before Dilla, before Kanye. He was about to kill it. I looked up to him a lot."

Shawn J. Period [Shawn Jones], the producer of the Mos Def singles leading up to the *Black Star* album, grew up in the suburbs outside of Richmond, VA. He had a moderately musical upbringing, including a stint in the high school band, but was an MC before he produced. "Production was a tool for me to write to," he explains. "It was a secondary thing, originally." He plays keyboards, but "not as an expert."

He continues, “I always made *hybrid* music, where there would be some live instrumentation and some sampling elements, chopping vocals or instruments. Even to this day, my strength is programming. Getting the essence of what I want to play, and then chopping or looping it. I’m a musician who programs, not vice-versa.”

Shawn’s work with Mos Def on his early Rawkus singles was not his first entrée into the world of hip-hop. In fact, he probably had more hip-hop “game” experience than Mos and Kweli combined in 1996. During his last year in high school through his first years at Virginia Commonwealth University, he was in a group called Down South: he and his cousin Jeremy [aka Soda Pop] were MCs, and their DJ was Myorr. They signed to Big Beat / Atlantic in 1992.

Shawn produced eight songs on their debut album, 1994’s *Lost In Brooklyn*, alongside the Beatnuts, T-Ray and Stretch Armstrong. He relocated to Brooklyn from Virginia in the early ‘90s, where he has been ever since.

“I came to New York to be an MC, not a producer,” he says. “But Reef Tewlow and Bobbito Garcia, who signed and mentored me during the Down South years, saw things in me as a producer that I hadn’t seen. Being around the Beatnuts also helped a lot.”

Album ad for Down South’s *Lost In Brooklyn*, from 1994.

Unfortunately the Down South album didn’t hit as much as anyone would have liked. The group was dropped by Big Beat, then it disbanded. But, as Shawn says, “I realized that, at my core, I was a producer.” He produced three tracks on fellow Virginian Mad Skillz’s album *From Where???* [Big Beat, 1996] and began working as a freelancer. “I really enjoyed being a [freelance] producer because it allowed me to be a part of various peoples’ careers, but I wasn’t tied to them,” he says. “I got the chance to go to different peoples’ ponds and fish in their waters.”

Shawn linked up with Mos Def thanks to his work on Da Bush Babees’ *Gravity* album, on which Mos was featured [Shawn did the intro and outro to the album, along with producing two other tracks]. Interestingly, the music used for Mos’ “The Universal Magnetic” single was originally offered to Da

Bush Babees. According to Shawn, it came too late in the album process, but Mos loved it and they developed it. "Body Rock" came next, and Shawn agrees that it's fair to say that that single was the "prequel" to what would become the *Black Star* album.

As for Shawn's take on how many songs he would produce on *Black Star*, he says, "I wanted to produce as much as I could, but there wasn't any understanding that I was going to do half of the tracks or anything like that. The difference with me and Mos [versus Talib and Hi-Tek] is that we weren't a group. They were a unit. Me and Mos were working together and we were tight, but he was working with other people as well. I didn't know Talib very much until we started working on the album."

Regarding his "conversion" during the *Black Star* recording era, Shawn explains: "I made a decision back then not to sample, because of spiritual reasons. I became a devout Christian at the time and I felt that 'the sampling people' *[Author's note: Assuming he means people at labels, who decide what they will clear and what they won't]* teach you to steal and then cover it up. It was just a personal conviction for me."

He continues, "I had no issue with samples that were cleared, of course. But most people weren't clearing back then, because it was costly. I mean, who wants to pay seven different people to take a piece of a song? But it's true that the *Black Star* album was about to start being recorded when I began to make the transition."

He does say, though, that his new feelings about sampling weren't the reason why he wasn't more involved. "Hi-Tek was just in a position to do more," Shawn says. "He was the group's DJ." He also states, "I don't necessarily wish that I had more songs on the album, because then the album wouldn't have been what it was. It was great to have all the producers who were involved. I'm very glad that it happened like it did."

An important chapter to the Black Star story was their early trip to Los Angeles, which was originally planned as the beginning of their actual recording sessions. "Before we went to Funky Slice in Brooklyn, we went to Los Angeles," Kweli remembers. "My friend Kendra Ross' father was a musician and he had a studio in his house out there. She said we could use the studio for free, and since I was watching our budget, I jumped on that idea."

He continues, "Mos was filming a movie in LA *[Author's note: Most likely the film 'Where's Marlowe,' which came out in 1998]*, so he was out there, in a hotel. Me, J. Rawls and Hi-Tek went and crashed in Mos' room. All of us, on cots. And we'd drive out to Kendra's father's house and record." Shawn J. says that he was there as well, and that different people in the crew were there at different times, not always overlapping.

The first songs they worked on during that trip included: "Brown Skin Lady"; "Definition";

"RE:DEFinition"; and, Kweli says, one other. Hi-Tek says he thinks the "other" song was "K.O.S. (Determination)."

"That trip to LA was a great bonding experience," recalls Hi-Tek. "I loved California, the energy, and it was great hanging out with all those guys. What I didn't like was the studio we were in. It was old-school, R & B, a not-hooked-up-right spot [laughs]. It had an ADAT, it wasn't all the way right. It was in his house, just in the living room. Some place in Sherman Oaks."

Tek continues, "We did some vocals there in LA but those sessions pretty much got lost. We had to re-do them in New York. With the ADAT there in LA, something wasn't recorded right. I still had everything in my MPC [sampler], but I had to re-track it. Kendra's dad went by Bobbalicious [laughs] *[Author's note: Unsure about spelling]*. There were bloods and crips both hanging out there, and this guy Charlie was the engineer. It wasn't perfect on the recording side, but it was still a great experience. I'll never forget it."

Shawn J. Period says, "Being out there put us in a great frame out mind. We were all out of our element. It was a great way to start the project." Neither of Shawn's two songs on the album – "Children's Story" and "Hater Players" – were worked on during the LA trip, they were done back in New York.

Kweli recalls, "We came back with those songs in November, 1997, and then went into Funky Slice, with some stuff done at Platinum Island [in Manhattan]."

The New York sessions, after having to re-record and correct some of the work done in California, were generally accomplished without much drama. "The sessions for the *Black Star* album went pretty well," says Kweli. "Funky Slice was a good place to record. It was in Downtown Brooklyn, near the Albee Square Mall. A lot of people had recorded there: MC Lyte, Stetsasonic, Big Daddy Kane. Honestly, the reason I chose Funky Slice was because I saw it listed in a bunch of different liner notes over the years. It probably closed a year or two after we did our album."

He says they did most of their Funky Slice sessions from midnight to 8 a.m., to save money with "night owl" rates. "To be honest, the only distraction making that album was just to try and stay within the $30,000 budget that Rawkus gave us," Kweli explains. "When you're talking about how that album actually got done back then, it was basically all me. I booked the studio time, I wrote contracts. And don't get me wrong, I'm not mad about it. Mos had a lot going on, and I basically had nothing else to do in my life at that time except to make that album happen."

Stress magazine, March / April 1998 cover feature on Rawkus. Issue included flexidisc of "Definition."

Tek agrees: "Mos was real in and out during that album. Honestly, if it wasn't for me and Kweli, the album wouldn't have gotten done. It was a time where I just took it upon myself to do things, and so did Kwa."

Kweli also describes an interesting discrepancy in their approaches to how lyrics were generally recorded: "My recording style and Mos' were very different back then. He's very organic and natural. He hears a beat and starts singing and rapping. With me, I've gotten to be more like that over the years. But, back then, I needed to be writing to a beat for at least a couple weeks. I had to be super-prepared, or I'd freak out."

In the late '90s, considering the growing "anti-pop-rap" sentiment in the indie underground that the duo – and Rawkus, keeping in mind that rabble rousers Company Flow had released their explosive *Funcrusher Plus* in mid-1997 – was surrounded by, Kweli was put into a strange predicament. "The way that I saw music was very different than many of our fans at the time," he recalls. "I was a Jay-Z fan, I remember 'Hawaiian

Sophie' [a single by Jaz, from 1989, which featured a young Jay-Z], I was rooting for him. I was friends with Lauryn Hill [of the Fugees]. I knew Puff Daddy."

"I didn't think of us as being a big part of the hip-hop industry, but I also didn't see us as being separate," he continues. "When [New York hip-hop station] Hot 97 started playing us, I realized that we could compete in the industry. But a lot of Rawkus fans wanted us to be against major label artists. When we had shows, people would be yelling, 'Fuck Jay-Z! Fuck Puff Daddy!' It was interesting, because I didn't share those same sentiments. Either way, it was impossible to escape the fact that we had come to symbolize a new hope for hip-hop, a rebirth."

Mos Def [Yasiin Bey] & Talib Kweli, 1998.
Photo © Eddie Otchere, www.genius-land.com.

The album was completed in March of 1998. Once it was, Kweli remembers, "It felt good. It felt like I was doing the right thing. It was a proud moment, where I could bring it to my parents and say, 'I made the right decision by dropping out of NYU and following my dream.'"

Although, he adds, "On the day our album came out, Outkast, The Roots, A Tribe Called Quest and Brand Nubian all put records out. I remember thinking, 'Shit, I'm not going to sell one record today!' I really thought that. It's my first album and I'm competing with all of my heroes." Luckily it didn't work out as badly as he thought.

The album hit stores in late August 1998, and featured two commercial singles: "Definition / Twice Inna Lifetime" and "Respiration," as well as the promo-only radio single "RE:DEFinition." It charted well but surprisingly, considering its influence, never went gold. Still, it remains one of the most influential and most-fondly-remembered hip-hop albums of the late '90s. They entered the recording of the album with things still to learn and exited feeling like veterans.

"In 1997 and 1998, labels were trying to phase out vinyl, but Rawkus wasn't part of that trend," Kweli says. "And our packaging was definitely influenced by jazz liner notes from earlier eras. I think that's pretty obvious. For the CD, unfortunately Rawkus only printed the more extensive 10-page booklet for the first run, however many thousands of copies that was. After that it was just a one-page insert. I remember them being like, 'We're not doing that [printing the longer booklet],' and we forced them to. It was a two-month argument and that was the compromise." *[Author's note: The original vinyl features a four-page fold-out booklet with photos and comments / commentary from Kweli and Mos Def, in addition to ads for future Rawkus releases].*

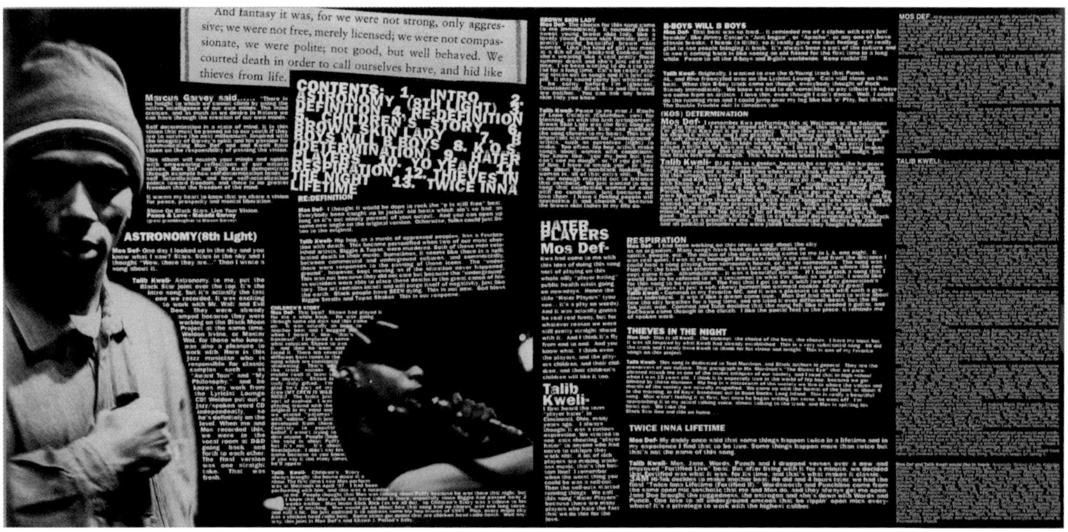

LP liner notes, interior pages

As for how the album was received, Kweli states, "It got a lot of critical acclaim, which blew me back a little bit. I wasn't necessarily ready for the pressure that came with all the expectations people had for us. Some reviews even said that the album was supposed to be some kind of 'second coming' for hip-hop. These were just rhymes that I had in my head, and we picked beats and made an album. We didn't want to represent a movement, we just wanted to rhyme. But you can't control how your fans use your music."

And, listening now, he says, "All the producers we used were definitely cut from the same cloth. So from that respect, I think that everything holds together really well. We were very focused on the themes we presented. And the album wasn't too long. It sounds pretty pure to me."

"I was curious to see how the album would do when it first came out, definitely," recalls Hi-Tek. "I looked at Mos and Kwa as regular dudes, and I was just there with them. It was a new thing for all of us. After it hit, I was pleasantly surprised at how people embraced the album. It felt like we were breathing new life into hip-hop. That felt great."

Hi-Tek adds, "I think its strength is because it has a Midwest production sound *[Author's note: Obviously not completely, since Hi-Tek only produced half the tracks]*, with New York rappers. That really helped them be more than your average New York guys. It could have had that regular boom-bap sound: Pete Rock or Premier. It still would have been dope, but the mix helped them stand out. The *sound* was different."

Black Star producers at album mixing session, Platinum Island NYC, 1998.
L to R: 88-Keys, DJ Hi-Tek, mix engineer Ken "Duro" Ifill and Shawn J. Period.
Photo courtesy of DJ Hi-Tek.

"The thing that really makes that album stand out is that the approach was pure," explains Shawn J. Period. "The way that it came together was very natural. It was a herald from the streets, but not just gun-play and the like. It was two people articulating what was going on, speaking about solutions, and not being pretentious about it."

"I'm really proud of that album," Bey says. "*Black Star* was a place where the things that me and Kweli were trying to do and the ideas we were trying to express as individuals were done as a group. It was two individuals agreeing with each other about a perspective on sound, ideas and textures; but also to an assertion of identity. That identity was as artists, but ultimately as people, as men. We were saying to the world at large: 'We're a lot more dynamic than what you might assume.' It was another perspective, showing that there are more narratives besides the macho narrative, the self-congratulatory narrative, and whatever others. Those weren't *our* narratives."

He continues, beaming and energized by looking back on what they accomplished: "The album was listenable, but it also had abstract parts that weren't heavy-handed. It was approachable, but strange upon inspection. We got away with some unusual things. Things were beautiful and arranged well, but also raw. We were addressing issues, we weren't just super-rappin' people to death. It was a commentary not only about the world we was livin' in, but about a world we thought was possible. The world that we needed."

Japanese "Rawkus Showcase '98" tour poster

TRACKS

Intro

[Producer: DJ Hi-Tek; co-producer Talib Kweli]

DJ HI-TEK: Kwa brought the spoken-word part of that. I did that beat on my own. We didn't really talk about it, I was just like, "We need an intro." I did that at Funky Slice. I had a beat that I had been working on at home for a while, and I had some scratches.

TALIB KWELI: Hi-Tek made that beat. The sampled person speaking on there, that's from my father's record collection. I guess I got co-production since I brought that in for Tek to sample. With poems and sound-bites on the album, I was very into skits, the glue between songs on albums. I'm not so much into it anymore because I feel that you can create a classic without that. But I always carried around a bag of records and movies that we could grab snippets from. I think the vocal stuff on there is either Nat or Cannonball Adderley, but we didn't clear it. Rawkus basically cleared what they felt they had to clear.

Astronomy (8th Light) [featuring Weldon Irvine]

[Producer: Mr. Walt; scratches: DJ Evil Dee]

YASIIN BEY: That time was really dynamic. Dave Chappelle was doing stand-up in the Village and we had mutual friends. Or The Roots would be at Electric Ladyland, recording with Common. Everybody was in each other's strata. And ['60s and '70s jazz keyboardist] Weldon Irvine was coming around. I might have met him through Hi-Tek. He was so interested in what we were doing, so interested in hip-hop. At the time, a lot of people from his generation were down on hip-hop culture. Some of the complaints might have been valid, but to see somebody who was a real musician say, "This is real music, this is art," was big for us. He was a great ally. He would listen to what we were working on. We let him hear "Astronomy" and he started playing to it, and it just added this whole other element. I was really eager to have it be on the album. I can't remember if we asked him to play along or if he volunteered, but either way we were so impressed that we put it on. That's a special song. Those types of [Miles Davis] *Sketches Of Spain* embellishments just added an extra level of sophistication. Melody and harmony wasn't being used like that in hip-hop at the time.

TALIB: That's the last song we recorded for the album. Rawkus had just done a deal with the Beatminerz [Evil Dee and Mr. Walt, known for production work with Black

Moon and Smif-N-Wessun] and Rawkus asked if they could do something on our record. I didn't really know them personally, but I loved Black Moon so I said, "Sure, tell them to send us some tracks." They sent three or four and we picked that one. Weldon Irvine was in the studio with us a lot, so he jumped on that, on keyboards. When he did that, that's when it came to life, for me. At first, I picked the music because I was trying to be nice to Rawkus. It was a good beat, but I wasn't sure if it would make the album. But Weldon did his thing and we jumped on and started rapping, and it became magical. And we knew that would be the song to set the album off. Weldon was on the spoken-word scene back then, he would show up at events and perform as Master Wel. He was the oldest dude in the fuckin' room, but his thing was that hip-hop was an exciting new music and he needed to be involved with it. Like how Miles Davis was involved with Easy Mo Bee and them. I met Weldon at Nkiru first. He was around a lot of our sessions. What impressed me most is how he was doing what elders are *supposed* to do, but not a lot of people his age were doing at that time. Once we recorded it, we realized that it was perfect to describe who we are. I like the back-and-forth vocals on there, we did those like that on purpose.

Definition

[Producer: DJ Hi-Tek]

TALIB: There was a *Stress* magazine cover that had a big impact on the success of the *Black Star* album. They had a story on Rawkus and the indie underground scene. On the cover they had me, El-P, Mos, Shabaam Sahdeeq and Sir Menelik. And in the middle of the cover was an acetate of the "Definition" single. *[Author's note: The March / April 1998 Stress magazine has a cover article about Rawkus, with photos of Talib, Mos and the aforementioned label-mates, along with a flexi-disc of "Definition."].* So all these DJs wanted that song and they started playing it early, in mainstream clubs and on the radio. That was the first single we put out. It was trendy to go "back to the old school" at the time, and we got on that, too. We had BDP [Boogie Down Productions] stuff, Double Trouble references, Slick Rick. Mos was really into that, he was very influenced by B-Boy culture. "Definition" came from Mos saying, "Our first single should be '1, 2, 3, Mos Def and Talib Kweli'," to the "Remix For P Is Free" beat [from 1987's *Criminal Minded*]. Then Hi-Tek went and made his version. We did the first version of that out

in California, early-on. That song and style was the first idea we had for *Black Star*. I also loved that video, that was my idea. I spent my whole life in Dollar Vans when we were recording that album. So I said, "We should get a Dollar Van, put Black Star on the side of it, and drive up and down the street, picking people up." It turned out really well.

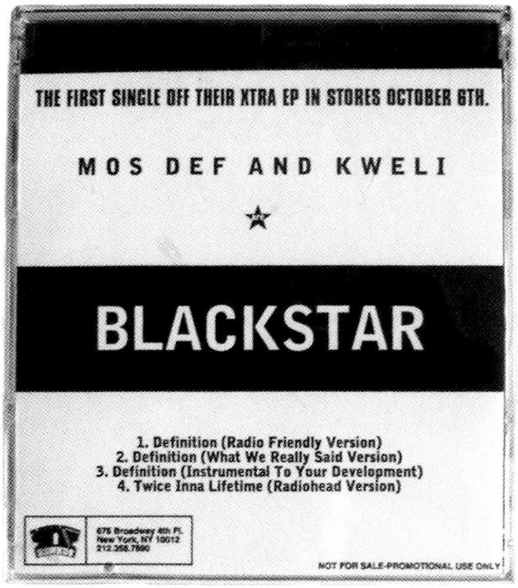

SHAWN J. PERIOD: That's my favorite song on the album that I didn't produce. I really like the energy of that one. I've always had a lot of respect for Hi-Tek's work. The vocals on there are excellent, too.

HI-TEK: Kwa gave me the sample for the intro to that song, too. The "Hello, everybody" part. When we were in New York, before we went to Cali, when they were signing the album and all that, Mos told me he wanted to do a BDP [Boogie Down Productions] thing, to re-make that beat. To me, that was easy, I could knock that out with no problem. So I went back to Cincinnati before Cali and did that "Definition" beat. I made it in MOOD's studio, which was called the Synagogue. Then I flew to Cali and let Mos hear what I did, and he loved it. We didn't think it was weird to do a BDP tribute even though KRS-One was still doing his thing at the time. There was still something original about what we did, so you couldn't knock it. It wasn't a cover. We never heard anything from KRS as to whether he liked it or anything. I was really glad to be in that video. Honestly I was sometimes a little worried about being left out. But Mos and Kwa always made sure that I was involved. So I was there in the video, driving the van. I knew that for my city that was a good look. And that video was dope, I like it still to this day.

YASIIN: I remember I said to Tek, "We should do something with 'The P Is Free,'" *[Author's note: Technically the song they re-do is titled "Remix For P Is Free" or "The P Is Free (Remake)" – it says both on the original album, in different places]* and he said he was down. Then a few days later, he had the beat. I was like, "Wow, that was fast!" And it was dope, it was much different. The BDP original is the original, but he did something new. He didn't just loop it, it was more dynamic. He added his energy into it. It was a very Brooklyn record. We wanted to have some presence on New York radio and that was a good one for that. It was raw and a great tribute to KRS-One, who was a major influence on me. That's one of my favorites on the album. It was just recognizable, I knew people would respond to it.

RE:DEFinition

[Producer: DJ Hi-Tek]

TALIB: Hi-Tek remade that BDP over [for "Definition"] and he did a damn good job. But with his ego as a producer, that didn't sit right with him. He wanted to do his own thing. He took the same beat as "Definition" and Hi-Tek-dified it. We couldn't decide which one we liked better, so we just rapped on both of them. It was really a six-minute song called "Definition" and we turned that in as our first single. The song is six minutes long, but the beat changes halfway through. And Rawkus was like, "No way." So they cut it in two for the single. But on the album it plays as one song ["Definition" and "RE:DEFinition"]. We actually did a $400,000 video for "RE:DEFinition" that was so awful that we never put it out. I probably have a copy of it somewhere. It just sucked, it was a horrible idea. And I had told them that from the get-go. It was the van from the "Definition" video and it gets into a car crash and the video takes place in the seconds when all of the stuff from the back of the van flies to the front, super-slow, over the course of the song. So it's fast-rapping but we're in a car crash in slow motion, with someone throwing eggs, and a cat in there. The director was a friend of the guys who owned Rawkus and he had just gotten a job at MTV, so they said they could guarantee MTV play. I guess that money must have come out of our pockets.

YASIIN: I thought we was just going to do "Definition" but we were in LA at Kendra Ross' dad's studio, and I was taking a nap. I could hear Tek doing something as I was dozing off. I woke up and he had "RE:DEFinition." We heard it and were like, "Whoa!" We were already wowed by "Definition" but "RE:DEFinition" was something else. I think Hi-Tek provided jazz sophistication with his sonics. It was melodic, and it also had a knock to it.

HI-TEK: I remember everybody fell asleep and I was working on more stuff, music that would become "RE:DEFinition." The original ["Definition"] was just too simple for me. I always wanted to do something different, to put a stamp on my beat. The original was BDP's shit, even though you could hear me in there. So I took the same drums, flipped 'em and added a different sample, added the strings. It was a real intense groove. I remember Mos waking up and being like, "Yo, that shit is *crazy*! Let's do it." So they did different vocals. It was basically like a remix done ahead of time. Mos was working [on a movie] when he was there in LA so he was a little bit in and out, but he did a lot with "Definition" and "RE:DEFinition" out there.

Children's Story

[Producer: Shawn J. Period]

YASIIN: Yeah, Slick Rick! That one wasn't necessarily supposed to be a solo track [as it ended up being]. I was such a Slick Rick fan. At the time, people were taking the favorite hits of their childhood and straight loopin' them *[Author's note: Puff Daddy aka P. Diddy was a prime example of this]*. In my eyes, that was a cheat. So I wrote somethin' about it. I really liked that Shawn J. beat. At the time, I was learning how to play bass and I liked that pattern so much. It was funky and unusual [he hums the strings line]. It was topical at the time, talking about a cultural habit in hip-hop. And it kind of still happens, to a certain degree. Raiding the hit parade of yesteryear. It's OK if it's done in a unique and original way, like how Tek did "Definition." I tried to trace Rick's cadence as much as I could [from the original "Children's Story," released in 1988], while speaking about a completely different subject matter. It was a lot of fun for me to write that rhyme. It was like a puzzle. I was happy with the outcome. Kweli wasn't on there, but that wasn't a big thing. At some point we were keen to show that we could come together, but we could also do things separately. We both didn't have to be on every song. He had "K.O.S. (Determination)," even though I'm on the chorus.

SHAWN: That was originally just the intro to a beat I had showed to Mos. He kept gravitating to the intro instead of the actual [full] beat. I tried to talk him out of it, but he really just liked the intro, so we made that the whole song. He was reading a book at the time that was talking about how string instruments or horn instruments could conjure up evil spirits, and he was wrestling with new information. I remember the original version had a bass sound on it and he asked me if I could rework it without the bass. So I re-programmed it with a Rhodes [keyboard]. That was the same with "The Universal Magnetic." For "Children's Story" I ended up taking a really thick rubber band and I mic-ed it and got a great note from it. Then I pitched it down so that the tone was lower, and messed with it some more. The rubber band is on "The Universal Magnetic," too. Earlier on, Mos would perform "Children's Story" over the original music I had, with the intro he liked. But then I reworked it for the version that appeared on the album.

TALIB: That was a song that Yasiin was already performing in his set, part of some songs that he and Shawn J. already had. It was such a good song that we had to put it on the album. I remember one time at the Lyricist Lounge, Puffy showed up. He was there all the time earlier on, but now he was Puff Daddy and he was an international superstar. Mos performed "Children's Story" and afterwards Puff came backstage and said, "Yo, what was that song about? Was that dissing me?" And Mos was like, "No, that's about the state of the industry in general, it's not about you specifically." But it was an interesting moment, because I knew Puff years before I worked with Mos and now I'm up on stage at an event, or at least with a crowd at the event, that is supposed to be anti-Puffy.

Brown Skin Lady

[Producer: J. Rawls]

TALIB: That was the second song we did. J. Rawls came out to LA, and honestly – now that I think about it – J. didn't even belong there in those sessions. Yasiin didn't know him well, I just liked the work he was doing with [J. Rawls' group] Lone Catalysts. They didn't even have a deal, he was a kid going to the University of Cincinnati. He was originally from Columbus, but he was at all those MOOD sessions. I would play his beats for Yasiin and he thought they were cool. We had invited a bunch of producers to LA, and besides Hi-Tek, I think J. was the only one who made the trip *[Author's note: Shawn J. Period says he was in LA as well]*. The movie quote at the beginning? I don't know if we'll get in trouble for it, but it's from this amazing movie called "Chameleon Street." It's out-of-print, but it's amazing, from the '80s. I knew that movie from Nkiru, we used to sell and rent rare black films. I remember J. Rawls played that beat in a car on our way to a session. I think Mos already had that song in his head, because as soon as Mos heard it, he started singing, "Brown skin lady…." And that was it, we just put it together.

B Boys Will B Boys

[Producer: G-ology; scratches by DJ Hi-Tek]

TALIB: I wasn't a B-Boy or into graffiti growing up. That was Mos. I was appreciative of it, but I didn't participate. G-ology produced that one, but Hi-Tek does some scratches. I remember I chose that track because it sounded like some B-Boy shit to me. Lyrically, I followed Yasiin's lead, those were his references. I didn't know the whole Rocksteady Crew roster like that. I saw [the graffiti / b-boy movie] "Wild Style," but I didn't know the Double Trouble routine by heart.

HI-TEK: I did scratches on that. I actually never liked that song [laughs].

K. O. S. (Determination) [featuring Vinia Mojica, with Mos Def on Rhodes electric piano]

[Producer: DJ Hi-Tek]

HI-TEK: That was actually a song we had for our Reflection Eternal EP, it was an early-on song. The original version had Talib rapping over 24-Carat Black. I still have the original version somewhere. We never used it anywhere. I used to always do remixes to songs beforehand, so that people could decide which ones they wanted to use. So, the other version was with that Minnie Riperton ["Baby This Love I Have"] chop. Before we actually released it, he re-recorded the vocals and put Vinia Mojica on it. We were all in love with Vinia back then [laughs]. We would get her into the studio just to look at her [laughs]. "Hey Vinia, we need you to sing on something..."

TALIB: That was my solo joint on the album. When I first started working with Hi-Tek, one of the first things we did was that song. That song existed back in the MOOD days, it was something I used to perform at my [solo] shows. Once Mos had "Children's Story," we both felt like I should have one of my own. Vinia Mojica… [pauses]… ahhh. As you probably know, all the hip-hop guys back then had a crush on Vinia. She was, to me, on another level. Someone I knew had her phone number, I don't remember who. It wasn't Mos. So I cold-called her. She didn't know who I was, but she said, "I'll come to hear the song, sure." She came to the studio and we had lunch, it was great. After that she became a really great friend of mine. But that was me living out a childhood fantasy: to call up Vinia Mojica.

Hater Players [featuring Apani B Fly Emcee]

[Producer: Shawn J. Period]

SHAWN: That was recorded at Funky Slice. It was a cool studio, it was good to have something there in Downtown Brooklyn. That one was first done [musically] when the Fugees had hit, and I really loved what they were doing, and what Salaam Remi was doing with their production. I wanted to make a beat with them in mind, maybe one that they would even use. I did that on the SP-1200 [sampler], using techniques like time-stretching, then I added some sounds. If I remember correctly, I let Talib hear it, and he liked it and had the vision for it. Then Mos heard it and agreed. I think I played the song for Talib when they were recording at Platinum Island. That song was really the only time I worked with Talib. I didn't think Apani needed a verse, as opposed to her just talking, as she does on there. That was just what they wanted to do. It was to give her respect, and I think she added a great part.

TALIB: I love Apani as a lyricist, I'm not sure if Mos knew as much about her back then. And with Black Star, it had to be a mutual thing, if someone was going to get on a song. I wanted her on the song because I love her voice, it's very unique. I wanted a cool girl's voice on there. I guess you could say that song is in the same vein as "Definition." Just done by Shawn J. Period.

Respiration [featuring Common, with guitar by DeChown Jenkins.]

[Producer: DJ Hi-Tek]

YASIIN: That was a really special song, and to get Common on it at that time was big. That's when I knew we had somethin'. I met Common during [the recording sessions for De La Soul's] *Stakes Is High*. He was the first dude I met in hip-hop who was close to my age but who was also a hero of mine. De La were older brothers, but Common was more like an older cousin. It was big when he said he'd be on there. The song was special, the beat was special, and I wrote my verse from a very inspired place. The live instrumentation was amazing on there, too. We recorded Common's part in Chicago. We have a picture of that session and I'm just beaming, I'm so happy.

TALIB: That is probably my favorite song on the album, and that one was definitely a labor of love [laughs]. Common was my favorite MC at the time and Mos knew him. But Mos wasn't the type to be chasing somebody down, so I ended up having to do it. Common had a show at Tramp's [in New York], that that's how I met [future manager] Corey Smyth, trying to get on Common's tour bus. Corey brought me on there. I told Common I had a beat and I wanted to use it with him and Mos. In the end, it was used for a song I did later with dead prez called "Sharp Shooters." But at the time, I gave Common the beat and he was into it. Three months later, Common had a show in San Diego and I hustled my way backstage to remind him, and I gave him the beat again. Then a couple months after that, Mos had a show in Chicago with Common, so I took a train out there. I performed with Mos during his set and that night Common said we could record, after the show. So I booked Streeterville Studios in Chicago and we went in. But I was really frustrated because after all that I had been through, no one was feeling that beat! I was like, "What the fuck?!" Hi-Tek was there, too, and Mos and Common liked the other [final] beat better. Which I guess was fine, but I wasn't as good at writing on the spot back then. My verse had been written to the old beat. I knew the "new" Hi-Tek beat already, from hearing him mess with it before, but I hadn't written anything to it. In the end, I was wrong about the original beat, because that song came out incredible. So I learned a lot by that process. I think we did Common's verse in Chi and the rest of the beat and our verses in New York.

HI-TEK: I was there for most of that journey. I was there that first day when Talib asked Common, on his tour bus. I didn't go on the bus, I waited outside. I don't even know if any beat was done at that point, at least not the final one. The original one they picked, I didn't like it that much. I liked it when I made it, but it needed more. Me, Mos and Kwa went to Chicago and we were in the studio, I think it was called Streeterville. I don't think Common had even arrived yet. I told them I didn't love the beat, so they told me to do something else, so I started chopping something up. I did all the programs, those breaks, the drops in the studio with Common, after they had laid vocals already. I think Mos and Kwa had to leave for some reason, so it was just me there with Common. I was a little star-struck but I knew it was an opportunity for me. The final beat was the same sample as the original one, it wasn't night and day. I chopped it differently and stretched the sample out over the track. And I changed the drums. We did all the final work in New York, but when we were there in Chicago, I needed Common to put his vocals down. I remember we was just kickin' it, drinking Heinekens. He dropped his vocals and asked me what I thought. He said, "Don't be scared to tell me what you think, on an honest level." It was a dope experience because we were both from the Midwest. It said to me that what I was doing was destined to be. I just had to work even harder. The guitarist [DeChown Jenkins] was from Common's [live] band. We laid the guitars in New York. I asked Common if he knew any guitar players to add something to the track and he said, "Hell yeah, use my man!"

Thieves In The Night

[Producer: 88-Keys]

YASIIN: That was a very thoughtful song, with a lot of elegance.

HI-TEK: That's my favorite song on the album that I didn't produce. I like the feel of that one. 88-Keys is super dope.

TALIB: That song is definitely slept-on. We have actually started to add that to the set-list when we do shows these days [as Black Star] because people always yell it out from the audience. That is 88-Keys' only track on the album. He was working with Q-Tip back then. He was really young, like 17 or 18, still living at home in Long Island. So we took the LIR [Long Island Railroad] out to his parents' house and he was there down in the basement. Mos wasn't sold on that beat, he didn't think it was strong enough. But when I recorded my verse, which is 16 bars, he got into it and did like 32 bars. He went off. I think we re-did vocals or some ad libs at Platinum Island later on. But the initial recording was at 88's house.

Twice Inna Lifetime [featuring Jane Doe and Punch & Words]

[Producer: DJ Hi-Tek]

HI-TEK: I went ham on that beat! We worked all night on that, I think we was at Electric Ladyland, Room C. I forget the original beat, but I ended up remixing it right there, that night. When Mos dropped his verse, it was the first time I had ever seen someone do a verse without writing it down. That's a real mistake you hear in the song. I was like, "Keep that, punch in right there, Mos." And he did it, and it came out crazy. I remember me going crazy on the MPC with that one. I was always trying to be the Beethoven of the MPC. I don't even remember what I didn't like about the original. That song was one of my favorites, the way the whole thing came together. It sounds like a real actual freestyle.

TALIB: That song was born out of the fact that Mos was spending a lot of time back then with Q-Tip, and Tip had this idea that he was going to form a group with Jane, Punch, Words and Mos. If you listen to the Tribe album that came out that same day as ours [*The Love Movement*], there's a song with all of them on it ["Rock Rock Y'all"]. I think Q-Tip was actually supposed to be on "Twice Inna Lifetime," but he was busy or something. I didn't know Jane that well, but I knew Punch and Words from the Lyricist Lounge. So I thought it was a dope idea to do a song together. Hi-Tek did the beat. What's interesting about that song is that Jane Doe is a fantastic MC, but we didn't like her first verse. And it was the first time I ever had to ask someone to re-do a verse. But she re-did it, and killed it. I think the cipher brought out some more edge in me. It was about bars on there.

[Much respect and many thanks to Jean Daval aka Preservation for interviewing Yasiin Bey for this chapter!]

NAUGHTY BY NATURE

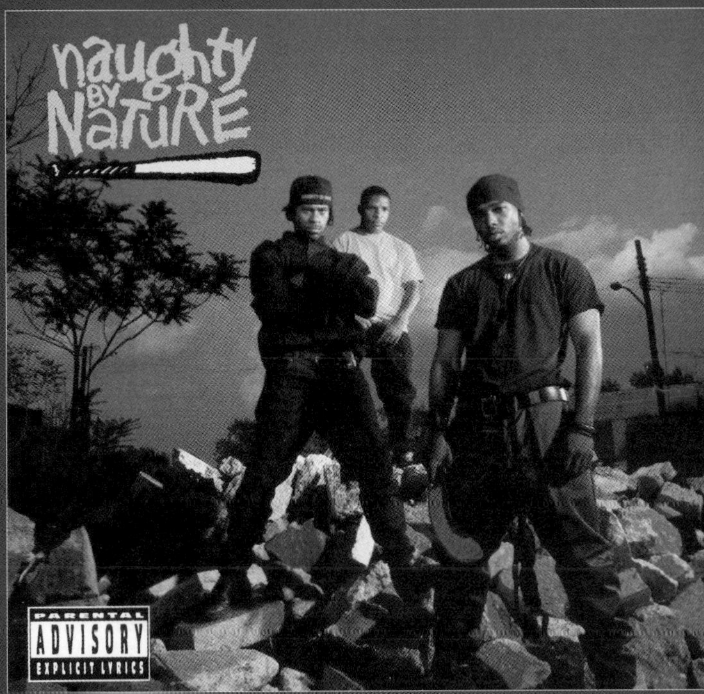

Naughty By Nature
Tommy Boy, 1991

"I never wanted to cut out any of the words, because I felt that it was all gonna mean something," says Treach [Anthony Criss] of Naughty By Nature, when asked about his quick-tongued style.

He does have a point: there weren't many words left off the group's self-titled 1991 album, which went platinum-plus on the strength of the crossover smash "O.P.P." But the group was much more than a one-hit wonder, as shown in the album's depth, musical range, and Treach's masterful flow and powerful lyrics. The combination led them to gold and platinum successes into the 2000s.

The group – with producer and DJ Kaygee [Keir Gist], and second MC Vinnie [Vincent Brown] – went to junior high and high school together in East Orange, right outside of Newark, New Jersey. "Vinnie and Kaygee were good friends back then," Treach says. "Vin used to beatbox and breakdance, and Kay DJed. He had a whole system and everything. Me, I was the little homie that bounced from clique to clique, rhyming and trying to find my space out there."

"Back then we all knew each other, but everybody was from their own little part of town," explains Kaygee. "I'm from 18th Street and Vin was from 15th, so we basically grew up together. We even went to the same elementary school."

He continues, "It was all about having fun when we were kids. We'd make our own tapes down in the basement, we were just loving the art of hip-hop. I also wrote graffiti and did some breakdancing. By high school, we were getting a lot more serious about it. Treach was already rhyming full-time and he was a furious rapper, which is why I went after him. I was DJing and starting to get into producing, so I was dead serious, too."

Treach, who was known as Tiny T as well as Double T Treachery back then, adds: "Everybody had their cliques and crews in our high school, but once we got together we really stood out. And we decided that us three were going to make a name for ourselves before we left. So we started doing talent shows." Kaygee graduated East Orange High School in 1987; Treach and Vinnie followed in 1988.

"When I started rhyming, my biggest influence was LL Cool J. I sounded a *lot* like him,"

Treach says. "Then there was a homie from the 'hood who also had an impact on me called The Almighty Mike C. To this day he's one of the illest ever. He spent a lot of time incarcerated, so he never got his chance to shine. But his style was so advanced back then, he made me step my shit up. And on top of it all, I had a strong reggae and dancehall influence. My quick-rhyming style comes from that."

Naughty's neighborhood running partners were the 118th Street Posse, and the name had multiple meanings. "That was our crew from 18th Street," Treach explains. "The 118 thing *[Author's note: Street numbers in East Orange only go into the 20s]* had two different meanings. Adding the '1' was because we were so strong, so far uptown. And the second meaning was like there was 100 of us motherfuckers from 18th Street."

Kay still remembers their talent show debut, while they were all still in high school: "We first performed live at the senior talent show in 1987, and we didn't even have a name for the group. I cut up that Beastie Boys song "It's The New Style" [from 1986], and everyone just started calling us The New Style after that. From there on, we built on that routine and did a lot more shows."

Aside from their school auditorium gigs, they entered other talent contests, many of them at a spot in East Orange called Club 88. "They had to retire us there because we won so many times," laughs Treach.

It's a lesser-known fact, but Naughty By Nature's 1991 smash on Tommy Boy was *not* their debut. The trio, as The New Style, released a full album after catching hip-hop record mogul Sylvia Robinson's ear in 1989. It was called *Independent Leaders* and was released on Bon Ami, a division of Robinson's Sugar Hill Records [which was distributed by MCA]. There was one single: "Scuffin' Those Knees."

Looking back at the deal and the experience, Treach and Kaygee don't have many good memories. At the time, they had no idea that Sugar Hill was an empire in decline. "Because of the legend of Sugar Hill, we thought that we was about to blow up," says Treach. "But we was basically just a write-off to them. We sat on the shelf, and we didn't see no money."

He sighs, continuing, "We did the dummy move and just signed whatever paper came in front of us, without a lawyer. After the record died, we was out on the streets, hustling. It was like we had been robbed and forced to go back to doing something we didn't wanna do. After that, we knew the rap thing wasn't guaranteed."

"Sugar Hill was on its way out at that point," Kaygee agrees. "We found out later that the deal they had with us was part of some kind of settlement. So we were set up to fail from the start. MCA wasn't going to promote us, because Sugar Hill was suing them at the time."

According to both Treach and Kaygee, the record received zero promo support, and quickly slid from the "out now" shelves into cut-out bins. But despite the album's retail failures, Kaygee says that it wasn't all for naught: "That album had a lot of good, conscious tracks. It basically showed that we knew how to make an album, even before we got a chance to make a *real* album. We had no real record company, no so-called industry people helping us out. But we still made an album, right out of high school. It was the blueprint that proved that we could do it. And I didn't have any [recording] equipment at the time, so I was able to learn about all that stuff in the studio. That was very important."

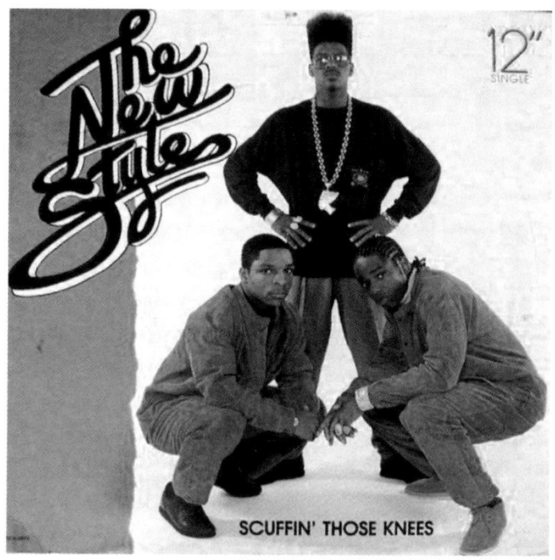

Treach also has some positive things to say, in hindsight. "I like that first record, even though I'm glad that our first actual exposure was on the second album," he says. "Let's put it this way: we never would have come out like we did as Naughty if we hadn't gone through all that other stuff first."

After the Bon Ami / Sugar Hill episode and now back at square one in many ways, the trio remained positive and kept on moving. As fortune would have it, by 1990, they had caught the ears of the newly-established Flavor Unit organization, which was based nearby, in northern New Jersey. This new music industry force was built on Queen Latifah's recent successes; helmed by manager Sha-Kim Compere; and anchored musically by DJ Mark The 45 King.

"Back then we were still doing lots of showcases around the area, to keep our name out there," Treach explains. "We did one at Upsala College in East Orange, where we rented out a hall and invited everybody. And before that, we had gone down to Mark The 45 King's basement and freestyled. He taped it and showed the video to the rest of the Flavor Unit, and they were impressed, so there was a buzz around us. After that show at Upsala, we got signed up with them [for management]."

"Sha-Kim saw potential in us," says Kaygee. "That brought some important business structure to what we were doing."

When they were The New Style, the group was – to be kind – *confused* on the image front. On-stage they even wore, Kaygee admits, "Zoot suits. Our style was wack! Sha-Kim said, 'Y'all just need to be *y'all*.' We'd all be out on 18th Street, just chillin', wild in the streets. So he said we should stop with the suits and just act like *us*."

"That's when the braids came in, the Dickies wear, the boots and the grimy Jersey shit," Treach adds. "No more hi-top fades."

They also adopted a new name, which was the title to a song that Treach had penned [but wasn't on The New Style's album]: Naughty By Nature. At first, though, Kay wasn't sure. "I thought we needed something shorter," he remembers. "But Treach knew it was hot. Because it doesn't only represent us, it represents *everybody*. We slept on it for a night, came back the next day, and that was it."

Leveraging Flavor Unit's growing influence, Sha-Kim shopped a demo including "O.P.P." and "Ghetto Bastard" [aka "Everything's Gonna Be Alright"], and had several labels interested in the group – most notably Hollywood Records – before they landed at Tommy Boy.

But they didn't land at Tommy Boy right away. They were actually first signed by Benny Medina at Warner Bros. "Benny wanted us on the spot," Kaygee recalls. "He didn't want Hollywood Records to get us. He basically put a deal on the table, and we had paperwork in three or four days."

Warner Bros. was Tommy Boy's parent company at the time. And, interestingly, Tommy Boy had initially taken a pass on their demo. After a second listen, though, Tommy Boy realized they had missed something good, and finagled the album back from Warner Bros.

"We originally chose Warner Bros.," explains Kaygee. "I don't think Tommy Boy listened much the first time around, maybe because of the image [confusion] thing. Benny didn't care about giving the album back to them, because he was still Executive Producer either way. He knew that Tommy Boy was a street label and they understood what we were doing as Naughty By Nature. So I guess it was just meant to be." Their advance,

Treach says, was $250,000.

"Before we got signed," Kaygee says, "We basically had 90% of the record done. But we didn't have the image straight." Treach, who was working as one of Latifah's roadies while Sha-Kim shopped the demo, says, "We had Flavor Unit behind us, and Latifah was so successful that we all knew things were bound to go well."

Kay remembers Treach's roadie days: "He was doing that because he was runnin' around wild in the neighborhood, and his mom had kicked him out of the house. Sha-Kim wanted to get him out of trouble, and being on the road kept him busy."

Album ad, fall 1991.

Treach has one memory about his early Tommy Boy dealings that still doesn't sit well with him. "Tommy Boy called me in, by myself, and tried to get me to drop Vinnie," he recalls. "They said, 'Let's just put out Treach, not Naughty By Nature.' And that was a problem for me. They were disrespecting the soldiers that I came up with. I told them to shove that contract up their ass if it wasn't with all of us. They really thought I'd go for the money [as a solo artist]. But after that, for the most part it was a beautiful relationship, because we all made millions."

Treach explains the group's studio dynamic: "Kaygee was 85 or 90% of all the music. He came with the tracks and we would all add things and finish it up. I wrote all the rhymes, even though it might say on the album that the group wrote them. That was my family and we was all gonna eat. We hustled together and we was all equal partners." Kaygee agrees on this division of labor: "At the time, the majority of the lyrics were Treach, and the majority of the music was me." *[Author's note: The album credits list all production by Naughty By Nature].*

"With *Independent Leaders*, most of that production was loops, nothing played live, nothing complicated," Kaygee adds. "Musically, I didn't understand as much. But I grew up very fast when we were working on the second record." He says that engineers and musicians David Bellochio [who played keyboards on the album] and Van Romaine [who played drums on the album] were very helpful as he continued to master studio equipment and techniques.

After re-touching and re-recording songs from the group's demo, the album was released in September 1991, exploding behind the double-platinum success of "O.P.P.": a single that mixed street smarts and slang, cheeky sexual innuendo and an irresistible Jackson 5 sample. "Before we came along, when you came to the hook in a song you'd just scratch over it," Treach explains. "But our call-and-response choruses changed the game."

With only two official singles [the second was "Everything's Gonna Be Alright," which is titled "Ghetto Bastard" on the album], the album nearly hit double-platinum, and cemented Naughty By Nature as one of the most influential hip-hop groups of the era.

"O.P.P." single ad.
Courtesy of the Adler Hip-Hop Archives / Cornell University Hip-Hop Collection.

Treach says, "We took it to a level where you didn't have to look like Vanilla Ice to do those kinds of numbers. You could be true to yourself and be thugged-out and change the game. You don't gotta dress up like the Five Heartbeats. We was thugged-out niggas with braids, boots and Dickies, and we had crossover pop appeal."

Even since, only a handful of groups have been able to capture their mix of lyrical wizardry – almost all Treach's; Vinnie was more of a hype-man at the time, rhyming on only one album track – and charismatic-yet-rugged pop prowess. "We always thought that we was gonna be a Brand Nubian type of group," Treach says. "Hot shit, borderline gold, but loved by the streets. We never expected to do the kinds of numbers that we did."

"Most people don't even get a first chance," muses Kaygee. "But we got a second chance, and a fair one at that. I'm really proud of everything on *Naughty By Nature*, because the journey was such a struggle, and such an up-and-down thing. We put all our cards on the table, everything we had, and it paid off."

And Treach sums it all up nicely, in classic Naughty By Nature form: "We're respected and we're feared, even if we're slept-on. What more can you ask for?"

Naughty By Nature, back of CD.

TRACKS

Yoke The Joker

TREACH: That voice saying "new style" on there is actually Latifah. We sampled a record with her voice saying that. We wanted to let people know where we came from, since that was our old name.

Wickedest Man Alive [featuring Queen Latifah]

TREACH: Latifah was mad beautiful when she was doing that reggae chanting on there. It was a great combination. Even though that song was the flip of the "O.P.P." single, it still got plenty of play.

O. P. P.

KAYGEE: I was just scratching that Jackson 5 "ABC" section one day, and Treach heard it and wanted to build on it. Everybody is saying these days how sample clearance is so high, but we sampled that in '91 and Jobete [Motown's publishing arm] took 75% of the publishing on that song. But we knew that it *made* the record, so we had to have it. 100% of nothing is nothing, and 25% of two million sold is a lot. We knew that it was gonna be huge, so we didn't care. At that time there was so much hardcore stuff out, but people weren't using pianos and melodic stuff, like on "O.P.P." When we first did the demo, our people around the way knew it was a hit, and that's all we needed to know.

TREACH: That was recorded in the first ¼ of our recording. We didn't try to make a pop hit, it just happened. It was the [Melvin Bliss "Synthetic] Substitution" beat and a Michael Jackson [technically, The Jackson 5] sample. It's a call-and-response song and we're talking about fuckin' other niggas' bitches. The record probably would have been banned if radio had known what we was talkin' about. It took them a year or two to figure out what it meant. If you weren't listening or weren't really into hip-hop, it wasn't easy. After we heard it on playback, I just hoped that mo'fuckas would be up on it. I was trying to make the record so to-the-point where mo'fuckas would figure out what I was talkin' about. I didn't want the meaning to get lost, I wanted people to understand. Since I was fast [with his rhymes], people had to catch on to my flow, and catch on to what the record really meant. I thought a lot of it was over peoples' heads. Most of the rest of the album is more hardcore, street type of shit. But we knew that we had to have something that radio wasn't scared of when we came out. I don't think the success of that song hurt the other songs on the album. In fact, it helped them. People who love hip-hop know "Guard Your Grill" and "1, 2, 3." Those never got lost.

TREACH: We was out on a promotional run, and the video for "O.P.P." came out when we were on the road. During the first half of the tour we could go wherever, and nobody knew us. But then the single heated up, it went gold, platinum, double-platinum. Then we went into malls and security was like, "Yo, don't *ever* come in here again without tellin' us." Because it was a mob. We had to run out the back door to get away. One other thing: we changed the whole Video Music Box game back then, because that channel would play whatever you called for. They had to change the whole format, because you wouldn't see nothin' but "O.P.P.," all day and night. There wasn't nobody else getting any video play!

Ghetto Bastard [aka Everything's Gonna Be Alright]

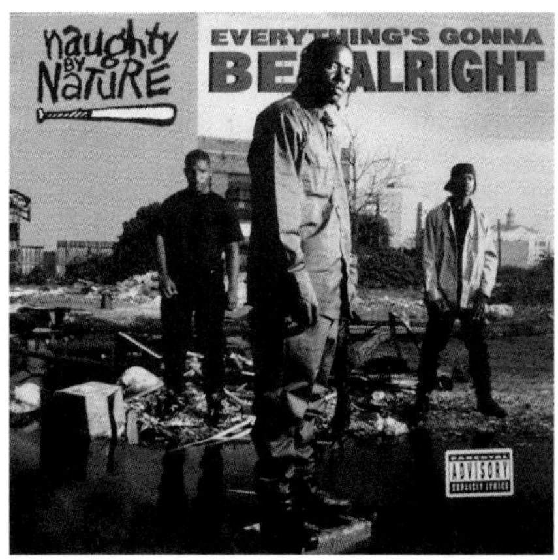

TREACH: After the "O.P.P." single, we didn't want another party anthem to follow it, so we released "Ghetto Bastard," which was more gutter. Back in the day that kind of a phrase was a curse. So when it was gonna be a single, because a lot of people was feelin' it, we didn't want anything that would make radio *not* play it, or ban it. So we called it "Everything's Gonna Be Alright." I didn't mind changing the title, because that phrase was in the hook. It made its mark either way, because people still love that song. That was easy to write because it was a true story. It was my life, so it came out real natural.

KAYGEE: When the "Everything's gonna be all right" [vocal] comes in on the chorus, that's me scratching it, not a loop. I was just scratching it in the studio one day and Treach was like, "Let's make a record on that theme." And he wrote his life story to it. I didn't mind that the title of that song got changed, because I was starting to understand the politics at that point. The hook said that anyways, and records are usually titled by whatever is repetitive in them. If a title is different than the call-and-response in the song, it gets complicated.

Every Day All Day

KAYGEE: That was a newer track that we did after we got our deal, it wasn't on our demo. It was a challenge with the live playing on there *[Author's note: Andy Schnitzer plays saxophone]*, but it was fun. At the time, I was still learning how to make all of that stuff work.

Guard Your Grill

TREACH: That was one of the first songs we did, maybe the first one, after we changed our name from The New Style to Naughty By Nature.

1, 2, 3 [featuring Lakim Shabazz and Apache; produced by Luis "Louie Louie" Vega]

KAYGEE: Louie Vega did that whole song, I didn't have anything to do with it. I love that one because it was a Flavor Unit Posse record, with Apache and Lakim. When I heard that beat I knew we had to do something with the Flavor Unit on it. I had never met Louie before. The album wasn't about me doing every track, it was just about us doing a great album.

Strike A Nerve

TREACH: That's the first song where you really hear Vinnie on the album. At that point in time, Vinnie was just the second MC, the back-up man, the beatboxer. Eventually, people got to hear more of him and he started being in the mix more and more.

KAYGEE: Vinnie never rhymed much, even in high school. He just did the beatbox. But beatboxing was getting phased out at that time, so Vin became a back-up man, and then a #2 rapper. I think he and Treach collaborated on the lyrics he rhymed on that one.

Rhyme'll Shine On

TREACH: That was a different track, musically. Basically we didn't know how people was gonna take this record, or the album as a whole. We just did *us*. Back then there were no records with that kind of range.

Uptown Anthem

[included on later editions of CD; released as a single off the "Juice" movie soundtrack on SOUL Records, 1991]

KAYGEE: That wasn't on the original album. We basically did it right after our album was done and out. By then, I had equipment. I had an MPC-3000 [sampler] and was making beats at my house. I used to be up all night every night, making beats. People loved that song so much that Tommy Boy tacked it onto re-pressings of the CD. Treach was in "Juice" and was hanging out with Tupac and [director] Ernest Dickerson, and they said we could be on the soundtrack. So I played Treach all these beats, and then, finally, the drums for "Uptown Anthem." Treach really wanted them, even though I didn't even care about using those. Treach knew that was it, and took a tape home. He came back the next day with the song. I just started adding music, and the rest is history.

NICE & SMOOTH

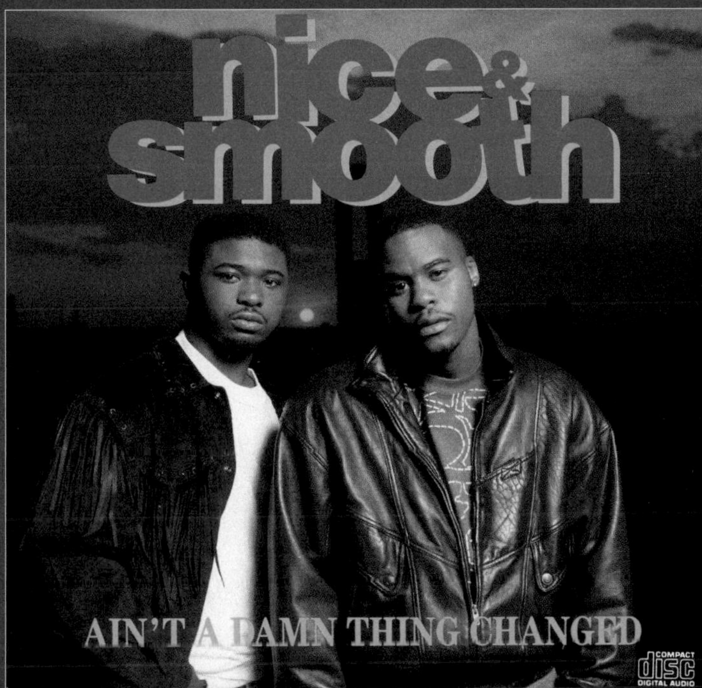

Ain't A Damn Thing Changed
RAL / PolyGram, 1991

For those who *really* know late '80s and early '90s hip-hop, the words Nice and Smooth, said in order, have a very special meaning. The group was influential and meaningful for a very simple reason: they came from – and embodied – an era of the rap game where originality was not only a plus... it was essential. Greg Nice explains this, bluntly, "If you weren't original back when we started, you had no chance."

Greg [sometimes spelled Gregg and / or Nyce; last name Mays] was an unpredictable and vastly entertaining MC who jumped from topic to topic and rhyme to rhyme, always armed with his wit and his echo pedal [an effect used at the end of most of his lines, one of his trademarks]. Smooth Bee [Darryl Barnes] was exactly as his name stated, finessing rhymes with the skill he also used to woo the ladies. Musically, their tracks were top-shelf, always catchy and upbeat, bringing levity to heavy times in the post-Reagan era.

Perhaps fittingly – at least considering his stage name – Smooth Bee broke into the music business with none other than R & B bad-boy Bobby Brown, first appearing as part of the stage show for Bobby's *King Of Stage* album in 1986. But Smooth wasn't from Boston, like Bobby, nor did he have an R & B background. He was from the home of hip-hop: the Bronx.

"I grew up around 165th Street, but really all over the Bronx," he says. "I saw my first Grandmaster Flash jam when I was 11 years old, at Taft schoolyard. Back then I used to breakdance. I did some *floorwork*, you know?"

Once Bee hit his mid-teens, he was rapping every chance he had. He worked with a DJ named Holiday, who was affiliated with the group UTFO. Through Holiday, Bee met UTFO's DJ, Mix Master Ice. Bee was younger, but he wasn't completely unknown at the time, having earned a bit of a rep in the Bronx.

Bee says, "I was known around the way back in '86, through battles and talent shows at the Disco Fever, Latin Quarter and Union Square. I was paying my dues. My whole shit back then was 'sing-rapping.' I had mad flows, but I always tried to put them in song form, with hooks and all that."

Bee caught a big break one day when Ice was unavailable at a session for recently-defected New Edition member Bobby Brown. "Ice was writing a song for Bobby and doing scratches for the album, but he couldn't make it to the studio," Bee remembers. "So I filled in for him and finished up the song. That was the song 'King Of Stage.' I did background vocals on that and also for a song called 'Girlfriend.' The next thing I know, I was writing damn near the whole album. I wrote all of Bobby's raps on that first one [*King Of Stage*, MCA, 1986]."

That was all he needed, a foot in the door. "Bobby Brown was the man who brought me into the music game, and it just took off from there," Bee explains. "After I started writin' for him it was like, 'Boom.' Next thing I know, I'm on tour with him. I wasn't producing, just writing rhymes and doing some raps and backups on-stage. Bobby took me straight and direct, fast lane. One minute I'm in the 'hood and the next I'm in Hollywood, meeting the Jackson 5. It was crazy. Everything was just stepped up mad notches."

Bee even moved to LA in 1986 for a spell, since Brown had relocated. Bee was only 17, and he was being groomed to be the Next Big Thing to come out of the Bobby Brown camp. Bee says, "With Bobby, I was rapping on-stage and he'd even give me my own little five-minute segment during his show. Bobby would beatbox for me while I was rhyming. He'd always tell people that he was going to produce my solo album, when it came out. But we never really got to that point."

Like Smooth Bee, Greg Nice was also born and raised in the Bronx ["Back and forth, over the 155th Street Bridge, near Yankee Stadium"] and had also been building his rep and resume in the mid-'80s. His early claim-to-fame was as a beatboxer, not a rapper. He was a DJ early-on, as well. "I had turntables since I was nine or 10 years old," he says. "My whole thing is about performance, any way I can. It's what keeps me breathin'."

In 1984 and 1985 he was involved in the background for a group called the Nasty Comedians, who put out two singles on their Home Boys Only label in 1985 and 1986. Greg recalls, "They would just snap on people in the crowd. It was all about jokes, and I was in there with them." Greg had also won beatbox competitions at talent shows in the same timeframe. "In 1985 I won a contest at a Mike & Dave party [party promoters in the early and mid-'80s in New York]," he says. "That's where I met Biz [Markie, also well-known for his beatboxing, as well as rapping]. We had a run-off and I beat him. I got a trophy and everything."

Greg had two other important associations during that era, both which involved his beatboxing talents: influential mid-'80s Bronx MC T La Rock; and lesser-known MC June Love. The T La Rock association was an important one, although at the time Greg was young and used exclusively as a beatboxer, not a rapper or producer. Greg says, "I met T when I was beatboxing at a house party, around the time when 'It's Yours' [T's huge hit, from 1984 on Def Jam / Partytime] was out. He and his brother Special K [from the Treacherous Three] were there."

Greg is featured on beatbox throughout T La Rock's 1987 album *The Lyrical King From The Boogie Down Bronx* [Fresh Records] and is even credited on the front cover. He also toured with him in 1986 and '87. But, ultimately, it wasn't the musical situation that he was looking for. He explains, "I was producing tracks back then, but they wasn't paying any attention to me. I'd hang out with T's people, do shows, talk to all the Sleeping Bag [Records, who owned Fresh, T La Rock's label] people, then go home and work on my own music, with my own friends."

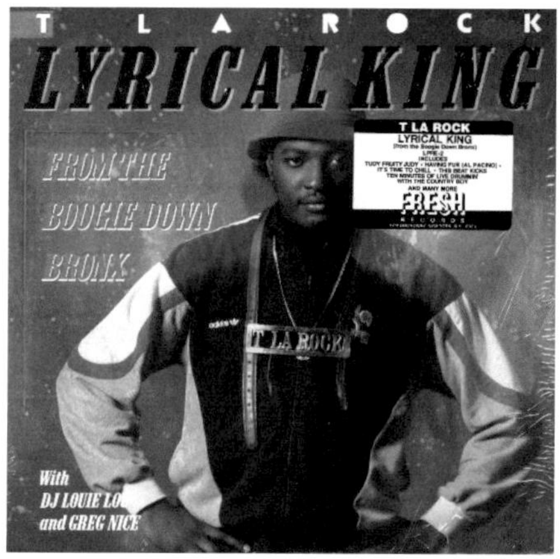

By 1986, Smooth Bee had started hearing about Greg Nice from a member of Bobby Brown's crew named Lance Romance [Greg says, of the situation, "Me and Smooth lived in the same neighborhoods growing up, but it took a guy from Texas [Lance] to introduce us!"]. Bee had no plans to leave Bobby's comfortable umbrella at the time, but he was curious about Nice, considering what he had heard about his beatboxing and producing skills.

Bee says, of his and Greg's working relationship when they first met: "In '86, Greg was traveling overseas with T La Rock and I was rolling with Bobby. So when we met, we had a lot in common. Like, 'You're rolling with a legend, I'm rolling with a legend."

"The connection was definitely a strong one when I first met Smooth," remembers Greg. "I'd go and see him at Bobby Brown shows and he'd play me the demo that they were working on [for Smooth's solo album]. Then I'd play them my demo, and he was like, 'Damn, who made that beat?!?' And I'd be like, 'I did.' Eventually he rhymed on my beats, and it made sense. I mean, he was already Smooth and I was already Nice, so that was a good start right there."

Aside from T La Rock, Greg's other important artistic association in the pre-Nice & Smooth years was with Bronx MC June Love. "I did music and beatbox for him," Greg says. "He was always the MC and he wanted me to rhyme, but I just let him do it. His flow was so unique, definitely more laid-back than I am." The two were working on tracks together, but before June and Greg had a chance to put out anything on wax – Nice says they were on the verge of signing a contract at the time – June was tragically killed. Smooth says it was on Valentine's Day, 1987.

Bee recalls, "I was on tour with Bobby when June got shot. I came back and Greg and I did a song that was dedicated to June. Greg wanted to just do beatbox on it, but I pushed him to rap on there, to keep June's memory alive. I was like, 'That flow can't die.'"

"I kept June's style going somewhat, but his style was a whole lot more laid-back than my own," Greg says. "I took what he was doing to another, different level. The laid-back thing was actually more like Bee's style."

After June's passing, Greg and Bee decided it was time to finally break out on their own, together. And so, off to the studio they went, to embark upon the next chapter in what was already a pretty interesting career for each man.

The first Nice & Smooth single appeared in the fall of 1987: Greg Nice & Smooth Bee "Dope On A Rope" / "Skill Trade," on their one-release-only Strange Family label [both songs would also appear on their debut album in 1989]. Bee says that they pressed up 1,500 copies of the record, and that it was played on the radio frequently in New York at the time, by DJs including Red Alert, Chuck Chillout and the Awesome 2 [DJ Teddy Tedd of the Awesome 2 did scratches on Nice & Smooth's first album].

"That was the first single we did for the public," Greg recalls. "We had recorded a couple things before that, but they never came out. That single was just an acetate at first, for the radio people [a very limited pressing, usually around 10 copies – he may also mean a test-pressing, which is simply a vinyl single without a commercially-printed label]. We pressed up more copies once it took off."

As they began to do shows as a duo, one clear Nice & Smooth calling card was the heavy attention paid to their stage show and live theatrics. And a big reason for this was from Smooth Bee's tenure with Bobby Brown. "Bobby showed me so much shit on the professional level back then," Bee explains. "New Edition were trailblazing pioneers for everything that's happening today, and with Bobby moving on from there it made me realize that you can't take this game lightly. Bobby taught me professionalism, focus and the importance of practice."

Bee also mentions another, lesser-known side of the Bobby Brown experience: "People had a perception of R & B mo'fuckas being soft, but I saw more guns with Bobby than any of these rappers today even *talk* about on their records. There were more gangsters behind with scenes with Bobby than cats can even imagine. I was like, '*This* shit is *very* real!' [laughs]. It was crazy!"

Shortly after the Nice & Smooth single on Strange Family hit, the duo became more serious as an actual group. Part of this was due to the duo being offered a single deal by Fresh Records, an imprint of Sleeping Bag. "I was already at Sleeping Bag with T, so that was an obvious choice," Greg says. "Apparently Smooth had already gone there trying to get a deal, but they turned him down. They might have even forgotten about that when we brought it in as Nice & Smooth."

Greg Nice & Smooth Bee.
Photo © Koi Sojer.

Nice & Smooth's second single hit in early 1989, this time with Fresh Records' rep and muscle behind it. "More & More Hits" / "Early To Rise" featured an ultra-catchy sample of the theme to "Fat Albert" and would still have a great chance at charting if it were released today. At that point, there was no turning back for the pair. Bee says, "I can't even really explain it, it was just some real shit between me and Greg. There was just like a gravitational pull. That first single on Fresh just matriculated into an album and the rest is history from there."

Aside from the funky production that Greg provided for the duo, one major vocal trademark was using an echo effect at the end of many of his lines. "Everybody did that in the late '70s and early '80s in the park, so I just brought that into my own style and made it mine," he says. "One important thing, though, was that the echoed word always had to *rhyme*. People forget about how to rhyme these days, but back then it was required."

Once Nice & Smooth were official, Bee's involvement with Bobby Brown began to fade into the rear-view mirror, much to the surprise of Bee's friends and associates. "Everybody thought I was motherfuckin' crazy for leaving Bobby Brown back then," he recalls. "They was like, 'What the fuck are you doing? You're starting over again?' But it wasn't starting over. It was about moving forward."

Bee's resolve had indeed been tested heavily in 1988, in between their first and second singles, as Bobby Brown's second album, *Don't Be Cruel*, spawned the worldwide smash "My Prerogative." Bobby still wanted Bee on the road with him, and still wanted to produce his solo album. But it was not to be.

Greg gives his take on the situation: "With Smooth leaving Bobby Brown, it made plenty of sense, at least to me. If you have talent, you want to do your own thing. Let's say your parents are rich. If you're a good kid, you don't want to live off your parents' money. You want to get your own."

Bee's instincts were solid, as proven by the success of Nice & Smooth's self-titled debut album, which hit later in 1989 [Fresh / Sleeping Bag]. "Nobody sounded like us that year," Bee says. "That first album did really well from the get-go, it was just so different."

As mentioned previously, the duo also expanded their popularity by giving one of the best live shows in hip-hop. "From 1989 to 1995, nobody was fuckin' with our stage show," brags Bee. "Our dancers were like acrobats. We had four background singers, five dancers, two DJs, a bass player and a drummer with us. Motherfuckers flippin' through the air, doin' some shit like in a karate movie. When we did 'Yo! MTV Raps' we just tore it down. BET 'Rap Summit,' all that."

Smooth Bee continues, "Our show developed like that because we had to get our paper [money from performances] up. We had to make our vision manifest. We wanted the illest show, because we was just fans of hip-hop at heart anyways. We always took our showmanship very seriously. And as a result, we were in a league with R & B cats who had big shows back then. Jodeci, Boyz II Men, Mary J. Blige. Motherfuckers was like, 'We're not going on after them.' So that made us headliners after a short time."

Their debut album was a perfect showcase for the duo, with songs like "Funky For You," "Early To Rise," and "No Delayin'," with ultra-catchy production work by Greg Nice that still managed to keep a street edge. Bee runs down the group's production at the time: "Basically, Greg did the music and I did my lyrics. Sometimes I would even write some of Greg's lyrics, because he was busy making the beats. He'd just tell me what he wanted to say. We feed off each other like that. I know his vibe. He might spit eight bars and be like, 'That's all I'm getting right there.' Then I'll add some shit at the end. And when it came to credit, everything was 50 / 50, 'cause we was family. Sometimes I'd bring in something for Greg to sample, but most of that was him. It all worked out."

Nice & Smooth, front and back cover of first LP. Fresh Records, 1989.

Things were moving quite nicely for the group as 1990 rolled on. But there was a serious snag heading their way, which was beyond their control. "In 1990, we was at a point where they was playing every one of our songs from that album on the radio," Bee says. "It was like they'd put the needle on it and just let it run. Then, next thing you know, Sleeping Bag folds. We had no idea it was going to happen. We came to the offices one day and there was a note taped to the door. Everything just went dead."

He adds, "We sold 300,000 copies of the album before the label folded and we had to wait years for it to be certified gold." *[Author's note: The RIAA website does not confirm Bee's claim about the album's gold status, although it may have not been officially certified].* According to Bee, Priority Records took over the record's distribution in 1993 or 1994.

Despite the downfall of their label, the group still had two things: their amazing live show that was commanding top dollar at the time; and the respect of hip-hop fans everywhere. "Sleeping Bag folded, but we were bangin' in the streets back then, doing shows everywhere," Greg recalls. "So it was still all good to us. That record rocked my peers and my people, and that's all I cared about. That's all I've ever cared about. When you're rockin' the motherfuckin' streets, sales and labels and all that other stuff is bullshit."

The group kept on building their reputation and Greg kept working on music. With their momentum still rolling, by early 1991 they were back in the game. Bee says, "Russell Simmons came along and got us back on track." Def Jam bought the group's contract from Fresh and they began work on what would be an even stronger record: *Ain't A Damn Thing Changed*. It would soon appear on the recently-minted Rush Associated Labels imprint.

The title let fans and potential doubters know what to expect: more funky, danceable, jump-around beats, some which were influenced by the "new jack swing" movement popularized by Teddy Riley. And, of course, the witty one-two lyrical punch from both MCs. Bee even flexed some R & B vocals whenever he could slide them in. "By the second album, we were seasoned into what we were doing as a group," Bee says. "We knew that it was real."

Bee continues, "I had a fun time making *Ain't A Damn Thing Changed*. That record was the real deal." He says it took about eight months to record, mostly laid down at Unique Recording in Manhattan.

Gang Starr's "DWYCK," featuring Nice & Smooth, 1992.
B-side of "Take It Personal" 12-inch, Chrysalis.

Aside from the tight-knit duo, they also brought friends along, as heard on the posse cut "Down The Line," which featured Gang Starr, among others. This song would be the predecessor to a track for which Nice & Smooth are still known to this day, although it is not under their own name: Gang Starr's "DWYCK." Bee says it was originally supposed to come out with Nice & Smooth, but instead first hit in 1992, on the B-side of Gang Starr's "Take It Personal" single on Chrysalis.

Greg says, when asked about his fondest memories of *Ain't A Damn Thing Changed*: "I don't really remember much about recording that second one, except that I had a great time. We didn't have a budget for it, really. I've never had a big budget for albums I've recorded. We had POs [purchase orders, billed directly to the record label] that got sent to the label. Any advance money we got from Def Jam was very minor."

Bee describes where they were as a group when their second album hit: "When we did that album it was make-it-or-break-it for us, because we bounced back from our label going out of business. That let us know that there's nothing promised to you. It was a new beginning for us, in a way, and we did it our way, with style. The album was more universal in a way, because of the music and the topics that we touched on. We definitely wanted to step it up."

Ain't A Damn Thing Changed album ad, fall 1991.

"I'm here today, so those first two albums obviously did pretty well," Greg reasons. "We wouldn't have done the second one if the first one wasn't such a great record. And Russell Simmons wouldn't have bought our contract if he didn't like what we were doing. But basically, I never paid attention to a lot of business details, because I'm not here to *talk* about my music. I'm just here to make music and to destroy shows."

And Smooth Bee closes things out with his usual enthusiasm, stating: "We had fun with *Ain't A Damn Thing Changed*! We had motherfuckers fucked up in the game back then!"

TRACKS

Harmonize [featuring Pure Blend and Horace "Fly" Hampton]

SMOOTH BEE: People really didn't have musical hooks in songs back then, at least in hip-hop. Their hooks would be their own voice sampled from a previous record, or some other sound used with a scratch. We came in with the harmonizing, which was a throwback to original pioneers like the Fantastic Romantic Five, the Cold Crush Brothers and the Force MDs. I was like, "We gotta bring that shit back and step it up." And of course Bobby Brown was influential with that as well. Pure Blend was on that song, on vocals. They were my dogs, a singing group from Brooklyn. I met them at a talent show at Norman Thomas High School [in Manhattan]. They won the "Top Dog" award five years in a row at the Apollo Theater. They also went out on the road with us, as background singers. Horace Hampton played keyboards and he was our bass player, too. We used to call him "Horace Fly."

Cake & Eat It Too

BEE: I wrote that song in 1984. Exact same shit, lyric for lyric. I wasn't gonna put it on the album. To tell you the truth, I tried to sell it to the Force MDs [laughs]. It was about this chick who fronted on me, trying to tell me she wanted to mess with me and this other dude. So I said, "Yo, baby, you can't have your cake and eat it, too," and hung up. I was sittin' at the table tryin' to figure out how I was gonna handle that shit, so I said, "Fuck that, I'ma turn this into a hit." It didn't matter that it was an old track, because like Greg said, "What's old to you might be new to the world." He put music to it and when I heard the track I knew that it would work. People didn't even believe that it was me singing on that track! I had to sing in the office because Russell [Simmons] didn't believe it was me! A lot of times labels didn't understand us. We had their heads fucked up, with two motherfuckers that can rhyme in different styles, and then we were singing, too? It was crazy.

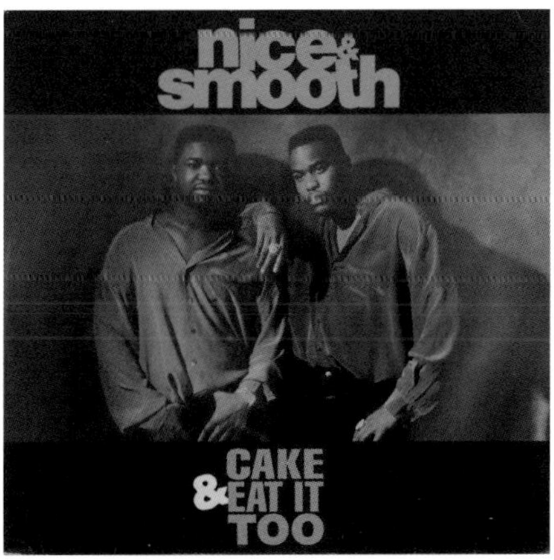

Down The Line [featuring Gang Starr, Bass Blaster, Asu, Melo T and Preacher Earl]

GREG NICE: Those guys on there were just our friends, so we brought them along. Bass Blaster was so eager to do anything with us that I just stayed away from that [makes sound like a dog panting]. Preacher Earl is doing some shit on the corporate side now. He and one of my old lawyers put out that song from a couple years back, [he sings chorus of the song "My Neck My Back" by Khia, from 2002]. I knew Earl from like '83 or '84, he was my boy from way back.

BEE: That song was on the B-side of the "Cake & Eat It Too" single. Bass Blaster is Irish, you hear me? We had the first bad-ass white boy on a record, man. You hear how he flows? We found him in Connecticut. My man Ray used to run with Bobby Brown and he had Bass Blaster and Melo T in his crew. Preacher Earl is on there, he's ill. He's from the Bronx. DJ Premier did the cuts.

Sometimes I Rhyme Slow

BEE: We used Tracey Chapman's "Fast Car" for that. Greg and I both bought that album, but I never listened to it. Greg used to ride around with that shit in his car every day, like it was a fuckin' Eric B. & Rakim album [laughs]. He whipped up that beat and we had someone come in and play it live. It wasn't a sample. For my rhyme, I took three different relationships and formed them into one. That was a serious joint. I was like, "Yo, I'ma take that emotional vibe from all that bullshit I've been through and put it all in one joint." I called it the "Jane Doe."

GREG: Yeah, I did really dig that Tracy Chapman album back then. I took the music and just tried to do something original with it.

Paranoia [produced by Louis Vega, co-produced by Nice & Smooth]

GREG: I knew Louie Vega from around New York, all over the place. I knew all kinds of dance motherfuckers. Stevie B, Information Society. I had messed with Don Barron [who does background vocals on the song] on different tracks before, but that was the first thing that ever came out.

BEE: Greg introduced me to Louie Vega. I gotta find that guy again. We used to blaze mad trees, so we just started blazing. You know, smoking up to such a level sometimes, you get mad paranoid! [laughs]. Don Barron was on there on background vocals, doing some reggae shit. He was from the Bronx, down with Jazzy Jay, Masters of Ceremony and Brand Nubian.

Sex, Sex, Sex

GREG: Who was more of a player? Just listen to his name, man! Smooth was the man. I'm just into rippin' shit down on the mic, makin' the fellas and the girls go crazy. When we'd tour I'd have one bag [of clothes] and Smooth would have like five, for all his stuff.

BEE: People have asked if that was a Schoolly-D tribute, but I didn't think it was, really. At the time with all the playa shit, I had to ease back! It was getting out of control [laughs]. I had to put away my pimpin' shoes. I was rollin' with Bobby [Brown] back in the day, and it wasn't even my shit, I was catching what he couldn't handle. Then when I had my own spoils, when Nice & Smooth blew up, it was a blessing that I had been through all that with Bobby already. Because I could hold my head better. That's why I never over-freaked myself. But man oh man, you could make a movie about all that shit!

How To Flow

BEE: That shit came off the top of my head, like butter. It was 1991, during the [first] Gulf War and on the way to the studio there were demonstrators all over the streets, with signs. It was so crazy. Then we get to the studio, go up in the lab, and KRS-One was there, and we was watchin' CNN together. It was time to throw down, and I said – these were my exact words – "Yo Greg, I don't know what the fuck is gonna come of this, but if this ends up being the last record we make, we gotta give it like that." We spit on that record like it was the last one. And once Greg got to his lyrics on there it was just a wrap. People to this day don't know how serious it was in the studio that day when we made that record.

GREG: I can't remember exactly how that one went down, but I do remember that we recorded it on the same night that we went to war with Iraq. I wouldn't say that I was trying to do New Jack Swing stuff on that song, or the album. It just happened the way it happened.

Hip Hop Junkies

BEE: That was a big single off the record. I bought that Partridge Family record [1970's "I Think I Love You," which was sampled] for 99 cents, on cassette. I used to watch that shit on TV. I heard the beginning part and gave it to Greg and he said, "Oh, *hell* yeah." He walked into the pre-production studio next door to where I was staying, in New Jersey, and 20 minutes later came back with that motherfucker looped to perfection. The rest was history. That was just the magic of making records back then, it was so spontaneous. Bobby Brown loved that song [which re-creates the chorus from "My Prerogative," with different words]. On the real, I was kind of like a ghostwriter for [the Bobby Brown version of] "My Prerogative." So it was like, "OK, let me take some of my funk back, let me swing it over here, on a rap level." Bobby re-paid the favor by singing on the original version of our song "Return Of The Hip-Hop Freaks" on our third album, but we couldn't put it out because of record label politics. We did a Spanish version and separate video for that song, with all the hooks sung in Spanish. You can find it on the "maxi-single" version of that single. The Spanish version of the video was shot on Orchard Beach [in the Bronx's Pelham Bay Park]. We had a huge Latin audience, and I wanted to give something back to them. We did a show at Roseland back then and the whole crowd was Latin. Those motherfuckers loved it so much that they almost turned the whole stage over! It was swaying from side to side. Before that I had no idea that we had such a big Latin following. Def Jam didn't believe that it was us rhyming in Spanish, either! So I had to go into the office and rhyme it for them [rhymes the Spanish version]. Lyor Cohen was like, "That can't be you guys rhyming." They thought we were crazy.

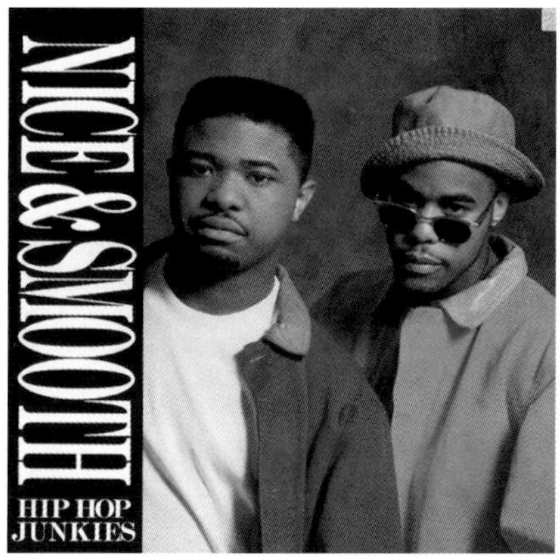

GREG: Yeah, Smooth had that [Partridge Family] album and I took it and ran with it. And with the Spanish stuff, just being from the Bronx, it was natural to have a Puerto Rican fan-base. The Bronx was full of them! We had the opportunity to break out of the Bronx and we used it any way that made sense. It was my idea to do the remix. The record company didn't see that vision, to do a separate video, but they do it all day like that nowadays. We still appreciated everything that Def Jam [Rush Associated Labels] did for us back then.

Pump It Up

BEE: When we were comin' up, you had to dig deeper, 'cause if you used someone else's shit, you were bitin'. We would only fuck with somebody else's beat if we really, really liked it and knew that person. Like the way we used what Craig G used on "Droppin' Science" [from 1988, produced by Marley Marl, on Cold Chillin'] for "Pump It Up." We flipped it and used a Smokey Robinson sample, too. We knew Craig G, he came to the studio when we did that song. He loved it and he told Marley about it, and Marley played it on his radio show all the time. A lot of mo'fuckas don't follow those rules these days. Using those rules is the only way you're gonna have any kind of respect.

Step By Step

BEE: Kisha Black was on the chorus on that [along with the Black Flames]. She's one of my artists, actually. I'm still gonna bring her out. We always wanted to use [the theme from] "Sanford & Son," so we did that on there. There's endless shit to use from those TV shows from when we was kids.

[CHEF] RAEKWON

GUEST STARRING TONY STARKS [GHOST FACE KILLER]

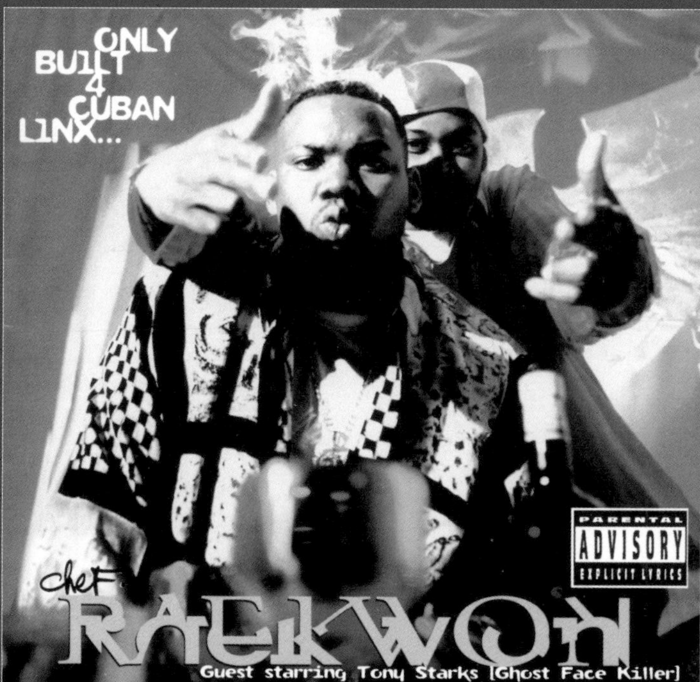

Only Built 4 Cuban Linx…
Loud / RCA, 1995

"I've always been talkin' sexy, since the '80s, baby."

It's hard to argue with those words, when they come from the mouth of Raekwon the Chef [Cory Woods]: a true MC's MC, and an artist who remains relevant and popular more than two decades after he first put his voice to tape.

"I started doin' my thing when I was like 15 or 16. We used to do it 'hallway style,' in the staircases," he remembers, with pride. "It was a hobby back then. I was gettin' in mad trouble, but we'd have fun going out and rhymin' in the hallway. You know, punch the beatbox with your face towards the wall and all that."

Originally hailing from Brownsville, Brooklyn, Raekwon landed in Staten Island when he was about 10 years old. Even at a relatively early age he claims to have been all-city: "At around 14 or 15 I was already movin' through every borough. I wasn't a Staten Island-bound nigga."

In his early MC days, dreams of fame were far from the young Chef's mind. "Rhyming was definitely recreational," he says. "That was even the name of our crew back then, the Rec Posse." He was aware of future Wu-Tang comrade Method Man doing similar intramural MCing nearby, although Meth wasn't part of Rae's crew.

Stylistically, Raekwon explains, "I've always been a boaster. My style is gangsta, all my life with it. I had slang even back then, but I was really a braggin' MC. It was about gettin' fly and gettin' fucked-up. Always talking about luxury shit. Shit I wanted to have."

As for MC influences, Raekwon cites two important figures. "Rakim was from Long Island, but he was always a Brooklyn nigga to me," he says. "And Slick Rick was my man also. He was the storytelling king. Once GZA and RZA came in, that caused an abomination, that's how The Chef got made. I studied Islam and at the same time I was a wolf, in the streets. You put those together and that's what came out of me."

Speaking of GZA and RZA, it would, of course, be a dereliction of duty to not discuss Rae's membership in hip-hop's biggest dynasty of the '90s: the Wu-Tang Clan. "I came into the Wu-Tang fold before the Clan even got built, when I was 16 or 17," he says. "By that time, in the late '80s, I was taking my rhymes more serious and I was already in the slacks and golden ring era, along with Slick Rick and them. I was also out in the street, livin' the Kool G Rap lifestyle."

He extrapolates further about his Wu-Tang mentors, and their influence upon his style: "The RZA had a notebook that was so old it had grey hair [laughs]. Back then we was always into words. RZA was the type of artist that said every word at least one time. And GZA and Rakim made me more of a magnetic MC. It's like being with the Super Friends – you have powers but they're not the same as the next super nigga [laughs]. You build off that."

Once RZA's plan was hatched for what would become the nine-member Wu-Tang Clan – RZA, GZA, Raekwon, Ol' Dirty Bastard, Inspectah Deck, Ghost Face Killer, Method Man, U-God and Master Killer – Rae was a fully-formed MC, ready for whatever was next. He says, "Back then it was a skill thing. If you had a little bit, you was gonna get heard. We really started goin' hard in '91, we had tapes circulatin'."

"We always felt like we was the underdogs, and that people slept on Staten Island," he continues. "We showed niggas that shit was real on Staten. And when it came to putting in work, I was always the first one to wake up and the last one to go to sleep on the mic. I would always feed you more than I had to. That's how I was taught – to feed you well."

After the Wu-Tang's world-changing debut in late 1993, *Enter The Wu-Tang (36 Chambers)* [Loud / RCA], individual MCs from the crew started to drop solo albums at a rapid pace. "We always planned solo projects before the Wu-Tang album, that was definitely premeditated," Rae says. "We was organized, built from the ground up. My deal came after *Enter The Wu-Tang* took off."

By 1995 Method Man and Ol' Dirty Bastard had both dropped their debuts [both produced chiefly by RZA, "The Abbot"]. And then came Raekwon's turn.

"With rhyming, I was takin' it back as a hustle to survive. That's where I was at," he says. "Once I got the deal I knew this would be my way of taking care of myself and my family. I took it like you'd own a spot on the street, where people can't disrespect you. People will deal with you based on the power you hold. And I can't even say that things changed drastically with me once I started working on my record, because I always managed to be the same type of cat. I was just talking about a description of my life at that time. Whips, money, guns, and whatever else."

The album was recorded in early 1995, mostly in the basement of RZA's newly purchased duplex apartment in Staten Island. Before settling in, though, there was a prelude trip, to escape the Wu-Tang hype and focus on the important task that lay ahead. "Me and Ghost, we packed up all our beats and went to Barbados for a minute before we did the album," Rae remembers. "Just to look at the water and all of that. We wrote some of the album there."

Tropical working vacations aside, most work was put to tape in Staten. Differing from most MCs with their debuts, most of Rae's lyrics weren't from old rhyme books, but were instead written on the spot. "Back then I never had a [writing] pad," he explains. "I was a paper plate writer, I would write on a back of a pizza box and catch a line out of the blue and just put it in. A lot of songs we did, I might have had the beat for a long time, but not the lyrics. I never owned a [rhyme] book, because I always felt like, 'Yo, I can kill you right *now*. I don't have to have my shit on paper.'"

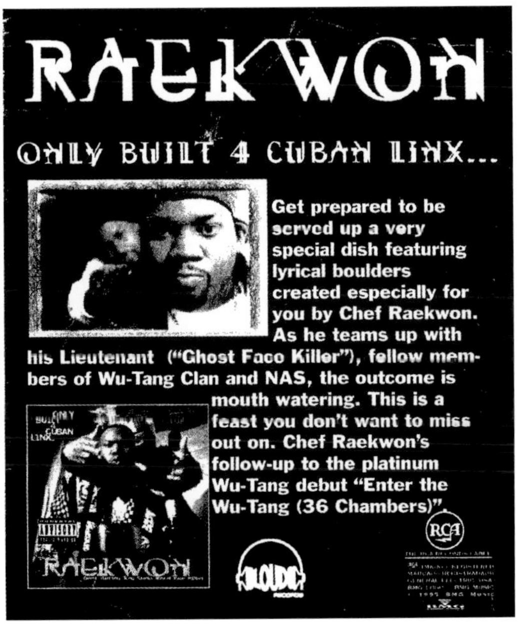

Loud promo sheet, 1995.
Courtesy of the Harvard Hip-Hop Archive.

1995 was a ridiculously busy time in the Wu-Tang universe, with other solo albums waiting to be recorded, but focus was impressively achieved. This didn't mean that inter-Clan battling wasn't still necessary at times. Even though Rae claims that RZA was pumping out "10 beats a day of the illest, craziest shit," Wu members had to scratch and claw for theirs. "Sometimes we'd have to fight for RZA beats," he grins. "Whoever's sword is the sharpest, wins. A lot of people got beats I wanted, and vice-versa. But we always looked at everything as a collective effort anyway."

As some liner notes watchers will recall, *Only Built 4 Cuban Linx* was actually co-billed, reading "guest starring Tony Starks," in appropriate feature-film language. And rightfully so, since Wu-Tang's Ghost Face Killer [Dennis Coles] shines on 12 of the album's original 17 album tracks. "Me and Ghost could adapt to doing the same types of things back then," Rae says. "We went to school together when we was younger, we had many similarities, and it just clicked."

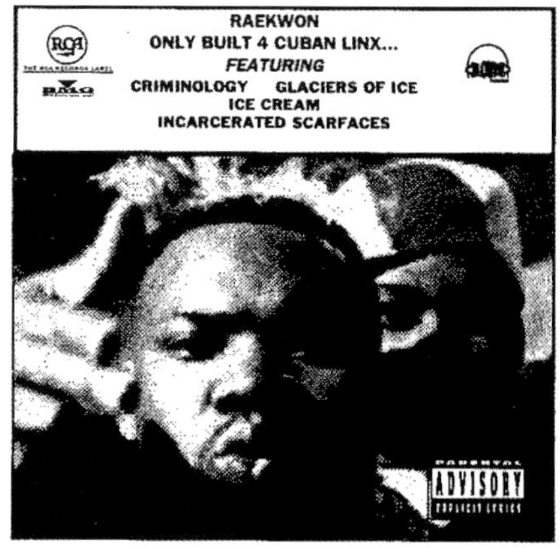

Loud promo card, 1995.
Courtesy of the Harvard Hip-Hop Archive.

Filled with movie quotes and overt themes from gangster flicks like John Woo's "The Killer" and the Al Pacino classic "Scarface," Raekwon and Ghost created a guns-and-money-filled world for listeners, interlocking intricate rhyme styles and very conspicuous wealth. "We was some street scholars who came from the underworld, where if you didn't represent, you didn't survive," Rae says. "With the mafia stuff and names, we was just into movies like that." He says that the movie snippets used were the result of combined input, from RZA and himself.

As for RZA's role, Raekwon says, "The album would have definitely been a lot different if RZA wasn't in the camp, of course. He had the illest shit back then, he was crazy with beats. It's like a scientist knowin' what it takes to make your shit work. It's a little bit of you creatin', a little bit of him creatin'. He's so versatile that it's basically how you apply what he has. I wouldn't take everything he gave me, it was always very collaborative. Sometimes he'd have to explain some of his outer-space shit to me and I'd be like, 'I need shit that'll hit me in like 14 seconds.'"

"Heaven & Hell" single ad, early 1995.

On the album's street date of August 1, 1995, as the legend goes, the first 10,000 cassette buyers ran home and opened their plastic cases to discover something special: the tape itself was a stunning shade of lavender. They, of course, didn't know how scarce these were at the time. *[Author's note: Despite research undertaken to verify the number of purple tapes produced, it was never confirmed 100%].*

Regarding this Willy Wonka-esque tactic, Raekwon told writer Julian Kimble, "It was my decision to do the Purple Tape. I wanted to make sure that the average cat who would listen to it had something special in his cassette deck. Like, out of all his tapes, my shit was private; my shit was for special people. I wanted to separate it from everybody else's. I was gonna do it olive green, 'cause green is my favorite color, but they couldn't do that color. Then they *[Author's note: Assumedly Loud Records]* was like, 'Blah, blah, blah and purple.' At first I was like, 'A lot of niggas might think purple is for girls.' But I liked the color because it stood out. So I said, 'Fuck it, let's go with purple.'"

After the initial purple versions, Loud switched to standard clear plastic for the cassette. The early version became an instant collector's item, a Holy Grail for Wu-Tang disciples, coveted by those who could then claim to be the earliest, or at least most fervent, devotees of Raekwon's lyrical genius. The album is even still called "The Purple Tape" to this day, by Raekwon and other Wu-Tang members.

Boasting five total [and four commercially-available] singles – "Heaven & Hell"; "Glaciers Of Ice" [promo only]; "Criminology"; "Ice Cream" / "Incarcerated Scarfaces"; and "Rainy Dayz" – the album was revered from the get-go, earning 4.5 out of 5 Mics in the *Source* [retroactively upgraded to 5 Mics in 2002] alongside raves in publications from *SPIN* to the *Los Angeles Times*. It went gold in two months and has since reached platinum status.

Looking back on the album today, The Chef philosophizes: "We really needed that album at the time. A lot of rappers wasn't being creative, and we came with a potion that just shocked the game. We introduced shoes back to the game, we brought about different names and aliases. And we talked about a lot of shit out in the streets."

He continues, beaming with pride: "That record inspired maybe 95% of the game's lyrics afterwards, and [it showed] integrity about just making music, period. People from our era know how real it is. It'll always be in my Top 5. It's timeless. It had an impact on the whole game."

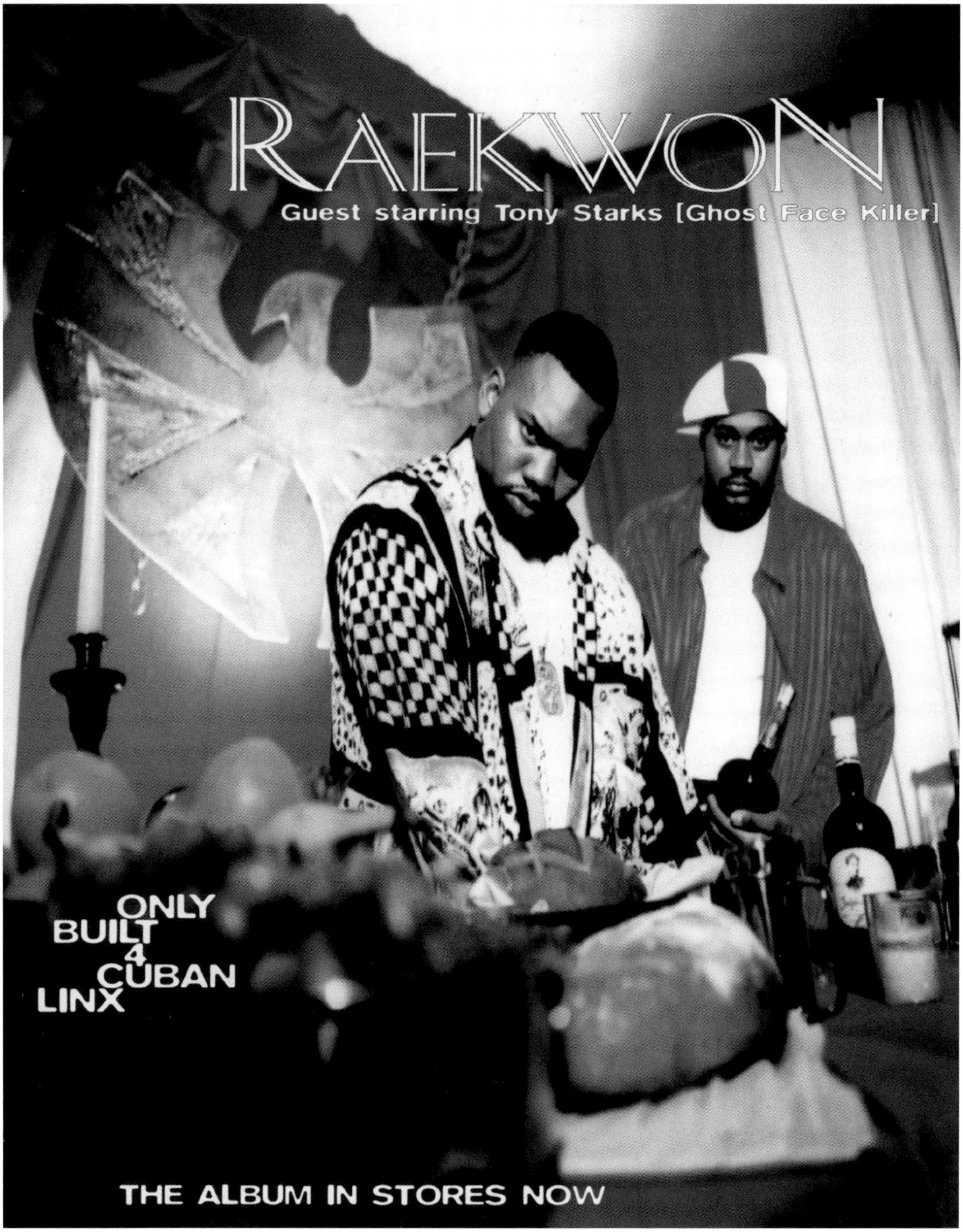
RAEKWON
Guest starring Tony Starks [Ghost Face Killer]
ONLY
BUILT
4
CUBAN
LINX
THE ALBUM IN STORES NOW

TRACKS

Knowledge God

That was RZA who decided to pan the music from left to right [on the vocals at the end of the track]. He was the maestro, he knew what kind of sound was needed, always.

Criminology [featuring Ghost Face Killer aka Tony Starks]

That must have been the first single, it's definitely one of my favorites. Any nigga who comes with a dart, you better wrap it up when Ghost and I start spittin' that joint. That song and "Glaciers" showed niggas how we get busy, then "Scarfaces" came and just knocked it out of the ballpark. Back then, me and Ghost was on some real M-O-B [spells word out] shit, we had the names poppin' off. We was wearin' silks, and shoes. Back then it was weird to see a rapper with shoes on. But we was just those types of dudes. It goes back to our history channel of where we came from. The video for that song was off the hook. Ghost had the robe on. He was so fly that he didn't have to buy clothes no more! The video was all scenery, it was like we was paid before we was paid. We had our image down pat.

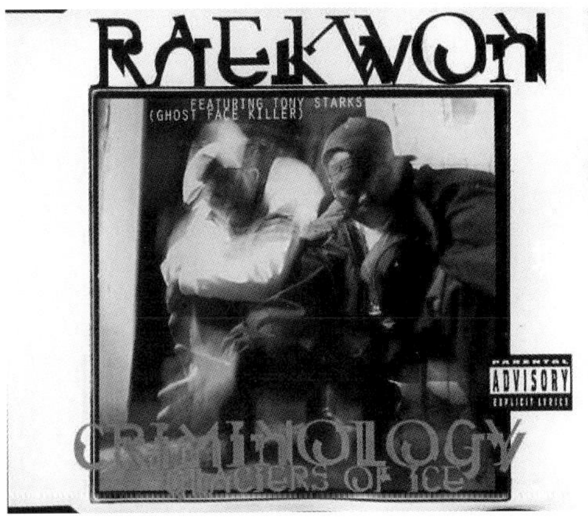

Incarcerated Scarfaces

Everybody likes that one. I wrote that song in like 20 minutes. If I don't add that one on there as one of my favorites, I'm playin' myself. That was basically to all my niggas locked the fuck up, it was more or less comin' up with a hook for niggas who got so much struggle in they way. It was me just talkin' about how I feel, like talkin' about cab drivers that be musty, know what I mean? Talkin' about a green Land. If you had a Land Cruiser back then you was a strong individual. I was grazin' on some luxury shit.

Rainy Dayz [featuring Ghost Face Killer aka Tony Starks, and Blue Raspberry]

With those female vocals on there [by Blue Raspberry] we wanted it to be a female who needed a man, but her man just gotta be out in the street doin' what he gotta do. At that time we was livin' like that. Women wanted more time from us, but we didn't have the time. For every sunny day you're gonna have a rainy day where shit ain't happenin' right.

Guillotine [Swordz]

[featuring Ghost Face Killer aka Tony Starks, Inspektah Deck aka Rollie Fingers, and Genius]

I think that song was originally a little piece of Method Man's album [*Tical*, from 1994], as a skit. I always told RZA that I wanted to use that beat. Meth used it as an interlude, I used it as a whole song. Genius [GZA] was on there. He's like my older brother, he's been gettin busy with it for longer than me.

Glaciers Of Ice

[featuring Ghost Face Killer aka Tony Starks, and Master Killa aka Noodles. Vocals by Blue Raspberry, and 62nd Assassin of Sunz of Man.]

That's probably my favorite song on there. The beat that RZA did had a weird type of sound. It always made me feel like it was a gun festival type of song. Like a fiesta, with all nines out.

Verbal Intercourse

[featuring Ghost Face Killer aka Tony Starks, and Nas aka Nas Escobar]

That one, with me, Nas and Ghost on it, that was a head-banger for niggas, too. We was rhymin' off all type of beats back then. Nas and me both came in the game around the same time, and we was feelin' each others' styles. We had a relationship back then. He'd come to Shaolin, and I was going out to Queens. We put that track together and history was made.

Wisdom Body [featuring Ghost Face Killer aka Tony Starks]

That track was just Ghost Face on there. I don't think I even came in that day [to the studio]. And I guess Ghost spit that and I fell in love with it, and it stayed as just being his track. *Only Built 4 Cuban Linx* was his album, too. We were both puttin' in 200%.

Ice Cream [featuring Ghost Face Killer aka Tony Starks, Method Man aka Johnny Blaze, and Cappachino]

To me, that wasn't even the biggest song. I didn't care about it too much at the time. It was to serve females, and at the time I wasn't tryin' to do that. I didn't really know the meaning of doing a record for a dancing crowd or a party crowd. I was more into my shit. I might have fought for that *not* to be the single, but RZA knew it should be. After a while it grew on me. The concept was just us buggin' out, thinkin' of shit to call bitches. Cappadonna [Cappachino; real name: Darryl Hill] had his debut on that joint. He's on "Ice Water," too.

Heaven & Hell [featuring Ghost Face Killer aka Tony Starks]

I can't remember if that was the first track we did for the album. Maybe it was. That was a maxi-single for the "Fresh" soundtrack. Then I guess maybe they white-labeled it for promo. It was definitely a slower track, it was a reminiscing type of beat. When that beat was brought to the table back then there was only one man that would try to take it, and that was me. I stepped up to it and we moved forward from there.

SMIF-N-WESSUN

Dah Shinin'
Wreck / Nervous, 1995

"We just painted a picture for people to see Bucktown. That's all we really wanted to do. We was just sayin', 'This is the town that most of y'all are even scared to come to.'"

– Tek

Hip-hop had a hell of a lot of variety in 1994. From aggressive gangsta to softer pop and multiple sub-genres in between, there was truly something for any fan out there, whether they were casual or die-hard.

As a result of the ever-growing fan-base that hip-hop enjoyed, the avaricious pop music industry had fully embraced the genre and was clearly in the process of fully exploiting it. Major labels were tempting its creators – or these creators were studying and learning how – to give in to lowest-common-denominator formulas: '80s bubblegum samples [as heard with the advent of Bad Boy Records and Sean Combs' mid-'90s productions]; sexy R & B hooks; hiring popular MCs or singers as mercenaries to help an artist reach new audiences in one quick step; and copying rhyme styles, since biting was apparently no longer frowned upon. To be fair, many producers and artists were all too happy to follow these short-cut routes, and made a lot of money along the way.

But that approach wasn't for everyone. Take, for instance, the duo Smif-N-Wessun, which consisted of MCs Tek [Tekomin Williams] and Steele [Darrell Yates, aka General Steele]. Neither MC wanted any part of the sell-out or short-cut game. Instead, they burrowed deep in the opposite direction, celebrating and detailing the darkest, dirtiest corners of their home turf of Brooklyn. Their early 1995 Beatminerz-produced debut, *Dah Shinin',* was a hard, cold and focused triumph, whose fans appreciated the group that much more because of their one-mindedness and rejection of the pop world's allure.

Tek and Steele were throwbacks, in a way. To a style of tag-team MCing, to be sure. But also to a steadfast, blinders-on dedication to telling tales about their 'hood. There were no dance songs (in fact, it would be nearly impossible to dance to anything on *Dah Shinin'*); no wooing or even dissing of females; no overt political rabble-rousing; no MTV-crossover videos.

And whether they did it in their hometown or on stages around the world, when it came to repping your borough, they – with musical brothers Black Moon – did their homeland of Bucktown very proud. Which is why NYC boom-bap diehards worship their debut, along with '90s platters by M.O.P., the Wu-Tang Clan, Jeru The Damaja and Mobb Deep.

First heard as a duo as part of two songs on Black Moon's gangsta lean *Enta Da Stage* in 1993, Tek and Steele – who were, for a time in the late '90s and early 2000s, known as the Cocoa Brovaz, thanks to a lawsuit from the gun-maker Smith & Wesson – expanded that crew's vision with their own debut. Executive Producer and future Duck Down label co-founder Dru Ha explains, "*Dah Shinin'* was an extension of *Enta Da Stage* because it was recorded with no time in between, and with the same production team."

They also introduced more members of the newly-solidified Boot Camp Clik, including Heltah Skeltah [Ruck aka Sean Price, and Rock] and the Originoo Gunn Clappaz [Starang Wondah, Top Dog and Louieville Sluggah].

Tek, Steele and Black Moon's lead MC [and Duck Down co-founder] Buckshot all met at different times, linked by Tek's cousin [and group road-manager] Cookie Head, and Buckshot's sister. Steele, Tek and Cookie all went to the same high school, along with Sticky Fingaz from Onyx: the High School of Graphic Communication Arts in Manhattan. "We was the original Partnaz 'n Crime," says Steele.

"Steele is the thinker of the crew," explains producer Evil Dee. "I always knew about him because Buckshot was talking about him the first time I met him. Then when I met Steele, he was definitely crazy on the mic. He influenced Black Moon a lot back when we were recording *Enta Da Stage*. And Tek was his right-hand man."

Raised in Brooklyn's Brownsville neighborhood [Seth Low Houses] until he was 18, at which time he moved to East Flatbush, Steele was – and still is – Smif-N-Wessun's leader. In many ways, he is also the leader of the entire Duck Down and Boot Camp Clik crew. His leadership skills stemmed from an early gang affiliation, with the all-city Decepticons.

"That was a big influence for me and Tek in high school," Steele says. "It was an interesting brotherhood. We was some of the smaller guys in there, just on the team. But they was a serious gang in the mid-'80s. It wasn't good [laughs]. They originated in Brooklyn but spread to all boroughs. They had guys and females. My vision of Boot Camp was absolutely an outgrowth of my experience in the Decepticons. With Boot Camp, I wasn't the boss or anything. That was a family thing, even if I was the one talking about it early-on."

Mr. Walt of the Beatminerz states, emphatically, "Steele is the reason why Boot Camp even exists. Don't let anyone tell you different. He's the one who put everything together. He was also an inspiration to Buckshot. He was his mentor in a lot of ways."

Steele started rhyming in high school. "I got into it thanks to a guy named Chase," he explains. "I was partners with Chase first, Tek wasn't even rapping back then. He was more security and in the entourage. Slowly but surely, Tek started to show more interest in writing rhymes and recording. And Chase didn't stick with rapping for too long." Steele's Decepticons name was Steel Punch, which begat his later MC name.

The artist formerly known as Steel Punch was, in fact, the first member of the Boot Camp / Duck Down crew to make it onto wax, although it's not anything he is particularly proud of today. He – credited as MC Steele – had a song called "Still Moving Strong," originally released on a 1990 compilation called *Inn The Mirror* on Jody Records, then re-released in 1992 on another Jody collection called *Native New York Rappers*. Since it was his only release at the time, he would perform it on bills with the earliest version of Black Moon [which, at the time, also included MC Finsta Bundy].

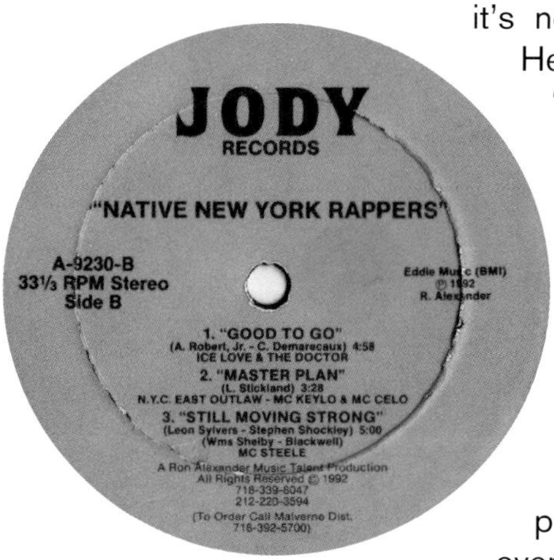

"That was my first recording, we paid out of our pocket to go into the studio," Steele recalls. "We even did a video for it, although I don't have a copy. It's not something I would go back and watch. I had a bald head. I'm sure people would love to see that, though! [laughs]. Rockness Monster [Rock], who grew up across the street from me in Brownsville, was dancing in the video, and Tek was in there playing an engineer."

He continues, "It was never a single, it was just on a compilation. I was signed to a production company, but they was trying to pull a fast one on me. It left a bad taste in my mouth, so I moved on."

Around that same time, Steele also created a group name of MOST: Man [or Men] of Steel. Soon thereafter it morphed into Major Organized Sound Troopers. "That was me, Tek, Supreme from The Representativz, and Rockness Monster," he explains. "We would congregate at my aunt's house, freestyle and make tapes. This was the early '90s, right before *Enta Da Stage*." Tek says another name for their street crew was PM, for both "Power Masters" and "Perfect Man."

Tek, who is about two years younger than Steele, grew up in Bed-Stuy ("I'm the only Bed-Stuy champion in the Clik"), not far from one of his childhood idols, Big Daddy Kane. "I liked Kane, but I was a retarded Kool G Rap fan," he says. He also cites Slick Rick's storytelling style as an early influence.

Steele and Tek were drawn into the forming Duck Down universe by their friendship with Buckshot, an up-and-coming MC who grew up chiefly in Crown Heights and started out as a hip-hop dancer, not an MC. Steele met Buckshot through Buckshot's sister, with whom he attended night school in the early '90s. Buck's sister was a dancer as well. Steele had a show at the Apollo for a Wednesday "Amateur Night" [booked by his soon-to-be ex-manager Ron Alexander] and he needed extra dancers. Buck and 5 FT from Black Moon, who were both younger than Steele, showed up. "At the time, I don't even think either dude was rapping," Steele recalls.

From that point on, they all began hanging out, and the formation of Black Moon and Smif-N-Wessun was only a matter of time. Although Steele had to force Tek into the spotlight a bit. "Tek was always with me, we was partners before he even rapped," he says. "But he got up to speed with rhyming very quickly. He's quiet and he analyzes things more than most people. He also has a lot of music in him because his dad is a musician."

"At first I wasn't even trying to be an MC," states Tek. "I was tryin' to be behind the boards, doing engineering and production. My moms is a minister and my pops was a musician, a rock-and-roller. He always had a recording set-up in the basement. I play drums and I dabble on bass. But I was just around Steele and other MCs so much that it just jumped off for me on the mic. Once I got in the studio with Black Moon, it really became an MC thing for me."

Evil Dee recalls, "When I met Tek the first time, I didn't even know he could speak [laughs]. He *never* said anything. And the first time I ever heard him speak was when he rhymed. And he was *dope*. Tek is more street, and Steele is more conscious, in their styles and approach. Tek says crazy shit and Steele will make you think. I didn't know Tek wanted to be an engineer back then, honestly. Although now that I think about it, he was always checkin' out what we was doing."

One notable and important facet to the duo's rhyme style is the intertwining of their vocal lines, hearkening back to early crews like the Cold Crush Brothers as well as more contemporary groups [in the mid / late '80s, that is] like Run-DMC and EPMD. "That comparison makes a lot of sense to me," Steele says. "With me and Tek as younger, smaller guys in Decepticons we formed a close bond, and it came out in our rhymes. We didn't try to emulate a group like Run-DMC on purpose."

"That back-and-forth style shows that they're cool with each other and that they have chemistry," explains Evil Dee. "You can't manufacture that. They was homeboys who happened to rhyme. They definitely always reminded me of Run-DMC in that way. When we recorded them, it was with two mics in the same room, looking at each other. Our engineer Kieran Walsh knew that it was breaking the rules, but we both said, 'Fuck it.' No one was really doing that at the time. I didn't care if the vocals bled into each other a little bit, I wanted them to sound as natural as possible. And it worked. We did that for the whole [*Dah Shinin'*] record."

Mr. Walt says, "For me, Steele is the core of the group, but they remind me a lot of EPMD. Two rappers in a group, but they aren't lopsided. On one song, this dude will be hot. On another song, it's the other guy. With the back-and-forth stuff, I was the one who encouraged them to do that. I said, 'You're a duo, so take advantage of it.' There wasn't that much of that going on at the time, and they jumped right into it."

Once Black Moon began work on their *Enta Da Stage* debut in 1992, Tek and Steele – along with other members of the Boot Camp Clik crew – were there with them. And they got their first shots on the mic as a duo on two songs: "Black Smif-N-Wessun" and "U Da Man."

Steele was the vet of the crew, but as the younger Black Moon rose to prominence, he took it all in stride. "Even though I had recorded before, I never looked at it like I knew more than anyone," he says. "I knew that we all had things to teach each other. That's why the Boot Camp Clik is so strong. No one is bossy. We all started off humble and built a family around it." He also points to his earlier association with the well-organized Decepticons as something that gave him a more serious outlook and allowed him to be more organized than others his age.

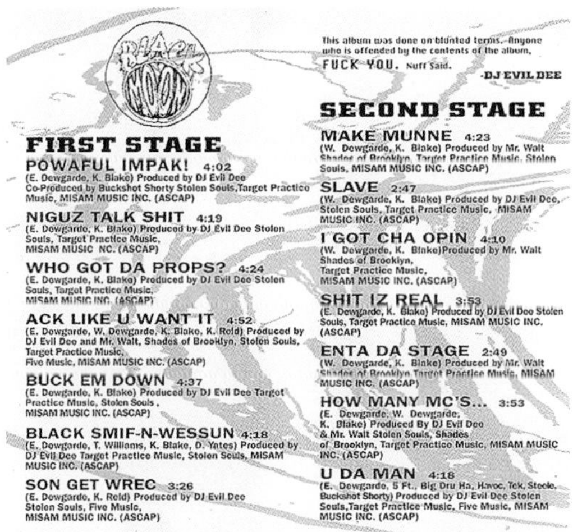

FIRST STAGE

POWAFUL IMPAK! 4:02
(E. Dewgarde, K. Blake) Produced by DJ Evil Dee Co-Produced by Buckshot Shorty Stolen Souls, Target Practice Music, MISAM MUSIC INC. (ASCAP)

NIGUZ TALK SHIT 4:19
(E. Dewgarde, K. Blake) Produced by DJ Evil Dee Stolen Souls, Target Practice Music, MISAM MUSIC NC. (ASCAP)

WHO GOT DA PROPS? 4:24
(E. Dewgarde, K. Blake) Produced by DJ Evil Dee Stolen Souls, Target Practice Music, MISAM MUSIC INC. (ASCAP)

ACK LIKE U WANT IT 4:52
(E. Dewgarde, W. Dewgarde, K. Blake, K. Reid) Produced by DJ Evil Dee and Mr. Walt, Shades of Brooklyn, Stolen Souls, Target Practice Music, Five Music, MISAM MUSIC INC. (ASCAP)

BUCK EM DOWN 4:37
(E. Dewgarde, K. Blake) Produced by DJ Evil Dee Target Practice Music, Stolen Souls, MISAM MUSIC INC. (ASCAP)

BLACK SMIF-N-WESSUN 4:18
(E. Dewgarde, T. Williams, K. Blake, D. Yates) Produced by DJ Evil Dee Target Practice Music, Stolen Souls, MISAM MUSIC INC. (ASCAP)

SON GET WREC 3:26
(E. Dewgarde, K. Reid) Produced by DJ Evil Dee Stolen Souls, Five Music, MISAM MUSIC INC. (ASCAP)

This album was done on blunted terms. Anyone who is offended by the contents of the album, FUCK YOU. Nuff Said.
-DJ EVIL DEE

SECOND STAGE

MAKE MUNNE 4:23
(W. Dewgarde, K. Blake) Produced by Mr. Walt Shades of Brooklyn, Target Practice Music, Stolen Souls, MISAM MUSIC INC. (ASCAP)

SLAVE 2:47
(W. Dewgarde, K. Blake) Produced by DJ Evil Dee, Stolen Souls, Target Practice Music, MISAM MUSIC INC. (ASCAP)

I GOT CHA OPIN 4:10
(W. Dewgarde, K. Blake) Produced by Mr. Walt Shades of Brooklyn, Target Practice Music, MISAM MUSIC INC. (ASCAP)

SHIT IZ REAL 3:53
(E. Dewgarde, K. Blake) Produced by DJ Evil Dee Stolen Souls, Target Practice Music, MISAM MUSIC INC. (ASCAP)

ENTA DA STAGE 2:49
(W. Dewgarde, K. Blake) Produced by Mr. Walt Shades of Brooklyn Target Practice Music, MISAM MUSIC INC. (ASCAP)

HOW MANY MC'S... 3:53
(E. Dewgarde, W. Dewgarde, K. Blake) Produced By DJ Evil Dee & Mr. Walt Stolen Souls, Shades of Brooklyn, Target Practice Music, MISAM MUSIC INC. (ASCAP)

U DA MAN 4:18
(E. Dewgarde, 5 Ft., Big Dru Ha, Havoc, Tek, Steele, Buckshot Shorty) Produced by DJ Evil Dee Stolen Souls, Target Practice Music, Five Music, MISAM MUSIC INC. (ASCAP)

Black Moon *Enta Da Stage* tracklist from CD, with "Black Smif-N-Wessun" and "U Da Man." Nervous, 1993.

Steele remembers, "We had to watch *Enta* be recorded, be humble and wait our turn. We knew what potential we had, we saw the progression. It wasn't easy to be patient, but we did it."

They also began building with their future producers: Evil Dee and Mr. Walt. "We didn't really know those guys when we started recording with them, so there wasn't a lot of playing around," says Steele. "And there was no weed smoking in Mama Dewgarde's crib, God rest her soul [the Beatminerz's pre-production studio was in their family home in Brooklyn]. So we'd have to go across the street to a park, between the monkey bars, to smoke enough bud and go back to the crib to write our raps. I remember some very cold-ass nights out in that park."

"When we got with the Beatminerz, there was respect there," he continues. "My previous recording sessions had no structure. But with E and Walt, they were giving us an opportunity, so we had to respect their establishment."

After the success of *Enta Da Stage*, by early 1994 Nervous Records was keen to have Tek and Steele release a "test the waters" single, and they recorded three demo songs at the Beatminerz lair. Those were "Bucktown," followed by "Let's Git It On" and "'Nothin' Move But The Money' [the latter didn't make the album or any singles]. Steele recalls, "On 'Nothin' Move' we was still on some gang-banger, tough guy shit. We tried to say we was sticking up the industry. It was a cool song, but it wasn't worthy of a single."

"Bucktown" with the flip "Let's Git It On" was released on Wreck / Nervous by spring of 1994, and did very well at radio. Partially, of course, because it was a strong, anthemic hip-hop track. And also because they were riding high on their association with Black Moon, who – along with Wu-Tang and Nas – were bringing "New York Rap" back from the recent ascension of Dr. Dre and others out West. With favorable sales and with the Black Moon / Beatminerz / Boot Camp Clik starting to gel, Nervous gave the green light for an album.

But first they had to clear up a small issue: Evil Dee and Walt didn't want to record any more tracks that would come out on Nervous Records, with whom they were in a dispute over Black Moon royalties. Evil Dee explains, "At first, me and Walt weren't going to do anything with the Smif-N-Wessun album, because we was beefin' with Nervous. But I didn't want to leave those guys hanging."

According to E, there was also another suitor for the group. "Chris Lighty wanted to sign them at Def Jam," he says. "But with Nervous, since they was an independent label, we could drop singles quickly. We didn't have to wait months. I would record on Monday and we'd have test pressings by that Friday. We was also the only hip-hop group at Nervous who was selling any records, so we got priority. If they had gone with a big label like Def Jam, I don't think there would be a Boot Camp Clik like there is now. In certain ways, being with Nervous helped them."

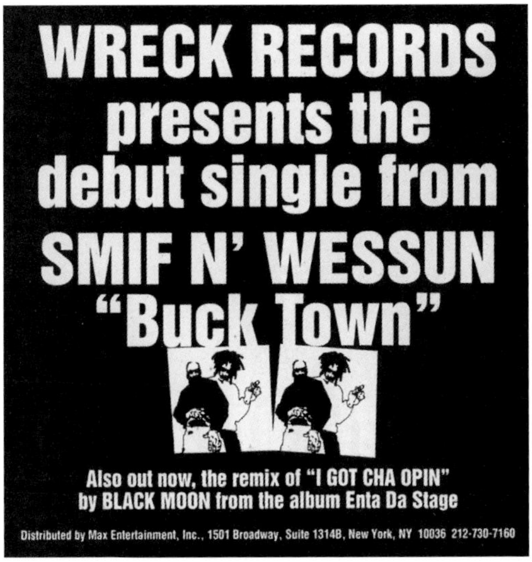

Before the sessions for the Smif-N-Wessun album, Mr. Walt had been in Atlanta working on Phife's [from A Tribe Called Quest] solo album. "We hadn't seen a dime from Nervous for Black Moon," Walt says, "So I told E not to start on the Smif-N-Wessun album until we had a deal with Nervous that looked good."

This created some tension, between Tek, Steele and the Beatminerz; and most definitely between the Beatminerz and Nervous. But, soon enough, a deal was reached that made Walt and E feel comfortable enough to dive in. Still, Walt says, "In reality, we did that album for Tek, Steele and the fans, not because the deal was a great one. I will do anything for Steele, until the day I die."

"We didn't record any tracks while we were waiting for E and Walt," Steele recalls. "We were just hoping it was going to work out. We were concerned about working with Nervous, too, seeing what had been happening with Black Moon, but keep in mind that we was coming from the streets. We didn't have much to lose."

To make matters worse, though, Tek and Steele had signed a bum contract with Nervous thanks to bad legal advice. But they always knew that they would figure out a way to make it work. "We had a love / hate thing with Nervous," Steele says. "[Label owner] Michael Weiss' dad groomed him to act the way he did with artists, so I don't even blame Michael."

Album sessions officially began by mid-year 1994. As noted earlier, just about everyone involved felt that – beyond the fact that Buckshot's and 5 FT's voices weren't heard on almost all tracks – Smif-N-Wessun were stepping up to the plate to continue where Black Moon's album had left off.

"*Dah Shinin'* was definitely a continuation of *Enta Da Stage*," says Tek. "One was definitely playing off the other. Buckshot came to almost every studio session of ours, and vice-versa. Everybody just fed off each other and gave each other energy. We got the deal going up to Nervous and just freestyling. When we was that young in the mind, we didn't know what we was lookin' for when it came to our careers. It just happened that the Most High was lookin' out for us."

Page from Steele's '90s scrap-book, with concert flyer.
Courtesy of General Steele.

Evil Dee's and Walt's production on *Dah Shinin'* was significantly different from their work on *Enta Da Stage*, for a couple important reasons. First off, with Black Moon, Evil Dee was lead producer, since that was, according to both Walt and E, "his group." E took lead, while Walt helped out and gave them beats and sample elements. He was the older brother, more of an observer and advice-giver. With Smif-N-Wessun, on the other hand, it was a partnership between the two, with Walt as "head" Beatminer.

Secondly, both E and Walt had learned a great deal working on *Enta Da Stage*, some by trial and error. And even though there wasn't much time in between the two records, they both felt like it was a new era for them. Evil Dee recalls, "Back with *Enta*, we didn't know the equipment, so we had to tell people [for instance, engineers] how to do what we wanted to do. By *Dah Shinin'*, I had my own equipment; I had an SP-1200 and an Akai 950."

"I had also learned a lot about how samples worked the second time around," E continues. "Everybody wanted a pay-day. I learned how to sample records so it didn't cost too much to clear. And also, when I did sample something that we would clear, how to get my money's worth; how to use it to the maximum." He concedes that he also masked many samples so expertly that there was no need for clearance, as the original authors would never figure them out. Of course we won't mention which ones those are, on the record.

E adds, "I was making beats at home and at the studio. So I was much more in control when I got to the studio. We knew how to work in the room at [their new studio of choice] D & D, so *Shinin'* had a better sound, overall. Half of *Enta* was done at Calliope and it wasn't the best place. The second half of *Enta Da Stage* and all of *Dah Shinin'* was done at D & D. For what we was doin', it was the best studio."

Located in midtown Manhattan, not far from the West Side Highway on 37th Street, D & D Studios – named for the first initials of '90s owners David Lotwin and Doug Grama – was known more as a dance music studio before it was "discovered" by Gang Starr's DJ Premier in the early '90s [the Fat Boys recorded there in the '80s, but it was far from a hip-hop haven in that era]. Premier's first song there was the classic 1992 Gang Starr posse cut, "DWYCK." From there on out, the master producer commandeered Studio B, effectively putting the room on permanent lock-down for his own use whenever he was in town.

"Premier's room, Studio B, had a small vocal booth and a big control room," E explains. "The studio we used, Studio A, had a big vocal booth and a small control room. Buckshot and 5 FT would always bring eight million people with them into the vocal booth, and I didn't want all these people in the control room with me. So it worked out great."

"E and Walt did all pre-production at their house," remembers Tek. "For the most part, they just gave us CDs with beats and then we went home and put our heads together. We'd come up with a song name and then go to work. Most of the time, we wrote right away, on the spot. It would only take us a couple hours to get a song together [lyrically]."

According to E, "With the earliest demos for tracks on *Dah Shinin'*, we would do them in advance, at our crib. But after we were actually doing the album, I would make the beats at D & D and play them for the guys there. Walt only really does his beats at home, he's more comfortable there. But I usually make mine in the studio. I had like four crates of records at D & D. I would go record shopping for each project and just keep stuff there."

As fans are aware, almost every song on the record is at a comfortable, head-nod or walking pace, and also stripped down, so that the lyrics are always front-and-center. "We did that on purpose, and still do that to this day, because people should always focus on what the MC is saying," explains Evil Dee. "Too many producers clutter their beats. They forget that an MC's voice is an instrument, too."

"Working with the Beatminerz definitely strengthened us," says Steele. "It put us on a more serious level, because they was already doing stuff. We [Steele and Tek] was brothers in Decepticons, but E and Walt was brothers for real! There was a lot of respect. No one had ever given us beats before, and their beats were bangin'."

Walt details one big change in the crew's recording habits from Black Moon's debut to Smif-N-Wessun's: daytime sessions. "For *Enta*, we did that all at night, midnight to 6 a.m.," he says. "I know Tek and Steele hated me for it, but I just wasn't havin' it no more. For *Dah Shinin'*, we booked D & D sessions starting at noon, which would run until whenever."

Page from Steele's '90s scrap-book, with photos. Bottom photo with Dru Ha. *Courtesy of General Steele.*

Walt continues, explaining his logic: "When we finished *Enta Da Stage*, we left the studio in the morning and would go to master the records right then. We was dead tired and a lot of shit would slip. Also, when we recorded during the day there were less guys hanging out at the studio. Boot Camp is a nocturnal crew. I admit it, I fucked the vibe up [laughs]. But my ears were clearer, so it was better overall."

Steele remembers the daytime sessions very well. "Oh yeah, I remember that," he says. "Smokin' weed in the daytime is kinda crazy [laughs]. In the end, I do think that recording during the day was a good thing, because it made us be like, 'Time to get up and go to work!' D & D also doesn't have any windows, so when you're in there, time stands still. Day or night, it didn't matter. The time passed pretty quickly."

No matter what time they recorded tracks for the Smif-N-Wessun platter, E and Walt are in full agreement about one thing, which E puts very simply: "*Dah Shinin'* is sonically better than *Enta Da Stage*, no question."

"On *Dah Shinin'*, some of those records were sampled in stereo," E elaborates. "You can hear the difference. On *Enta* it was mono and it was all about turning the bass up. But by the time we were doing Smif-N-Wessun, I had learned to listen to stuff differently, and to make a better-sounding record."

"There was a lot of friendly competition between us and guys like Pete Rock, Q-Tip, Lord Finesse and Buckwild back then," Walt explains. "We was trying our best to flip our samples better than anyone else. In those days, producers were fans of other producers. That's what made that era so dope. We were all emulating each other with our own twists. We all wanted to do it better. People don't compete with each other these days."

After recording for a total of eight or nine months ["That wasn't a long time to do an album back then," says Evil Dee], Walt says that the final product hit stores in January 1995. The single "Wreckonize" was released alongside the album.

While the Beatminerz were the main producers on the record, they did have some help from two members of their record-digging family: Baby Paul [Paul Hendricks, also spelled Babee Pall] and Rich Black [Richard Nurse, aka Rich Blak]. Paul produced "Wipe Ya Mouf" and co-produced "Wreckonize" and "Home Sweet Home"; and Rich co-produced "Wontime."

"Wrekonize" single and *Dah Shinin'* album promo sheet, late 1994.
Courtesy of the Adler Hip-Hop Archives / Cornell University Hip-Hop Collection.

The record went to extremes listing producers and writers in the liner notes, which Evil Dee says was done by Dru Ha. "I actually just wanted it to say 'Produced by the Beatminerz' for everything," E says. "It was cool the way Dru did it, but I just wanted to be more secretive." Walt would have also voted against all the specificity in the credits, but also has no huge issues with how things were listed.

The album yielded four strong singles: "Bucktown" with "Let's Git It On" early-on; with "Wreckonize"; "Wontime"; and "Sound Bwoy Bureill" to support the full-length. There were also videos for all five songs. "Nervous had no choice, because of how people were responding," says Tek.

"We were coming right off the success of *Enta*, so budgets had loosened up a little bit," recalls Dru Ha. "We knew we were going to do at least three videos right off the bat. Keep in mind, the budgets were still moderate, especially when you consider that major labels back then would spend $250,000 on a video without even blinking. We were more like $30,000 to $50,000. But overall, we weren't beefing with Nervous over our videos."

"Wontime" single promo sheet announcing "Yo! MTV Raps" appearance, April 1995.
Courtesy of the Adler Hip-Hop Archives / Cornell University Hip-Hop Collection.

The group performed frequently before and after the album's release, usually with Black Moon. But not as often in their hometown as Tek would have liked. He explains, "Back then, Brooklyn didn't have too many places to rock, unless you was on the corner, or you was walkin' down the street saying, 'Yo, check out the shit I just wrote!' There weren't too many [live venues] because shit was always getting shut down early."

If they did perform in New York, it was in Manhattan, at clubs like The Muse, The Fever or 2000. Tek also says that they never had their own DJ in the early years, they would either use Evil Dee or DJ Logic, whomever was working on-stage with Black Moon at the time.

And, like Black Moon, Smif-N-Wessun say that they weren't thrilled with their Nervous dealings overall. "Nervous didn't know what they had," Tek says. "Remember, they was a dance label. We brought the hip-hop in there. We were eventually able to get out of there. We had our eyes open at that point, we was learnin' the business at the same time we was playin' the game."

Looking back at the album now, Walt says: "The reason that I love *Dah Shinin'* more than *Enta Da Stage* is because by the time we got to Tek and Steele, we had already done the muddy shit. *Shinin'* was brighter, and the album title made sense too, as a result. It showed growth for all of us. I didn't feel like I knew what I was doing until we started Tek and Steele's record. That record just fit in perfectly with what hip-hop was all about in 1995."

"*Dah Shinin'* is just an album that speaks from what we saw," explains Tek. "We gave people the plain truth, with a little blue here, a little orange there, to color it up. We rhymed about the way it was goin' down out where we lived. Girls liked us because we looked good and guys liked us because we were saying shit that they wanted to hear."

Test shot for *Dah Shinin'* album cover.
Photograph by Gary Spector, courtesy of General Steele and Gary Spector.

Steele sums up his feelings about *Dah Shinin'* by stating: "When we came out, we was regular guys who knew the neighborhood, but weren't derelicts. We were average guys out there on the street, so I think we appealed to regular folk. And having a partner like Tek definitely kept me and the crew grounded. It was a fun record to make."

Album ad, early 1995.

"At first listen, Tek's and Steele's lyrics can appear to be straight hardcore," says Dru Ha. "But if you go deeper, they tell a lot of life lessons and give inspiration. And Da Beatminerz created such a distinct sound on that album. They were like a basketball player who couldn't miss a shot. Production was so important to that album, and the Beatminerz kept finding loops and samples that created vibes that were truly unique. The album was right there in the rebirth of the East Coast, with Wu-Tang, Biggie, Nas and Black Moon."

And Evil Dee gets the final word: "When I listen to *Dah Shinin'*, there were no mistakes. We sat down and perfected everything before it went out. Tek and Steele were in their lane, and they stuck with it. I was definitely happy with the way everything came out. They brought back tag-team rhyming, that was number one to me. When that record was done, I was happy because I felt like I really knew how to make the most of a studio environment. I knew if my future albums could sound like this one, I'd be good. That was a lot different than when *Enta Da Stage* hit. If I had it to do again today it would be exactly the same."

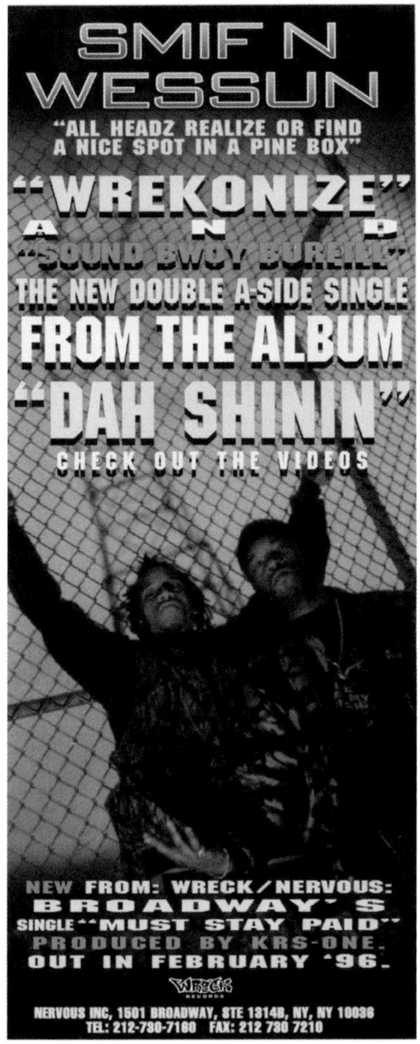

"Wrekonize" and "Sound Bwoy Bureil" single ad, late 1995.

TRACKS

[All songs produced by Da Beatminerz unless noted]

Timz N Hood Chek

DRU HA: The lyrics to that were the first verses Tek and Steele kicked for me when I met them. I didn't need to hear another verse from either of them to know how talented they were and that they needed a deal. I had gently pursued them to lay those down on the album somewhere, and when they put them on that track, I got it.

STEELE: When it came to who went first on any given track, it was like any other team: basketball, football, whatever. Strongest hit goes first. So I guess I was hottest there on that one. Me and Tek always made those decisions, not E or Walt.

TEK: That wasn't even gonna go on the album. It was one of the shortest tracks, like we was doing an experiment. We took that version right from the freestyle tape it was goin' to go on. That was one of the finishing touches on the album, making that intro.

EVIL DEE: That was the intro to the album. For the first version, it was a one-take thing. D & D had a third studio, Studio C, which was an editing studio. When our room was full of people recording, I would rent Studio C and use it to make beats. It was like $30 an hour. So I would make beats in there. I made the beat for "Timz N Hood Chek" in Studio C, one take, straight to DAT. One track, with the scratches done live. When the guys heard it they was like, "Yo, that's an ill intro!" I was thinking it was something they could put on at shows when they were coming out on stage. They also wanted to rhyme on it, so I had to redo the track and they laid down their rhymes. I still have the original DAT of that beat somewhere.

Wrektime

STEELE: We mention Boot Camp on there. It was an idea from the very beginning. It was a family. Top Dog is my brother. Starang, Louieville, Rock, we all lived in the same project. Sean Price [Ruck] lived in the Brownsville Projects. We all knew each other, we were in the trenches together. With a lot of guys, I never knew they could rhyme until they got on the mic the first time. That song pretty much speaks for itself. That's exactly what we was doing at the time, smoking mad lah [laughs].

Wontime [produced by Mr. Walt and Rich Black]

MR. WALT: Rich Black did production on that one with me. Rich was one of the most dangerous producers I ever met. He never had equipment, he always borrowed. But the way he would make beats was just crazy. He could always make records sound totally different. The eerie sound on that song was all him. He put the [James Brown] "Funky President" in there, and the way he tuned it was crazy. He was a genius. He did other stuff, for Shadez of Brooklyn, but he never took off. He didn't like the business side of the game. I put the Spoonie Gee in there [vocal sample] and I fine-tuned the "Funky President." But everything else was Rich. He's one of the dopest producers I ever heard.

STEELE: Rich was important in what we were doing, he did one of the dopest songs, "Wontime." Ruck and Rock are both on the chorus there. And Ruck [Sean Price] *hates* doing choruses. When I got him on there it was a miracle. I don't know why he hates them, I guess he just loves to keep rapping. Rich Black struck me as a visionary. He didn't talk a lot. He made that track just for us, it wasn't on a beat tape or anything.

TEK: That was the introduction to Heltah Skeltah, on the chorus there.

EVIL DEE: I love that one. Rich Black was our boy, he was a Beatminer. He was ill. He didn't have equipment, but he just thought crazy. He was a genius. He's still around, but I don't think he's doing music anymore.

DRU: That is definitely my favorite video on the album, and it was the most expensive one to do. As I recall, the single and video hit right when the album was coming out. Marcus Turner directed it. I wrote the treatment for it at first. I remember me, Tek and Steele were in LA and we just sat down on the floor of their hotel room and wrote everything out. The album was obviously called *Dah Shinin'* so doing the video that way was an obvious play [using inspiration from Stanley Kubrick's 1980 film "The Shining"]. The three of us just built everything out and gave the ideas to Marcus. He added some stuff, too. He found that unbelievable location, it was an old abandoned music hall or movie theater in Brooklyn. I found the maze, at a botanical garden. I'm really proud of what we did with that one. We were all very hands-on. We really wanted the bartending scene in there, where Tek would be serving himself a drink [also influenced by "The Shining"]. The weight-lifting stuff was in there because they were supposed to be in jail. It was about how being locked up can mess with your mind. It was just so amazing that we could have all these ideas and actually make them happen. I still get the chills today when I see that video, from the lighting to the little boy on the tricycle, to the typewriter.

Wrekonize [produced by Baby Paul]

WALT: For the remix of that, Tek and Steele wanted to use a Grover Washington, Jr. sample ["Just The Two Of Us"] and asked me to loop it up. And I was fighting them on it, like, "C'mon, we can't do something so *regular*." So they ended up doing it themselves, and people liked it.

STEELE: Baby Paul was an important part of our record, he produced that song. I produced the remix of that song, on the single. I think the Beatminerz hated that [laughs], they just never liked doing remixes. Nothing is better than the original, but the remix is good, people dig it. We talk about snakes and critics on there, that's just something we deal with in our community. It wasn't about magazine critics. Baby Paul was more jovial than the Beatminerz, he didn't have as much pressure as they did. We would hang out and he wouldn't just play me beats. He would play me *music*, he'd make me cassettes of stuff. Producers don't always like to reveal their sources, but Paul never cared. I never really had access to records growing up. I lived with my dad at the time and he was somewhat of a bad guy. He had hella records but I couldn't touch 'em.

DRU: I'm pretty sure Rolando Hudson directed that video, those were a lot of his ideas in there. We [Steele, Tek and Dru] didn't work as much on the treatment for that song as we did with others. There was definitely an influence from [A Tribe Called Quest's] "Oh My God" [video] on there, and some Spike Lee stuff, too.

Sound Bwoy Bureill

DRU: That song can set or change the mood in a club. To this day, breaking that song still sticks out to me as a great memory. We knew it was something special, but it actually took a full year for it to penetrate clubs and mix-show radio after we put it out. The video was a lot of fun to do. Marcus Turner directed it. We basically took over a playground, I think it was uptown [Manhattan / Harlem]. We just had a party, and kept playing that song over and over, and filming it. People were loving it. The kids you see there at the fence really wanted to come in, so we just opened the fence and let them in. I don't think we got any permits to shoot that one. The unfortunate thing about that video was that BET wouldn't clear it, because of some of the [anti-gay] language in the lyrics. BET was huge back then, so we lost that exposure.

WALT: I didn't really think about how long it took for that song to break, I wasn't involved with that side. All I know is that with anyone I played it for, it stood out. The only resistance I got with "Sound Bwoy" was with Ruck and Rock, because I originally made that beat for Heltah Skeltah. I played it for them and they didn't like it, but Tek was like, "*Yo*, let *me* get on that." And the rest is history. Who knows what Heltah Skeltah would have sounded like on that. I did 90% of that song, but that was also one of the most collaborative tracks on the album. E put the [makes moaning sound] undertones on there. And Steele added the wind sound. I think Tek came up with the title. With my reggae sound, that's just something I always put in my music. Our family is from Jamaica. I had this old reggae record that I wanted to fly in and I did it on all the hooks, just to make it sound different. We brought [reggae vocalist] Jahdan in for the remix. That MC talk-over [sample] was Fuzzy Jones, from an old "sound-clash" record that I got at the Music Factory [the famed record store in Queens where Walt used to work]. People weren't doing shit like that at the time. Here, I found the record [plays it over phone]. Jahdan is an artist who worked with Biggest Gord from Gang Starr Foundation. He was always around in D & D and he and Steele became friends. Kanye just used a Fuzzy Jones [sample] for his "Mercy" song with Pusha T [and Big Sean and 2 Chainz]. Kenny Parker told me that when KRS-One heard "Sound Bwoy Bureill" he lost... his... mind. [laughs].

TEK: With the reggae stuff we did on there, people was lookin' at us like, "Hold up – how y'all talkin' like this one minute and then in mid-sentence switch up to bumba-clots or somethin?!" People were feelin' it, but were scared to accept it at first. It took a minute for people to catch on. But once they did, it was a wrap. I don't think that people expected us to go that route at all. Both me and Steele have West Indian roots, so it's all in the family.

STEELE: Top Dog [from O.G.C.] is the one who influenced me on the reggae side. That's from him and my uncle. When we were doing the song I knew we had to get him [Top Dog] on the joint. We wrote his verse, the "Boom bye bye" one [on the remix]. At times, that song seems bigger than "Bucktown." Brooklyn is such a West Indian-influenced culture. My uncle Guy brought me up in a lot of different ways, and he used to buy Betamax videotapes of these Jamaican sound-clashes. I'd come home from school and he'd be watching them on the TV. Either those, or Kung Fu movies. So, I grew up with that. When my mom and dad thought I was doing homework, I was watching sound-clashes and Kung Fu. Roots and culture is dear to my heart.

EVIL DEE: I have no idea why that song took so long to finally impact with people. The record was really dark, that probably had something to do with it. Once it hit, though, shit would go crazy when it would come on in a club.

K. I. M.

WALT: That's my favorite song on the album. I love the way it sounds and the way it came out. I had just come from a [Tribe Called Quest] *Midnight Marauders* session before I started that, and had just heard "Oh My God." Those drops that Tip did, how he would drop the beat out. That blew me away, and I tried my version of that with "K. I. M." I just love the way that song came out. My engineer Kieran [Walsh] did a superb job.

Bucktown

TEK: That was one of the first songs we recorded when we got professional, before *Enta Da Stage* was even out. It came out as a single in early 1994. It didn't take too long for that to catch on. It's what people was lookin' for at the time.

STEELE: Once we did that song and it did well as a single, we started to see the power that we had [as a group]. When we did the two joints with Black Moon [on *Enta Da Stage*], Nervous – Michael Weiss and his father Sam – told Black Moon, "You can't use those songs." But they were two of the dopest songs on the album. They said they couldn't use them because me and Tek wasn't signed to Nervous. They was trying to get over on us. So we signed with them, we didn't want to stop production on our brothers' album. They signed us for more than an album, but later on we fought for our freedom. *Enta Da Stage* was like going to school, and "Bucktown" was like graduating. It was like we were on our own, using what we learned in school. We didn't know if that song would be big or not, we were just doing our best.

EVIL DEE: We started working on "Bucktown" and "Let's Git It On" at our house, right after *Enta Da Stage* came out. Probably November or December 1993, on a 4-track. That was the first beat I gave them. We tested "Bucktown" on the road during Black Moon shows. Tek and Steele were traveling with us. One thing about that song is that the beat is a little bit "off." It's a lazy beat and that played into its sound. The loop is a little bit off [he re-sings it]. It added to the song. I could have corrected it, but I didn't want to. When we were testing "Bucktown" on the road, after the demo but before we went to D & D, I noticed how the chorus built up. The first time, it's just them. The second time, there are a couple more people. Then the third chorus was a whole crowd, just like at the club. So when we went into D & D, we duplicated that. The last chorus was like ten dudes and I probably doubled or tripled it [by multi-tracking]. I always knew that song would build as it went along. I did the beat for that but for some reason, whenever it came time to mix it, I would get sick. So Walt mixed it for me, and I approved the mix over the phone.

DRU: Rolando Hudson directed that video, he also did the video for "Let's Git It On" and had done a few of the Black Moon videos for *Enta Da Stage*, including "How Many Emcees." It was done a bit guerrilla style, I don't think we got permits for most of those locations. I remember that one of the guys from the group was late to the shoot that day, and we ran out of light, so we didn't get as many outdoor shots as we wanted. I won't say which guy [laughs], I don't want to get in trouble. Rolando was going crazy, he saw his daylight slipping away. I think "Bucktown" and "Let's Git It On" were the two most popular videos off the album.

Stand Strong

EVIL DEE: That's one of my favorites, I like the way they flowed over that sample. That [samples] an Isaac Hayes record, one that I had always wanted to use. At the end of the loop you hear that flute come in, just a little bit. For about two hours I was trying to take that flute out, in the studio. And finally I was like, "Wait, what the hell am I doing? That shit is hot!" I'm glad I left it in there.

Shinin... Next Shit

EVIL DEE: I made that first part in Studio C, in the editing room. They never rhymed to it, so we just used it there for the intro [of the second side of the album]. "Next Shit" is Walt's.

WALT: I was fucking with the pianos on that one. I would do a loop and then chop little stuff over it to make sure it sounded different. That uses the Power of Zeus drums, those were the drums of the moment back then. I think we used those twice on the album.

Cession At Da Doghillee [featuring Buckshot, Heltah Skeltah and Originoo Gunn Clappaz; mixed by Tek and Steele]

STEELE: Ahhh! The Doghillee. That was my mom's house, but I wasn't living there at the time. I was going over there, though, like Sergeant Slaughter, reg-u-latin'. Top Dog lived there and that was basically home base for all the scragglers. Ruck lived there for a while, Tek for a minute. It was just a place for us to congregate and build. My moms was a beautiful lady, she had me when she was a teenager, so I guess she could relate to things that we was doin'. There wasn't no house rules, but I'd keep things in line. People couldn't hang there if they was cuttin' school. It was a place where we could go to become better individuals. There'd be like eight to 12 people there, you'd be steppin' over bodies. When we did that song, we [Tek and Steele] wanted to mix it because it was more personal to us. We wanted to arrange it differently, and E wasn't with that at first. We didn't mix that song as much as we arranged the music. Everyone from Boot Camp is on there, and Buckshot is on the chorus. Nervous tried to do the same thing with the rest of the guys that they did with us, to sign them [to a contract, just to be on the song]. I stood up to Michael Weiss, I said I'd fuck the whole office up. So they backed down.

TEK: That was the introduction to the rest of the Boot Camp Clik. The Doghillee was Steele's ma dukes' crib in East New York, on Linden Boulevard, where everyone lived. When a nigga was really on hard times, living on the street, Steele's mom took 'em in. That track really showed the people that Boot Camp had an arsenal.

EVIL DEE: Buckshot always wanted our crew to be an army, back when he was shopping Black Moon. And we were all definitely into it. Buck was adamant about it. And on that song, it was clear that we really had a dope crew. I chopped up the sample on there to the point that you don't know what it is. Tek and Steele wanted to mix that record, and at first I said no. But I had to realize that this was their album, I couldn't control everything. So I stepped back and let them do it. And they did a good job. We both did a mix of that song and I liked theirs better. It taught me that I need to step back sometimes.

WALT: My brother was on some other shit with that. I have no idea how he put those two records together to make that beat. I don't understand it. I think Starang even rhymed on the wrong part of the record, but it was still hot.

Hellucination

TEK: That's my favorite track on the album. That really spoke of how it went down in the 'hood. How police was fuckin' with people.

EVIL DEE: I love Minnie Riperton, I love her voice. Sorry, but Mariah Carey is no Minnie Riperton. I looped that high note. That track is my "Lyrics To Go" [referencing the Tribe Called Quest song]. That tempo was a little faster. I also love that the original production [on the record that was sampled – Riperton's "Only When I'm Dreaming"] had all those layers. The bass, the nice mids and the highs.

Home Sweet Home [produced by Baby Paul and Steele]

TEK: That song is one of my favorites. Roy Ayers was a big musical influence on us. Steele came up with the album cover [a tribute to Roy Ayers Ubiquity's 1972 album *He's Coming* – "Home Sweet Home" also samples the Ubiquity song "We Live In Brooklyn Baby," from that album]. The song was paying homage to Roy Ayers and Brooklyn at the same time. We loved Roy Ayers' music, it just made it that much easier to identify with.

STEELE: I co-produced that song. I chose the Roy Ayers record and the part to use, but I didn't push no buttons or anything. My dad liked Roy Ayers, the Commodores, stuff like that. When we were doing that song and "Wreckonize," we went over to Baby Paul's place in East Flatbush, and he had records all over the place. He had that one Roy Ayers album [*He's Coming*] and first of all, the cover captivated me. I was just gone over the cover. So much so that we used it on our own. If I hadn't gone to his crib, our cover wouldn't have looked like that. It was dope to build a relationship with someone like Paul.

DRU: That's one of my favorite songs on the album. The lyrics to that song were based on actual events and Tek and Steele narrated them so well.

WALT: That song was Baby Paul's idea. That is definitely one of my least favorite tracks on the album, though. Paul was one of my good friends. I met him when I was working at the Music Factory. We hung out all the time and we would go beat shopping together. I'm the oldest in the crew, Paul is maybe a year older than E.

Let's Git It On

EVIL DEE: Walt produced that, and it's one of my favorites. When I heard it, I was like, "Yo, that shit is crazy!" And I asked him who it was for. Then they got Rock from Heltah Skeltah to do the intro. Maybe I helped on the mix, but that was really all Walt, no matter what the credits say.

WALT: We did that song and "Bucktown" first, for their demo. On the original demo we sampled "Stop On By" by Chaka Khan and Rufus. We couldn't clear the sample so I went in and did a whole new beat, which was darker.

TEK: I remember with that song, it was the first time I heard myself on the radio. I was getting some pussy when that song came on. I got up and was bangin' on doors, telling everybody. It was on 98.7 FM, maybe Red Alert.

STEELE: When you said the title of the song right there, I got goosebumps. That might be my favorite on the album. I'm not sure, but it gave me goosebumps. Walt did another version that never came out. So I guess the album version is technically a remix. I'm not sure which one I like better. I can say that I like what the original music made us come up with for lyrics. I hear our youth on there, for sure.

DRU: That is a pretty amazing video, one of the more popular ones. Rolando Hudson directed it.

P. N. C.

TEK: We did that song for Sean Grady, aka Rambo, who was a brother of ours who got gunned down. He was a suave kid. It was specifically to him, but we all have fallen Partnaz 'N Crime. It was about moving on with any bullshit and static in your life. I lost a brother who drowned in a pool, I lost cousins. My first baby's mother, my girlfriend got hit by a bus.

STEELE: That's a very personal song. Partnaz 'N Crime was our crew. In Decepticons we had a mini-crew called Power Masters or Perfect Men, at 16 and 17 [laughs]. So

Perfect Men evolved into P. N. C. Rambo was one of the most beautiful guys I ever knew. He was a hardcore brother, he loved his family. He was murdered way before his time. Let me sum it up: Rambo is the reason why Tek, me and Cookie Head even know each other. We all went to high school together. They were all Bed-Stuy, I was the only Brownsville cat.

WALT: That's my second favorite track on the album, lyrically. E did that one.

EVIL DEE: I didn't know Rambo. I met Tek and Steele after he had passed.

STETSASONIC

In Full Gear
Tommy Boy, 1988

"The general concept of the album was, 'We're in now, we know what we're doing and we can do whatever we want to do. We can do everything.'"

– Daddy-O

"I think the whole vibe of the In Full Gear *sessions was 'We're gonna get our respect.' Seeing what groups like LL Cool J, Whodini, Jazzy Jeff & The Fresh Prince and Eric B. & Rakim were doing made us realize what was out there. And we knew what we could accomplish."*

– Prince Paul

In the music game, groups – for our purposes here, more than two people – can be highly complicated and potentially volatile animals. When they are working in unison, a collection of musicians in any genre can be incredibly powerful. But it can also be difficult to keep a unit focused and working towards the same goal over time, with egos in the proper places.

Rock music has given the world more groups than soloists. Hip-hop is the opposite, even though many pioneering hip-hop entities from the late '70s and early '80s were indeed groups: including the Cold Crush Brothers, the Fantastic Five, the Sugar Hill Gang and Grandmaster Flash and his Furious Five.

But as the '80s progressed, hip-hop was becoming more minimal, with a trio starting to become a crowd. Groups were seemingly less and less necessary, as a DJ could team up with an MC and make a run as a self-contained unit. Less hassles, less money splits.

Daddy-O [Glenn Kareem Bolton] came from the late 1970s pioneer days and, to put it bluntly, never really bought into the solo or duo game. Thankfully, his persistence made the group he led, Stetsasonic, into one of the most innovative and powerful hip-hop forces of all time.

Stet was Brooklyn to the core, and each member had a voice in making the group so unique. The group also stayed consistent, personnel-wise, throughout the decade.

Aside from Daddy-O, Stetsasonic included: MC Delite [Marvin Shahid Wright]; MC Fruitkwan [Arnold Hamilton, now known as Frukwan]; DJ Prince Paul [Paul Huston]; keyboardist and DJ DBC [Martin Nemley, often listed as Marvin, the "Devastating Beat Creator"]; human beatboxer aka "Human Mix-Machine" Wise [Leonardo Roman]; and drummer Bobby Simmons.

"I'm from East New York and Brownsville," states Daddy-O, proudly. "Pretty much both. There's a bridge at Julius Street and Van Sinderan [Avenue], a trestle for the L [subway] train that divides the two areas. I was born and bred from right there."

Daddy-O was first introduced to the music game in high school, at Thomas Jefferson High in East New York, where he attended school with future music mogul Kedar Massenburg. He was about 15 years old. "I had a friend named Reggie who was a DJ and did parties in Brooklyn," Daddy explains. "When people today say 'disco,' most of them think [the movie and soundtrack] 'Saturday Night Fever.' But for us it meant Loleatta Holloway and First Choice, the soul and funk music that came just before hip-hop took hold."

"I remember Reggie had a gig at Erasmus Hall High School in Flatbush [Brooklyn], and he had an MC with him who was called Barshan D," he continues. "This was around 1979, it was a Labor Day party. I'll never forget that night. I used to write poetry back then, and hip-hop was becoming more popular. I had started hearing Grandmaster Flash tapes from the Bronx, and I wanted to figure out how to make my poetry rock like Melle Mel, or the Funky Four. I never thought about doing the rhymes myself, I would write them for other people. So I wrote this rhyme for Barshan. And this kid was *horrible* with my rhyme. At that point I said that I'd never give another rhyme away."

And, with some foreshadowing, he explains, "So I started writing my own rhymes and developing my own identity. At the time, all my heroes in hip-hop were in *groups*."

The group idea was partially built on how to maximize live performances, even before Stet existed. "Basically, I knew what was wack and what was good from an early age," Daddy says. "I always just knew what bands should sound like. James Brown was the ultimate, obviously. The first group in hip-hop that I ever fell for was Melle Mel and the Furious Five, on live tapes I would hear. He was very influential on me. At the same time I loved the Temptations as a group. And it's kind of ill when I think about it, but that's kind of the way I ended up dealing with Stetsasonic. The group thing, one singer had a high voice, one had a low voice."

Around this same time, Daddy-O had been building with a friend named Marvin, who also went by Shahid. Shahid was from South Jamaica, Queens but moved to Brooklyn for a period of time in his late teens. Daddy-O still lived in Brooklyn, but worked in

Queens, so they would cross paths. By the early '80s, they were both loosely involved in a DJ and MC crew called Mass Communications. Shahid decided it was about time he took on an MC name: Delite.

"Delite became one of my best friends, and he was into the group idea, so we just started doing it," Daddy-O says. "At first it was just us two, practicing and getting the back-and-forth routines down." He adds, "We went through a *lot* of people until we got someone for that third MC spot [laughs]. The first dude was my man Crown Supreme. Then it was my man Del, then a guy Shamel. A lot of guys."

Daddy-O explains that the name Stetsasonic followed a fairly byzantine route before it was finally confirmed. Back in 1980 or early '81, when Daddy was calling himself Dr. On, there was an MC crew from Long Island ("Wyandanch or Freeport") called The Stetson Brothers. "They used to battle, and they actually beat Flash and them once," Daddy recalls. "Some of them, from the second generation of that group, used to hang out on the corner in my neighborhood because they used to hustle, selling coke. They knew me because I always had my box out with me."

According to Daddy, the second generation Stetson crew helped him in three ways: first, by telling him to be more aggressive with his rhymes and MC demeanor. Secondly, by naming him Daddy-O, after he graduated to tough-guy-on-the-mic status. And, finally, by bequeathing their group name to him.

"After I got my new rhyming style, I started making moves," he explains. "I got a DJ and I asked the Stetson guys to be down with me. I wanted to get things poppin' with hip-hop, but they just wanted to keep hustling. I asked them if I could use the name, and they gave it to me. I guess you could say they passed the legacy to me. So me and Delite took it from there, as the Stetson Brothers, probably in early 1981."

Daddy continues, "Our DJ was my man Master Mike Bushon. He was the best DJ in the neighborhood back then. We got a stage show together and made up t-shirts. The DJ crew was called Stetsamation. I would rap hard over slowed-down Barry White songs at parties. No one had ever heard shit like that before."

By 1982, Delite had modified the Stetson moniker to fit the new age, and it became Stetsasonic. "He figured that Stetson meant style and sonic meant sound, so why not?," Daddy says.

When the Fat Boys burst onto the scene in 1983, Stet quickly came up with someone who could rival the beatboxing skills of the Boys' phenom Buffy. "Our friend Kevin Porter, who was a dancer, introduced us to Wise, the Human Mix-Machine," recalls Daddy-O. "When we met him, he was scratching with his mouth, he did all the heavy-breathing stuff. So we put together a routine with him in it and he became an important part of what we were doing from then on."

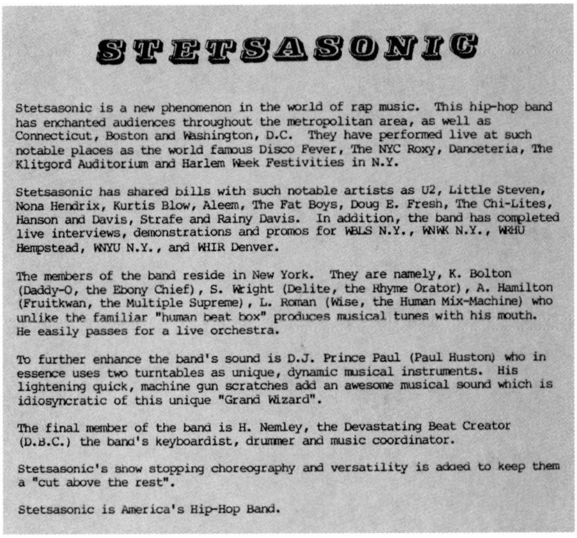
STETSASONIC

Stetsasonic is a new phenomenon in the world of rap music. This hip-hop band has enchanted audiences throughout the metropolitan area, as well as Connecticut, Boston and Washington, D.C. They have performed live at such notable places as the world famous Disco Fever, The NYC Roxy, Danceteria, The Klitgord Auditorium and Harlem Week Festivities in N.Y.

Stetsasonic has shared bills with such notable artists as U2, Little Steven, Nona Hendrix, Kurtis Blow, Aleem, The Fat Boys, Doug E. Fresh, The Chi-Lites, Hanson and Davis, Strafe and Rainy Davis. In addition, the band has completed live interviews, demonstrations and promos for WBLS N.Y., WNWK N.Y., WRHU Hempstead, WNYU N.Y., and WHIR Denver.

The members of the band reside in New York. They are namely, K. Bolton (Daddy-O, the Ebony Chief), S. Wright (Delite, the Rhyme Orator), A. Hamilton (Fruitkwan, the Multiple Supreme), L. Roman (Wise, the Human Mix-Machine) who unlike the familiar "human beat box" produces musical tunes with his mouth. He easily passes for a live orchestra.

To further enhance the band's sound is D.J. Prince Paul (Paul Huston) who in essence uses two turntables as unique, dynamic musical instruments. His lightening quick, machine gun scratches add an awesome musical sound which is idiosyncratic of this unique "Grand Wizard".

The final member of the band is H. Nemley, the Devastating Beat Creator (D.B.C.) the band's keyboardist, drummer and music coordinator.

Stetsasonic's show stopping choreography and versatility is added to keep them a "cut above the rest".

Stetsasonic is America's Hip-Hop Band.

Pre-Tommy Boy Stetsasonic bio.

Courtesy of the Adler Hip-Hop Archives / Cornell University Hip-Hop Collection.

During this time, there were some unfortunate personnel issues. "Our DJ, Bushon, dropped out," Daddy explains. "And our third MC, Crown Supreme, was really not that good. But we never wanted to be a duet. I had always loved the idea of having a third MC."

Enter Frukwan, another friend of Kevin Porter's. Daddy says, "I had never heard of him before we met. He was from the other side of East New York, the Breukelen Projects. When he came over and rhymed, me and Delite looked at each other and said, 'If we don't add this guy to the group, it's going to bite us in the ass.' He was the only other guy we knew who was rhyming that hard back then. He had an ill voice and we were a group that was predicated on the 'ill voice' thing."

Frukwan was definitely a perfect complement for the still-forming Stet crew. Aside from the "ill voice thing" – he does indeed possess one of the most distinctive voices and flows in all of hip-hop – he was a strong conceptualist, with many great ideas to bring to the table.

Frukwan recalls, "Around 1974 and '75 I was listening to these underground rap stations late at night when I was supposed to be resting up for school the next morning. I was just fascinated by the new-sounding music I was hearing. I could definitely relate to it. I start writing rap lyrics right around that time."

"In my [housing] project, Breukelen, there was a DJ crew called Phase III Disco, older cats," he continues. "They had equipment and speakers and they'd throw block parties. I would rhyme over their breakbeats, and I also did some breakdancing back then, too. I wouldn't just stay in Brooklyn, I'd go up to jams at the Armory in the Bronx and places like that. I was influenced by MCs who had any sort of consciousness in their rhymes."

Back before he joined up with Stet, Frukwan was planning on being a solo MC. He recalls his first meeting with Daddy-O and Delite: "My brother Calvin Cash had told me someone was asking about me, and I went to Daddy-O's crib. He had a beatbox and speakers and a recording set-up there. When I rhymed for them, I came out of left-field, I wasn't trying to sound like nobody else. My battle rhymes was crazy back then." Daddy-O and Frukwan both agree that the MC's acceptance into the group, which knocked Crown Supreme out, was a quick and decisive action.

Stet continued to build their camaraderie and they rehearsed as much as they could throughout 1983. "After I joined up, we started doing talent shows and stuff like that," Frukwan recalls. "With the rehearsals we were doing, the main focus was on crowd participation, staying energetic and never letting the crowd get bored. That stayed the same for years. We would be on tour with LL and Run-DMC and we were competing with them. We had to look great, we had to be energetic and we had to be in synch when it came to the lyrics."

He adds, "We had a great chemistry, starting early but building as we went on. It was 'One band, one sound.' When I came into the group, I had to recalculate my solo lyrics to fit into group songs. I had to narrow things down. It was an all-for-one thing, I made the choice to be in the group instead of just being a solo MC. It was a strong group. I mean, we was the first hip-hop *band*."

Despite being without a DJ at the time, the group's big break came in 1983, with a connection provided by New York radio legend Mr. Magic, on WBLS. By some accounts, Magic sponsored a talent show through his radio show and the first prize was a record deal with Sugar Hill Records. Also in mix were Pop Art and Tommy Boy Records.

"It was a contest on Magic's radio show," Daddy-O says. "We won different rounds in other boroughs and then we won the final, hands-down, at Coney Island [in Brooklyn]. It was a routine we had with Wise. We were so good that all three of the labels wanted us."

Future group DJ Prince Paul and Tommy Boy's Monica Lynch have different recollections about how the group got to Tommy Boy. Lynch – who was had been with Tommy Boy since late 1981 and was one of the top people at the label, aside from owner Tom Silverman – says: "I honestly don't recall if they won a talent show for the deal or not, but I do know that a talent show took place at Coney Island. But the most important thing was that Mr. Magic steered the group towards us. That was the first time I had ever heard of Stetsasonic. The fact that Magic walked them in to us meant that there wasn't a lot of debate as to whether we should sign them or not."

"Daddy-O said that we had a deal with Sugar Hill, but a lawyer looked at the contract and said it was bad," recalls Paul. "So the plan was for us to make a demo and shop it. I didn't even know what a demo was. Honestly, I didn't even know what shopping to labels meant [laughs]." According to Paul's recollection, the demo they made got played on Magic's radio show and Tom Silverman heard it and signed them from there.

No matter how the deal came about, Daddy-O says: "We never really gave Pop Art a chance, but we went to the Sugar Hill offices and studio and it was *so* pretentious. They had all these rented Benzes in the parking lot. Then Melle Mel came out with two girls on his arm. To this day, me and Delite believe that it was all staged. So we ended up choosing Tommy Boy, because they had Afrika Bambaataa [the song "Planet Rock" had become a worldwide smash the year before]."

"Sugar Hill was strong at that time, but then again they had a whole roster of people, so we would have had to wait in line," explains Frukwan. "If Tommy Boy was willing to give us an equal situation and we didn't have to wait, then that appealed to us. They also had links to the Zulu Nation [via Bambaataa], and that was important, too."

Lynch says, "1983 and '84 were interesting years at Tommy Boy, because those were the post-electro years. The Run-DMC sound had taken over, and we were in a bit of a lull. Our next phase hadn't come yet. So Stet arrived at a great time. I think my first impression of the group was, 'Wow, that's a lot of guys!' [laughs]. But I definitely thought the 'hip-hop band' angle was a really interesting one. Stet really helped us get to our second big period of success, in the late '80s and early '90s."

The Tommy Boy deal was, of course, great news for Stet. But the group still had no one to mind the turntables. "Once we won the contest, we knew things were really going to break out, and quickly," Daddy recalls. "Now we could really work Frukwan into the group even more and breathe a little easier, because we knew we would have records out. But we still had to get a DJ."

"I joined up with Stet in 1984," says Prince Paul. "I was in 10th grade, going into 11th." The future production guru grew up in Long Island; Amityville to be specific, about ten miles outside of Queens' Eastern border. "My whole thing at the time was what people today call 'Turntablism.' Behind-the-leg, show-off type of stuff. Not many people were doing that back then."

"A friend of mine from Amityville was going to a block party in Brooklyn, because his mom lived there," Paul continues. "And my grandmother lived in East New York, Glenmore Plaza, not far from Daddy-O. So I knew it pretty well. I almost didn't go, but at the last second I decided I would, and I brought my equipment. I was killin' it at this party and Stet rolled up on me. All I remember is that Daddy-O had really long braids and Delite had a spiked collar around his neck. Wise was there, I think he had just joined up a week before, and this guy Crown Supreme was with them, although that's the last time I saw him."

Daddy remembers the same incident, with a chuckle: "When we asked Paul to come over, he probably thought we were going to beat him up because we looked so mean [laughs]!"

A young Prince Paul, with Stetsasonic jacket.
Photo courtesy of Prince Paul.

"Those guys came running up, saying, 'That's him!,'" Paul says. "And I thought they was gonna kick my ass. But Daddy-O said they were looking for someone like me to DJ for the group. So I said, 'Yeah, let's give it a try.' I remember they came to my house to meet my mom and tell her the plan about me joining. Daddy-O said, 'Your son's a genius' and everyone in my family was like, 'Who, Paul?!?' [laughs]."

Paul adds, "When I first met Daddy-O and went to his house, I was in awe of him. He used to rhyme and I'd get the chills. He was charismatic and outspoken and he was definitely always the leader of the crew, even though in the early days it was more of a collaborative effort than it became later on."

Paul had been making beats from a young age, out in Amityville. Daddy-O even claims that Rick Rubin and Russell Simmons "borrowed" a Paul beat from a demo he sent them for LL Cool J's 1984 smash hit "I Need A Beat." And although he didn't get to shine as much on production until a couple years later, on *In Full Gear*, Paul was another important part of the group's sonic mix, both in the studio and on-stage.

The final piece of the Stet puzzle at the time was a relatively easy one. Daddy says, "After Paul joined, a friend of mine and Delite's said, 'My brother does music for rappers.' He was talking about DBC, who was mostly a keyboardist at the time. He was originally from Queens, but he moved outside of the city. So we put him in, too, which made us a six-man band."

It should be noted that the make-up of Stetsasonic the Hip-Hop Band in 1984 didn't yet have a drummer. DBC was on keyboards and had drum machines. Wise was an instrument, too, of course. Drummer Bobby Simmons, from Brownsville, would not enter until a couple years later.

Rehearsals for the group were very important to Daddy-O. Paul remembers them quite well: "I didn't have to practice and learn routines as much as the rest of them back then. I worked a lot at DJing and, to be honest, I was pretty nice. But when I did have to rehearse, Daddy-O would send me letters – if anyone can remember the days before email – with instructions about how each song would go. He'd write all the song structures out."

"In reality, though," Paul adds, "practice for me meant that I had to lug two turntables, a mixer, headphones and records on the train in a huge bag, all the way from Amityville to Brooklyn. Then I'd have to lug the bag through all these crime-ridden areas. It was crazy."

After more rehearsing and some quality time in the studio, the group launched their first single, which hit on Tommy Boy in 1985: "Just Say Stet." It was a stark song, featuring all of the elements for which the group would become known: hard, three-way rhymes; keyboards; skillful DJ cuts (finessed with a flanger effect); and beatbox skills. "DBC programmed the [drum machine] beat for that song and played the keys," Paul says. "That was my first time doing anything on wax. It was all new to me and I was loving it."

Early logo, sticker from "Just Say Stet" single, 1985.

The group's debut album followed after the success of "Just Say Stet," although not immediately. It was chiefly recorded at Calliope Studios in Manhattan, titled *On Fire*, and it hit in late 1986.

"We were proud of that record," Daddy recalls. "Maybe blindly proud. At the time, we had no focus on sales at all. We were just glad to have a record out. It was really more of a local New York record, not a big national thing. The only other first record that I can compare to *On Fire*, technically and sonically, is Boogie Down Productions' *Criminal Minded* [from 1987]. And, sonically, I think we even beat them."

Daddy continues, "In 1985 and 1986, we weren't afraid of anything, it wasn't 'beginner's luck.' A lot of those songs for *On Fire* were first [vocals] takes. With [1988's] *In Full Gear*, it was a little bit different, I would be trying to figure out which voice I was going to use. The loud Daddy-O or the mild guy. On both records, we knew that what we had was dope and we were just going for it."

"*On Fire* was our introduction," Frukwan explains. "At that time, Rakim had his first stuff out. Run-DMC and LL had albums out. And most of them were solo rappers. [The single] 'Go Stetsa I' is a classic. Even the song 'On Fire,' Dirty South rappers still use that style today. People still recite and re-format the rhymes we did on that album."

On Fire, back of LP. 1986.

"I had zero expectations back then," Paul says. "Basically we were all on a mission, to make great songs. The whole thing was a great experience, even though I never felt that the music on *On Fire*, aside from one or two songs, really pushed the envelope. I mean, 'Just Say Stet' was a Run-DMC bite in a lot of ways. I loved 'Go Stetsa I,' though, that's my favorite."

Monica Lynch opines, "*On Fire* is a fantastic album. The group was wildly adventurous and advanced as a band. Honestly, they might have been too advanced for the scene that was thriving at the time. Sales-wise, it definitely did well enough for us to want to do a second album. The singles off that one were 'Forever My Beat'; 'Faye'; and 'Go Stetsa I,' which everyone loved."

Daddy-O recalls, "Back then, with the first album, having live instrumentation was almost a sin *[Author's note: Run-DMC had used live playing on significant hits just a couple years before, so it could be argued that this wasn't necessarily true]*, because hip-hop was such a DJ culture. But because of our ages, we wanted to pick up instruments and be like Mandrill, War, or Earth, Wind & Fire. We were caught in the middle. Either way, on the first album, we only had live drums on one song. It was keyboards and then mostly drum machines and beatbox."

The standout track on the album, discussed previously, is "Go Stetsa I," which was released as a promo in late '86 and then commercially available in 1987. The reason for its uniqueness is the fact that it blends many elements of the group [minus keyboards and beatbox], including the use of live drums, drum machines and Paul's DJ skills. It's

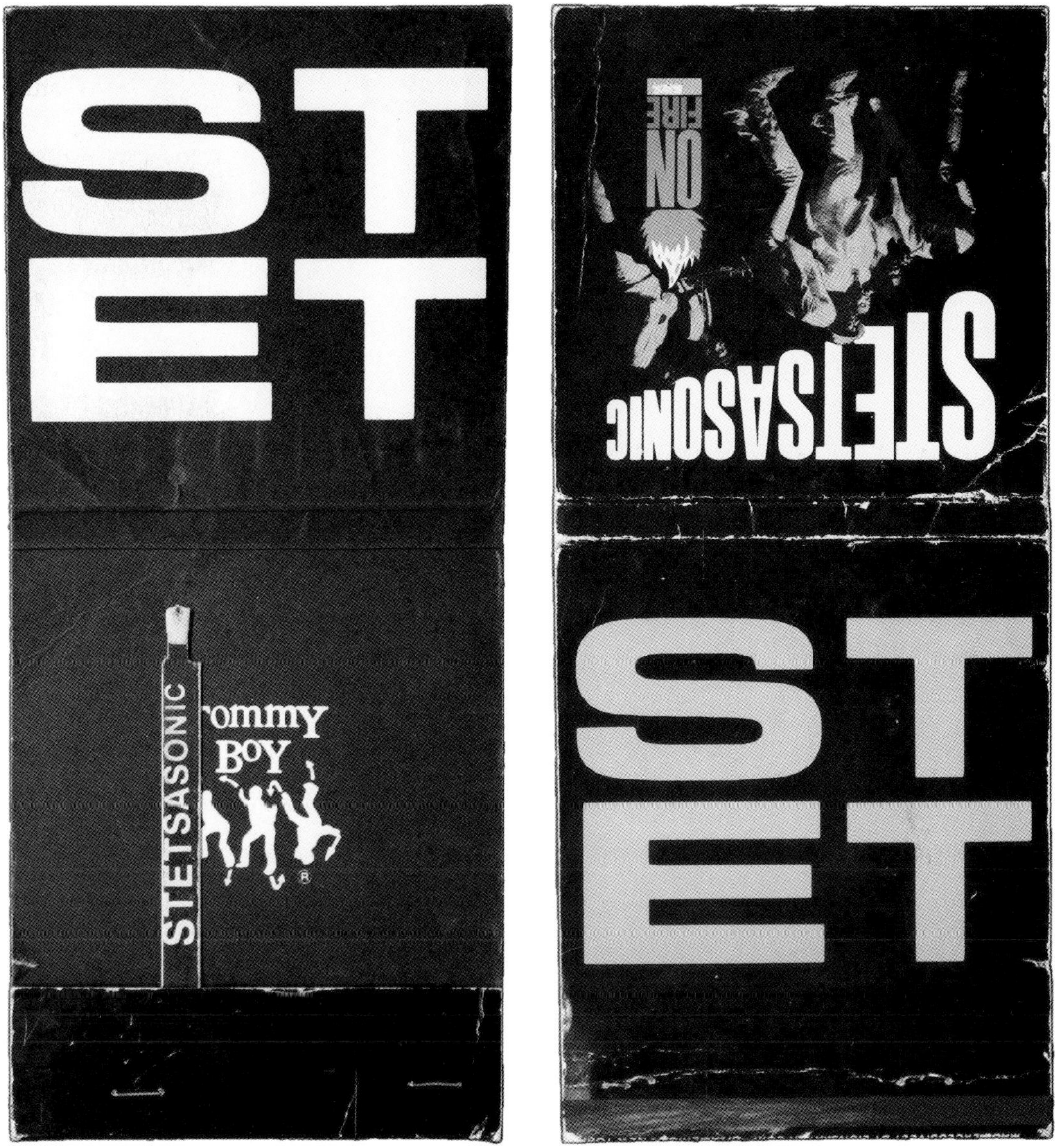

On Fire promotional matches, interior and exterior, 1986.
Courtesy of the Adler Hip-Hop Archives / Cornell University Hip-Hop Collection.

basic, raw and real, shooting a cannonball across the bow of Run-DMC, who were ruling the hip-hop charts at the time.

Before he goes into the story of "Go Stetsa I," Daddy points out two things, relating to percussion: "The drummer on 'Go Stetsa I' *wasn't* Bobby Simmons, it was my and Delite's friend Nawthar Muhammad. And although we had live drums on some of our records from the beginning, we weren't using live drums in performance that early. Bobby started performing with us on-stage after the *On Fire* album [1986] and before *In Full Gear* [1988]."

"Go Stetsa I" single, 1986.

"Tom Silverman [owner of Tommy Boy] would let us use the conference room at Tommy Boy to work on our rough tracks," Daddy-O says. "He had a LinnDrum [drum machine] in there and that's where we started 'Go Stetsa.' The original beat was basically a James Brown breakbeat, and we wrote the whole song to that, programmed on the Linn. Then Prince Paul found the Tom Jones break ['Looking Out My Window'] that we sampled. We originally wanted to use a drummer to just do some fills, not the whole beat."

He continues, "We recorded that song at Calliope Studios and Nawthar played throughout the whole song. I had hand signals in the booth which told him when to do fills and drum-rolls. One time I said to the engineer, 'Don't bring up the LinnDrum, let me hear how it sounds with the drummer.' And it sounded crazy. So we used that instead of the Linn. One of the mics we used for the drums was in the bathroom that was right near the vocal booth. It was a different way to do things. Bob Power did most of the engineering work on 'Go Stetsa I' but he was too anal for our taste, so we didn't work with him after that."

Going back to Daddy-O's earliest dreams of what a group he would lead could be, things were always based on how good its live performances were. And Stet rarely disappointed, even if they weren't always given as much high-marquee billing as they should have received.

"During our first two tours, we had both Paul and DBC on turntables," Daddy says.

"DBC also had his drum machine and keyboards. We'd have DBC battle Paul, and they would both battle Wise. Or they'd all do routines together. There was always something going on. Nobody was messing with our live show back then, it wasn't even close. Other acts were great live, but they didn't have what we had: a band. The whole concept for us, from the beginning, was to be as versatile as possible. To be able to do all sorts of ill stuff at the drop of a dime. Things that you could never do with just two turntables."

In New York, they wowed crowds at mid-'80s hotspots like their second home, the Latin Quarter, in addition to venues across the country, usually as part of Russell Simmons-booked package tours with Run-DMC, Public Enemy, LL Cool J and others. By 1987, Stet was part of the RUSH Artist Management umbrella, which brought them alongside some of the world's elite rap talent.

Frukwan especially remembers the group's '87 and '88 Latin Quarter shows. "Those were like practice," he explains. "It was a chance for us to try new things. When we were headlining, our show could be like two hours long, because we had so many elements. We could extend songs, MCs could take a rest, Wise could take a rest. I mean, if you do human beatbox for 30 minutes, your lips will go numb [laughs]. Groups were always worried about going on after us."

Stetsasonic and DJ Red Alert backstage at The Latin Quarter 1986.
Photo © Paradise Gray, Courtesy of The Paradise Collection Hip-Hop Archives.

"[Drummer] Bobby Simmons really made Stet's live show special," Lynch remembers. "Having a live drummer sounded amazing. Those guys had everything. Wise was incredible, too."

"During 1987, when *On Fire* was out, we opened for LL Cool J on the *Bigger And Deffer* tour," Paul recalls. "That was a big deal to us. Although we called it the 'Dis Jam Tour,' because we were the opening act. So when we were on, people were literally walking in and getting popcorn, like, 'Who are *these* guys?' Everyone else had big stage props and we had like a picnic table. We were on the RUSH roster, but we were always on the lowest rung. I will say, though, that it made us work harder on our stage show, because we thought that we were just as good – or better – than any other acts out there."

Daddy-O is ambivalent about Tommy Boy's support of the group throughout the '80s, especially regarding video budgets and tour support. "If you look at Def Jam back then, even the smaller artists on that label got paid, there was no argument," he says. "They took care of their artists. Lyor [Cohen, from RUSH, which was linked to Def Jam via Russell Simmons] tried to find money for Stetsasonic *[Author's note: For instance, extra marketing or advertising when they were touring, or better stage set-ups]* but he only had so many sources to tap into. Tommy Boy just never wanted to get up off the money. Although I know Tom Silverman supported us in other ways. It's not like they didn't want to help. He really did encourage us a lot."

Frukwan agrees with the lack of monetary support, at least compared to artists on rosters like Def Jam: "We didn't have huge ad campaigns or anything, but we made the best of the situation. I was still thankful to be on the RUSH roster. We also got to do outside campaigns like the 'A.F.R.I.C.A.' single [from 1987 on Tommy Boy, a collaboration with the Reverend Jesse Jackson and the Africa Fund] and the 'Self Destruction' project as well [from 1989, on Jive, technically the 'Stop The Violence Movement']. Wherever we were, when we got on stage we wanted to take everyone else out and show them what we had."

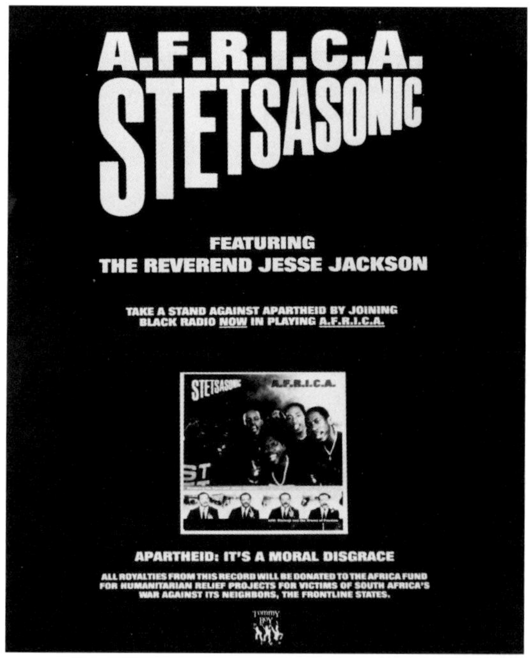

Trade magazine ad for "A.F.R.I.C.A." single, 1987.

"No matter what, we always split everything equally," Daddy-O adds. "When we went on tour, we'd just economize, share rooms or whatever." If you look at the way the group's publishing is still split up, Daddy's claim seems to bear this out, with all six main members listed as writers on tracks going back to *On Fire*.

After almost a year of touring behind *On Fire*, it was time to go back into the studio and show the world what Stetsasonic was really all about. "When we got ready to start recording *In Full Gear*, competition was a big influence on us," Daddy-O recalls. "We wanted to make records that were comparable to other records put out by our peers, or even better than theirs. There were so many more hip-hop artists putting out great music in 1988 than in 1986. We had a bigger budget for our second record, and we had more time to make it how we wanted it to sound."

As for the groups Daddy-O was keeping sonic tabs on, he says: "We couldn't compete with how dope Public Enemy was, but we had some similar group situations and we recorded in some of the same rooms, so we gave it a shot. We really wanted to be like EPMD, though, and we also wanted to keep up with Ced-Gee and Ultramagnetic MCs."

Lyrically, there was some competition as well, and it came from within the group. But, as members note, it was friendly and healthy. "We almost always wrote our rhymes together," Daddy-O says. "One person would spark the original rhyme, and everyone else would go off that." Frukwan adds, "There was definitely competition with the other MCs. Not aggressive competition, because there was no hate amongst us. We just wanted to kill the song, any way we could."

Stetsasonic, 1988.
Photo © Janette Beckman.

Daddy says, "By 1988 we had also fully settled into the concept of us being a *band*. We were going to be Sly & The Family Stone and P-Funk. And we wanted our music to match that. We wanted it to be *big*. The sound had to be bigger and better, and if there was something we wanted to try, we were going to figure out how to try it."

"Sonically, *In Full Gear* was influenced by us going abroad, as well," Daddy-O points out. "Me, DBC and Prince Paul are some of the biggest record junkies in the whole world, so when we went overseas to tour, we started finding all of these rare grooves. It was ridiculous. That was like finding a whole new set of [the famed breakbeat compilations] *Ultimate Breaks & Beats*. We had never heard of a lot of the stuff we found, and it had an influence on the album's sound, for sure."

Paul agrees. "I think a lot of the sound on *In Full Gear* had to do with us seeing the country and realizing that New York wasn't the only place that had hip-hop," he says. "It definitely opened our eyes, and led to songs like 'Miami Bass.' We shaped our music and made it broader. But as we did that, it also started to lack some of the raw, gut feeling that we had with *On Fire*. It was a bit of a trade-off. But it was still a lot of fun to make that album."

[Author's note: Paul, of course, would very soon take a side-trip to produce De La Soul's groundbreaking album, 3 Feet High And Rising, which hit in 1989, also on Tommy Boy.]

"In general, with our group evolution, everybody's ears got better as well," Daddy explains. "We had good ears with *On Fire*, but by *In Full Gear* we had great ears. You could walk in and say, 'That hi-hat is too loud,' and that would make the difference in the song."

In Full Gear album ad, 1988.
Courtesy of the Adler Hip-Hop Archives / Cornell University Hip-Hop Collection.

Daddy-O estimates that recording for the album was between six and eight months, starting in mid-1987. Laid down at both their home-base of Calliope as well as Chung King, Bob Coulter was their head engineer [listed in the credits as "console magician"] for just about all of the sounds created.

"Recording *In Full Gear* was an all-day thing when we hit the studio," says Frukwan. "We always blocked out time. There were no excuses, and we couldn't wait to record. It was a family thing, too. I brought my little girl in there and was changing her diapers right in the studio. We were all just in sync, everybody got along. There was unity."

Daddy-O notes that whereas "Stetsasonic" was given group production credit for all *On Fire* tracks, by *In Full Gear* they started to designate which specific group member was pulling more weight on any given song. "It didn't change the royalties, because our contracts didn't change," he explains. "It just gave people in the group time to loosen up and get their own thing on."

According to Daddy-O, Prince Paul – aside from producing some excellent songs on the album [credited and uncredited, according to him, see below] – was in charge of album sequencing. Daddy says, "Because we had Paul, sequencing was never a problem. He also titled the album."

"The recording was so much more relaxed for *In Full Gear*, because with *On Fire* we always felt like we had to finish everything up during that session," Daddy-O explains. "We didn't rush as much later on, we knew what we were doing and we were going to take our time."

"*In Full Gear* was the real birth of Stetsasonic, in my opinion," says Frukwan. "It was an incredible album, there were so many sounds on there. Different flows and different topics. It was a great time back then."

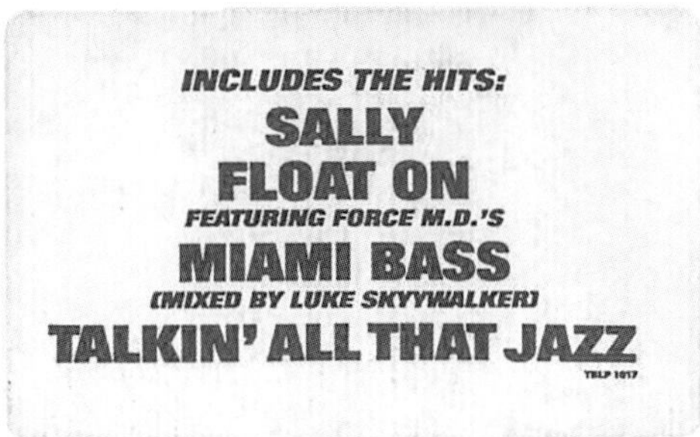

Album sticker, 1988.

Daddy mentions one tidbit that will certainly interest die-hard fans: "We ended up cutting as many tracks as the number that made the final album [15 on the LP edition]. Bobby Simmons has most of the ones that we cut somewhere. Maybe we'll put them out someday. I remember there was one called "We Got A Beat," with Wise rhyming on it. It used Donna Summer's 'Love To Love You Baby' bassline."

The album came out in the summer of 1988 and boasted three singles: "Sally"; "Talkin' All That Jazz"; and 1989's R & B-tinged "Float On." Daddy-O says he thinks the album should have reached gold status after all these years, but the RIAA has not officially designated it as such. Monica Lynch, without any confirmed numbers, estimates sales of the album through the late '80s at, "Not more than 200,000, most likely less."

Regarding the Janette Beckman-shot cover and interior photos, Daddy-O recalls, "We knew exactly how we wanted the album cover to look. There was that sign [on concrete, on the front of the album, reading "East New York"] at Pennsylvania Ave and Pitkin [Avenue], it says 'East New York Industrial' something. We shot the cover right against that wall. And all the inside photos were in Alabama Park, my old stomping grounds."

Lynch remembers the photo shoot as well, at least for the back cover [where the group stands in front of a "Stetson Hats" storefront]: "Those shots were done in the Fulton Street Mall [in Brooklyn], on a Sunday. We knew it would be quieter in the morning. As you can see, the guys all had their new gear, they were super-fresh for those pictures. I love those."

Looking back at Stet's heyday, Daddy-O says, "I do feel that a lot of people leave us out when they discuss the best hip-hop groups of all time, but I don't think they'll leave us out forever. And we're not the only ones. The only thing I really regret, the big reason why I think we never blew up like we should have, is that we never had enough videos. We fought tooth and nail, and those would have changed so much for us. But that just never happened."

Lynch doesn't necessarily agree with Daddy-O's assertion about the group's videos (or lack thereof). "I'm not convinced that doing more Stet videos would have dramatically changed how much success they had," she says. "The Tommy Boy criteria back then for doing a video wasn't to first do a video and make it a hit. It was the opposite: 'Let's see if we have a hit, and then we'll do a video, to expand on it.' We did this with hits from the Jonzun Crew, Afrika Bambaataa & Soulsonic Force and other artists. Tommy Boy just didn't have a ton of money back then. This was pre-De La Soul and pre-Queen Latifah."

"Sally" single release party (with early performance by De La Soul). April, 1988.

Courtesy of the Adler Hip-Hop Archives / Cornell University Hip-Hop Collection.

Beyond videos, budgets or anything else, Paul says, regarding what is generally considered Stetsasonic's masterwork: "*In Full Gear* was big for us because people around the world finally got to hear who we were. We finally got a video ['Talkin' All That Jazz'], which got played a lot. And 'A.F.R.I.C.A' was cool, too. That album was big overseas, we even headlined a European tour. The album might not have gone gold back then, but I think we really got stepped up in how much respect people had for us."

Frukwan, looking back, beams, "I honestly liked all the songs on *In Full Gear*. We made a whole new universe, something that nobody else had ever done in hip-hop. Our live show spoke for us, and sold us records. We were blessed to tour a lot, and fans always knew who Stetsasonic was when the show was over."

"I'm still not sure that they get the recognition they deserve," laments Monica Lynch. "Maybe they were a bit too advanced or abstract for a marketplace that wanted its hip-hop more direct and in-your-face. No matter what, *In Full Gear* is a great album, it was so varied. And I agree that it was the true birth of Stetsasonic in a lot of ways. We were very proud to put it out."

"Stetsasonic definitely shaped what I might call the independence of hip-hop," says Daddy-O, in summation. "People always knew that Stet was a group that did what we wanted, and I think that had an impact on everything. Our influence on other artists was maybe bigger than our influence on fans, because a lot of times fans only embrace what is pushed on them. Musically, we opened up a whole bunch of things in terms of what could be done. And performance-wise, we showed that hip-hop could be taken to that other level."

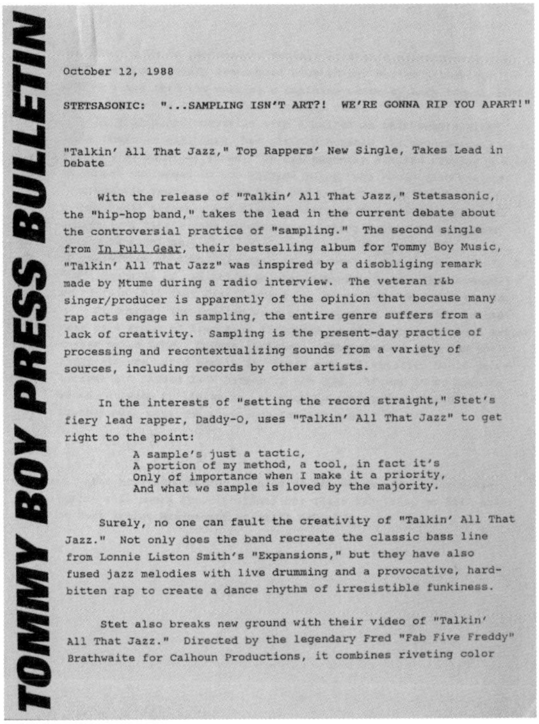

TOMMY BOY PRESS BULLETIN

October 12, 1988

STETSASONIC: "...SAMPLING ISN'T ART?! WE'RE GONNA RIP YOU APART!"

"Talkin' All That Jazz," Top Rappers' New Single, Takes Lead in Debate

With the release of "Talkin' All That Jazz," Stetsasonic, the "hip-hop band," takes the lead in the current debate about the controversial practice of "sampling." The second single from In Full Gear, their bestselling album for Tommy Boy Music, "Talkin' All That Jazz" was inspired by a disobliging remark made by Mtume during a radio interview. The veteran r&b singer/producer is apparently of the opinion that because many rap acts engage in sampling, the entire genre suffers from a lack of creativity. Sampling is the present-day practice of processing and recontextualizing sounds from a variety of sources, including records by other artists.

In the interests of "setting the record straight," Stet's fiery lead rapper, Daddy-O, uses "Talkin' All That Jazz" to get right to the point:

A sample's just a tactic,
A portion of my method, a tool, in fact it's
Only of importance when I make it a priority,
And what we sample is loved by the majority.

Surely, no one can fault the creativity of "Talkin' All That Jazz." Not only does the band recreate the classic bass line from Lonnie Liston Smith's "Expansions," but they have also fused jazz melodies with live drumming and a provocative, hard-bitten rap to create a dance rhythm of irresistible funkiness.

Stet also breaks new ground with their video of "Talkin' All That Jazz." Directed by the legendary Fred "Fab Five Freddy" Brathwaite for Calhoun Productions, it combines riveting color

"Talkin' All That Jazz" press release, page one. October, 1988.
Courtesy of the Adler Hip-Hop Archives / Cornell University Hip-Hop Collection

TRACKS

In Full Gear

[Produced by Prince Paul]

PRINCE PAUL: I didn't love the production on that one. I remember I had a Sequential Circuits Tom drum machine I used, and a cheap sampler. I did a rough of it and they decided to use it on the album. The song we sampled from was called "Shifting Gears" [by Johnny Hammond] and Daddy-O changed that up on the chorus. I wasn't cutting the words "In Full Gear" on the chorus [from a previous record], it's just them saying it. We sampled that. I'm cutting "Gear" from the original Johnny Hammond record, and our MCs are saying "In Full" over the top.

DADDY-O: For a whole year, that was the song we opened up our live show with. That was such a fun record. We didn't always know that would be the album title. Paul came up with it. The main sample was "Shifting Gears," and we changed it. The guy from the Masterdon Committee, Master G *[Author's note: He may mean Gangster G]*, is singing on there. The guy who sang "Funkbox." He's singing "In Full Gear," double-tracked, harmonizing with himself. That's not live bass on there, it's a sample. It was just a great track to start off the album. I love that line, "I've been fully baptized in the river of Stet." Once I wrote that, it got Delite and Frukwan started.

DBC Let The Music Play

[Produced by DBC]

FRUKWAN: DBC produced that track, of course. He brought an element of supreme-ness to the group, you know what I'm sayin'? Besides being a keyboard player, he produced a lot of tracks. We all related to his form of brainstorming. He was from Long Island, like wayyyyy out Long Island. He'd carry his keyboard with him all that way, on mass transit. Even if it was snowing, DB was there, he was dedicated to the utmost. DB also helped with the live sound, he'd be there at the soundboard, to make sure it was just what we needed. He played a very important role.

DADDY-O: DBC had a studio in his house and we'd record stuff there. What convinced us about him was when we recorded "My Rhyme" at his place [from *On Fire*]. We loved that and knew he was the guy. Paul didn't learn much production from DBC, but I did. He was a great [drum machine] programmer. He wasn't just a producer, he called himself a "Beat Creator," to show that he was a musician. We all loved old hip-hop records when MCs would talk about their crew. That would always entice us. [He recites an old Kid Creole live rhyme, talking about the Furious Five]. And we'd always do that, too, because we had so many people to talk about. So that track was all about DBC. There were a lot of different versions of that track. Eventually we found a mix that worked for it. There's a different version on the B-side of the "Sally" single. Wise rapped on there. He always wanted to rap, but we'd just tell him he couldn't. It's not that he wasn't good, it's just that he was facing tough competition. We had three great MCs, and why would we put a fourth on if we didn't have to? He was an amazing Human Mix-Machine, so we wanted him to stick to that. But we put him on a couple songs.

Freedom Or Death

[Produced by Daddy-O]

DADDY-O: That's my ode to the late, great Sonny Carson. His son, Lumumba [aka Professor X, from X-Clan], was a good friend of mine, and we did a lot of things together, early on. He was kind of our early security. That was Sonny's statement, "Freedom Or Death," So I made that song for him. They say that phrase in some X-Clan records, too. My brother Aasim came up with this ill conga thing in the studio one day, and I wanted to use it. He was pretty surprised that I liked it, actually. I think the political side of Stet is one of the main things that people remember. We really prided ourselves on making music for the mind, body and soul. That was part of our stage dialogue. That song might get overlooked, but not our political side in general. Articles would come out back then talking about me, KRS-One and Chuck [D].

FRUKWAN: I met Sonny Carson and I knew Lumumba. Sonny was a wise man and he did a lot for our people.

Float On [featuring the Force MDs]

[Produced by Vincent Bell]

DADDY-O: That took a while to become a great record. Me and Paul did an early version of that with the [Honeydrippers'] "Impeach The President" beat, and it sampled the Floaters [who did the original "Float On," in 1977]. Monica said we should get the Force MDs to sing on it. Basically, we just wanted to do a ballad. That was one of Delite's great ideas, and at first I thought it was crazy. Once he said, "Float On," I realized we could make it work. We wanted to prove something, musically. We didn't want to just be part of rap. We wanted to be part of *music*. And everybody in the group was equally down with it. That song was definitely a bugged-out thing to do. But our fans loved it, and they'd get mad when we wouldn't perform it. We only ever did it once live. We didn't make that song to perform it. It was way too slow and way too long, and we wouldn't have the Force MDs to help with it when we toured. We actually shot a video for that song, but I *hated* it. Tom Silverman allowed me to destroy the tape. It was like, "I'm going Sly Stone on this *[Author's note: Referring to some of Sly's studio antics in the There's A Riot Goin' On era]*, destroy it!" Of course, now I wish I had the tape. But I watched it being destroyed, we ripped it up. It really was *that* bad. I had an idea and that idea went south. I wanted to look like the Four Tops and the Temptations in the video, and it just didn't look right. A & M Breakout paid for it, Tommy Boy didn't pay anything. But Tom could have put it out anyways, and he didn't. We shot the video in England. If you find a copy, let me know. Someone's got it I'm sure!

PAUL: I didn't have anything to do with that final version. I liked the original and I understood why Daddy-O wanted to do a ballad, because that was big back then. With LL's "I Need Love" and all that. But I always thought slow songs were cheesy. Vincent Bell [the song's producer] was an R & B type of cat and I remember that Daddy was really excited about getting him to produce it.

MONICA LYNCH: I don't remember a video for that, or anyone destroying it!

FRUKWAN: When I first heard that song, I of course first thought of Force MCs [aka Force MDs – early on, the MDs went by the Force MCs, known for their harmonizing as much as their group MCing]. It was definitely going to be an interesting challenge to re-make that as a rap song. That was just a classic R & B song. We made a video that was for Europe, to be released over there. I don't know anything about destroying any video copies. I'm sure that video is on YouTube anyways [laughs].

Stet Troop '88!

[Produced by Wise]

DADDY-O: Overall, that's my favorite rhyme, all the way through. I could listen to that record over and over. I don't even know how I did that on there. I killed it. I would consider that the "anti-Doug E. Fresh" record. We really wanted to show people what

Wise's beatbox could sound like on a record. Other beatboxers would cheat when they recorded, they'd put stuff up underneath the beatbox. When I talk about getting into a fight with a cop on there, it wasn't literally the night before. It was a while before, at the Roxy, this cop was fucking with us, and Frukwan's face got shoved in a puddle. It was fucked-up.

Pen And Paper

[Produced by Prince Paul]

PAUL: Those aren't live drums on there, that's me programming them [on a drum machine]. I was really getting into programming at that point, I was fucking with shuffles and drumrolls. I did that one on the Sequential Tom machine. "Pen And Paper" was a loop from a breakbeat record I had. I made the demo for the group and we decided to make a song of it.

Music For The Stetfully Insane

[Produced by Prince Paul]

LYNCH: I always loved that song! [laughs]. That one and "Talkin' All That Jazz" are my two favorites on the album. "Stetfully Insane" was a precursor to Paul's genius [as a producer and solo artist].

PAUL: That was when I first started to show my bizarre side. I'm actually surprised that they allowed me to put it on the album. I did it at home, played it for them and they wanted it. I was like, "Really?!" I always loved that Funkadelic "Atmosphere" track [from *Let's Take It To The Stage*]. I didn't really sample it, I was cutting the different parts in. I played pretty big chunks of the original. Back then there weren't any sampling laws, so we'd just go for it.

This Is It, Y'All (Go Stetsa II)

[Produced by Daddy-O]

FRUKWAN: That was a great song, another classic.

DADDY-O: We used that Billy Preston ["Will It Go Round In Circles"] loop on there and I loved that. We all loved the beat on that song so much that we knew we had to use it, even before we knew what the song would be about. We named it "Go Stetsa

II" because it had a similar drum pattern as the first one [from *On Fire*]. And the concept was just to talk about all the things we did while we was on tour. The interview at the beginning was from a Long Island station, WBAU, the one that Hank [Shocklee] and Chuck [D] was on [as DJs, in the early '80s]. The intertwining vocals we used on there were set when we did "Just Say Stet" [also from *On Fire*], if you ask me. It was always something we tried to do, and it's one of my biggest beefs with groups out there now. All you have to do is listen to EPMD one time to see how it makes sense. That song definitely sounds laid-back, and that was on purpose.

Extensions

[Produced by Daddy-O]

DADDY-O: That was written by a friend of mine, Mike Chin, who went by Finesse. He got killed. We used to work together. He had a group, Finesse and TLC, from East New York, and they used to just do rhymes like that all the time. I wanted to put that rhyme on the album, so they came in and did it for us.

Sally

[Produced by Daddy-O]

PAUL: That started as a "Just Say Stet" remix and was supposed to be on the *On Fire* album. I came in with the beat and I had everything programmed, then Frukwan did the drum beat programming. Those were all my samples, but when the album came out I didn't get any credit. It should have said, "Written by Prince Paul and Frukwan, with lyrics by Daddy-O." I programmed the kick and the snare for that on the SP-1200. Then Frukwan added some stuff, and Daddy came in and was like, "I've got a concept for that" and he wrote all the lyrics for it. It was a tribute to the B-Boys [song] "Girls," in a way. That song was recorded earlier than other songs on the *In Full Gear* LP.

FRUKWAN: That was the hottest beat on the album, to me. And I basically produced that track. That was the epitome of what songs for females would become. Everybody wanted to hear that one, even our [fellow] touring artists on Def Jam. I don't remember that being started as a remix, it was just something that was put together and wasn't completed. I ended up triggering the beat for it and we laid down some lyrics, to make it spicy. The Dyke & The Blazers sample came in later. I think each MC spit eight bars. I wish we had had a video for that one, it could have taken us to another level.

DADDY-O: That was the first single off the album. The basic idea was already really done on the Dyke & The Blazers original ["Let A Woman Be A Woman – Let A Man Be A Man"]. Basically, when you live in the projects there are girls who have walks that just stop cars. Some people are haters about it. It wasn't as much of a B-Boys [whose song "Girls" is sampled] tribute, it was just about chicks in the projects. Some of them, when you see them walk, you wanna fuck 'em. That's exactly what it was. We always played "Sally" last when we performed, it was the show closer. We made a beginning, middle and end to the story and we really loved how it turned out. Frukwan did most of that. Paul might have brought in the 808 [drum machine] and a couple other things, with me saying move this here, move that there. Frukwan didn't really produce it, so he didn't get the credit. He did the beat and me and Paul took it from there. I really think that it would have helped us so much if we had gotten a video for "Sally." I think we could have blown up like Run-DMC or Whodini. But Tom and Monica really thought that videos just didn't sell records.

LYNCH: That song did well, but we didn't do a video. I don't remember numbers, but that was a bit of a hit. It went to #25 on the [*Billboard*] "Hot R & B / Hip-Hop" singles chart, as I'm looking at my reference book right now.

Talkin' All That Jazz

[Produced by Delite]

DADDY-O: That was the biggest hit on the record, definitely. It was a simple concept: Delite had an idea to use Lonnie Liston Smith's "Expansions" to show the correlation between hip-hop and jazz, which we could all see. At the time, I was producing a single for the Audio Two: "Make It Funky," with the B-side "Top Billin'." And the guys' father, Nat Robinson, called and told me how [jazz multi-instrumentalist and producer] James Mtume was on the radio talking about how rap was creating a whole generation of non-creative musicians. It was on Bob Slate's show, called "The Week In Review," Sunday mornings on Kiss 98. And then I went on Bob's show and re-butted what Mtume said. We made the song up as a routine like we used to do back in the day, and I wrote the parts for everyone and put it all together. I was pissed off at Mtume and that song is me going off on him. And it's funny because he and I are good friends now. He knew it was about him. And I met him at the "Self Destruction" video shoot [in 1989]. He said, "Hi, I'm the narrow-minded guy." [laughs]. That was our first commercial video, after "A.F.R.I.C.A." Fab 5 Freddy [who directed] came up with the concept for the video, he knew it was about sampling. We didn't want to do a typical performance, but we said he could film us on stage if he wanted. We shots part of it at a jazz club downtown. And Freddy came up with some great older footage, too. I don't know where he found that.

PAUL: That song still sounds great today, people still love it. I looped that beat. Delite had the idea to use "Expansions," he knew that would be big. And I got Don Newkirk to play keyboard. I never got credit on that song for my production. I guess it's partially my fault, because I didn't study about the music business back then. I never knew that you were the writer if you did the beat. No one told me. I learned all about it, though, when Daddy-O got a big healthy check for "Talkin' All That Jazz" and I didn't. I didn't get anything, actually. I guess he gave Delite [production] credit because he was so adamant about using that "Expansions" loop.

LYNCH: That's a masterpiece of a song, really. It's very much ahead of the curve in using jazz in a hip-hop context. That song definitely had an appeal beyond hip-hop. In fact, it didn't blow up with hip-hop fans in places like Houston or Miami. But dance crowds got into it in a way that they might not have gotten into a Stet song like "Sally." Everybody at Tommy Boy liked that song the most [off the album] but I think we also thought it would be a hard sell at black radio outside of the Northeast, New York and Philly. Honestly, there was not a hands-down smash on the album. I'm looking it up now, and it was #22 on the [*Billboard*] "Dance Music / Club Play" chart, and #34 on "Hot R & B / Hip-Hop." Fab 5 Freddy directed the video, I haven't seen that in a long time. We did that video before the song became a hit, unlike other videos we would do. There was sufficient enthusiasm at the label so that we didn't have to wait. [She pulls up video on YouTube]. I love this! I forgot how great it was [laughs several times as she watches it]. Freddy did a great job. Coati Mundi is the bartender. The vintage dance footage is amazing. And of course Freddy has a cameo [laughs]. James Mtume was very much an activist against hip-hop back then.

FRUKWAN: That was something that Daddy-O was experimenting with and we added on to it. That was definitely a favorite off that album, it was very radio friendly.

It's In My Song

[Produced by DBC]

PAUL: I like that one a lot, that's definitely one of my favorites. Those were all my cuts on there, not DBC. DBC produced it. DBC was more about programming the music and playing keyboards. That's why he was brought in [to the group].

DADDY-O: That's one of my favorites, because I did my rhyme with scratches. No one had ever done that before. I wanted to do even more than I did. I think that's my favorite rhyme I ever said on a record, after "On Fire." We went overseas and found an instrumental cover version of [Sly & The Family Stone's] "Sing A Simple Song" and that's what we used for that. [Engineer] Bob Coulter is playing guitar on there, over the cover that we were sampling.

Miami Bass

[Produced by Prince Paul and Daddy-O]

FRUKWAN: That was a song we did for the South, and it did well in LA too. We had done shows with 2 Live Crew back then, and we definitely rocked that in our live shows all the time.

LYNCH: That song and "Sally" were more commercial than other tracks on the album, for sure.

PAUL: I remember looping that up, I forget the song [that was sampled], throwing the 808 on it and scratching on it. Daddy-O was really into 2 Live Crew at the time, so he linked up with them. It wasn't a typical bass song, it was more like throwing Brooklyn and Miami together. Nobody in New York was listening to Miami Bass back then, so it helped spread that sound. I loved the first 2 Live Crew album, and after that I didn't listen to them as much.

DADDY-O: We went down there and heard what was going on and just loved it. Luke [Skyywalker aka Uncle Luke, from 2 Live Crew] approved that record, we kept sending him new drafts of it along the way. Luke and [2 Live Crew member] Mr. Mixx basically just turned the bass all the way up. That's a really fun record. It was our own version of what they were doing. 2 Live Crew and guys from the South never got any respect in New York. That's why Luke loves Chuck D and me to this day. We were the only ones. Same with Eazy-E. We told people in New York, "Look, it's not gonna be just us anymore. It's not just about us, it's about *everybody*."

Rollin' Wit Rush

[Produced by Prince Paul and Daddy-O]

DADDY-O: Paul came up with that sample, I don't know where he got it. But I knew I wanted to rhyme on it. Frukwan killed me on it! We did the track and then I decided to put the "Rollin' With Rush" from the beginning of the Eric B. & Rakim record ["Paid In Full"] at the end. I thought it would be something that would get Russell a little bit more on our side [laughs].

BONUS

[Song is not on *In Full Gear* album]

A.F.R.I.C.A. [Released as a Tommy Boy single in 1987]

[Produced by Stetsasonic, Chris Irwin and the News Dissector for the A.F.R.I.C.A. Project]

DADDY-O: That was never supposed to come out on any album, it was just a single. Norman Cook [aka Fatboy Slim] did that remix [released as a single on Go Discs, 1990], and that got the song in front of a lot more people. It was a side project, but that song might be the thing that I'm most proud of doing, ever. Danny Schechter worked for ABC "20/20" at the time, I might have met him through [RUSH and Def Jam publicist] Bill Adler. Danny was working with the Africa Fund in South Africa and he got us involved. Me and Frukwan wrote that whole song and the Africa Fund paid for it *[Author's note: The back cover of the record says, "All royalties for this record will be donated to the Africa Fund for humanitarian relief projects for the people of the Frontline States"]*. I got to tour with the Africa Fund behind that. They only took me. And that's what started my public speaking career. We went to the United Nations with Jesse Jackson. But since Tommy Boy hadn't supported it or paid for it, I wasn't going to put it on their album.

WILD STYLE BREAKBEATS

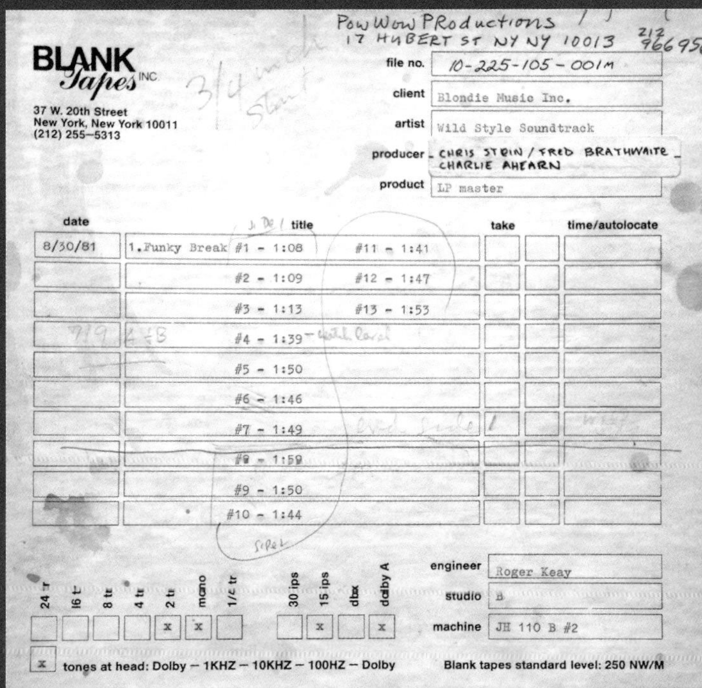

Pow Wow Productions
17 HUBERT ST NY NY 10013 212 966956

BLANK Tapes INC
37 W. 20th Street
New York, New York 10011
(212) 255–5313

file no. 10-225-105-001M
client Blondie Music Inc.
artist Wild Style Soundtrack
producer CHRIS STEIN / FRED BRATHWAITE CHARLIE AHEARN
product LP master

date	title		take		time/autolocate
8/30/81	1.Funky Break #1 - 1:08	#11 - 1:41			
	#2 - 1:09	#12 - 1:47			
	#3 - 1:13	#13 - 1:53			
	#4 - 1:39				
	#5 - 1:50				
	#6 - 1:46				
	#7 - 1:49				
	#8 - 1:59				
	#9 - 1:50				
	#10 - 1:44				

24 tr	16 tr	8 tr	4 tr	2 tr	mono	1/2 tr	30 ips	15 ips	dbx	dolby A
				x	x			x		x

engineer Roger Keay
studio B
machine JH 110 B #2

x tones at head: Dolby – 1KHZ – 10KHZ – 100HZ – Dolby

Blank tapes standard level: 250 NW/M

Recorded 1981

"I loved hearing DJs like GrandWizzard Theodore cut up classic hip-hop beats like [Thin Lizzy's] 'Johnny The Fox' or [Cerrone's] 'Rocket In The Pocket.' There was a 'flavor of the month' at any given time, such as 'Heartbeat' by Taana Gardner, which the Treacherous [Three] used for 'Feel The Heartbeat.' Everybody in 1981 was rapping over that song. We didn't want to be dependent on the hit of the month but, more importantly, I was afraid of [filming] MCs rhyming off a pile of records that I wouldn't be able to clear."

– "Wild Style" Director Charlie Ahearn

"At first, I thought it was crazy," says the legendary GrandWizzard Theodore.

Charlie Ahearn has referred to it as a "ridiculously ambitious plan."

And guitarist Chris Stein, with three decades of hindsight, proclaims that Ahearn's idea was "brilliant."

When reminiscing these days, the band of merry men involved in creating perhaps the most obscure 22 minutes in hip-hop music history – the infamous *Wild Style Breakbeats* – do indeed use adjectives like *crazy* and *ridiculous*. What they were attempting back in the summer of 1981 hadn't been done before. But keep in mind: hip-hop as a "culture" didn't exist just a decade prior. In fact, as Ahearn's co-conspirator Fab 5 Freddy points out, until press interviews about the film appeared, no one had even used the term "hip-hop" to describe what was going on in New York's clubs, parks, rec centers and street corners.

In a story that is well-known to true-blue hip-hop fans, as the '80s broke, New York City-based film director Charlie Ahearn set out to make the first full-length movie about this exciting youth culture. What is lesser-known is that, to go along with the film, he also had a vision about the movie's backbone: instrumental music that would be used in the film to replace breakbeats that DJs in New York were rocking at the time. In a sense, he wanted to concoct personalized funky soul in a lab, instead of wrestling it out of dusty record crates.

The plan easily could have crashed, burned and / or fizzled out if the planets and players had not been properly aligned. But, fortunately for Ahearn and the hip-hop world, the research scientist called upon to complete the task happened to be the hippest doc on the scene: the aforementioned Fred "Fab 5 Freddy" Brathwaite.

"Basically, we weren't going to use current breakbeats," Freddy explains. "It was very smart on Charlie's part, because we might have gotten in trouble down the road [with clearance issues]. I myself wanted to use the current breaks. But he said we should create our own, so I went and did that."

Fab 5 Freddy.
Photo © Bobby Grossman, www.bobbygrossman.com.

This all sounds straightforward enough, except for one thing: Freddy wasn't a music producer. But he did have some funky friends to lean on. As it so happened, most of them came through the infamous NYC public-access show "TV Party," launched in 1978 on Manhattan Cable by journalist and scenester Glenn O'Brien. Freddy was, in fact, the show's cameraman. And in the show's Orchestra – a term used facetiously by anyone involved – were Leonardo "Lenny Ferrari" Ferraro, a jazz-raised R & B drummer, Vietnam vet and recent NYC transplant from Pittsburgh; and guitarist and occasional co-host Chris Stein, from the band Blondie.

"'TV Party' was just for fun, it was like 'Our Gang' or a Vaudeville show," says Ferrari today. "It was loose, anything went. And it became my favorite thing to do in New York. It was absurd and we were a family. That show pulled everyone together."

Ferrari, aside from his drumming duties – which were usually carried out without an actual drum kit – also played the role of "bad magician," The Great Luigi Ciccolini, on the show. O'Brien said, on TVParty.org, "Lenny was a great drummer, but an even greater personality… he invented the 'TV Party' drum kit, which consisted of a music stand, small cymbals and [a copy of] the *New Yorker*."

Chris Stein also remembers the Orchestra family fondly: "With 'TV Party' we couldn't really make too much noise with the music, so Lenny had to use a magazine for a snare drum. Lenny was great, he was always doing sessions and out in the scene. He was the go-to drummer for a lot of projects and different artists."

Freddy details his own experience with the show: "I was the cameraman around 1979, and a regular [on-camera] guest. 'TV Party' was important because Glenn was a mentor to me, he gave me a lot of advice. Being involved with the show was the first significant thing I had done in the media, so it was a great training ground."

Lenny Ferrari.
Photo © Bobby Grossman, www.bobbygrossman.com.

Considering all of the above, when it came to Freddy's "Wild Style" music production task, making personnel choices was a no-brainer. "I went to the people I knew," he says. "Those guys were instrumental in putting the *Breakbeats* together. No pun intended." Stein adds, "The musician choices were all from Freddy and Charlie [Ahearn]. We all knew Lenny. It was all very casual. Honestly, I don't think that a lot of forethought went into any of this. It was more about: 'Who's around?'"

Ferrari remembers, "I loved Freddy and I advised him a little bit on the production. But he's a great producer, because he pulled it all together. He saw it through." Freddy adds one important point: "I was the only one in the group who had a real sense of what was appropriate [for the *Breakbeats*], based on what was being played at the parties."

Hip-hop lore has generally perpetuated the myth that Chris Stein was the producer of the *Wild Style Breakbeats* sessions. But Stein never made this claim, and wholeheartedly agrees that Freddy was in charge. Stein would play the producer role on the songs "Wild Style Theme Rap 1" and "Wild Style Theme Rap 2," which used the Breakbeats music and featured Grand Master Caz on vocals and DJ Charlie Chase on cuts. Both songs appeared on the movie's soundtrack in 1983, and as a 12-inch single [on Stein's Animal Records label].

"Wild Style Rap" 12-inch cover.
Animal Records, 1983.

Freddy does point out one reason for publicizing Stein's name more conspicuously after the *Breakbeats* were made in 1981, but before the movie was released in 1983: "We put Chris' name prominently in the mix because we were struggling to get financing. He was a big-name star and he worked with us, advising and helping however he could to get the movie made. So with his name and the fact that he was involved, people assumed [his leadership with the *Breakbeats*] was larger than it was. But in reality, for the *Breakbeats* he was just a session guy."

Chris Stein.
Photo © Bobby Grossman, www.bobbygrossman.com.

As they embarked on their studio journey, Freddy put a plan together. "The idea when we started was to create a series of what I felt were breakbeats that DJs would cut up [in the movie]," he explains. "They would be very short, a minute or a little more. The idea wasn't to even name them. They were going to become what they became once the DJs scratched them and the rappers rhymed on them."

For production nerds, a notable fact about the recording of the *Wild Style Breakbeats* is that each instrument and element was recorded on its own. In fact, none of the three principal instrumentalists [drums, bass and guitar] even saw each other face-to-face. This goes against traditional studio norms, where band members typically "shed" together, develop grooves and then finalize a plan before hitting the record button. Freddy admits, "What I learned later on was that I should have had the rhythm section playing together. At the time, I just didn't know. I was feeling it out and trying to make it happen as best I knew how, making it up as I went along."

According to Freddy, the instruments went in this order: "I had Lenny lay down the drums first. Then David [Harpur] played the bass parts. And Chris Stein came in with guitar and different effects and gadgets."

"It was all done so quickly," Stein says today, looking back. "All of that music for the *Breakbeats* probably took three days to put together."

Freddy says of Ferrari, who was first up to bat, "Lenny was a drummer who had a lot of soul and rhythm. He appreciated the drummers who paved the way before him. So I went to him, first off." Ferrari says that his drum tracks were recorded "record-breakingly fast," once the studio sound was set.

"I think the whole budget for those sessions was about $1,000," Lenny adds. "And I might have gotten half of that."

To add to the disjointedness, all parts weren't even laid down at the same recording studio. The first location came via both Stein and Lenny Ferrari: Blank Tapes, located at 37 West 20th Street in Manhattan. Operated by a gentleman named Bob Blank, it wasn't the fanciest spot; but it was certainly good enough for the *Breakbeats*.

"I hooked up the studio because that was my second home at the time," Ferrari says. "I also made sure we got the right engineer for the drums, a guy I had worked with before named Butch. I can't remember his last name. He understood where the bass and snare should be, and he knew funk."

BLANK Tapes INC

37 W. 20th Street
New York, New York 10011
(212) 255–5313

Ferrari continues, "We spent most of the time on that first day just getting the right drum sound. After that, it was a piece of cake. I walked in and knocked off the drums pretty quick, mostly in one take. I mean, they were just a minute each. Honestly, a minute was a long time for what we needed. What I was doing was what you would call 'fatback' drums, like [Otis Redding's and Carla Thomas'] 'Tramp.' That's the ultimate example of what a hip-hop drum break was."

An interesting extra component of the *Breakbeats* recording equation is that – most likely since Ferrari was not a park-jam attendee or hip-hop denizen – for the drums he laid down, he was first given a "cheat sheet" via cassette. "Before the session, I had asked Freddy to get one minute of the DJs' favorite grooves, the stuff they liked to cut up," Lenny recalls. "I wanted to use those as a reference. I don't remember the song names, I didn't recognize any of them. All 13 of those drum recordings we made were based on beats I heard. It was my version of other artists' breaks. I told him, 'Just figure out the beats you want, and I'll knock them off. Then you can build the layers.'"

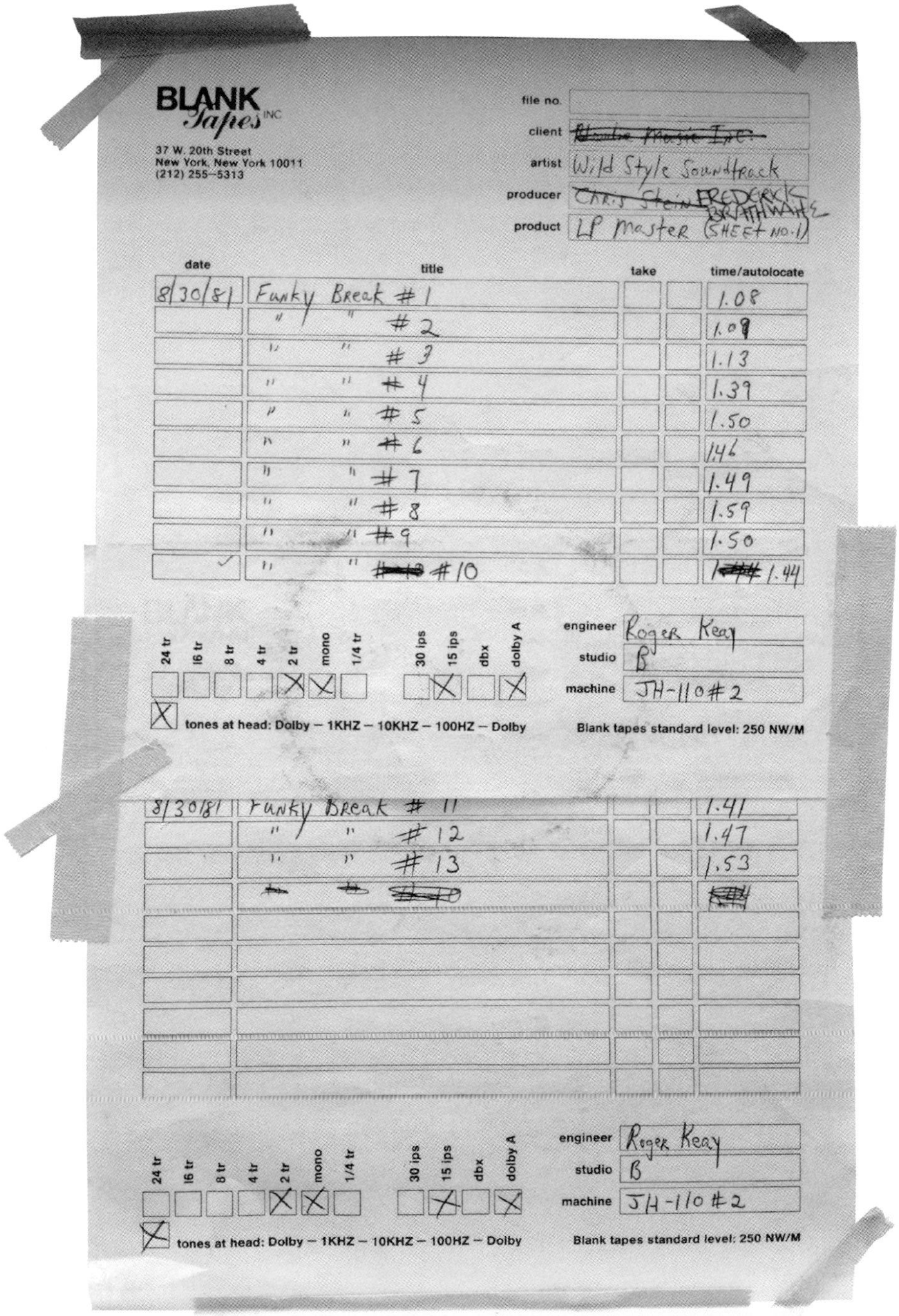

BLANK Tapes INC
37 W. 20th Street
New York, New York 10011
(212) 255–5313

file no.
client ~~Blondie Music Inc.~~
artist Wild Style Soundtrack
producer ~~Chris Stein~~ FREDERICK BRATHWAITE
product LP Master (SHEET NO. 1)

date	title	take		time/autolocate
8/30/81	Funky Break #1			1.08
	" " #2			1.08
	" " #3			1.13
	" " #4			1.39
	" " #5			1.50
	" " #6			1.46
	" " #7			1.49
	" " #8			1.59
	" " #9			1.50
✓	" " ~~#10~~ #10			~~1.44~~ 1.44

24 tr · 16 tr · 8 tr · 4 tr · 2 tr [X] · mono [X] · 1/4 tr · 30 ips · 15 ips [X] · dbx · dolby A [X]

engineer Roger Keay
studio B
machine JH-110 #2

[X] tones at head: Dolby – 1KHZ – 10KHZ – 100HZ – Dolby

Blank tapes standard level: 250 NW/M

date	title	take		time/autolocate
8/30/81	Funky Break #11			1.41
	" " #12			1.47
	" " #13			1.53
	~~" " #10~~			~~1.44~~

24 tr · 16 tr · 8 tr · 4 tr · 2 tr [X] · mono [X] · 1/4 tr · 30 ips · 15 ips [X] · dbx · dolby A [X]

engineer Roger Keay
studio B
machine JH-110 #2

[X] tones at head: Dolby – 1KHZ – 10KHZ – 100HZ – Dolby

Blank tapes standard level: 250 NW/M

Mastering sheets for *Wild Style Breakbeats* session, August 1981. Chris Stein's name is crossed out as producer, replaced by "Frederick Brathwaite."

Image courtesy of Kenny Dope and Charlie Ahearn.

DJ GrandWizzard Theodore confirms this: "Before they recorded the *Breakbeats*, they [Freddy and assumedly Charlie Ahearn as well] came to my house and I put a bunch of breaks on a cassette for them." Unfortunately, Theodore doesn't recall any of the specific breaks that he gave them.

"I had different breakbeats that people were using, and tapes from early [hip-hop] parties," Freddy adds. "I would play the stuff for Lenny, and I would imitate other breaks and rhythm patterns with my mouth for him to lay down his parts. It was a combination."

Does Freddy remember which classic breaks on Theodore's mix-tape match up with their *Wild Style Breakbeats* offspring? "I don't remember that for any of them," he says. "The songs weren't that direct. In the creative process, the musicians started laying stuff down, and I would say 'Play this' or 'Play that.' And it changed. So the original breaks were just guides for feel and attitude, more than to try and actually re-create the full original break, or even the [original] sound."

The mix-tape guide seemed to do the trick on the drums side, since Ferrari recalls, "I remember seeing Freddy dancing while I was playing. I could see him through the control room window. It felt good to know that I could pull it off for him, that he had chosen the right guy."

Three decades later, the facts from all parties involved are fuzzy, but at some point after Ferrari's Blank Tape recordings, the sessions moved to another studio: one that no one seems to remember very well, except for the general GPS coordinates. "It was one of the cheapest per-hour places that I could find," Freddy recalls. "It was on Broadway, near the Beacon Theater [Broadway & 74th Street], maybe on the same block. I remember that the mixing board had tubes inside of it, which I could see glowing when I walked around the side. Blank Tapes was slicker, they had transistors in their board!"

And so, further uptown, in the glowing tube light of this mystery studio, the next phase of their musical journey began.

For bass duty, Freddy enlisted a session player named David Harpur, or at least that is how it has usually been spelled *[Author's note: Freddy concedes that it could also be spelled "Harper"]*. Freddy was the only one involved with the *Breakbeats* who knew him, and he's not sure where the bassist is today. "I knew him from Brooklyn," Freddy says. "He was involved with a lot of Philly groups like First Choice and other soul groups. Stuff right at the beginning of disco, before it was really disco. He was a good friend at the time."

Chris Stein recalls, "The bass and drums were already done when I got there. I was probably just there for a couple of hours and I put guitar on pretty much all of the Breakbeats, as I recall. All the stuff I did was based on what they had already done; how I was inspired by the grooves they did. Anything with straightforward, traditional guitar is me, and I did those weird synth melodies with a very early Roland synth guitar."

Freddy and Stein both confirm that no one played formal keyboards on the sessions. Freddy says, "Chris had a lot of effects and synthesizers and things that he didn't get to use a lot [in Blondie], so he laid down different things, to give tracks a different personality. Chris could make all kinds of weird sounds with those."

Even though the different instruments were recorded separately, Freddy built the vibe as the layers unfolded. "Once the musicians started to play their parts, I'd ask them to try different things," he explains. "The tracks were evolving. Once I heard something I liked, I'd say, 'Go with that!'"

The final audio icing was done by Freddy himself, mad scientist style. "There was a sound effects record that had all these weird sounds, like the military stuff," he recalls. "The studio just had it there for people to use. I put those parts in." Chris Stein remembers the extra icing fondly: "Freddy put all those crazy buzzing noises and sound effects on. I can't remember if he did any of them while I was in there or afterwards, but none of those were my doing."

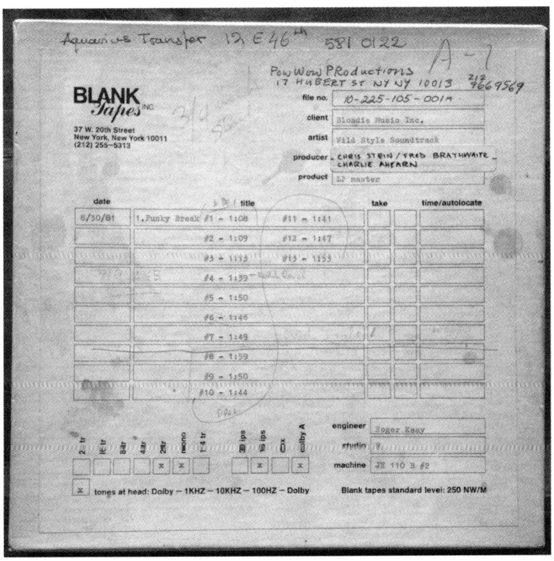

Tape box listing 13 *Breakbeats*, all titled "Funky Break," dated August 30, 1981.
Image courtesy of Kenny Dope and Charlie Ahearn.

After the quick recording and subsequent mixing and mastering, by September of 1981 the quartet's work – which produced 13 short compositions, all titled "Funky Break" – was ready for its next phase. But, not for public consumption. Because perhaps the most unique thing about the *Wild Style Breakbeats* is that they were only ever intended for the DJs in the movie to use for live scenes [and, later, for incidental / score music]. For this reason, the songs didn't even require proper names.

Regarding the song titles, Freddy says. "I haven't looked at a copy of them for years, but there was 'Cuckoo Clocking'; 'Military Breakbeat' [aka 'Military Cut']; and, of course, 'Down By Law.' I named them at some point, just so we could have some form of reference."

He continues, "I think I just hand-wrote the early original ones I gave to the DJs. I don't remember listing the songs on those, because it was more about the DJs figuring out which tracks they liked." Theodore remembers it the same way: "When I first got my copies they had no song names, it just said '*Wild Style Breakbeats*.'"

Since the DJs needed the records for upcoming live scene recordings, Freddy and Ahearn pressed up a very limited number of platters and gave them to the jocks, only to hear some bad news. Freddy recalls, "We pressed up *acetates* instead of vinyl, and those are really heavy." Theodore says, "I think at first they gave me four pieces of vinyl, but they were very heavy. I was like, 'You can't cut with these.'"

Next stop: a vinyl pressing plant, placing a rush order for the minimum. 100 copies.

Freddy claims that after giving out copies from this batch of white-label vinyl to DJs in the film [seven, which would be 14 pieces of vinyl, or 28 if each got two sets]; some VIPs; and keeping some for emergencies, "That was it." He adds, still remaining a bit mysterious, "It wasn't like we knew these would become a greatly-treasured thing."

No matter who got them initially, or who found them in a record bin or traded a treasured object for them years later, there weren't many to be had in the first place. Which, of course, only led to furthering their legend.

Thankfully, the vinyl did arrive into the DJs' hands in time for filming. And it was put to good use, even though almost every DJ in the film gravitated towards one single Breakbeat: "Down By Law." Freddy says, "It didn't work out exactly how we had envisioned. They all used 'Down By Law.' It was just something that got locked in stone. I think it was because the DJs were just very competitive. Like, 'They're using it, I want to use it and do my thing.' I couldn't dictate which ones they were going to use, although I do recall them all wanting to know from me what the others would be using, and I told them that Flash liked 'Down By Law.' I wanted to let it be organic, and they all used one, for the most part [laughs]."

[Author's note: When pressed, Freddy acknowledges that "Down By Law" is his own personal favorite, so he might not be able to give the DJs too hard of a time about their choices!].

And what exactly *did* Freddy and Charlie Ahearn hope that DJs would do with the *Breakbeats*? "We wanted to have variety," Freddy says. "What I envisioned was like a party. This guy plays this beat, then goes into a different one, and this other one after that. We wanted to make it interesting, to give the DJs the tools they would need to re-create the cutting and mixing vibe that went on at these parties, with obscure records."

From the film DJs' perspective, Theodore still remembers his first listen to the *Breakbeats*. "When they gave them to me, I was like, 'These breaks are kind of dry,'" he says. "They weren't like anything I had heard before. So they had to grow on me, and I think it was the same with the other DJs too. If [Freddy and Charlie] had had some of the DJs in the studio when they were making the *Breakbeats*, they probably would have been more authentic, overall."

Flyer for May 1, 1982 "Amphitheatre Jam," where live scenes from "Wild Style" film were taped, using *Wild Style Breakbeats*.
Courtesy of the Charlie Ahearn Hip-Hop Archive at Cornell University.

According to Theodore, the reason that "Down By Law" was put into heavy rotation was simple: it was the closest to a *real* breakbeat that DJs were already using in parks and clubs. "It was that break, it was that groove," he explains. "That and 'Military [Cut]' were the closest to *actual* breakbeats. That's why we used them. When we first got the breaks we only had a week or two to pick out the ones we wanted to use. And as soon as I listened, I knew mine would be 'Down By Law.'" He also says that he didn't know which *Breakbeats* other DJs from the film would be using ahead of time, which runs contrary to Freddy's "competitive" theory.

Theodore says that before "Wild Style" hit in theaters in 1983, his copies of the *Wild Style Breakbeats* remained buried in his crates after filming. But after the fan-fare of the film spread, "They eventually became part of my regular set."

It should be noted that DJ Charlie Chase broke from the pack and used the "Subway Theme" break with the Cold Crush Brothers in the film. And Grandmixer D.ST [aka GrandMixer DXT] used "Cuckoo Clocking" with Rammellzee and Shock Dell, to stunning effect. Overall, though, out of 13 Breakbeats made, only about half of them were ever used in relation to the film itself.

Chris Stein says, "'Down By Law' was the track that everybody gravitated towards for the film, but there were other great ones that people didn't grab onto. That was too bad. I always liked the one that had a rolling drum thing that almost reminds me of [Kanye West's and Jay-Z's 2011 song] 'No Church In The Wild' *[Author's note: Stein is likely referring to 'Jungle Beat']*. But no one gravitated to that one."

"Wild Style" hat and film canister.
Courtesy of the Charlie Ahearn Hip-Hop Archive at Cornell University.

Even though initially it wasn't something that crossed anyone's mind – since they were scraping and clawing simply to get the film financed and completed – Freddy does acknowledge the *Breakbeats*' "Holy Grail" status amongst hip-hop collectors since 1983. "I'm well-aware of the mystery surrounding the *Breakbeats* among record nerds and beat junkies," he admits. "Years later it became a great hunt for people to try and find where those beats came from. I was fascinated by that. And even when people bootleg them, I still appreciate the nerdy obsession that people have with them. The #1 question I would get when I would meet significant DJs in the '90s was, 'Where did those records come from?' It was a big thing to a lot of people."

Freddy continues, underscoring an important parallel to the funk breaks that made up the backbone of the original '70s Bronx jams: "The kind of breakbeats that were popular in the early years sounded so obscure, even if you were a DJ, because jocks would soak the labels off so people couldn't figure out what they were playing. The *Wild Style Breakbeats* became a similar thing."

White-label bootlegs of *Wild Style Breakbeats*, year unknown.
Courtesy of the Charlie Ahearn Hip-Hop Archive at Cornell University.

Chris Stein sums up his "Wild Style" experience, three decades later: "While the film was being made, I knew it was going somewhere, because I was really aware of what was going on in the hip-hop world back then. I can't say I knew the full significance of what it would become at the

Ad for "Wild Style" film, December 1983.

beginning [of filming] and I definitely didn't know that four years later I would have guys in the UK begging me for white labels of the *Breakbeats*. But when I finally saw the movie, I was really impressed. I told them, 'This is going to get knocked off by Hollywood immediately.' Within six months, there was 'Beat Street.'"

"Charlie and Freddy had the vision," says Lenny Ferrari. "They knew hip-hop was becoming a revolution. Most people didn't. I was just honored to be involved. That movie helped to bring hip-hop to the world."

And bringing it 360, back to Theodore's original thought about Charlie Ahearn's plan being "crazy," the legendary DJ says: "Even after Charlie explained it, I still didn't see it. But as time went by, I understood. I think he saw something that I didn't."

Track-list for first official release of *Wild Style Breakbeats*.
Kay-Dee / Get On Down, 2014

SHOUT OUTS!

This is my third time around the block with one of these crazy books, and each time I am even more indebted to those who help me make them happen. Many of the people listed here have stuck with me since *Rakim Told Me* came out in 2005 (or much earlier), and for that I will always be grateful.

As always, my first and deepest thanks go to my beautiful and amazing wife Margot. She puts up with a lot, much of it extending far beyond any of my publishing endeavors. Thank you from the bottom of my heart.

My family is also a never-ending source of encouragement and support, including Rich and Sally Coleman, Darcie, Hope, Sadie, Jenna, Raziyah, the Ohio Shaws, the Pennsylvania Colemans, as well as Paula, Alexis, Janet, Nate and many other great people on the Edwards and Menn sides of the family.

James Blackwell deserves a huge thank you for a ridiculous amount of "above and beyond" hard work with book design. It has been a pleasure working with someone who not only has the skills to make these pages look amazing, but who also has a passion for and knowledge of the hip-hop covered in these chapters.

Because of the newsprint it would entail, I am not going to thank each of the 80-plus people interviewed for this book separately. But please allow me to state the obvious – if it weren't for the time they gave me in sharing their stories, none of this would have been possible. I thank you all, for your generosity and for your inspiration.

I will, though, point out a couple of interviewees who were extra patient and generous, humoring my additional questions and/or giving me some killer visuals to use: Prime Minister Pete Nice, General Steele, Prince Paul, Dante Ross, Joe Mansfield, Jamieson Grillo, DJ Jazzy Jeff, Fab 5 Freddy, Mr. Len, Lord Finesse, Teddy Tedd and Will Socolov.

Others who helped me in crucial – but very different – ways along the path to *Check the Technique Volume 2* include: Bill Adler, for encouragement and for allowing me early access to his mind-boggling Hip-Hop Archives at Cornell University; Adam Mansbach, for friendship, support and a kick-ass Foreword; Romanowski, for the eye-popping visuals on the book's cover and for all the amazing music I have enjoyed for years; Paul Williams, for book production and packaging knowledge and advice; and iocolor in Seattle for making things look purdy.

Also, to Jeff Chang, Dan Charnas, Adam Bradley, Questlove, Dave Tompkins, Harry Allen, Ronin Ro and Elijah Wald: thank you for letting me know over the years that I was doing something worthwhile, at least for music nerds like us. To Chris Faraone, Tim Linberg, O'Neal Rowe, all my peeps at Traffic and Get On Down [Matt Welch, Papa D, DJ 7L, Lou Mansdorf, Luca Iannino, Alfredo Rico-Dimas, Mike Q, Lee Martin], Pacey Foster, Trevor KARMA Gendron, Dan McCormack, Peter Fiumara, James Sullivan, Dana Scott, DJ Nomadik, Dart Adams, DJ Knife, Marty Caballero, Carly Carioli, and Mike Monestime, for years of friendship and Boston-based support. Sean Westergaard, I owe you for the JPEGs [three times!!!]. To Michelle Mercer and Ed Nawotka, you guys have helped more than you know. Big-ups to Soren Baker and Jake Paine: top-shelf journalists I am proud to call friends. To Katherine Reagan and Ben Ortiz at the Cornell Hip-Hop Archive, thanks for letting me soak in what you are both doing there – it is truly inspiring. And I appreciate Noah and Jen Uman, for being Noah and Jen Uman.

Many world-class photographers were kind enough to license and/or grant me permission to use their incredible work to make these chapters come to life: Geoff Spear, Gary Spector, Bobby Grossman, Eddie Otchere, Janette Beckman, Paradise Gray, Brian "B+" Cross, Koi Sojer, Debra DiPaolo and Linda Covello.

Some of my most important literary and journalistic inspirations have remained steady over the years: David Toop, Nelson George, Steven Hager, Ishmael Reed, Dave Marsh and the late, great Tim Haslett. I also want to thank some top-shelf academics, most who are also accomplished and inspiring authors: Murray Forman, Joe Schloss, Stephen Webber, Bill Banfield, Emmett Price, Mark Katz, Solomon Comissiong and Carleton Gholz, who present the hip-hop artform to young people the right way. And thanks to some of my past boosters and comrades who helped in various ways to bring my first two books into the world: Adam Korn, Porscha Burke, David Dunton, Matt Nicholas and Paula Breen.

And here is a big list of very important people who I salute, for book help either direct or indirect... My two favorite Ds: Schoolly and Chuck. Wes Jackson, Peanut Butter Wolf, David Lopes, Adisa Banjoko, Makeba Mooncycle, Koe Rodriguez (thanks for the friendship and the 3rd Bass photo!), DJ Rob Swift, DJ Eclipse, James Hughes, DJ Mick, Hua Hsu, DJ Platurn, Z-Trip, Gina and Tony Gervino, Billy Jam, Jean "DJ Preservation" Daval, Donwil and Von Pea from Tanya Morgan, Theo Haumesser, Mitch Myers, Alex Engelen, Stephen Szillus, Jeff "Mr. Lif" Haynes, Andre "Insight"

Todman, Roy Christopher, Paul Edwards, Chris Vognar, Noah Schaffer, Eric Arnold, Domino, Rob Reilly, Sara Rosen, Ian Wallace, Jacob Bronstein, Andre Sirois, Rubix, Neil Nice, Darcel Turner, Marcyliena Morgan and Ally McGinty at the Harvard Hip-Hop Archive, Dru Ha, Jeff Ladd, David Ma, Jamel Shabazz, Jack Hamilton, Michael Brown, Torsten Schmidt, Nicole Arruda Palumbo, Lynette Townes, Maya Wilson, Adam Blumenkranz, Carly Mann, Richard Smith (appreciate the Lord Finesse assists!!!), Gary Bond, Andy Shih, Donna Dragotta, Dawaun Parker, Gabriel Alvarez, Cookie Amare, Rebekah Foster, Clarissa Robinson, Peter Agoston, Michelle McDevitt, William D'Jan Hernandez, Jamison "DJ Prestige" Harvey, Brendan Canning, Fubz, Oliver "O-Dub" Wang, DJ Babu and the Beat Junkies, S.H. Fernando, DJ Mighty Mi, Michaelangelo Matos, Riggs Morales, Reef Tewlow, Greg Mack, Adam Leaventon, John McGregor, Frank "The Butcher" Rivera, Neil and Paul Bennun, Jason Gloss, Dan Leroy, Vince Kamin, John Rhodes, Omar Albertto, Davide Bortot, Dave Hofer and the wonderful spirit of Jan Dizdarevic.

And, finally, merci to the faceless but hugely helpful online research assistance of Discogs.com, BMI.com and ASCAP.com.

I'm sure I missed some people. It happens. So.... if you are mad, then that must mean I thank you as well, and ask for your forgiveness. I owe you a Biz Markie 12-inch somewhere down the line.

INDEX

BOLD = *Interviewed in book*

2 Live Crew *59, 182, 204, 495*

2*2*4 (group) *34*

24-Carat Black *381, 403*

3 Def Notes *184-186, 203*

5 FT (artist) *448, 451, 453*

510 South Franklin (studio) *241-242, 244, 250*

62nd Assassin *442*

88-Keys *382, 395, 405-406*

A Nubian Notion (store) *201-202*

A Tribe Called Quest *34, 36, 43, 46-48, 50, 86, 193, 287, 296, 393, 406, 451, 461, 463, 466*

Aaberg, Michael *102, 104*

Ace & Quan [Daquan] *198-199*

Aceyalone *203*

Adler, Bill (and Adler Hip-Hop Archives at Cornell University) *10, 17, 37, 49, 67, 137, 143, 219, 222-223, 290-291, 312, 347, 413, 455-456, 473, 479, 484, 486-487, 496*

Africa Fund, The *482, 496*

African Identity (artist) *108*

Afrika Baby Bam (Jungle Brothers) *34*

Afu-Ra *269, 273*

AG [aka Andre The Giant] *119, 336-338, 340, 342*

Ahearn, Charlie *498-500, 503-509*

Akai 612 (sampler) *187, 352, 358*

Akai ASQ-10 (sequencer) *187*

Akai S-950 (sampler) *225, 452*

Al Cohen Studio (see also: Cohen, Al) *351-352*

Allah, Dawud *112*

Almighty R.S.O. *201*

Alpert, Herb *54*

Andersen, Andy [aka Andyboy] *177*

Animal Records *501*

Ant Live *316*

Anti-Pop Consortium *68*

Anton (see: Pukshansky)

Anttex [aka Darren Johnson] *58-62, 65, 68*

Apache *417*

Apani B Fly Emcee *403*

Apollo Theater *12, 14, 49, 51, 267, 335, 429, 448*

Arguillen, Orlando *370*

Arrington, Steve *113, 242, 250*

Askew, Reg Reg *219-221, 223, 228, 230*

ASR-10, Ensoniq (keyboard / sampler) *231-232*

Atlantic Records *260, 301, 321, 325, 362, 387, 389*

Automator, Dan The *157-180*

Awesome 2 *185, 189-194, 198, 200-201, 205, 423*

Ayers, Roy *206, 466*

Azor, Hurby "Luv Bug" *7, 322-326, 328-329, 331*

Azor, Steve *323, 326*

B. B. King *371*

Baby Paul [aka Babee Paul] *455, 461, 466-467*

Baker, Jon *216-233*

Bambaataa, Afrika *59, 116, 187, 232, 345, 475, 486*

Barron, Don *430-431*

Barry, Steve *183-184*

Bass Blaster *430*

Battery Studios *134-136, 138, 146*

Bayside Studios *324-325*

B-Boys (group) *492-493*

Beastie Boys *9-10, 19, 24, 29-30, 41, 143, 376, 409*

Beatminerz *397, 446-468*

Beavis & Butthead *108*

Beckman, Janette *483, 485*

Bell Biv Devoe *243, 256*
Bell, Archie (& The Drells) *189, 194, 208-209*
Bellochio, David *412*
Benson, George *99, 149*
BET "Video Soul" *206-207*
BET [Black Entertainment Television] *102, 202, 206-207, 317, 425, 462*
Bey, Yasiin (see Mos Def)
Big Arm Management *59, 60, 66*
Big Daddy Kane *53, 143, 239, 275, 308-309, 318, 326, 333-334, 342, 364, 376, 392, 448*
Bigg Jus *57-90*
Biggest Gord *462*
Biz Markie *84, 126, 140, 193, 218, 225-226, 232, 308, 311, 318, 364, 421*
Black Moon *208, 264, 398, 446-452, 454, 456, 458, 463-465*
Black, Kisha *433*
Blank Tapes Studio *502, 504*
Bliss, Melvin *178, 415*
Blondie *499, 505*
Blow, Kurtis *33, 47, 208-209*
Blue Raspberry *442*
Blunt Records *379, 381-382*
BMS (rapper) *66, 83-84*
Body Count *292*
Body Rock Crew *184*
Bohannon, Hamilton *189, 200-201, 208*
BOMB Records / Magazine *159*
Bomb Squad, the *2, 15, 21, 23-24, 29-30, 70, 74, 235-262, 329, 345*
Bon Ami Records *325, 409-410*
Boogie Down Productions *70, 74, 191, 253, 376, 398-400, 477*
Boot Camp Clik *446-447, 449-451, 454, 459, 465*
Boston Goes Def (compilation) *183-184, 187*
Brand New Heavies *365*
Brand Nubian *80, 118, 123, 282, 296, 393, 413, 431*
Brother K [Keith McArthur] *113*
Brown, Bobby *420-425, 429-430, 432*
Brown, James *147-148, 152, 198, 201, 205-206, 250, 329-330, 339-340, 460, 471, 480*
Brown, Reggie *107*
Buckshot *446-448, 451-453, 465*
Bulk Recordings *167-168*
Busy Bee *117*
B-Wiz *64*
Byrd, Bobby *330*
Byrd, Donald *148*
C.I.A. (group) *236-237*
Cage *65, 83, 84, 299*
Calder, Clive *135, 152*
Calliope Studios *20, 49, 283, 286, 453, 477, 480, 484*
Cameo (group) *146*
Capitol Records *117-118, 158, 160-162, 176, 272, 358*
Cappachino [aka Cappadonna] *443*
Carli, Ann [aka Tokyo Rose] *133-155*
Carson, Lumumba [aka Professor X] *6, 489*
Carson, Sonny *6, 489*
Casio SK-5 (keyboard) *381*
Cathedral Projects (Boston) *201*
Cazal Boys *128*
Ced-Gee *158, 329, 483*
Cenobites *81*
Cerrone *498*
C-Funk *97*
Chameleon Street (film) *402*
Chapman, Tracy *430*
Charbonnet, Pat *260*
Chase, Charlie *500, 507*
Chavis, Dr. Benjamin *206-207*
Chemistry Records *118-119, 121, 188, 190*
Chi-Ali *35-36, 52, 55*
Chin, Brian *190-192, 196, 199, 204*
Chrysalis Records *202, 266, 277, 427*
Chuck D *14, 199, 235-260, 495*
Chung King Studios *8-9, 13-14, 49, 134, 286, 289, 484*
Circus Records *108*
CMOB (artist) *301*
Cocoa Brovaz *446*
Cohen, Al *351-352, 354, 356, 358*
Cohen, Lyor *5, 8-9, 11, 17, 20, 29, 100, 239, 432, 482*
Cold Chillin' Records *305, 307-308, 312-313, 363-367, 371, 433*
Cold Crush Brothers *115, 127, 154, 179, 225-226, 231, 429, 448, 470, 507*
Collins, Lyn *329*
Coltrane, John *387*
Common *35-36, 397, 404-405*
Compere, Sha-Kim *410-412*
Conscious Daughters *101*
Constipated Monkey(s) (crew) *285, 287, 294, 299, 301*
Cook, Norman *496*
Cookie Head *446, 468*
Corona (Queens) *33, 36, 39, 304, 306, 311, 312, 322*
Cortes, Lisa *49, 52*
Coulter, Bob *484, 495*
Craig G *129, 305, 364, 433*

Cybotron *154*

D & D Studios *267, 453-454, 459, 462, 464*

D.J. Polo *304-320*

Da Bush Babees *379, 383, 389-390*

Daddy-O *214, 470-496*

Dajani, Geeby *282*

Dan The Automator (see Automator)

Dana Dane *2, 7-8, 141, 322-323, 329*

Danceteria *346, 348*

Davis, Betty *242, 254*

Davy DMX *347*

DBC *471, 476-477, 480, 483, 488-489, 495*

De La Soul *14, 30, 35-36, 43-44, 50-51, 111, 158, 212-213, 216, 218-219, 222, 226, 230, 238, 282, 287, 383-384, 404, 484, 486*

dead prez *101, 404*

Decepticons (gang) *446-449, 454, 467*

Dee, Charlie *355, 357*

Def Jam Records / Recordings *2, 4-5, 9, 10-11, 13-15, 19-20, 22, 26, 29-30, 70, 100, 116, 130, 202, 216, 221, 239, 281-282, 307, 313, 422, 427-428, 432-433, 451, 482, 492, 496*

Def Jef *198-199*

Def Row (compilation) *184-186*

Definitive Jux *57*

Del Tha Funkee Homosapien *110-111, 238*

Delfonics *121, 204*

Delicious Vinyl *198, 365-366*

Delite (rapper) *471-476, 480, 488-489, 493-494*

Depeche Mode *24, 31, 93*

Dere, Karen *113*

Dew Doo Man Records *212-213*

Diamond D *115-124, 188, 190, 333-334, 336, 340-342, 382*

Diamond Two *351, 355, 357*

Dickerson, Ernest *418*

Digital Underground *95, 104, 205*

Disco P *183-184*

DITC (Diggin' In The Crates) *116, 119, 333, 338*

DJ Chilly Chill *260-262*

DJ Cruz *184, 188-189, 203-204*

DJ Cut Creator *304, 307, 311*

DJ Daddy Rich [aka DJ Richie Rich] *2-31*

DJ Doc (see: Rodriguez, Ivan)

DJ Hi-Tek *380-406*

DJ Jazzy Jay *116-118, 123, 334, 431*

DJ Jazzy Jeff *126-155, 182, 254, 317, 470*

DJ Mark The 45 King *123, 337, 410-411*

DJ Mike Smooth *334, 336-337, 341*

DJ Premier *117, 157, 202, 205, 264-277, 333-343, 382, 395, 430, 453*

DJ Q-Bert *166, 170-179*

DJ Red Alert *4, 44-48, 55, 376, 423, 467, 481*

DJ Shadow *159, 169, 177, 179, 356, 375*

DJ Supreme (Bronx) *116*

DJ White Nite / DJ Nite *11, 12*

DJ Word *11, 12*

DJO *94, 98*

DNA International *220*

Dogday Records *103-105*

Dominant Species *64, 69, 77*

Down South (group) *389*

Downtown Records *346-348, 355*

Dr. Butcher (DJ) *311-319*

Dr. Dre *27, 110, 115, 157-158, 235-240, 242, 244-246, 248, 254, 261, 264, 270, 368, 450*

DreamWorks Records *162, 165, 169-170, 175*

Dres *43-55*

DRS (group) *272*

Dru-Ha *446-468*

Duck Down (Records / Management) *446-448*

Dyke & The Blazers *493*

Eady, Howard *250*

Earthquake *299*

East New York (Brooklyn) *46, 264-266, 270, 465, 471, 473, 475, 485, 492*

Eazy-E *27, 237-238, 240, 253-254, 256-257, 496*

ED O.G. [aka Edo G] *182-210*

Edifice *110*

Electric Ladyland Studios *397, 406*

Elektra Records *5, 279, 281-284, 289, 291-293, 297-298, 302*

Ellis, Jay *185, 203*

Elmcor Center (Queens) *306*

El-P *57-90, 398*

Emax, Emu (sampler) *187*

EMI Records *99-100*

Eminem *113*

EPMD *110, 262, 448-449, 483, 492*

Eric B. *24, 29, 126, 143, 191, 267, 299, 304-307, 310-311, 316, 318, 322, 364, 381, 470, 496*

E-Roc *94, 96-99, 101-102, 106, 109*

Evil Dee (DJ) *397, 446-468*

Eyce *365-366, 369, 371-372*

F.T.S. (group) *110*

Fab 5 Freddy *494, 498-509*

Faber, Shane *118, 123-124*

Fairlight (synthesizer / sampler) *134, 136, 146, 148, 151*

Fashion [aka Al Tariq] *36-38, 41*

Fat Beats Records / Distribution *67, 77, 383*

Fat Boys *82, 87, 140, 145-146, 452, 472*

Fat Joe *115, 117, 119, 121, 123, 336, 340*

Fatman Scoop *123*

Female Funk (group) *97*

Fender Rhodes (keyboard) *329*

Fernando, S.H. "Skiz" *229*

Fine, Stu *95, 99-100, 109, 335-336, 342*

Finesse & TLC *492*

Finsta Bundy *447*

Firehouse Studios *217, 367*

Flatlinerz (group) *221*

Flavor Flav *243, 252, 256-257*

Flavor Unit *122, 410-412, 417*

Floaters, The *489*

Fondle 'Em Records *285, 293-294, 302*

Force MDs [aka Force MCs] *429, 489-490*

Forest Houses *115, 119, 333*

Forté, John *377, 379-381, 383*

Foxxx, Freddie *316*

Freddy Krueger *145-147*

Fresh Prince, The [aka Will Smith] *126-155, 182, 254, 470*

Fresh Records *205, 422, 424-427*

Freshco *336*

Friedman, Glen E. *195*

Frukwan [aka Fruitkwan] *212-233, 367, 470-496*

FTI [Fresh To Impress] (group) *183-184, 187-189*

Funk Lab All-Stars *97*

Funky Ass Records *158, 162*

Funky Slice Studios *7, 12, 28, 388, 390-392, 397, 403*

Gamble, John *282-283, 288*

Gang Starr *204-205, 208, 264-271, 274-275, 277, 335-338, 367, 427, 430, 453, 462*

Garcia, Bobbito *7-8, 22, 29, 67-68, 77, 80, 83, 161, 285, 293-294, 298-299, 380, 383, 389*

Gardner, Taana *498*

Gaye, Marvin *258, 315*

Gee Street Records *216-223, 228, 367, 379*

Geffen Records *100, 109, 296*

Ghost Face Killer *435-443*

Gillespe, Dizzy *39*

GLC Studios *218, 227, 229, 232*

Glue Factory (studio) *159, 162, 164*

G-ology *402*

Goodman, Dana *130-131, 133-134, 139*

Goodman, Lawrence *130-131, 133-134*

Gossett, Dave *49, 52, 55*

Gottfried, Gilbert *22*

Graham, Chris *103*

Grand Master Caz *154, 225-226, 500*

Grand Puba *118, 121, 123*

Grandmixer D.ST [aka DXT] *507*

Greene Street Studios *28, 218, 239, 241, 243-245, 252, 283*

Gregg Nice [aka Greg Nice] *420-433*

Grillo, Jamieson *120, 191, 195-196, 203, 208*

Group Home *265-267*

Guru *182, 202, 208, 264-268, 272, 335-336, 340*

GZA [aka The Genius] *272, 435-436, 442*

H2O [aka Hard 2 Obtain] *301*

Hammond, Johnny *488*

Harpur [aka Harper], David *502, 504*

Harris, Pete Q. *135-155*

Harris, Ricky *254*

Harrison, Greg *151-152*

Hashim *154*

Hassan, Elijah [aka Elijah Baker] *109*

Hastings, Daniel *274*

Hawkins, Yusuf *318*

Hayes, Al "Purple" *252*

Headhunters *149*

Heller, Jerry *238*

Heltah Skeltah *446, 460, 462, 465, 467*

Holy Mountain, The (film) *81*

Honeydrippers, The *489*

Horace "Fly" [Hampton] *205, 429*

Hot 97 *75, 123, 229-230, 393*

House Party (film) *147*

Hudson, Rolando *461, 464, 467*

Hyde Street Studios *104*

Hypnotic MCs *129*

Ice Cream Tee *133*

Ice Cube *51, 196, 221, 234-262, 370*

Ice-C *128-129*

Ice-T *182, 240, 292, 308, 316, 341*

Idlers Records *4, 216*

Ill Kid Records *267*

In-A-Minute Records *103*

INS (studio) *348-349, 351, 359-360*

Inspectah Deck [aka Inspektah Deck] *436, 442*

Invisibl Skratch Piklz *138, 166, 174*

Irvine, Weldon *397-398*

Island Records *216, 228, 367*

J. Dee (Lench Mob) *241, 245, 253, 258*

J. Rawls *382, 390, 402*

Jackson 5 *413, 415, 421*

Jackson, Jesse *482, 496*

Jackson, Milt *387*

Jahdan *462*

Jam Master Jay *3, 22, 306*

James, Bob *147, 200, 275, 329*

James, Rick *150*

Jane Doe *406*

Jay-Z *273, 392-393, 508*

Jenkins, DeChown *404-405*

Jeru The Damaja *86, 264-277, 446*

Jive Records *131-138, 141, 145-147, 149, 151-153, 216, 337, 482*

Jive Rhythm Trax *135*

Jobete *415*

Jody Records *447*

Joe Control *121*

Johnstone, Magnus *184*

Jones, Fuzzy *462*

Jones, Tom *480*

Jonzun Crew *486*

J-Treds *72, 77, 79, 86, 88*

Juice Crew, The *304, 308, 313, 345, 364*

JuJu *33-41*

June Love (artist) *422-423*

Jungle Brothers *4, 33-35, 37, 46, 287*

Juno (keyboard) *231, 355-356*

Just-Ice *6, 80, 254*

K2000, Kurzweil (keyboard) *175*

Kain, Gylan *288, 298, 301*

Kalvert, Scott *141, 147, 150 151*

Kango Crew *2, 7*

Kaygee *408-418*

KDAY (Los Angeles) *26-27, 93*

K-Dee [aka Kid Disaster] *236*

Keak Da Sneak *108*

Keller, Rich *39, 286-302*

Kid 'N Play *7, 126, 322-323, 326, 329-330*

Kid Capri *205, 340*

Kid Destroy *127*

Killah Priest *219, 227-229, 231*

King Shab *265*

KISS FM (New York) *4, 29, 46, 493*

Klein, Dave "Funken" *47*

KMD *20, 22, 279-302*

Kool & The Gang *330*

Kool G Rap *36, 275, 304-320, 322-323, 326, 333-334, 364, 436, 448*

Kool Keith *81, 156-180*

Kool Moe Dee *134, 136, 139, 151, 179, 304*

Korner Boys *128*

Krasilovsky, William *63, 71*

Krasnow, Bob *292-293*

KRS-One *55, 83, 193, 269, 275, 318, 333, 337, 380, 399, 431, 462, 489*

Kru-Cut Records *237*

Kubrick, Stanley *460*

Kurious [Jorge] *225, 285, 293, 299*

Kut Masta Kurt [aka Kutmasta Kurt] *158-164, 166, 170, 174, 176-177*

Kwamé The Boy Genius *322-331*

Kweli, Talib *375-406*

Ladd, Mike *68-69*

Lady B *132*

Lakim Shabazz *122, 417*

Large Professor *124, 274, 296, 310-319*

Latief *365, 370*

Latin Quarter (club) *5-6, 46, 143, 185, 420, 481*

Latin Rascals *345, 355-356*

Lavelle, James *169*

L-Brothers *179*

Leete, Lisle *49*

Lench Mob *241, 245, 253, 258, 262*

Lethem, Blake *5, 7-8, 12, 16, 28*

Levy, Alain *51, 54*

Lewis, Parker *300*

Lewis, Ramsey *53*

Libra Records *58, 59, 61-63*

Lighty, Chris *35, 47, 52, 55, 384, 451*

Lil' Dap *265-267*

LinnDrum *136, 480*

LL Cool J *19, 142, 238, 304, 307, 311, 322, 342, 408, 470, 474, 476, 478, 481, 490*

Lollapalooza *170*

Lone Catalysts *402*

Lord Digga *365, 372-373*

Lord Finesse *115-117, 119, 333-343, 455*

Lord Sear *299*

Lynch, Monica *474-496*

Lyricist Lounge *381, 383-385, 401, 406*

M.C. Shan *198, 305-308*

Mack, Charlie *139, 146, 149*

Mack, Greg *26, 27*

Mad Skillz *389*

Mandre (group) *154*

Mansfield, Joe *186-210*

Mantronik, Kurtis [see also: Mantronix] *345-361*

Mantronix (group) *5, 127, 345-361*
Marley Marl *4, 25, 129, 304-309, 311, 313, 320, 337, 341, 345, 363-364, 366, 370, 433*
Marquis [aka Brother Marquis] (2 Live Crew) *204*
Martin, Lionel [aka The Vid Kid] *16, 22, 25, 29-30, 272*
Masekela, Hugh *147*
Massenburg, Kedar *471*
Masta Ace [aka Master Ace] *232, 324, 363-373*
Master Killa *442*
Master Rob *116-118, 334*
Masterdon Committee *488*
Masters of Ceremony *116, 118, 431*
Mau Mau Rhythm Collective *95*
Mays, Dave *185, 203*
MC Hammer *18-19, 21, 26-27, 150*
MC Serch *2-31, 99, 218, 226, 280-282, 299*
MC Tee *345-361*
MCA Records *117, 243, 409-410, 421*
Medina, Benny *364, 411*
Melle Mel *304, 335, 347, 471, 475*
Mercury Records *47-49, 52, 54, 118-119, 188, 191, 196-197, 202, 207-209*
Metal Face Records *295, 302*
Method Man *435-436, 442-443*
MF Doom (see Zev Love X)
MF Grimm *299, 301-302*
Mike G (Jungle Brothers) *34*
Mikey D *336*
Mista Lawnge [aka Mr. Long] *43-55*
Mister Cee *84, 366*
Mister Man [aka Mr. / Lord Khaliyl] *379*
Mister Rogers (TV show / personality) *255-256*
Mix Master Ice *420*
Mo Wax Records *165, 169*
Mobley, Hank *38*
Mojica, Vinia *403*
MOOD (group) *380-382, 399, 402-403*
Mooncycle, Makeba *378-381, 383, 387*
Mos Def [aka Yasiin Bey] *117, 375-406*
Moxey, Patrick *266-268, 378*
MPC-2000, Akai (sampler) *89*
MPC-3000, Akai (sampler) *418*
MPC-60, Akai (sampler) *13, 38*
Mr. Len *59-90*
Mr. Magic *4, 153, 305, 347, 376, 474-475*
Mr. Mixx *59, 495*
Mr. Sime *225, 231-232*
Mr. Walt *397, 447-468*
Mtume, James *493-494*
MTV [see also: "Yo! MTV Raps"] *40, 202, 230, 254, 400*
Murphy, Eddie *152, 334, 339*
Music Factory, The (record store) *462, 467*
N.W.A. *27, 51, 96-97, 126, 182, 235-243, 246, 250, 254, 256, 258, 261, 270, 367, 369*
Nardone, Mike *161*
Nas *264, 304, 338, 442, 450, 458*
Nassau Coliseum *148*
Nasty Comedians (group) *421*
Nation of Gods & Earths *78, 92*
Native Tongues *14, 34, 43, 48, 50, 55, 95*
Nelson, Havelock *291*
Nervous Records *449-452, 455-456, 463, 465*
New Line Cinema *145-147*
New Music Seminar (MC and DJ Battles) *4, 12, 48, 132-133, 335-336, 341, 343, 382*
New Style, The (group) *409, 411, 417*
New, Bryan "Chuck" *135-136, 139, 148, 155*
Newkirk, Don *232, 494*
Nicolo, Joe "The Butcher" *130-155*
Nightmare On Elm Street (film) *145-146*
Nkiru Books (store) *377, 379, 398, 402*
Notorious B.I.G. [aka Biggie Smalls] *223, 229, 249, 273, 375, 458*
Nunez, Chep *355, 357*
O'Brien, Glenn *499-500*
Official Recordings *57, 62-66, 69-70, 72, 81, 89*
Ogrin, Dave *123*
Onyx (group) *275-276, 286, 324, 446*
Onyx (member of KMD) *280, 283, 297*
Orchard Park Projects (Boston) *201*
Originoo Gunn Clappaz *446, 465*
Overbrook High School (Philadephia) *129*
Ozone (Management / Music) *68-70, 72, 80, 87, 89-90*
Pam The Funkstress *96-113*
Parker, Kenny *462*
Parliament - Funkadelic [aka P-Funk] *108, 204, 252, 483, 491*
Partridge Family, The (TV show) *432*
Patterson, Aaron "Moose" *104*
Paul C (producer) *324, 329*
Paul's Coffee Shop (studio) *215*
Payday Records *267, 276, 378, 383*
Percee P *340*
Perez, Dave ("Shady") *40*
Perry, Paula *365, 371-372*
Pete Nice, Prime Minister *2-31, 281-302*
Pete Rock *203, 212, 274, 282, 382, 395, 455*

PF Cuttin' *266*

Phife Dawg *451*

Pianosaurus (instrument) *177, 179*

Pinkett, Jada *228*

Platinum Island Studios *384, 391, 395, 403, 406*

Pleasure (group) *148*

PM Dawn *79, 216, 223*

Poetic (rapper) *212-233, 367*

Polemic Records *94*

Pop Art Records *129-130, 305, 474-475*

Poppo, John *349-351, 354, 356, 359-360*

Porter, Kevin *472-473*

Power Of Zeus (group) *465*

Power Play Studios *191-193, 201, 203, 206, 210, 312, 315*

Power, Bob *480*

Powers, Herb *349, 360*

Preston, Billy *491*

Prince (artist) *61, 92-93, 327*

Prince Paul *15, 17, 20-21, 28, 212-233, 367, 470-496*

Priority Records *238-239, 255, 261, 426*

Prism Records *364-365*

Professor Griff *235, 239, 246, 257*

Professor Rock *184*

Progressive Labor Party *92-93*

Psycho Les *33-41*

Public Enemy *14, 19, 30, 92, 95, 126, 143, 149, 235, 238-239, 241-244, 251, 256-258, 262, 275-276, 345, 376, 481, 483*

Publison Infernal Machine 90 (keyboard) *259*

Pukshansky, Anton *310-311, 315, 319*

Punch & Words *406*

Pure Blend *204-205, 429*

Purple Tape, The *438-439*

Pushead (visual artist) *167*

PWL America *118, 188, 190-192, 195-196, 199-201, 208*

Q4 (artist) *301*

Q-Tip *34, 124, 385, 405-406, 455*

Queen (group) *89-90*

Queen Latifah *46, 410, 412, 415, 486*

Raekwon *435-443*

Raheem *334, 340*

Rakim *24, 29, 107, 126, 143, 191, 267, 299, 307, 316, 318, 333-334, 340-341, 364, 376, 381, 435-436, 470, 478, 496*

Rammellzee *84, 507*

Ratner, Brett *40*

Rawkus Records *71-72, 74-75, 86, 379, 383-385, 387-389, 392-394, 397-398, 400*

Raybin, Marc *191, 202*

Readyrock Records *295, 302*

Reflection Eternal (group) *381, 384-385, 388, 403*

Reid, Vernon *227*

Resident Alien (group) *212, 216*

Reynolds, Marthe *191, 195-196, 202, 207, 209-210*

Rich Black [aka Rich Blak] *455, 460*

Riley, Boots *92-113*

Riperton, Minnie *403, 466*

RNS (artist) *228-229*

Robinson, Nat *493*

Robinson, Smokey *433*

Rodriguez, Ivan "DJ Doc" *191-192, 198, 201, 203-204*

Romaine, Van *412*

Ross, Dante *5, 8-9, 19, 279-302*

Ross, Kendra *390, 400*

Rossi, Terri *291-292*

Roxy, The (club) *216, 353, 359, 491*

Rudy Ray Moore *107*

Rufus & Chaka Kahn *330, 467*

Run-DMC *3, 5, 78, 87, 96, 131, 142-143, 149, 183, 236, 275, 286, 306, 316, 345, 353, 356, 358, 376, 448-449, 474-475, 478, 481, 493*

RUSH Artist Management *4, 5, 8, 281, 481-482, 496*

Rush Associated Labels (RAL) *212, 427, 433,*

RZA, The [aka Prince Rakeem] *212-233, 272, 367, 435-443*

S.O.S. Band *198*

Sadat X *122*

Sadler, Eric "Vietnam" (see also: Bomb Squad) *23, 235-262*

Salt-N-Pepa *7, 97, 237-238, 322-323, 326, 328-329*

Sanford & Son (TV show) *433*

Santana, Omar *355*

Schechter, Danny *496*

Schoolly-D *182, 254, 431*

Scientific Shabazz [aka Shabazz The Disciple] *219, 228-229, 231*

Scientifik *188, 202, 207*

Scotty Hard [aka Scott Harding] *216-218, 222-223, 227-228, 232*

SD50 Studio *283*

Sequential Circuits Studio 440 (drum machine) *163*

Serch (see MC Serch)

Sermon, Erick *22, 193, 210*

Servin' Generals *7-8*

Sever, Sam *2-31, 239*

Shannon *154*

Shawn J. Period *382-406*

Shecter, Jonathan *185, 371*

Shock Dell *507*

Shocklee, Hank (see also: Bomb Squad) *23, 30, 235-262, 492*

Shocklee, Keith (see also: Bomb Squad) *23, 30, 235-262*

Showbiz *48, 115-117, 119, 121-122, 333, 336, 340*

Silverman, Tom *474-475, 480, 482, 490*

Simmons, Bobby *471, 476, 480-481, 485*

Simmons, Russell *4, 5, 8-9, 11, 17, 19-20, 24-27, 30, 142, 152, 220, 353, 427-429, 476, 480, 482, 496*

Sir Jinx *51, 234-262*

Sir Menelik *160, 162, 165-166, 173, 176-178, 398*

Skyywalker, Luke *204, 495*

Sleeping Bag Records *345, 348, 350-351, 353, 355, 422, 424-427*

Slick Rick *2-3, 15, 19, 126, 130, 141, 183, 203, 236, 323, 329, 398, 401, 435-436, 448*

Sly & The Family Stone *259, 483, 490, 495*

Smith, Lonnie Liston *493*

Smith, Roger Guenveur *108*

Smith, Will (see Fresh Prince)

Smooth Bee *420-433*

Smooth Ice Gee *188, 207, 209*

Smyth, Corey *404*

Socolov, Will *345-361*

Solesides Records *159, 375*

Son of Bazerk *251-252, 258*

Sonic Sum *68*

Soul Train (TV show) *207, 209*

SP-12, Emu (sampler / drum machine) *233, 343*

SP-1200, Emu (sampler / drum machine) *13, 153, 310, 343, 403, 452, 492*

Special K (Awesome 2) *185-210*

Spice 1 *94-95, 97, 109, 111*

Spoonie Gee *460*

Staple Singers *329*

Steady B *130*

Steele [aka General Steele] *445-468*

Stereo Crew *236-237*

Stetsasonic *6, 212-214, 219, 265, 392, 469-496*

Stetson Brothers, The *472*

Stimulated Dummies *282, 301*

Strafe *319*

Strange Family Records *423-424*

Streeterville Studios *404-405*

Stretch & Bobbito Show (radio show) *8, 77, 83, 161, 299, 380, 383*

Stretch Armstrong *7-8, 67-68, 74, 77, 83, 161, 299, 380, 383, 389*

Strong City Records *116-117*

Studio 4 (Philadelphia) *130-131, 137, 139, 148, 153-154*

Style Wars (film) *371*

Sub Verse Records *294-296, 302*

Subroc *22, 279-302*

Such-A-Sound Studios *337*

Sugar Hill Records *324-325, 349, 409-410, 470, 474-475*

Swift, DJ Rob *33, 35*

Synclavier (synthesizer / sampler) *136-137*

T La Rock *116, 301, 422*

Tascam 8-Track (recorder) *217, 226, 352*

Tash *385*

T-Bone *241, 245, 258, 262*

Teddy Tedd *185-210, 423*

Tek *445-468*

Temptations, The *471, 490*

Terrors Of A New Breed *187*

Tewlow, Reef *389*

The Shining (film) *460*

Thin Lizzy *498*

T-Nyne *184, 188, 190*

Tommy Boy Records *5, 9, 213, 216, 220, 227, 281, 409, 411-412, 418, 474-475, 477, 480-482, 484, 486, 490, 494, 496*

Tommy Hill (DJ) *265, 267*

Tompkins, Dave *81*

Tone Loc *208-209, 365*

Tony D [Anthony Dick] *3-5*

Tony! Toni! Toné *96, 109*

Too $hort *92-97, 109, 254*

TR-606 Drumatix, Roland (drum machine) *346, 350*

TR-808, Roland (drum machine) *136, 146, 187, 201, 345-346, 350-351, 353-354, 359-360, 493, 495*

TR-909, Roland (drum machine) *153, 350*

Treach *408-418*

Treacherous Three *422, 498*

Treggiari, Jo *103*

True Master *265, 269*

True Mathematics *255*

Tucker, C. Delores *220, 228, 291*

Tupac [Shakur] *74, 89, 95, 97, 110, 158, 375, 418*

Turner, Marcus *460-461*

TV Party (TV show) *499-500*

Twilight Zone, The (TV show) *160, 174*

Ultimate Force *117, 121, 334*

Ultramagnetic MCs *158-160, 165, 168, 176, 178, 324, 329, 483*

Uneek *365-366, 369-371*

Uni Records *117, 334*

Union Square (club) *46, 131, 140, 143, 149, 153, 420*

Unique Recording Studios *427*

Urban Thermo Dynamics [aka UTD] (group) *378, 383*
Ussery, John *226*
UTFO *4, 6, 420*
Uzoigwe, Amaechi *64-90*
V.I.C. [Victor Padilla] *36, 39*
Vega, Luis "Louie" *417, 430-431*
Vicious Lee *381-383*
Video Music Box *30, 272, 378, 416*
Vinnie (rapper) *408, 412-413, 418*
Vocoder (instrument) *356-357,*
Waits, Tom *27, 28, 232*
Wake Up Show *113, 161*
Walsh, Kieran *449, 463*
Warlock Records *3-4, 216*
Warner Bros. Records *92, 308, 363-364, 411*
Washington Jr., Grover *208, 461*
Waterman, Pete *191*
Watley, Jody *297*
WBAU *229, 492*
WBLS (New York) *4, 25, 153, 205, 267, 275, 305, 347, 474*
Weiss, Barry *133, 145*
Weiss, Michael *451, 463, 465*
WHBI *185, 297*
Wheeler, Carl *96, 102, 104*
Whistle (group) *6, 153*
Whodini *3, 96, 133-134, 136, 145, 356, 470, 493*
Whole Darn Family, The *232*
Wild Pitch Records *95-96, 98-100, 102, 105, 109, 117, 266, 335-336, 340*
Willesden Dodgers *135*
Williams, Alonzo "Lonzo" *236*
Williams, Hype *221, 230*
Williams, Saul *68-69*
Willis, Wesley *162*
Wise The Human Mix-Machine *471-472, 474-476, 480-481, 485, 489-491*
Witchdoctor [aka Witchdoc] *365*
Witkin, Christopher *219*
WKCR (Columbia University) *7-8, 67, 77, 299, 380*
WKTU *355*
Word Up Records *130-134*
World Class Wreckin' Cru *236*
World Trade Center *84-85, 348*
World's Famous Supreme Team *297*
Wreck Records (see also: Nervous Records) *450*
Wright, Bernard *203*
Wu-Tang Clan *73, 217-221, 226, 229-232, 264-265, 272, 275, 286, 304, 313, 367, 435-437, 439, 446, 450, 458*
Wynnefield (Philadelphia) *128, 130*
X-Clan *6, 34, 92, 95, 209, 243, 262, 376, 379, 489*
X-Files, The (TV show) *167*
Yamaha DX7 (keyboard) *163*
Yo! MTV Raps (TV show) *196, 201, 425, 456*
York, Dr. Malachi *285-286*
Young Comrades *100-101, 107, 109, 111*
Yo-Yo *259-260*
Zev Love X [aka MF Doom] *20-22, 279-302*
Zomba *135*
Zulu Nation *116, 122, 475*

ABOUT THE AUTHOR

Brian Coleman is a music journalist and historian who has previously authored two acclaimed, nonfiction music books: *Check the Technique: Liner Notes for Hip-Hop Junkies* (Villard / Random House, 2007; Shinko [Japan], 2008) and *Rakim Told Me: Hip-Hop Wax Facts, Straight From the Original Artists. The '80s* (Wax Facts Press, 2005). Before that, he promoted avant garde jazz and moonlighted as a hip-hop journalist for more than a decade, contributing hundreds of articles and reviews to publications including *XXL*, *Scratch*, *Wax Poetics*, *URB*, *CMJ*, the *Boston Herald*, *Metro Newspapers*, and many more.

He resides in Boston and is the sole employee of Good Road, which encompasses a PR agency, apparel brand and record label.

For more information, visit www.BrianColemanBooks.com and www.Good-Road.net.